T3-BGV-815

Religion on the American Frontier 1783–1840

Vol. IV

The Methodists

Religion on the American Frontier · 1783-1840

Vol. IV

The Methodists

A Collection of Source Materials

By

WILLIAM WARREN SWEET

The University of Chicago Press

Chicago · Illinois

The University of Chicago Press · Chicago 37
Agent: Cambridge University Press · London

 Published 1946. Composed and printed by the University of Chicago Press, Chicago, Illinois, U.S.A.

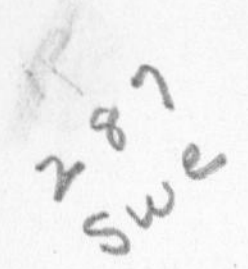

PREFACE

THE central theme in this volume is the Methodist circuit-rider. The principal purpose in compiling these original documents is to illustrate the kind of man he was, the methods he used in accomplishing his purpose, and the influence he exerted in bringing the refining influence of religion to bear upon a rough, uncouth society. It will be necessary, in order properly to appraise him and his work, to understand the ecclesiastical system within which he labored and of which he was the most important part. For this reason a chapter on the Methodist system appears in Part I, and extracts from typical annual and quarterly conference minutes have been included in Part II. The bulk of the materials here assembled, however, are personal documents and consist primarily of journals and letters of the men who were typical of those at the center of Methodist activity in the great new country in process of settlement beyond the Allegheny Mountains from the close of the War for Independence to the middle of the century.

The amount of published biographical and autobiographical material of frontier Methodism is very large—larger by far than that of any other religious group to be found at work in the early West. There are three factors which help to explain this fact. The first is that the Methodist preachers naturally followed the example of their great founder and his associates—John Wesley, George Whitefield, Thomas Coke, and Francis Asbury—all of whom kept daily records of their activities in extensive journals which were published and widely circulated.[1] A second factor was that, with the extensive circuits, necessitating their preaching in different localities for several weeks, they could use the same sermon over and over, relieving them of the necessity of preparing new sermons week by week. Thus they had more time for journal-keeping than would have been the case had they been under the necessity of preaching continually to the

[1] Wesley encouraged his preachers to keep journals and to write autobiographies. He raised the question of journal-keeping at his first conference in 1744, with the question: "Should all our Assistants keep Journals?" The answer returned was: "By all means, as well for our satisfaction as for the profit of their souls" (N. Curnock, *The Journal of the Reverend John Wesley, etc.* [8 vols.; London, 1909–16], III, 143–44; see also T. W. Herbert, *John Wesley as Editor and Author* [Princeton, N.J., 1940]).

same congregation. A third reason was that they were constantly meeting new people and having new experiences, which, in themselves, made for a larger incentive for recording daily activities.

None of the material in Part II has appeared in print, with the exception of the documents relating to the Kansas Indian missions. These appeared contemporaneously in the *Christian Advocate* and were reprinted in the *Collections of the Kansas State Historical Society* (Topeka, 1925). The unpublished minutes of conferences, journals, and letters were so abundant that we have been compelled to exercise our best selective judgment in choosing from among them those materials which seemed best suited to portray the manner in which the circuit-rider functioned. The extracts from James Gilruth's "Journal," for instance, are taken from a nineteen-volume manuscript journal, while the Dromgoole Papers, in the library of the University of North Carolina, contain some two thousand items.

As in the other volumes of the series *Religion on the American Frontier,* I have been assisted in the preparation of this book by numerous graduate students who have worked with me in my seminars. Among them I mention particularly Dr. George H. Bost, Dr. Felix J. Schrag, Dr. William C. Walzer, Miss Sally Lucas, Mr. Robert E. Ledbetter, Dr. Harold E. Bernhard, Dr. James Edward McEldowney, Mr. Frederick I. Kuhns, Mr. Arthur A. Azlein, Mr. Millard G. Roberts, Mr. William E. Cassell, and Mr. W. K. Shown. And, finally, I wish especially to acknowledge the assistance of Mr. Donald H. Yoder, Fellow in Church History at the University of Chicago, 1943–45, who served as my research assistant in putting the manuscript in its final form. More than in any other volume of the series, I have relied on such research assistance as Mr. Yoder has furnished. In fact, without his careful and scholarly editing, the volume would have been indefinitely delayed. I have prepared all the introductory chapters and have gathered and selected all the manuscripts which have found place in this volume. The publication of these volumes has, from the beginning, been a co-operative enterprise and has been made possible by the encouragement and financial assistance generously furnished by the University of Chicago.

WILLIAM WARREN SWEET

SWIFT HALL
January 1, 1946

TABLE OF CONTENTS

PART I. GENERAL INTRODUCTION

PART II. DOCUMENTS ILLUSTRATING THE WORK OF METHODISTS ON THE FRONTIER

BIBLIOGRAPHY

INDEX

LIST OF ILLUSTRATIONS

PART I

General Introduction

CHAPTER I

Methodism Gains a Foothold in America

IT HAS been suggested by Edward Eggleston that Methodism was to the West what Puritanism was to New England.[1] Considering them both historically, they are sublime; neither would be agreeable to live with today. Both have left a permanent impress upon the nation. Puritanism has been given, and rightfully, a prominent place in the history of America, and its great contributions are well understood. Methodism, on the other hand, neither has been understood nor have its contributions received adequate historic recognition. Yet no single force had more to do with bringing order out of frontier chaos than the Methodist circuit-rider, and among no other class of men was the heroic element more "finely displayed."

Of all the religious bodies in America at the close of the American Revolution, the Methodists were the most insignificant, in point both of numbers and of influence. They had obtained a foothold in America in a haphazard kind of way some ten years before the Declaration of Independence. No one had planned for their coming. John Wesley had taken no steps to send any of his preachers across the Atlantic. In fact, there is no evidence to show that he had been thinking of America as a possible field for the expansion of his movement until he learned that some of his preachers had voluntarily gone to the New World and that, through their labors, Methodist classes had been formed. Three had come at about the same time, around 1766, but none of them had sailed primarily to spread Methodism. The lure of cheap and fertile land and the greater opportunities in America, together with the oppression of Old World greedy landlords, brought Robert Strawbridge and Philip Embury from Ireland; while Captain Thomas Webb of the British army, one of Wesley's own recent converts, came as a result of the new policy adopted by the English government of sending troops to America.

[1] *The Circuit-Rider: A Tale of the Heroic Age* (New York, 1878), p. 159.

By 1768 a rude log chapel had been built on Sam's Creek in Maryland as the result of Strawbridge's activities, and, growing out of Philip Embury's preaching, steps had been taken to erect a chapel in New York City. Captain Webb assumed the leadership in the raising of funds for the new building and himself headed the subscription list with the largest contribution—thirty pounds. But he was not satisfied with limiting his activities to New York. It was he who brought the Methodist gospel first to Philadelphia as well as to New Jersey, and it was his foresight and generosity which enabled the little Methodist class in Philadelphia to purchase (1769) a half-finished church begun by a German Reformed congregation, now the oldest Methodist church still in use in America. In 1768 came another voluntary recruit, Robert Williams, and the following year John King.[2]

By 1768 Wesley had been well informed of what had been taking place in America. He had received a long letter in April of that year from a Thomas Taylor, one of the trustees of Wesley Chapel in New York, in which the work there was described and an appeal made for preachers, promising to "sell our [their] coats and shirts" in order to pay the passage, if they could not be procured otherwise. In the autumn Dr. Charles Mangus von Wrangel, the provost of the Swedish churches on the Delaware and a sincere pietist, visited Wesley in Bristol on his way to Sweden and pleaded that he send preachers to America. Of Robert Strawbridge and his work in Maryland, Wesley seems to have known nothing at this time; at least there are no traces of any appeal to him for help. It may well have been that the independent Strawbridge felt no need of Wesley's help, as the work was going forward under his bold leadership.

It was at the conference of Wesley's preachers which met at Bristol in August, 1768, that the first call for help from America was officially received. This plea was laid before them and was left for their consideration until the next yearly conference. At the conference at Leeds the following August (1769), Wesley stated from the chair: "We have a pressing call from our brethren of New York (who have built a meetinghouse) to come over and help them. Who are willing to go?" This appeal brought an immediate response, and Richard

[2] W. W. Sweet, *Men of Zeal: The Romance of American Methodist Beginnings* (New York, 1935). This is the most recent account of Methodist beginnings in America, based on all the available sources.

Boardman and Joseph Pilmoor, the first official missionaries sent to America by the English Methodists, were on their way within three weeks, with funds to pay their passage and an additional fifty pounds to help pay the debt on the New York meetinghouse. These first two of Wesley's missionaries remained in America until January, 1774, confining their work largely to New York and Philadelphia, though both made extensive journeys—Boardman to the north as far as Boston, and Pilmoor to the south as far as Whitefield's orphanage in Georgia.[3]

Altogether Wesley sent to America eight missionaries. At the conference of 1771 another call was made for help to America, and, of the five who volunteered, Francis Asbury and Richard Wright were chosen. A year later, as the result of a personal appeal to the conference by Captain Webb, Thomas Rankin and George Shardford were sent. In 1774 came James Dempster and Martin Rodda. Meanwhile Joseph Yearby and William Glendenning had also come out as volunteers but on their own responsibility. From the standpoint of the future of American Methodism, Asbury alone, of these eight official missionaries, is of any great importance. From the beginning he seems to have been determined to make America his home, and he never wavered in that determination. By 1778 all of Wesley's missionaries except Asbury had returned to England. Of them, Thomas Rankin was the oldest, and, as Wesley's assistant, he was responsible for the calling of the first Methodist conference in America, which met in Philadelphia in 1773. There ten preachers were assigned to circuits, ranging from New York to Petersburg, Virginia. American Methodist statistics have been faithfully kept from that time to this, a fortunate fact for the historian, but perhaps unfortunate also,[4] to a certain degree, in that it has made the Methodists inordinately conscious of statistics.

The departure of the English preachers in the midst of the Revolution was a blessing in disguise for American Methodism. All of them were staunch Loyalists, as was John Wesley. This, of course, was nothing against them, but for Loyalist preachers to have remained in

[3] See the "Journal of Joseph Pilmoor" (MS), Methodist Historical Society, Philadelphia; transcripts in University of Chicago Library.

[4] See *The General Minutes of the Methodist Episcopal Church,* Vol. I: 1773–1823 (New York, 1840), and subsequent volumes to the present.

America at this time would have done far more harm to the cause than good. Wesley's political pamphlets upholding George III's policy toward the colonies put all Methodists in America under suspicion as Tories, and even Asbury did not fully establish himself in the confidence of his American brethren until the close of the Revolution.

The departure of Wesley's missionaries gave the American Methodists an early opportunity to develop an indigenous movement, for, during the course of the war, Methodism was compelled to carry on, if at all, under the leadership of native preachers. The first of the native preachers were "raised up" under the independent activities of Robert Strawbridge. Strawbridge undoubtedly was a thorn in the flesh of both Rankin and Asbury, who, as Wesley's assistants, had the responsibility of administering discipline. Wesley insisted that the American Methodists receive the sacraments at the hands of the Episcopal clergy. This Strawbridge disregarded, and, though unordained, on numerous occasions he administered them himself. Though guilty of "irregularity," to use Asbury's term regarding him, Strawbridge was an effective instrument in spreading Methodism, especially in Maryland and Virginia. His energetic, fiery, and fluent preaching won converts and attracted numerous young men as itinerants; in fact, the first native preachers were his spiritual sons. It would be difficult to see how Methodism could have carried on during the Revolution without William Watters, Philip Gatch, Daniel Ruff, and Freeborn Garrettson, to say nothing of the numerous local preachers and exhorters whom Strawbridge had been instrumental in bringing into the movement.

Though nominally a movement within the Anglican church, early Methodism found little encouragement and less co-operation from the Colonial Episcopal clergy. Wesley, however, continued to insist, even throughout the Revolution, that Methodists receive the sacraments from the church clergy and that, in places where there were Anglican churches, Methodist meetings be held at such times as not to conflict with the church services. In an extended journey through the southern colonies in 1773, Joseph Pilmoor records attending numerous Episcopal services and not infrequently being permitted to preach in Anglican churches. In fact, he finds much good to say of the English church clergy and little to criticize.[5] But, as the Methodist movement made its way into Maryland and Virginia, it met opposition from the Anglican church clergy. In fact, only one Anglican clergyman in all Colonial America gave the Methodists full co-operation and assistance. That clergyman was Devereux Jarratt,[6] of Bath Parish in Dinwiddie County, Virginia. Jarratt's importance in the establishment of American Methodism has been largely overlooked by Methodist historians, though in recent years he has for the first time received more adequate attention, both from Methodists as well as from Episcopalians.

From the beginning of his long ministry in Dinwiddie County in 1763 to his death in 1801, Jarratt was indefatigable in preaching the evangelical doctrines of repentance and conversion. His preaching, in fact, had created a widespread revival of religion in his own extensive parish years before any of the Methodist revivalists had appeared in America. Himself a convert in the Presbyterian awakening in Virginia, he had entered the ministry because of his firm belief in personal and experimental religion. His Sunday services were crowded with strangers from far and near. He held meetings in private homes and visited extensively among the people, and for the first time poor people were reached and brought into relationship with the church.

With the coming of the Methodist itinerants into the region of his parish, Jarratt welcomed them and was soon working in close co-operation with them. Robert Williams was the first Methodist preacher Jarratt had ever seen. He came into Jarratt's parish in 1773 and remained a week in Jarratt's house. Williams assured Jarratt that the Methodists "were true members of the Church of England" and that "their design was to build up and not to divide the church."[7] He stated that the Methodist itinerants were not ordained men and that they therefore looked to the parish ministers for the ordinances of

[5] "Journal of Joseph Pilmoor" (MS).

[6] See E. Clowes Chorley, "The Reverend Devereux Jarratt, 1732–1801," *Historical Magazine of the Protestant Episcopal Church,* V, 45–64. See also "Devereux Jarratt: Forerunner" in Sweet, *op. cit.,* pp. 19–47, and W. M. Gewehr, *The Great Awakening in Virginia* (Durham, N.C.: Duke University Press, 1930), chap vi: "Devereux Jarratt and the Methodist Movement."

[7] *The Life of the Reverend Devereux Jarratt, Rector of Bath Parish, Dinwiddie County, Virginia, etc.,* ed. John Coleman (Baltimore, 1806), pp. 107 ff.

baptism and the Lord's Supper. The importance of this evangelical Anglican clergyman in helping Methodism gain a foothold in America may be summarized as follows: From 1776 to 1783 Jarratt visited twenty-nine counties in Virginia and North Carolina, preaching and administering the sacraments to Methodists, at the same time carrying on the work of his own parish. During this period the number of Methodists increased in this region from a few hundred to more than four thousand; in fact, two-thirds of the total number of Methodists in America at the close of the Revolution were to be found in this area.

In the year 1775–76 a flaming revival swept over the whole of Jarratt's parish and throughout the surrounding counties.[8] Jarratt and the Methodists co-operated wholeheartedly in this work, and Jarratt particularly testified to the permanent effect for good.

The rapid increase in the number of Methodists in Virgina and the physical impossibility of Jarratt's covering the whole region led to a movement in 1779, fostered by a group of native Virginia preachers, to ordain one another and assume the full functions of clergymen. This movement would have resulted in a division in Methodism had not Asbury, aided by Freeborn Garrettson and William Watters, persuaded the Virginia preachers to surrender their right to administer the ordinances. For the next several years Jarratt redoubled his efforts to "remedy the complaint of the want of ordinances, and to render them steady to the church in the future." "All which," he said, "I did without fee or reward, and I continued so to do as long as the Methodists stood to their profession" of being loyal to the Anglican church. At the conference of 1782 held in Sussex County, Virginia, which adjoined the county in which Jarratt's parish was located, Jarratt was present and opened the conference with a sermon. He also preached each day of the conference and agreed "to satisfy the just wants of the people, to 'visit all the circuits he could,' to administer the sacraments of baptism and the Lord's Supper." The conference in turn "acknowleded their obligation to Rev. Mr. Jarratt, for his kind and friendly services to the preachers and people" and

[8] Jesse Lee, Devereux Jarratt, Thomas Rankin, and Francis Asbury all wrote contemporary accounts of this revival. Jarratt's account, however, is the fullest description. Asbury placed this account and also Thomas Rankin's account in his *Journal* (New York and Cincinnati, n.d.), I, 208–30. See also Sweet, *op. cit.*, pp. 36–43.

particularly for attending the Sussex conference, and the preachers in the South were advised "to consult him and take his advice, in the absence of Brother Asbury."[9]

Jarratt's co-operation ended when the Methodists formed an independent ecclesiastical body in 1784, and for a time there was some unpleasantness. It seems, however, from letters of Jarratt's recently found, that the estrangement was due more to the Methodists than to Jarratt. In a letter of May 31, 1785, he states that his absence from the conference was due to his failure to receive an invitation from either of the superintendents and not from the "want of inclination" on his part. He further states that he had written both to Coke and to Asbury to visit him before they left the state. To this invitation Coke did not even vouchsafe a verbal reply, and Asbury made only "a very slight one." "If ever I was worthy of the love and esteem of Mr. Asbury and any Preacher in connection with him," he writes, "I am so still. For I am the same both in principle and practice as I was the first Day he ever saw me."[10]

Another Anglican clergyman who gave considerable assistance to the early Methodists in America was Charles Pettigrew of North Carolina. Letters which have recently come to light reveal that a particularly friendly relationship existed between Pettigrew and Caleb B. Pedicord, a Methodist preacher of great earnestness and eloquence. Pettigrew, though a native of Pennsylvania, was educated in North Carolina and in his early life was a schoolteacher. On his determination to enter the ministry of the Anglican church he journeyed to England for ordination just as the Revolutionary War was beginning (1774–75). During the war he was the only Anglican clergyman who remained in the colony, and it was at this time that he got in touch with the Methodist itinerants. He frequently entertained the Methodist preachers in his home, attended their confer-

[9] *Minutes of the Annual Conference, 1773–1828, I* (New York, 1840), 17.

[10] Devereux Jarratt to Edward Dromgoole, May 31, 1785 (Dromgoole Papers, University of North Carolina; microfilm at the University of Chicago). A letter written to Dromgoole on March 22, 1788 (Dromgoole Papers), would indicate that Methodist criticism and denunciation of slaveholders was a cause of estrangement. Jarratt was a slaveholder, though in this letter he states that he is not "writing .... to prove the innocency or lawfulness of Slavery..... I love the Methodists for their Works sake. And if some of their Conduct towards me has been unkind & childish, I bear it very well; I was once a child myself."

ences, and carried on an active correspondence with Jarratt, Edward Dromgoole, and Caleb Pedicord. In a letter to Pettigrew dated August 13, 1782, Jarratt states:

I was glad to hear of your attendance at a later Quarter-Conference & of the Friendship you show & the assistance you give to the Methodists. They are the only people, that I know of, whose labours are considerably blest to the salvation of Souls; and they have given the most striking & indubitable Testimonies of their love & adherence to that Church of which you and I have the Honour to be ministers. They therefore claim a right to our Patronage, Countenance & Assistance. Some no doubt, may view us with an evil Eye for so doing & we may forfeit the good opinion of the worldly wise & great. . . . But what of this? If we seek to please men we are not the servants of Christ. If we can do good or be a Means by our Counsel, Direction, or Aid of helping others to be useful in the work of promoting the best Interests of Mankind—can we live to better purpose?[11]

A letter later the same year from Pedicord to Pettigrew furnishes further evidence of Pettigrew's interest in and co-operation with the Methodists.

I am authorized from Mr. Asbury to give you an affectionate invitation to our Conference in the Spring, his modesty prevents him from writing you. He has heard of your disinterested acts of friendship; and your labors among us, which gives him great satisfaction.

In April of the following year Pedicord writes Pettigrew an account of his labors on his circuit and of his inner desires for himself and people and extends to him an invitation to "our Quarter Conference" and also expresses the hope that he will attend the conference.[12]

As in Virginia, Methodism gained its early foothold in Maryland, Delaware, and New Jersey as a result of the work of a group of remarkably able native preachers. Freeborn Garrettson, William Watters, Philip Gatch, and Caleb B. Pedicord were all natives of Maryland and not only were active in that colony but extended their work into Delaware and New Jersey. In many respects the most unusual char-

[11] "Charles Pettigrew Letters" (MSS) (University of North Carolina).

[12] Pedicord to Pettigrew, December 29, 1782, and April 2, 1783 ("Charles Pettigrew Letters"). See also the letter from Pedicord to Pettigrew, dated September 6, 1784 (*ibid.*).

acter in early New Jersey Methodism was Benjamin Abbott. Converted under the preaching of Philip Gatch, he began at once to tell others of his transformed life and soon was attracting multitudes to hear him preach. Though ungrammatical, he had the gift of coining unusual sentences, and great emotional excitement was often occasioned as a result of his rugged eloquence. Southey in his *Life of Wesley* devotes three pages to Abbott.[13]

Asbury, who heard Abbott preach (February 14, 1781), remarked that his "words came with great power" and that "people fall to the ground under him, and sink into a passive state, helpless, stiff, motionless."[14] Methodism in New Jersey was also encouraged by Uzal Ogden, an Episcopal minister at Newton. In a letter to Asbury, April 11, 1783, Ogden states that he had recently come in contact with some of the Methodist preachers and had given them such "countenance and advice" as he deemed expedient and expressed the hope that "they and their successors in this country" might be instrumental in "turning many souls from darkness to light, and from the power of Satan unto God." He adds that "your preachers here do honour to the cause they profess to serve."[15]

Of the forty-two circuits reported at the conference in the spring of 1784, thirty-four were located in Virginia, North Carolina, and Maryland, and eight in Delaware, New Jersey, Pennsylvania, and New York. The total membership in Methodist societies was 14,988, and, of this number, only 2,589 were to be found north of Maryland.

[13] Robert Southey, *The Life of Wesley and the Rise and Progress of Methodism* (2 vols.; London, 1864), II, 261.

[14] *The Journal of the Rev. Francis Asbury* (3 vols.; New York, 1821), I, 420.

[15] The *Methodist Magazine* (New York), Vols. V and VI (1822 and 1823), published a series of seventeen letters from Rev. Uzal Ogden. In a long letter dated December 13, 1782, to Joseph Lyon, Essex County, he clearly sets forth his evangelical views. The letter to Asbury is found in *ibid.*, V, 424. Ogden was one of four missionaries of the Society for the Propagation of the Gospel in New Jersey who remained at their posts during the Revolution. On the organization of the Protestant Episcopal church, Ogden was elected the first bishop of New Jersey but was never consecrated because of a ruling (canon) that no bishop should be consecrated for a state unless there were at least six presbyters resident within the state (W. M. Manross, *History of the American Episcopal Church* [Milwaukee, 1935], p. 204).

CHAPTER II

The American Methodists Secure Their Ecclesiastical Independence

UNTIL the year 1784 American Methodism was a lay movement within the Church of England. Up to that time none of the Methodist itinerants had been ordained nor did they consider their societies real churches, their places of worship being called "chapels" or "meetinghouses," never "churches." Wesley was insistent throughout the Revolution that the American Methodists maintain the relationship with the Church of England, and Asbury exercised all the influence he possessed to keep down any movement that would in any way precipitate a break. Wesley's vigorous support of the policies of George III and his condemnation of the American "rebels," in his several political pamphlets, brought embarrassment to his spiritual children in America.[1] The long years of war wrought far-reaching changes in the attitude of the American Methodists toward the Church of England and even toward their venerable founder. After 1778, with the exception of Francis Asbury, their principal leaders were native Americans, thoroughly imbued with American ideals. They were devoted to the great cause for which Methodism stood and still had great veneration for Wesley, but they believed that they knew better than he what was needed to meet the new situation which an independent America presented.

At the end of the war Wesley had not fully sensed this changed situation and undoubtedly expected to continue his control in America, even though the former colonies were now an independent nation. As the war neared its close, there began to be evident concern among the American preachers as to what Wesley would attempt to do in regard to the changed situation in America. Would he displace Asbury with some other leader, such as Dr. Thomas Coke, to be

[1] For a summary of Wesley's political views and their effect upon the American Methodists see W. W. Sweet, "John Wesley, Tory," *Methodist Quarterly Review,* LXXI (1922), 255–68.

sent over from England? This concern is indicated in a letter written to Wesley by Edward Dromgoole, one of the preachers then residing in Brunswick County, Virginia, dated May 22, 1783.[2] Evidently this is the first letter Dromgoole had ever written Wesley, for he devotes a major portion of it to an account of his life and conversion and infers that he is a friend of Devereux Jarratt's and resides not far from his parish, thus establishing himself as a person to be relied upon. He reports that Methodism in America had made decided progress in spite of the war, and the final paragraph, which undoubtedly is the essential part of the letter, explains Asbury's importance to the American work.

> The preachers are united to Mr. Asbury, and esteem him very highly in love for his work'[s] sake; and earnestly desire his continuance on the continent during his natural life; and to act as he does at present, (to wit) to superintend the whole work, and go through all the circuits once a year. He is now well and has a large share in the affections of both; therefore they would not willingly part with him, or submit to any other to act in his place, until they have good proof of his integrity. If any of our brethren should be appointed to come from England to help us here, we shall gladly receive them; as there is now a great and effectual door opened, and a blessed prospect of great good being done. I remain, with great respect, your humble servant.

Here is implied a fear lest Asbury be displaced by an Englishman, unfamiliar with America, and a warning that such a step would be resented by the preachers and people.

That Wesley took this letter in good part is indicated by his reply, dated September 17, 1783.

> Bristol, Sept. 17, 1783
>
> My dear Brother,
>
> The more sensible we are to our own weakness the more strength we shall receive from above. As long as we feel that we are helpless and blind and poor, our strong helper will be always at hand. I am glad to hear, that notwithstanding all these Commotions, He is carrying on his work in America. It is a peculiar Blessing, that the Labourers are connected together, so as to act in concert with each other: And that God has given you all, to be of one heart and one mind that you may "kindly think and meekly speak the same." One would have imagined, that y*e* "fell monster

[2] *Arminian Magazine,* XIV (1791), 218–19.

War," would have utterly destroyed the work of God. So it has done in all Ages and Countries: So it did in Scotland a few years ago. But that his Work should increase at such a season, was never heard of before! It is plain, God has wrought a new thing in the Earth, shewing thereby, that nothing is too hard for Him.

I had not heard anything concerning Mr. Jarratt for a long season, You send me welcome News concerning him: I am glad to hear, that his Love is not grown cold. It is well, that you "agree to disagree" in your opinions concerning Public Affairs. There is no end of disputing about these matters. Let everyone enjoy his own persuasion. Let us leave God to govern the world: And he will be sure to do all things well. And all will work together for his glory, and for the good of them *yt* love Him.

When the Government in America is settled, I believe some of our Brethren will be ready to come over. I cannot advise them to do it yet: First let us see how Providence opens itself. And I am the less in haste, because I am persuaded Bro: Asbury is raised up to preserve Order among you, and to do just what I should do myself, if it pleased God to bring me to America. Go on in the name of *ye* Lord and in the power of his might! I am

Your Affectionate Brother

J. WESLEY[3]

If Wesley had been contemplating displacing Asbury, this letter shows that that step was no longer in his mind and that he was perfectly satisfied that Asbury was doing all that possibly could be done in keeping the American Methodists in order.

Less than a month later Wesley wrote to Jesse Lee a characteristic letter, dated October 3, 1783, giving four definite instructions relating to America:

1. The American Methodists must determine to abide by the Methodist doctrine and discipline as found in his *Sermons, Notes on the New Testament* and the *Large Minutes*.

2. He warns them against preachers coming from Great Britain and Ireland without recommendations from him, stating that three preachers desired to come, but he could not approve them because they were shaky

[3] This letter is reproduced in full, since it has never before been published. It was recently discovered in the collection of the Dromgoole Papers at the University of North Carolina. It is undoubtedly a reply to the letter written by Dromgoole on May 24, 1783 (*ibid.*). See below, facing p. 719.

Bristol
Sept 17. 1783

My Dear Brother

The more sensible we are of our own Weakness, the more Strength we shall receive from above. As long as we feel, ~~that we feel~~ that we are helpless & blind & poor, our strong Helper will be always at hand. I am glad to hear, that notwithstanding all these Commotions, he is carrying on his work in America. It is a peculiar Blessing, that the Labourers are connected together, so as to act in concert with each other: And that GOD have given you all, to be of one heart & one mind that you may "kindly think & sweetly speak the same." One would have imagined, that "the fell monster War" would have utterly destroyed the work of GOD. So it has done in all Ages & Countries: So it did in Scotland a few years ago. But that his Work shd increase at such a season, was never heard of before! It is plain, GOD has wrought a new thing in the Earth, shewing hereby, that nothing is too hard for Him.

I have not heard any thing concerning Mr Jarratt for a long season. You send me welcome News concerning him: I am glad to hear, that his Love is not grown cold. It is well, that you "agree to disagree", in your Opinions concerning Public Affairs. There is no end of disputing about these matters. Let every one enjoy his own persuasion. Let us leave GOD to govern the world: And he will be sure to do all things well. And all will work together for his glory, & for the Good of them yt love Him.

When the Government in America is settled, I believe some of our Brethren will be ready to come over. I cannot advise them to do it yet. First let us see, how Providence opens itself. And I am the less in haste, because I am persuaded Bro: Asbury is raised up, to preserve Order among you, & to do just what I should do myself, if it pleased GOD to bring me to America. Go on, in the name of ye Lord & in the power of his might. I am

Your Affectionate Brother

J Wesley

on discipline and doctrine and he suspicioned that they wanted to get away from his supervision.

3. He further warns them against receiving anyone, no matter by whom recommended who refused to be subject to the American Conference and who does not cheerfully conform to the Minutes of the American and English Conferences.

4. He does not wish any to be received in America who make any difficulty of receiving Asbury as the General Assistant. He thinks that the greatest danger to the work in America is from preachers coming from Europe or who will arise in America, bringing in new doctrines "particularly Calvinism."[4]

Among the letters which passed between Wesley and his American preachers during the autumn of 1783 is one from Asbury dated West Jersey, September 20, 1783. After reporting on the religious situation in the Jerseys, stating among other things that the Calvinists and the Universalists "very much retard the work of God in Pennsylvania and the Jerseys" by keeping people from seeking "heart religion," he takes up the matter of the "ordinances." While professing his reverence for the ordiances, Asbury believes that other things are more important and suggests that the people should be advised that, where the ordinances can be obtained, they should take advantage of them, but, if not, "there can be no guilt" in not attending them. He thinks that if "young men of our connection should get ordained, it will not do well," for no person, he adds, "can manage the Lay Preachers here so well, it is thought, as one that has been in the raising of the most of them. No man can make a proper change upon paper to send one here, and another [there] without knowing the Circuits and the gifts of all the Preachers, unless he is always among them." There is no doubt but that Asbury is here suggesting the continuance of his own authority and pointing out the impossibility of any kind of long-range control. The letter closes with the suggestion that if Wesley is to send preachers to America, "let them be proper persons . . . . ; for it would be better for us not to have [English] preachers, than to be divided."[5]

[4] *The Letters of the Rev. John Wesley, A.M. Sometime Fellow of Lincoln College, Oxford,* ed. John Telford (8 vols.; London: Epworth Press, 1931), VII, 191.

[5] *Arminian Magazine,* XIV (1791), 385–87.

The following spring (March, 1784) Asbury wrote Wesley from North Carolina, describing the progress of Methodism particularly in Virginia and the Carolinas, where many converts had been won and even "a few Presbyterians and Baptists" had been "lifted out of the Calvinian and Antinomian quicksands." In the course of the letter he states:

> *Dear Sir,* we are in great need of help. A [ordained] minister, and such preachers as you can fully recommend, will be very acceptable: without your recommendation we shall receive none. But nothing is so pleasing to me, Sir, as the thought of seeing you here: which is the ardent desire of thousands more in America.

That Wesley had in mind the possibility of his coming to America is here hinted, and this is further supported by the passage in the newly discovered letter to Dromgoole noted above, where he states: "I am persuaded Bro: Asbury is raised up to preserve order among you, and to do just what I should do myself, if it pleased God to bring me to America."

Asbury closes his letter with these adroit words:

> You know, Sir, it is not easy to rule: nor am I pleased with it; yet it seems that necessity is laid upon me. O pray for me, that I may be filled with light and power; with zeal and Prudence; and above all, with humility and a single eye. In so doing you will greatly oblige.
>
> Your dutiful son in the Gospel,
>
> Francis Asbury[6]

Such were the negotiations which passed between John Wesley and his American preachers which led to the formation of an independent ecclesiastical organization in America. Wesley does not seem to have given his American preachers any forewarning as to just what he planned to do to meet their critical situation, though they knew well enough that something momentous for them was pending. Just when Wesley made up his mind to ordain preachers for America is not known. When he did at last so decide, he kept it a secret, even from his brother Charles, for he was well aware that, once it was known, it would create a storm of protest from the Established Church clergy who were working with him. But, once having made up his mind,

[6] Asbury to Wesley, March, 1784 (*Arminian Magazine,* IX [1786], 680–82).

he acted quickly. There is evidence that Wesley had had Dr. Thomas Coke in mind for some time to head an American mission and had consulted him about it.[7] Coke was perfectly willing to undertake the work and urged Wesley to do everything possible "this side the water," and from this time forward Coke seems to have been the real leader in the plans for America. Wesley, having come to the conclusion that, historically, he, as a presbyter, had ordaining powers, proceeded on September 2, 1784, assisted by Coke and James Creignton, both Church of England clergymen, to ordain Richard Whatcoat and Thomas Vasey, the two preachers who had been selected. On September 18, 1784, Coke, Whatcoat, and Vasey sailed for America, arriving in New York on November 3.[8]

Of the three members of Wesley's delegation to America, Whatcoat was the eldest, being forty-eight years of age. Dr. Coke was thirty-nine, and Vasey was thirty-four. Coke was a Welshman and a graduate of Jesus College, Oxford, and later had received a doctorate of civil law from the university. He was an ordained clergyman of the Church of England, had become a Methodist in 1777, and within a few years was one of Wesley's most valued helpers. He had inherited a small fortune from his father, and in all his varied activities for the advancement of religion he was completely self-supporting. Small of stature, somewhat inclined to corpulency, with ruddy complexion, piercing eyes, and melodious voice, he did not always make the best impression upon the American preachers, who were inclined to consider him effeminate. His life furnishes irrefutable evidence of a generous heart and complete consecration, but these fine qualities were accompanied with an ambition to lead, and the height of his ambition was to be a bishop.

Once in the New World, Wesley's delegation soon made themselves known to the American Methodists. They at once sought out the Methodist preaching-house in New York—Wesley Chapel—and

[7] Henry Moore (*The Life of the Rev. John Wesley* .... [2 vols.; New York, 1825], II, 272–73) states that Wesley informed Coke of his plan for America at least a year before the ordinations took place. No sources are given for this statement.

[8] A detailed account of the steps taken by Wesley in regard to the American Methodists and Coke's relation to them is told in detail by John Alfred Faulkner in *Burning Questions in Historic Christianity* (New York: Abingdon Press, 1930), chap. xiii: "Did Wesley Intend To Found the Methodist Episcopal Church?"

Coke was soon telling John Dickins, the Methodist preacher in charge there, about the plan for forming the American Methodists into an independent body. We are told that Dickins heartily approved the plan and is credited with having suggested the name finally adopted for the new body—Methodist Episcopal church. Two days later Coke and Whatcoat left by stage for Philadelphia, where the two Episcopal clergymen in the city called upon them, with Coke accepting their invitation to preach at St. Paul's Church the following Sunday morning and afternoon. In the evening he preached in the Methodist Chapel (St. George's Church). Later Coke was to feel some twinges of conscience for accepting the invitation to preach in an Episcopalian pulpit without having said anything to the clergymen about the impending separation of the Methodists from the mother-church. The following Wednesday he drank coffee with the governor of Pennsylvania, and on the succeeding Sunday we find him in the pulpit of Barrett's Chapel in Delaware, where, after preaching, he administered the sacrament to "five or six hundred" communicants. "After the service," he tells us, "a plain, robust man came to me in the pulpit and kissed me: I thought it could be no other than Mr. Asbury and I was not deceived." Asbury tells us that, as he had had no opportunity of conversing with Coke before the service, he was "greatly surprised to see brother Whatcoat assist by taking the cup in the administration of the sacrament." When told of the plan to form an independent Episcopal church, Asbury was shocked. But evidently the sense of shock soon passed as Dr. Coke outlined the plan he and John Wesley had perfected.

In the comfortable home of Mrs. Barrett (Judge Barrett had died a short time before), located about a mile from Barrett's Chapel, the two Methodist leaders, destined to be the first Methodist bishops, held their first consultation relative to Wesley's plans for the new American church. Asbury soon disillusioned Dr. Coke of any notion he may have had that the new church could be formed by the mere dictum of John Wesley. This was the first lesson Coke had of what the achievement of independence had done to the American Methodists. Instead of receiving Wesley's plan without question, Asbury insisted that the way to proceed was to call all the preachers together; after they had fully discussed the plan, they would then determine by a majority vote whether or not it was to be accepted. This would, of course, cause delay, for the preachers must be summoned to a conference, and the summoning must be done by a man on horseback. Freeborn Garrettson, a young Maryland Methodist preacher of Anglican background, was given this task. To use Coke's picturesque words, he was sent "like an arrow, from North to South .... [to] gather all the preachers together at Baltimore on Christmas Eve."

In order that the sleek little Doctor might have some real American experience before the conference convened, Asbury arranged a preaching tour for him of nearly a thousand miles, to be covered from November 14 to December 24. The journey took him through Delaware, along the eastern shore of Maryland, and into Virginia. Everywhere he was greeted by throngs, the Methodists flocking from all directions to receive the sacraments from the first Methodist preacher in America who had the right to administer them. And Coke enjoyed it, expressing himself as charmed by the spirit of the American brethren.[9] Meanwhile Asbury was giving Richard Whatcoat and Thomas Vasey their first experience in American itineracy in western Maryland.

Some twelve miles north of Baltimore stood "Perry Hall," a "most spacious and elegant building," the residence of Henry Dorsey Gough, one of the few wealthy Methodists in America, reputed to be worth a hundred thousand pounds. It was in this spacious mansion that the Methodist preachers began to gather on December 17. Dr. Coke had a "noble room" all to himself, and here it was that he and Asbury, Whatcoat and Vasey, with the other preachers present, talked over plans for the ensuing conference. On the morning of December 24 the whole body left their comfortable quarters at Perry Hall and by ten o'clock had arrived at the Lovely Land Chapel in Baltimore, where the conference opened with Coke in the chair.[10]

[9] *Extracts from the Journals of the Rev. Dr. Coke's Five Visits to America* (London, 1793), pp. 13–16, 17–23.

[10] The preachers certainly in attendance were Thomas Coke, Francis Asbury, Richard Whatcoat, Thomas Vasey, Freeborn Garrettson, William Gill, Reuben Ellis, LeRoy Cole, Richard Ivey, James O'Kelley, John Hagerty, Nelson Reed, James O. Cromwell, Jeremiah Lambert, John Dickins, William Glendenning, Francis Poythress, Joseph Everett, William Black, William Phoebus, Thomas Ware, Thomas Haskins, and Edward Dromgoole—twenty-three in all. Until recent years it was not known that Thomas Haskins was present. His presence was revealed by the discovery of his manuscript "Journal" in the Library of Congress. It is probable that thirty-two other preachers were also present, since their standing in the Methodist movement and the proximity

The "Christmas Conference," as the organizing body of American Methodism has been generally called, was made up largely of young men.[11] Many of them were under thirty years of age, and not a few had been active itinerants less than five years. The very youth of the members made them the more willing to cast aside precedent and to create innovations in church government. Indeed, it may have been their lack of knowledge of other forms of church polity that accounts in part for what they did and for their willingness to turn their backs upon precedent, though they, through Wesley's guidance, found in the past firm standing-ground. But, whatever may have been the influences which guided their action, their finished work, which came out of ten days of deliberation, has lasted the Methodist church in America for more than a hundred and fifty years. Besides Asbury, one of the most experienced preachers at the conference was the Irish itinerant Edward Dromgoole, upon whom much new light has been thrown by the Dromgoole Papers now at the University of North Carolina.

Thomas Coke was, at least outwardly, the leading figure at the conference, since he more than any other represented Wesley, though it may be assumed that Asbury exercised the largest influence. As Ezra Squier Tipple has phrased it, "Rarely has so important a task been accomplished with such comparative ease."[12] The reason was that John Wesley had sent over with Coke a general form for the organization of the new church, and little besides a resolution accepting it was required. Unfortunately, there are no official records of that gathering. Richard Whatcoat has left us the most satisfactory summary:

On the 24th we rode to Baltimore; at ten o'clock we began our Conference, in which we agreed to form a Methodist Episcopal Church,

---

of their circuits would naturally cause them to respond to the summons to attend such an important conference (John Lednum, *The Rise of Methodism in America, Containing Sketches of Methodist Itinerant Preachers from 1736 to 1785, etc.* [Philadelphia, 1859], p. 413). See Abel Stevens, *History of the Methodist Episcopal Church in the United States of America* (4 vols.; New York, 1864), I, 235–40, for an account of the Gough family and their relation to early Methodism.

[11] Stevens (*ibid.*, II, 187–88) discusses the age and experience of the several members of the conference.

[12] *Francis Asbury: The Prophet of the Long Road* (New York, 1916), p. 151.

in which the Liturgy (as presented by Mr. John Wesley) *should be read,* and the sacraments administered by a superintendent, elders, and deacons, who shall be ordained, by a presbytery, using the Episcopal form, as prescribed by the Rev. Mr. John Wesley's prayer book. Persons to be ordained are to be nominated by the superintendent, elected by the Conference, and ordained by imposition of the hands of superintendent and elders; the *superintendent has a negative voice.*

Although Wesley had appoined Coke and Asbury superintendents, Asbury knew that such arbitrary procedure would not find favor with the preachers, since America was not taking orders any longer from Englishmen, even from their own spiritual father, John Wesley. He accordingly insisted that the superintendents be chosen by the vote of the preachers, and thus Wesley's desires were accomplished in a democratic manner. Asbury was then ordained deacon by Coke, assisted by Whatcoat and Vasey, and on successive days he was ordained elder and consecrated superintendent. Twelve of the older preachers were also ordained, first as deacons and then as elders, and thus it was that American Methodism secured both an independent ecclesiastical organization and an ordained ministry.

In addition to the above action, the conference adopted the Twenty-four Articles of Religion, which Wesley had formulated from the Thirty-nine Articles of the Church of England; and it accepted both the Sunday service and hymns which Wesley had prepared and published as the liturgy of American Methodism and the order that the service be read in all Methodist congregations on each Sabbath. A discipline, based upon Wesley's *Larger Minutes,* was adopted, with certain enactments suited to America to be added later, and rules governing slaveholding in the Methodist church were formulated. It fixed the annual allowance for single preachers at $64 and at $128 for married ones. It voted that the mode of baptism was to be determined by the candidate, and it formulated rules governing class meetings and also regulations discouraging ministers from marrying "unawakened" persons. And, finally, it adopted elaborate plans for founding a college.

At least one Methodist preacher who attended the Christmas Conference doubted the wisdom of separating from the Episcopalians. This was Thomas Haskins, whose "Journal," now in the Manuscript

Division of the Library of Congress, only in recent years has come to the attention of historians.[13] He was disturbed as to the expediency of an immediate separation from the Episcopalians and suggested that final action should be delayed. He further suggested that, since the Methodists had professed themselves to be dutiful sons of the Episcopal church, the Episcopalians should have been consulted before separation and that as many Methodist preachers as possible should attend the next meeting of the General Convention of the Episcopal clergy in Philadelphia. He feared that, unless the Methodists moved cautiously, they would be accused of being "hunters after power and disturbers of the peace and good order of the Church and State." He even feared the possibility of civil broils and advised his brethren to "move with the utmost caution and deliberation."[14] On January 1, 1785, the day the conference ended, Haskins wrote in his "Journal": "Our Conference ended, I feel myself uneasy. Oh how tottering I see Methodism now—But thou Oh Lord art able to make her strong and establish her on the top of the Hills. Keep Oh Keep us from dissentions among ourselves, here our danger lies." Fortunately, young Haskins' forebodings of disaster for Methodism proved to be unfounded.

The withdrawal of the Methodists from the Episcopalian communion was naturally very displeasing to Devereux Jarratt, who through many years had co-operated so effectively with them. He felt that he had been deceived. He resented the rules against slaveholding adopted by the organizing conference and the harsh things some of the preachers were saying against slaveholders, since he was the owner of twenty-three slaves. Coke states that he feared that Jarratt would do infinite hurt "by his opposition to our Rules."[15] Two Jarratt letters recently found—the first dated May 31, 1785, and the other

[13] For a brief description of the manuscripts see W. W. Sweet, *Men of Zeal: The Romance of American Methodist Beginnings* (New York, 1935), pp. 169–70. For a sketch of Haskins' life see Lednum, *op. cit.*, pp. 356–57.

[14] Thomas Haskins, "Journal" (MSS) (photostats in the library of the University of Chicago).

[15] Thomas Coke, *Extracts of the Journals of the Rev. Dr. Coke's Five Visits to America* (London, 1793), p. 33. Coke further states: "On the 7th passed by the house of Mr. Jarratt that violent asserter of the propriety and justice of negro slavery" (*ibid.*, p. 39).

March 22, 1788[16]—show conclusively that his attitude toward the Methodists had not greatly changed. In the first letter (May 31, 1785) he wrote:

My not being at the Conference, was not owing to want of inclination, but not being invited by either of the Superintendents, I imagined my company was not desired; and since I have been more convinced of it, for I wrote to Dr. Coke intreating him and Mr. Asbury to pay me a visit before they left the State, to which the Doctor did not even vouch safe a verbal answer and Mr. Asbury a very slight one. If ever I was worthy of the love and esteem of Mr. Asbury or any Preacher in connection with him, I am so still. For I am the same in principle and practice as I was the first Day he ever saw me. I have suffered no change at all, I love and honour those who fear the Lord, let their station in life be what it will; but my peculiar attachment has been to the Methodist[s]: and considering the Persecution I have suffered on their account, the many miles I have rode thro' all Weathers and at all Seasons to serve them in every respect, I cannot conceive how I have deserved to be treated so coldly, to say the least.

The letter dated March 22, 1788, also to Edward Dromgoole, is devoted largely to a discusion of slavery, in which Jarratt sets forth the scriptural argument for slaveholding.

In spite of the fact that he is aware that the Methodists condemn him roundly for his slaveholding and that they have written him "many a keen letter" on the subject, Jarratt says:

I love the Methodists for their Works sake. And if some of their Conduct towards me has been unkind & childish, I bear it very well; I was a child once myself. . . . . Once Mr. Asbury seemed to think Nothing could be done so well without me—but now he thinks I have done more harm than all the Preachers have done good—but I know to the contrary—Franky ought to have been the last Man to say This for I don't believe he can produce one Soul for all his travels & preaching in Virginia. But, blessed be God, he has given me many who I trust will be my Crown of rejoicing at last.[17]

[16] These letters were written to Edward Dromgoole, one of the older Methodist preachers and a neighbor of Jarratt's (Dromgoole Papers, University of North Carolina).

[17] Devereux Jarratt died on January 29, 1801, and Bishop Asbury preached his funeral sermon. Jarratt's *Autobiography*, originally written in a series of letters to Rev. John Coleman, was published at Baltimore in 1806, and Asbury was therefore unaware at the time of Jarratt's harsh criticisms of the Methodists. Let us hope that even if

It may not be out of place at this point to consider the wisdom of the action taken by the Methodists in forming an independent ecclesiastical body. Would it not have been a wiser course for John Wesley to have explored further the possibility of Methodism's remaining within the fold for the Church of England? In 1780 Wesley had written a long letter to Robert Lowth, bishop of London, taking him to task for his failure to ordain a Mr. John Hoskins, a London Methodist who had introduced Methodism into Newfoundland in 1774 and had opened a school there. Wesley had urged his ordination upon the bishop, who had evidently refused on the ground of Hoskins' lack of education. Wesley held up to scorn such a reason. "Your Lordship," he states, "did not see fit to ordain him; but your Lordship did see good to ordain and send into America other persons who knew something of Greek and Latin, but who knew no more of saving souls than of catching whales."[18]

The final paragraph of Wesley's letter "To Our Brethren in America," dated September 10, 1784, which he had intrusted to Dr. Coke, and which formed the basis of the action of the Christmas Conference in organizing an independent religious body in America, reads:

It has, indeed, been proposed to desire the English bishops to ordain part of our preachers for America. But to this I object; (1) I desired the Bishop of London to ordain only one, but could not prevail. (2) If they consented, we know the slowness of their proceedings; but the matter admits of no delay. (3) If they would ordain them now, they would likewise expect to govern them. And how grievously would this entangle us! (4) As our American brethren are now totally disentangled both from the State and from the English hierarchy, we dare not entangle them again either with the one or the other. They are now at full liberty simply to follow the Scriptures and the Primitive Church. And we judge it best that they should stand fast in that liberty wherewith God had so strangely made them free.[19]

Asbury had known of Jarratt's criticism, it would have made no difference in his judgments of his old friend and fellow-laborer. See Nathan Bangs, *A History of the Methodist Episcopal Church* (3d ed.; 4 vols.; New York, 1839), II, 128–30, for a reasoned judgment of Jarratt and his relation to the Methodists.

[18] *The Letters of the Rev. John Wesley, A.M.*, ed. Telford, VII, 29–31. The letter is dated August 10, 1780.

[19] *Ibid.*, p. 39.

Wesley was evidently clear in his own mind that it was absolutely hopeless to expect any assistance or aid from the bishops of the Church of England. Was there any chance for increased co-operation from the Episcopal clergy in America? The sincere interest and assistance of Devereux Jarratt has already been noted. The two other Episcopal clergyman, Charles Pettigrew of North Carolina and Uzal Ogden of New Jersey, also expressed their interest in the work being done by the Methodists and doubtless would have gladly entered into some official relationship with them if they had reason to think such co-operation would have pleased the Anglican authorities. Shortly after the Christmas Conference and the formation of the Methodist Episcopal church, Coke and Asbury were interviewed by two Anglican clergyman, John Andrews and William West, both in charge of parishes in Baltimore County, who suggested that when Episcopal bishops were secured in America, special bishops might be consecrated for the Methodists. Both Coke and Asbury rejected the proposal, and later, when Andrews again urged the plan upon Coke, he replied that he saw no advantage to the Methodists from the suggested proposal.[20]

By 1791 Thomas Coke had evidently changed his mind in regard to American Methodist relationship to the Episcopal church. In the spring of that year he wrote a letter to Bishop William White of Philadelphia in which he proposed a reunion of the Methodists with the Episcopalians. In this letter he stated:

> .... I am not sure but I went farther in the separation of our church in America, than Mr. Wesley, from whom I received my commission, did intend. He did indeed solemnly invest me, as far as he had a right to do, with Episcopal authority, but dd not intend I think, that an entire separation should take place.[21]

He further stated that he had no doubt that Wesley would favor reunion, "if a readiness were shown by the bishops of the protestant episcopal church to reunite." The great obstacle to reunion, on the

[20] W. W. Manross, *A History of the American Episcopal Church* (New York and Milwaukee, 1935), p. 205.

[21] Letter from Coke to "The Right Rev. Father in God, Bishop White," in *Memoirs of the Protestant Episcopal Church in the United States of America, etc.* (Philadelphia, 1820), Appendix, pp. 424–29. Letter dated April 24, 1791.

part of the Methodists, he believed, would be the attitude of the preachers. The ordained preachers would not give up their right to administer the sacraments, but he did not believe that "the generality" of them would object to reordination. The unordained preachers, who constituted a great majority, would not agree to reunion if it would cut off the possibility of their "rising up to ordination." He thinks, however, that all these matters might be ironed out and asks for an interview. He further states that he has written a "penitential letter" to Devereux Jarratt to make amends for his sharp criticism of him published in "our magazines." He also offers apologies to Bishop White and Dr. Magaw for the use of their churches "six years ago on my first visit to Philadelphia, without informing you of our plan of separation from the church of England." He advises that secrecy regarding these matters "is of great importance in the present state of the business, till the minds of you, your brother bishops, and Mr. Wesley be circumstantially known."

In his reply to this letter, Bishop White agreed to a meeting with Coke and promised to keep the whole matter secret. Though recognizing difficulties standing in the way of reunion, he thought that they were not "insuperable, provided there be a conciliatory disposition on both sides."[22] Doubtless Bishop White had in mind his attempt in 1787 to have an interview with John Wesley when he had been in England to obtain consecration. He had brought with him a letter of introduction from Joseph Pilmoor, but he had received such a cool reply from Wesley that he gave up the attempt.[23] He did, however, have an interview with Charles Wesley, who, as is well known, disapproved of what his brother had done in assuming the right to ordain.[24]

A few weeks after his letter to Bishop White, Thomas Coke addressed a similar one to Bishop Samuel Seabury (May 14, 1791). In this letter he proposed that he and Asbury be consecrated

as bishops of the Methodist Society in the Protestant Episcopal Church in these United States (or by any other title, if that be not proper), on the

[22] *Ibid.,* pp. 430–31.

[23] Manross, *op. cit.,* p. 205.

[24] Charles Wesley once stated: "All the difference between my brother and me was that my brother's first object was the Methodists and then the Church; mine was first the Church and then the Methodists."

supposition of the reunion of the two Churches, under proper mutual stipulations, and engage that the Methodist Society shall have a regular supply, on the death of their bishops, and so *ad perpetuum,* the grand difficulty in respect to the preachers would be removed—they would have the same men to confide in whom they have at present, and all other mutual stipulations would soon be settled.[25]

The letter closes with: "I most cordially wish for a reunion of the Protestant Episcopal and the Methodist churches in these States. The object is of vast magnitude."[26] Seabury evidently did not agree in the matter of its "vast importance," for he failed to reply. Of the early Episcopal bishops in America, Bishop James Madison of Virginia (consecrated September 19, 1790) seems to have been the only one who fully appreciated the seriousness of the withdrawal of the Methodists.[27] This is easily understood, since, of all the Episcopal dioceses in America, his suffered most from the secession of the Methodists, and he was concerned about the growing religious indifference so evident everywhere at the time. In the General Convention of 1792 he submitted to the House of Bishops a sweeping proposal which was undoubtedly motivated by the hope that Coke's proposals to reunite the Methodists with the Episcopal church might find sufficient support to warrant further steps. The proposals are so catholic in spirit that they deserve quoting in full.

The Protestant Episcopal Church in the United States of America, ever bearing in mind the sacred obligation which attends all the followers of Christ to avoid divisions among themselves, and anxious to promote that union for which our Lord and Saviour so earnestly prayed, do thereby declare to the Christian world that, uninfluenced by any other considerations than those of duty as Christians, and an earnest desire for the prosperity of pure Christianity and the furtherance of our holy religion, they are ready and willing to unite and form one body with any religious society which shall be influenced by the same catholic spirit.

[25] C. C. Tiffany, *A History of the Protestant Episcopal Church of the United States of America* (New York, 1895), p. 407. See facsimile of Coke's letter to Seabury in *Fac-Similes of Church Documents of the American Church, 1874–79,* No. 55.

[26] E. E. Beardsley, *Life and Correspondence of the Right Reverend Samuel Seabury, etc.* (Boston, 1881), pp. 400–401.

[27] Tiffany, *op. cit.,* pp. 388–89.

And in order that this Christian end may be the more easily effected, they further declare that all things in which the great essentials of Christianity and the characteristic principles of their church are not concerned, they are willing to leave to future discussion, being ready to alter or modify those points which, in the opinions of the Protestant Episcopal Church, are subject to human alteration. And it is hereby recommended to the State Conventions to adopt such measures or propose such conferences with Christians of other denominations as to themselves may be thought most prudent, and report accordingly to the ensuing General Convention.

The proposals were agreed to by the bishops and were submitted to the House of Deputies. Evidently there were few laymen in the House of Deputies who knew anything about the correspondence between Dr. Coke and Bishops White and Seabury, and Bishop Madison's proposal found little support. In fact, it was generally considered by them as "preposterous" and "tending to produce distrust of the stability of the system of the Episcopal Church, without the least prospect of embracing any other religious body." Following such a cool reception in the House of Deputies, the proposition was withdrawn.

The fact that Coke had carried on his negotiations with the Episcopal bishops entirely without Francis Asbury's knowledge would indicate that it was a personal scheme and did not have the support of the American Methodists. There is no doubt but that Coke was greatly disappointed in his relations with the American Methodists. He had come to America with the expectation of taking a leading role in their direction, but he soon found that Bishop Asbury occupied first place in the affections of the American Methodists and outranked him in the minds of the preachers. Asbury's experience was far wider than his own and his will stronger. At one of the general conferences, probably that of 1796, Coke introduced a matter which seemed dictatorial to some of the preachers, whereupon one of the preachers, an Irishman and a convert from Roman Catholicism, cried out, "Popery, Popery, Popery!" Angered at the interruption, Coke in huff tore up the paper containing his resolution, remarking as he glanced about the conference, "Do you think yourself equal to me?" Whereupon Nelson Reed, a leading minister, arose and, addressing himself to Bishop Asbury, remarked: "Dr. Coke has asked whether we think ourselves equal to him—I answer, yes, we *do* think ourselves equal to him, notwithstanding he was educated at Oxford and has been honored with the degree of Doctor of Laws—and more than that, we think ourselves equal to Dr. Coke's king." Coke's anger was now completely cooled, and he remarked, very blandly, "He is hard upon me." Asbury then remarked, "I told you our preachers were not blockheads."[28]

The following sentence in Coke's letter to Bishop Seabury would indicate, moreover, that his plan to unite with the Episcopalians was intended to give him equal rank with Asbury.

> I love the Methodists in America, and could not think of leaving them entirely, whatever might happen to me in Europe. The preachers and people also love me. Many of them have a peculiar regard for me. But I could not *with propriety* visit the American Methodists, possessing in our Church on this side of the water an Office inferiour to that of Mr. Asbury.

This frank statement forces the conclusion that Coke was at least partly motivated by his desire to add to his own authority and at the same time counteract the influence of Asbury.

In his letter to Bishop White, Coke had expressed the desire to settle the whole matter of reunion with the Episcopalians before Wesley's death, for he believed that the latter's approval would determine the issue. Wesley died on March 2, 1791, changing the entire picture, and Coke hurried back to England, perhaps with the hope that he might step into Wesley's place of leadership, and from that time on Coke's influence in American Methodism steadily declined.

As Tiffany has suggested, there was a lack of genuine interest in Coke's plan for unity on the part both of the Episcopalians and of the Methodists.[29] The Methodists were distrustful of the sincerity of the Episcopalian clergy, whom they deemed generally unconverted, while the Episcopalians were contemptuous of the Methodists, whose preachers they considered ignorant laymen. Though having many things in common, the gulf between them had become too wide to bridge. Although the smallest and most humble religious body in America, the Methodists were the first to secure an independent national ecclesiastical organization. This was achieved at a strategic

[28] W. B. Sprague, "Nelson Reed," *Annals of the American Pulpit,* VIII (New York, 1865), 68–70.

[29] *Op. cit.,* p. 408.

moment in the history of the American nation—at a time when Christianity in America was facing two momentous tasks. The first was a part of a world problem—that of combating forces which were openly aligned against all religion and morals, a movement which had grown out of the social and political upheavals of the latter eighteenth and early nineteenth centuries. The second task was primarily an American one—that of following the restless and moving population as, in ever increasing streams, it pushed westward and that of helping to save the ever advancing American frontier from barbarism. Though having a part in the meeting of both these problems, Methodism, for the next three-quarters of a century, was to make its greatest contribution in dealing with the problems of the West. A reunion with the Episcopalians would have undoubtedly cramped and hindered the kind of work the Methodists were best equipped to perform, and for that reason, if for no other, it was best that both should go their separate ways.

CHAPTER III

The Methodist System

THE Methodists believed that there was no one form of church government prescribed in Scripture. This was the position to which John Wesley came thirty-eight years before the formation of the American Methodists into a separate ecclesiastical body. He did not arrive at this position quickly and easily. Indeed, it was not until 1746, after reading Lord King's *Account of the Primitive Church,* that his High Church views in regard to the gospel requirement for bishops as a distinct order of the clergy began to be shaken. Later these views were confirmed by his reading of Bishop Edward Stillingfleet's *Irenicon.* Wesley defined a visible church as a congregation of faithful men, "in which the pure Word of God is preached, and the Sacraments duly administered according to Christ's ordinance."[1] He held that doctrines and sacraments were essential but that church government was of secondary importance. In a letter to the Reverend James Clark, an Established Church clergyman, written July 3, 1756, Wesley makes clear his matured position on church government. He states:

I still believe "the Episcopal form of Church government to be both scriptural and apostolical"; I mean, well agreeing with the practice and writings of the Apostles. But that it is prescribed in Scripture I do not believe. This opinion (which I once heartily espoused) I have been heartily ashamed of ever since I read Dr. Stillingfleet's *Irenicon.* I think he has unanswerably proved that neither Christ or His Apostles prescribed any particular form of Church government, and that the plea for the divine right of Episcopacy was never heard of in the primitive Church.

But were it otherwise, I would still call these "smaller matters than the love of God and mankind." . . . .[2]

[1] Umphrey Lee, *John Wesley and Modern Religion* (Nashville, 1936). Chapter x is an excellent discussion of Wesley's doctrine of the church.

[2] *The Letters of the Rev. John Wesley,* ed. John Telford (8 vols.; London, 1931), III, 180–83.

It was a fortunate circumstance, from the standpoint of the propagation of Methodism in America, that the movement was not handicapped by rigid views in regard to church government. This fact enabled the Methodists readily to adjust their system of organization to meet the needs of a changing frontier situation. A rigid system or set of ideas, of any sort, whether in church or state, in a society in motion would find itself sorely handicapped. The experience of Presbyterianism in the West well illustrates this fact. When such a system comes in contact with a mobile society, the system must give way or be broken into fragments. And this is just what happened.[3]

I

Methodism began in England as a paternal system, with John Wesley in complete control, and it remained so, with little change, until the end of its founder's life.

At the conference at Leeds in 1766, Wesley explained at length how his system of personal control over the Methodists in England and Ireland arose. This he did in the usual form of questions and answers. The question in this case was:

Q. But what *power* is this, which *you* exercise over all the Methodists in Great Britain and Ireland?

A. Count Z(inzendorf) loved to keep all things closely. I love to do things openly. I will therefore tell you all I know of the matter taking it from the very beginning.

At first, he states, a few people in London came to him (November, 1738) and desired that he advise and pray with them. This he promised to do. Soon other groups in Bristol, Kingswood, Newcastle, and

[3] W. W. Sweet, *Religion on the American Frontier,* Vol. II: *The Presbyterians* (New York, 1936), particularly chap. iv, "Revivalism and Presbyterian Controversy," and chap. v, "The Operation of the Plan of Union and Frontier Controversy." Jonathan Dickinson, perhaps the outstanding Colonial Presbyterian, stated in a sermon in Boston in 1722: "All the essentials of Government are left upon record in the Word of God and are unalterable by any Human authority—As Christ is sole King and Legislator to his church. It is an uncommunicable Jewel in his Crown, to give all Laws and all Ordinances thereof; and it would therefore be an egregious Reflection on his Faithfulness, to suppose any Case that can possibly occure unprovided for" ("Sermon Preached at the Opening of the Synod of Philadelphia, September 19, 1722," pp. 11, 13–14, 15).

in other parts of England, Scotland, and Ireland desired his assistance. This, he points out, was *their* desire, not *his*. This was the beginning of his power—"namely, a power to appoint when, and where, and how, they should meet; and to remove those, whose life shewed that they had no desire to 'flee from the wrath to come.'" This power remained the same when the number had increased to thousands. Soon some suggested that they subscribe money to pay for the lease of the Foundary and put and keep it in repair. This he allowed them to do. The necessity of keeping account of the money subscribed led to the beginning of another of his powers—that of appointing and removing stewards. The next step was that of directing certain young men who had come to him desiring to "serve me as sons and to labour when and where I should direct." Here arose his power to appoint and direct his preachers. He is at pains to point out that these powers came to him not as a result of his own choosing but as a consequence of others' insistence.

The first conference, that of 1744, came about as a result of Wesley's desire to have the advice of his preachers. "They," the preachers, he stated, "did not desire this meeting, but *I* did," for he held that "in the multitude of councellors there is safety." Later, when the number increased to such an extent that they could not all meet conveniently, he invited only certain ones to come. Still later he "gave a general permission that all who desired it, might come." These conferences were begun to "advise" him, not to "govern" him, nor did he at any time divest himself of any part of that "power" which the "providence of God had cast upon [him], without any design or choice of [his]."

He next takes upon himself to justify his having and retaining such power. He states that "several gentlemen are offended" at his having so much power. This he answers by stating: "If you can tell me any one, or any five men, to whom I may transfer this burden, who *can* and *will* do just what I do now, I will heartily thank both them and you."

Again some of his helpers say that he is "shackling free-born Englishmen" and demand a "free conference" to be attended by all the preachers, where all matters shall be determined by a majority vote. To this he counters that such a thing might take place after his death but not while he lives. To him, alone, he says, "the Preachers have engaged themselves to submit, ... to serve me as sons in the gospel," and not to anyone else. To him likewise, the people, he says, "will submit, [but] they will not yet submit to any other." As for his shackling freeborn Englishmen, he says, anyone may leave him who desires to do so. But those who choose to stay with him stay on his terms. He admits that this is *arbitrary* power if by arbitrary power is meant power exercised *singly*. But if by arbitrary power is meant "unjust, unreasonable or tyrannical" power, then, he insists, "it is not true." To the charge that he is making himself a pope, he replies:

> The Pope affirms, that every Christian must do all he bids, and believe all he says, under pain of damnation. I never affirmed anything that bears any, the most distant resemblance to this. All I affirm is, "The Preachers who choose to labour with me, choose to serve me as sons in the gospel." And "the people who choose to be under my care, choose to be so, on the same terms they were at first."[4]

Wesley refused to consider any change in his system of personal rule until toward the end of his life, when his thought for the survival of the movement began to cause him concern. As the number of societies and preachers increased, Wesley found it necessary to appoint certain of the more experienced among them "assistants." These he considered his personal representatives to supervise the work of the "helpers." The assistants accompanied the circuit preacher once each quarter as he made the round of his circuit, when love feasts were held and members were admitted or expelled from the societies. The advisory conferences were held annually and were made up entirely of preachers.

II

As far as possible this system of personal rule was transplanted to America and continued to function until the disturbed conditions brought on by the Revolutionary War and changing personal attitudes on the part of the American preachers compelled a change. Wesley's first "assistant" in America was Richard Boardman. Boardman was succeeded by Francis Asbury, and Asbury in turn by

[4] *Minutes of the Methodist Conferences, from the First Held in London, by the Late Rev. John Wesley, A. M. in the Year 1744,* I (London, 1812), 58–61.

Thomas Rankin, who was the first to be a "general assistant." The general assistant, as Wesley's representative, had the power to station the preachers, as did Wesley in England.[5]

Until 1773 what little business the American Methodists had was conducted in quarterly meetings. In that year Thomas Rankin, the newly appointed general assistant, called the first conference. It was modeled after Wesley's conferences in England and, like them, was advisory only. From this time forward until 1784 such conferences were held annually. Thomas Rankin acted as general assistant until his departure for England in 1778, and from that time onward by a vote of the conference Asbury acted as general assistant. It was not, however, until late in 1783 that Asbury received a commission from Wesley, naming him general assistant.[6]

The Wesley system of control and management, however, encountered snags in America from the very beginning. The general assistant acting for Wesley was never very popular. Joseph Pilmoor had serious objections to Boardman's management,[7] and Thomas Rankin's rule brought near-rebellion, because he "assumed too much authority over the preachers and people." Even Asbury chafed under it.[8] Bangs observes that Rankin's sternness of character, while sustaining him in the exercise of discipline, was not suited to "the genius of the American people as was the more gentle yet equally firm disposition of Mr. Asbury."

Robert Strawbridge was the principal thorn in the flesh to Wesley's assistants in America. In fact, he paid little attention to them and went his own way very much as he saw fit. Wesley and his assistants always insisted that the Colonial Methodists receive the sacraments at the hands of the Established Church clergy. Owing to the lack of Episcopalian co-operation, this was impossible in any adequate sense. Strawbridge, evidently without authority from anyone, administered

[5] For a discussion of the titles "general assistant," "assistant," and "helpers" see Nathan Bangs, *A History of the Methodist Episcopal Church* (3d ed.; 4 vols.; New York, 1839), I, 74.

[6] *Ibid.*, p. 128.

[7] See Pilmoor's "Journal" (MS) in the Methodist Historical Society, Philadelphia (transcript in the University of Chicago Library).

[8] Bangs, *op. cit.*, pp. 86–87.

the sacraments as and when he saw fit.[9] News of his death in 1781 brought a sigh of relief from Asbury, and he wrote in his *Journal* (September 3, 1781): "He [Strawbridge] is no more: upon the whole, I am inclined to think the Lord took him away in judgment, because he was in a way to do harm to the work." This was, I think, a false judgment on Asbury's part, as the next few years were to prove. As a matter of fact, Strawbridge was ahead of his time, and he may well be called "the first real American Methodist leader."

As for the other preachers from England, with the possible exception of Asbury, it was an unmixed blessing when they decided to return to England. One of the things that Strawbridge was doing more effectively than any other Colonial Methodist preacher was the "raising up" of native American preachers. William Watters, Philip Gatch, Daniel Ruff, and Freeborn Garrettson, all spiritual sons of Strawbridge, had achieved places of leadership by 1778, the year the last of Wesley's missionaries had departed. The very fact that Colonial Methodism made the most rapid progress in the regions where Strawbridge's influence was the most widespread seems to indicate that his "irregularities," as Asbury called them, were more effective than the "regular" procedure which Asbury and the former assistants were attempting to carry on.

Wesley undoubtedly never understood the situation in America. The colonists, as Stevens has well pointed out, "had no traditional attachment to the Anglican Church," and both Wesley and his assistants in America were too Anglican to recognize that fact.[10] Strawbridge fully perceived it, and, "being an Irishman, he shared not in the deferential sympathies of his English brethren for the Establishment." This spirit of independence manifested by Strawbridge and his "sons in the gospel" came to a climax in the midst of the Revolution. Wesley's *Calm Address to the American Colonies* and his other *Calm Addresses*—none of which were calm—in which he took a very strong anti-American position, put a decided strain

[9] For an account of Strawbridge and an estimate of his work see W. W. Sweet, *Men of Zeal: The Romance of American Methodist Beginnings* (New York, 1935), pp. 73–79.

[10] Abel Stevens, *History of the Methodist Church in the United States* (4 vols.; New York, 1864), I, 164.

upon Colonial Methodist attachment to him and led Asbury to remark: "I.... am truly sorry that the venerable man [Wesley] ever dipped into the politics of America."[11]

Asbury's supervision of the Methodist societies in the colonies was interrupted in the midst of the Revolution by his confinement to the state of Delaware from the fall of 1778 to the spring of 1780, owing to his unwillingness to take the oath of allegiance in the colonies where it was required. Delaware was his place of refuge, since it did not require an oath of ministers. A committee of preachers was appointed by the conference of 1777 to have general oversight over the societies during Asbury's forced retirement. During this period the work had gone forward even better than it had previously, especially in Virginia and the Carolinas. Sixteen preachers from New Jersey, Delaware, and the eastern shore of Maryland met with Asbury in a "preparatory conference" in April, 1779, and went on record as confirming Asbury's authority over all the Methodist societies in America. The next May a much larger number of Virginia and Carolina preachers met in a conference at Fluvanna, Virginia, and, contrary to the well-known wishes of both Wesley and Asbury, decided to form a presbytery and ordain preachers in order to secure the sacraments for the growing number of Methodist people being gathered in the expanding societies.[12]

This action greatly distressed Asbury, and it looked for a time as though American Methodism was to suffer a serious division. At the conference in 1780, however, it was finally agreed to suspend the administration of the ordinances for one year until Wesley could be consulted. Undoubtedly this near-division in the ranks of the American Methodists was one of the factors which helped Wesley decide to ordain men for America, once the war was at an end. The suspension of the action of the Fluvanna conference was only a temporary return to personal rule, and that fact Asbury well understood, for, when Dr. Coke arrived in 1784, with instructions from Wesley, he was

[11] Francis Asbury, *Journal* (New York and Cincinnati, n.d.), pp. 1176–77. For an account of Wesley's attitude toward the Revolution see W. W. Sweet, "John Wesley, Tory," *Methodist Quarterly Review,* LXXI (1922), 255–68.

[12] For a fuller account of these happenings see Sweet, *Men of Zeal,* pp. 144–49; see also Sweet, *Methodism in American History* (New York, 1933), pp. 93–97.

soon informed that the American preachers would not accept any longer even John Wesley's directions and that matters must be determined by majority vote.

III

The organizing conference at Baltimore was a new kind of Methodist conference. It was not an advisory body and had been called to determine what course Methodism was to take in an independent America. It decided all matters by majority vote; thus was introduced the *governing* conference into the American Methodist system. Asbury refused to accept his appointment as superintendent from Wesley and insisted that the preachers' wishes in all matters be followed. Neither Wesley nor Coke had visualized the necessity for such procedure, but Asbury was fully aware of its necessity. This marked the end of Wesley's personal rule in American Methodism, but its influence was to last until at least the end of Asbury's life.

The formation of a separate ecclesiastical body of the American Methodists changed the whole character of the Methodist conference. It now had the power to elect deacons and elders and to admit men into the ranks of the ministry and into conference membership. As Methodism expanded geographically and the number of preachers increased, it became necessary to divide the annual conference into sections. From 1785 to 1787 the conference met in three sections; in 1788 it was held in six sections; and by 1791–92 the number of sections had become seventeen. These sectional meetings were not separate conferences but sections of one undivided conference held in different localities for the convenience of its members. The sectional conferences were created at the discretion of the bishops to accommodate their itinerant schedule. Legislation was carried from conference to conference by the bishops, and it required a majority of all to make it valid. The minutes were recorded as of one conference.

In 1796 six separate annual conferences with definite boundaries were formed—the Eastern (New England), the Philadelphia, the Baltimore, the Virginia, the South Carolina, and the Western. This fixed the pattern of the annual conference, which has remained substantially the same from that day to this. The rise of the annual conference is a good example of the way in which the organizational structure of American Methodism developed to meet the new demands of an expanding society.[13] Still another development was the rise of the "general conference," which came into existence in 1792. Before it emerged, however, a council, made up of the bishops and presiding elders, was tried out as a substitute for a general conference, since the rapid increase in the number of preachers was complicating the situation.[14] This had been proposed by Asbury as a superbody to oversee the affairs of the church. Never popular with the preachers, because of their suspicion that it tended toward the centralization of power, it held but two meetings—1789 and 1790.

Jesse Lee states that the establishment of the council did serious injury to the "Methodist connection," since it served as the starting-point for the opposition to Asbury on the part of James O'Kelley because of the power Asbury exercised, which finally led to what has come to be called "the O'Kelley schism."[15] Since the presiding elders were all the appointees of the bishops, the council therefore was a hand-picked body and very much under the thumb of the bishops and especially of Asbury. Asbury was reluctant to give up the council, but the antagonism to it was too powerful to resist, and to meet the crisis the first general conference was called to meet in Baltimore in November, 1792. Here it was agreed that thereafter a general conference was to be held every four years.

It was at this first general conference that the O'Kelley schism occurred. O'Kelley had introduced a resolution providing for an appeal to the conference by any preacher who felt himself injured by the appointment assigned him by the bishop. It was when this motion was lost by a large majority that O'Kelley and his followers withdrew. It seems strange from this distance that James O'Kelley did not receive larger support in his attempt to further democratize the

[13] For the boundaries of the first annual conferences see Robert Emory, *History of the Discipline of the Methodist Episcopal Church* (New York, 1844), pp. 211–12. In 1820 the number of conferences had grown to twelve and by 1840 to thirty-four. The thirty-fourth was in West Africa and was called the "Liberia Conference" (*ibid.*, pp. 225–28). The conferences from 1796 to 1816 were called "yearly" conferences; since 1816 they have been called "annual" conferences.

[14] Jesse Lee was one of the strong opponents of the council. See his account in *A Short History of the Methodists in the United States of America, etc.* (Baltimore, 1810), pp. 149–59.

[15] See Lee's account (*ibd.*, pp. 176–93).

Methodist system.[16] There is no doubt but that the O'Kelley plan would have weakened the effectiveness of the system, and the known opposition of Asbury to any change was doubtless one of the principal factors in its defeat.

The rise of the office of presiding elder is another example of the way in which Methodist organization kept pace with frontier demands. The office of presiding elder was established by action of the first general conference (1792), although before that time the term is found applied in the minutes of the conferences to men appointed by the bishops to supervise a group of circuits. The duties of the new official were to have oversight of all the preachers in his district, both traveling and located; to change, receive, or suspend traveling preachers in the absence of the bishop; to be present as far as possible at all quarterly meetings of the circuits in his district; and to preside in the district conference in the absence of the bishop. The need for the new official was obvious. Methodism was a rapidly expanding movement. From 1784 to 1792 the number of preachers had increased from 83 to 266; the circuits from 42 to 135; and the membership from 14,988 to 65,980. Though officially there were two bishops, Francis Asbury and Thomas Coke, the latter was never fully accepted by the preachers; and in 1787 he had agreed to limit his activities in America. Thus the superintendence of the growing church was largely in the hands of Asbury, a task too large for one man. Hence the necessity for the new official, the presiding elder.[17]

At this early period only a relatively small number of the circuit preachers were ordained. Of the 266 preachers in 1792, only 78 were fully ordained and qualified to administer the sacrament of the Lord's Supper. As a consequence, it became one of the recognized functions of the presiding elder to administer the sacraments when he made his quarterly rounds of the circuits in his district. The rise

[16] For the development of the O'Kelley movement see *ibid.*, pp. 202–6.

[17] *Ibid.*, p. 183. See also Samuel Drew, *The Life of the Rev. Thomas Coke, LL.D., etc.* (New York, 1818). In the year 1787 Wesley had written directing that Richard Whatcoat was to be ordained joint superintendent with Asbury. The conference refused to carry out Wesley's wishes, though Coke argued that it was under obligation to do so, since it had been agreed at the Christmas Conference to obey Wesley "in matters belonging to Church government." The preachers answered that they were not "ready now to obey his command" (Sweet, *Methodism in American History,* p. 115).

of the office of presiding elder made it possible to carry on the work of expansion without increasing the number of bishops. Thus Asbury carried on as the only full-time bishop from 1792 until Richard Whatcoat was elected to that office in 1800. The direct and close supervision of the circuits performed by the presiding elders was therefore of great importance and was one of the principal reasons why Methodism was more effective than any other religious body in the entire nation in the period of great population movement.[18]

By the year 1808 the church had grown so large and the number of preachers had so increased that it was no longer practicable for all of them to attend the general conferences.[19] Accordingly, at the general conference of that year a plan for a delegated body was adopted, which provided that there should be one delegate for every five members of each annual conference to be chosen either by seniority or choice, according as each annual conference should determine. It provided also that the general conferences were to meet every four years on the first of May. The conference was to have full power to make all rules and regulations for the church under six restrictions, which, however, might be altered by a joint recommendation of all the annual conferences and a majority of two-thirds of the succeeding general conference.[20] One of the principal reasons for the adoption of a delegated lawmaking body was that under the old plan the annual conferences near the seat of the general conference sent a great majority of the members. Thus at the general conference of 1804 the Philadelphia and Baltimore conferences had two-thirds of the total members present, while the conferences remote from the place of convening were inadequately represented. The memorial for a delegated general conference was presented by the New York conference

[18] Resulting from the controversies in the 1820's, which finally led to the formation of the Methodist Protestant church, district conferences were authorized, to be called at least once a year in each presiding elder's district and to be composed of all local preachers in the district who shall have been licensed at least two years. It possessed the right to grant and renew licenses of proper persons to be local preachers and to recommend candidates to the annual conference for orders in the local connection or for admission on trial in the traveling connection. It also possessed power of discipline over its members (Emory, *op. cit.*, pp. 166–67).

[19] In 1792 it was provided that all traveling preachers in full connection shall be members of the general conference. In 1800 the additional qualification was added that they shall "have travelled four years" (*ibid.*, p. 111).

[20] *Ibid.*, pp. 111–14.

and was indorsed by three other conferences—the Eastern (New England), the Western, and the South Carolina.[21] The memorial urged a delegated conference in the interest of "equal representation" and also as a means of saving expense and loss of time, as well as the loss to the church, which resulted when all the preachers throughout the country attended the prolonged sessions of the general lawmaking body. These arguments were unanswerable, and, although there was considerable opposition at first, it eventually carried when presented item by item. Bangs states:

> I suppose some voted against it from fear that, if adopted, they could never attend another General Conference; and others were jealous of their rights, fearing to intrust the affairs of the Church to so few hands; while some opposed it from opposition to Bishop Asbury, with whom it was a favorite measure, for notwithstanding his great merits, he had his enemies.[22]

The action of the general conference of 1808 in providing for a delegated general conference with the statement of the powers belonging to that body, together with the so-called "restrictive rules," has been called the constitution of the Methodist Episcopal church.[23] This marks the beginning of a new era in American Methodism, since it provided for the stabilization of Methodist church government. Thus Methodism became more and more "like a drilled army ready for the charge."

IV

More than any other single factor, "itineracy" was responsible for the rapid spread of Methodism throughout the United States in the frontier period. This type of ministry had its origin in early English

[21] For the memorials, etc., presented to the general conference of 1808 favoring a delegated conference see *Journals of the General Conference of the Methodist Episcopal Church,* Vol. I: *1796–1836* (New York, 1855), pp. 76–78, 79, 82–83. See also J. M. Buckley, *Constitutional and Parliamentary History of the Methodist Episcopal Church* (New York, 1912), chaps. xvi–xviii.

[22] Abel Stevens, *Life and Times of Nathan Bangs* (New York, 1863), p. 171; Buckley, *op. cit.,* p. 109.

[23] For a discussion of constitution and the restrictive rules see Buckley, *op. cit.,* pp. 121–234. See also H. M. Du Bose, *Life of Joshua Soule* (Nashville, 1916), chap v, and J. J. Tigert, *Constitutional History of American Episcopal Methodism* (Nashville, 1904), chap xii.

Methodism. In a real sense, Wesley himself was the first Methodist itinerant, when in 1739 he began to shuttle between London and Bristol. Wesley never had a parish or a settled ministry, except his brief experience as his father's curate at Wroote, a part of Epworth parish, and his two years at Savannah, Georgia, may be so called. As a result of his own experience and the success which attended the work of his early helpers, Wesley was soon convinced that the itinerant ministry not only was best suited for providing spiritual guidance to converts but was also supported by apostolic example, for had not Paul followed such a plan in Christianizing the Roman world? Indeed, as Ezra Squier Tipple tells us, "the Itinerant preacher is in apostolic succession." Wesley came to believe that the English parish system was entirely inadequate for the time and opposed it for Methodists. When suggestions were made that some of his preachers be settled, he invariably turned a deaf ear. Commenting on one such proposal made in 1756, he stated:

> Be their talents ever so great, they will ere long grow dead themselves, and so will most of those that hear them. I know, were I myself to preach one whole year in one place, I should preach both myself and most of my congregation asleep. Nor can I believe it was ever the will of our Lord that any one congregation should have one teacher only. We have found by long and constant experience that a frequent change of teachers is best. This preacher has one talent, that another. No one whom I ever yet knew has all the talents which are needful for beginning, continuing, and perfecting the work of grace in an whole congregation.[24]

Noting the failure of the societies in Glasgow to show any increase, he placed the blame on the fact that "one preacher stays here two or three months at a time, preaching on Sunday mornings and three or four evenings in a week. Can a Methodist preacher preserve either bodily health or spiritual life with this exercise? And if he is but half alive, what will the people be?"[25]

Not only was the circuit system and the traveling ministry effective

[24] From a letter to Samuel Walker, a Church of England clergyman, in answer to a letter from him (August 16, 1756) urging Wesley to take steps to bring the Methodists closer to the Church of England, proposing that some Methodist preachers be ordained and others "be fixed to certain Societies" (*Letters of John Wesley,* ed. Telford, III, 192–96).

[25] N. Curnock, *Journal of John Wesley* (8 vols., 1909–16), VI, 19–20.

in eighteenth-century England, but, transplanted to the New World, they soon proved ideally suited to the American situation. When Francis Asbury appeared on the American scene, he found that there was a tendency on the part of Boardman and Pilmoor to center their activities in New York and Philadelphia. He states in his *Journal:* "My brethren seem unwilling to leave the cities, but I think I will show them the way." Immediately he set about forming a circuit, preaching anywhere and everywhere opportunity offered. He has been credited with saving the itinerant feature of Methodism for America, and he himself was probably "the greatest itinerant of the Christian Centuries."

His home was on "the road." He had no other. When he came to America he rented no house, he hired no lodgings, he made no arrangements to board anywhere, but simply set out upon the Long Road, and was traveling forty-five years later when Death finally caught up with him.[26]

The circuit system and the itinerant ministry belonged together.[27] The particular advantage of itineracy and the circuit system where population is sparce was that a single circuit preacher could supply a plurality of societies. On any new frontier where population was scattered and settlements far between, the circuits were vast in extent, often a hundred and even more miles around, and the number of preaching places numbered anywhere from twenty to thirty, sometimes even more.[28] This necessitated preaching every day in the week, with the possible exception of Monday, when the circuit-rider rested from the especially heavy duties of the Sabbath, for, on the early frontier, there developed what was called the "two-day" meeting, held at some one place on the circuit, lasting from Saturday afternoon to Sunday evening.

As Abel Stevens puts it: "The usual stationary ministers wait for

[26] Ezra S. Tipple, *Francis Asbury* (New York, 1916), pp. 158–59.

[27] Abel Stevens, *An Essay on Church Polity, etc.* (New York, 1847), esp. chap. ii, "Itineracy," pp. 138–60.

[28] As late as 1825 the Vincennes Circuit in Indiana had twenty-one preaching places (W. W. Sweet, *Circuit-Rider Days in Indiana* [Indianapolis, 1916], p. 42). In 1805–6 the Miami Circuit in Ohio had twenty-seven preaching places (Lakin MSS, "Preaching Places on the Miami Circuit, Ohio, 1805–1806, of Benjamin Lakin," with texts of his sermons and accounts).

the call of the people. . . . ; the Methodist ministry goes forth to call the people." The story of the establishment of any new circuit on the American frontier would verify the truth of this statement. The circuit-riders were constantly adding new preaching places to their circuits, and the presiding elders were continually on the lookout for new settlements in the process of forming.[29] To these new settlements preachers would be sent and new circuits formed at any time of the year, under the supervision of the presiding elders. Since one of the duties of the presiding elder was "to change, receive, or suspend preachers in his district during the intervals of the conferences, and in the absence of the bishop," he had power to act immediately, without waiting for the authorization of the conference.

Generally at least two preachers were sent to the larger circuits, a younger man usually being associated with an older, designated junior and senior preachers. The younger man profited from the older man's experience, for there were no formal schools in which the circuit preachers might receive training, except the school of experience. The early trans-Alleghenian circuit-riders were graduates of "Brush College," which, according to John Strange, was "more ancient though less pretentious than Yale or Harvard or Princeton." The curriculum was constituted of such subjects as "the philosophy of nature and the mysteries of redemption," while the library consisted of the "Word of God, the Discipline and the hymn book, supplemented by trees and brooks and stones, all of which were full of wisdom, and sermons and speeches; and her parchments of literary honors were the horse and the saddle bags."[30]

The fact that the Methodist had become the largest Protestant body in America by the 1840's is proof, according to Abel Stevens, of the "remarkable superiority of the Methodist economy."[31] In 1844 just sixty years had elapsed since the formation of the Methodist Episcopal church. Some of the American churches had been operating in the New World more than two hundred years, and others more than a hundred, yet by 1844 the Methodists, with 1,068,525 members, 3,988

[29] For an account of the forming of the Whitewater Circuit in Indiana in 1806 see Sweet, *Circuit-Rider Days in Indiana,* pp. 5–7.

[30] J. C. Smith, *Reminiscences of Early Methodism in Indiana* (Indianapolis, 1879), pp. 38–39.

[31] Stevens, *An Essay on Church Polity,* p. 148.

itinerant preachers, and 7,730 local preachers, outnumbered by nearly one-half any other Protestant body. The Baptists ranked next with 632,200 communicants. Even in New England, the thorniest soil for Methodist circuit-riders in the whole country, the Methodists had become second only to the Congregationalists in numbers, and according to Stevens, "first in progress."

The learned and accomplished Presbyterian, Robert Baird, who probably knew more about organized religion in America than any other man of his time, stated in his *Religion in America* published in 1843:

> The whole land is covered with a network system of [Methodist] stations and circuits, and the Gospel is carried into thousands of the most remote as well as the most secluded and thinly-peopled neighborhoods. This denomination has made great exertions to increase the number of its church edifices within the last few years. But its itinerating ministers preach in thousands of places where no such buildings are yet erected, or at least none belonging to that denomination. In these cases they hold their meetings in school-houses, court-houses, and private houses.
>
> No American Christian who takes a comprehensive view of the progress of religion in his country .... will .... fail to recognize in the Methodist economy, as well as in the zeal, the devoted piety, and the efficiency of its ministry, one of the most powerful elements in the religious prosperity of the United States, as well as one of the firmest pillars of their civil and political institutions.[32]

Itineracy was a sacrificial system in that it called for constant change and movement on the part of the ministry, but its hardships were "abundantly indemnified by its singular usefulness." It enabled the Methodists to bring the gospel to the poor throughout the length and breadth of an expanding America, and, to use Stevens' phrase, "its fruits are like the herbage of the fields."[33]

By the end of the third decade of the nineteenth century there was a growing trend toward a stationed ministry, which caused great concern among the older ministers. In Peter Cartwright's opinion it tended "to locality and congregationalism," and it would have been

[32] *Religion in America, or an Account of the Origin, Relation to the State and the Present Condition of the Evangelical Churches in the United States, with Notice of the Unevangelical Denominations* (1st ed., 1843; New York, 1856), pp. 496–97.

[33] *Ibid.*, p. 154.

far better for the Methodist church had it never had a station. His advice was: "Put all the work on circuits, and put on as many preachers as the people need, and are able to support, and let the church be blessed with the spice of variety and a constant interchange of preachers."[34]

With the rapid increase of urban population in the United States after the middle of the century, it came to be generally believed that itineracy was not suitable to the larger towns and cities, though the circuit system and the traveling ministry continued effective in rural sections and on the new frontiers. While this change was going on in America, the Wesleyan Methodists in England still persisted in maintaining the circuit system even in their largest cities, and to this day English Methodism maintains it successfully.[35]

V

One of the most important functions of the Methodist circuit-rider was that of co-ordinating the activities of the class leaders, the exhorters, and the local preachers. These constituted the local ministry, as contrasted with the traveling ministry. Like the itineracy, the use of lay preachers originated with John Wesley, and, as has been noted, it was through this type of ministry that Methodism was brought to America. After American Methodism became a separate ecclesiastical body, with an ordained ministry, the local ministry continued to operate, though with somewhat different functions. Like the circuit system and the itineracy, the local ministry—the class leader and the local preacher—were easily adapted to American frontier needs and occupied an important place in the success of frontier Methodism.

The local unit in American Methodism was the class, made up of a few "believers" in a given community, over whom a class leader was placed. The class met at frequent intervals, generally once a week, and on the frontier in the homes of the members. It was the duty of

[34] Peter Cartwright, *Autobiography* (New York, 1856), p. 503. See also Stevens, *An Essay on Church Polity,* chap. v, "Objections to, and Dangers of, the Itineracy."

[35] During a four months' residence in Cambridge, England, in 1937, I was privileged in getting some acquaintance with the Cambridge circuit. It consisted of twenty-three churches and chapels, five ordained ministers, who gave all their time to the circuit, and over one hundred lay preachers, who took their turn in supplying the preaching in the chapels, under the supervision of the "head of the circuit."

the class leader to "carefully inquire how every soul in his class prospers; not only how each person observes the outward rules, but how he grows in the knowledge and love of God."[36]

The exhorter represented the next step above the class leader in the local ministry, the third step being the local preacher. All these officials were under the direct supervision of the circuit-rider and the quarterly conference. The circuit-preacher met the classes on each round of his circuit and at least once a quarter examined into the faithfulness of each of the leaders. The quarterly conference was made up of all the traveling and local preachers of a circuit, together with the exhorters, stewards, and class leaders. The presiding elder was its presiding officer. The quarterly conference licensed the exhorters and local preachers, and it was a requirement that licenses be renewed each year. After 1789, local preachers might receive ordination as deacons, and at the general conference of 1812 local deacons were made eligible for elder's orders. Both offices were carefully guarded to prevent unworthy men from securing ordination.[37]

One of the hardships of the itinerant system was the difficulty on the part of the circuit-riders in maintaining homes and families. The first four bishops—Asbury, Whatcoat, McKendree, and George—were all unmarried and had no homes of their own. The poverty of the frontier also meant that the people could not adequately support a married ministry. The organizing conference of 1784 had fixed the circuit-rider's salary at "twenty-four pounds (Pennsylvania currency)." At the general conference of 1792 it was placed at $64 and traveling expenses, which included such items as ferriage fees, horseshoeing, and provisions for the circuit-riders and their mounts. To the

[36] In the Preamble to Wesley's *General Rules,* published in 1743, occurs this statement as to the classes and the duties of class leaders: "That it may the more easily be discerned, whether they (the members) are indeed working out their own salvation, each society is divided into smaller companies, called Classes, according to their respective places of abode. There are about twelve persons in every class: one of whom is stiled *The Leader*. It is his business, to see each person in his class once a week at least, in order, (1) to enquire how their soul prosper. (2) To advise, reprove, comfort, or exhort, as occasion may require. (3) To receive what they are willing to give towards the relief of the poor" (Emory, *op. cit.,* pp. 177–80). In English Methodism there was a still smaller unity known as the "band" made up of the more spiritually minded (*ibid.,* pp. 183–86). The band system, though introduced into America, never developed here.

[37] *Ibid.,* pp. 144, 164–74.

question, "What shall be annually allowed the wives of married preachers?" the answer was, "Sixty-four dollars if they be in want of it." The minutes of the Western Conference lists the deficiencies of the preachers year by year, and it was seldom that a circuit-rider received the full amount due him.[38] Two entries in the minutes for 1803 will illustrate the attitude of the bachelor preachers toward their married brethren. William Burke, the secretary of the conference, reported a large deficiency, hoping to receive some financial help from the Chartered Fund.[39] The conference, however, took the following action: "We judge that it is right for Bro. Burk to pay board for his wife, and that the people, if they please, may pay the board for him, but that he has no Just claim on the Conference for it." At this same conference session Benjamin Lakin reported a deficiency of $28.95, regarding which the conference stated:

> But it appears that the Circuit maintained Bro. Lakin's wife and her Beast; gratis. It is therefore our opinion, that it is ungenerous in him to bring a demand on Conference; and seeing there are others more needy, it is our judgement that he ought not have anything.

In consequence of this situation, marriage was discouraged among the traveling preachers, and, when marriage did take place, it often meant that the preacher was soon forced to "locate." In the early years the "located" preacher automatically lost his conference membership, but he generally continued to function in the locality where he settled

[38] The manuscript "Minutes of the Western Conference (1800–1811)" are at Ohio Wesleyan University. They were published with introduction and notes in W. W. Sweet's *Rise of Methodism in the West* (New York, 1920).

[39] The general conference of 1796 had authorized the creation of "the Chartered Fund" for the relief of "distressed traveling preachers, their families, worn-out preachers, and the widows and orphans of preachers." The fund was to be supported by voluntary gifts and was to be under the direction of a board of trustees. Incorporation was secured through the legislature of Pennsylvania. For a number of years Thomas Haskins was the treasurer of the Chartered Fund (Emory, *op. cit.,* pp. 251–53). Previous to the establishment of the Chartered Fund, Asbury had been collecting what he termed a "mite" subscription for the relief of the preachers and their families. No one was to give more than a dollar. The "mite" subscription manuscripts are in the library of Drew Theological Seminary. There was also established a "preacher's fund." Preachers paid into it $2.67 on admission to the conference and thereafter $2.00 annual dues. This was to provide for worn-out preachers and for their widows and orphans (John F. Hurst, *The History of Methodism* [7 vols.; New York, 1902–4], IV, 323).

as a local preacher. The great loss of traveling ministers through their "location" is shown by the fact that, of the 1,616 preachers received into the conferences from the beginning of American Methodism to 1814, 821 had located, most of them within a relatively few years after their admission; 131 had died in the service; 34 had been expelled; and 25 had withdrawn. As late as 1809, of the 84 preachers in the Virginia Conference, only 3 had wives.[40]

The Methodist system functioned effectively, not so much because of its mechanical perfection, but rather because of the self-sacrificing devotion of the circuit-riders, who, like Paul, counted not their lives dear unto themselves.

[40] This information is obtained from Bangs, *History of the Methodist Episcopal Church,* II, 421–54. Here are lists of all the preachers received to 1814.

CHAPTER IV

Methodist Growth and Expansion, 1784–1850

THE rapid expansion of Methodism westward, beginning immediately following the achievement of Independence, was a matter of major importance for the future of the new nation. Fortunately, American Methodism began its independent existence with a national view of its task and with an organization suited to an indefinite geographic expansion. It was not handicapped, as were the Presbyterians, Congregationalists, and Lutherans, each of whom were primarily concerned not with frontier society as a whole but with particular groups. The Congregational missionary in the West sought out New England settlements, and thus western Congregationalism was largely a transplanted New England. The Presbyterian frontier preacher tended to limit his activities to people of Presbyterian background and to Scotch-Irish or Scotch communities. The Lutherans were largely concerned with people of German ancestry. The Methodists and Baptists, on the other hand, went forth into the western wilderness to win people of all kinds to the Christian way of life. Neither felt any special commitment to any one class or group but thought in terms of western society as a whole. This one fact helps to account for the wide distribution of these two bodies throughout the nation today.

As has already been noted, at the time of the formation of the Methodist Episcopal church at Baltimore, completed on January 10, 1785, there were 14,988 Methodists in the United States, 83 preachers, and 43 circuits, covering the region from New York City on the north to the Carolinas on the south. The major proportion of the members were found in Delaware, Maryland, and Virginia. New York, New Jersey, and Pennsylvania contained only some fifteen hundred Methodists gathered into seven circuits. The region lying north of Long Island Sound had not as yet been entered, but within six years after American Methodism had become an independent body the entire settled part of the nation east of the Alleghenies had been potentially covered with a network of circuits. The very nature of Methodist organization, combined with the burning zeal of the circuit-riders under Bishop Asbury's devoted supervision, made Methodist expansion a natural and inevitable consequence.

Outside a narrow fringe of population along the Atlantic seaboard the entire nation was in 1785 a frontier, though we are primarily concerned in this chapter with the expansion of Methodism in the great region between the Alleghenies and the Mississippi River from the close of the Revolution to the year 1850.

Methodism first made its way over the Allegheny Mountains in the population movement pushing westward from Virginia and North Carolina, into eastern Tennessee and Kentucky during and immediately following the Revolution. In the year 1782 there were circuits forming on the headwaters of two of the rivers that flow together to form the Tennessee—the Yadkin and the Holston—the circuits taking the names of the rivers. Two years later the Redstone Circuit in southwestern Pennsylvania appeared in the minutes, and in 1786 these three earliest trans-Alleghenian Methodist circuits reported a combined membership of 1,210, of whom 11 were colored. The same year the Kentucky Circuit was formed, with James Haw and Benjamin Ogden as circuit-preachers. Haw was a fully ordained preacher and had previously served several circuits in Virginia. Ogden was a native of New Jersey who had served in the army during the Revolution, and his appointment to the Kentucky Circuit with Haw began his itinerant ministry. Both ceased the "traveling ministry" after a few years because of marriage, as was true of a great proportion of the early western Methodist preachers. Haw left the Methodist church to become an O'Kelley disciple and later a Presbyterian. Ogden also became involved in the O'Kelley schism, though later he was readmitted to the conference and to the active ministry.[1]

I

How a circuit-rider succeeded in securing a foothold for his work in a new country is illustrated by the early activities of Benjamin Ogden. Ogden probably came to Kentucky by way of the Ohio River, landing

[1] For the most recent account of the beginnings of Kentucky Methodism see W. E. Arnold, *A History of Methodism in Kentucky* (2 vols.; Winchester, Ky., 1935), I, 35–45.

at Maysville. Making his way to Simon Kenton's Station, about three miles to the southwest, he found the cabin of Thomas Stevenson and his wife, Methodists from Maryland. There he was welcomed and there the first regular Methodist preaching took place. Ogden visited among and prayed with the families in the station, and before he left for central Kentucky he had formed a class, evidently with Stevenson as the class leader. At the end of the first year ninety members were reported from the Kentucky Circuit.

By 1800 there were at least fourteen circuits west of the Allegheny Mountains: six in Kentucky, two in Tennessee, two in the Ohio Territory, two in southwestern Pennsylvania, and one each in western Virginia and western North Carolina. Ohio Methodism dates from 1798, when John Kobler, the presiding elder of the Kentucky District, crossed the Ohio River and preached in the cabins of Kentucky Methodists who had recently moved across the river. The first Ohio circuit was the Miami; the second the Scioto, which included settlements along both banks of those rivers. Methodism did not reach Indiana Territory until after the turn of the century with the formation of the Whitewater Circuit in 1805. Methodist preachers, however, had crossed the Ohio into Indiana as early as 1801, when regular preaching was begun in what was known as Clark's Grant. One of the first Methodist preachers to cross the Ohio into what is now Indiana was Benjamin Lakin. He and Ralph Lotspeich were the preachers on the Salt River and Shelby Circuit in Kentucky. Lakin thus records in his "Journal" his first crossing into Indiana:

Sat and Sund. [April] 9 and 10 [1803]. Preached in the Ilenois grant with some liberty, on Sund. morning. I felt God to be with me here in this wilderness, we had near 30 communicants and a melting time. This place has for some time lain on my mind. I had thoughts of takeing it into the circuit. (Which we have since done, there is a prospect of good being done. Some have been converted and others are under good impressions)....[2]

Lakin's career was typical of many other frontier circuit-riders. A native of Maryland, his family moved to the Redstone country in southwestern Pennsylvania. Here, under the preaching of Richard

[2] "Journal of Rev. Benjamin Lakin" (13 manuscript booklets), No. 3, p. 78. These journals are now in the possession of the University of Chicago. Extracts from Lakin's "Journal" constitute chap. vii of this volume.

Whatcoat, he was converted in 1791, when he was twenty-four years of age. Two years later the family moved to Kentucky, and almost immediately Lakin felt the call to preach, and, after licensure, he began his ministry in 1794. We have no information as to his formal education. His marriage in 1798 caused him to locate and settle on a farm. Restless and dissatisfied, he sought admission to the newly formed Western Conference in 1800, where he was ordained deacon and assigned to the Limestone Circuit. He continued in the active itineracy until 1817. Benjamin Lakin's "Journal" in thirteen small manuscript booklets, together with several hundred miscellaneous papers, including plans of circuit, lists of sermons preached, and notes on books read, have recently come into the possession of the University of Chicago. They show that he was a sincere and capable preacher. He became one of the recognized leaders of his conference. His level of intelligence was high, as is indicated by his relatively wide reading and the simplicity and clarity with which he expressed himself.

Allen Wiley, who later became a leading Methodist preacher in Indiana, gives the following account of a sermon he heard Lakin preach in 1806 or 1807. Wiley grew to manhood in southeastern Indiana, his family having migrated from Kentucky to the Whitewater Valley in 1804, and was seventeen or eighteen years of age when he heard Lakin preach at a quarterly meeting, or it may have been a "two-day" meeting, held at McCarty's, one of the preaching places on the Whitewater Circuit.[3] In the midst of his sermon the preacher suddenly paused and said in a most impressive manner, "I feel an impression that there is some young man or woman in this house who will be tramping in hell before this time next year." Immediately, as Wiley tells us, "all the young people whom I could see became deathly pale; and I suppose myself among the rest; for I felt as awful as death, judgement and eternity could make me."[4]

The first circuit to which Peter Cartwright was assigned by the Western Conference in 1804 was the Salt River and Shelby Circuit in

[3] See the Lakin manuscript.

[4] Allen Wiley, "Methodism in Southeastern Indiana," *Western Christian Advocate,* 1845–46. Reprinted in *Indiana Magazine of History* in the four issues of Vol. XXIII (1927). The above account is found in the *Western Christian Advocate,* December 5, 1845; in the reprint *Indiana Magazine of History,* p. 21.

Kentucky, with Benjamin Lakin as the senior preacher. It was a six-week circuit, which meant that it took six weeks to make the rounds of the preaching places once, and extended from the Green River on the south to the Ohio River on the north and across the Ohio into Clark's Grant in the present state of Indiana, then a part of Illinois Territory. Benjamin Lakin had charge of the circuit, while the youthful Cartwright's duty was to preach, meet the classes and visit among the people, and especially among the sick, and "then" he states, "to my books and study."[5] A part of the duty of the senior preacher and the presiding elder was to see that the young junior preachers had some acquaintance with books and did some studying.

Looking back over fifty years to the early experiences of his ministry, Peter Cartwright thus describes the backwoods Methodists of that early day.

> The Methodists in that early day dressed plain; attended their meetings faithfully, especially preaching, prayer and class meetings; they wore no jewelry, no ruffles; they would frequently walk three or four miles to class meetings, and home again, on Sundays; they would go thirty or forty miles to their quarterly meetings, and think it a glorious privilege to meet their presiding elder, and the rest of the preachers. They could, nearly every soul of them, sing our hymns and spiritual songs. They religiously kept the Sabbath day; many of them abstained from dram-drinking, not because the temperance reformation was ever heard of in that day, but because it was interdicted in the General Rules of our Discipline. Methodists of that day stood up and faced their preacher when they sung; they kneeled down in the public congregation as well as elsewhere, when the preacher said, "Let us pray." .... Parents did not allow their children to go to balls or plays; they did not send them to dancing-schools; they generally fasted once a week, and almost universally on the Friday before each quarterly meeting.[6]

The settlement of Ohio was begun at Marietta at the mouth of the Muskingum in 1788 by a Connecticut Land Company, and the community was dominated religiously by Congregationalists. There the first Congregational church in the West was formed in 1796.

[5] *Autobiography of Peter Cartwright, the Backwoods Preacher,* ed. W. P. Strickland (Cincinnati and New York, 1856), pp. 74–80, 167.

[6] *Ibid.*, pp. 74–75.

Methodism found its first foothold in Ohio in the southwest corner of the state among the settlers along the Miami and Mad rivers. John Kobler, presiding elder of the Kentucky District, crossed the Ohio in 1798, looking for Kentucky Methodists who had moved into the new territory. Two years previously a class had been formed in what is now Cincinnati by a local preacher, Francis McCormick, a Virginian, who had migrated to Ohio by way of Cincinnati. The Miami Circuit appeared first in the minutes in 1799; in 1800 a second Ohio circuit, the Scioto, appeared; and in 1804 two additional names, Muskingum and Hockhocking, were listed among the Ohio appointments. That year also an Ohio district appeared, composed of five circuits, two of them extending into what is now West Virginia and Kentucky.

Early settlements in the West were along the streams, and, as a consequence, when circuits were formed, they took the names of the creeks or rivers along whose banks the settlers were to be found. In 1806 the Whitewater Circuit was formed along the banks of the river of that name, in the southeast corner of what is now Indiana. Though its course lies mostly in Indiana, the Whitewater empties into the Ohio River just across the boundary line in the state of Ohio. By 1805 two settlements had been formed on the east branch of that river, one by people from Kentucky, a little south of the present city of Richmond, the other by South Carolinians, just above the present town of Brookville. Among the settlers in both settlements were Methodists who were anxious to have regular preaching. A petition was sent to John Sale, the presiding elder of the Ohio District, which covered the whole southern part of Ohio and two circuits across the Ohio River.[7] In response to the petition, Sale sent Joseph Oglesby, a young man just beginning his ministry, to minister to the Whitewater settlers.[8] Oglesby started out at once for his new field in the spring of 1806, and by the time the conference met in September he had formed a four-week circuit along both banks of the Whitewater,

[7] The following were the circuits in the Ohio District in 1806; Miami, Mad River, Scioto, Hockhocking, Muskingum, and in Kentucky the Little Kanawha and Guyandott (see the John Sale letters in chap. vi).

[8] See the Wiley article in the *Western Christian Advocate,* October 17, 1845. In this letter Wiley quotes from a letter of Joseph Oglesby in which the story of the founding of the Whitewater Circuit is told in detail. The Whitewater Circuit appears in the minutes first in 1807 and is miscalled the White River (*Indiana Magazine of History,* XXIII, 21–23). Oglesby later became a physician in Madison, Indiana.

had organized numerous classes, and had appointed class leaders, and at the conference he reported sixty-seven members.

The forming of the Whitewater Circuit will serve as a typical illustration of the way in which the Methodist system made it possible to keep pace with moving population. Not infrequently a Methodist circuit-rider called at the cabin of a settler before the mud in his stick chimney was dry or before the weight poles were on the roof. "It [Methodism] alone was so organized as to be able to follow step by step this moveable population, and to carry the gospel even to the most distant cabin. It alone could be present whenever a grave was opened, or an infant was found in its cradle."[9]

Methodism was not only expanding westward in the latter years of the eighteenth and the early years of the nineteenth centuries, but it was pushing out in all directions. In the 1790's New England was invaded, and about the same time it began its march into central and western New York. In 1797, at the South Carolina Conference, Bishop Asbury sent Tobias Gibson to the Southwest, and he became the founder of Methodism in the territory that is now the states of Mississippi and Louisiana.[10] A native of Georgia and a man of considerable wealth, Gibson gave up a life of ease to proclaim the gospel in the wilderness. He had been a member of the conference since 1792, when as a young man of twenty-one he began his itinerant ministry. Though already broken in health, he volunteered for the whole lower Mississippi Valley and after the conference of 1799 started off alone on horseback for the Cumberland River. On reaching its banks, he sold his horse and, securing a canoe, paddled down the Cumberland to the Ohio, and thence down the Ohio to the Mississippi and then seven hundred miles down the Mississippi to the city of Natchez. The first year on this vast wilderness circuit he reported sixty members. To use the words of Nathan Bangs: "Four times he traveled the wilderness, a distance of six hundred miles, being conducted by some

[9] This quotation is taken from a lengthy review of Peter Cartwright's *Autobiography* which appeared in the *Revue des deux mondes* (Paris) by A. Cucheval-Clavigny, translated and reprinted under the title "Peter Cartwright and Preaching in the West," *Methodist Review,* LIV, 556–77; LV, 69–88.

[10] Abel Stevens, *Memorials of the Introduction of Methodism into the Eastern States, etc.* (Boston, 1848).

friendly Indians on his devious way. The burning love of God which impelled him on this work, filled his mouth with persuasive arguments in behalf of the gospel."[11] Though worn down by excessive labors, Gibson came to the Western Conference in 1802 and so successfully pled the cause of the lower Mississippi that he was given an assistant, Moses Floyd. Thus it was that Methodism made its way into every corner of the land, carried forward by the indefatigable zeal of an ever increasing army of circuit-riders.

The year following Tobias Gibson's death in 1805, Elisha W. Bowman answered Asbury's call for volunteers to go to Louisiana, which only two years before had been added to the territory of the United States by purchase from France. Bowman was assigned to the Appalousas (Opelousas) Circuit, a region lying west of the Mississippi, a hundred miles or more south of Natchez. He made his way by horseback to New Orleans, which, he said, he found as filthy as a pigsty and in a state of moral corruption. He obtained permission from the governor to preach in the city hall, but, on going to the hall on the Sabbath, he found it locked against him. The same thing happened the following Sunday. His only recourse was to preach to a few straggling people on the street. Hearing of an American settlement some two hundred miles to the west, he turned his face in that direction, though the way led through a country intersected with innumerable streams and bayous. He finally secured two large canoes from some Spaniards, built a platform on them for his horse, and thus succeeded in reaching the Opelousas country. Here he found some Catholic people and some churches and priests, which he considered little better than nothing at all, as far as religion was concerned. He found that the non-Catholic Americans knew no more about religion than the untaught Indians. After hearing him preach, he was asked what he meant by the fall of man, and when it was that he fell. In traveling between the settlements, with rain falling in torrents, he was often dripping with water from morning until night. "What I have suffered in body and mind," he writes,

[11] Nathan Bangs, *History of the Methodist Episcopal Church* (4 vols.; New York, 1842), II, 81–83; see also A. G. Jones, *A Complete History of Methodism as Connected with the Mississippi Conference of the Methodist Episcopal Church, South* (2 vols.; Nashville, 1887), I, 24 ff.

"my pen is unable to communicate."[12] But even in the face of such difficulties the work continued, and in 1811 the Mississippi District contained eight circuits and a membership of 639 whites and 150 colored.

The name "Illinois" appeared first among the list of appointments in 1803 when Benjamin Young was sent to the settlements on the eastern side of the Mississippi from the Kaskaskia River on the south to Wood River, where the city of Alton now stands. He found Kaskaskia very cool toward the Methodist gospel, and the "bulk of the people given up to wickedness of every kind." He reported that, of all the places he visited, "it is the worst for stealing, fighting and lying."[13] On the way to his distant circuit, the young preacher's horse was stolen by the Kickapoo Indians, and he was compelled to hire another until his own had been recovered. At Kaskaskia he paid two dollars for the rental of the room in which he preached, while two days' board in the town cost twenty shillings. He ran out of money and was compelled to sell his books. His clothes were worn, and he had no money to buy others. Despite such difficulties, he reported sixty-seven members in five classes on the new circuit at the end of the year.

Two years later (1806) the name "Missouri" appears among the appointments of the Western Conference, with John Travis assigned to the new circuit. Travis seems to have come from that region, for the "Ellenoies" quarterly conference recommended him for admission on trial. By 1811 the two circuits farthest west, the Illinois and the Missouri, reported a membership of nearly seven hundred.[14]

The years covered by the life of the Western Conference, which had been created by the action of the general conference in 1796, was from 1797 to 1811, though from 1796 to 1800 the western circuits

[12] William H. Milburn, *Lance, Cross and Canoe: Flatboat, Rifle and Plow in the Valley of the Mississippi* (New York, 1892), 357–60. The author was for many years chaplain of the United States Senate and also of the House of Representatives. See his biography in the *Dictionary of American Biography,* Vol. XII. See letter of Bowman's dated "Opelousas, January 29, 1806," quoted above.

[13] From a letter dated "Randolph County, Indiana Territory, June 1, 1804." Quoted in James Leaton, *History of Methodism in Illinois from 1793–1832* (Cincinnati, 1883), pp. 34–37.

[14] The minutes of the Western Conference from 1800 to 1811 are found in W. W. Sweet, *The Rise of Methodism in the West* (New York and Nashville, 1920), pp. 73–207. The manuscript minutes are in the library of Ohio Wesleyan University.

were generally designated as the Kentucky District. At the beginning of the century the total number of Methodists in the region west of the Alleghenies was 2,622 white members and 179 colored; twelve years later, or in 1811, there were 29,093 white and 1,648 colored members. The number of circuits had increased from nine in 1800 to sixty-nine in 1811. In 1800 Bishop Asbury had assigned fourteen preachers to travel these western circuits; in 1811 Bishop McKendree stationed one hundred preachers within the bounds of the Western Conference.

These early years of western Methodism are rich in personalities, some of whom deserve a permanent place in the history of the western movement. In the year 1808 the Western Conference elected the following men to represent them at the general conference meeting in Baltimore: William McKendree, William Burke, James Ward, Benjamin Lakin, Learner Blackman, Thomas Milligan, and John Sale. Although the general conference was not yet a delegated body, 1812 being the first delegated conference, the men serving the faraway trans-Alleghenian circuits saw the necessity of a delegated body. Of the seven delegates chosen, William McKendree was outstanding. A native of King William County, Virginia, a Revolutionary soldier, and with little formal education, McKendree had large native ability and a commanding presence. He had some slight religious training in the Episcopal church, and during the Revolution, when nineteen years of age, he came in contact with Methodism and joined a Methodist society. It was ten years, however, before he began to preach, having been recommended to the Virginia Conference without his knowledge. He began his ministry just at the time James O'Kelley was at the height of his influence, and in 1792, when O'Kelley withdrew from the Virginia Conference, McKendree refused to take an appointment. Owing to Asbury's tact in inviting him to accompany him in his episcopal travels, McKendree was saved to the church and in 1800 was placed in charge of the supervision of the western circuits.

Since his ministry had been largely in the West, McKendree was little known among the eastern brethren. At that time there was no church periodical in any denomination, so that there was little chance of a man in one section becoming known in another. On the first Sunday of the general conference, McKendree was assigned to preach in the Light Street Church, in which the conference was meeting. The church was filled and many conference delegates were present.

McKendree's appearance was not prepossessing; though tall and commanding, his clothes were coarse and homely, his movements awkward, his manners rustic. The first part of his sermon seemed tame, and his sentences were broken and disjointed. A change came when the sermon was half-finished, and soon the congregation was carried away with him "into the regions of experimental religion." When he came down from the pulpit, the people gazed upon him "as they might at some messenger from another world" while the preachers said one to another, "That is the man for a bishop." So it was on May 12, 1808, McKendree, the first native American, was elected to the office of bishop in the Methodist Episcopal church. No man in the church was better fitted than William McKendree to follow in the footsteps of Francis Asbury, for he had already learned the ways of the wilderness, and American Methodism's future was tied up with the then great unoccupied wilderness which was the West.[15]

The second name in the list of those chosen as delegates to the general conference of 1808 from the Western Conference was William Burke. He was the secretary of the Western Conference throughout its entire twelve years. Like most of the other preachers, his formal education was limited, though he attended school until about his sixteenth year. He possessed a high degree of intelligence and was clearheaded and capable. As the minutes show, his penmanship was excellent, though his orthography followed no rule, not infrequently spelling the same word several different ways on the same page. A native of Virginia, born in Louden County in 1770, his family was substantial and well-to-do, and he was baptised in the Episcopal church. There being no minister in the parish during his boyhood, Methodist preachers were permitted to use the parish church, and as a consequence his father and mother became Methodists. The family moved to North Carolina in 1787, and in the new surroundings young Burke became, as he says, "very profligate and vain, and entered fully into all the amusements of the day." A change came, however, in 1790, when he was awakened under Methodist preaching, and the next year he began to preach in the neighborhood as a local preacher. In 1792 he was admitted on trial in the conference

[15] Robert Paine, *Life and Times of William McKendree* (Nashville, 1922), pp. 119–24. See the account of the general conference of 1808 in Bangs, *op. cit.*, II, 236–38. See also the article in the *Dictionary of American Biography*, Vol. XII.

MAP I

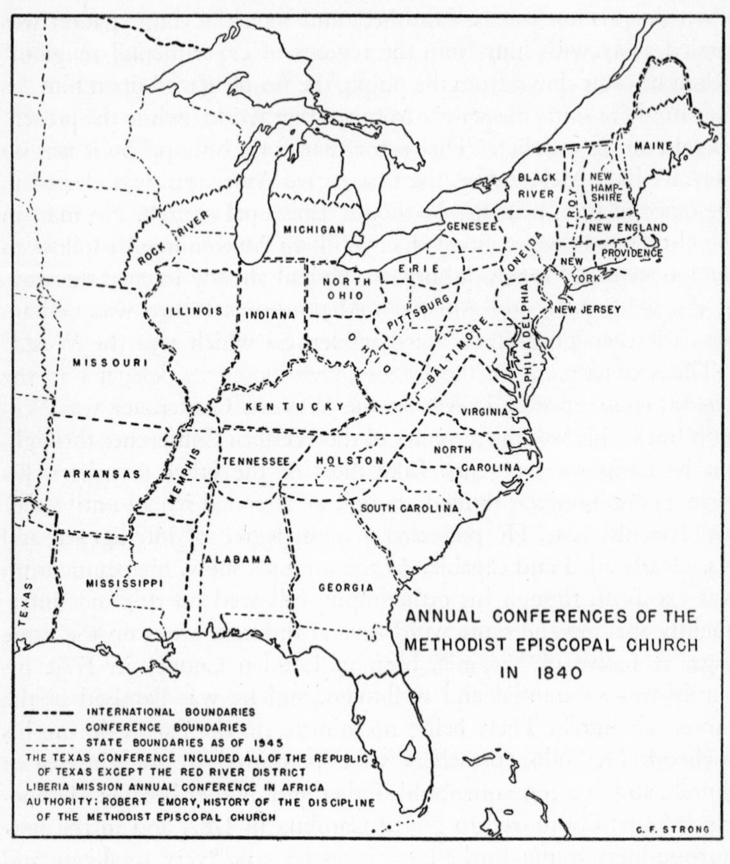
MAINE
BLACK RIVER
NEW HAMPSHIRE
TROY
NEW ENGLAND
PROVIDENCE
GENESEE
ONEIDA
NEW YORK
MICHIGAN
ROCK RIVER
ERIE
NORTH OHIO
PITTSBURG
NEW JERSEY
ILLINOIS
INDIANA
BALTIMORE
PHILADELPHIA
OHIO
MISSOURI
KENTUCKY
VIRGINIA
TENNESSEE
HOLSTON
NORTH CAROLINA
ARKANSAS
MEMPHIS
SOUTH CAROLINA
ALABAMA
MISSISSIPPI
GEORGIA
TEXAS
ANNUAL CONFERENCES OF THE METHODIST EPISCOPAL CHURCH IN 1840
INTERNATIONAL BOUNDARIES
CONFERENCE BOUNDARIES
STATE BOUNDARIES AS OF 1945
THE TEXAS CONFERENCE INCLUDED ALL OF THE REPUBLIC OF TEXAS EXCEPT THE RED RIVER DISTRICT
LIBERIA MISSION ANNUAL CONFERENCE IN AFRICA
AUTHORITY: ROBERT EMORY, HISTORY OF THE DISCIPLINE OF THE METHODIST EPISCOPAL CHURCH
C. F. STRONG

and was assigned to the New River Circuit. This was a four-week circuit, between four and five hundred miles around, and extended on both sides of the Allegheny Mountains, much of the circuit lying at high altitudes. No better picture of Methodist beginnings west of the Alleghenies can be found than is contained in Burke's "Autobiography" covering particularly his early career.[16]

Burke tells us that he was the first preacher in the West who continued to travel after marrying. His marriage took place in 1796, and at that time the sum of sixty-four dollars was the amount fixed as the salary of traveling preachers, and there was no allowance for wives. He met with every discouragement, for preachers and people alike told him that he had better locate. Burke, however, continued his active ministry until failing health caused him to locate in Cincinnati, where he was appointed postmaster, which position he held for twenty-eight years. Burke, however, as did many other "located" men, continued to preach. At the Ohio Conference of 1813, charges were brought against him for treating the elder with contempt, and in 1818 he was "suspended from all official services in the M.E. Church" and two years later was expelled. After a long-continued investigation Burke was restored to full standing in the Ohio Conference in 1836.[17] From this distance such treatment of a man who had served so faithfully for so long seems harsh and unjust, for he was never accused of anything more than failing to adhere to the more or less arbitrary authority of the presiding elder. This case, however, serves to illustrate the attitude of the Methodist church toward regularity and order at a time when law and order were none too highly respected in the western country.

The general conference of 1812 divided the Western Conference into two new conferences, the Ohio and the Tennessee. The Ohio included within its boundaries western Pennsylvania, the southwest corner of New York, all of Ohio, southeastern Indiana, western Virginia, the eastern half of Kentucky, and, later, all the Territory of

[16] J. B. Finley, *Sketches of Western Methodism, Biographical, Historical and Miscellaneous*, ed. W. P. Strickland (Cincinnati, 1855). For Burke's "Autobiography" see *ibid.*, pp. 22–92.

[17] See the "Minutes of the Ohio Conference, 1813–1836" (photostats in the library of the University of Chicago). Cf. W. W. Sweet, *Circuit-Rider Days along the Ohio* (New York, 1923), pp. 53–54.

Michigan. The Tennessee Conference included western Kentucky, the Illinois Territory, except what is now southeastern Indiana, the entire state of Tennessee, and the whole region of the lower Mississippi. As the population movement continued, the territory west of the mountains was divided and redivided until by 1840 there were fifteen annual conferences west of the Alleghenies, and the entire populated part of the nation was covered with a network of conferences, districts, and circuits.[18] The membership, now the largest of any denomination, was 852,908, and the traveling preachers numbered 3,587, with 6,393 local preachers.[19]

During the first fifty years the Methodist Episcopal church was served by twelve bishops, or general superintendents.[20] Of these, Thomas Coke, though named by Wesley as superintendent for America and elected to that office by the organizing conference in 1784, never actually functioned in a full capacity. This was due to the fact that the preachers were unwilling to be under the supervision of an Englishman. Asbury never permitted him to preside at an annual conference without his being present, and in no instance did Dr. Coke assign the preachers to their appointments. The next four bishops in order of their election—Asbury, Whatcoat, McKendree, and George—were all unmarried men, however, not because they were opposed to a married episcopacy but because the very nature of their work in supervising a ministry constantly on the move made the establishment of a home a practical impossibility. The first married bishop was Robert R. Roberts, who in 1819 established his residence on a farm in Lawrence County, Indiana, and in a sense was

[18] Methodism entered Michigan in 1823; Minnesota in 1824; Wisconsin in 1826; Kansas in 1830; Oregon in 1834; and California in 1847. The following is the order of the formation of new annual conferences in the West from 1812 to 1850: In 1812 the Ohio and Tennessee conferences were formed; in 1816 the Missouri and Mississippi conferences; in 1820 the Kentucky; in 1824 the Pittsburgh, the Illinois, and the Holston; in 1832 the Indiana; in 1836 the Michigan and the Arkansas; in 1840 the Rock River, the Memphis, and the Texas. In 1844 the Iowa and the Texas conferences were divided into Eastern and Western conferences.

[19] *Minutes of the Annual Conferences,* Vol. III: *1839–1845* (New York, n.d.), p. 156. The total number of conferences in the entire country was thirty-two.

[20] The first twelve bishops in order of their election were: Thomas Coke and Francis Asbury, 1784; Richard Whatcoat, 1800; William McKendree, 1808; Enoch George and Robert R. Roberts, 1816; Joshua Soule, 1820; Elijah Hedding, 1824; James O. Andrew and John Emory, 1832; Beverly Waugh and Thomas A. Morris, 1836.

the first bishop completely to identify himself with the West. Of the twelve bishops, three were Englishmen—Coke, Asbury, and Whatcoat—four were natives of Virginia, two of Maryland, two from New England, and one—James O. Andrew—was from Georgia, and it was Andrew whose marriage to a slaveholding wife helped precipitate the slavery schism in 1844–45. Of the twelve first bishops, only two were college graduates—Thomas Coke, who graduated from Jesus College, Oxford, in 1768, and John Emory, who graduated from Washington College in Maryland in 1804.

The election to the episcopacy in the Methodist Episcopal church in the early 1800's did not mean the settling-down in a comfortable episcopal residence but rather it was a call to a nation-wide circuit. Each bishop took his turn at presiding over the annual conferences, and during each four-year period between general conferences every bishop was expected to have made the complete round of the entire church. This meant constant travel. Nor was the remuneration attached to the office an inducement to the materially minded. The early bishops received the same salary as the humblest circuit-rider—$64 a year and traveling expenses.[21] This was raised to $80 in 1800, with the same amount for preacher's wives and an allowance of $16 for children under seven and $24 for children between seven and fourteen. In 1816 the sum of $100 was fixed as the salary of all preachers and their wives; in 1836 this was made $200. Differences in preacher's salaries began to appear after 1848, when the general conference ruled that the "table expenses" of preachers "shall be subject to the action of the quarterly meeting conference." In 1832 it was ruled that the annual conference in which a bishop resides is to estimate the episcopal "table expenses." Thus the Indiana Conference estimated Bishop Roberts' "table expenses" at $250 from 1832 to 1836; at $300 from 1836 to 1840; and at $400 from 1840 to his death in 1843.[22]

II

It has been assumed quite generally that Methodist leaders gloried in ignorance and actively opposed an educated ministry. It is true

[21] See Robert Emory, *History of the Discipline of the Methodist Episcopal Church* (New York, 1857), pp. 20, 42, 272, 282.

[22] See W. W. Sweet, *Circuit-Rider Days in Indiana* (Indianapolis, 1916), p. 83.

that many uneducated preachers were utilized in the raw frontier period and that there was undoubtedly an abiding fear among the leaders that formal ministerial education would chill the ardor and enthusiasm of the preachers. But education as such was never opposed. The first book of discipline adopted by the Methodist Episcopal church in 1784 directed the preachers to study five hours a day and to preach at intervals on the subject of education. This was in line with Wesley's admonition to his English preachers.

The organizing conference of the Methodist Episcopal church (1784) made elaborate plans for a college to be established at Abingdon, Maryland, to be called Cokesbury, and in 1792 the college opened its doors to seventy students. Three years later (1795) the building was destroyed by fire, and, although there were three attempts to revive it, none was successful. It was undoubtedly a premature attempt, promoted largely by Dr. Coke, and was never wholeheartedly supported either by Asbury or by the preachers.[23] Asbury now began to urge the establishment of what he called "district schools," and a number of Methodist academies were organized, all of which, however, were short lived. Their failure was due to the policy of locating them in out-of-the-way places and to the poverty and indifference to education of Methodists generally.[24] Not one of the schools which Asbury had a hand in establishing became a permanent institution. It was not until 1820 that the Methodist church adopted a general educational policy.

The general conference of that year (1820) recommended to the annual conferences that they establish as soon as possible literary institutions under their control. This conference also provided that thereafter bishops might appoint traveling ministers as officers and teacher in colleges. Previously the church had frowned upon ministers leaving the active ministry to become teachers. The response to this

[23] The fullest account of the founding of Cokesbury College is given by Bangs (*op. cit.*, I, 229–42). Cf. W. W. Sweet, *Methodism in American History* (New York, 1933), pp. 207–28, and W. B. Posey, *The Development of Methodism in the Old Southwest, 1783–1824* (Tuscaloosa, Ala., 1933), chap. v.

[24] Among the academies established under Asbury's leadership were Ebenezer Academy, Brunswick County, Va.; Bethel Academy, Jassamine County, Ky.; Cokesbury School in western North Carolina; the Wesley and Whitefield School in Georgia; and Union Seminary in Uniontown, Pa. (A. W. Cummings, *The Early Schools of Methodism* [New York, 1886]).

legislation was immediate, and the next twenty years saw the beginning of a school- and college-building program among the Methodists, which continued through the next two decades with increased tempo. By 1860 thirty-four permanent colleges had been established in nineteen states, a majority of them being located west of the Alleghenies.[25] Besides these, several colleges had been founded in the twenties which had eventually failed.[26]

While one of the principal motives in the establishment of Methodist colleges was to train ministers, there long remained a prejudice against college-trained preachers in the annual conferences. Thomas A. Goodwin was the first college graduate to enter the Indiana Conference. He had received his A.B. degree from Indiana Asbury University (now DePauw University) in 1848. The presiding elders were afraid of showing too much favor to a college man, and on a number of occasions he was actually demoted for no other reason than that he was a college graduate.[27]

Peter Cartwright has often been quoted as opposed to education for the ministry, yet he had a hand in establishing two colleges, McKendree and Jacksonville Woman's College now (MacMurray College), in Illinois, and as a member of the Illinois legislature he introduced the first bill for the establishment of a state university. He did not undervalue education, but he had little use for the college- and the seminary-trained eastern missionaries who came West and tried to use their manuscript sermons on the western people. So many of these "educated preachers," he states, "remind me of lettuce growing under the shade of a peach tree, or like a gosling that had got the straddles wading in the dew." The older circuit-preachers were particularly hostile to the theological seminaries. Cartwright did not understand why such institutions were necessary when colleges

[25] D. G. Tewskbury, *The Founding of American Colleges and Universities before the Civil War, with Particular Reference to the Religious Influences Bearing upon the College Movement* (New York, 1932), pp. 103–11. See also W. W. Sweet, *Indiana-Asbury-DePauw University, 1837–1937: A Hundred Years of Higher Education in the Middle West* (New York, 1937), chap. i.

[26] Two of the colleges founded in the 1820's which failed were Augusta College, Augusta, Kentucky, which was chartered in 1822 and continued to 1849, and Madison College, Uniontown, Pennsylvania, which opened in 1827 and closed two years later (Sweet, *Methodism in American History,* pp. 211–14).

[27] Joseph Tarkington, *Autobiography* (Cincinnati, 1899), pp. 15–16.

abounded. But what Peter Cartwright and Alfred Brunson and others like them particularly feared was the creation of a type of ministry that would not be willing to ride great circuits and undergo the hardships entailed by the traveling ministry. They all felt that the future of Methodism depended upon the continuance of the circuit system. Cartwright thus expresses this fear:

> Multiply colleges, universities, seminaries and academies; multiply our agencies, and editorships, and fill them all with our best and most efficient preachers and you localize the ministry and secularize them, too; then farewell to itineracy.[28]

III

Though originating among frontier Presbyterians in the James McGready revivals in Logan County, Kentucky, in the latter years of the eighteenth and the early years of the nineteenth centuries, the camp meeting soon became, to a large degree, a Methodist institution.[29] The regular Presbyterians threw it overboard because of their distrust of innovations and their inability to control it. The Cumberland Presbyterians and the Baptists, to a limited degree, continued its use, but it was the Methodists who developed it into the most important social institution of the frontier. The development of the camp meeting among the Methodists may be traced by turning the pages of Asbury's *Journal* from 1800 onward. On December 12, 1805, he lists a whole series of camp meetings in Maryland, Virginia, and North Carolina at which many hundreds professed conversion. In 1806 he notes a camp meeting at Long-Calm in Maryland, held in October, at which five hundred and eighty were "said to be converted." In August, 1808, at Deer Creek in Ohio, there were twenty-three traveling and local preachers present, at a great camp meeting where there were a hundred and twenty-five tents and wagons and about two thousand people.[30] By 1816, the year of Asbury's death, there were

[28] *Autobiography*, p. 81.

[29] For recent appraisal of the importance of camp meetings in the Methodist system see W. W. Sweet, *Revivalism in America, Its Origin, Growth and Decline* (New York, 1944), pp. 129–33. See also Posey, *op. cit.*, chap. ii, 17–34; Elizabeth K. Nottingham, *Methodism and the Frontier: The Indiana Proving Ground* (New York, 1941), pp. 61–70.

[30] Francis Asbury, *Journal* (New York and Cincinnati, n.d.), III, 210–11, 286, 316, 321.

at least six hundred Methodist camp meetings held in various parts of the country.

Many who have written on frontier camp meetings, in recent times particularly, have overemphasized their importance. The camp meeting was never recognized as an official Methodist institution, and the name "camp meeting" does not appear in the indexes of the general conference *Journals* or in the Methodist discipline. Such writers as Homer C. Loud in his *Evangelized America* and Gilbert Seldes in his *Stammering Century* and numerous others have assumed that the camp meeting represented about all there was of Methodist influence and activity in the early West. The camp meeting did become a widely used frontier institution, but always as an extra occasion in the economy of Methodism. There gradually came to be, however, certain general ideas as to how camp meetings should be best organized and regulated, and camp-meeting manuals were published, though they were never officially adopted by any church body.[31] There were special camp-meeting hymnbooks also published, but they, too, were never officially recognized by the Methodist church. Many of these songs were the crudest doggerel, but others were dignified and worshipful. The American Methodists from the beginning have had an official hymnal, the first one prepared by John Wesley and approved by the organizing conference in 1784.

The emotional excesses of camp-meeting revivalism have been greatly overstressed, while too little attention has been given to the routine work of the frontier churches and the circuit preachers. Every Methodist preacher throughout the country was a distributor of religious literature. In fact, that was one of his most important functions. Chapter xiv in this volume, dealing with Methodist publishing activities and the distribution of literature in the West, furnishes specific facts as to the wide extent of this type of Methodist activity. This was a part of the circuit-riders' duty, and they were encouraged in it by the fact that they received a percentage on their sales. The Methodist Book Concern was organized in 1789 and was located in New

[31] B. W. Gorham, *Camp Meeting Manual: A Practical Book for the Camp Ground* (Boston, 1854) is an example. See also Orange Scott, *The New and Improved Camp Meeting Hymn Book, etc.* (Brookfield, 1832); Seth Mead, *Hymns and Spiritual Songs* (Richmond, 1807); see also the camp-meeting rules taken from the "Journal" of James Gilruth (below, chap. ix).

York. In 1800 the general conference passed the ruling that every presiding elder was to see that his district was fully supplied with books, and it also stated that every preacher was to see that his circuit was duly supplied. In 1817, 1,203 books were sent to James B. Finley, the presiding elder of the Ohio District, to be sold in his district, and the same year Benjamin Lakin sold 236 books on the Limestone Circuit in Kentucky.[32] Some idea of the extent of the circulation of Methodist books throughout the nation in 1817 may be realized when it is understood that there were at that time more than four hundred and fifty circuits.

The first national Methodist paper was the *Christian Advocate and Journal,* which began publication in New York in 1826. The circuit preachers were likewise the agents for its circulation, and by 1828, to quote John B. McMaster, it "had a weekly circulation of fifteen thousand copies, the largest, it was claimed, then reached by any newspaper in the world, the *London Times* not excepted."[33] It was also one of the first papers in the United States to have a nation-wide circulation. In the year 1831–32 there were fifty-two subscribers who received the *Christian Advocate and Journal* through the post office at Jacksonville, Illinois, which was twice the number of subscribers of any other paper. In 1828 a western branch of the Book Concern was opened at Cincinnati, and six years later (1834) a second Methodist weekly began publication, the *Western Christian Advocate.* In 1836 the Western Methodist Book Concern was made independent of the New York Concern and four years later began the publication of one of the first women's magazines published in the United States, the *Ladies Repository and Gleanings of the West.* The *Western Christian Advocate* soon had a circulation of 15,000, while the *Ladies Repository* exercised a cultural influence outside as well as within Methodist circles.

[32] See below, chap. xiv.

[33] *History of the People of the United States* (8 vols.; New York, 1904), V, 274–75.

PART II

Documents Illustrating the Work of Methodists on the Frontier

CHAPTER V

The Journal of Bishop Richard Whatcoat August 1, 1789—December 31, 1790

RICHARD WHATCOAT (1736–1806), third bishop of the Methodist Episcopal church, was born of Anglican parentage at Quinton, Gloucestershire, England. Orphaned as a child, and bound out at an early age to learn a trade, he had but meager opportunity for formal education. After completing his apprenticeship, he settled in Wednesbury, Staffordshire, where his conversion occurred in 1761, under Methodist preaching.

His friend, the Reverend Samuel Taylor, vicar of Quinton parish, had been in full sympathy with the Methodist movement and had attended the first Wesleyan conference in 1744 as well as later conferences. The influence of this "Methodist" vicar and the Christian home of his childhood were undoubtedly factors in bringing Whatcoat to a conversion experience. After several years' experience as band leader, class leader, and steward of the Wednesbury society, he began to preach in 1767. Determining to devote himself entirely to preaching, he began his work in 1769 as an itinerant under John Wesley's direction. After serving circuits in England, Ireland, and Wales, he was selected in 1784 by Wesley as one of the delegation of three to come to America to organize the American Methodists into a separate ecclesiastical body.

In America he served until 1800 as circuit-preacher and presiding elder. He was chosen bishop in 1800 and for the following six years shared with Francis Asbury the arduous task of supervising the rapidly expanding Methodist work in America. During his years in America he kept a brief "Journal" of his travels in the ministry, only fragments of which remain. Portions of this "Journal" are now at Garrett Biblical Institute and in the Library of Congress, covering the following periods: August 1, 1789—May 25, 1791; January 30, 1792—August 25, 1793; May 23, 1794—June 7, 1796; August 13, 1797—August 13, 1798; and August 16, 1798—May 30, 1800. Microfilms of all these extant portions are at the University of Chicago.

The excerpt from the "Journal" here printed for the first time covers the period from August 1, 1789, to December 31, 1790. Whatcoat was during this period presiding elder over circuits on the eastern shore of Chesapeake Bay, including parts of Maryland, Delaware, and Virginia. In the early part of the year 1790 he accompanied Bishop Francis Asbury on an extended preaching tour which reached as far south as Georgia and as far west as Tennessee and Kentucky. En route they held conferences for the preachers in certain areas, such as South Carolina, Georgia, Kentucky, and Virginia. At the conference in Philadelphia in September, 1790, Whatcoat was stationed at Philadelphia and was appointed presiding elder of the district centering about the city.

Whatcoat seems to have given little time to journal-keeping, much less than did Asbury, though it must be remembered that Asbury was writing for publication. The parallel selections quoted from Asbury's *Journal* show the comparative merits of the two documents. Whatcoat's short, laconic phrases reveal the pressure of his work. His labors were ceaseless, despite ill-health. Obviously, the "Journal" was never revised. Blanks were left that the writer never took the trouble to fill; naïve and erratic spellings were never corrected. But on its pages is revealed the plain, humble man that was Richard Whatcoat, who, though not so great an organizer and administrator as Asbury, was a zealous father to American Methodism and seems to have been beloved and respected by preacher and laymen alike.

The chief biographical studies of Whatcoat are William Phoebus' pioneer work, *Memoirs of the Rev. Richard Whatcoat* (New York, 1828); S. B. Bradley, *The Life of Bishop Richard Whatcoat* (Louisville, 1936); and W. T. Wallace, "Richard Whatcoat, Early Methodist Bishop" (M.A. thesis, University of Chicago, 1941). Shorter sketches will be found in the *Minutes of the Annual Conferences of the Methodist Episcopal Church,* Vol. I: *1773–1828,* pp. 145–46; William B. Sprague, *Annals of the American Pulpit* (New York, 1865), VII, 92–101; and the *Dictionary of American Biography,* XX, 36.

Aug*t** 1—1789 F[rancis] asbury Bro*r* willis[1] & I Rode To Cornal [Colonel] Barrotts F asbury preach*d* I Exhorted

*[Note.—Owing to typographical necessity, all superscript letters in the original manuscript are set, throughout this volume, in on-the-line italics.]

[1] Henry Willis (? –1808), a native of Brunswick County, Virrginia, was in 1789 presiding elder of the Philadelphia district (*Minutes of the Annual Conferences of the Methodist Episcopal Church,* Vol. I: *1773–1828,* p. 34). Note that, throughout this document, references in the notes to appointments of preachers in 1789–90 are from this source. The appointments for 1789 are found on pp. 33–34; those for 1790, on pp. 37–38. For a biographical sketch of Willis see George C. M. Roberts, *Centennial Pictorial Album: Being Contributions of the Early History of Methodism in the State of Maryland* (Baltimore, 1866), pp. 45–49.

2 Rode To Jo*s* Cressups C[hapel][2] F asbury preach*d* I Exhorted Bro*r* Willes Spoke from Nathanie[l] The word was with weight May it be Lasting

3 Rode To Fort Cumberland Stopt at Joshua Scritchferlds F asbury preach*d* Bro*r* Willis Spoke from the Gift of the Spirit I Exhorted we Rode [to] Bro*r* Fosters & Dined &C

The Second of August I Joined in the Bands of Matrimony Thomas Brown and Milley Rolings of the place Called uper old Town Hundred washington County State of Mary land (Baptized Six] They were published by the Rev*d* Mr Crossley

4 F asbury preach*d* I Exhorted &C Rode To [Old] T[own]

5 F preach*d* I Exhorted Bro*r* willis preach*d* f[irst] at old Town

6 Rode To Tho*s* Williamses &C—

7 Rode To the Springs Took our horses To Arther Wigginses Brought our things to Sisters Adams and Morrises &C—

9 F asbury Re[a]d the Morning Servis[3] I preach*d* F asbury preach*d* at three in the afternoon

11 Bro*r* Haggerty[4] Came To Bath &C—

15 Bro*r* willis Came and preach*d* a funarl Sermon over —— agustans Child &C—

16 Bro*r* Willis Re[a]d the Servis I preach*d* & also at Archible Wiggens at three & Bro*r* Haggerty Exhorted Bro*r* Willis preach*d* & Bro*r* adams[5] at the Springs in the afternoon &C— Truly it apears that [like] Light & Darkness the Children of God & the Children of the wicked Can have But Little fellowship to gether

in this place about two hundred houses & Cabbins are Built for the Inhabitant[s] and Conveniance of them that attend the Season for the Benifit of the waters [There are] about thirty

[2] Note that hereafter unexpanded "C." means "Chapel" or "Church."

[3] The practice of reading a modified form of the Anglican service, as well as the wearing of clerical gowns, had been recommended to American Methodist preachers by Wesley, through imperfect knowledge of American conditions. Because of frontier exigencies, the practice was soon discarded.

[4] George Hagerty, appointed to Bath Circuit, Virginia, 1789.

[5] Evidently a local preacher.

familys that Reside here after Stoping at the Springs twelv Days Brother asbury finding himself Very poorly and the famalys we Lodged with Leaving the Springs we Rode to

19 Marg*t* Strowds &C—

20 We Rode To Bengamin Bordstons[6] Bro*r* Willis Rode To Sheperdstown & preach*d* in the Evning

21 Bro*r* willis preach*d* in the Evning at Tho*s* Bordston[s] I Exhorted &C— [The] Daughter of —— —— found peace with god

22 F asbury and I Rode to John Milburns

23 F asbury preach*d* I & Bro*r* Fleming[7] Exhorted &C F asbury & Fleming Rode To Winchester &C— I Rode to Henery parns & preach*d* with freedom Met the Class Baptized one &C— the power of the Lord was Sencably felt—

24 F asbury preach*d* a powerful Discours &C—

25 We Rode To Ja*s* Strowds F asbury preach*d* in a Large Barn To A few unawakned people

26 We Rode To John Rees*s* F asbury preach*d* I Exhorted But the Roks were hard. We Called at the Sulfer Spring about 10 or 12 Miles from Sheperds Town the water Looks of a Bluish Cast Clear as Cristial Tasts Strong of the Sulpher Tinkterd with Cole I Drank five Small Glases which helped forward my Lax

27 I Took about 38 Grains of Ruburb which worked me about forty houers Rode to John Hights F asbury preach*d* I was not able To attend

28 Rode to Benjamin Bordstons F asbury preach*d*

29 Q[uarterly] Meeting Began at Sheperds Town But I finding Myself unfit to attend having A Great opression and Sickness on my Stomack I Took 20 Grains of Ipecacuanha which Gave me Some Ease

[6] Benjamin Boydstone, a local preacher.

[7] Thornton Fleming (1764–1846), a native of Williamsburg, Virginia, was a pioneer itinerant in Virginia and western Pennsylvania. He spent fifty-eight years in the itinerancy without "locating." His colleagues wrote of him in 1846: "Our venerable father was the oldest member of the Pittsburgh Conference, and a man and minister of rare endowments and great usefulness" ("Memoir," *Minutes,* Vol. IV: *1846–1851,* pp. 139–40).

30 finding myself unfit to for [*sic*] publick worship I Rested at home at Diner I Eat Some Salt meat which opresed my Stomack Greatly and caused my Lax to Return with Duble Violence Such a Nights Labour I think I never had before

31 I Cried Right Early unto the Lord and he Delivered me tho there was but one Step between me and Deth Took My Leav of Bro*r* asbury willis Thomas[8] &C—Rested Comfortably this night

Sept*r* 1, 2. 1789 Gained a Little Strength &C—

3 Rode With Sister Bordston & Sist*r* wood To Sister Willises &C

4 Called To See Bro*r* Odal & Nancey Jeferis who had Lost her Speech four Days & Nights But God was with her She Saw A Glorious place and heared heavenly Music; and also Heard the Screeks & Crys of Damned Souls She Said Oh if Siners Did See the joys of Heaven they would Leav the plesurs of this world or if thay knew the Misery of the wicked they would not go on in Sin we held a praye[r] Meeting in the Evning one woman Brok oute in prayer with all her Might in Dutch

5 Very weak and I Lay Down Most of the Day

6 finding my Self much Beter I preach*d* at Tho*s* odals at Eleven and [in] Sheperds Town at four the word Seemed waity on the people &C—I got but Little Rest this Night I supose owing To the Exersizes of the Day

1789 July the Twenty third in Tho*s* Odals Class three were justified and Nine Santified Glory to God By a Letter To Benjamin Bordston I was informed that Seventeen found peas [peace] with God and five purity of Heart; and also one Bla[c]k man [was] powerfuly Struk to the ground under Conviction in his Return from Q Meeting when the Lord Spoke peace to his Soul, he Spoke of Seeing the Narrow way his Master was walking in And also the way his Mistres was in ——

Sept*r* 7 Rode with Tho*s* Bordston To Ja*s* Sargants preach*d* To A Little Congregation with freedom

8 Rode To Samuel philipses preach*d* with Liberty

9 Rode To Fredrick preach*d* at Ja*s* wiliamson[s] with freedom Lodged at Fredrick Bierlys

[8] James Thomas, appointed to Allegheny Circuit, western Virginia, in 1789.

10 Rode To Liberty Town [and] preach*d* at Benjmin Musgrove[s] Held prayer Meeting at Daniel Dorceys

11 Dined & Lodged at Ephr*m* Howerds Drank Tea at upton Sheradins Esq*r*

12 preach*d* & Met Class at Liberty Town

13 preach*d* & Gave the Sacrament at Lingon Ore. C. it was A Time of Refreshing

14 Rode [to] John Evanses[9] preach*d* it was A quickening Time Baptized one Rode to Elis Joneses

15 Rode To Baltimore as Bro*r* Cooper[10] Did not Come So Soon as was Expected I joined in the Bands of Matrimony Samuel Vincent and Mary Hands of Baltimore by Virtew of Licence from the Cl[er]k of the Same C[ounty] which I Left with Ezekel Cooper To Give in To the Tresurer of the Western Shore preach*d* with Moderat freedom &C

16 Rode To the Stone Church Heard F Asbury preach I Exhorted we Rode To Charles Carnans[11] Doct*r* —— Tarried with us

[17] as it was A Wet Day we Kept Close quarters

18 Rode To Baltimore Held a prayer Meeting at Grace Wrights &C—

20 preach*d* at 10 and at 3 at the point and at Seven at the New Church[12] welfil[l]ed Oh My God what hast thou Don[e] for this people Go on Glorious Redeemer Till the Little Leven Shall Leven the whole Lump

21 Viseted Some friends Met Class at Bro*r* Haukins Held a prayermeeting at Sist*r* Burlys

22 Visited Sist*r* Simson; and Mary Hilling Dying in the Triumph of faith preach*d* &C

[9] The Evans family were converts of Robert Strawbridge and members of the first Methodist society in Baltimore County, Maryland.

[10] Ezekiel Cooper (1763–1847) was a native of Caroline County, Maryland, and had joined the traveling connection in 1785. At the time of Whatcoat's visit Cooper was serving Annapolis. After John Dickins' death in 1798, he became head of the Methodist publishing interests in Philadelphia and New York ("Memoir," *Minutes*, Vol. IV: *1846–1851*, pp. 104–5).

[11] Charles Carnan, of Baltimore County, Maryland, a cousin of Governor Ridgley, was a prominent Methodist layman.

[12] Light Street Chapel, frequently the seat of the Baltimore Conference in later years.

23 Held a watch Night at the point I preach*d* Bro*r* Reed[13] & Cooper Exhorted &C I Left Between Ten and Eleven 5 or 6 found peace

24 Held a watch Night in Town I preach*d* & Retiered Bro*r* Cooper & Reed Exhorted &C Six [were] Connverted Glory Be to God &C

25 Rod[e] To Abingdon F Asbury preach*d* &C

26 I preach*d* Bro*r* Chambers[14] & Asbury Exhorted prayed &C—

27 I preach*d* at Eleven F asbury at four &C

28 Rode To Captin Ridgleys[15] Held A watch Night the Rev*d* John Coleman[16] was Closeing his Discours as I arived I preach*d* Bro*r* Forster[17] Exhorted &C The Fier Brok out then there was Crying praying and [....] through the asembley which Continued til Twelv Then I Dismised the Congregation But Some Remained in Distress and Som Continued in prayer &C Till three I Supose 10 or 12 found peace if Not More (I Supose I [*sic*] there were Ten or twelv Hundred people)

Sept*r* 14 at Ston[e] Church 9 found peace 15[*th*] at Hooks Town 5 at Baltimore the 20[*th*] four 23[*d*] at the point 5 at Baltimore the 24*th* Six 25*th* Twenty 27[*th*] thirty Blesed be the Lord God who Doth wondrous things

[13] Nelson Reed (1751-1840), a native of Anne Arundel County, Maryland, preached widely in Virginia, Maryland, Delaware, and Pennsylvania. In 1789 he was presiding elder of the Baltimore District. For biographical data see William B. Sprague, *Annals of the American Pulpit* (New York, 1865), VII, 68–70; also "Memoir," *Minutes,* Vol. III: *1839–1845,* pp. 153–54. His "Journal," covering the years 1778–82, is the property of the American Methodist Historical Society, Baltimore.

[14] Evidently a local preacher or exhorter.

[15] Charles Ridgley of "Hampton," Long Green, Baltimore County, Maryland, was a friend and patron of Strawbridge (John Lednum, *A History of the Rise of Methodism in America* [Philadelphia, 1859], p. 22).

[16] John Coleman (1758–1816), a native of Dinwiddie County, Virginia, was educated by Devereux Jarratt, evangelical Anglican rector of Bath Parish in Dinwiddie County. The American Revolution prevented his going to England to take orders in the Church of England, but he became a Methodist lay preacher in 1780. Five years later he left the Methodists and in 1787 was admitted to orders by Bishop White. In 1789 he was minister of St. John's and St. James' parishes in Baltimore County, Maryland. He is remembered for publishing in 1806 *The Life of the Reverend Devereux Jarratt* (Sprague, *op. cit.,* V, 220).

[17] Thomas Foster, appointed to Fell's Point, Maryland, in 1789.

29 Dined at perry Hall[18] Rode To Capt. Kells Exhorted &C

30 Rode t[o] Abingdon Dined at Lambert Wilmore[s][19] Rode To Josiah Dallams[20] &C—

Oct*r* 1 Rode To John Fords [at] Turkey point

2 Rode To Robert Hearts preach*d* Some were powerfuly Wrought on—

3 Held a Short watch night I preach*d* &C—

4 I preach*d* Bro*r* Everit[21] Exhorted Gave the Sacrament To about Sixty Crost over To the Court house Bro*r* Everit preach*d* I Exhorted Gave the Sacrament To about Sixty it was a powerful Time Crost in a Buttow [bateau] to —— Keggs &C——

5 Rode to Benj. Herseys[22] Bro*r* Everit preach*d* I Exhorted &C—

6 Rode to Gilbert Simmons Bro*r* Everit preach*d* I Exhorted Bro*r* Roberts[23] & Moor[24] prayed &C Rode To John Days[25]

7 Rode To New Town Bro*r* Everit preach*d* I Exhorted &C—

Oct*r* 8—1789 Bro*r* Everit & I Being poorly we Rode to Samuel Dudleys[26] Staid Tow [two] Nights

[18] Perry Hall, on the Bel Air Road twelve miles from Baltimore, was the seat of Henry Dorsey Gough, convert of Asbury, and his wife Prudence (Ridgley), a sister of Governor Ridgley of Maryland.

[19] John Lambert Wilmer, wealthy planter of Kent County, Maryland.

[20] The Dallams of Harford County, Maryland, were among the "first fruits" of Methodism in Maryland. A society was formed at their home prior to 1773.

[21] Joseph Everett (1732–1809), a native of Queen Anne's County, Maryland, was "awakened" during the Whitefield revivals and joined the Presbyterian church in 1763. After serving in the Revolutionary army, he commenced itinerating on Dorchester Circuit, Maryland, in 1780, and was admitted on trial into the traveling connection in 1781. In 1789 he was Whatcoat's assistant on the Peninsula District. His ministry was spent chiefly in New Jersey, Pennsylvania, Delaware, Maryland, and Virginia ("Memoir," *Minutes,* Vol. I: *1773–1828,* pp. 179–81; Sprague, *op. cit.,* VII, 71–73.

[22] Benjamin, Isaac, and Solomon Hersey were early converts in Cecil County, Maryland.

[23] Benjamin Roberts, appointed to Cecil Circuit, Maryland, in 1789.

[24] George Moore, a native of Delaware, was appointed, with Benjamin Roberts, to Cecil Circuit, Maryland, in 1789.

[25] John Day was a local preacher at Thomas' Chapel on the Peninsula.

[26] Samuel Dudley, of Kent County, Maryland, had entered the traveling connection in 1781 but "located" in 1788 through family concerns.

10 I Retu[r]ned to Town &C—

11 preach*d* at Eleven & in the Evning I think the people felt the power of the word

12 Bro*r* Everit preach*d* I Exhorted &C—

13 Rode To Church Hill Drank Tea at Benj. Ritchersons preach[*d*] at John Johnsons To A Crowded audinance Some felt the power &C—

14 Rod[e] To W*m* Brufs preach*d* his wifes funeral who about three Days before She Died Said She walked to Sister Stories about three Miles and Conversed with her tho at the Same Time unable to Sit up in her Bed and Sister Story Said She Conversed with hir at the Same Time who also was Veri ill and Likly to Die and Not only So But She was Sensable of the Time M*rs* bruf Departed and Spoke of it to her famaly!

15 Rode to Chopthank Bridg preach*d* in their New Church &C—

16 Rode To Benjamin Blunts preach*d* Met Class it was a Time of Refreshing From the presance of the Lord Rode with Bro*r* Merich[27] To —— preach*d* to a Little house full of people

17 Rode to Dover opened the Q Meeting Bro*r* Asbury preach*d* A Great Sermon Bro*r* Everit & Bro*r* Moor Exhorted &C Bro*r* Everit preach*d* in the Evning &C—

Oct*r* 18—1789 Lovefeast Began About halfpas[t] Eight I & Bro*rs* Ratclif[28] [and] Boyour[29] Exhorted Bro*r* Asbury prayed &C &C the Lord was powerfuly presant Jacob Brush[30] and W*m* Jesup[31] were ordained Elders Bishop asbury preach*d*

[27] John Merrick, appointed to Elizabethtown Circuit, New Jersey, in 1789.

[28] William Ratcliffe, appointed to Milford Circuit, Delaware, in 1789.

[29] Caleb Boyer, a native of Kent County, Delaware, was converted under Freeborn Garrettson and entered the traveling connection in 1780 but located in 1788 and settled near Dover, serving thenceforth as a local preacher (Lednum, *op. cit.*, pp. 304–5).

[30] Jacob Brush (1762–1795), a native of Long Island, New York, was appointed to Dover and Duck Creek, Delaware, in 1789. His conference brethren wrote in their pious memoir of him in 1795: "He was an active man of God, a great friend to order and union. . . . . We entertain no doubt but he rests in Abraham's bosom (*Minutes,* Vol. I: *1773–1828,* p. 66).

[31] William Jessop (? –1795), a native of Sussex County, Delaware, was appointed to Wilmington, Delaware, in 1789 ("Memoir," *Minutes,* Vol. I: *1773–1828,* p. 66).

A Great Sermon I Exhorted Bro*r* Everit preach*d* &C— I preach*d* in the Evning at M*r* Basits Esq*r*[32]
19 Rode to Calob Boyers preach*d* & Baptized three Rode To —— Dills [at] Fredericka I preach*d* at —— Wakemans in the Evning
20 Rode to Milford Sung & prayed, F asbury preach*d* I Exhorted the Shout of A King was heared in our Camp &C &C— Rode [to] —— Williamses the Old Man had A Violent feaver How Dos Afflictions Abound
21 the old Man was Considerably beter this Morning he thought the Lord heard [his] prayer we Rode to Milford F Asbury preach*d* Several preachers Exhorted &C the Lord was presant
22 Rode to Johns Town As Bro*r* Asbury was unwell (I preach*d* [and] Bro*r* Ev*t* Exhorted) this Night he was Very Restless with A Cold Sore throte & feaver &C—
23 he Sat up A Little but renewed his Cold
24 he kept his Bed & was a Little Easier
25 kept his Bed Mended A Little I preach*d* & Took Cold by the wind Beating in on my head
26 Kept his Bed
27 Sat up A Little—
28 Rode to Lowery[s][33] 12 M[iles]. Rode to Isack Herseys 9 M.
Oct*r* 29 Rode to Isaac Vinson[s] 17 M. Dined Rode to W*m* Waricks 16 M. pokamoke Hundred Somerset County Maryland
30 as it Rained we Stopt till two oh Clock then Rode to Stevenses Ferry 8 M. [thence] To W*m* Downings 12 M. in the Rain Took Some Cold Arived at 1/2 past Six

Nov*r* 1 Rode to Accamack Court house Dined at the Wido Robinsons 21 M. Rode to Cornal parromors 7 M. Rested in peace
2 Rode To Garitsons C. F asbury [and] I Exhorted &C Bro*r*

[32] Richard Bassett (1745–1815), of Dover, Delaware, and Bohemia Manor, Maryland, was a prominent Methodist layman and founder of Wesley Chapel, Dover, in 1784. He was a member of the Constitutional Convention, 1787; United States senator from Delaware, 1789–93; governor of Delaware, 1798–1801; and judge of the United States District Court for Delaware (*Dictionary of American Biography,* II, 39–40).

[33] James Lowery, early Methodist, lived at Lowery's Mill at the head of Nanticoke River.

Evrit Gave the Sacrament to About three hundred F asbury preach*d* &C ordained Cristepher Spry[34] & Conner Simpkins[35] Deacons I Exhorted Bro*r* Evrit prayed &C we had two Mighty Gusts of the power of God one at the Love feast & the other at the Close of our Meeting Glory to God for Ever we Rode to Conner Simpkins 22 M. I Rested with Bro*r* Everit F asbury Rode to John Stratons preach*d* & Returned 38 M.

3 Rode to Johannes Johnsons 4 M. F asbury preach*d* I Exhorted Bro*r* Everit Exhorted Bro*r* Causden[36] prayed &C we Dined at John Goy[s] we Rode [to] Cor. parromors 28 M. (this Day five years I Landed at New Yark) Thanks be to God that I have Seen the plesure of the Lord prosper in these parts

4 Rode to Accamack Courthouse F asbury preach*d* I Exhorted &C &C Rode to Curtises

5 Rode to W*m* Downings F preach*d* I & Bro*r* Evrit & Bro*r* Spry Exhorted &C—

Nov*r* 6 1789 We Gave the Sacrament to 150 F asbury preach*d* I Bro*r* Evrit &C Exhorted we had A Mighty Gust of the Spirit after giving the Sacrament &C— we Rode to Littleton Longs 11 Miles

7 Rode to Curtises C. I Bro*r* ward[37] asbury Evrit &C Exhorted to A Small Congregation

8 at Nine we Gave the Sacrament to Near two hundred people But one of the preachers Mightely Exhort[ed] the people So that the power of God Came Down and interupted in Giving the Elements which Continued Neare two hours at Eleven F asbury preach*d* to Maney More then [than] the house Could Hold at the Close of his Discource the power of the Lord Came Down upon the people So that Maney began to praise the Lord Call upon his Name and Exhort the people &C I

[34] Christopher Spry, appointed to Northampton Circuit, Virginia, in 1789.

[35] Evidently a local preacher.

[36] Jeremiah Cosden, appointed with Christopher Spry to Northampton Circuit, Virginia, in 1789.

[37] William Ward, appointed to Annamessex Circuit, Maryland, in 1789.

hope Meney will Date their Conversion from this Q Meeting we Rode to Solomon Longs Dined [at] Bro*r* ward[s] and Rode to princes anns I preach*d* in the Court house at Early Candle Light to about 70 or 80 quiat Hearers Lodged at W*m* Lowbers &C—

9 F asbury preach*d* in the Court House at ten to about fifty people, we Rode to tho*s* Garitsons F asbury preach*d* to about forty I & Bro*r* Everit Exhorted &C there apeared to be Some Move at preaching & prayermeeting in the Evning Glory To God &C

10 Rode with Capt. —— Conaway to quant[i]co I preach*d* Bro*r* Reed,[38] Wallis, asbury, [and] Everit Exhorted &C—with Spirit and power to A Small Congregation—we Rode with John Dunlap To Sarah Nutters Slept in peace Lord Bless this famaly &C

Nov*r* 11 we Gave the Sacr[a]ment to about Fifty at half past nine F asbury preach*d* at Eleven I Bro*r* Everit &C Exhorted &C— it was a Refreshing Time to Most &C— Rode with Bro*r* Reed To Tho*s* Fletchers

12 Rode to the Wido Heamey[s] preach*d* Rich*d* Heameys Funeral [They] Gave Me 2—1 To A Smal Atentiv Congregation &C Dined Rode to Isaac Herseys Bro*r* asbury preach*d*

13 F asbury preach[*d*] [and] ordained Campbell St Cleir[39] Deacon Gave the Sacrament to about forty and to Isaac Herse[y] Who was Very Ill Rode to Ja*s* Lowery[s] I preach*d* F asbury Exhorted

14 our horses Left us So we had a Littl [search] in the Night

15 I preach*d* at Jacob wrights to A Large Congreg[a]tion

16 Rode [to] Tho*s* Whit[e]s[40] Called at H. Y. Dickensons He

[38] Eliphalet Reed, appointed to Somerset Circuit, Maryland, in 1789.

[39] Evidently a local preacher.

[40] Thomas White (1730–95) was reared in the Anglican church but converted to Methodism in 1778. Several early Methodist conferences were held in his home. Asbury, who had "lived days, weeks, and months in his house," called him one of his "best friends in America" and wrote of his active benevolence: "He was a friend to the poor and oppressed; he had been a professed Churchman, and was united to the Methodist connection about seventeen or eighteen years. His house and heart were always open; and he was a faithful friend to liberty, in spirit and practice; he was a most indulgent

being taken ill on his Return from Baltimore I Left the List of persons I Joined in Matrimony Since My Last return with M*is* Dickenson his Eldest Daughter

17 Called at Doct*r* whites[41] Rode to Church Hill preach*d* at John Johnsons

18 preach*d* [and] Met Class Rode to Chestertown

19 preach*d* to A Small But atentive people

20 Viseted Some of our friends Rec*d* their Blessing Towards our Charity School Rode to John Days

21 Rode to Cisel [Cecil] Court house preach*d* to A Moderat Congragation Considering the wetness of the Day

22 Began our Lovefeast Near ten the Lord was powerfully presant preach*d* at twelv to A house well fil*d* Notwithstanding the Rain it was A powerful Melting time Bro*r* Moor Exhorted Slep at John Fords &C—

Nov*r* 23 1789 Rode To Samson Curriors preach*d* To a Small Congregation Met Class preach*d* again in the Evning to a few more

24 Rode To peter Hukills (North west point)

25 Preach*d* To A Small Congregation Rode [to] John Fords

26 Rode To Harts Mill preach*d* & gave the Sacrament to [a] Small Congregation the Rain preventing the people Rode to Nathan Ierlands preach*d* & gave the Sacrament To his Black famaly the Lord was presant

27 Rode to John Fords &C—

28 Heard the Rev*d* M*r* Couden preach A practical & Experimental Discource on Rev 22 He Invited me to Spend a Night with him I Rode to John Carnans or Isaac Allmans

29 preach*d* at jess Hukills to a ful House with freedom Met Bishop asbury at governor Claytons[42]

---

husband, a tender father, and a most affectionate friend" (Abel Stevens, *History of the Methodist Episcopal Church in the United States of America* [New York, 1867], III, 61).

[41] Edward White, of Kent County, Delaware, later of Dorchester County, Maryland, was an early patron of Methodism. He was a nephew of Judge Thomas White (see above).

[42] Dr. Joshua Clayton (1744–98), physician and statesman, was an early convert to Methodism. He served as president of Delaware, 1789–92; governor of Delaware, 1792-98; and United States senator from Delaware, 1798 (*DAB,* IV, 186–87).

30 Rode to Abindon with Tho*s* white Mr Basit Alin Mc-Lane[43] Bro*r* asbury & Bro*r* Everit

Dec*r* 1 the Studiant[s] where [were] Examined & performed their orations I think Much to their Credit

2 Dined at perry Hall Rode to Baltimore

3 Opened our Council[44] with Much prayer &C preaching Every Night on Tusday the Eight[h] at our watch Night about Eleven found peace

11 our Council Broke up in Great unanimety

13 I preach*d* at the point

14 F asbury Bro*r* Reed &C Rode To Thos Cromwel[ls][45] F asbury gave them Two Exhortations &C— we Rode To anop-

[43] Allan McLane (1746–1829) was an influential layman of Smyrna, Kent County, Delaware, where he gave land for Asbury Chapel. He was the father of Hon. Louis McLane, a member of Jackson's cabinet and minister to England, and grandfather of Hon. Robert McLane, minister to France (*DAB,* XII, 112–13; Lednum, *op. cit.,* p. 260).

[44] The Council was a general ecclesiastical body, composed of bishops and presiding elders, designed to give union to the church by counteracting the division of the work into separate annual conferences, which had necessarily occurred due to the inexpediency of calling all the preachers to one central yearly gathering. James O'Kelley, in opposition to this newly constituted central authority, withdrew from the connection in 1793 to form the Republican Methodists. In 1792 the council resolved into the historic general conference of the Methodist Episcopal church. Asbury writes of this session: "*Thursday, December* 3 [1789]. Our council was seated, consisting of the following persons, viz.: Richard Ivey, from Georgia; R. Ellis, South Carolina; E. Morris, North Carolina; Phil. Bruce, North district of Virginia; James O'Kelly, South district of Virginia; L. Green, Ohio; Nelson Reid, Western Shore of Maryland; J. Everett, Eastern Shore; John Dickens, Pennsylvania; J. O. Cromwell, Jersey; and Freeborn Garrettson, New-York. All our business was done in love and unanimity. The concerns of the [Cokesbury] college were well attended to, as also the printing business. We formed some resolutions relative to economy and union, and others concerning the funds for the relief of our suffering preachers on the frontiers. We rose on the eve of Wednesday following. During our sitting we had preaching every night; some few souls were stirred up, and others converted. The *prudence* of some had stilled the noisy ardour of our young people; and it was difficult to rekindle the fire. I collected about twenty-eight pounds for the poor suffering preachers in the West. We spent one day in speaking our own experiences, and giving an account of the progress and state of the work of God in our several districts; a spirit of union pervades the whole body, producing blessed effects and fruits" (*Journal of Rev. Francis Asbury* [New York, 1852], II [1787–1800], 66).

[45] Thomas Cromwell lived in Baltimore County, Maryland. This seems to have been the home of Joseph and James O. Cromwell, early Methodist preachers (see below).

olas [Annapolis] F asbury preach*d* I Exhorted Several prayed &C—

15 Brekfast at the Wido Smalls Dined [at] Ebeneazer Ridgley[s]

16 Rode [to] —— Wimses [at] Fishin Creek arannald [Ann Arundel] County Mary Land A Rainey Day few people atended parson —— has ofishiated at fishing Creek Church three years

17 Rode through the Rain to John Childs[46] [in] Calvert County

Dec*r* 18 Rod To —— Greys F asbury preach*d* To about fifty people Bro*r* John Childs & I Exhorted Near patapcico Calvert County we held a prayer Meeting with the Bla[c]ks in the Evning it was A Time of Refreshing

19 we Crosed patapsico (3/4′) at Bonific[s] Rode through Newport Charleses County Maryland Crosed patomack at Hows Ferry M*rs* How Entertained us that Night Gratis!

20 We Crost at Modock[s] Ferry and Mattoxs Bridg[e] Rode by Roundhill Church just as parson Low had Ended his Servis, passed by Mattoxs Church Rode To Laronce popes [in] westmorland County Virginia

21 Bro*r* asbury preach*d* in the Evning To a few people

22 we Rode To Rich*d* Sanfords Near Stratford House I preach*d* Bro*r* Asbury Exhorted &C To A few pepol

23 Rode To the Widow —— Hutts we Exhorted &C To A few people in the Evning

24 Bro*r* Asbury & I Rode To Nomeny Hall[47] and Spent the afternoon Cheifly in Conversation with Cornal Robert Carter & M*r* Dauson A Baptis[t] preacher & Doct*r* Hearington Bro*r* Asbury Ex[p]ounded & I Exhorted in the Evning the famaly [on] how hardly Shall A Rich Man Enter the Kingdom

[46] John Childs (? –1829), a native of Calvert County, Maryland, was admitted on trial and appointed to Montgomery Circuit, Maryland, in 1789. He returned to farming the same year, but in 1816 he was readmitted to the Baltimore Conference ("Memoir," *Minutes,* Vol. II: *1829–1839,* pp. 76–77).

[47] Nomini Hall, seat of Robert Carter (1728–1804), was in Westmoreland County, Virginia. Carter was currently a Baptist, though later he accepted Arminian views and embraced Swedenborgianism in his last years.

25 Bro*r* Asbury preachd at the Widow Hutts Bro*r* Bruce[48] & I Exhorted &C and Rode to the Widow Wolands

26 Rode To Lancaster Court House preach*d* in the Church Formerly A presbytearion M[eeting] H[ouse] the House was fil[l]ed with atentive hearers Bro*r* Asbury Tomson[49] & Bruse Exhorted &C— We Slept at John Diggses

December 27 we Began our Lovefeast Between Nine & Ten it being A Wet Day Many were prevented yet the house was ful at publick worship Bro*r* Lunsford[50] & Tomson Exhorted Bro*r* Asbury preach*d* from if thou Seporate the preciouce From the Vile thou Shalt be as My mouth I & Bro*r* Bruce Exhorted there was A great Melting among the people we Gave the Sacrament To I Supose To [*sic*] about Two hundred Dined at Capt. Diggs, Spent the Evning with Cor*l* Gordon

28 Called at Capt. Diggs Rode To Mary Tapscott[s] Bro*r* Asbury preach*d* I & Bro*r* Bruce Exhorted To A house filled with atentive hearers we Rode To the Wido —— Balls &C—

29 Rode To urebannah [Urbana] York River Ferry about Ten O. C. About four we Got Safe over tho with Some Dificulty Crost pops or Turks Ferry about the Tim[e] that Twylight Lef the Sky But the Horses had liket To have Sunk the Skew to[o] Deep But thanks be To Kind providence we Got Safe To the Wido Dugleses about Eight Oh Clock the Calmness and Clearness of the Evning Made our Traveling Tolerable Chees Cake Gloster County Virginia)

30 I preach*d* Bro*r* asbury [and] Bro*r* Bruce Exhorted &C— Some of the people were Like Botles fil[l]ed With New wine Both at publick Servi[s] and Sacrament. we Rode To Jo*s* Bellam[y]s

[48] Philip Bruce (1755–1826), a native of North Carolina, was presiding elder of the North District of Virginia in 1789. His ministry was spent largely in Virginia and the Carolinas. ("Memoir," *Minutes,* Vol. I: *1773–1828,* p. 541; Sprague, *op cit.,* VII, 73–76).

[49] Amos G. Thompson, appointed to Lancaster Circuit, Virginia, in 1789.

[50] Isaac Lunsford, appointed with Amos G. Thompson to Lancaster Circuit, Virginia, in 1789.

31 Bro*r* Asbury preach*d* I & Bro*r* Bruce Exhorted Bro*r* Scott[51] prayed &C Some were Deeply Efected

Jan*y* 1 1790 Crosed York River [at] Capehoshe Ferry 3 M*s* in a Calme fine Morning Rode To —— Weldons For four or five Months in the former part of the Last year My Spirit had Great Conflicts with the powers of Darkness as tho the waight of the people Lay on me for there Seemed to be A Cloud over Six out of Nine of the Circuits I had the Oversight of; tho the preachers Laboured faithfuly the Camp of Isarial Moved forward Very Slow But it was a Time of Sifting. But Glory be to God in April the Cloud Brok and the pilors of Hell Began to Tremble Since Then I think I have Seen more of the Down pouring of the Spirit then [than] I have in the cource of Twenty years Before I Bless God For almost an uninterupted peace and Comunion with God through the Courrce of the Last year But I want to Sink Deeper into God and To Bring fourth [forth] More frute Lord Help

2 Bro*r* Asbury preach*d* To A few Peopl I & Bro*r* Bruce Exhorted &C Some felt A Softening power

3 we Rode To Cheekahomany Church Bro*r* asbury & I preach*d* Bro*r* Brown[52] Exhorted Bro*r* Bruce &C prayed &C the people felt the power of the word Bro*r* Bruce preach*d* at friend Browns [and] I at Bro*r* Weldons in the Evning Bro*r* Asbury Exhorted & I hope this Days Exersise will be Remembered for Good by Some precious Soles

4 Crossed Jameses River at Swan point Ferry in a fine Calme Morning (But we Narowly Escaped being Run upon by Two Bridgs [brigs].) Rode to Henery Mooring[s][53] [in] Surry County Virginia

[51] Thomas Scott (1772–1856), a native of Maryland, was appointed to Gloucester Circuit, Virginia, in 1789. He located in 1795 and subsequently served as judge of the Ohio Supreme Court.

[52] Benjamin Brown, appointed with Thornton Fleming to Berkeley Circuit, Virginia, in 1789.

[53] Christopher S. Mooring (1767–1825), a native of Surry County who entered the traveling connection in 1789, was of this family.

5 Spent [in] pr[i]vat Exersises &C—
6 Bro*r* Asbury preach*d*, & I in the Evning the word was with power To Many Souls
7 Rode to W*m* Elises Bro*r* Asbury preach*d* I gave A Exhortation Alls[o] Bro*r* asbury Met the Bla[c]k peopl in the Evning &C— the people felt the presance of the Lord
8 Being a Rainy Day I Stayed at Bro*r* Elises To Nurs My Sore Leg Susix County, V[irginia].
9 Rode To —— Ross[es] Bro*r* Asbury preach*d* I & Bro*r* Bruce Exhorted &C— and Gave the Sacrament &C &C—
10 Rode To Rob*t* Jones's Bro*r* Asbury preach*d*
Jan*y* 11 Rode To Mayburys Church Bro*r* Asbury['s] Horse Got Loos Bro*r* Bruce & I went forward But Mist the way but we arived before Bro*r* Asbury had finished his Discource the Sacrament was given &C—&C— we Rode to the widow Mayburys they Gave me A pare [pair] of Legings as My Boots oprest My Sore Leg
12 Rode To woolseys C. Bro*r* asbury preach*d* I Exhorted &C Rode To B. Drumgolds[54] &C
13 Sacrament & Lovefeast began [at] half past Nine paup[55] was ordained Deacon Some Spoke feelingly Bro*r* Bruce & B. asbury preach*d* at the End of the Latter the power of God brought Some to the Ground I hope Some found peace &C We Rode To W*m* Owings & Slept in peace
14 Rode to Roan Oak C. Bro*r* Asbury preach*d* Bro*r* Bruce Exhorted &C Slep at Stephen Shels [in] warrin County [North] Carolina.
15 Rode To the Wido pig[r]ams Bro*r* Asbury preach*d* Bro*r* Bruce Exhorted &C Gave the Sacrament the power of the Lord was presant &C We Slep at John falkons &C [in] Warin County
16 Rode To Roger Jones[es] [in] Franklin County.

[54] Edward Dromgoole (1751–1835), a native of Ireland and a convert from Roman Catholicism, came to America in 1770. He entered the traveling connection in 1774 but located in 1786, settling in Brunswick County, Virginia. For further biographical data see the introduction to "The Edward Dromgoole Letters" in the present volume (chap. vi).

[55] John Paup, appointed to Mecklenburg Circuit, Virginia, in 1789.

17 Sacrament & Lovefeast [at] half past Nine it was A precious Time Some profest the Lord had Santified their Souls it was A General quickning Bro*r* Asbury preach*d* and Rode To pop[e]s C. preach*d* in the Evning Bro*r* Bruce & I Rode with James lester

18 Rode To —— Bruce's Bro*r* Asbury preach*d* I & Bro*r* Bruce Exhorted &C—&C

Jan*y* 19 Rode to Tho*s* Tomalinson[s] [in] Weake [Wake] County on Nuce [Neuse] River

20 Rode with Rubin Elis[56] To W*m* O Keleys Refresh*d* Man & Beasts Bro*r* Asbury preach*d* at New hope Church I Exhorted Bro*r* anderson[57] prayed feelingly Some of the Stones Melted A Little we Slep at W*m* —— on N[ew] H[ope] River [in] Chatham County.

21 Rode To Sarah Snipes [in] Chatham County B asbury prech*d* To [a] Smart Congregation But hard Enough I Exhorted Bro*r* anderson prayed &C—

22 Rode To Wm Renys [Raineys] Esq*r* [in] orange County &C—

23 Sacrament & Lovefeast at Nine O Clock &C— Bro*r* Asbury & I preach*d* Bro*r* Elis Exhorted &C— Tho*s* Anderson Was Ordained Elder &C— We Rode To Garrald Burrough[s] [in] Chatham County. it Was A Wet Journy

24 Rode To W*m* M*c*Masters [in] Chatham County

25 Rode To W*m* Bell[s][58] on Deep River [in] Randolf County Who Entertained us Kindly &C—

[56] Reuben Ellis (? –1796), a native of North Carolina, was, in 1789–90, presiding elder of the South Carolina District. His official memoir (1796) mentions his having been "about twenty years in the travelling connection, during which time he travelled and preached through Pennsylvania, Maryland, Virginia, North and South Carolina, and Georgia. A man of slow, but very sure and solid parts, both as a counsellor and a guide . . . . a man of simplicity and godly sincerity . . . . he sought not himself. During twenty years' labour, to our knowledge, he never laid up twenty pounds by preaching: —his horse, his clothing, and immediate necessaries, were all he appeared to want of the world. . . . . It is a doubt whether there be one left in all the connection higher, if equal, in standing, piety, and usefulness (*Minutes,* Vol. I: *1773–1828,* p. 67).

[57] Thomas Anderson, appointed to New Hope Circuit, North Carolina, in 1789.

[58] William Bell was the stepfather of John McGee (Methodist) and William McGee (Presbyterian), preachers closely connected with the Great Revival in Kentucky and the rise of the camp meeting. Asbury wrote of this visit: "Went to Mr. Bell's, on Deep River, and were received in the kindest manner; before I left the house, I felt per-

26 Bro*r* asbury Elis & I Mounted our Steeds About Sun Riseing and Rode through A Dreary Hilley & Stoney Road about Fifty Two Miles To Tho*s* Chields who Received us Friendly w[h]ere we arived about Ten Oh Clock we had a few Flying Showers But Soon after we Got Shelter it Set to Rain[ing] Very hard

27 But it Cleared of[f] Time Enough for a people To Gether Bro*r* asbury & I preach*d* We Met A Little Company in the Evning &C.

28 Rode To Doct*r* Miles Kings [in] Montgomery County Bro*r* Asbury preach*d* —— Crarks funerel &C To A Large Company

29 Rode To Nights C. Bro*r* Asbury preach*d* I Exhorted &C the power of the Lord was presant A few people Rec*d* the Sacrament We Rode To Jacob Abit[s] [in] S[outh] Caroline Where we were Kindly Entertained

Jany 30 A Beutiful Day Inclined To heat B asbury preach*d* I & John Elis[59] Exhorted To A housfull of people I believe thay Felt the word Hard as thay were we Rode To —— pryers

31 Bro*r* Asbury preach*d* after the Lovefeast I Bro*r* Humfris[60] & John Elis Exhorted &C— Surely these Ex[c]ursions Cannot be in Vain

Feb*y* 1 I preach*d* Bro*r* asbury & Elis Exhorted &C Bro*r* wood Told me the Baptis preacher that has Long been Exclaiming against the Methodists After Servis was over with Tears in his Eys [and] Confesed they were the people of God. how Long will this Conviction Last. we Rode To Frederick Joneses [in] prince Georges parish Who was Born 1702 & his Wife is 77

2 Bro Asbury preach*d* I & Bro*r* Elis Exhorted &C— the power of the Lord Was presant one found peace Bro*r* Elis preach*d* in the Evning at 7

---

suaded that that family would come to experience the power of religion" (*Journal,* II [1787–1800], 70; see also W. L. Gissom, *History of Methodism in North Carolina* [Nashville and Dallas, 1905], I, 330–31).

[59] John Ellis, appointed to Anson Circuit, South Carolina, in 1789.

[60] Thomas Humphries (? –1820), a native of Virginia, was appointed to Little Pee Dee Circuit, South Carolina, in 1789.

3 Rode To Volantine Rowel[s] C. on Catfish. I Bro*r* Asbury & Elis Exhorted to about Eleven people that Much Need it We Were Very Wet But Rode To the Wido ports in Safety tho one of the horses Geting his hind feet over the Side of the Boat Made it Dangorous for the others &C—

4 Bro*r* asbury preach*d* in Britians Neck—I allso Gave them A Short Discource &C [and] we Returned. (W*m* Balson Died Soon after we Left the House)

5 Bro*r* —— preach*d* his funeral Gave the Sacrament and Gave A Strong Exhortation to the Black people in the Evning On Great pee Dee

6 Rode To George Town Never Do I Remember Riding Forty miles on So fine and Levil a Rode [Road] Shaded by Statly pines a Great part of the way George Town has About one hundred and Twenty Famalys in it. [It is] on the Wakamaugh [Waccamaw] a Sort of A Bay [made] by Black River [and] pe Dee which join together we Slept &C at W*m* Wayne[s]

7 Bro*r* asbury Re[a]d the Morning Servis I preach*d* we Gave the Sacrament to about forty B asbury preach*d* at three & I again in the Evning we Drank Tee at M*is* Judey Raggs

8 we Visited Some of our friends B. asbury preach*d* an Alarming Sermon in the Evning I Gave A Exortation the people felt the power of the Word &C—

9 Rode To George St Capers B. asbury preach*d* &C—

10 Rode To Charl[e]ston Slep a[t] John huses &C—

11 I preach*d* at five in [and] again in the Evning the waters were Trubled A Little. We B[reakfasted] at M*rs* pattons, D[ined] at Bro*r* Cooks T[ea][61] at Bro*r* huses &C—

12 B. [at] —— Seavers D. at Capt. Dorals

13 D. at Capt Doral[s] Rubin Elis preach*d* &C—

14 Bro*r* asbury preach*d* Morning & after Noon and Ordained Tho*s* Hunpheris Elder & Gave the Sacrament I preach*d* in the Evning we D at Bro*r* —— Welses

15 B at Bro*r* Huses D a[t] Seavers T. [at] M*rs* Wrights Spen[t] A Little Time With M*r* M*c*Gowin &C—

[61] Note that hereafter unexpanded "B," "D," and "T" mean "Breakfast," "Dinner," and "Tea," respectively.

16 B.D.T. at Bro*r* Huses we Held A Short watchnight Bro*r* Asbury Re[a]d an Extract of Some Letters Conserning the Revival of Religion at New York Baltimore &C I Gave an Exortation the power of God Came Down A Great Shaking Trembling & Mo[u]rning was heard through the Asembley I Beleive Charlston Never Saw the Like before Ride on Glorious Redeemer

17 B. at Bro*r* Huses D. at Jonathan Cooks on the Warf (Amen Street or Ragg aley) Bro*r* —— preach*d* &C &C— (Great Crys and Meltings among the people)

18 B.D.T. at John Huse[s] I preach*d* to A Crowded Congregation Bro*r* asbury Exhorted So we Concluded our publick Servis in Great Solemnity (Oh that thay May improve their gratiouse Visitation)[62]

19 Rode through Dorchester To philip Gibham[s] B. A[sbury] preach*d* I Exhorted &C [to] A few people Hard Enough

20 Rode To Jacob Linders I preach*d* B. A. Exhorted &C

Feb*y* 21 Rode To Kettle Creek C. Bro*r* Asbury prech*d* I Exhorted four or five went to prayer Satans Bulworks are Very Strong we Slept at Bro*r* Berrys

22 We Crost Edisto at —— Ferry Rode to George Burtons I & B. asbury preach*d* To [some?] to[o] Nere Akin to the Antinomians

23 Rode To Joneses C. B Asbury preach*d* to a Smart Company the Stons were Very hard we Rested at John Ridgdals (Orang County)

24 Rode to David Chesters I & B Asbury preach*d*

25 Rode to M*r* peukets [Puckets] Mr asbury preach*d* [to] A Few people it Being Taxgethering Day we Gave Notis that we would meet the Neibours in the Evning three Came two [too] Much in Licker

[62] Asbury wrote of this conference, held in Charleston for the Carolina preachers: "Our business was conducted in great peace and love. The business of the council came before us; and it was determined that the concerns of the college, and the printing, should be left with the council to act decisively upon; but that no new canons should be made, nor the old altered, without the consent of the conference; and that whatever was done on this head, should come in the shape of advice only. We had some quickening seasons, and living meetings. Several young people come under awakenings" (*Journal,* II [1787–1800] 73).

26 Rode To M*r* Tredaw[a]ys thirteen Came I preach*d* B asbury spoke A Little we Rode to Doct*r* Fulors &C [at] Blubery Hill

27 Rode to W*m* Guyins [at] Cam[pb]el[l] to[w]n B. Asbury preach*d* in the Evning &C—

28 B asbury preach*d* & I. to A Large welbehaved Congregation At Eleven &C— I preach*d* again in the Evning Lord Bless thy wor[d] to them

March 1 Crosed Savanah at Agusta, B. asbury preach*d* [at] W*m* Lees C. Rode to Joel Walkers I preach*d* in the Evning &C—

2 We Rode To old Sandy Run Church B asbury preach*d* &C I preach*d* at Tho*s* Wyches in the Evning the Lord was powerfuly presant &C—

3 I preach*d* at Gaulphin[s] old town C. we had a Solom time Rode to Elijah padgets B asbury Gave A Exhortation in the Evning &C—

4 Rode to Salam C. B asbury preach*d* &C— Rode To Charles Hudsps— prayermeeting[63]

5 Rode to arthra Forts C. B. Asbury preach*d* &C

6 Rode To Heths C. F. Asbury preach*d* &C— Rode to Ja*s* threets &C—

7 Rode To —— Harveys I & B Asbury preach*d* we Rode To ——

March*d* [*sic*] 8 Rode To —— New C. B Asbury preach*d* we Rod[e] to Corl. Bostick[s]

9 Rode To Stars I preach*d* B asbury Exhorted we Rode To —— Grants

10 Conference Began[64] I & B. asbury preach*d* five or Six

[63] On the same date, Asbury wrote of the conditions under which they were traveling: "We have been exercised in public night and day; frequently we have not more than six hours' sleep; our horses are weary, and the houses are so crowded, that at night our rest is much disturbed. Jesus is not always in our dwellings; and where he is not, a pole cabin is not very agreeable. Provisions for man and horse we have plenty of. Our journeys are about thirty miles, day by day; but under all these trials I enjoy peace and patience, and have much of the love of God" (*ibid.*, p. 75).

[64] With this meager account of the Georgia Conference, compare Asbury's: "*Wednesday,* [March] 10 [1790]. Our conference began at Grant's. We had preaching every day, and there were some quickenings amongst the people. Our business was conducted in peace and unanimity. The deficiences of the preachers, who

prayed &C— we have Rode About one hundred and Seventy four Miles through the State of Georgia from Agustia &C to the forks of Ogochea [Ogeechee]

11 I preach*d* there was A Melting among the people

12 B Asbury preach*d* & [read] Some Letters Several prayed Br Hull[65] preach*d* in the Evning three found peace one purity &C— the Conerence Ended in Great unanimety

13 Rode through the Rain to Cok[e]sbury C. and preach*d* there was A Considerable Melting Among the people, Rode To John wingfield[s] (falling Springs wilks County) Bro Haris[66] preach*d* in the Evning &C—

14 it was A wet Morning But the House was fil[l]ed at our Love feast B Asbury preach*d* I Exhorted &C— we Had A Shower of Blessings in our Lovefeast and publick Servis Lord water the Seed &C—

15 Veued the Land perposed to Build A Colege on

16 Rode To Cross Roads Near Basdels Ferry B Asbury preach*d* I Exhorted there was A Little Melting Among the people We Rode To Isaac Herbit[s] we have Rode about 211 Miles thro the State of Georgia &C—

17 Crossed Savanah & Little River[s] rode To patrick Coughwons Where we were kindly Entertained

---

receive a salary of sixty-four dollars per annum from this conference, amounted to seventy-four pounds for the last year.

"*Thursday,* 11. We had a rainy day, yet a full house, and a living love-feast. Some souls were converted, and others professed sanctification. I had some opening in speaking from Ezek. ii, 7. We have a prospect of obtaining a hundred acres of land for every one hundred pounds we can raise and pay, for the support of Wesley and Whitfield school. On *Monday* we rode out to view three hundred acres of land offered for the above purpose. My soul has been much tried since conference began. I must strive to keep from rising too high, or sinking too low" (*ibid.,* pp. 75–76).

[65] Hope Hull (1763–1818), a native of Worcester County, Maryland, was appointed to Savannah-Town, Georgia, in 1790. A carpenter's apprentice as a youth, he was largely self-educated. After pioneering as a Methodist preacher in Georgia, he located in 1795 and founded a Methodist school in Wilkes County. In 1796 he married a daughter of John Wingfield, a Virginian residing in Wilkes County, mentioned below. Hull later became a member of the board of trustees of the University of Georgia and at one time was acting president (Sprague, *op. cit.,* VII, 112–17).

[66] Matthew Harris, appointed to Washington Circuit, Georgia, in 1790.

18 Cauled at John Hambletons [at] Abervel Courthouse who Fed our horses G[rati]s Likewise by Gabril Smutherses who Shewed kindness, So on To Hugh porters B Asbury preach*d* I Exhorted

19 Cross[ed] at the forks of Seludoy Rode To Wido Bowmans

March 20 Dined at —— Moors Sister foster pilated us To Kerseys

21 B Asbury preach*d* I Exh*d*—&C Rode to Smiths [and gave] an Exhortation or tow [two] &C I believe the Lord was presant to awaken one Soul A[t] Least

22 we Rode to Nickolis waters[67] Near Union Courthouse South Caroline

23 B. asbury preach*d* I Exh*d* tow [two] More prayed &C— B asbury preach*d* Againe in the Evning &C

24 Crossed Broad River Near Smith[s] Ferry in A Conew & Swam our horses I preach*d* at Josiah Smiths in the Evning &C N[orth] C[arolina]

25 B Asbury preach*d* in the Evning thunder Litening & Tempest Came hevey upon us &C—

26 our Dear Friend Smith Rode 16 or 18 Miles with us and Caried A feed for Man & beast Soon after we parted A Mighty Tempest met us we arived at Cor*l* W*m* Grehams (on Little Broad River) Very Wet we were Entertained with Great Hospetality til the Rain was Near over tho it Continewed more than Sixty houers with Very Little intermition

29 We Rode To George Moor[s] I preach[*d*] in the Evning

30 Bro*r* Asbury preach*d* I gave an Exhortation in the Evning We Sang prayed & Exhorted a few that Came in the Evning

31 Rode to —— H[a]mptons Near —— Courthouse B Asbury preach*d* A Strong pointed Sermon from By Grace are ye Saved through faith &C I Exhorted

April 1st we Rode Near fifty Miles over A Mountainous Road—we Arived at W*m* Whites Esq*r* on Johns River about Eight in the Evining

2 Rested &C—

[67] Nicholas Watters (1739–1804), a native of Anne Arundel County, Maryland, had entered the traveling connection in 1776. He was the elder brother of William Watters, the first native Methodist itinerant in America ("Memoir," *Minutes,* Vol. I: *1773–1828,* pp. 126–27).

3 I preach[*d*] & B asbury [and] Bro*r* Anderson[68] Exh*d* &C it was a quickening time tow [two] found peace Sacrament Began about Nine O Clock

4 I & B asbury preach*d* Bro*r* anders*n* Exhorted & it was A Time of Refreshing we Rode Ab[o]ut Twelv Miles & B Asb*y* preach*d* Eliz. Biggerstafs funeral But the people were Near all Gon Before we arived

April 5 we Crost the Blew [Blue] Ridg and Stop*d* at Beaver Dam [This was] the first time I Remember Being honered with Lieing in the woods we had no Sooner kindled A fier then [than] we where [were] Saluted with A Tremendious Storm of Lightnin thunder & Rain witch [which] almost put out our fier Oh that we May Reign with Christ in his Glory[69]

6 we Crost Stone & Iron Mountains and Lodged at M*r* Grears

7 we Rode to W*m* Nelsons I preach*d* B As*y* and anderson Exhorted &C

8 we Came To Stephen Heasly[s] about Eleven oh Clock

9 We Crost the North fork of holston at Smiths Ferry and and [*sic*] Arived at Capt. Eameys Near Sun Set a plase well prepared for Travilers

10 We Rode To Robin Beans at the fork of Cumberland & Kantukky Roads [in] Hukin County Near Klinch Mountain [in] Grasey Valey Heare we had Exercise for faith and patience as we had Nothing but Grein for our Horses we Let them Run in the woods

11 Ten persons Made Serch for them but found them Not A Smal Company Came in the Evning with Whom we intended to Venter through the wilderness the Next Day but

12 our horses not Coming to hand thay Left us So we gave our Corn to those that went forward and Laid our things on a Horse and Walked about ten Miles up the River To Lawer Cok's where we where [were] kindly Entertained and about

[68] Thomas Anderson was at this time presiding elder of the East District of North Carolina.

[69] Of this night passed in the wilds of Tigert's Valley, Asbury wrote that they "slept at the Beaver Dam in a cabin without a cover, except what a few boards supplied: we had very heavy thunder and lightning, and most hideous yelling of wolves around; with rain, which is frequent in the mountains" (*Journal,* II [1787–1800], 78).

Four oh Clock T[w]o Boys brought our Horses; we Rested that Night in peace

13 Rode To Capt. Eamis and waited two

14 Nights & one Day for A Company &C—

April 15 1790 We Road [rode] About fifty Miles and To Jas Karrs & arived about Ten in the Evning Beaver Creek Washington County V[irginia].

16 We walked To John Owens B asbury preach*d* To A few people I Exhorted & preach*d* in the Evning at Ja*s* Karrs B asbury Exhorted &C—

17 we Rode by Washington Courthouse To Michel Half Hakers it Was [a] Wet Day &C—

18 Rode To General Samuel Russels[70] I preach*d* &C— Since we Left Baltimore we have Traveled Two thousand five hundre[d] & Seventy Eight Miles in Eighteen weeks.

19 Bro*r* Asbury Being Much Indisposed Took Some Immatic Which Gave him Great Relief

20 We had A prayermeeting [with] Two Exhortations &C—

21 Five Days thick and Rainey Wether &C Hail and Snow Lies on the Mountains

22 we Rode To Stephen Keywood[s] held a prayermeeting

23 Rode To Michel Halfacers held a prayermeeting &C

24 Rode To John M*c*Hendrey[s][71] Meney Came to our prayer Meeting in the Evning

25 Bro*r* Asbury and I preach*d* the Generals house was Crowded I hope the Seed will not all Fall To the Ground

26 I was Glad to find the Salt works Brought to Such perfection it Must be A Great privilidg to these back partes as they Can bie it Nine Shilings a Bushel in produce &C we Rode To Rich*d* prices [on] Klinch [in] Russel County

27 B Asbury & I preach*d* To About Ninty people Lord Raise the Ded

[70] Russell lived in western Virginia. He and his wife, who was a sister of Patrick Henry, had been converted to Methodism at the conference held in the Holston country in 1788 (Thomas Ware, *Sketches of the Life and Travels of Rev. Thomas Ware* [New York, 1839], pp. 152–53).

[71] John McHenry of Washington County, Virginia, was the father of Barnabas McHenry (see below).

28 We Rode To Cap. Charles Beckels [at] Castles woods B Asbury preach*d* & I Exhorted To about Seventy people Some felt the word

29 Caled at Ja*s* Ausbands B Asbury preach*d* I Exhorted To About Seventy people I I [*sic*] joined in the Bands of Matrimony John Alley & Mary porter of Russel County Virginia we Rode To Jo*s* blackmors on Klinch River Lord pity the people in thes Back wood[s] tho they Live [in] jeperdy Every Day yet the Greatest part of them Seem to have no more Religon then [than] the Savage Tribes

30 We Road [rode] About twelve Miles through A wilderness To Mockason Gap as Ruf & uneven as Most I Ever Traveled, Stephen Heasly & Tho*s* Rubey Met us & Conducted us to Bro*r* Heasleys

May 1 B asbury Took Some Salt[s] which Operated Strongly on Me [*sic*] we held A pr[a]yer Meeting in the Evning.

2 B Asbury preach*d* I also preach*d* first To about 70*ty*

3 B Asbury preach*d* I Exhorted To about Seventy Maney Came To prayer meeting in the Evning. Last Night Bishop Asbury Dreamed that A Company Was come To conduckt him to —— through the Wilderness and that Two Sedate men Came up To him Where he was: Which was Exactly So About four Oh Clock this Day[72]

4 Got —— Bul To put our Horse Shose in Order Kantuckey Rode To Tho*s* Rubey[s] &—

5 Rode To Cap. Emis about thirty two Miles

6 Rode To Jo*s* Crabs [in] Grassey Valley

7 we Rode To the New Station Ne[ar] Cumberland Gap Slep at Jo*s* Lewises

[72] Asbury's version: "Sabbath night, I dreamed the guard from Kentucky came for me; and mentioned it to brother W[hatcoat]. In the morning I retired to a small stream, for meditation and prayer, and whilst there saw two men come over the hills: I felt a presumption that they were Kentucky men, and so they proved to be; they were Peter Massie and John Clark, who were coming for me, with the intelligence that they had left eight men below: after reading the letters, and asking counsel of God, I consented to go with them" (*Journal,* II [1787–1800], 82). Asbury's account of this journey across the Alleghenies to Kentucky shows the wild and semisettled condition of the area. The Massie-Clark party were engaged not only as wilderness guides but as protectors against the Indians. Asbury mentions Indian troubles within the past year (1789).

8 Rod[e] to the Rich Valley
9 Rode to Near the Hazel patch
10 Rode To W*m* Maguyer[s] Near Mattoson [Madison] Courthouse
11 Rode To Henery Renolds
12 B Asbury preach*d* I Exhorted &C &C we were Comforted Together we Rode To Morgan Brions
13 Rode to Lexin[g]ton Courthouse. B Asbury preach*d* I Exhorted &C we Rode To Rich*d* Mastersons[73] Near Lexington
14 Conference Began I preach*d* Bro*r* Williamson[74] Richards[75] & Bro*r* Haw[76] Exhorted &C—&C
May 15 Bro*r* Asbury preach*d* To About 3 hundred And ordained wilson Lee[77] & Barnab[a]s M*c*Kendree[78] Deacons A powerful Meeting in the Evning

[73] Richard Masterson (? –1806) moved about 1784 from Virginia to Fayette County, Kentucky, where he erected the first Methodist meetinghouse in the state (William E. Arnold, *A History of Methodism in Kentucky* [Louisville, 1935], I [1783–1820], 46–47). Asbury writes of this first Methodist conference held in Kentucky: "Our conference was held at brother Masterson's, a very comfortable house, and kind people. We went through our business in great love and harmony. I ordained Wilson Lee, Thomas Williamson, and Barnabas M'Henry, elders. We had preaching noon and night, and souls were converted, and the fallen restored. My soul has been blessed among these people, and I am exceedingly pleased with them. . . . We fixed a plan for a school, and called it *Bethel;* and obtained a subscription of upwards of three hundred pounds, in land and money, towards its establishment" (*Journal,* II [1787–1800], 84–85).

[74] Thomas Williamson, appointed to Cumberland Circuit, Kentucky-Tennessee, in 1789, and to Danville Circuit, Kentucky, in 1790.

[75] Evidently a local preacher or exhorter.

[76] James Haw was appointed to Lexington Circuit, Kentucky, in 1789, and to Cumberland Circuit, Kentucky-Tennessee, in 1790. He located in 1791, joining O'Kelley's Republican Methodists, and later entered the Cumberland Presbytery. For his ministry in that body see W. W. Sweet, *Religion on the American Frontier,* Vol. II: *The Presbyterians, 1783–1840* (New York, 1936), pp. 282–305).

[77] Wilson Lee (1761–1804), a native of Sussex County, Delaware, was appointed with James Haw to Lexington Circuit, Kentucky, in 1789 and, in 1790, also with Haw, to Cumberland Circuit, Kentucky-Tennessee. Until 1793 his labors were chiefly west of the Alleghenies ("Memoir," *Minutes,* Vol. I: *1773–1828,* pp. 127–28; Sprague, *op. cit.,* VII, 90–92).

[78] Barnabas McHenry (1767–1833), a native of North Carolina, was appointed to Danville Circuit, Kentucky, 1789, and Madison Circuit, Kentucky, 1790. He preached chiefly in West Virginia, Tennessee, and Kentucky and died a member of the Kentucky Conference (James B. Finley, *Sketches of Western Methodism* [Cincinnati, 1855], pp. 143–53; Sprague, *op. cit.,* VII, 143–45).

16 the Lord was powerfully preasant I Trust To Justify & Sanctify &C B Asbury preach*d* To I Supose five hundred people and Ordained wilson Lee Tho*s* Wiliamson and Barnabas M*c*Hendery Elders & Gave the Sacrament yesterday the Bisness of the Conferance Ended Ja*s* Haw & Joshua Hartly[79] Desist [from] Traviling About three hundred pounds was Subscribed Towards Bethel S[c]hool[80] To be Built in the District of Kantuky

17 Called at Charles Whites [at] Lexington who Lat[e]ly Came from New York we Rode To Benjamin Colemans C. B Asbury preach*d* I Exhorted & the Lord was powerfully presant we Dined at Bro*r* Colemans and Rode To John Lewis[es][81] on Kantucky River About twenty Miles from Lexington [in] Fiatte [Fayette] County

18 B Asbury preach*d* I Exhorted &C—

19 Rode through Danvil To Francis Clark[s][82]—

20 Bro*r* Asbury preach*d* I Exhorted &C &C the Sacrament was Given it was A Time of Refreshing from the presance of the Lord

21 Rode To Willis Greens[83] on salt water River B Asbury preach*d* Bro*r* Poythres[84] & I Exhorted &C—

[79] Joshua Hartley, appointed with Thomas Williamson to Cumberland Circuit, Kentucky-Tennessee, in 1789.

[80] Bethel Academy in Jessamine County, Kentucky, was the first Methodist school in the state. For its history see Arnold, *op. cit.,* I (1783–1820), 81–86.

[81] John Lewis was donor of the ground upon which Bethel Academy was built. Asbury describes Lewis, who lived on the Kentucky River, as "an old acquaintance, from Leesburg, Virginia; I was pleased to find that heaven and religion were not lost sight of in this family. Brother Lewis offered me one hundred acres of land for *Bethel,* on a good spot for building materials" (*Journal,* II [1787–1800], 85).

[82] Francis Clark (? –1799), with "John Durham, a class-leader, and a few of their neighbors, with their families, removed from Virginia about 1784; and Clark organized the first Methodist class ever formed in what was then called 'the far West,' about six miles from where Danville [Kentucky] now stands" (J. F. Wright, in *Western Christian Advocate,* March 7, 1866). He may also deserve credit for preaching the first Methodist sermon in Ohio, since there is some indication that he preached in Fort Washington (Cincinnati) in 1793 (Stevens, *op. cit.,* II, 317–18).

[83] Willis Green, Kentucky legislator and Methodist layman of Lincoln County, Kentucky, served as trustee both of Transylvania Seminary and of Bethel Academy. He was a native of the Shenandoah Valley of Virginia. A son, the Rev. Lewis Warner Green, D.D., a Presbyterian minister, became president of Hampden-Sydney, Transylvania, and Center colleges (Arnold, *op. cit.,* I [1783–1820], 27).

[84] Francis Poythress (1732–1810), a native of Virginia and a convert of Devereux Jarratt, entered the itinerancy in 1775. His first appointment (1776), with Dromgoole

22 Rode To Absolom Browns I & B asbury preach*d* we had a Mighty Move

23 Rode To [....] I & B asbury preach*d* To A [crowd of] I Supose Six or Seven hundred people the word [had] Some Considerab[le] waight on the Asembley we Rode To the Crabb Orchard Kantuckey is Near T[w]o hundred [miles] in Length & Breadth (Settled) A Rich*d* [*sic*] Soile Heavy Dews Much on the Level Suposed To have Not Less than forty thousand Souls in it the Gospel is Now Taking Root in the Light And power thereof about 13 hundred have Joyned in Con[tuck]ay

May 24 we Started from the Crab Orchard Near Forty in Company [and] Encamped Near the Hazle patch the first Night[85] the Second at Cumberland River [and] the third at powels [River] at old peevis

27 Rode To Capt. Emis

28 we Rode a Little in the night as we Lost our Road we Turned into A Little Cabin and Slep under the widows Roof

29 We Rode About fifty Miles Slep at Mickel Half Acours

30 Rode To General Russels B Asbury preach*d* I Exhorted &C Since We where [were] here Last the General & his Lady I Believe they have found peace with God we had Dry wethe[r] Going & Coming through the Wilderness [and] Good Order in our Company [with] Much peace and Solemnity in My own Soul

31 Rode To Michel Lees on New River

June 1 Rode up Cripel Creek Slep at —— armstrong[s] Near the Flower Gap

22 Rode To George McNights on the yead kin [Yadkin] [in] Rowin County North Caraline

---

and Tatum, was "[North] Carolina." He served the connection as presiding elder in Virginia, North Carolina, Kentucky, and Tennessee and was a founder of Bethel Academy, Kentucky. In 1789–90 he was presiding elder of the Kentucky or Western District. His active ministry was terminated by mental derangement after 1800 (M[atthew] H. Moore, *Sketches of the Pioneers of Methodism in North Carolina and Virginia* [Nashville, 1884], pp. 83–92).

[85] For Asbury's description of the return journey across the mountains through Tennessee to North Carolina see *Journal,* II (1787–1800), 85–86.

3 Conferance Began[86] I preache*d* To A ful house

4 I Rod[e] To Adom peathree[s] To Get the horses Shod

5 B Asbury preach*d* I Exhorted &C— the power of the Lord was presant to Wound and To Heal Glory To God &C— five were ordained Deacons

6 B Asbury preach*d* And ordained Seven Elders I Bro*r* Anderson & Low[87] Exhorted the Convinceing and Converting power of God Came Down it was Suposed that Twelv found peace we Rode To John Hills

7 we Rode To Isaac Lowes [in] Rockingham County

8 Caled To Refresh our Selvs at Nathan Wiliamsons Lodged at Ja*s* Rice*s* [in] Cazwell County

9 Caled at Gabril Lees, Lodged at John Cannons [in] Granvil County

10 [At] Cor*l* Samuel Smiths Crossed at Taylors Ferry Rownoak Lodged at Tignal Jones[es] in Macling Burg [Mecklenburg] County Virginia

June 11 Cauled at Jo*s* Speeds Lodged at Isaac Johnsons [in] Macklingburg County

12 Cauld and fed at Ropers Tavern Caled at Capt. Ed*d* peagrams Near Dunweedey [Dinwiddie] Court house Rode To peaters Burg Lodged at Grissifh [Gresset] Davises

13 B Asbury preach*d* to A Large Congregation I Exhorted the Word was With power

14 Conferance Sat[88] I preach*d* &C—

15 parson Garat[89] preach*d* A Laboured Discors Bishop asbury ordained I think 16 deacons

[86] *Ibid.*, p. 86.

[87] Isaac Lowe, appointed to Guilford Circuit, North Carolina, in 1789.

[88] For this Virginia session of the Methodist Conference see Asbury, *Journal,* II (1787–1800), 87.

[89] Devereux Jarratt (1733–1801), evangelical Anglican rector of Bath Parish, Dinwiddie County, Virginia, long worked in co-operation with the pioneer Methodist preachers. Asbury wrote of him in 1781: "I am persuaded there have been more souls convinced by his ministry, than by that of any other man in Virginia" (*Journal,* I [1771–1786], 435). His "Life" was published by the Reverend John Coleman in 1806 (*DAB,* IX, 616–17).

16 B.A. preach*d* and ordained [....] Elders &C I preach*d* David Tuckers funeral
17 I preach*d* with plainness & Liberty
18 Ira Elis[90] Gave us a plain Discours
19 I preach*d* with freedom &C—
20 B. A. preach*d* Morning and after Noon I Exhorte[d] We Drank Tae at Rich*d* Garatsons[91] Called at —— Hardens Monday the fourteenth Some Delagats from the Baptis Church atended our Conferance T[o] aske our asistance To Petision for an Act to Sel the Gleebs[92] &C— But our preachers Chose To be Neuters
21 & 22 I had Exercise for patience Til the Gethering Broke[93]
23 Got Some Eas and Took A Dose of Salts
24 Rode To Rob*t* wallthalls the Lord was powerfuly presant in famaly prayer
25 Bro*r* Asbury preach*d* I Exhorted &C at old amelia Courthouse we Rode through A thunder Gust To Tho*s* Joneses &C—
26 Rode To John Davis[es] I preach*d* at prid[e]s C. &C— Rode To Rob*t* Good[s] [in] prince Edward County
27 Rode To Samuel Strongs [in] Cumberland County Bro*r* Asbury & I preach*d* Bro*r* Minter[94] Exhorted To A Large

[90] Ira Ellis, a native of Virginia, was in 1789 assistant to his brother, Reuben Ellis, presiding elder of the South Carolina District. In 1790 he was appointed presiding elder of Richmond District, Virginia. Like many of the early preachers, he "located," on account of marriage, in 1795 (Stevens, *op. cit.*, II, 110–11).

[91] Richard Garrettson, a brother of Freeborn Garrettson (see below), was a native of Maryland who had itinerated from 1778 until his location in 1783.

[92] In Colonial Virginia each parish of the Established (Anglican) Church was granted by the government a tract of land ("glebe") purchased with public funds. After independence, dissenting church bodies looked upon the continuance of this last vestige of establishment in Virginia as violation of the state law establishing religious freedom (1785). The Baptists led the struggle for the sale of the glebes, the money from which was to be applied to public use. In 1802 this was accomplished by act of the assembly.

[93] Asbury writes: "[June 20] My dear old friend and fellow-traveler, W[hatcoat], is smitten with boils, so that he cannot go on" (*Journal,* II [1787–1800], 88).

[94] Jeremiah Minter, appointed to Brunswick Circuit, Virginia, in 1789, and to Mecklenburg Circuit, Virginia, in 1790.

Congregation of Atentive hearers in the Woods it was a Melting Time I Beleive one Woman found peace at family prayer in the Evning

June 28 I preache*d* Bro*r* Asbury Exhorted at the widow Lacklands it was A Refreshin Time

29 Rode To —— Martins I & B. A. preach*d* &C— the Lord was presant to Comfert us &C—

30 Rode To W*m* Swiney[s] [in] prince Edward County B asbury preach*d* To About forty Hard Enough

July 1 B asbury preach*d* at Holts Schoolhouse [on] pilat Mountain [in] Cam[p]bel[l] County To about Sixty Most of them apeared To be unawakned About Twelv Rec*d* the Sacrament Some apeared to be Tuched with the presance of God I preach*d* at Robert Mosleys in the Evning to About Twenty From We Know that we are of God &C—

2 Rode to Charles Calaways [in] Bedford County

3 B Asbury preach*d* and Gave the Sacrament to About Ten peoule Lord Revive thy Work

4 Rode To Jo*s* Wilsons &C— I & B Asbury preach*d* to A Large Congregation the Word Was with power to Some; we Rode To John Murphys

5 Rode To John Ayers B Asbury preach*d* I Exhorted the word was atended with a Softning power

6 Rode To Liberty Dined at —— Marcle[s] I preach*d* in the Courthous to Sixty or Seventy people with freedom we Rode with Henery Ogburn[95] A Cross the peaks of Auta [Otter] [and] Down Geninses [Jennisons] Creek To James River and arived at Ja*s* Michels About Eleven o Clock Botitot [Botetourt] County

7 B. Asbury & I preach*d* Gave the Sacrament

8 Rode to Ed*d* Mitchel[s][96] B Asbury & I preach*d* And Gave

[95] Henry Ogburn, of Lunenburg County, Virginia, was a Methodist itinerant from 1779 to 1790. In 1795 he settled near Carrollton, Kentucky (Arnold, *op. cit.*, I [1783–1820], 175).

[96] Edward Mitchell, a local preacher of Botetourt County, Virginia.

the Sacrament. Bro*r* poythers's Sister found peace it was A powerful time

9 Crost Creags Creek & on Rich patch Mountains I preach*d* & B Asbury Exhorted & Gave the Sacrament to 20 at Jo*s* Carpenters the power of the Lord was presant we Slep at Ja*s* Wright[s] on patses [Pott's] Creek

10 Rode To the Church B Asbury preach*d* John Tunels[97] Funarel from Phil. 1:21—And Gave him an Exalted Caricter which I Trust he was worthy of we Slep at Sam. Dews

11 Rode To the Sweet Springs B Asbury preach*d* in Botitot Circuit Courthouse we Rode To James Mosses &C W[h]ere John Tunil Died on thursday the Eighth of July 1790

12 Drank of the Sweet Spring water

14 D[itt]o & Got our horses Shooed &C—

15 Rode To Ed*d* Keenan[s][98] I preach*d* B Abel[99] & Asbury Exhorted &C— Gave the Sacrament at Rehobath C. the Lord was presant Greenbrye[r] County

16 Rode To Greenbryer Courthouse B Asbury preach*d* I Exhorted &C— Lord Visit them with thy Salv[a]tion We Rode To Ja*s* Watts & Dined

17 I &C B Asbury preach*d* to [a] Large Congregation With Freedom I hope Some felt the power of the word we Rode

[97] John Tunnell (? –1790) was buried at Dew's Chapel, Hampshire County, Virginia. Asbury says of him: "[July 10, 1790] It is fourteen years since brother Tunnell first knew the Lord; and he has spoken about thirteen years, and travelled through eight of the thirteen States: few men, as public ministers, were better known or more beloved" (*Journal,* II [1787–1800], 90). His labors as presiding elder in New York, New Jersey, North Carolina, and the Holston region are significant ("Memoir," *Minutes,* Vol. I: *1773–1828,* p. 37; Moore, *op. cit.,* pp. 131–35).

[98] Edward Keenan, originally a Roman Catholic, gave the land for Rehoboth Chapel in Greenbrier County, Virginia. Stith Mead, describing in his "Journal" the conference held May 21–24, 1792, at "Brother Edward Keenan's at Rehoboth Chapel, Sinks of Greenbrier county," writes: "This is a rough, uncultivated country in soil, ways, and manners; the Conference was held in a log-body cabin-house, the residence of Brother G. [E.] Keenan, of Irish national descent. Our accommodation was the best in this part of the world" (quoted in William W. Bennett, *Memorials of Methodism in Virginia* [Richmond, 1871], pp. 306–8).

[99] Jeremiah Abel, appointed to West New River Circuit, Tennessee, in 1789, and presiding elder of the Western District of Virginia, 1790.

about Twenty Two Miles To John M*c* Neals[100] on the Flats of Greenbrier

18 B Asbury preach*d* I Exhorted To the N[ew] C[hapel] Near Ful of people Lord Move the Rocks &C—

19 We Rode fourteen Miles To [....]

20 We Crossed the Mountains To Turkey Valey Lodged at M*r* Nelsons [in] Tigurs [Tygerts] Valey

21 Rode To M*r*. Wilsons B. asbury preach*d* To A Small Congregation Rode with Bro*r* Fidler[101] To Esq*r* Maxwels and Slept in peace

22 Rode To Z Osmans in the Cove B Asb*y* preach*d* To About Twenty people

23 Rode To Ja*s* Coburn[s] About 36 Miles We have Rode About one Hundred and forty Mil[es] [over] As Ruf a Road as I Ever I [*sic*] Traveled So interupt[e]d With Mountains Hils Trees Waters &C—

24 B Asbury preach*d* A Long Nervous Discours Against Strong Delusions I Exhorted & preach*d* in *y*e afternoon

25 we Slep at W*m* Lenham[s] Sadlor [of] Morgan Town we Gave the Sacrement & held our Lovefeast at Seven O Clok B Asbury preach*d* About Ten &C— Mr —— Marshal a presbytearian at Twelve I at half past Two M*r* Marshal at four We had a Comfortable Time I hope profitable also we Dined at John Stealey[s] Tan[n]er

July 26 Rode To Tho*s* Batting[s] B asbury preach*d* I preach*d* in the Evning at [....] we Slept at Joshua Browns

27 B asbury preach*d* at John Hudsons we Rode To the Widow Murphys[102] &C—

28 I preach*d* at Union Town in the Evning

[100] John McNeil was a pioneer Methodist of western Virginia, a convert of Strawbridge; his wife was a Welsh Methodist.

[101] Daniel Fidler, appointed to Ohio Circuit in 1790.

[102] Ann Murphy was one of the founders of Methodism in Uniontown, Pennsylvania.

29 Bro*r* Caluhan[103] preach*d* at Sun Rising B asbury at Twelv B Green[104] at Night

30 We observed as A Day of fasting & prayer I preach*d* at Eleven O Clok Several of the preachers joined in prayer Some Met in the Evning &C

31 Bro*r* Green preach[*d*] at Twelv at three B Asbury preach*d* on Education; Some Met in [the] Evning and the Lord was powerfuly presant Both in Town and Cuntry &C—

Aug*t* 1 the Lord Gave us A Comfortable & powerful Visit at our Sacrament & Love feast B Asbury and I preach*d* To I Supose five hundred people Bro*r* Lurton[105] Conaway[106] and Calua-

[103] George Callahan, appointed to Pittsburgh Circuit in 1790. A humorous rhymed letter written about this time by Caleb Jarvis Taylor (1762–1817), Methodist frontier hymnist, then a schoolteacher near Morgantown, (West) Virginia, to friends in and about Uniontown, chides Callahan for his marriage:

"That once illustrious Callahan,
That fear'd not devil, no, nor man,
Has felt the marriage fever;
A gentle fair hangs on his arm—
Thus he cries out, caught by the charm,
'Circuit—farewell—for ever!' "

The same poem alludes to Burton, Banning, Murphy, Bonham, Hill, Peck, Chambers, Stoneham, Matthews, Cook, and Connaway ([Thomas S. Hinde], "Short Sketches of Revivals of Religion among the Methodists in the Western Country," *Methodist Magazine,* XI [1828], 191).

[104] Lemuel Green (1751–1831), a native of Baltimore County, Maryland, served as joint presiding elder with Henry Willis of the Philadelphia District in 1789; and was appointed to South River Circuit, Maryland, in 1790 ("Memoir," *Minutes,* Vol. II: *1829–1839,* p. 161).

[105] Jacob Lurton, appointed to Clarksburg Circuit, (West) Virginia, 1789; and Kanawha Circuit, (West) Virginia, 1790. Cartwright, who heard him as a boy in Logan County, Kentucky, *ca.* 1793–94, describes him as "a real son of thunder" (William P. Strickland [ed.], *Autobiography of Peter Cartwright, the Backwoods Preacher* [Cincinnati, 1860], pp. 23–24). After his location in 1795 he settled in Jefferson County, Kentucky, and late in life moved near to Alton, Illinois, where he died (Arnold, *op. cit.,* I [1783–1820], 115).

[106] Charles Conaway served the Pittsburgh Circuit in 1789, and was appointed presiding elder of Pittsburgh District in 1790.

han were Ordained Elders; Bro*r* Dodridg[107] Matthews[108] Banning[109] Cocheran[110] &C—Jo*s* Cheuvront[111] Deacons. Bro*r* Conaway [was] Elected for The Counsil So we Concluded in Great Love

2 Crossed the Mountains Lodged At Mountains

3 Rode To Cornal Barrots B Asbury preach*d*

4 Called at Jo*s* Crisups parted With Bishop Asbury Bro*r* Green & I Rode To John Forsters I preach*d* To A few people &C—

5 Rode To John Jacobs Esq*r*[112] Bro*r* Green preach*d* I Ex[horted] [Also] Bro*r* Bruse &C the power of the Lord was presant

6 Rode To Arther Wigens I preach*d* &C—

7 it was A Wet Day So we Rested &C—

8 I preach*d* at the Springs At Ten &C B*r* Green at at [*sic*]

[107] Dr. Joseph Doddridge (1769–1826), a native of Bedford County, Pennsylvania, was appointed with Jeremiah Abel to West New River Circuit, Tennessee, in 1789; and Pittsburgh Circuit, with George Callahan, in 1790; but he withdrew from the connection in 1791 to enter the Protestant Episcopal church. Thenceforth he labored as a physician and Episcopal missionary in West Virginia and Ohio. He was the author of *Notes on the Settlement and Indian Wars of the Western Parts of Virginia and Pennsylvania* (1824) (*DAB,* V, 342–43).

[108] Lasley Matthews (1758–1813), an Irish Catholic, dated his conversion to Methodism from 1781, while in the Revolutionary army, "through the instrumentality of brother Joseph Chieuvront [see below], who used to carry a Bible in his pocket and read to him, and converse with him on the great things pertaining to the kingdom of God" ("Memoir," *Minutes,* Vol. I: *1773–1828,* pp. 223–24). His ministry was spent mostly in and west of the Alleghenies. In 1789 he had ridden Clarksburg Circuit, (West) Virginia, with Jacob Lurton; this year (1790) he was appointed to Greenbrier Circuit, (West) Virginia.

[109] Anthony Banning, appointed to Dorchester Circuit, Maryland, in 1789, and to Randolph Circuit, (West) Virginia, in 1790.

[110] Simon Cochran (1755–1845) was a local preacher of Hampshire County, Virginia. He later (1799) settled in Kentucky and went from there to Ohio (Lednum, *op. cit.,* pp. 391–92).

[111] Joseph Chieuvront, a Frenchman by birth and a convert from Catholicism, then evidently a local preacher in Rockingham County, Virginia, was the spiritual father of Lasley Matthews, and the founder of Methodism in Clarksburg, West Virginia. Henry Smith, while on Clarksburg Circuit in 1794, attended a meeting "in backwoods style" at Chieuvront's. Only one man, he says, in describing the meeting in his reminiscences, had shoes on, and Chieuvront himself was wearing moccasins (Stevens, *op. cit.,* III, 324–25).

[112] John Jeremiah Jacob (1756–1839), a native of Anne Arundel County, Maryland, was a local preacher in Hampshire County, Virginia (Lednum, *op. cit.,* pp. 392–93).

Four. I think My God Will not thank the Gentlemen & Ladys that Attend thes Waters For their not Atending Divine Servis

Aug*t* 9 1790 I, Bro*r* Green & Simmons[113] [rode] About 25 Miles & Dined at the Widow Strowd[s] we Rode To Benj. Bordstons Bro*r* Green preach*d* I, Bror Lurton, parrot[114] and Bro*r* Simmons Exhorted &C the Lord was Presant

10 We Rode To Samuel philips's I preach*d* Bro*r* Green Exhorted &C— Bro*r* Simmons & parrot Rode To Fredrick

11 we Rode To Liberty Bro*r* Green preach*d* I Exhorted we Rode To Daniel Dorcys To Meet his Brother

12 I Rode To John Evan[es] & preach*d* To About 30 people

13 Rode with Bro*r* Green To Elis Jones[es] I preach*d* in the Evning &C—

14 Rode To Baltimore preach*t* in the Evning At Fel[l]s point Bro*r* willis Exhorted &C—

15 I preach*d* [in the] Morning Bro*r* willis & Hagerty[115] Gave the Sacrament, Also I prech*d* in the Afternoon To I Supose as many more as the house Could hold Left Bro*r* Willis Hagerty &C To Keep watchnight Which Continued Til one O Clock the power of the Lord was presant To Heal and justify I preach*d* in Town To A thin Congregation (perhaps the Clowds hindred

16 Rode To Abingdon preach*d* in the Evning we were Comforted Together I Slep at Jo*s* Toys[116]

[113] John Simmons, appointed to Frederick Circuit, Maryland, in 1790.

[114] Richard Parrott was traveling Little York Circuit, Pennsylvania, in 1790. On June 11, 1794, William Colbert, who in 1792 had succeeded Parrott on the Northumberland Circuit in Pennsylvania, visited Georgetown, D.C., and "called at Richard Parrott's, who was formerly a travelling preacher in the Methodist Church, and remarkable for his zeal and great usefulness, as a minister of Christ.—But he is married and commenced Merchant [*sic*], and is far from being the man he was, when climbing the mountains of Northumberland, in persuit of the purchase of the Redeemer's Blood. He used me well, but he appears to be absorpt in worldly business" ("Journal of William Colbert," II [1794–1798], 13 [Garrett Biblical Institute]).

[115] John Hagerty (1747–1823), a native of Prince George's County, Maryland, was appointed to Fell's Point, Maryland, in 1790. For biographical data see "The Edward Dromgoole Letters," Part I, in the present volume (chap. vi).

[116] Joseph Toy (1748–1826), a native of New Jersey, was at this time head of the mathematics department of Cokesbury College, Abingdon, Harford County, Maryland. In 1802 he entered the Baltimore Conference, which he served as secretary ("Obituary," *Methodist Magazine,* IX [1826], 438–39).

17 Rode To Josiah Delams &C—
18 Dined at W*m* Mackintears Slep at Sol*m* Hercys
19 Rode To Wilmin[g]ton Dined With W*m* Daugherdy[117] Bro*r* Felwels[118] D. T[ea] At Sister Matsons; preach*d* To A Smal Congregation in the Evning [with] Liberty
20 B[reakfasted] at Bro*r* Joneses D[ined] at Mary Witheys[119] Rode To philadelphia T[ea] at John Dickens[120] Slept in peace
21 B. & D. at Bro*r* Dickens T at Bro*r* Stuerds[121] Held A prayer Meeting at —— Rogers[es]
22 Dickens preach*d* in the Morning I at three and in the Evning Bro*r* Thomas[122] in the feilds at five the people apeared to be A Little moved one profesed to have found peace in the Evning

Aug*t* 23 1790 I Laid the Corner Stone of Ebenezer[123] &C— I atended the Rev*d* Doct. Wineburgs[124] funarel I Supose about 30 of the Clergey and Ministers were presant and A Vast number of Spectaters 4 or 5 Hymns or psalms were Sung; and A Exortation in Dutch and one Exortation in English on the Bur[y]ing Grond Good order was observed I Met Bro*r*

[117] William Dougharty, appointed to Chester Circuit, Pennsylvania, in 1789.

[118] John Thelwell was a native of Ireland and a schoolteacher in Wilmington, Delaware.

[119] Mary Withey (? –1810), innkeeper at Chester, Delaware County, Pennsylvania, was converted to Methodism in 1772. Asbury, who preached her funeral in May, 1810, said of her: "For the last thirty years [she had] kept one of the best houses of entertainment on the continent: in her household management she had Martha's anxieties, to which she added the spirit and humility of Mary" (*Journal,* III [1801–15], 336).

[120] John Dickins (1746–98), a native of England and a pioneer American Methodist preacher, was in 1790 superintendent of the printing and book business (the Methodist Book Concern) at Philadelphia (Sprague, *op. cit.,* VII, 63–65; *DAB,* V, 292–93).

[121] Duncan Stewart, a trustee of St. George's M.E. Church, Philadelphia.

[122] Either James Thomas, appointed to Milford Circuit, Delaware, in 1790, or William Thomas, traveling book steward.

[123] Ebenezer Church, opened in 1790 (see below), was the second Methodist church in Philadelphia.

[124] Dr. Casper Dietrich Weyberg, a Swiss by birth, was pastor of the German Reformed church at Philadelphia, 1763–90. During the Revolution he was imprisoned for some time by the British for having preached sermons favoring the American cause. For biography see Henry Harbaugh, *The Fathers of the German Reformed Church in Europe and America* (Lancaster, Pa., 1857), II, 100–108.

Manlys[125] Class in the Evning & we where [were] Comforted Together   Slep at Henery Manlys &C—

24 B & D. at Bro*r* manlys   T. at Bro*r* Gilberds   preach*d* in the Evning

25 B & D. at Bro*r* manlys   T. at Bro*r* Doughtys[126]   prayermeeting at Bro*r* Fetherbridg[es][127]

26 B & D. at Bro*r* manlys   T. at Bro*r* Dickens   preach*d* in the Evning—

27 B & T. at Bro*r* manlys   D. at Bro*r* Rogerses—

28 B.D. at Bro*r* manlys   T. at Bro*r* Rogers[es] & prayermeeting

29 I preach*d* at eleven & 8*t* in the C[hurch] at five in the field B.D. at Bro*r* manlys   T. at Mary Frisses. [....] at B*r* Stuards

30 B.D. at Bro*r* manlys   T. at John M*c*Neals   met Bro*r* Smiths Class

31 B.D. at B*r* manlys   T. at B*r* Swains   preach*d* at the Church &C—

Sept*r* 1 B.T. at B*r* manlys   D. at Rich*d* Allins, prayermeeting at Fetherbridges   My Soul was sweetly Drawn out in privet meditation and prayer &C—

2 B.D.T. at Bro*r* manlys   preach*d* in the Evning to A Small [congregation] this Day for the first time I saw his Exelency president Washington

3 D. with M*r* pilmore,[128] askins,[129] Thomas, & petherbrig, at

[125] During the first part of his stay in Philadelphia, Whatcoat seems to have made his home with Manly.

[126] James Doughty, a trustee of St. George's M.E. Church, Philadelphia.

[127] Mr. Petherbridge was a founder of Ebenezer M.E. Church, 1790, and the father of Richard Whatcoat Petherbridge of the New Jersey Conference.

[128] Joseph Pilmoor (1739–1825) came to America in 1769 as Wesley's first American missionary. In 1790 he resided at Northern Liberties, Philadelphia County, Pennsylvania, and was rector of the three united Episcopal parishes of Trinity (Oxford), All Saints (Lower Dublin), and St. Thomas (Whitemarsh), and assistant rector of St. Paul's, Philadelphia. Beginning in 1794 he spent ten years as rector of Christ Church, New York, returning to Philadelphia as rector of St. Paul's in 1804. He was honored by the degree of Doctor of Divinity by the University of Pennsylvania in 1807. His original "Journal," dealing with his part in American Methodist beginnings (1769–74), is owned by the Historical Society of the Philadelphia Annual Conference, Philadelphia (Sprague, *op. cit.,* V, 266–70).

[129] Thomas Haskins (1760–1816), a native of Caroline County, Maryland, was at this time a local preacher at St. George's. He had studied law but entered the traveling

B. Kenears[130] T. at Bro*r* Rogerses and preach*d* there in the Evning with freedom

4 B.D. at Bro*r* manlys with Jo*s* Cromwel[131] & Bro*r* Thomas Drank T. at Bro*r* Rankins held a prayer meeting at B*r* Rogerses

5 B. at Bro*r* manlys D. at Sister Dickens T. at Bro*r* Askins. P[reached] 3 T[ime]s

6 B. at Cornal procters D. at Bro*r* manlys T. at Tho*s* Armits[132] Met Class at Bro*r* Jolifs Bapt[i]zed a Child at the poin[t] of Deth

7 B.D. at Bro*r* manlys T. at M*r* W*m* Wyatt Fenthams. preach*d* on perfection

8 B. at Bro*r* manlys D. Bro*r* petherbridg[e]s T. at Ebenezer Swains held a prayermeeting at Hugh Smiths[133]—

9 B at Bro*r* manlys D. at george Crips. T. at Hughey Smiths preach[d] [in the] Ev*ng*

10 D. at Bro*r* Rogers, T. at Bro*r* manly[s], Met Class at Doct*r* Lusbys[134] &C—

11 B. at Bro*r* manlys D. at Corn. Norths,[135] T. at John Hoods,[136] prayermeeting [at] Roger's

---

connection in 1782, locating in 1786. He helped to found the Academy (or Union) and St. Thomas M.E. churches in Philadelphia. His "Journal" (1782–85) is in the Library of Congress (Lednum, *op. cit.*, pp. 356–57).

[130] James Kinnear, a trustee of St. George's M.E. Church.

[131] Joseph Cromwell was appointed to Salem Circuit, New Jersey, in 1790. Thomas Ware said Cromwell preached "with an authority few could withstand." However, after about sixteen years in the ministry, including Philadelphia and Baltimore stations, and the presiding eldership, he located in 1793; and in 1804 Asbury wrote that he had died a drunkard. His funeral sermon was, Asbury remarks, appropriately on the text: "Tell it not in Gath . . . ." (John Atkinson, *Memorials of Methodism in New Jersey* [Philadelphia, 1860], pp. 216–19).

[132] Thomas Arnatt, a trustee of St. George's M.E. Church.

[133] Hugh Smith, a member of St. George's M.E. Church, had joined Benjamin Abbott's class in Salem, New Jersey, about 1775. A granddaughter of his married Bishop Scott.

[134] Josiah Lusby, a trustee of St. George's M.E. Church.

[135] Caleb North (1753–1840), a native of Pennsylvania, helped to found the Academy (Union) Church, and with Thomas Haskins was joint founder of the "Chartered Fund."

[136] John Hood (1749–1829), a trustee, class leader, and local preacher at St. George's M.E. Church.

12 B. at Bro*r* manlys, D. at Tho*s* allyborn[s] T. at Sis*r* Dickins preach*d* 3. Times &C—

13 B. at Bro*r* manlys, D.T. at John Hewsons Met Bro*r* Doughtys Class &C—

14 B.D. at Bro*r* manlys, T. at Sist*r* Reeds Held a watchnight Til 10 O. C'k

15 B at Bro*r* manlys D. at Rich*d* Whiteheads T. at Lambert Wilmors[137]

16 B.D. at Bro*r* manlys T. at Bro*r* Kenears preach*d* in the Evning &C—

17 D. at Bro*r* manlys, T. at Bro*r* Herskins [Haskins], preached at Bro*r* Rogerses—

18 B.D.T. at Bro*r* Manlys

19 B. [at] Bro*r* Manlys D. at Bro*r* Haskenses T. at Bro*r* petherbridges.

Sept 19 1790 preach*d* at 11 & 7 in the Church at 5 New Arch feilds

20 B.D. at Bro*r* Manlys T. at Bro*r* Dickins*s* With B. A[sbur]y

21 B.T. at Bro*r* Dickins, D. at Bro*r* Manlys Bro*r* Cann[138] preach*d* I Exhorted Bro*r* Daugherdy prayed &C—

22 B.T. at Bro*r* Dickins*s* D at Bror Bakers,[139] [and] preach*d*. Bro*r* Cromwell Exhorted Bro*r* Asbury & Bro*r* Dickens prayed &C—[140]

23 B.T. at Bro*r* —— D. [at] Doct*r* Lusbys Ja*s* Cromwel[141] preach*d* &C—

[137] Lambert Wilmer (? –1825), a native of Maryland and a resident of Northern Liberties, Philadelphia County, Pennsylvania, was originally a member of St. Paul's Church, and friend of Dr. von Wrangel, provost of the Swedish churches in America. He was in 1790 a member of St. George's, and later a founder of the Academy Church (Lednum, *op. cit.*, p. 42).

[138] Robert Cann, appointed to Bethel Circuit, New Jersey, 1790.

[139] Jacob Baker, Esq. (1753–1820), joined St. George's in 1773 and was a trustee in 1789. He later helped to found the Academy Church and headed the board of trustees of the Chartered Fund (Lednum, *op. cit.*, p. 44).

[140] Asbury describes this Philadelphia session of the conference, which convened September 22, in *Journal,* II (1787–1800), 95–96.

[141] James Oliver Cromwell, a brother of Joseph Cromwell (see above), was a native of Maryland, and in 1790 was presiding elder of the New Jersey District. He had

24 T. at Bro*r* Haskins*s* Held A Lovefeast A Solom Time
25 B. at Bro*r* Dickins, D. at Corl. Norths, T. at Bro*r* Swains prayermeeting at Bro*r* Rogerses &C—
26 Bishop Asbury preach*d* in the morning at [....] at three Opned Ebenezer I preached in the Evening &C— this Morning I was informed that My horse was Drowned When I heared it I felt unmoved; But was soon led to Reflect thus why Lord has this hapened what have I Don[e] Shall I no more want A horse are my travils Coming to an End &C—
27 Rode to Burlington[142] B. Asbury preach*d* from Who are Setled on their Lees and [*sic*] to a Large Congregation Several prayed
28 I preach*d* at Noon B Asbury at Night &C
29 We had A Mighty Stur at our Lovefeast I preach*d* in the Evning And [there was] A Mighty Move under the Exhortation
30 Rode to M*r* Hitchensons & Dined Rode to M*r* jaquist[s]

Oct*r* 1 Rode To Elizabeth Town and Bro*r* Asbury preach*d* I & Aron Hutchinson[143] Exhorted &C—
2 We Were About Seven Hours going to N[ew] York
3 in the Morning I preach*d* Bro*r* Hutchinson Exhort[e]d at the New Church;[144] B Asbury at the old[145] & Gave the Sacrament in the Afternoon Aron Hutchinson preach*d* at the old & B. asbury at the New Church in the Evning I—at the old & B. Hutchinson at the New

---

been ordained an elder at the Christmas Conference (1784) and served during the years 1784–86, with Freeborn Garrettson, in Nova Scotia. After serving as presiding elder in Maryland and New Jersey, he located in 1793 (Atkinson, *op. cit.*, pp. 219–20).

[142] For the conference held here for New Jersey, see Asbury, *Journal,* II (1787–1800), 96.

[143] Aaron Hutchinson (1767–91), a native of Milford, Mercer County, New Jersey, was converted about 1786. He was one of four brothers who became preachers. In 1790 he was appointed to Trenton, New Jersey (Atkinson, *op. cit.*, pp. 412–15).

[144] The Forsyth Street M.E. Church was the second in New York City and was erected in 1790.

[145] The John Street M.E. Church, erected in 1768.

4 I preach*d* at the New Church—[146]

5 I preach*d* at the old Church B Lee[147] Exhorted

6 Jesse Lee & others were ordained we had the Shout of a King at our Lovefeast Some Souls were Set at liberty B asbury preach*d* in the Evening &C—

7 Closed the Conference in Great Love and unanimaty Took the packet about half past twelve Reached Elizabeth Town about five Slep at M*r* Morrals[148] &C—

8 Mounted our Steeds about half past Six M*r* asbury Bought a Horse at Brumsweek [Brunswick] we arived at Trenton about Six M*r* asbury preach*d* How has the power of the Lord been Manyfested here Since our Last visit

Oct*r* 9 Rode to philadelphia

10 it being [a] Very Rainey Day I preach*d* at Ebinezer 3 Times

11 B. at Bro*r* petherbridg[e]s D. at Bro*r* Keneurs with B. asbury Bro*r* Dickins—Willis Harskins & the Rev Jo*s* pilmore

12 B [at] Dickins, D. at Hugh Smiths B. Asbury preach*d* &C—

13 B. [at] Dickins, D. at Bro*r* manlys I preach*d* at Ebenezer

14 B. [at] Bro*r* Dickins, D. [at] Mary Witheys (in) Chester T at M*r* Bonds B. Asbury preach*d* to A little house ful of quiat hearers

15 I preach*d* With freedom and plainness of Speech &C—

17 I heard M*r* Bar preach A Labered Discource &C— I preach*d* in the after Noon and Night with freedom

18 Rode With M*r* Sutley To philadelphia &C—

[146] The conference for New York and New England sat on this date (see Asbury, *Journal,* II [1787–1800], 96–97).

[147] Jesse Lee (1758–1816), a native of Virginia, was converted under Devereux Jarratt and after the Revolution was admitted on trial into the traveling connection in 1783. This year (1790) he was appointed to Boston, Massachusetts. From his pioneer work in New England, Lee gained the title of Methodist "Apostle to New England." He is also remembered for producing the first history of American Methodism. In 1809 he was chosen chaplain of the United States House of Representatives and in 1814 chaplain of the Senate (*DAB,* XI, 112–14; Leroy M. Lee, *The Life and Times of the Rev. Jesse Lee* [Louisville, 1848]).

[148] Jonathan Morrell (1725–1805), Methodist layman, was the father of Thomas Morrell (1747–1838), who in 1790 was presiding elder of the New York District. His wife had been a member of the Embury class in New York, but after their removal to Elizabethtown in 1772, there being no Methodist class there, they joined the Presbyterians (Atkinson, *op. cit.,* pp. 381–82).

19 B T at Bro*r* Dickins D. at B. Manlys preach*d* in the Evning

20 This Day I Set apart for fasting and prayer, that God Might be with me and fit me for the Charge Comm[it]ted to [me],— & Revive his Work (I Neithe[r] Eat Bread nor Drank water) and preach*d* in the Evning at Ebenezer &C—

21 B.D.T. at Bro*r* Dickins, Went with Bro*r* Kenear and pether Bridg to Beg for the New Church preach*d* in the Evning &C—

22 B.T. at Bro*r* Dickins D at Bro*r* Kenears Continewed to petetion for the Church preach*d* at Jo*s* Rogerses &C—

23 B.D. at Bro*r* Dickins T. at Bro*r* Swains, [Went with] Doct*r* Lusby—Armit Kenear Stewart petherbridg wilmar & Dickins to hear the Acusation M*r* Millis brought against Jo*s* Rogers

24 I preach*d* at St M[ichael]s Morning & after Noon Bro*r* Dickens Morning at Ebenezer [and] night at St M*s* Bro*r* Willis Read prayers [and] preach*d* after Noon & Night at Ebenezer I Met the Society

25 B. at Bro*r* Dickins, D.T. at Bro*r* Kenears Traveled Market Street with Bro*r* Kenear & petherbridg To beg for Ebenezer, Met Class at B*r* Stewards

26 B. [at] Bro*r* Dickins D. at Bro*r* Manlys T. at Bro*r* stewards preach[*d*] at St Michils

27 B. at Bro*r* Dickins D.T. at Bro*r* petherbridg[e]s Gleaned frunt Street with Bro*r* Ditto; preach*d* in the Evning Dav. Exhorted

Oct*r* 28 1790 B. at Bro*r* petherbridg[e]s Called at a few places D.T. at Bro*r* Dickins preach*d* at the C[hurch] in the Evning

29 D. at Bro*r* Dickins T. at Bro*r* Stewards Bro*r* Abbott[149] preach*d* Some Smoke appeared &C—

[149] Benjamin Abbott (1732–96), a native of New York, was in 1790 serving Newburgh Circuit, New York. Converted in 1772, he devoted the rest of his life to evangelizing New Jersey, Pennsylvania, etc. His preaching powerfully affected his hearers. Asbury writes of him: "the people fall to the ground under him, and sink into a passive state, helpless, stiff, motionless. . . . . He is a man of uncommon zeal, and (although his language has somewhat of incorrectness) of good utterance" (*Journal,* I [1771–86], 420–21). In 1820 John Ffirth published the *Experience and Gospel Labours of the Rev. Benjamin Abbott,* one of the earliest of American Methodist biographies.

30 B.D.T. at Bro*r* Dickins, at W*m* Penn Chandler[s][150] prayer meeting

31 this Morning about four O Clock we were Alarmed by A Terable Cry of fier Which Consumed M*r* Rob*t* Ayrs Brew-house. I preach*d* Morning and Afternoon at Ebenezer [and at] Night in the old Church &C B.T. at Bro*r* Dickins. D. at Bro*r* Doughtys

Nov*r* B. D. T. at Bro*r* Dickins Met Class at M*r* patersons

2 B. T. at Bro*r* Dickins D. at Bro*r* Manlys preach*d* in the Evning (I was aflicted with a Sore Boile & a Chill of the Ague

3 B. D. T. at Bro*r* Dickins (Ditto—)

4 B. D. T. at Bro*r* Dickins I was a Little Better—

5 B. D. T. at Bro*r* Dickins

6 B T at Bro*r* Dickins D at Bro*r* Manlys was Much opressed With a Colection of Wind on My Stumoc[k]

7 I preach*d* in the Afternoon—

8 B D T at Bro*r* Dickins Kept House &C—

9 B. T. at Bro*r* Dickins D. at Bro*r* Manlys— Ja*s* Bell preach*d* in the Evning—

10 B. D. at Bro*r* Dickins T. at Bro*r* petherbridg[es] preach*d* &C

11 B. at Bro*r* petherbridg[e]s D. T. at Bro*r* Dickins, preach*d* &C

12 B. D. at Bro*r* Dickins T. at Bro*r* Bakers Met Class at Doct. Lu[s]bys

13 B. D. at Bro*r* Dickins T at Bro*r* Stewerds prayer meeting at Chandlers &C

14 B. at Bro*r* Dickins D. at Bro*r* Harskins T. at Bro*r* pether-bridg[e]s— (I Bro*r* Harskins & Bro*r* Willis at the old Church: Bro*r* Boid[151] I and Bro*r* Dickins preach*d* at Ebenezer &C—

15 B. D. T. at Bro*r* Dickins Met Class at M*r* pattersons &C— preach*d* at St Georges from Looking for that Blessed hope

[150] Dr. William Penn Chandler (1764–1822), a native of Charles County, Maryland, was a dentist and was studying medicine under Dr. Rush of Philadelphia when he entered the traveling connection in 1797. He located in 1813 (Sprague, *op. cit.,* VII, 287–90).

[151] Evidently a local preacher.

16 B. at Bro*r* Dickins D. [at] Bro*r* Manlys T. at John Rankins preach*d* at St. Georges from Looking for that Blessed hope &C—

17 B. D. at Bro*r* Dickins T. at Ja*s* pickerings Met Class at Robert Singers &C—

18 B. D. at Bro*r* Dickins Visited —— under Sentance of Death he apeared insencable of his Spiritual State

19 I Rode To Obediah Wileys With ——

20 I preach*d* Bro*r* M*c*Claskey[152] Hutchenson[153] Cooper[154] & Robinson[155] Exhorted we had A Genewing [genuine] out pouring of the Spirit

Nov*r* 21 at ower Sacrament and Love feast we had a Mighty outpouring of the Spirit Allso in publick Exortation &C Bro*r* M*c*Claskey preach*d* Some Continewed the Servis From Nine in the Morning Till Sun Set— I Suppose 10 or 12 were Set at Liberty Some Suppose twenty GLORY Be to GOD for Ever

22 B at obediah Wileys, D. T. at Bro*r* Dickins Met Class at Rich*d* Allins &C—

23 B at Bro. Harskins. D. [at] Bro*r* Manlys T. [at] Bro*r* Dickins

24 B. D. at Bro*r* Dickins T at Bro*r* Manly[s] prayer Meeting at Hugh Smiths

25 B. D. at Bro*r* Dickins T. at Bro*r* Manlys &C—

26 B. D. at Bro*r* Dickins

27 B. D. at Bro*r* Dickins T at Bro*r* Manlys prayermeeting at Bro*r* Chandlors

28 B. D. [at] Bro*r* Dickins T. [at] Bro*r* Manlys preach*d* at St georges Met class at —— Shutes preach*d* at Ebenezer

29 B at Bro*r* Manly[s], D. at Bro*r* Dickins Met Class at Bro*r* Smiths

30 B. T. at Bro*r* Dickins D. at Bror Manlys preach*d* [at] St. George[s]

[152] John McClaskey (1756–1814), a native of County Derry, Ireland, born of Anglican parentage, was in 1790 appointed to Wilmington, Delaware (Sprague, *op. cit.,* VII, 125–26).

[153] Either Sylvester Hutchinson, appointed with John Cooper to Chester Circuit, Pennsylvania, in 1790; or Robert Hutchinson, appointed to Bristol Circuit, Pennsylvania, in 1790.

[154] John Cooper, appointed to Chester Circuit, Pennsylvania, in 1790.

[155] Evidently a local preacher or exhorter.

Dec*r* 1 B. D. at Bro*r* Dickins T. at Bro*r* petherbridg preach*d* and Met Bro*r* Doughtys & Gilberts Classes

2 B. D. T. at Bro*r* Dickins preach*d* at St. Georges—

3 B. D. at Bro*r* Dickins T. at Bro*r* Manlys &C—

4 B. D. T. at Bro*r* Dickins

5 B. D. T. at Bro*r* Dickins. preach*d* 3 times Met a Class & the Society &C—

6 B. D. T. at Bro*r* Dickins Met Class at Bro*r* Stewards [....] profest to be Santified Glory to God

7 B. T. at Bro*r* Dickins, D. at Bro*r* Manlys preach*d* [at] St Georges

8 B. D. at Bro*r* Dickins T. at Bro*r* petherbridges preach*d* [at] Ebenezer

9 B. D. T. at Bro*r* Dickins preach*d* [at] St Georges &C—

10 B. D. at Bro*r* Dickins T at Bro*r* Manlys prayermeeting at Ebenezer

11 B. D. T. at Bro*r* Dickins &C—&C—

12 B. T. at Bro*r* Dickins, D at Bro*r* Harskins preach*d* Morning & Night at St Georges Bro*r* Willis afternoon and at Night at Ebenezer

13 B. D. at Bro*r* Dickins, T at Capt. Norths Met Class at Bro*r* Stewards

14 B. at Bro*r* Dickins D at Bro*r* Manlys T at Sist[*r*] watsons preach*d* at St. Georges

Dec*r* 15 1790 B. D. at Bro*r* Dickins T. at Bro*r* petherbridges preach*d* at Ebenezer to about forty Souls Colected for [new church] 30S 2d

16 B. at Bro*r* petherbridg[e]s D. T. at Bro*r* Dickins preach*d*

17 B. D. at Bro*r* Dickins T. at Bro*r* McKeens prayer Meeting

18 B. D. at Bro*r* Dickins T. at Bro*r* Jolliffs prayer Meeting [at] Chand[lers]

19 B. D. T. at Bro*r* Dickins preach*d* Morning & afternoon

20 B. D. T. at Bro*r* Dickins Met Class at Rich*d* Allins [One] Backslider healed: I began to Reed [read] M*r* Fletchers Checks

21 B. T. at Bro*r* Dickins, D. at Bro*r* Manlys preach*d* [at] St Georges [Went to] Hear the Cause between M*r*. & M*rs* Shryder and M*r* & M*rs* Hall

22 B. D. at Bro*r* Dickins, T. at Bro*r* Hoods preach*d* at Ebenez*r*

23 B. D. T. at Bro*r* Dickins preach*d* at St Georges—

24 D. at Bro*r* Dickins Gave the Sacrament To Bro*r* & Sist*r* Singer &C— T. at Bro*r* Wilmores

25 B. T. at Bro*r* Dickins D. at Bro*r* petherbridg[e]s preach*d* at Eb[eneze]*r* Re[a]d the burial Servis over Skinner Davis from Chinkateag [Chincoteague] Virginia Held A Love feast at three O Clock at St. G. the Lord was powerfuly presant two found peace Bro*r* Garritson[156] preach*d*

26 B. T. at Bro*r* Dickins D. at Bro*r* petherbridges preach*d* Morning & afternoon Bro*r* Dickins at Night Bro*r* Garritson preach*d* Morning and Night and Bro*r* Willis in the Afternoon at St. Georges [....] Were Set at Liberty at a prayermeeting

27 B. at Bro*r* Dickins D. at Rich*d* Allins T. at Cornal Norths Bro*r* Garritson preach*d* at Ebenezer at Night We Slept at Bro*r* Manlys &C—

28 B. at Bro*r* Bakers D. at Bro*r* Manlys preach*d*

29 B. D. at Bro*r* Dickins T. at Robert Busbys preach*d* at Eben[ezer].

30 B. at Bro*r* petherbridges D. T. at Bro*r* Dickins preach*d* &C

31 B. D. at Bro*r* Dickins T. at George Fox[es] and preach*d* there Bro*r* Dickins preach*d* Bro*r* M*c*Claskey Willis and I Exhorted five of our Leaders prayed We Concluded our Watch Night about one oh Clock But the Coldness of the Night Seemed to Move the atention of the people But I hope the Lord will Not Despise the Day of Small things

[156] Freeborn Garrettson (1752–1827), a native of Maryland, was in 1790 presiding elder of the North District of New York. Converted in 1775, he joined the conference in the following year and served the Methodists in America for half a century as traveling preacher and presiding elder. He is remembered for having been the "arrow" sent through the South to summon the preachers to the Christmas Conference (1784). The best biography is Nathan Bangs's *The Life of the Rev. Freeborn Garrettson* (New York, 1832). For condensed biographical sketches see Sprague, *op. cit.,* VII, 54–63; or *DAB,* VII, 166–67.

CHAPTER VI

The Edward Dromgoole Letters, 1778–1812

I. LETTERS FROM EARLY METHODIST PREACHERS (1778–98)

THE Dromgoole Papers in the Historical Manuscript Collection of the University of North Carolina Library consist chiefly of correspondence addressed to Edward Dromgoole, Sr. (1751–1835), a Methodist preacher of Brunswick County, Virginia, and to members of his family. Covering the formative years of American Methodism, and written as they are by several influential circuit-riders of the latter part of the eighteenth century, they afford a contemporary insight into the workings of Methodism as it expanded into many parts of the eastern seaboard. Part I includes those letters written in the period 1778–98 by such Methodist worthies as John Hagerty, Robert Lindsay, Reuben Ellis, Richard Ivy, William Watters, John Dickins, and others; biographical data concerning these correspondents are given in the notes. Part II comprises letters written from 1802 to 1812, chiefly from former Virginia Methodists who had removed to Ohio.

Edward Dromgoole was born near Sligo, in County Sligo, Ireland, in the year 1751. Reliable data concerning his early years are at a premium, but it is known that he was reared a Roman Catholic and was converted to Methodism by the Wesleyan missionaries in his homeland and joined the society in 1770. His public recantation of Catholicism at the time alienated his family and may well have been a contributing factor in his removal to North America. He sailed for America in May, 1770, and, landing at Baltimore, made his way inland to Frederick, in Frederick County, western Maryland, where his Christian experience was renewed under the ministrations of another native Irishman, Robert Strawbridge, who had planted the seeds of Methodism in western Maryland. He began preaching, probably on Frederick Circuit, in the year 1773. At the conference of Methodist preachers held in Philadelphia on May 25, 1774, he was admitted on trial to the traveling connection. His first appointment was with George Shadford, Richard Webster, and Robert Lindsay to Baltimore Circuit, embracing most of the western shore of Maryland. In 1775 he was admitted into full connection and thereafter, as an "assistant," served successively Brunswick Circuit in 1775; Carolina Circuit, 1776; Amelia Circuit, 1777; Sussex Circuit, 1778; Mecklenburg Circuit, 1783; Bertie Circuit, 1784; and Brunswick Circuit, 1785. His career as a traveling preacher came to a close at the conference of 1786, when his name was read out in answer to the question, "Who desist from traveling?"

Doubtless this step was prompted by his marriage and the cares of a growing family. On March 7, 1777, Dromgoole had married Miss Rebecca Walton (1753–1826), a daughter of John Walton of Brunswick County, Virginia, and one of the first-fruits of the revival on Brunswick Circuit in 1775. No provision was made at the time for supporting preachers' wives, and Dromgoole settled down in Brunswick County as planter and merchant, residing there until his death in 1835. All the remainder of his life he was active as a local preacher on the Brunswick and later the Greensville circuits, which included his neighborhood and the church at his home, which came to be called "Dromgoole's Chapel." He seems to have prospered in his temporal concerns and in his Brunswick home hospitably entertained circuit-preachers, presiding elders, and Methodist bishops. Bishop Francis Asbury records in his *Journal* several visits to the Dromgoole home. His last was on Sabbath, February 12, 1815, when, after preaching "in Drumgoold's house," the aged bishop "ordained Edward Drumgoold an elder in the church of God." Dromgoole, having entered the Methodist ministry before ordination was instituted in the separate church in 1784, and located soon thereafter, had never previously received ordination as elder. Rebecca Dromgoole died in 1826 and Edward in 1835, at the age of eighty-four. Of their family, Thomas, who attended Cokesbury College, and Edward became local preachers; and the youngest son, George Coke Dromgoole, served as member of Congress from Virginia. A daughter, Mary, died in 1835; and there were two other children, Richard and Rebecca. A grandson, the Reverend Edward Dromgoole Sims, was a distinguished professor in Randolph-Macon and LaGrange colleges and in the University of Alabama.

The letters contain a wide range of material pertinent to the Methodist economy of the day. Circuit-preachers and presiding elders wrote to their old friend, telling of their experiences and spiritual trials, of their personal health and the hardships they endured in frontier circuit-riding, of the rapid expansion of the work through recurrent revivals on the borders of settlement, of Methodist publishing interests, and of other topics. The several letters referring to Dromgoole's son's stay at Cokesbury College shed interesting light on the general setup of student life at that pioneer Methodist higher school. Withal they give us an intimate and incisive glimpse of early American Methodism at work.

I

January 19th, 1778

MY DEAR BROTHER IN CHRIST

Your obliging request[1] lays me under a happy necessity of calling to mind the past mercies of God. May every review of them bring thankfulness for past and present blessings and cause me to trust for future blessings.

Ever since I can remember I have had some conviction for sin at times. When I was about eight years of age[2] from hearing my Sister talk of the happiness she should receive after death and seeing her depart this life I was brought to fear that I was not prepared to die which caused me to be much in private prayer and [I] thought if I knew the will of God that I would do it.

About two years after the death of Father my soul was much distressed so that I though[t] if the Lord would prepare me for Heaven it was all that I desired. But after awhile this wore off and I took much delight in young peoples company and dancing which destroyed all my desires after heaven and happiness untill I was about eighteen years of age. At which time it pleased God to send Mr. King[3] among us. Under his preaching my Judgment was much convinced though I did not see I deserved Hell untill the 27th of March 1770. Then I heard Mr. Williams[4] preach on Rom[ans] 6 Chap. 1 verse. His words were as Arrows in my heart so that I was forced to cry out in the bitterness of my soul "Lord save or I perish." I went every opportunity to hear Mr. King which encreased my desires[.] He often spoke to

[1] Evidently Dromgoole had requested a written account of the writer's conversion.

[2] *Ca.* 1755.

[3] John King (1746–94), an English local preacher and alumnus of Oxford, was converted under Wesley and on his disinheritance by his father, who was bitterly opposed to the Methodist movement, came to America in 1769. He is remembered especially for establishing Methodism in Baltimore. Attending the conference of 1773, he was appointed with William Watters to New Jersey and later served Methodist circuits in Virginia and North Carolina (M. H. Moore, *Sketches of the Pioneers of Methodism In North Carolina and Virginia* [Nashville, 1884], pp. 51–56).

[4] Robert Williams (? –1775), one of Wesley's English preachers, came to America with Wesley's consent in 1769, arriving in August, two months before Boardman and Pilmoor, Wesley's first missionaries to America. He labored in Maryland from November, 1769, until about June, 1770, later preaching in New York and Virginia, where he formed Brunswick Circuit (*ibid.*, pp. 47–51; see also C. H. Crookshank, *History of Methodism in Ireland* [1885], I, 225).

me but I could not say much for weeping. He was going to the upper end of the county where I had an opportunity of hearing him that night. I was so distressed I thought I must die and soul and body would be cast into hell. The next morning Mr. Rollings[5] talked to me and mentioned that we all should receive our just reward, according to the deeds done in the body. I knew that if I did I should be miserable forever and was much tempted to make away with myself. Not long after this I returned home and was very desirous of hearing Mr. Williams which I soon did. That night I could not rest for I thought the earth would open and swallow me up. My Mother was much disturbed and said I would go beside myself and she was advised to keep me from hearing the Methodists preach which she endeavoured to do; but the Lord made a way that I heard them sometimes. I went again to hear Mr. Rollings and he in conversation desired me to tell him how it was with me. My answer was that the day of grace was past. He mentioned many promises but I could not believe they were for me. My Sister often spoke to me and encouraged me to trust in the Lord; but I told her God would not pardon my sins, she asked me why I thought so[.] I told her because I crucified the Lord afresh and put him to open shame[.] she asked me if I did not feel sorrow for sin[.] I told her yes; she said that was a sign God had not forsaken me and that He would pardon me. I told her that Esau found no place for repentance, though he sought it carefully with tears. Thus I was distressed untill sometime in October following I heard Mr King preach and received some comfort from this man. I spent that afternoon in reading and prayer and the Lord removed my burden, though I cannot say He had pardoned my sins. At times I was afraid I had lost my conviction and at other times I felt the drawing of the Spirit of God and so I continued untill the 11th day of December[.] When I was on my knees crying to God for a full Deliverance I heard a voice inwardly say "I have sealed the pardon of thy sins with my blood." I felt the truth of it in my heart and in a moment prayer was turned into praises. I wanted all the world to help

[5] Isaac Rollins (? –1783) was a member of the first Methodist society in Baltimore County, Maryland, and was admitted on trial to the Methodist traveling connection in 1774, with Edward Dromgoole, Robert Lindsay, and others (*Minutes of the Annual Conferences of the Methodist Episcopal Church,* Vol. I: *1773–1828,* p. 6; John Lednum, *A History of the Rise of Methodism in America* [Philadelphia, 1859], p. 389).

me praise my God. In a few moments I felt prostrate before the Lord [and] determined not [to] rise untill I knew the Lord had pardoned me and in a little while the same words were imprest on my mind more strongly than before. I was more assured of his forgiving love and enjoyed much peace in believing I now thought I never should sin more[.] My mind was taken up with God and I convers'd with Him as a Man with his Friend[.] My confidence was unshaken and my hope full of immortality. I was astonished when I heard any complain of Doubts & fears. But it was not long before the Lord shewed me the remains of sin that was left within which caused many doubts and fears and made my soul to mourn for a deliverance from them. I thought it would be a progressive work untill I heard you[6] read a Christian Letter which convinced me that it must be by simple faith and from that time I was enabled to press hard after it. I was kept watching unto prayer sometimes in much distress at other times in patient expectation of the blessing[.] for a fortnight I thought I should then receive it untill my Brother[7] was delivered and then I was filled with unbelief and my mind blinded. My cry was Lord I am oppressed undertake for me[.] My Brother asked for me and he believed I was convinced of the necessity of it and desired I would not rest untill I had obtained it[.] his words were with power to my soul for I could not rest that night. Tho' I had no doubt of the pardoning love of God and I knew that I did not love Him with all my heart, and that was a grief to my soul. That Scripture was often imprest on my mind "Without holiness no man shall see the Lord." I knew I was far from it for I saw so many things in me contrary to the will of God that I was afraid I should at last fall away. On Monday my distress was deepened and on Tuesday I thought my heart would break for it appeared as if all the powers of hell were engaged against me I never knew before as I did then what it was to be tempted. On Wednesday I thought I could believe the Lord would deliver me. I went to class meeting and soon after we begun my Brother broke out in praising God which greatly encreased my distress. It was imprest on my mind to kneel down and pray[.] I resisted it but it re-

[6] Dromgoole seems at this time to have been living in Frederick, Maryland (Lednum, *op. cit.,* p. 133).

[7] As early as 1772 a brother, Paul Hagerty, was a member of the Pipe Creek Society in Frederick County, Maryland, where Strawbridge had labored (*ibid.,* pp. 17–18).

turned the second time. I thought if I did not it would be the last time that the Lord would strive with me which caused me to cry mightily to the Lord for deliverance. I was in a short time enabled to lay hold on Jesus Christ and found salvation by simple faith. I believe He removed my sins as far from me as the east is from the west. I do not know if I have felt anything contrary to love since. For some months my soul was continually happy. Not a cloud did arise to darken the skies. But afterwards through my rest being much broken by a Motherless infant I found much coldness and backwardness; but Glory be to my God He has delivered me from it, so that I enjoy a constant peace, and have a conscience void of offence towards God and man. My soul is happy this moment, and I believe I shall be like Him, for when He shall appear I shall see Him as He is.

JNO. HAGERTY[8]

II

BALTIMORE TOWN Sep 15# 1778

MY DEAR BROTHER

The Love I feel to the People of God & a Consideration of that former socibleness that we had together when Traveling in Frederick Circuit has induced me to write these few lines tho it may be a matter of indifferency to thee Whether thee See or Hear from me or Not. As I have understood of Some of my Dear Friends that thee told them, they Need not be so Desirous of Seeing me as I have Left of[f] Preaching. But my Dear Brother, I would fain hope that thy Love is not so Narrowly Confin[e]d as to Reach only to those that Travels with thee in Connection or Are of the Same Society with thee. But Rather that it Extends itself in Complacency & Delight towards all God's Dear Children of every Denomination or Persuation, & in Pity Compassion & Tenderness towards the Whole Sinfull Race of mankind. I think that as Calvin said of Luther Whether He Calls me Dog or Devil, I Believe him to be a good Man (or words to that

[8] John Hagerty (1747–1823) was a native of Prince George County, Maryland, and a distinguished traveling preacher and presiding elder in the formative years of American Methodism. He began work as a local preacher *ca.* 1772 but entered the traveling connection at the Fluvanna Conference of 1779. For biography see "Memoir of the Rev. John Hagerty," *Methodist Magazine,* VII (1824), 209–12; see also William B. Sprague, *Annals of the American Pulpit* (New York, 1865), VII, 65–68.

effect). So Say I Whether thee think Good or evil of Me. I Feel a measure of Love to thee as a Follower of my Dear and Loving Jesus, Who was No Respector of Persons, But Extended his Love to all mankind as even to Lay Down his Life Freely as a Ransom for them and is Still Wooing of them by his mercies & Judgments, His Servants of Sin here & the Consequences of Sin Hereafter, By Believing in him & to become Happy in his Love & meet for a Happy Eternity. For my Part my Dear Brother Since I Saw thee I have mett with many Trials and Exercises of mind. Yet Blessed be God, that when I look back upon my Past Life, I find Great Cause of Praise & Thankfullness to Him that He has So wonderfully Preserved & Helped me Hitherto, tho with Shame I acknowledge that I have not made that Wise improvement of them as I might. Yet I Trust that they will, & in Some measure have been Sanctified to the Good of my Soul. As I Can Say it has Weaned me more from the World & has given me Greater Views of God's Providential Care over & His Fatherly Love towards me So that at times I seem to be almost Lost in Wonder, Love & Praise & am Ready to Say with the Psalmist of Old, O Come Taste & See that the Lord is Good. This Day it is Two Years Since I Left New York Owing to the English's Coming there Since which I have been at my Brother in Laws in Baltimore Town & amongst my Dear Friends in the Country. I follow No Business, But Live in Expectation of Seeing the Day when the English Shall find it Expedient to Leave New York & Let the inhabitants Enjoy their Rights & Privileges Unmolested[.] my Dear Brother I have seen by the minites of the Last Conference that thou art Still Traveling & labouring in a Public Manner in Our Dear Lord's Vinyard & I Trust thee have found that the Lord has Ownd thy Labours by Giving thee many Seals to thy ministrey, tho it seems to me at Present, as if Zion is become almost Desolate for the Church Seems to be Now in the Wilderness & Many of her members gets Scattered by the Storm yet I know Blessed be God for that Knowledge that those that Abides in Christ the Ark by Faith & Prayer will be able to Ride out the Storm & at Last Land Safe in the Port of Everlasting Rest, Where I hope to meet thee (if not before) & all those that Loves our Dear Lord and Saviour Jesus Christ in Sincerity. I Have been informed that thee have Changed thy Condition in Life[9]

[9] Dromgoole had married Rebecca Walton of Brunswick County, Virginia, on March 7, 1777 (*Methodist Magazine,* X [1827], 232).

& I hope it has Proved to be for the Best both temporally & Spiritually As the Wise Man Says "Two are better than one" And also Trust that Your Mutual & Affectionate Love one to the other under the Blessing of God will Cause You both to become As Trees of Life Planted by the Rivers of Water bringing forth Fruit Both Literally & Spiritually to the Glory of God & the Comfort & Joy of Each of Your Hearts. So I Shall Conclude for this time by Wishing thee & thy Loving Spouse every Blessing both Temporal & Spiritual which God in his Divine Wisdom Sees will Redown [redound] Mostly to his Glory & the Good of Each of Your Precious & Never Dying Souls

I Remain thy & thy Loving Spouse's Real
Friend & Brother in Christ
PHILIP EBERT[10]

N.B. If thee think Proper to Write I Shall be Glad to Hear from thee & of the Work of the Lord Amongst you all by Directing or Sending a Letter to the Care of B*r*[other] William Moore[11] or M*r* Henry Sheaff, Merchant in Baltimore Town

III

SLIGO [IRELAND] 18th May 1784

MY DEAR BROTHER

I wonder I have not been honoured with an answ[er] to my long letter before now. What is the matter? Have you forgotten the days of old? Or is it because you are a married man that you have let a whole year pass without writing to me? Well, I have at last taken courage, and on the 6th past, ventured into the holy state of matrimony! Jane Lawder, Daughter to Frederick Lawder of the County of Letrim, of an Antient and very respectable family in Ireland, is the dear companion of my life. This union is more honourable than I

[10] Philip Ebert, a native of the western shore of Maryland, joined the Methodist traveling connection in 1773 and labored in 1774 on Greenwich Circuit, New Jersey. While there, he was converted to Universalism by Abraham Whitworth, also a Methodist minister, and both were expelled in 1774 (*Minutes,* I, 6; Lednum, *op. cit.,* p. 121).

[11] William Moore was one of the pioneer Methodists in Baltimore, opening his home to Asbury's preaching in 1772; he was one of the trustees for the erection of Lovely Lane Chapel in 1774 (Lednum, *op. cit.,* pp. 88–89).

ever expected to be favoured with in this world, and I assure you that a fortune of £40 p[er] Ann[um] for ever is one of her least Accomplishments. But—O pity me! In securing the possession of my dear companion, I have step'd aside from the Minutes of Conference which forbids a Methodist preacher to marry a woman without the consent of her parents.[12] Here I stand exposed to any penalty my Brethren shall think fit to inflict upon me.

But I hope for a favourable issue. We dearly loved each other, and were determin'd to sink or swim together. Each of us Ventured much, but I hope to find more lenity from my Brethren than She is ever likely to find from her friends. Yet a few of them are well pleased with us, and wishes us a deal of happiness. Yesterday my dear companion was brought on a visit to M*r* Ornsby's of Commin, by her Brother & Young M*r* Ornsby. She was treated with the utmost respect, and they assured her of *yr* [their] constant friendship and love. I hope in God our union will be the cause of much peace & comfort to us both.

This day fortnight Doctor Coke[13] is to preach in Sligo. I imagine abundance of bitter invectives will be sent him ag[ains]t me, by my wife's friends, many of whom love the Methodists almost as much as they love the Devil. From the preachers I expect honour and respect, as I trust my choice will never put them to shame, tho' I suppose some of them will affect to blame the mode I pursued.—Should matters turn ag[ains]t us, I believe we shall set off for the [American] Continent next year, as my wife has a Sister Married to a Geo. Mason in Harlem near N[ew] York, in wealthy circumstances. But these matters are not yet ripe for determination.

[12] At the Wesleyan Conference of 1744 the following rule was adopted:

"*Q.* Ought any woman to marry without the consent of her parents?

"*A.* In general, she ought not: yet there may be an exception. For if, 1. A woman be under a necessity of marrying. If, 2. Her parents absolutely refuse to let her marry any Christian; then she may: nay, ought to marry without their consent. Yet even then, a Methodist Preacher ought not to marry her" (*Minutes of the Methodist Conferences, from the First, Held in London, by the Late Rev. John Wesley, A.M. in the Year 1744* [London, 1812], Vol. I: *1744–1798,* p. 13).

[13] Thomas Coke (1747–1814), later bishop of the Methodist Episcopal church, was on July 29, 1783, stationed in London, but made itinerant tours of the British Isles occasionally (*ibid.,* p. 162). Lindsay described him as follows in a letter to Dromgoole dated June 2, 1783: "D*r* Coke is about 34, of an open, I*n*ocent, child-like Countenance, M*r* Wesley's almost Ditto in person, and his true Son in the Gospel."

We have nothing among us very remarkable since my last except the downfall of two of our preachers this year. Indeed seldom a year passes without one or more dropping like blasted Stars. I fear it is the same with you, as I cannot fi[nd] by Br[other] Asbury's extract of your last Minutes more tha[n a] few of my old acquaintances travelling with you.

I have sent Br[other] Asbury an affadavit and Certificate of Sara[h] Baily being the wife of Ned. Baily, to recover the prop[erty] left by Ned when he died for the widow. This shall [later] be followed by a Letter of Attorney in order to force Ned's Brothers to deliver it up, should they refuse[.] do all you can for the poor widow. She has reared two children and has behaved extremely well since he left her.

My dear Jenny's best respects and mine waits on you & your beloved. Per adventure we may yet see you in the land of liberty. But we wait the command of our Sov'reign Lord in this as in all other matters.

My mind, formerly like the troubled Sea, is much composed. Troubles I expect to meet in every Station of life, but I trust my dangers will be far less than before. Shall I call you ungrateful for your long silence? No. Tho' I fear my patience will hardly hold out another season without some proof of how deservedly I remain your truly Affectionate and loving Brother

ROB[ER]T LINDSAY[14]

IV

YADKIN C[IRCUI]T, [NORTH CAROLINA] Aug. 30, 1786

MY DEAR BROTHER,

My unabating Love to you, moved me, tho at this distance to write —Being persuaded also that you would be glad to know how I fare. I am in a very rough part of the Country—The roads, in general, are exceeding bad—And the People, a few excepted, are rougher than the roads: and accomidations coarse enough—But I thank God, in

[14] Lindsay was admitted on trial in 1774 with Edward Dromgoole and appointed with him, George Shadford, and Richard Webster to Baltimore Circuit. He was an Irishman by birth and returned to his homeland during the Revolution, preaching until 1788 (*Minutes,* I, 6; Jesse Lee, *A Short History of the Methodists in the United States of America* [Baltimore, 1810], p. 322).

general I enjoy tolerable health—And, what is better, in common, I am much Comforted in my labours, which, I trust, have been blessed to a few Persons at l[e]ast—We have also great calls to streatch our lines towards the South, beyond where we now are—I think I never felt more desire to spread the Gospel, or more resigned to my sufferings for the Gospels sake, than I have lately—The Preachers, who labour with me[15] are all young—But I trust they are Humble, & truely ingaged, & some of them have considerable Abilities—One Obstacle in our way [is that] here as in other places there are a great many Baptists, & Presbyterians, who have fill'd the Peoples heads with Predestination. They have opposed pretty warmly sometime past, but at present they are pretty quick.—Indeed the Baptist Preachers, in these parts, are (from as best I can learn) grossly Ignorant of Controversy. So they can't do much.—Dear Bro[ther], I often, affectionately, think of you, in my retired moments, as I trust you do of me also—I hope also you do not cease to labour all you can for God! O how soon will the struggle be at an end! & we, if we are "Faithful to Death" "enter into the Joy of our Lord!" Farewell

Yours as ever
REUBEN ELLIS[16]

NB. Remember kindly to Sister Dromgoole, & your little ones. And also to others who Love our Lord Jesus Christ in Sincerity. Let me hear from you if you have opportunity. Br[other] Mason[17] is with me. He is well, & desires to be remembered to you.

V

DOVER CIRCUIT [DELAWARE] March 3 1787

MY DEAR BROTHER.

Grace, mercy & peace be multiplied to you & yours, altho I have been long silent, & have not wrote to you, I have not forgot you but

[15] The preachers in Reuben Ellis' district in 1786 were Thomas Williamson, Henry Bingham, Robert J. Miller, John Mason, Mark Whitaker, and Mark Moore, serving Salisbury, Yadkin, and Holston circuits in North Carolina (*Minutes,* I, 25).

[16] Ellis (? –1796) was a native North Carolinian who entered the itineracy in 1777 (Moore, *op. cit.,* pp. 196–204).

[17] John Mason was then serving Yadkin Circuit (*Minutes,* I, 25).

as ever do feel a cordial affection for you, & wish you all happiness in this & the world to come, hope you keep your head above water and are going on your way to the Kingdom, laying aside every weight and urging your way straight forward. I have gone thro many trials since I saw you, & have had many blessings, for the first part of this year my trials were great, having lost my dear friend Geo. Augure[.] he died the 10 of June suddenly, & I veryly believe is at rest in Abrahams Bosom, but my inward trials were greater than my outward, but thro mercy the cloud broke, & for these 6 months past have been very happy, & have the pleasure to inform you the work of the Lord prospers much in my round.[18] We have had a very great outpouring of Spirit in Talbot[19] between 5 & 600 have joined the Society. The work begins to break out in Dorchester Circuit. Last Sunday & Tuesday a week ago I never saw such a work I do not know how many were converted to God but I g[u]ess between 30 & 40. In Kent at the Q[uarterly] M[eetin]g the power of the Lord came down in a wonderful maner among the people, the door is opening in Cecil County, blessed be God we have comfortable times here among us. I hope my dear wife is well, but I have not seen her these 7 weeks, but expect to see her in a few days, I am disorder'd with a cold, but am resigned to the will of God. You'll excuse my scrawl. I have but a short time [to] write[.] accept of this as a token of love and believe me to [be] your very affectionate Friend & Bro: in Christ

JNO HAGERTY JR.

VI

BALTIMORE May 14, 1787

VERY DEAR BRO:

Yours of the 9 of April came safe to hand & by Bro: Poythress[20] I have an opportunity of acknowledging the reception thereof. I am glad to hear that you still keep your head above water, I hope it will

[18] In 1787 Hagerty was (presiding) elder over Caroline and Dorchester circuits on the eastern shore of Maryland (*ibid.*). The title "presiding elder" did not become official until 1792.

[19] Talbot, Dorchester, and Cecil circuits centered largely in the Maryland counties bearing those names; Kent included Kent County, Delaware.

[20] Francis Poythress (1732–1810), a native of North Carolina or Virginia, was in 1786–87 appointed (presiding) elder over Brunswick, Sussex, and Amelia circuits, Virginia (*Minutes,* I, 25).

still be the case with you, but the way of life you now are in will require a double degree of watchfulness. I have more of worldly matters in my hands at present than I want as I am left an executor to my Bro: in law Geo. Augure['s] Estate, but I know business m[a]y be passed through and our hearts and affections placed on things above. The Lord has been kind to me the past year. I have seen the Travel [travail] of the Saviour Soul coming home to God. there has been a great work in the circuits I have had under my inspection, my lott is now cast in Baltimore & its Vicinity,[21] & I feel a hope the Lord will still be my shield as well as my Preserver, we have had a good time at our conference upon the whole, we have concluded to have no more Superintendants than we now have & the Doct[or] (Coke) Exercises no Authority when out of the States[22] & when in them he [1] ordains. 2 presides in Conference as Moderator & 3 Travels at large, Mr Asbury acts as our Chief Ruler at all times & I hope God will smile upon [our] resolves. The Lord is before us[.] if we keep humble he will do all things in us & by us. Sally[23] has her health as well as common & joins me in love to you & yours. I hope you'll write when convenient & when it is well with thee Remember at the throne of grace your affectionate tho Unworthy Bro[ther] in Christ

JOHN HAGERTY

VII

DOWNPATRICK [COUNTY DOWN, NORTH IRELAND]
22d. March 1788

MY DEAR BROTHER

I sit down now to answer yours of Oct[ober] 26 with only a hope of its conveyance. My Circuit (Lisburn)[24] is rather remote from ports which send vessels to your country. I felt a Singular Satisfaction in receiving a renewal of our former friendship, which I trust com-

[21] As (presiding) elder (with Nelson Reed and Ignatius Pigman) over Frederick, Calvert, and Baltimore circuits in 1787 (*ibid.*, p. 28).

[22] The Conference of 1787 acknowledged Coke as "superintendent" "of our church for the United States" only "when present in the States" (*ibid.*, p. 26).

[23] Mrs. Hagerty.

[24] Lindsay was appointed with J. Burnet and F. Armstrong to Lisburn Circuit in Ulster, at the British Conference held at Manchester, July 31, 1787 (*Minutes of the Methodist Conferences .... Held .... by the Late Rev. John Wesley,* I, 196).

menced in that "Love" which will out last the "ruined Earth and Heavens." Yet I felt my mind somewhat agitated on your telling me you were "located."[25] But I dare not censure. Convinced you would not venture on a mode of living, inconsistent with *that* which a very peculiar providence had called you to, without clear evidence of its being the will of God. Yet I cannot help indulging a fear concerning You. Your present Situation, Your employment, your Connections; and above all, Your *cares,* cannot but direct your attention from the "Vocation where with you were called." May the Lord save you from what I fear concerning You!—I am really surprized that our Brethren on the [American] Continent has not adopted our mode of supporting Preachers wives and families. Here a wife has the same salary with her husband,[26] and £1 ann[ually] for every child till they are fit for Kingswood School.[27] In fact, our married preachers may live more comfortable than the Single ones. It is strange to me to see so few of my old acquaintances in the minutes. But you solve the difficulty at once. "*They are Married,*" So there is an end of them.

R[OBERT] LINDSAY

VIII

NEW YORK May 5th 1788

MY DEAR AND MUCH ESTEEMED [FRIEND],

Dont think, I love but little because I write but seldom. My hands are pretty full of opportunities; I might also add my great aversion to writing. I intended to have gone to the South this spring; but Providence has hindered by the indisposition of Br[other] Hickson,[28] who is now in a consumption and I have the whole charge of the Church.

[25] Dromgoole had located, i.e., left the traveling ministry, in 1786 (*Minutes,* I, 25).

[26] Provision for preachers' wives was made as follows by the British Conference of 1774: ". . . . 1. Let every Preacher's wife (except at London and Bristol) have £12. a year. 2. Every Circuit is to find her a lodging, coal and candles; or to allow her fifteen pounds a year" (*Minutes of the Methodist Conferences . . . . Held . . . . by the Late Rev. John Wesley,* I, 115). American support of ministers' wives was more grudging.

[27] Kingswood School was set up in 1741, first for Methodist children in general, but it gradually became exclusively a school to educate Methodist traveling preachers' sons.

[28] Henry Willis had been appointed with Dickins to New-York for the year 1787, but his place was taken by Woolman Hickson, who died of consumption during the year (*Minutes,* I, 30; J. B. Wakeley, *Lost Chapters Recovered from the Early History of American Methodism* [New York, 1858], pp. 310–11).

I am still very infirm though not more so than when I saw you last. My wife also continues poorly. But blessed be God for all things. I do not yet see whither I shall [bend] my course or what I shall do after next fall, when my present plan will expire, but I believe I have One above that careth for me all unworthy as I am. Probably he will take me to himself. His will be done. I should think myself very happy to enjoy your company as in former days, but hope we shall sit down together in our heavenly Father's kingdom.

I congratulate you on the happy times which God has given you to see not only in your country but also in your own house.[29] O may the blessed spirit be poured out in a much larger measure than heretofore, not only in Virginia not only in America, but on all the face of the earth.

I think I can venture to tell my dear friend that I am still endeavouring to press on in the narrow way—Oh *narrow* indeed! Many have been my trials since I saw you; but, I am persuaded that I experience the truth of the Apostle's words—The trying of our faith worketh *patience*—

I hope dear Sister Dromgoole is well. Should be glad [if] you would try to secure that piece of gold I sent Br[other] Marko. I have received but one letter from you that I can recollect.

My wife joins me in kind affection to you and yours. Farewell. I am, in sincere love, your brother and servant in [Christ],

John Dickins[30]

IX

Baltimore May 30, 1788

My dear Bro[ther]

I sent a case of Tracts by the packet to you with about 100 Minutes of Conference, to Petersburg to the care of Mr Hardy. But the Capt. Barbian by Name said he could not find Mr Hardy[.] if you have not received [them] please to inquire of the Merchant [to] whom the

[29] The Virginia Revival of 1787–88, centering in Amelia, Sussex, and Brunswick counties, was then in progress.

[30] John Dickins (1746–1798), a native of London, England, became a Methodist traveling preacher in America in 1777. He helped Asbury in planning Cokesbury College and was the chief founder of the Methodist Book Concern (see Moore, *op. cit.*, pp. 106–17).

packet from Baltimore is consigned. I expect Bro[ther] Ira Ellis[31] who favours me with the carriage of this line, sent from Philadelphia two Schrew Augurs for his Father[.] in this case, he will Enquire in Petersburg about it. I should be glad to hear from you. I think this case of tracts is very unfortunate, they have been about 2 years on the way between Philadelphia and Petersburg.

I have great cause to be thankful for the kind dealings of a Blessed Saviour to my body and my soul. I find the life of religion in my Soul and if I love at all I love God and his people and have found enlargement in preaching the word of truth of late. I bless God for trials[.] I have them of various kinds but hitherto the Lord hath helped, and they have been a means of driving me nearer to God. The work looks favourable in Annapolis. I have been there these 12 days past and had large serious congregations to preach to. My poor wife was near death the other night, but is recovered again and at present is as well as common for her to be, in her weak state of health. I hope she is aspiring after the life and power of Religion and enjoys the comfort of believing. I should be glad to see [you], but Whether this will be in this World I know not, but I trust we shall spend a blessed Eternity together. Remember me and my dear wife, and, with respect as ever am your Affectionate

Unworthy Brother in Christ
JOHN HAGERTY JUNR.[32]

X

BALT'ORE July 6 1788

DEAR BRO[THER]:

I have just time by brother Ogden[33] to inform you that we thro mercy are all on praying ground and in the Land of hope, favoured with every needful blessing for life and Godliness. I wrote to you and sent a case of tracts to your care and to dispose of them for me, but

[31] Ira Ellis was appointed to Kent Circuit, Delaware, in 1787, and Charleston, South Carolina, in 1788 (*Minutes,* I, 28, 30).

[32] Hagerty was in 1787, with Willliam Gill, (presiding) elder over Philadelphia and Little York circuits, in Pennsylvania, and was sent in 1788 to Annapolis, Maryland (*ibid.,* pp. 28, 31).

[33] Benjamin Ogden (1764–1834) was appointed to Brunswick Circuit, Virginia, in 1788 (*ibid.,* p. 30). In 1786 Ogden served with James Haw on the Kentucky Circuit (see chap. iv).

they did not come to Petersburg so soon as I expected. Bro. Tunnell[34] who is concerned with me in them wrote to me that he had received them and was distributing them among the Subscribers. perhaps the residue may be left in your hands. He informs me that they will not sell for more than *3d*. I am content with this. I would thank you for a line by the Packet or otherwise. I feel that time and distance does not wean my affections from the dear Children of God. I feel my regard for you the same as ever. O that God may unite us more and more to himself. I am favoured with comfort in the ways of God, I expect there has some unfavourable reports spread thro your country about the College,[35] but it may be relied on that things are not so bad there. I came from visiting it with Brother Reed[36] on Friday last. Mr. Otterbein[37] heard the boys examined by Doct[or] Hall[38] and they improve in their learning. we inquired into their Morrels also and can hear no evil at present except they are not so deeply engaged about their souls as could [be] wished.

With this I send you a Letter from our old friend Rob[er]t Lindsay. I received one from him with yours. he gives a favorable Acc[oun]t of the work of God in Ireland. &c but the work with you exceeds all I have ever heard of. I am in a great hurry and hope you'll excuse this line and believe me to be with the warmest sentiments of Esteem, Regard and Friendship, your Affectionate tho Unworthy

Bro[ther] in the Lord
JOHN HAGERTY

P.S. Sally (who is in a weak state of body) joins me in love to you and Sist[e]r Dromgoole

Farewell

[34] John Tunnell (? –1790) was (presiding) elder over the North Carolina circuits in this year (*Minutes*, I, 30).

[35] Cokesbury College had formally opened on September 17, 1787 (Matthew Simpson [ed.], *Cyclopaedia of Methodism* [Philadelphia, 1878], p. 236).

[36] Nelson Reed (1751–1840), a native of Maryland, as (presiding) elder over the circuits centering about Baltimore, was Hagerty's superior (*Minutes*, I, 31).

[37] Philip William Otterbein (1726–1813), was then pastor of the Independent German Reformed Church at Baltimore. He was cofounder of the Church of the United Brethren in Christ, a church for the American Germans patterned on Methodistic lines.

[38] Dr. Jacob Hall was the second president of Cokesbury College (Simpson, *op. cit.*, p. 236).

XI

BLAKES, W[ILKES] C[OUNTY] GEORGIA
Sep[tembe]r 26th 1788

DEAR BRO[THER]

Your letter by M*r*. W. came safe to hand for which I am thankful; and I cheerfully embrace this opportunity by Bro. R. Marlin to inform you of the glorious work that God is carrying on in the back-woods of Georgia. We've 3 circuits[39] and traveling preachers and between 1500 and 2000 members the greater part of which are changed in heart as well as life and the work of sanctification goes on sweetly and powerfully in the heads of many. Tho we've many em-pediments from the Antinomians in this country but the Lord helps us to out preach, out live, and out love them, and that in the judgment of those who are strangers to Religion. Our preaching Houses are but tolerable but we begin to improve and in time we shall by the blessing of God bring our cause in this Country to tolerable perfection. The Preachers[40] are in Health of Body and in high spirits and strive together for the faith of the Gospel; and several young men are likely to become useful as publick speakers, one of our dangers is gaining too fast though we gain only real friends. The more the better. The prospect in Augusta[41] is but gloomy and wins not by Savanna[42] yet, tho' expect to this fall. The people in general are kind and teachable and their objections against Justice & Sobriety are hardly as many and great as we might have expected; Lord hasten the time when Truth may outweigh Custom and which contribute[s] for salvation both here and here after. I feel myself unprofitable, but praise God my Soul pants for all the life of Faith and Love. Bro[the]r how does thy Soul, thy Family, and the people prosper in the way to the Kingdom. God forbid that the trifles of time should cause us to neglect the things of Eternity[.] with all get thy own Soul and the Souls of

[39] Ivy's circuits for 1788 were Burke, Richmond, and Washington (*Minutes,* I, 30).

[40] Moses Park, Bennett Maxey, Matthew Harris, Hope Hull, and James Conner (*ibid.*).

[41] Augusta Circuit appears in the *Minutes* of 1789 (*ibid.,* p. 33).

[42] The first permanent society in Savannah was founded in 1807 by Jesse Lee while on a missionary tour of the region (George G. Smith, *The History of Methodism in Georgia and Florida* [Macon, Ga., 1877], pp. 443–44).

Others to Heaven if possible—dear bro. J. M.[43] left the world in perfect peace without a sigh or a groan, Last April at Isaac Herbert['s] on Savannah. O that when we are cal[le]d, we may leave the stage of action with cheerfulness and enter into joys of our Lord. give my respects to all enquirers and fail not to write and pray for your affectionate bro[the]r in Christ.

RICH*d* IVEY[44]

XII

CHARLESTON Feby. 23, 1790

MY MUCH ESTEEMED BRO[THER]

I am thankful for an opportunity to write to you. And the more because I have good news. The Lord hath, I trust, begun a glorious work in this City. Our Conference[45] began on yesterday [a] week, and concluded on Wed[nesday]. All was harmony and love! This is good news, but this is not all. The public exercises were attended with such power as, I believe, was never seen here before, particularly on Tuesd[a]y, and Wed[nesda]y evenings; on the last mentioned Even'g, I think Bro. Asbury preached the greatest Sermon that ever I heard from these words Jer[emiah] 15 and 19 "If thou take forth the precious from the vile, thou shalt be as my mouth." And the word was indeed with power. A cry arose throughout the Church, almost; We turned into exhortation, and prayer, in different parts of the Church, where Mourners were crying for mercy, till near 10 O Clock. Satan mustered his forces also, there was a great noise in the street, and some in the Church, but no mischief done.[46] Since our Congre-

[43] John Major, a Virginian, called "the weeping prophet," had been serving Burke Circuit, Georgia, in 1787 (*Minutes,* I, 27). His memoir appears in the *Minutes* of the following year: "JOHN MAJOR,—a simple-hearted man; a living, loving soul, who died, as he lived, full of faith and the Holy Ghost:—ten years in the work; useful and blameless" (*ibid.,* p. 30).

[44] Richard Ivy was "eighteen years in the work; a native of Sussex county, in Virginia. He travelled extensively through Jersey, Pennsylvania, Maryland, Virginia, North and South Carolina, and Georgia. . . . . He died in his native county, in Virginia, in the latter part of the year 1795" (*ibid.,* p. 67).

[45] The conference convened at Charleston, Monday, February 15, 1790 (*ibid.,* p. 35).

[46] Asbury complained, in writing of these events: "But we have not a sufficient breastwork: our friends are too mute and fearful, and many of the *outdoors* people are violent and wicked, ... [but] I have hopes that some hundreds in this city will be converted by this time next year" (*Journal of Rev. Francis Asbury* [New York and Cincinnati, n.d.], II, 65).

gation has been much crowded but no extraordinary stir till last ev[ening] at a private prayer meeting when the Lord manifested his power, both to Wound and heal; several sinners were cut down and one mourner, if no more, fill'd with joy! As I have been much engaged in the exercise, I feel myself relaxed a good deal. Satan says spare yourself, you can't support under such labour; but if I die with the Philistines, I hope it will be like Sampson! And what is life worth if we can't do good. I have not a doubt but the Lord sent me back there, and I trust he will now cause me to Rejoice according to the time I have suffered affliction. Glory, Glory to his Name. I'm y'rs.

R[EUBEN] ELLIS[47]

My love to Sister Dromgoole

XIII

BALTIMORE, FELLS POINT
April 16 1790

VERY DEAR BROTHER

Yours of February 5 came safe to hand. The inclosed account I think is right, as to the books or tracts on hand[.] if Bro. Coe would take them at the price I charged them to you he would make as much by them as would pay him for his trouble. I would be willing to make them a little lower but could not abate much because I set them at a small profit expecting they would sell the sooner on that account. If I had them here I could now sell them fast, but the difficulty of getting them is great. They would hardly bear the expence beside, I will leave it to you to dispose of them, as you may see most convenient. If any of the preachers was to take a few of them at a time around their circuits they would make something by them and the people would be profitted.

I thank my God I still am thro grace in the way that leads to the Kingdom, we have had glorious times here this winter, since the 30 and 31 of Jan'ry there has been above 130 persons converted in Town and Point and near that No. that has joined the church. The work does not go on so rapid now as it has done, but it is still moving

[47] Ellis was appointed (presiding) elder for 1790–91 over the South Carolina circuits, including Charleston (*Minutes,* I, 37, 41).

forward. I have compared it to the dam[m]ing up water till it gets a head and then breaks down and carries all before it, we have I think every week some tokens of Gods love for poor Sinners, in their conversion. I have now moved to Fells Point, where my station is at present.[48] I think we have had now about 80 persons added to the Church here since the above named time.

I thought it would be better for me to be among the people when I labour and therefore came to this place yesterday. Bro. Willis[49] a dear Man of God is in Town, and preaches with great success—My wife has had her health better this Winter than common, by using the Elextricity[!] she is all on streach for Glory.—blessed be God I hope we shall arive safe in the Harbour of Eternal Rest. She joins me in much affection to you and Sister Dromgoole. Pray for us—and write when convenient to your affectionate Brother in the Lord.

JOHN HAGERTY

XIV

[PHILADELPHIA] NOV. 1791

MY DEAR OLD FRIEND AND BROTHER,

I received a short letter from you a short time past; for which I am thankful. But I was afraid the style of it indicated some jealousy that affection on my side had grown cool. I believe that you know that I am of a cool constitution and never shew much affection as many people do. But I think if I have a sincere regard for any Christian friend, I have for my old friend, Bro. Dromgoole; and should rejoice exceedingly to see you; which I humbly hope to do in heaven if not on earth—As far as I know myself, I am the same plain man that I was ten years ago. Living in these polite cities has not polished off any of my roughness. And, through grace, I endeavour to be the same Christian. O that I were a more holy one! However, I am not conscious that I have grown remiss in any act of private devotion. I speak in respect to the means—And I would be the same preacher, which the Lord knows is mean enough. But my voice

[48] Hagerty was appointed to Fell's Point (after 1826 called East Baltimore) for the year 1790 (*ibid.*, p. 38).

[49] Henry Willis (? –1808), a native of Brunswick County, Virginia, had been in 1789 (presiding) elder of Philadelphia district, but located on account of ill-health in 1790 (*ibid.*, pp. 36, 157–58).

greatly fails me. I am in no way to make an estate, neither do I desire it, but through kind Providence, I am in a way of comfortable support, with abundance of labour, from year to year. I am blest with 4 living children: the eldest, Asbury,[50] has been at the College about 2½ years; and has made considerable progress in latin—My wife and children are all in good health—She joins in the kindest Christian affection to you and S[iste]r Dromgoole,

with thine sincerely,

JNO. DICKINS[51]

XV

COKESBURY COLLEGE October 27 1793

DEAR FATHER,

It has been three Months since I have heard from you, & it makes me uneasy to think of not getting a letter only once a Quarter, you signified that you expected that we cou'd hear from each other about once every two Months; but I believe that we cannot hear from each other under 3 Months, I wrote to you some Time in Sept*r* when I expected the disorder that is now raging in Philadelphia[52] would get to this place, but it has never got here as yet; & I hope never will; a great many of the Inhabitants of Philadelphia have been carried off the papers say 6500 that can be given account by one or two Physicians of that City. I hope that the disorder will be stop[p]ed this winter.—

The Teachers and Students of this College are tolerable well, Mr Quarter's Son; from Manchester arrived here last Saturday; and has began to Learn the Latin Language; and expects [to] return next August to pay his Father a visit at which I wish (if you can make it convenient, to come to se[e] my Friends & Relations. I have not heard whether my Grand-Mother has got better or worse: pray write every Opportunity: as I shall do the same; I want some Things which

[50] Asbury Dickins, Esq., of North Carolina, served as secretary of the United States Senate from December 12, 1836, to July 15, 1861 (*A Biographical Congressional Directory* [1903], pp. 50–195, *passim*).

[51] Dickins was then "Superintendent of the Printing and Book Business" and stationed in Philadelphia (*Minutes,* I, 42).

[52] The yellow fever epidemic of 1793.

I will Mention on the other side; which you will please to send as quick as possible.

3 *pr* Drawers
1 *pr* Gloves for the winter } 4 Pocket Handk[er]c[hief]s &
2 Shirts of Cotton } 2 Night Caps
1 *pr* Breeches } or Stuff of the Annotto Dye to make them.
1 Jacket }
3 or 4 *pr* Stockings
1 *pr* Neat Shoes
& 3 or 4 *pr* of coarse D°

As for the Shoes I think it wou'd be best for you to write Mr Toy[53] word to supply me with them & you settle with him for them; for I think they come much cheaper in this town;[54] than you can have them made & send them here; I have been obliged to get a *pr* since you left me; I have bought 2 *pr* Stockings; & am in want of Stockings again: I shall want a *pr* of Shoe-Boots, this Winter which I can get here for 2½ Dollars: You'll Please to send the other Things with my Arithmetic & English Dictionary & Coper Plate, as I wish to learn how to write & not to forget Arithmetic. Please to send me Money; I must inform you that every Boy has to find his own wood & Candles or be turned away from the Fire; I bought 2 *pr* Shoes 14/. 2 *pr* Stockings 12/. Out of the Money that Mr. Hagerty[55] let me have. I received 5 Dollars from him & 5/. for the making of my Gown which made 31/. & I have purchased 1 Quire Paper 1/. my passage to Baltimore & back 5/. & 6*d* for Candles, & I have none left. I hope you'll send me as much as you think. If you'll speak to my Grand-Father or Uncle to send me a Barrel or two of Apples I will be much obliged to them if they will send them as it is seldom we can get Apples here & when we get them we pay at the Rate of 5/ or 6/ p[er] Bushel now & 'tis supposed they will be 15/. next Spring. Please to

[53] Joseph Toy (1748–1826) was a native of New Jersey and a convert of Captain Thomas Webb. He labored first as a local preacher and was for a time head of the mathematics department at Cokesbury College, but in 1801 he joined the Baltimore Conference, becoming its first secretary (James E. Armstrong, *History of the Old Baltimore Conference* [Baltimore, 1907] p. 475; John Atkinson, *Memorials of Methodism in New Jersey* [Philadelphia, 1860], pp. 35–36, 46–49).

[54] Abingdon, Maryland.

[55] Hagerty was then stationed at Baltimore Town, 1793 (*Minutes*, I, 51).

write as quick as Possible. my Love to my Mother Brother & Sisters with my Grand Father & Mother, no more just now

I Remain your dutiful Son
THOMAS DROMGOOLE[56]

NB. As to my learning I have made some Progress; & wish to know how long you can keep me at it: as I have a desire to learn French if it be agreeable to you

T. DROMGOOLE

XVI

BALT[IMO]RE Jan*r*y 11 1794

MY DEAR BROTHER

I rec*d* a letter a few days ago from Bro Everet[57] at the Colege that Tom[m]y was of an ungovernable & wicked turn so that he could be kept there no longer[.] last night, he with Mr McDowels' Son came to my house. & tomorrow I expect he will sail on a packet for Norfolk. I have advanced some money to convey him home, which is placed to your ac[count]. The tobacco you sent me is not sold. I have sold about 300 lb or a little more of the inferior kind at 5*d* our money & about 100 or a little more of the Superior, it at 1/6 & 1/10 in our Money. if it had been saleable it would have been sold long ago but we must make the best of it. I have advanced Money for Bro[ther] McCannons bill 9.7.6 & exceeded your orders one Dollar to Tommy when at the College[.] 5 Dollars is all he had, One Lattin Dictionary 18.9 One Morses Geography[58] 7/6 & a pocket Bible 8/4 all which are charged to your acc[oun]t. I have been negligent in writing to you[.] the hurry of Business has in a great measure prevented it.

We are much better in health at present than for some time past and I trust on our way to bliss & glory but I am much ashamed of myself for my ingratitude and unfaithfulness to God. I sometimes

[56] Thomas Dromgoole became a schoolteacher. On February 23, 1813, in Virginia, Bishop Asbury ordained "Thomas Drumgoold" a local deacon in the Methodist Episcopal church (Asbury, *Journal*, III, 343, 376).

[57] Joseph Everett (1732–1809), a native of Maryland, was appointed chaplain to Cokesbury College for 1794 (*Minutes*, I, 55).

[58] Jedidiah Morse's *American Geography* (1789) was the first widely used American text on the subject and dealt chiefly with the United States.

wonder that I live, & have desires to serve God, O may the work of grace revive in me. The work seems to have been at a stand and has rather declined till of late. it revives a little in Town.

I have heard that you was sick. I hope your affliction was sanctified. May God give you a heart to pray always for me and mine & believe me to be as ever yours

Affectionate

JOHN HAGERTY[59]

P.S. I have advanced 8 Dol[la]rs for Tommy. & hope that will convey him to Petersburg

XVII

16th May 1795

MY DEAR BRO:

It is long since I have heard any thing from you: but doubt not, but what you are more than ever resol[ve]d to live and die the Lords.

Through mercy I am blest with health, and in my poor faint manner am still making some fe[e]ble steps toward the kingdom.

It is a most remarkable de[a]d time in these parts as fare [far] round as I am acquainted: and we have had a good deal of uneasiness both in Town and country, between the trav[e]ling preachers and people. The preachers keeping in and turning out who they pleas[e]; not alowing Local preachers or people to have any thing to say in the business.[60]

The consequence is many people withdrew: [w]rote for M*r*. O Kelley[61] and he is now preaching through the neighbourhood while multitudes from every quarter flock to hear him.

As I conceive we ought not to discourage any one that sincerely preaches Christ; so neither ought we to encourage any one that dose [does] not.—I have though[t] it my duty to say but little till I am better enform'd.

My request theirfore is, that you will give me a full and perticular

[59] John Hagerty's name is listed in the *Minutes* for 1794 as one of those "under a location through weakness of body or family concerns," i.e., he had left the itinerant ministry, retaining a local status (*Minutes,* I, 54).

[60] For a similar complaint in a later period see below, Part II, Letter XVIII.

[61] The legend on the envelope of this letter, "Favourd by M*r* OKelley," reveals that O'Kelley was its bearer to Dromgoole.

an account of him, and his proseedings as you possibly can. Pray be very perticular, and let nothing be in the account but what you can prove, or at least fully depend on. My long acquantance with you influences me to make this extionery request. If you have not a ready and safe passage you will pleas[e] send your letter by post d[i]rected to the care of Mr. Charles Turner. Alexandria

I love you and wish it was with Methodism now in its advanc'd state in many respects as it was in its infincy. God bless you. Pray for me, who am

as ever yours in much love &c

Wm Watters[62]

XVIII

Philadelphia July 12, 1798

My much esteemed old friend,

Though our friendship is of long date, & much established, yet we correspond but seldom—And even now I have ventured to write, I am rather at a loss what to say—In this city[63] we had some revival last winter, though it is still to the poor that the gospel is preached with the greatest success—And in several circuits round about,[64] there is a good work of God going forward—But such is my infirmity by an affection in my breast, & weakness of body, that I seldom preach more than once a week, & that with difficulty—In respect to my soul, I believe there is very little change for the better or worse since I saw you, though perhaps I possess a greater degree of the passive graces—

[62] William Watters (1751–1827), a native of Baltimore County, Maryland, was the first native itinerant Methodist preacher in America. Converted in 1771, he became an exhorter in 1772 and toured Virginia with Robert Williams. He was admitted on trial to the traveling connection at the Conference of 1773 (Lednum, *op. cit.*, pp. 87–88; *Minutes,* I, 5; see also *A Short Account of the Christian Experience and Ministerial Labours of William Watters Drawn up by Himself* [Alexandria, Va., n.d.]).

[63] Philadelphia, where the writer (John Dickins) lived. He died there in September, 1798, of yellow fever. For memoir see *Minutes,* I, 79–80.

[64] A "gracious revival" was under way in neighboring Strasburg Circuit, Pennsylvania, and Cecil Circuit, Maryland, under the ministrations of Dr. William P. Chandler, one of the circuit preachers. Thomas Ware, the presiding elder, writes: "From this the fire began to spread to the south, and soon the whole peninsula was in a flame of revival. At the north also the influence was felt. Sparks were kindled in Middletown, Northumberland, Wilkesbarre, and quite up in the Genesee and lake country in western New-York" (Thomas Ware, *Sketches Of the Life and Travels of Rev. Thomas Ware* [New York, 1839], p. 230).

But I find myself a very poor creature and if it were not fear of arrogating too much humility to myself, I might adopt Mr. Wesleys description of that grace, & say, I am "little & mean & base & vile in my own eyes"—But I dare not make any great profession—Suffice it to say, I love God, & have no dependence on anything but the merits of Jesus Christ—But even while I am writing, I am ready to doubt of the prosperity [propriety] of saying so much about myself—However, I am writing to a particular friend, who I think would be glad to know—

A few days ago I had a letter from Mr. Asbury, who was then at New York & much minded by the means of abstaining from all flesh of every kind—

My wife is very weakly & we have six children who are for the most part pretty healthy—The expense of living in this city, where *everything* must be bought, is very great indeed; and I am sometimes amased at the kind Providence which has always made a way for our effort—

It was with great persuasion that I yielded to my friend, & entered into a little business to help in the support of my family, I would not have done it after all if I would have made out without it—And, though my family is large, I may perhaps venture to say, through grace, I am in a great measure away from [the] world, & am in some sense retired in the midst of this populous city—It affords me some satisfaction that I can serve the cause of God by promoting the circulation of our books—This I feel enclined to do for consciences sake—

It would afford me great satisfaction, if my oldest son were in a situation similar to yours; but it is not so yet, though very few possess better moral principles than he does—

I should be happy to receive some circumstances of you and yours—that you are crucified with Christ, and waiting all the days of your appointed time, till your change shall come—There is no doubt but you have both gained more & done more in religion than I have

My wife & children give in sincere affection to yourself & S[iste]r Dromgoole with all your offspring.

I remain your friend & brother,

JNO. DICKENS

II. LETTERS FROM OHIO, NORTH CAROLINA, AND TENNESSEE (1802–12)

The exploration and settlement of the Northwest Territory, with the development of its component states and the planting therein of religion and culture, is one of the great epic chapters of America's history. There a new generation of pioneers fought and won much the same battle for existence against the frontier that had been waged by their grandsires from Maine to Georgia. Settlers came from all parts of the East, many for the same economic reasons that had drawn their ancestors across the Atlantic. Religious motives entered into the emigration from the South; it was the exclusion of slavery from the territory by the Northwest Ordinance of 1787 which made the region attractive to those southerners who were opposed to slavery. The extensive Quaker migration to Ohio and Indiana from Virginia and the Carolinas, to escape the evils of the slavery economy, is not the only instance afforded by American history of the migration of a religious people in search of freedom from the curse of the slave system. The following letters show the same spirit among a number of Virginian Methodist families who came to Ohio for the reasons that impelled the Quaker migration. Part II of the Dromgoole Letters presents a selection of letters from such persons—friends of the Dromgoole family and former neighbors and associates of theirs in church affairs, who wrote to them from their new homes in Ohio.

Of these correspondents, Philip Gatch (1751–1835) made the earliest departure from Virginia. Like Edward Dromgoole, he had once been a traveling preacher, but upon his marriage he had located in Powhatan County, Virginia, later removing to Buckingham. He writes that he never felt favorable to slavery, and soon after his marriage he liberated his slaves. Finally, in 1798, he resolved to make the great trek northward to the free Northwest Territory beyond the Ohio. His memoirs and letters indicate that slavery was his foremost reason for locating in Ohio. He writes: "I viewed the evils of slavery at present as great, and apprehended more serious results in the future, if some effectual remedy should not be applied." Gatch settled on the Little Miami River in southwestern Ohio, in what became Clermont County, and, in the capacity of a local preacher, helped to plant Methodism in that part of the state. His natural abilities were soon recognized by his new neighbors, who elected him to represent Clermont County at Ohio's constitutional convention in 1802, and he was later chosen an associate judge of his home county. His honors in these respects show him to be a representative of that small but influential group of civic-minded Methodists such as Governors Tiffin, Trimble, and Worthington, who held high office in early Ohio.

By far the largest number of these letters were written by the Peter Pelham family, who had formerly lived in Greensville County, Virginia, and had attended class meeting in the Dromgoole neighborhood. In April, 1807, they journeyed to Ohio, settling in Greene County, near Xenia. There were at least three sons and five daughters in the family. Of these, Samuel, the eldest son, married Martha Bonner, a daughter of Frederick Bonner, a former Virginian and a neighbor of the Pelhams in Greene County; and Sarah (called "Sally" in the letters) married Edward Dromgoole, Jr., and returned to the South with her husband. Among the other correspondents from Greene County were John Sale, Bennett Maxey, and James Tawler, three Virginia preachers who had likewise sought new homes north of the Ohio.

Dromgoole himself suffered slight attacks of "Ohio fever"—enough to visit the pioneer state about 1807 and speculate in Ohio lands, which he managed by remote control from Virginia, they being leased through the Pelhams to some recent settlers. Despite his Ohio friends' frequent and impassioned appeals in the letters to join them in actual settlement, however, he remained in the Old Dominion the rest of his life. He wrote to Gatch in October, 1813: "We are still living in old Brunswick, and nearly in the common way of the country. I often think of Ohio, but can get no farther than a wish to be there..... My five oldest children are professors, and in society. Our youngest child is sixteen years of age. He is moral, but not a professor yet. May the Lord bring him into the fold! Two of my sons are preachers..... I am yet endeavoring to labor in my Master's vineyard."

In addition, several letters from James H. Keys, a North Carolinian who after a sojourn in Tennessee settled in Warren County, North Carolina, forty miles from Dromgoole's home, and one from a budding young preacher, Enos Scarbrough, have been included, since they illustrate problems of Methodist discipline, ministerial requirements, and anti-slavery views.

The value of the Ohio letters, which make up the main bulk of Part II, lies in their poignant descriptions of life in general on the Ohio frontier. They give us a cross-section of all phases of life in a developing community—political, social, economic, and religious. Prices of farm products and of lands, hardships of early settlements, means of communication—all are set forth in these letters. This "frontier history told by contemporaries" is especially valuable for the light it sheds on the unfolding religious life of the Ohio pioneers. In short, it shows how Methodism met the problems facing it on the Ohio frontier.

I

Clermont County,[1] Forks of L[ittle] Miami
Territory of the United States N.W. of the Ohio
Febr*y* 11th 1802

Dear Brother

Unexpectedly I received a letter from you dated [the] 26th of August. Oppertunity has failed in answering the same untill now. The Lord has been my helper since I saw you last thro a Dangerous Wourld, I hope I have been persevering untill now, in the work and ways of God[.] I shar'd in a considerable revival in Powhatan and also in Buckingham,[2] where I felt my self greatly attach't to the people and where I could have whish't to have spent my days but I felt unwilling to lay my Bones there, and leave my Children whom I tenderly loved in a land of slavery not knowing what the Evils there of would amount to in there [their] time. the Lord has conducted us in safety to this New Countrey, where we have been over three years, and I can say, that I believe our way has been of the Lord. this last summer we have had a stir of Religion[.] one of our children and a Black Boy of our Familey got converted, our three oldest daughters profess religion[.] my wife[3] I hope is devoted to God. we have Eight Children 4 sons, and 4 Daught[er]s.[4] One

[1] Clermont County was erected and organized in 1800 in the Little Miami Valley of southwestern Ohio.

[2] The Powhatan Revival took place during the latter years of the Revolution, while Gatch was a resident of Powhatan County, Virginia. He later removed to Buckingham County, where he shared in a revival initiated by Hope Hull and joined in by Baptist and Presbyterian ministers. Gatch writes of these co-operative efforts: "We dwelt together 'in unity'. We preached with and for each other, and the Lord again favored the neighborhood with his presence. A glorious revival took place, and Zion was greatly enlarged" (John McLean, *Sketch of Rev. Philip Gatch* [Cincinnati, 1854], pp. 88–89, 93–94).

[3] Gatch had married a Miss Elizabeth Smith of Powhatan County, Virginia, January 14, 1778. At her father's house was held the Methodist Conference of 1780. Three of Mrs. Gatch's brothers became ministers: a half-brother, George M., Separate Baptist; George S., a Regular Baptist of Kentucky; and James, a Methodist (*ibid.*, pp. 56–57).

[4] Gatch's sons were Conduce, Thomas, Philip, and Rev. George Gatch; his daughters: Presocia, who married (1) James Garland and (2) David Osborne; Martha, who married John Gest; Elizabeth, who married Aaron Matson; and Ruth, wife of Michael Swing (*History of Clermont County, Ohio* .... [Philadelphia, 1880], pp. 462–63).

Daughter married since we came to this countrey. the Lord is working in different parts in this countrey by the Methodists Presbeterians and Baptists, but we w[ant] more Labourers. may the Lord send them am[ong us] and give us grace to improve the favours of [his] hand. the Work of God has been wonderful in Kentuckey[5] the last year. I and a Brother[6] of mine from Baltimore was over a great deal of Kentuckey, last summer[.][7] we have a Brother living below Salt river whome we went to see and I held several meetings in different parts of the state. Is Br[other] Rob*t* Jones[8] still alive[?] if so my kindest Love to him and Familey and all my old Friends[.] I think numbers from your part of the wourld had better move to this countrey but they must judge for themselves—

This Countrey is far distant from you but I heartily whish you where [were] settled here with your Familey and all my old Friends that are out of the Spirit of Slavery[.] the Countrey is Beautiful in its situation and promices every advantage I believe that any Country in this Wourld can do[.] the L[ittle] Miami is a Beautiful stream[.] it [i]s clear summer and winter Flush and swift and the best stream for Mills I ever saw not excepting Brandywine[.][9] there is about near a Dowzen Mills on this stream and is sufficient for mills in a straight direction about sixty miles up it[.] I have been up it about 40 miles and there is a Mill still higher up[.] there are also many other good streams or mills in this Countrey that I have seen[:] Cezar [Caesar's] Creek, and Todds Forks, and Andersone Fork, these are good for Mills[.] the B[ig] Miammi I am inform'd is also good for Mills and Mad River also which empties into the B[ig] Miami[.] there is a number of fine springs, and salt springs and where springs are not the People get fine Wells of water[.] I can assure you that this Countrey is Possest of an excellent Boddy of Water for every purpose. I am settled about Ten miles distance from

[5] The Great Revival of the West had begun in Logan County, Kentucky, in 1797, and was still in progress.

[6] Nicholas Gatch, Philip's brother, settled in Clermont County, Ohio, *ca.* 1810 (*History of Clermont County, Ohio,* p. 464).

[7] For this trip to Kentucky see McLean, *op. cit.,* pp. 106–8.

[8] Robert Jones was a prominent layman of Sussex County, Virginia (John Lednum, *A History of the Rise of Methodism in America* [Philadelphia, 1859], p. 140).

[9] In Chester County, Pennsylvania, and Newcastle County, Delaware.

the Ohio and about Fifteen from Cincinnatta[10] a Flourishing Town on our side the Ohio. A considerable place of Trade[.] there was three Sea vessals Built on the Ohio and went down Loaded last year, great number of Boats also went down the River Loaded with Flower [flour] Bacon [....] Bear & so [....] floa[ted] down already and many more are going[.] I believe we shall not want for trade in this Countrey; when I came to the Countrey the land that I had bought before I came to the Countrey did not suit us to settle on, so I bought a small piece the 16th of Jan*ry,* we built our cabbins clear[e]d our ground and rais[e]d a plenty of Flax Hemp and Cotten for cloathing and Corn more than we needed for our own use and turnips. Pumpkins and potatoes in abundance[.] in short our Countrey is good for every kind of produce that Virginia and Maryland, Pennsylvania and the Jersies take in. The land is in common Rich and a great deal of it richer I expect than you ever saw. we have rais[e]d from 50 Bushells to 90 odd to the Acre of Corn, Wheat and Rye is wonderful in its gro[w]th and produce[.] Land is 2 Dollars and there abouts p[e]r Acre in the Woods, improved land 3–4, 5, 6, 7, 8 p[e]r acre. We have had two sickly Falls[11] since we have been in the Countrey, A Fever attended with great pain and Chills. our Familey was very sick with it the [Fall] before last[.] I thought [....].[12] I do not believe that the Countrey will [....]. yet on the Big watters it may be aguish, the [....] the up Lands are general[ly] healthey. I have [enjoyed] more real health for the length of time toge[ther since] I was in my Sixteenth Year; we have Iron, [....]. Iron about 9*d* p[e]r pound, Sugar we make, [and] want for no necessary article, Salt 2, and 3*d*[.] as to the Indians we feel no more affraid of them [than] you do there[.] the Countrey is setled above us 60 [miles. We have] been more affraid of the Negroes in Virginia [day] or Night than I have ever been in this Coun[try of the] Poor Indians[.] put it all together, tell Siste[r Dromgoole that] my Wife feels quite comfortable

[10] Cincinnati was at the mouth of the Great Miami River; Gatch lived at Milford, in Miami Township, Clermont County, on the Little Miami.

[11] For a description of health conditions on the Ohio frontier see *Autobiography of Rev. James B. Finley* (Cincinnati, 1855), p. 107; also William T. Utter, *The History of the State of Ohio,* Vol. II: *The Frontier State, 1803–1825* (Columbus: 1942), pp. 338–43.

[12] The right edge of this page has been torn off, which is the reason for the frequent gaps which follow.

here and say[s she is glad] she is out of Virginia. I think your best [route] will be to go to Redstone and so come down the O[hio] and Land at Col[umb]ia at the Mouth of the [....]. a stage Waggon [....] Boddy lengthe [....] for Yourself Wife [and ch]ildren. it will be n[ecessary to] have a Tent, and a good Road Waggon, so we where [were] first and made out very well in our journey—We have no Slavery as yet among us[.] some whish for it but I hope God will never permit it. I Pray against it, and talk against it, but I hope the greater part of our People are against it, at present our gover[n]ment is fleeting but I expect it will be more permanent and sufficiently garded against [slavery]. I and my Wife join in our Former Love to you and Your Wife God Bless you all if you dont come write again and pray for us

PHILIP GATCH[13]

II

June 1*st* 1805

D[EAR] BRO[THER:]

Yours I receiv'd by Friend Pelham,[14] and am well pleas'd with the contents, only that of your afflicted son, get two bands of pollished steal [steel], and confine one round each wrist, perhaps it may be of real service to the Child;—I am affread that the Young Men are discouraged in our new woodsey countrey, the Virginian[s] are so little

[13] Philip Gatch (1751–1835), pioneer Methodist evangelist in many parts of the Eastern Seaboard, was born in Baltimore County, Maryland, of German descent. He was converted to Methodism in 1772 and entered the traveling connection in 1773. After his marriage and location, he became a planter in Powhatan County and later in Buckingham County, Virginia. Because of his growing distaste for slavery and the slave culture of the South, he and his family, with his brothers-in-law Ambrose Ranson and Rev. James Smith—in all, a party of thirty-six—removed in 1798 to the valley of the Little Miami, in what was the Virginia Military Reserve of the Northwest Territory. He settled on the site of the present town of Milford, in Clermont County, where that same year he and his party joined a Methodist society founded in 1797 by Rev. Francis McCormick; this was the first Methodist congregation in Ohio. Gatch was chosen in 1802 a member of the Ohio constitutional convention, and in 1803 he was elected by the General Assembly one of Clermont's associate judges, an office which he capably filled for twenty-one years. In his home he frequently entertained Bishop Asbury and other Methodist dignitaries. He died at Milford, December 29, 1835 (McLean, *op. cit.;* William B. Sprague, *Annals of the American Pulpit* [New York, 1865], VII, 50–54).

[14] For the account of Peter Pelham's final settlement in Ohio in 1807 see below, Letter VI.

accostomed to labour, th[at] tho out of the spirit of slavery, they think they ca[nnot do] without them in this countrey. I will g[ive you an] historical account of our situation, and star[t] since here. we have now been in this countrey going on seven years. we had about six or seven hundred Dollars in money perhaps not so much, when we got here—Then we had 230 of that to give for land to live on, and the rest to go on; I have never repented our moving [to] this countrey at any time, tho we have had our [diffi]culties you may expect; and at this time, I think myself better settled and situated than I was in Virginia. we want Buildings, but that we are able to obtain if we saw good to erect them here. the most of our wealth I laid out in Lands before we moved, and they have been of no advantage to us as yet; we have had a though[t] of moving on a tract I have about 40 miles above this, but [since] I know not how it will be yet, we are undetermined. We enjoy all the common and necesary mercies of Life, as plentifully as we have ever done since we have been house keeping, for which I desire to be thankfull to God always. some of the contents as p[e]r former letter you have. my own health has never been better since I was a lad, than it has been since in this countrey nor as good, my wife has been as much so as could be expected[.] our Children have had afflictian, but are all still alive. two are Married, one has two children and the other one. they are married to industrous men. We have eight Children, four of each sort, six profess to be converted, our two young[est not.] the spread of religion has been great [in this coun]trey, many have been converted to God. we [have] about, I should suppose, seven hundred members in our Circuit, and their [there] are several circuits in our State.[15] we have about sixty members in our class.[16] I can assure you my Brother the Lord is good to us, and their [there] is no just cause for complaining amongst us. some

[15] The Ohio District of the Western Conference, of which William Burke was presiding elder, included, in 1804–5, the circuits of Miami and Mad River, Scioto, Hockhocking, Muskingum and Kanawha, and Guyandott (William Warren Sweet, *The Rise of Methodism in the West* [New York and Cincinnati, 1920], p. 99). On the Miami and Mad River Circuit for that year, which included Clermont County, was reported a membership of 722 white and 12 colored members (*Minutes of the Annual Conferences of the Methodist Episcopal Church,* Vol. I: *1773–1828,* p. 129).

[16] Gatch's class was located at his residence in Miami Township, Clermont County, Ohio. Henry Smith writes that in 1800 "Gatch's neighborhood was our headquarters, where we had the strongest society" (*Recollections and Reflections of an Old Itinerant* [New York, 1848], p. 337).

of our Members profess to be sanctified, and I hope are[.] we have good Preachers, that I do believe Love souls. Our Countrey at present is new, and our Counties are fil[le]d up with clerks, but if B[rothe]r Pelham is enclined to move to our State, no doubt God will provide. the Earth is the Lords and the fulness thereof. says David I never saw the Ri[gh]teous forsaken nor their Children beging their bread. I generally look at a mans Spirit more than his wealth. this may fail, but charity never failith, this includes the first and second command, which will abide forever. The young Men you wrote about have never been here as I know of, I got the letter by Post—You say you dont like to stay where you are. indeed my Brother I dont know how you do to stay there attall with your tender connection. You say what can we do in your new countrey, God will provide, none begg their Bread here. Farms here will rent for the third of corn and wheat, and the [....] which is more in common than your Far[ms] in Virginia. A Family that is supported in Virginia by a Farm and several Negroes can be supported by a Farm equally as well without a slave, only they must wait on themselves, which in Idea is more than to reduce it to practice. I perceive a remarkable temedity in the old Virginians owing to their customs. they dread that. that I have felt a pleasure in. we can generally sell here what we have for market. Corn at this time is plenty and cheap. the greater number are moving this spring than ever before, Methodists and Quakers are comeing here fast from different directions, and that is no bad omen.[17] the Coppy of the constitution[18] of our State, I hope you will receive. I shall be glad to here [hear] from you at every opportunity[.] remember me to my old Friends in Virginia. Trade here is extensive, and some make by it. Friend Pelham can give you considerable information on this subject. Our Bro[ther] love to you Sister and Children

PHILIP GATCH

[17] The Quaker immigration to Ohio had begun around 1800, chiefly from two sources, Pennsylvania–New Jersey and the South. Several monthly meetings of Quakers were organized in the Miami Valley about this time, beginning with Miami, at Waynesville, in 1803. At least one Quaker, Nathan Updegraff, had been a member of the Ohio constitutional convention of 1802 (Rufus M. Jones, *The Later Periods of Quakerism* [London, 1921], I, 411).

[18] Gatch had been a member of the constitutional convention of 1802, representing Clermont County, and was one of three ministers present (Utter, *op. cit.,* p. 9).

III

Near Murfress boro [Tennessee] October 22, 1805

My Dear Brother

I would have wrote you long ere now, had I not been prevented a heavy fit of sickness, which well-nigh carried me to my long home. I never before experienced the feelings of one apparently dying—about to meet an all powerful God, seated upon a throne of justice. Oh! My brother! it is awful. My very nerves *now* thrill [with] the recollection. And tho, ('thank God] I feel nothing, upon the most minute scrutiny, where of to accuse myself; still I experienced not those overflowings of the spirit of God—those sweet and consolatory feelings,—those beams of heavenly bliss, that so frequently, and so usually evidence themselves to the children of grace, particularly when on the threshhold of eternity, about to wing their flight into the presence of God. I am so weak now, that I can with difficulty write to you. Yet I can truly and justly say, that my affliction has been a blessing to me. It has taught me, for ever hereafter, to live nearer to God, more obedient to the will of my master, and more subservient to his holy law. We don't remember a more sickly fall than this, in many years. Indeed there are very few families about, that are not somehow afflicted. Mrs Keys has been very unwell, but, I thank the Lord, she is geting over it. Several of my negroes are confined, and I doubt not I shall lose some; but the will of the Lord be done: he knows what is best for us.

I've had a letter sometime back from a dear country man of ours, Doctor Niblick, who lives some where in your country. He has given me a warm invitation to that part of the country, and I doubt not would be glad to see me. He is a wild dog: but we've all had our day. I have been informed, that he has been lately very ill, and given out by his physicians. Poor fellow! It may be a blessing to him perhaps; a time never to be remembered, but with sensations of gratitude to his Lord and Maker. Lord, humble us, if nothing else will do! Lord, do with us whatever is consonant to thy will! We are passive in thy hand, willing to submit to the utmost, can we only bask in the rays of thy reconciled countenance, whensoever it may be thy will and pleasure to summon us from *here!*

Will you be so obliging, brother, as to inform the Doctor of my situation, either by letter or otherwise; for I am evidently too weak at this time to write him. Let him know, that I shall, if in my power, pay him a visit this winter or spring; at which time also I hope to have the pleasure of spending a day with my dear brother, Drumgold.

Lord, brother, I wish I never owned, or was master of negroes! They are a hell to us in this world, and I fear they will be so in the next. But what to do with them, I know not. We can't live with them or without them; and what to [do] is a question. If they make a little, they steal it as soon after as they can; and unless the whip is forever on the creatures backs they do nothing [and] Therefore become a charge. Is this a life for a christian to lead? I wish some good advice upon this head. I think it is full time to conclude my letter, for this is the 3d day since I began it. Pray make my love and comp[limen]ts to sister Drumgold; also to doctor Niblick, should you see him or be acquainted with him.

D[ear] Brother, yours affectionately I am

James H. Keys[19]

IV

Febr*y* 20*th* 1807

D[ea]r Bro[ther:]

It would be Vanity to attempt a relation of every thing that has pass'd with me since we saw each other—suffice it to say I love God, his people and cause more than I did when I parted with you. I enjoy good health. My Wife and little son are well & the Lord provides for us[.] Glory to God is my song[.] O help me to Sing—We had five or Six Camp meetings[20] last fall. The Lord attended them all. A No were convicted, converted & Sanctified how many I cant tell—I be-

[19] James H. Keys was in 1790 a resident of Hillsboro, Orange County, North Carolina. As this letter shows, he had later removed to Murfreesboro, Rutherford County, Tennessee, where on February 12, 1807, Bishop Asbury writes: "I lodged at Doctor Key's" (*Journal of Rev. Francis Asbury* [New York and Cincinnati, n.d.], III, 215). Keys must have been a recent acquaintance of Dromgoole's, since he addressed the envelope: "Rev'd *Daniel* Drumgold Brunswick Virginia."

[20] The writer (John Sale) was in 1806–7 presiding elder of the Ohio District of the Western Conference (Sweet, *op. cit.*, p. 122) and in that capacity attended the camp meetings in the circuits under his care.

lieve that God will own the Methodist[s], so long as they maintain their Union with Him, and each other—A holy disintrested Ministry has been the Glory of the Methodist Church, & great care should be used to keep it so. One designing man may do more harm than 10 unlearned but sincere Preachers will do. The Purity of our doctrines is to our prosperity as the main spring of a watch is to its constant run[n]ing. I hope you and Family are we[ll and some] years nearer Heaven than when I saw you. My love to *yr* son Tho*s* & all the Family Meacham[21] bee—

I have been told you have had thought of coming to this country[.] we have a fertile soil & Sallubrious Air that is not contaminated with *Slavery;* perhaps you may live as well in Virg[ini]a & better as it respects luxuries, But I doubt whether you enjoy more peace & Tranquillity in every respect. If you were here in the Mercantile line you could get goods from Baltimore or Philladelphia[.] if you sold for Cash you could make your remittances when you went or sent for goods[;] if you sold for the produce of the Country you could send it down the American Nile (i e) the Ohio[.] A[aron] Burr has not yet put himself in possession of New Orlean[s.] We enjoy all the privileges of Sosciety that you can enjoy as it respects X*tn* [Christian] Fellowship. I still continue to Travel ar[ound t]he Neighbour hood where I live when at home[.][22] we have a good Society[.] I expect this State will be as the Garden of God & it is pleasing to me to live in a Country where there is so much of an Equallity & a Man is not thought to be great here because he possesses a little more of this Worlds rubbish than his Neighbour[.] I have many things to say but have not time or room on my sheet[.] I must conclude by craving an intrest in *yr* prayers: This from your Truily Loving Bro. in Xt [Christ] Jesus

John Sale[23]

[21] One James Meachem of Virginia had been a traveling preacher from his admission on trial in 1788 until his location in 1797 (*Minutes,* I, 30, 73).

[22] Sale after his marriage lived at Union, near Xenia, in Greene County, Ohio (James B. Finley, *Sketches of Western Methodism* [Cincinnati, 1855], p. 191).

[23] John Sale (1769–1827) was born in Virginia and was received on trial in the traveling connection in 1795. He was one of the founders of Methodism in Cincinnati and a distinguished presiding elder in the early days of Ohio Methodism, serving the Ohio and Miami districts. He had come to Ohio with the Bonners and Pelhams and had married one of Frederick Bonner's daughters (Sprague, *op. cit.,* VII, 256–58; Finley, *Sketches of Western Methodism,* pp. 185–92).

MAP II

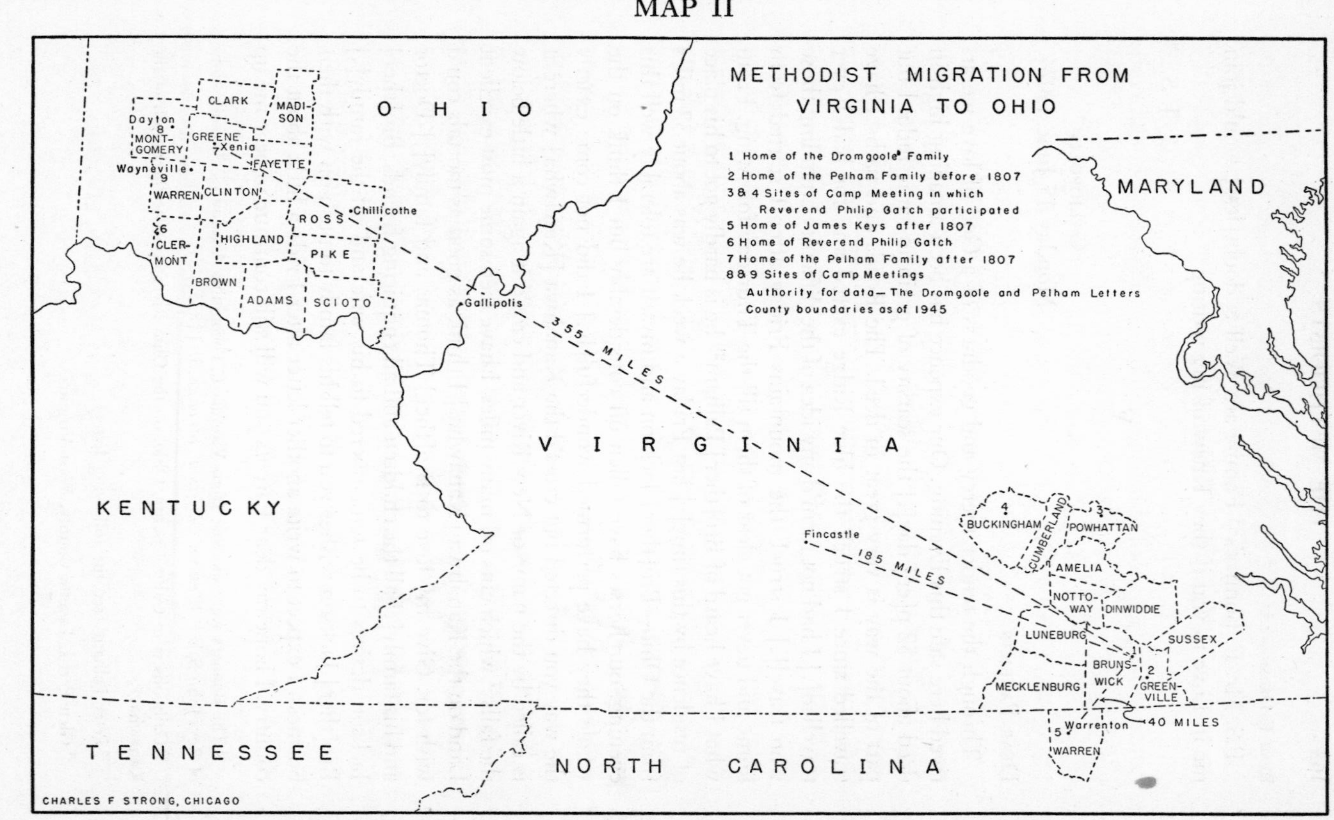

METHODIST MIGRATION FROM VIRGINIA TO OHIO
1 Home of the Dromgoole Family
2 Home of the Pelham Family before 1807
3 & 4 Sites of Camp Meeting in which Reverend Philip Gatch participated
5 Home of James Keys after 1807
6 Home of Reverend Philip Gatch
7 Home of the Pelham Family after 1807
8 & 9 Sites of Camp Meetings
Authority for data— The Dromgoole and Pelham Letters
County boundaries as of 1945
OHIO
CLARK
MADISON
Dayton
8
MONTGOMERY
GREENE
7 Xenia
FAYETTE
Wayneville
9
WARREN
CLINTON
ROSS
Chillicothe
6
CLERMONT
HIGHLAND
PIKE
BROWN
ADAMS
SCIOTO
Gallipolis
355 MILES
MARYLAND
VIRGINIA
KENTUCKY
4
BUCKINGHAM
CUMBERLAND
3
POWHATTAN
Fincastle
185 MILES
AMELIA
NOTTOWAY
DINWIDDIE
LUNEBURG
SUSSEX
1
BRUNSWICK
2
GREENVILLE
MECKLENBURG
5 Warrenton
40 MILES
WARREN
TENNESSEE
NORTH CAROLINA
CHARLES F STRONG, CHICAGO

REV*d* E DROMGOOLE

P.S. M*r*. F. Bonner's[24] Family are Well & doubt[less] would join me in Love to you if they Knew of my writing

J. S.

V

GALIOPOLIS[25]
Monday 15 June 1807

DEAR PARENTS

Through the tender mercy and goodness of a God of love we arrived here safe this Evening. Our expence has been amazing high in deed about $2 p[er] day[.] the scarsity of grain in same indeed but part of the way is very great in deed. The Roads and paths I have travelled since I struck the blue Ridge exceed any for bad I ever travelled[.] I had not form'd any idea of the difficulty attending those who travel[.] I struck the mountains Friday after I started from home and never got clear of them till the Thursday following. From what I have heard of Bro[ther] Palham[26] he is hardly got to his place of residence by this time[.] last Friday a week he was about 32 miles from the Ohio—Bro[ther] Jackson and myself are tolerably well this evening. our horses have fallen off considerably but I think on the whole they have performed wonderful[ly.] I did not come exactly the way you directed but cross'd the Kanahwa [Kanawha] where it is called by the name of New River and cros'd it again a little below the falls[27] which cuts off many miles. I have seen some most excellent Land on the Kanahwa [Kanawha.] I think as good as mortals cou'd wish for. Give my love to Bro[ther] Thomas and family[,] Doctor and his family[,] all the children and all enquiring friends. Bro[ther] Jackson desires to be remembered to his wife and all the family[.] Bro[ther] Jackson wishes you to tell his family to push on with their business. I expect to write another letter after I ride a little about the country. I hope my dear Parents you will still continue to bear me up

[24] The Bonners were likewise from Virginia ("Theophilus Arminius," "Recollections of Rev. John Sale," *Western Christian Advocate,* II [1835], 8).

[25] Gallipolis is in Gallia County, Ohio, on the Ohio River opposite the mouth of the Kanawha.

[26] Peter Pelham (see the following letter).

[27] Glen Ferris, Fayette County, West Virginia.

in the arms of prayer that God may bring me back to my native land again in peace and safety. I have met with difficultys on my way the only chance I had to pray in secret very often was in the stable or the woods. Sunday after I started I spent at a camp meeting on craggs creek[28] and the next sunday I rested[.] Some part of my way I have been greatly troubled with flies gnats & muscheters.

I remain your loving Son
EDW*d* DROMGOOLE[29]

VI

GREEN[E] COUNTY,[30] OHIO, 20th June 1807 Saturday

MY DEAR BROTHER,

After a tedious & fatigueing Journey of 9 Weeks one Day & a few hours my family & self thro' the mercies of our good & gracious God, safely arrived at our new Habitation in the Woods (which we have named Shunam)[.] our arrival here was on Thursday last after taking Dinner with our old friend & Brother Bonner & family who live about 1½ mile from us, and where I receiv'd your letter of the 23*d* of April together with those from Polly [Dromgoole] to Nancy & Sally [Pelham], for which you will both be pleased to accept of our thanks, as also for your particular expressions of your friendship to me, of which for a number of years I have experienced, and never had the least reason to doubt, tho' unworthy of it: however this you may be assured of, that I am not in debt to you on that account, (I mean in real sentiment) tho' never able to perform my wishes to express, & perform my desires for your satisfaction, but be assured there is no families I have left behind me, that I so ardently wish to be neighbours to me (in this happy Country & Neighbourhood) as yours & your Children & their Con[nect]ions. Since I have been at home

[28] Craig's Creek flows through Montgomery and Botetourt counties, Virginia.

[29] Edward, second son of Edward Dromgoole, Sr., was born in Brunswick County, Virginia, February 2, 1788. On February 22, 1813, Bishop Asbury writes that he ordained "Edward Drumgoold" a local deacon in the Methodist Episcopal church (*Journal*, III, 342, 376).

[30] Greene County was erected and organized in 1803; it is located in the upper valley of the Little Miami.

Brothers Maxey,[31] Heath[32] [. . . .] & Sister Malone have been to see us. Br[other] Sale inform'd me, [as] also did Br[other] Bonner that the Land[s] you have given a list of, lie about 50 miles from Xenia & some not very far from Chilicothe, but they are at present under some incumbrances, and doubtful whether they or any of the Tracts can (at present) be safely purchas'd. Br[other] Sale intends to [go to] Chilicothe in 3 or 4 weeks when he will enquire of M*r* Massey,[33] M*r* McNiel's agent, after which you will receive information from Br[other] Sale, who told me, yesterday, he would write you on the subject.

There is about 1½ mile from me a Tract of 400 acres of good land for sale with two small improvements on it, and adjoins the 370 acres that was David Bonner's, which I bought of youn[g] George Smith, last March, and where I expect my son Samuel will hereafter reside, the above 400 Acres I think of buying for you immediately if Mr. O'Neal[34] (*an honest Quaker*) & myself can agree on the terms after Samuel or both of us have view'd the Land; in this purchase I shall have regard to your future temporal interest as well as *the happiness* of being your *near* neighbour. the title is, and can be made *good,* as I have been inform'd by Br[other] Bonner as far as I recollect from the short & hurry of conversation I had with him on the subject.

[31] Bennett Maxey of Virginia was admitted on trial to the Methodist itinerant ministry in 1788 but located in 1797. Later rejoining, he served until a second location in 1835. One Horatio Maxey, perhaps a brother, had come from Powhatan County, Virginia, to Greene County, Ohio, in 1804 (*Western Christian Advocate,* II [1835], 44).

[32] "As early as 1803 and 1804, four adjoining surveys of land were made and settled by the Bonner, Sale, Butler, Davis, Heath and other families from Dinwiddie County, Virginia, and to the entire settlement was given the name of Union. These families were joined by others from the Old Dominion" (*Greene County, 1803–1908* [Xenia, Ohio, 1908], p. 53).

[33] Nathaniel Massie (1763–1813) of Virginia had served in the American Revolution and at its close settled in Kentucky. In 1790 he was appointed deputy surveyor to Colonel R. C. Anderson, in whose charge was the surveying and opening-up of the Virginia Military Reserve in Ohio. Massie founded Chillicothe in the Scioto Valley, which became Ohio's first capital. He had served as member of the territorial legislature and Ohio senate, of the Ohio constitutional convention, and as presidential elector in 1804. One of the largest landowners in the state, he necessarily was interested in furthering immigration (*History of Ross and Highland Counties, Ohio* [Cleveland, 1880], pp. 218–19).

[34] One Abijah O'Neall was the moving spirit in the emigration of the entire Bush River Monthly Meeting of Friends from Newberry County, South Carolina, to Warren County, Ohio, in the Little Miami Valley, in 1800–1810 (Jones, *op. cit.,* I, 409).

If Br[other] Neddy[35] sets off for this *fine Country* the first of September next let it be time enough to meet me at [the Western] Conference to be held in Chilicothe on the 17th of that month, where I hope to be with part of my family, if the Lord so permit, and expect M*r* Asbury to come home with us. I wrote to B[rothe]r Edm*d* Heath[36] when I was at Cincinnati, and to send you the Letter for your Reading. you have in that something of my happy feelings on setting my feet on a Land of *Liberty*. if ever you arrive here my dear Br[other] may you and yours feel at least, and I pray much more of the Goodness & presence of God that I felt on that happy Day. I know I have made a great sacrifice of *some things* in order to reach *this place,* and am in the woods with only one House & that not finished, but thank God I do not repent of it, and live in hopes I never shall.

My wife, and our children *do wonderfully,* we had our Dinner yesterday, our supper last night and our breakfast this morning on a ne[at] Cherry 4 foot square Table, and in neat and [much] better order than in old Virginia, and that *too without one black person to wait on us*. We Rest in peace, we Eat in peace & Glory to God we, in general[,] live in peace. O that we may spend our Days in peace with God, and at last come to Eternal rest. Xenia is a growing Town, about 2½ miles from me, and there is now a full store of goods. there are several Lots yet for sale there & I have it in contemplation to purchase one or two for myself, and if you think proper to speculate on any vacant Lots in Xenia you will please to write me, and I will endeavour to comply with your directions. However, I really think from the number of persons settled here in our neighbourhood you might find a support from Merchandize without living in Town if you should prefer a Country life after looking about you. I read part of your Letter to me to Brother Bonner and he says there is no doubt but you may get people both men & maid to do services for you. This I believe to be the case for this morning two men have been with me to employ them to open & clear some Land, and are to come next Monday to do some, and thereafter to work till the fall, in order to get some ground ready to sow wheat. I need not apologize to you

[35] Edward Dromgoole, Jr.

[36] Edmund Heath lived in Greensville County, Virginia, in 1810 (Jesse Lee, *A Short History of the Methodists in the United States of America* [Baltimore, 1810], p. 398). This family produced several early Methodist preachers.

for unconnexion in this as you know I generally write as things occur to my weak Mind, but what I do write tho' in a poor manner, is to my dear friend & that satisfies me on that head, and if my pen cou'd move with my poor tho' quick ideas you wou'd have several sheets, instead of two or three pages of paper. The great emigration to this and different parts of the State not very far from here this Spring together with the small crops made last year in comparison with former [years] has rais'd the price within a few days past from 2/. to 3/ V[irgini]a money p[e]r Bushell, which I am oblig'd to give for 30 Barrels purchas'd last Feb*y* by Son Sam*l* but he could not then fix the price, which has made a difference of 25$ against me, and would have been saved had we only got home 4 or 5 Days earlier. The growing Crops of wheat are really beyond my conception for fineness, and expected to be 50 cents p[e]r Bushel, or perhaps less. We have pass'd thro' a variety of climates as to Vegitation since I left old V[irgini]a. In the course of one Days travel of only 8 or 10 Miles, I have seen fine wheat & Corn growing and then at other pa[rt] the trees as barren of leaves, except a few buds, as [in the mon]th of January. This occur'd about the middle of last month, at which time we camped on little Sewall Mountain,[37] and some travellers who were then with us (strangers) said it Snow'd a little on the top of great Sewell only about 6 or 7 miles back from us at that time, which was on the 17th [of] May. Br[other] Bonner & family are well as also the neighbours in general as I have been informed, and this is said to be a healthy neighbourhood. We have had some afflictions on our Journey, and I was thro' amazing fatigue in driving my Stage, together with 4 or 5 Days sickness from the water greatly reduced and weaken'd in body about 4 or 5 weeks past, after which recovery I have gain'd flesh and weigh'd yesterday ¼ pounds more than I did the Day before we left V[irgini]a by the same Steelyards. Betsy weigh'd 2 lbs more Nancy 10 lbs, Sally 2—in short all have gain'd something in weight except Mary who is not at present quite so well as she has been, tho' keeps in general about business in the House, and my wife has fatten'd much on the Journey. My walking and riding on Horse back I think has not exceeded 30 Miles in the whole journey.

Br[other] Sale is acquainted with Br[other] Sims and thinks he

[37] In Fayette County, now West Virginia.

would do well in this Country & Neighbourhood, as there is only one physician in Xenia, and he not much approved of.

We all join in love to you, our dear Sister Dromgoole, & the family at your house, Br[other] Tommy D[romgoole] & family, Br[other] Sims & family, &c, &c Please to communicate such part of this Letter to our Sister Jane Fisher with our love to her, as you think proper, as also to Br[other]s Rideout, Heath & family & all my dear former class at the Camp meeting House[38] whom I dearly love in the Lord, and Bless God I forgot them not in my Evenings retirements at the Throne of Grace and hope never shall while I live. Dear Br[other] pray for us, many years have I prayed for you, and I do not know whether I have been 6 hours at a time without thinking of you and your situation, and the sweet conversation we have had together, except when I have been lock'd in the arms of sweet repose.

For the present I bid you Adieu, Aduir my Dear Brother.

Yours sincerely as ever
P[ETER] P[ELHAM][39]

P.S. Br[other] Sale has mention'd me to Br[other] Gatch to succeed Mr Paul[40] the present Clerk of this County who has thoughts of removing out of the County. Three Judges appoint the Clerk of the Court, and I have Thoughts of seeing some of them next Week on the

[38] Camp meetings were introduced into Virginia from the West in the spring of 1803. The first seems to have been held in Brunswick County at a new meeting-house which, Jesse Lee writes, "was named *Camp Meeting House,* that it might be remembered in future, that the first camp-meeting in that part of the world was held at that place" (William W. Bennett, *Memorials of Methodism in Virginia* [Richmond, 1871], p. 417).

[39] The Pelham family, of which Peter was head, lived originally in Greensville County, Virginia, near the Dromgooles, who lived in neighboring Brunswick County. Bishop Asbury had visited Peter Pelham's home in Virginia as early as 1802 (*Journal,* III, 53); and in Ohio for the first time on August 23, 1808 (*ibid.,* p. 248). They seem to have been progressive pioneers, with interests in developing Ohio's industries and good government, and they are said to have edited and published Xenia's first newspaper in 1810 (William Mills, *Centennial Historical Address Greene Co., O.* [Xenia, Ohio, 1876], p. 49).

[40] Colonel John Paul, the founder of Xenia, Ohio, was a delegate to the Ohio constitutional convention of 1802 and a state senator (Utter, *op. cit.,* p. 8). In 1809 he moved to Indiana, founding the town of Madison (*Greene County, 1803–1908,* pp. 32, 74–75).

subject. should M*r* Paul leave the County, perhaps I may succeed, unless prejudice in favour of some former acquaintance of the Judges, instead of having regard to a Person from a great number of year[s] experience in that business in your & Greensville County should prevail in the choice. I want to be doing a little here while I live, and for me to attempt the cutting down some of those large trees about my House &c would be folly indeed. The Land we live is *very rich,* fine and level, and do expect in future if the Lord spares me to have a fine *farm.*

Br[other] I am happy I am contented, Glory to God, but expect to have many things to attend to.

VII

GREEN[E] COUNTY STATE OF OHIO
June 24, 1807

DEAR PARENTS

The day after I wrote to you I left Galiopolis and reached Chilicothe Wednesday and staid with Doctor Tiffin,[41] he has resign'd being Governor. Mr. Massie was not at home. I talked with Doctor Tiffin about the Land offered for Sale by Mr. McNiel[.] The Doct[o]r says it is not wirth my while to go look at the Land on Brush Creek as it is not good. Left Chilicothe on Thursday Morning came through the Quaker Settlements in highland county[42] and so on to Bro. Bonner['s] on Thursday Evening and have been in this Neighbourhood ever since. I was well pleased with the land in High land County but had by far rather live in this neighbourhood. The land is excellent

[41] Edward Tiffin (1766–1829), a native of Carlisle, England, settled in Virginia in 1786 and received an M.D. degree from the University of Pennsylvania in 1789. Removing to Chillicothe, Ohio, in 1798, he served as speaker of the territorial house of representatives in 1799, was a member of the Ohio constitutional convention of 1802, and served as Ohio's first governor, 1803–7. In 1807–9 he served in the United States Senate; in 1812–14 was commissioner of the General Land Office; and from 1814 until 1828 was surveyor-general of the Northwest Territory. He was a Methodist local preacher, and one of a coterie of distinguished Methodists who held high offices in frontier Ohio's civil government (*A Biographical Congressional Directory* [1903], p. 843; see also Finley, *Sketches of Western Methodism,* pp. 260–87).

[42] Highland County lay in southwestern Ohio, occupying, with Fayette and Clinton counties, the territory between the Scioto and Little Miami rivers.

here, good neighbours, christian friends meet[ing] convenient & this part of the country healthy and [we]ll watered. I shall next week close a bargain for land[.] the tract contains 450 acres has two log cabbins on it and about 16 acres clear. One of the houses is very good has two Rooms below stairs. It has also a very good spring. This neighbourhood pleases me far better than any I have seen, and I think if you was here you wou'd like the country[.] such bodies of good Land I never see[.] I had not form'd any idea of it. I rode Thursday Friday & Saturday on most excellent land indeed & I have [not] seen any poor land Since I left Salt lick creek 13 miles before I got to Chilicothe except a small part on a creek and that was something like a mountain. When I first entered this State I was much discouraged for I travelled about a day and a half on much hilly very poor Land [with] Muscheters [mosquitoes] and flys—but after I got clear of that I was much encouraged. With respect to this Country's being a Muschoteo [mosquito] country I do not think it is[.] in [some] places on water courses and [swampy] land there is a good many[;] in some other places there is some[,] but I am informed that as people settle and get the Land cleared they are not plauged [plagued] with them after that only on some of the water courses. As I cannot write you everything about the country what I have must suffice for the present. Bro. Pelham and his family only got home last Thursday Evening. I hope they will do well in this country. I have been to see them[.] they are [well] except the old Lady and she has something of the ague & fever, wh[i]ch perhaps may make you believe that the country is favourable for that complaint. I talk'd with Doctor Tiffin about the complaints most prevailing in this country which are plourisies which the Doctor thinks is partly owing to their exposing themselves so much when they first come here, and some people have the ague while [....] is owing to the change of climate[.] after they get over that they are generally healthy.

Bro. Jackson is so wonderfully pleased with this country and says that if he had his family here he would never see old Virginia again. As for my part I feel willing to spend my days here. Bro. Jackson and myself are tolerably well or was when I parted with him. I left him with his friends the Quakers. You need not look for me home till the 20th or 23th of August as my horse is poor[.] his back [is] sore and

I must get him [in shape] before I start or I fear he will not be able to bring me back. I expect to start to a Camp Meeting on Friday next within 4 miles of Bro. Bonners. I still feel bound to find my way to heaven and do what good [I can]. Pray much for me. Nancy & Sally Pelham desire to be remembered to the family and no doubt the rest of Bro. Pelhams would send their Love if they know I was writing. Bro. Bonner sends his Love to you. Give my Love to all my friends as if nam'd and believe me to be your affectionate dutiful loving and unworthy Son

EDWARD DROMGOOLE JUN*r*

VIII

GREEN[E] C[OUN]TY OHIO
July 19th 1807

MY DEAR BRO[THER] DRUMGOLE

Thanks be to God for the peace and tranquility of mind which I have felt since I came through all the difficulties that attended my removal to this Land of Liberty and Equality?—

Your former request I thought was fully answered by Br*o* Gatch & John Sale who was much better acquainted than myself with this Country; I was very fortunate in my purchase of Land in this Country[.] the situation is Healthy & quite agreeable the Land very fertile yielding plentifully with little labour. the land on this side the Ohio is generally good but greatly varied by hills & flat[s] & swamps barren[s] & prairies, therefore you should be cautious in your purchases; Lands are rising[.] the migrations to this country surpasses anything I ever expected.

In a space of country above and below me where there was perhaps not more than 30 or 40 families last winter 3 years ago there are now 3 or 400 now setled & yet there is room[.] Why will you tarry in Sodom because there are 5 righteous found there & God withholds his fierce wrath[?]

By your letter I find you wate [wait] to be driven from that country of oppression & wrong by some Ju[d]gment. Oh! Bro. Drumgole the Lord provided for the Vertuous sons of the Eastern States in the liberty of State of Ohio—the thing speaks for its self[.] The CALL IS LOUD. I know there are difficulties not only in preparing to start but also on the way; but thanks to the Lord there is no red Sea in the way; no phar[a]o[h']s host to pursue us while traveling to the American Canaan & as for our Jordon (I mean the Ohio) it is easy to cross and (whats better) when once planted here our children are saved from the harmfull practice of trading on their fellow creatures in the manner I understand some of our old Friends have done in the state, when Slavery exist[s] & whats worse they take protection under General Conference.[43] LORD have Mercy on the Methodists cause and Fix it on a firm basis—When the Legislature of V[irgini]a has determined against liberty[44] & our preachers & people will be purchasing Slaves without a prospect of liberating them what can we think will be the condition of the church in the state when slavery is encouraged & liberty suppresst, in a few years[.] With respect to our health thank God we enjoy that inextimable blessing better than we did in V[irgini]a. Glory to God[!] David Chappele Paley & Eliz*er* has found the Lord since we came here[.] David & Nancy are Married and are blesst with a prospect of doing well as there [their] own labour & are glad at heart that I ever brought them to a land where they are not to be troubled with slaves; We are highly favour*d* with good society having 51 in class at my house & have good times indeed—As for the Mercantile business at present it is thought to be profitable[.] the cost of Geting Mer[chan]d[ise] from Philadelphia here is about $9 p[e]r hundred & it is sold for Cash pork &.....

When you make up your mind about coming to [Ohio] you [must] write to me & let me know the conclusion

My wife & Family Join me in love to you & yours Adieu

FREDERICK BONNER[45]

[43] The General Conference urged emancipation of slaves, but, in cases where this was precluded by state laws, church membership was still allowed to slaveholders.

[44] Restrictions were placed on manumission of Negro slaves by several of the southern states, as Virginia and North Carolina.

[45] The Bonner family produced several Methodist circuit-riders, among them John, who was received into the traveling connection on trial in 1790. Frederick Bonner (1759–1827) was a friend and traveling companion of Philip Gatch when the latter served Sussex Circuit, Virginia, in 1777 (McLean, *op. cit.*, p. 55). In his tours of Ohio, Bishop Asbury usually visited the Bonners, as in August of 1808 (*Journal*, III, 248). In August, 1815, he writes: "On our route [through Ohio] we called upon many of our old friends, Buck, Sale, Bonner, Smith, Butler—they treated us like presidents" (*ibid.*, p. 390).

IX

July 27. 1807 A Rainy Day

MY DEAR BROTHER

The above[46] is in answer to part of your Letter I rec*d* by your son Edward, which came to hand the Sunday morning after we arriv'd at our new habitation in this happy Country, and, the neighbourhood we are bless'd with.

I have been at a Camp Meeting about 6 miles from home where were suppos'd to be about 25 Converted. The Congregation on Sunday consisted of only about 600 persons. We have Circuit preaching[47] about 1½ mile from us at Br[other] Bonners, where and at some other places of public worship I have attended, and thank God my soul has thro' the goodness of God been much refresh'd & blessed at those places in particular; and thank God I am in general happy in the peace [and] love of God in our new habitation; and also have been bless'd with the Company of Br[other]s Sale P[residing] Elder,[48] McGuire,[49] and Quin[50] who are travel[in]g preachers. Br[other] Sale's Cabin is about 7 Mile from ours; & Br[other] Maxey who lives a little further, and whom we frequently see. As to our situation in those respeck [respects] it is as agreeable as I cou'd wish, and thank God we are in health and happy; and are glad we ever came to this fruitful Land, and place of LIBERTY.

My wife and Children, thank God, do wonderfully, and bear their respective burdens in the family with cheerfulness and frequently mention how much better to do their family business of Cooking &c themselves, than to have any black ones about them. When we want

[46] Pelham sent an extract from the revised code of Ohio on "State Tax on Land," which is here omitted.

[47] The circuit was Mad River, to which Adjet McGuire and Isaac Quinn were appointed for 1807 (see below) (*Minutes,* I, 149).

[48] Sale was still presiding elder of the Ohio District.

[49] Among those admitted on trial to the Western Conference of 1803 was "Adjet McGuire, who travelled the Limestone Circuit [Kentucky] nearly 12 months past, was well received, and useful; and came recommended according to rule" (Sweet, *op. cit.,* p. 84).

[50] Isaac Quinn received his first appointment in the Western Conference in 1806. Though his name is absent from the list of those received on trial in that year, it appears among those who were continued on trial in the following year (*ibid.,* p. 122; *Minutes,* I, 153).

washing done we get assistance from one of our young Sisters to assist, and business carried on with cheerfulness and good humour. From what little I have seen and experienc'd here, I wou'd not be situated to spend my Days where I came from, for half the State of Old Virginia. We are daily improving our settlement, and to Day two young men have come to clear me ten Acres of Ground to be *seeded* next fall in wheat, and afterwards to clear me some ready for Corn next Spring. Harvest labourers are plenty here and wages from 4/6 to 1 Doll[ar] p[er] Day. We have had a very wet season during the harvest here, but thank God, it is expected there will be plenty of good wheat &c for the supply of the neighbourhood and to spare. The growing Corn is in a most beautiful and flourishing state, and bids fair for abundance of that Commodity. I wrote to you the Day before Neddy arrived, and have since purchas'd for you the Land I mention'd in that Letter (which by survey and exchange of part with David Bonner for other lands adjoining for the better accommodating both parties) amounts to 433 Acres as it now stands, 418 being the part purchas'd at 3$ 12½ Cents p[er] acre. This will be more fully explain'd to you by Neddy who with my wishes and approbation, conducted the business, as I considered the exchange beneficial to you & what I shou'd have done had I purchas'd the tract for myself, and indeed should have done it myself for you, if Neddy had not been here to attend to it, so that I flatter myself this part of my conduct will meet your approbation.

I cou'd not get the Land for less than 3¼ Dollars if I had advanc'd the balance in Cash. The amount paid for the Land was 1306$ 25 Cents—As my collections while in Virginia fell far short of my expectations, if convenient I will thank you to enclose by Mail 300 Dollars in Virginia B[ank] Notes, for I am rather afraid I shall want more than I have before Sammy can go to, and return from Virginia. The Tract of Land that joins mine on C[a]esarsville please to let me know if you wish to have it or not, Br[other] Maxey & others say it is very good, and may be had for 3$ p[er] acre, the owner or agent lives about 16 miles from this and when I hear from you I will try to comply with your command.

If I recollect right I think I have in a good measure in my former Letters answered your last to me, in giving you what information I cou'd that I thought might be useful for you to know.

I do sincerely sympathize with my former fellow Citizens of Greensville and Brunswick in their distresses, and do not forget daily to emplore the Almighty to provide & make some way for their support in the time of their calamities, and I hope the Lord will supply them and support their lives with the necessaries, altho' it may appear from scarcily improbable if not impossible to human nature, and may their present distresses & the Judgments of God be sanctified to them, and the Nation in general. May you my dear Brother be still supported with wisdom and strength from on high to continue in the work of the Lord, and I pray God that you may speedily see the fruits of your labours to the Glory of God and the great comfort & peace of your own soul. O my dear Br[other] there is no family in Virginia that I so ardently wish to be near Neighbours to me as you and yours, and "if I am not your friend I am no ones below the Sky," and if I was as worthy of your friendship, as you are of mine & all who know how sweet it wou'd be to be.

My wife and Children join in love to you and yours with D[ear] Br[other] yours affectionately

P. Pelham

P.S. Neddy can tell you how we are accommodated, and how we are going on, in order to get comfortably fixed against the approaching fall and winter. I am the only one of the family that have little that I can do, yet let me tell you I have cut more wood for fires than I thought I ever should be able to do, thank God for the health & strength I have which is more than I have enjoy'd for years past. Pray for us.

X

July 27 1807

My dear Bro[ther]

I recie[ve]d your kind letter and was glad to find that you and your family are still on your pilgrimage to the Land of reste. Yet I find that you are not sattisfide to live in the land where you now are—if I knew the cause of your dissatisfaction & could the better give you mine opinion, whether you had Beste stay where you are, or come to the Land of liberty[.] are you dissatisfied because you have not nor cannot make money enuph for your Children and Grand children—if so, I shall not say come—altho I believe the fare [far] greater parte that have come from Virginia have ad[d]ed fore [four] fold to their property with industry and frugality[.] They live as well as heart could wish for[.] Or is it because you live in a land of Slavery and have you[r] doubts whether it be right in the sight of God for you to die there and live [leave] your children and grand ch[i]l[dren] In that land of oppression, When there is a fare [far] more excellent place provided and that you might be the happy instrument under God to plant them in this good land Where that evil is not and from every possible circumstance the free born sons Of Ohio will never admit it [slavery]. If this be the cause I say Come in the Name of the Lorde. no doubt but your sacrifice there will be great—yet the pe[a]ce of mind and the smiles of a good providence will reste on you and be with you on your jurney—and if the good God should bring you to this land you will join your Brethren and say, that you now possess that sattisfaction and peace of soul you eve[r] was a stranger to—

I have been in this country now fore [four] years[.] I am well pleased with it[.] if my family was in the old settlement and I knew as much of this country as I know now—there is no object as I know of that would keep me away from the ohio—in my opinion This is a helthy country. We have had but little or no sickness since I moved to the state—as to the good quality of these Lands, I know not what the reports have been with you—but I'll tell you that there is the largest body of good land in this state that I ever saw anywhere and it is [of] a superior quality.

You may do well by keeping a retail store in this country[.] three years ago our merchents began the wourld with little or nothing. This spring they opened there [their] stores with a large assortment. You may git farmers to cultivate your land

Is slavery a morel Evil—is not all morel Evil of a damning nature—Can a child of God live in a damning sin

My wife joins me in love to you and Sister Dromgoole and invit[e]s you all to this good land

BENNETT MAXEY[51]

[51] Bennett Maxey, a convert of the Powhatan revival in Virginia, was received on trial to the traveling connection in 1788 and located from the Virginia Conference in 1835 (McLean, *op. cit.*, p. 89; *Minutes*, I, 30).

XI

CHILLICOTHE Sept. 16, 1807

MY DEAR BROTHER DROMGOOLE

Last Saturday I arr[ive]d here in Company with our Br[other] Sale. The Conference[52] was open'd on Monday, we have had good preach[in]g Day & Night, and as yet only one poor soul converted, who it is said was the vilest white woman in the Town, she profess'd to be very happy indeed, and I believe was so, she has a hard and persecuting husband, Mother & Sister—poor Creature; the Lord grant her grace to stand fast. 13 preachers received on Trial—Yesterday & Deacons ordained—to-day 7 Elders ordained—increase of Nos [numbers] at this Conference 2200.[53] The Night before last was a very powerful and happy time, at which time the above woman got converted. Mr. Asbury is as well and in as good spirits & cheerful as usual—he intends to go home with me. I left my family in usual health—since I came here I am not so well as when I left home owing to having taken some cold, but thank God I am well enough to attend the meetings, and the Lord refreshes my poor soul, and I sometimes am at liberty to shout aloud as in Days past; Glory to God[!] I feel I have taken a fresh start for the Heavenly Canaan, and I don't doubt but my dear Br[other] & Sister D[romgoole] are on their journey, and in pursuit of Crowns of immort[ality]—. I am at Br[other] Tiffen's, where I [have] been treated above my deserts Br[other] & Sister Tiffin are kind, plain, and affible—He has (unasked) promis'd me, if any thing should turn up at Congress, wherein he can serve me, he will do it.

I wrote to you by Br[other] James Wyche,[54] who left this Town last Friday morning. Samuel is preparing to go into Housekeeping this fall and to take Patsy B[onner] with him as his Spouse, so that I have only Jesse and Peter with me (of the boys) except such as I hire: these I can [hire] plenty of as long as my money lasts. Please

[52] The Western Conference met at Chillicothe, Ohio, on September 14, 1807 (Sweet, *op. cit.*, p. 123).

[53] Bishop Asbury writes of the proceedings: "There were thirteen preachers added, and we found an addition of two thousand two hundred members to the society in these bounds; seven deacons were elected and ordained, and ten elders: two preachers only located; sixty-six preachers were stationed" (*Journal*, III, 233).

[54] James Wyche lived in Brunswick County, Virginia, in 1810 (Lee, *op. cit,* p. 397).

write to me; and also give my love to Sister D[romgoole] and all that appertain to your family:—To Br[other] Jackson and tell him I was sorry he went off without coming again to see me. I wish to be re-m[embere]d [to] Br[other] & Sister Coe—Br[other] Rideout & family &c. &c. &c all in love.

I am really thine
P. PELHAM

How happy should I be were you here now but alas we are *too far* apart; Shall I hope for us (if we live) ever to be near enough again to visit each other? But in order to effect this my dear Br[other] you must *come to me,* for *I cannot go to you.* Adieu

P. P.

17th. Thank God I feel better, and am in my usual state of good health this morning. We had a comfortable meeting last night—but no new Converts that I know of.—This Town [Chillicothe] contains about 2000 Inhabitants, and there are several new buildings on hand, some will be elegant, when finished, both of Brick, and wood. Our meeting House is of Brick 40 × 30 with Galleries on 2 sides & one end, which contains a pretty large No [number] of people who crowd to our Night meetings. Continue to pray for me and mine, & I do not forget you and yo[urs]

P. P——

XII

GREEN[E] COUNTY Nov. 19, 1807

MY VERY DEAR BROTHER,

Yours of the 31 Aug*t* I rec*d* on the 11[*t*]*h* of last Month. Your Tenant was not at home nor has he been at home since, he is gone about 80 miles from this neighbourhood to prepare a place for himself and family for the next year. He had a pretty good crop of Corn growing when he left it, but it has all (except a few bushels) been destroyed by the Squirrels during his absence, how I shall secure the rent due you I know not at present, but when he returns, which is daily expected, I shall endeavor to effect it for you. It is difficult sowing wheat in Corn ground in this Country unless the Corn is all taken away first and the stalks clear'd from the ground, and your Tenant not being at home as above ment[ione]d nothing has been done in that matter. Let me know whether you wish to rent out the place next year or not, or to reserve the Cabin, if the land be rented to cultivate.

Mr. D[avid] Bonner was to have gotten a deed for your Land as also for his own purchas'd of Mr O Niele, but has not yet done [it], however both will I expect be effected before long, and the Lands are as secure at present as if deeded, so that you may make yourself easy on that subject.—There have no Lands been sold in this neighbourhood, except [the] James Spain Tract of 50 Acres since I wrote you & what that sold for I have [not] certainly heard or whether it is certainly sold to Baker Pashim of Virginia or not, however we have heard he is removing out here with his family.

Mr O'Neile is answerable for the present year's los[s]es of your land, as I have been inform'd but if of right you ought to pay them, I shall discharge the legal demand when made. The ground is now cover'd with Snow, and it has been snowing this Morning. The weather is now cloudy and moderately warm, but we have had smart frosts the 9& 10th of Sept. also sometimes in Oct. and the present month some severe freezing weather—Ice about 1½ Inch thick in one night last week.

Thro' mercy we are all in the Land of the living but have been made subjects of the general affliction of the Influenze so prevalent (excepting wife & one or two others of the family, otherwise, thank God, we have generally good health since we have been in this State.

This will be conveyed as far as Fincastle by a Br[other] Hipes[55] who stayed with us last Night, and is from that Neighbourhood looking a place to remove to next Spring or fall. About 2 weeks [ago] about 3 or 4 families came from Virginia, and are gone to settle on the Waters of Derby Creek.

We all join in love to you and yours &c. wishing peace, health & prosperity to attend you. Bishop Asbury came home with me from Conference.[56] I show'd him some of your Letters to me, and he said

[55] Henry Hypes (1775–1854), a native of Rockbridge County, Virginia, moved near Xenia, Greene County, Ohio, in 1811 (*Portrait and Biographical Album of Greene and Clarke Counties, Ohio* [Chicago, 1890], pp. 880–81).

[56] The bishop left the conference "with a determination to visit the frontier settlements on the Great-Miami River" and writes that on Saturday he "got into C[a]esarsville, and stopped with Peter Pelham . . . ." (*Journal,* III, 233). Samuel Pelham wrote

he was glad to find you so far advanced toward imigrating, and observ'd that this was the Country for all such as *you and me*. He was pleas'd to find us so well off here as he did, and thought we had great things for the short time we had been in the Country. He intends to call and see you on his way from So[uth] Carolina Conference.[57]

We wish to hear from you. In haste yours as ever

P. PELHAM

Excuse errors & neglects, as I have no time just now to correct or add.

XIII

GREEN[E] COUNTY, OHIO Oct*r* 22*d* 1808

MY DEAR BROTHER—

I rec*d* yours of the 27 Aug*t* & 23*d* Sept[ember] last Tuesday, which thro' the goodness & mercy of God found us all in health, except some slight indispositions (among some of us) from Colds, which at present is pretty general in our Neighbourhood tho' not violently bad in any family & is the only complaint any of our Neighbours, or my own family has experienced since you left us, that I know of.

I am glad to find the Lord is still carrying on his work of Salvation in old Virginia. I pray God it may never stop till the whole bend to the mild sceptre of our blessed Savior. We have had some glorious times since you left us. Mary & Caroline got converted at our Camp meeting near Xenia, which began on the 9*th* Sept*r* where about 25 souls profess'd to get converted. The fortnight before I was down at Br[other] Gatch's at C[amp] Meeting where it was suppos'd 30 or 50 (some say more) Souls got converted. Glory to God for his abundant Grace.

I shall write to Br[other] Robbins agreeable to your request, and send by Br[other] Sale when he goes on his next Tour to Chillicothe &c which I expect will be in a few days.

I am not surprised to find from what quarter your removal to this

---

to Edward Dromgoole, Jr., October 21, 1807; "Old Father Asbury stayed one night at Papas, one at M*r* Bonners & one at M*r* Sales and then left us, saying he rec[k]oned he must come this way again it looked so much like old Virg[ini]a. . . . ."

[57] The South Carolina Conference was to be held at Charleston, December 28, 1807 (*Minutes*, I, 152).

Country prevents[.] it is no more than what I have often thought wou'd be the Case, owing to my dear Sister D[romgoole]'s almost constant indisposition, but flatter myself it is the only reason with her, and should it please God to restore her to sound health (which I pray God may soon be the case) and we should all be spar'd I hope to see you and yours yet in this fertile Land of LIBERTY. As there is no present prospect of your coming out next Spring, can't you and Sister D give up my Br[other] Thomas [Dromgoole] and family to come out then, where we can furnish him with a School of 30 Scholars or more, and a House to live in, where Dempsy McDaniel now lives, and which Br[other] Davis will give up for that purpose. We are now erecting a School House 30 × 20 feet, to [with] two fireplaces in the same Room also to answer for the Temporary preach[in]g House till a better can be erected. If Br[other] Thomas will come we will try to do all we can for him, for his comfort and satisfaction, and I think, if he should come, he would not repent it. This is the wish of Br[other] Maxey & others, who are Trustees, to the School, with myself. I shall apply to M*r* Galloway[58] for the papers, if he has not sent them already to Doct[or] Tiffin, and forward them to him by the Mail to Washington, if he cant get them before he leaves Chillicothe. In regard to renting out your place, I shall attend to your desires respecting the same.

I wish you to forward me some money, if you can make any collection for me—put the Letter in the P[ost] Office Hicks' Ford [Virginia].

You wish to know how our Crops have turn'd out. Crops of wheat [are] but small. None have gather'd Corn yet, but our fields look pretty full of Ears. It is judg'd my new ground (notwithstanding the great number of Sugar Trees in it) will bring between 40 & 50 Bushels to the Acre, some of it more than 50 Bushels, altho' we never had Rain to wet the ground 1½ Inch deep from the time you left us until the 14*th* of Sept*r*.

Thank God this will leave us in pretty good Health, with love to you & family and all my Vi[r]g[ini]a friends. Yours as usual & ever

P. PELHAM

[58] James Galloway, Sr., settled in 1798 on the Little Miami two miles north of Oldtown. James Galloway, Sr., was Greene County's first treasurer, and his son James its first surveyor (*Greene County, 1803–1908*, pp. 39 and 41).

P.S. I wrote to Br[other] E[dmund] Heath the begi(nni)ng of this month I think & for him to pay to you what money he may Collect for me. P. P.

Br[other] Davis has rais'd and cover'd with weather Boards, a framed House, and is ready to be shingled—and expects to get it ready to go in this fall. You may Read my Letter to Br[other] Heath when you see him.

Last Monday 3 weeks on that Night we had a pretty small frost, & several times since tho' not severe till last Monday night, the latter kill'd our sugar Beans, & potatoes tops, and standing Fodder. To day a very rainy one. *23d* Fine pleasant clear weather for the Season. We are to have meeting here to Day, and expect to deliver this to Br[other] Towler[59] to be put in the Mail next Tuesday.

XIV

OHIO, GREEN[E] COUNTY, Monday 15th May 1809

DEAR BROTHER

Yours of the 12th of last month, came to hand by mail, this Day [a] Week with its contents, for which you will please to accept my thanks. I wrote to you the 27th of March last, which I expect has come to Hand before this time. The Dutchman I rented your land to was not willing at last to come on it, but I have rented it to George Morgan on the same terms I mentioned in my letter above and he is now living on it. Br[other] Bonner made allowance for cleaning up the field to be 3 B[ushe]lls corn, so that the rent corn to you will be 17 Blbs. I have heard nothing from Br[other] Robbins about your lands near Paint [Creek].[60] I shall apply the 20 dollars as you express. I saw Mr Galloway, not long since, and he told me he had not rec[eive]d the papers from Anderson's Office,[61] but should go down soon, himself, and get them with other business he has to do there. As soon as I get them I shall do the best to obtain the Patents, after Samuel has

[59] See below, Letter XVI.

[60] Paint Creek was a western branch of the Scioto River, rising in Madison County, near the source of the Little Miami.

[61] Colonel Richard Clough Anderson was appointed in 1783 to oversee the location and survey of the Revolutionary bounty lands for Virginia in Kentucky and Ohio. The Virginia Military District in the latter state included Greene County.

seen the plots and approves as you mentioned in your letter to him. Br[other] Tiffin has resigned his seat in Congress, and is [married to] a Miss Polly Porter, formerly of Delaware State.[62] Sammy has some thoughts of going to Virg[ini]a once more for me; for I am apprehensive I could not well endure the fatigue of the Journey. Lands are, and have been, of dull sale. One hundred acres with a Cabin, and about 15 acres clear'd land of excellent quality, sold last fall about 3 miles from me at 4$ per acre, one half in money, and the other (what is here called) in Trade.

We yet have comfortable, tho, at present, not very powerful times at our Meetings, no new Converts of late but the people attend meetings pretty well. Our prayer meetings are kept up on Sunday afternoons at different places. At my House yesterday evening there were between 40 and 50 present and a comfortable time. Glory to God for his mercies and blessings to poor Sinners.

My family are all about, but my wife is somewhat indisposed from a cold and fevers at times.

The Lord has thought proper to take our Daughter Nancy Bonner from the evils to come; which event took place on the 2nd Day of last Month, and Glory to God she departed triumphant in the faith, and said a little before she died, if she had strength of voice, she could shout, Victory—Victory! Our little Grand Daughter, Baptized Anne Pelham, is well and grows fast, and is a pretty little girl. I should be glad if you and all yours were happily and comfortably situated here among us entirely to all your satisfactions.

You will please to continue to do what you can for me till Sammy comes to Virginia.

I have been informed 11 fa[milies], removed from No. Carolina to the Neighborhood of [....] Drakes, last fall, and several others in different parts of the State. Br[other] Joel Drake had Circuit Preaching and a class of 9 or 11 Members at his House, which has greatly comforted him and his, *once dissatisfied* wife.

We join in love to you, your family and all our friends of your Neighborhood, and wishing you all happiness,

I remain Yours sincerely

P. Pelham..

[62] Tiffin's first wife had been Mary Worthington of Charlestown, Berkeley County, Virginia, sister of Governor Thomas Worthington of Ohio (Utter, *op. cit.*, p. 12).

P.S. We have had upwards of 3 weeks dry weather; the Roads are fine, and pleasant travelling. The weather is now very cool, and the ground very dry. We began to plant Corn the Day before Yesterday, and shall finish to Day. Some have not begun yet, and some of your neighbors have finished. My Wheat much more promising than this time last year.

Be[c]ky wrote to Sister Rebecca Sims last Mail.

I have got a Hand Bill from Petersburg expressing the situation of our affairs with Great Brittain, which came by the last mail.

XV

OHIO. GREEN[E COUNTY], Sept. 8. 1809

MY DEAR BR[OTHER] DROMGOOLE—

Yours arrived in the P[ost] Office the 17th [of] July I rec[eive]d the 14th. of the month, being some Days previous to Neddy's arrival here, owing to his long stay in Chillicothe. You say "pray for you as usual, and write on all subjects that are expedient." The former part of this request, thank God I have never fail'd, I think, to do for many years, and hope thro' grace so to continue; but the latter part of the request; I feel myself too barren to comply with, as I could I wish for your satisfaction. Accept of my thanks for your attention to the business you undertook for me, and for the returns made by Neddy which were cordially and timely received; by which I have been enabled to purchase some land warrants for upwards of 2000 acres a[t] 35 p[er] c[en]t—but this is not the best news to inform you of. Last week we had a Camp Meeting about a mile from Xenia [with] about 22 preachers, (Travelling and Local) [and] a very large Congregation in general for our part of the Country, and on Sunday about 1000 people attended, powerful times, and in the Evening my Son Peter, blessed be God, got powerfully converted I believe. On Monday last 38 joined society, and 45 professed to get converted during the C[amp] Meeting—but I think there were between 50 and 60 new Converts several having gone away before the meeting broke up. My dear Children are all in Society, and all profess religion but poor Sarah who still remains as when you saw her last, but I am not without hopes for her. We expect Mr. Asbury,[63] Br[other] McKendree,[64] and Br[other] Beahm[65] in our Neighborhood next Week. Appointments are made for Mr. A[sbury] to preach in Xenia tomorrow week and at our M[eeting] House the next Day which is a little more than ½ mile from us. Neddy has not been able to let out your place but is to leave a power with me to do so which I shall endeavor to comply with. The present years rent corn he has empowered me to dispose of or take for myself (If I choose) at the market price in the fall. Our Crops of Wheat in general are light, but a great prospect for large Crops of Corn thank God.

"You say you wish well to Ohio so long as the practice and spirit of Slavery is rejected;" I hope you will never have reason to wish otherwise: for should a change in that respect take place, perhaps, I might in vain, wish to be situated as I was in the beginning of the Year 1807. But I flatter myself there will be no cause for uneasiness on that account, and am sorry the horrid practice still continues, and is likely to continue in your Country, and I am the more so, as I expect if life last[s] one of my Children will become an inhabitant of your Country again, a thing I never expected when we left old Virg[ini]a. but I wish to be resigned, and to meet all trouble and trials with true Christian patience and fortitude while I stay in this world: and should the circumstance alluded to take place, *I know I am clear* from persuasions or advice on the occasion. Yet I believe (as you do) that a Heaven may be secured in any place or condition and that divine porvidence shall place us in. "Yet there may be situations and circumstances more advantageous than others." I suppose you mean (by

[63] On Wednesday, September 13, 1809, Asbury "stopped at Petham's [Pelham's]," where he remained for several days, reading Wesley's sermons. Of the Philip Davis family in the neighborhood, he writes: ". . . . this is an old Virginia family, and here are brethren and sisters whom I have known, some twenty, others above thirty years" (*Journal,* III, 275).

[64] Bishop William McKendree (1757–1835) was a native of King William County, Virginia, and was converted during the Brunswick revival of 1787, joining the traveling connection soon thereafter. In 1800 he superintended the expanding Methodist work west of the Appalachians and in 1808 was elected bishop of the Methodist Episcopal church, the first native American to hold the position.

[65] Henry Boehm (1775–1875), a Pennsylvania German, was Bishop Asbury's traveling companion. He was a son of Martin Boehm, who was, with Otterbein, cofounder of the Church of the United Brethren in Christ.

this) in order to obtain Heaven; if so, on weighing all circumstances and situations, don't you *believe,* that a Land of Liberty must be preferable to a Land of Slavery for the purpose? Yes you do believe that Ohio is preferable to Virginia, but alas too many hindrances, and inconveniences to struggle with; well Br[other] if we never meet here to pray with and for each other, let us continue our prayers to God that we may meet at the right Hand of God to behold our Jesus and join the Celestial Band in Eternal praises to the Triune, One God over all blessed forever more. Glory to God[!] I hope myself and family are still in the Heavenly Road, and I trust if we continue we shall meet our good and Gracious God in Peace and Happiness. We all join in love to Sister D[romgoole] &c and Dr. Sims &c and T[homas] D[romgoole] &c and Sister Wyche &c and D[....], Br[other] Hobbes &c— and all our friends as opportunity offers, and pray God to grant that when we fail on earth we may meet in Glory, is the prayer of your aff[ectionat]e unworthy Brother

P. PELHAM

XVI

XENIA OHIO Sep[tember] 11. 1809

DEAR BROTHER

By the hands of your son forwarded from Chillicothe while he [was] there [....] I rec[eive]d your letter m[entioning] the business we had some conversations on while you were out here[.] I thot as you did not expect to move into this state it would not suit you to settle my business & take land. I have the greater part of the land still unsold. if the way should open you can have it.

You wished to know something of Xenia, except [for] the finishing [of] the court house the improvements have been inconsiderable. The principal alteration that has taken place, which is of far the greatest consequence is a religious revival, but mostly among the young people[.] Our Town society has increas[e]d to 30[.] as brother Edward [Dromgoole] was at our late camp meeting about one mile from this place, I need say no more about it: but permit me & join me in praises to our all bountiful God for his increasing [favors and his] mercies crowd our favor[e]d state, potentially free I pray God we may be free from sin & folly. I make the best use of our precious priviledges.

I frequently think of and tremble for my native state. May the God of wisdom open some way to relieve her from the Most dangerous & formidable enemy she has under heaven [which is,] I sincerely believe, the *slaves*. One sentence in your letter has frequently sensibly impressed my mind "that we should all members of the church act as if the prosperity of the whole depended on the single fortunes of each member." When I retrospect my life I groan under the view of my inactivity for God, how apt we are to suffer the chaff to blind us, while we neglect the more important concerns of the salvation of our fellow men, selves, & the glory of God; time passes but never re[turns, and we] neglect those duties that if perf[ormed] would have brought comfort to our own souls, & souls probably to God & honor to our Master & the favorable opportunity returns no more forever; It is my unfortunate lot to be under the powerful necessity of claiming the above character, I feel at times at the age of 40 odd as if I had the business of my whole life to do now, and I know not where to begin[.] a thousand things as it were present themselves to me at the same instent, & I stand astonished I look on I know not what to do. I in some measure at times work, but have to own the labor vain and then cry out O when shall I be able to cease to work in my own strength.

These things, together with my temporal concer[n]s bearing on me, & my way yet blocked up in a considerable degree make many of my hours very serious & in a considerable [....], when you read this [ask] God for Christ['s] sake to have mercy on me & continue with me thro the Seventh & last trial. Amidst all the storms of life I am comfroted that the time is come & coming for the Lord to favor Zion. I behold the church coming forth as the morning fair as the Moon & will be I hope ere it be very long clear as the son [sun] and as terrible to the powers of darkness as an army with banners. O Lord let thy salvation come that all the people may praise Thee. May you & I be faithful to our Master live the life of the righteous with all within the bounds of Gods mercy, & die their death & meet them in heaven to praise God eternaly for Christ sake amen

James Tawler[66]

[66] James Tawler, a Methodist preacher from Petersburg, Virginia, located in the newly established town of Xenia, Greene County, Ohio, in 1804 (*Greene County, 1803–1908,* p. 47).

XVII

OHIO, GREENE [COUNTY] April 16th 1810

MY DEAR BR[OTHER] DROMGOOLE,

Your long silence had thrown me into numberless (vain) thoughts, as they have turn'd out to be, concerning my lost letter to you by Neddy, fearing I had written somewhat too freely, so as to have given you offence unintentionally in some of the subjects, ment[ione]d therein and caus'd your not writing to me till Neddy's return to our Country, but your Letter has freed my Mind fully on the subject. Neddy found us all thro' divine mercy in a tolerable degree of health, and expect Neddy and Sally will leave us the Day after to-morrow in that respect the same, but in sorrow and grief at our parting. but I hope our good and gracious God will give us supporting Grace, in the distressing, and future hours of our lives.

We have had very happy times of late in waiting on God at the Meeting House, and our prayer meetings, which we keep up regularly twice a week; Every Sunday Evening at my House and Wednesday Evenings at Br[other] Sales'. Two Souls have profes'd to find the Lord at one of our me[e]tings at my House not long since. Neddy preached[67] yesterday at our M[eeting] H[ouse] [and] had great liberty, and I think did justice to the subject, it was a time of great power, many Xtians [Christians] happy, and one poor Sinner pricked to the Heart, and roared out for mercy, and before we all left, profess'd to have some comfort, and said he loved God. Our Society has increas'd to somewhat about, or above 90 members and is divided into three Classes, for convenience of the preachers to examine them. I am sorry to find by your Letter that you have had no revival among you since we left V[irgini]a—May the Lord shew the hind'ring cause, and may it be speedily removed, and the power of God displayed in the Conversion of Souls, as in the Glorious years 1787 & '88.[68] O the blessed Religion of Jesus, may it spread its glorious influence speedily to Earth's remotest bounds till there shall not be a sinner left to blaspheme the God of Heaven. Thro' mercy I feel I am on my way to the New Jerusalen, my Soul is happy my God & Savior

[67] In the capacity of a local preacher; he never joined the traveling ministry.

[68] Revivals in Sussex, Amelia, and Brunswick counties, Virginia.

is with me, and I have taken a fresh start for the Kingdom, and if I never more see you & yours in this vale of tears & sorrow, I hope to meet you all in Bliss & Glory. Yet while I am here I must give God the praise and Glory, for that my joys as far exceed my troubles and sorrows, as the brightness of the Sun outshines that of the Moon.

I have not yet rented out your place, altho' I have advertised it three different times in Xenia, but it is not yet too late[.] perhaps I may yet rent it; if not I have had a thought of getting it sown in Oats. I have sold 42½ Bushels of your Corn for Seven Dollars & ten Cents the whole. The balance being 38½ Bushels (after pay[in]g 4 Bus[he]ls for wagonage) I have here and will do the best I can with it for you.

Neddy can inform you of the Law relating to non-residents' Lands, and what I have advised him to do as the most certain to save the 100 p[er] c[en]t on the taxes, which would be due if not punctually paid.

Br[other]s Sandford, T. Bonner, David Bonner, J. Sale & myself have joined in Company to erect and carry on a Woolen and Cotton manufactury (at David Bonner's) by water, which we flatter ourselves, under providence, will be of advantage to our Neighbourhood, Country, and ourselves. We expect to make up about 2000$ to begin with, exclusive of cutting a Race, and erecting the Buildings necessary; We are in hopes of having it to work early in June.

I shou'd rejoice cou'd you be with us a month or two at this time, tho' writing answers many good and great purposes yet it don['']t answer all my ends; concerning my desires of conversation with you, nothing will fully supply that—May peace and happiness forever attend you and yours, and our young Couple.[69] We all join in love to you and family &c and enquiring friends. I am and hope ever to be, thy unworthy, but most aff[ectionat]e Brother

Pray for us.

P. Pelham

P.S. The Money is not yet due for the Corn, sold, but as Neddy has Debts to collect for me in V[irgini]a he may pay you the 7.10/100 d[ollar]s, of which you will inform me when done.

[69] Edward Dromgoole, Jr., son of Edward and Rebecca Dromgoole, was married in Greene County, Ohio, March 28, 1810, by Rev. Bennett Maxey, to Sarah C., daughter of Peter and Parthenia Pelham (Bible record, Dromgoole Papers).

XVIII

JERICHO, [WARREN CO., N.C.], August 3*d* 1810

DEAR BROTHER.

It is not from any desire of not continuing my correspondence with you, that I have not wrote to you before now, but from a delicasy, or rather from an apprehension, that my letter wou'd in some sort give you pain. I was in some degree conscious, that the steps, that my companion and myself had taken since we had the pleasure of seeing you, w[oul]d from your respect and feelings for us, produce on your part uneasiness, but how the motives producing such changes may meet your approbation or disapprobation, I cou'd not conjecture; altho I had every reason to believe, from your christian experience, knowledge and long standing in life, that you wou'd pass a righteous judgment. Believe me, brother, when I inform you, that I had nothing more at heart, than to conform to the advice you had given me; that is, to speak to Early[70] before preaching, and to request, that he wou'd lay the business before our next [Quarterly] Conference, and in the interim proceed as [no] farther. But when he made his appearance in the house, his countenance exhibited so many marks of passion and ill humour, (tho' perhaps nothing more than the man's natural looks) that I was deprived of all my former resolutions, and determined with myself to let things take their course. However, just as he had enter'd his pulpit, brother John Mayfield called him out; and, as I have been since informd, requested him not bring the business forward, but lay it before Conference, that such was y[ou]r request & [....] informed him, that as for his part, he cou'd not consent to turn M*rs* Keys out for such a cause, nor did he suppose any of the class would do so &ca But so far was the message sent him, or the advice of bro: Mayfield from having any good effect upon him, that he appeared to get doubly charged with, I fear, the spirit of the evil one, and said, that he w[oul]d go on, and if it went against him, as respected the class, that he w[ould] appeal[.] After sermon, *acd* to one he appear'd to express with a degree of accimoney [acrimony];

[70] John Early (1786–1873) was in 1810 serving Caswell Circuit, Raleigh District, Virginia Conference (*Minutes,* I, 185). His surprising lack of tact in this instance is unusual in the light of the fact that he later became a presiding elder and a bishop of the M.E. Church, South.

and in class-meeting, he behaved to my wife with a great degree of disrespect; and in a very authoritative manner asked her if she had laid aside her ring &ca I saw her embarrassed situation, and requested I may be heard upon the occasion. I read him the article upon dress in our dicipline,[71] and M*r* Westley's fuller explanation thereof in the 4*th* vol[ume] of his sermons pa[ge] 100 &ca I observed, that M*r* W[esley's] language was by way of advice, not a positive command.—that he was a man of too much good sense; too well versed in the knowledge and spirit of the word of God, as to make that a cause, in his discipline, of expulsion from the church here below, that wou'd not exclude from the kingdom of glory—that it is possible a woman may die with 20 gold rings upon her fingers, and still be possessed of living faith—that all the church has to do was, in such cases, to curtail a member of some of the privileges; such as tickets[72] &ca When, however, I found nothing w[oul]d answer, and that he was bent on expulsion, I desired that we may no longer be considered as members of the society, and to take our names off the class-paper. I told him, that I was exceedingly sorry he had ever come amongst us. Now, brother, it might be said, that I was rather hasty. Perhaps it may be so. But before a man can be a good judge of any case, he ought to understand it thoroughly—he ought to put himself in my place. Now, what place was that. I will tell you, brother. On the one hand stood my wife, in as plain attire as any woman cou'd appear in, wreathing [writhing] under the last [lash] of an ignorant, stubborn, coxcomb; whose place would be best fill[e]d at the tail of a plough, than as a guide or director of civiliz[e]d people; then on the other hand stood our spiritual guide (Oh, perversion of terms!) as swoln and as big as the frog in the fables, exercising an authority he had no right to exert, and looking as big as an Eastern Nabob.—Tis a great pity, brother, that we can't have some old experienced men among us, who are acquainted with the rules, and the feelings of mankind. And tis also a great pity to give the managem[en]t of a circuit to a man no better acquainted with his rules than he appears to be. I am told that he said, that he was inform'd of my wifes' ring

[71] Cf. the *Discipline* of 1784: "Give no tickets to any that wear high heads, or enormous bonnets, ruffles, or rings."

[72] Lovefeast or class tickets.

long before he came into the circuit, and that it hurt a great many of the society! Why, to be sure, Their sensibility was extreme; but, it appears, their ignorance was more so. Is not this, bro: something like straining at gnats, and swallowing of camels? Perhaps those who felt so exceedingly unhappy in the contemplation of my wifes' wearing an innocent ring, that injured no man, w[oul]d not feel themselves equally unhappy and miserable in the possession of property illegally acquired, or under the idea of having destroy'd the peace and happiness of an innocent neighbour. Brother, unless there be some steps taken to lop the extravigances of young preachers, (for the old, almost to a man, have left us) the sober and sensible part of our societies will get disgusted, and others will be prevented from coming among us. Should there not be a day, or a part of a day set apart, at every yearly conference, for the benefit especially of young and inexperienced preachers? shou'd the rules be not read and explained to them, and not suffer every man to put his own construction upon them? I have long thought, and a note that I made in our book of discipline in the y[ea]r 1800 will say so; I have long thought I say, that circuit preachers were no advantage to us, & that there is much more good done by our local preachers.

Brother I have 10,000 things to say, but it appears the more I have to say the less I can say, for I have a man at my elbow hurrying me along to see a patient, so that you'l please to excuse the incoherent manner in w[hi]ch I have dictated and wrote this letter. You request my attendance at y[ou]r camp-meeting. I will if I can do so, but consider it will be at a very sickly time. Therefore, if I don't attend, don't blame me. oh, brother, I am mortified, that I can't realy call you brother; and, tho hard the judgment, can't help thinking and saying, that I believe Early an instrument in the hands of the [Devil] to draw M*rs* Keys and myself from a people of God,—from a people with whom we wished to live and die and with whom, of all christian people upon earth, we shou'd elect to cast our lot in this world and in the world to come. I have given y[ou]r love & comp[limen]ts to my wife, and desire I may return them two fold. Rem[embe]r me to sister Dromgoole and the family.

Am, brother as usual Y[ou]r friend & brother

JAMES H. KEYS

Remember me to bro: Lee.[73] shoud you see him I shou'd be glad to know where Niblocks book and medicine are to be sold

JHK

XIX

GREEN[E] COUNTY August 30th 1810

MY DEAR SISTER SALLY[74]

Thro' the mercy and goodness of God we are yet in the land amongst the living and trying thro' grace divine to prepare for Death; I had a severe attack of something like the pleurisy last June; which brought me very low indeed, but thank God I am as well at present as common; I think M*r* P[elham] has enjoy'd his health better this summer than he ever has of a summer since we've been married. Tho[ma]s is well and grows tolerable fast, and begins to talk tolerable smart

Sister Betsy Pelham has been very poorly for some time. I think its been four weeks that she has been confin'd to her bed, but thank the Lord she is better than I ever expected to have seen her again but is still confin'd to her bed, and set up with of nights, the rest of the family are as well as usual—My Father's family is well at present, my mother had a very severe attack of the pluerisy in July she was so Ill four or five days that we expected every day to be the last, but thank God about the ninth day she began to mend and is now as well as common. Brother Davids family is tolerable well[.] they had a son in July they call him Joseph Reynolds, Bro. Sales family is well except Tho[ma]s he's very sick. Bro[ther] Chappell is well; Sister Polly poorly but keeps about, Cousin Betsey P[elham] very poorly, the rest of the neighbours tolerable except Bro. Heath who was taken last saturday with pleurisy, and is now very ill. he don't think he can stand it long without an alteration for the better. I never [k]new nor heard of as much sickness in the country as I have this summer. I

[73] Jesse Lee (1758–1816) was for 1810 presiding elder of Meherren District, Virginia Conference (*Minutes,* I, 185).

[74] Sarah (Pelham) Dromgoole, wife of Edward, Jr.

hope this will find you and my dear Bro. Edward well. O my dear sister I often think of you and want to see you very much indeed, but I hardly expect we shall meet in this world again. But O Salley if we never meet below, I hope we shall meet above where parting will be no more; there all tears will be wiped away by the soft tender hand of Jesus and we praise God and the Lamb forever more. I have seen some good times since I saw you. I was up at Mad River at a Camp Meeting (in June last) where we had a glorious time[.] I dont think I ever saw such a time before, there was 30 or 40 converted and great many mourners, and the Christians appear'd to be happy in the Lord.

There has been a smart revival about Ceasar'sville this summer and [a] good many converted among the rest Sarah Bell, Nancy West, Betsey Saunders, & Wilson McDaniel who is expected to make a preacher[.][75] we have some precious times in this neighbourhood particularly when we meet at our prayer meetings[.] the presence of the Lord is generally felt amongst the people and they are enabled to rejoice with that Joy which is unspeakable and full of glory. I feel sometimes like there wou'd not be one sinner left in this settlement to serve the Devil. I pray God almighty may hasten the happy time when all shall experience his pardoning love shed abroad in their hearts—I have nothing more at present, but must conclude—my Fathers Family and Mr. Pelham joins me in love to you and Brother Edward and father Dromgooles Family

I am as ever your sincere friend and sister—

MARTHA PELHAM[76]

P.S. Sister Betsey strain desires to be remembered to you. She is well and says she feels determined to try thro' the assisting grace of God to meet you on that celestial Hill, where sorrows are no more—You must be sure to write to me and tell Bro. Neddy he must too—

P[ETER] P[ELHAM]

[75] McDaniel never entered the traveling ministry, though he may have labored locally.

[76] Mrs. Samuel Pelham, formerly Martha Bonner.

XX

BERTIE CIRCUIT[77] NORTHCAROLINA
Ye 18*th* February 1811

REV[EREN]D & HONOUR[ED] SIR

Two days past a letter from you was put into my hand; upon opening & seeing its date I found that it had been wrote Something more than Two Months; I observ*d* Its contents but found It impracticable to comply with Its request in as short Time. However, I feel it incumbent on me to write you, in order to let you know—What I am doing & trying to do: After I wrote you the 1*st* & 2*nd* Letter & recieving no Answer: I felt my Spirits Much dejected; & concluded that I was in the Estimation of all my Old Brunswick friends Buried. As I had wrote too [to] Several & found that they were Silent.—Perhaps they might in the Language of one of old, say: Lord we have seen & heard what havoc he has done & made in thy church. & altho, he may not have letters from the Governor; yet he may discimulate; having Sinister ends in View.—But None of these things Mov*d* Me, Neither count I my life dear unto myself So that I may finish my course with Joy; & the Ministry Which I have Reciev*d* of the Lord Jesus: To Testify the Gospel of the Grace of God. Yet my mind was Much agitated respecting the Will of God Towards me. I felt in myself that I must Preach Jesus to my fellow Travellars to Eternity & Somtimes Concluded that I would Travel at Large & freely Spend & be spent in the Service of God; indeed my feelings are only known to God. I at that time liv*d* in a place Singularly wicked but in the Midst of My Exercise I remember & it was not all well with me that I owed Money & I*d* no other way to Get It but by these hands; for after I began to preach in the Neighbourhood an old Baptist Preacher Said that Scarbrough was Preaching for Applause & his ends are sinister[.] Some of the Church which had heard me several Times said with tears in their eyes they thought not. Some said one thing & some another. I was then in no Society, but thought I would go & join the Methodist[s]; I did so and applied to the [Presiding] Elder for Li-

[77] Bertie Circuit was in Norfolk District, Virginia Conference, of which James Boyd was presiding elder in 1811. Humphrey Wood and W. M. Elliott were the circuit preachers (*Minutes,* I, 199).

cense to preach which he refus*d* telling me in a very Cool tone of Voice that I was too recently a Member to Preach[.] Great God Give me Brace.—For what are we all coming to. I wonder if a child is to be just 14 Months old before he calls the name of his parents—Here I was sorely try*d* for one of the old Trav[e]ling Preachers & myself had somewhat of Talk about the business (& he told me in what Manner the Said Elder was rec*d* at Conference) here I again concluded to Travel & preach at large. But upon Second thought found that my way was heddg*d* on Every Side[.] one said I was too recently a Member, & the other That I was running the race of popularity—None but those who have had the live Exercise can form an Idea. In all this time I was alone being a Stranger Which drove Me to the wounds of a Crucify*d* Jesus—I thought if I could sell you my Horse I would Give the rest of my days on earth Entirely to the Service of God But Not Geting any Answer from you Still kept me in dispair not knowing What was best for me to do. I try*d* to sell my Horse for cash but could not & so I was forc*d* to sell him on a credit[.] I also have taken a School for the same year[.] I've 14 Schollars at $11 p[e]r schollar & now Sir I am on my knees & pray you to have patience & I will pay you the Last farthing, Should God See fit to Spare my unprofitable Life. My debts Tender me more uneasiness than all things else on earth for I hope the time is at hand that God will make my Enemies to be at peace with me! I look*d* at your letter as an honour confer*d* on me thats to[o] unworthy to receive any Good—I thank you for your Good wishes & pray Jehovah to remember you & all that pertain unto you, for Good: May your Sun Set with a Smiling Countenance, & you & me when the Storms of life are blown over; be convey*d* by Angels to Sit down in the Kingdom of our Heavenly Father With all the Patrearch[s] & Prophets old & with that innumerable Company of Happy Spirits that no Man c[o]uld Number.——

I feel a Great Propensity To Preach once at the Olive Branch[78] To those with whom I once Lov*d* If Providence See fit—

I hope you will be more fortunate in Geting these lines than I was in geting yours. & could you think it worth your while to stoop so

[78] The Olive Branch Meetinghouse, also called Branch Chapel, or Dromgoole's Chapel, was in Brunswick County, Virginia, near the Dromgoole plantation (Asbury, *Journal,* III, 161). The Virginia Conference of 1803 was held there (Bennett, *op. cit.,* p. 407).

low as to Answer this Letter It would be thankfully receiv*d* by one that wishes to be a Lover of Mankind. I Remain in Sincerity yours until Death

ENOS SCARBROUGH[79]

XXI

PLEASANT RETREAT GREEN[E COUNTY], OHIO
June 21 1811

DEAR EDWARD,[80]

Yours & your father's Letters written in Petersburg with one from Sally *safely* arrived yesterday by Mail. They found us in our usual health, & Betsy somewhat better than she has been lately, but she dispairs of a perfect recovery, & is still thro' Grace perfectly resign'd to her situation[.] The relation about Betsy Rideout & Br[other] [....]et's family brought tears from mine Eyes, & I really sympathize with them in their distressed situation.

From yours & Sally's Letters I feel some hope if the Lord spares us all a while longer, we shall all be living, together, in a land of Liberty, peace & plenty. Give my love to Br[other] Dromgoole & family; tell him I shall attend to what he has written to me, & that I wrote to him on the *29th* last Month, wherein I had express'd the same. Tell Sally, Peter says he don't think it will do for him to go to Carolina to stay till you come out here, for fear he might get good for nothing, as a farmer he means, during his stay there.—We all should be glad to see you &c &c but we wish it be here rather than in Virg[ini]a or Carolina; so that you & Sally &c must try to get out among us, and clear your skirts, if possible, from the polution of *Slavery* and that as soon as possibly you can.

Br[other] Towler & myself are concern'd together in a small Grocery line of business in Xenia, and wish to extend it to a truly Republican Store of altogether American Manufactures, this we are trying to do, and if you cou'd come out you might make one with us I expect. In order to carry on the above my dependance is on supplies from the debt due me in Virg[ini]a which I hope you will exert your-

[79] The writer never joined the conference.

[80] Edward Dromgoole, Jr.

self as much as you can, and forward as heretofore, unless you meet with a safe private opportunity.

Tell Sally, James Fiers was converted at a Camp Meeting near Dayton[81] last week together with about 20 others. Our Camp Meeting on Br[other] Towler's land[82] comes on the *23d* August we expect good [times]. Sally Bell was married yesterday to a Son of Sister Cornwell's. Br[other] Sanford & Gen*l* Worthington[83] have erected works in Chillicothe, to the amount of 6 or 7000$ for manufacturing of Cotton, Wool & Flax, worked by Horses. Tell Polly I cant spare Jesse to go so far to see big parthe[nia][84] this year. I cannot tell how it may be the next year.

We have comfortable Meetings yet thro' mercy divine, a happy time at our prayer meeting last Wednesday Night. I still try to get to some of them, and last Wednesday Night, I felt a fresh start for the Kingdom of Heaven. Glory to God for it. To day is our Class Meeting at the M[eeting] H[ouse] where we generally have comfortable times, & sometimes shouts of praises to the Redeemer. This I want to finish & take with me to meeting to be carried by Br[other] T. Davis to Chillicothe, who sets off to-morrow with his Sister Nancy to go there to see their Sister Hannah (who is at Br[other] Sanford's) Married on Tuesday next, to a Br[other] Gregg who is a *rich merch[an]t* about 50 years old, & a pious Methodist. James & Sam*l* Gowdy have a Capital Store of Goods in Xenia, bro[ugh]t out this Spring from Philadelphia, & receiving Cash Daily.

A few weeks past a sloop arriv'd in Cincinnatti of C. A. Tone burthen, from Orleans, with Sugar, Cotton &c We have some of the Sugar for Sale a 25 Cents Pr it cost 18 3/4 Cts. in Cincinnati.

We all join in love to you, Sally & our little (big) Parthenia,[84] and

[81] Dayton is in Montgomery County, Ohio, near the mouth of Mad River, on the Great Miami.

[82] At Xenia.

[83] Hector Sandford and Thomas Worthington were both members of the Chillicothe Methodist Church. Sandford was admitted on trial to the Western Conference in 1806 (Sweet, *op. cit.,* p. 113). Thomas Worthington (1773–1827) was a native of Virginia who settled in the Scioto Valley in 1798. He served as United States senator from Ohio, 1803–7, 1811–14, and governor of Ohio, 1814–18 (*A Biographical Congressional Directory* [1903], p. 896).

[84] The writer's granddaughter, Parthenia Brown Dromgoole, born January 28, 1811, in Halifax County, North Carolina (Bible record Dromgoole Papers).

say you must kiss her much for us all. Sam*l* Patsy & Tho[ma]s are [in] usual health. Sam*l* has mov'd to his new [house], & Patsy in the way to increase the [....]. Adiew my Children

Your affectionate [fath]er
P. Pelham

XXII

Ohio, Green[e] County, July 28th 1811

My Dear Sister[85]

I once more take my pen in hands to write you a few lines, informing you that we are all yet in the land of the living, bless'd with a tolerable degree of health and strength, except Sister Betsy[.] she is yet alive but is in a very low state of health and has lost all hopes of recovery[.] she appears to possess patience, and resignation to the will of God—We are all in a world [of] afflictions, troubles and we have many things to encounter with. May the Lord give us supporting grace that we may prove faithful and at last come to reign with him forever—We were very sorry to hear that Betsy Rideout had done so bad as to be put in jail. I think her father and mother must be very much distressed to think that one of their daughters should do so. Dear sister you wrote word that I must go and live with you untill you come to this country. you also wrote that when brother Edw[ar]d saw how the world went he wish'd he was out here. you ought not to have wrote in that manner if you wanted me to go live with you, for may be so it would be the ruin of me as I am very young. so therefore my sister I must decline going there to live—Mama says that she prays that you and Brother Edw[ar]d would come out here to live for Ohio has got much better than it was once. she sends her love to you, and sister Betsy sends her love to you all. With respect to religions in this neighbourhood we dont have quite such good times as what [we] have had[.] at times we have happy meetings and at other times dull and cold. I was at camp meeting near Dayton last June and it was supposed there were between thirty and forty converted[.] Eighteen join'd society and there were twenty one mourners. On friday next a Campmeeting is to begin near Waynesville.[86] I forgot to tell

[85] Sarah (Pelham) Dromgoole.

[86] Waynesville is in Warren County, Ohio, on the Little Miami River.

you James Fires got converted at the Campmeeting, and seems to enjoy the love of God in his soul—There has some joined society and are turn'd out again on account of bad conduct—We have had a very dry spell in some parts of the state not far from this[.] some crops look very indifferent. But ours and some of our neighbors crops look very promising at present. Now I beseech you myself to try and wind up affairs and come and live here where we can see you as well as hear from you sometimes. I dont know that I have wrote all I want to write but as I cant think of any more at present I must conclude with sending my best love to you all individually and enquiring friends. Mary Caroline and all join me love to you

Adieu Adieu my dear sister Sally—

PETER A. PELHAM[87]

P.S. do write to me if you please my dear sister and I shall esteem you.

P. A. P.

XXIII

GREEN[E] COUNTY, OHIO, May 3, 1812

MY DEAR LITTLE DUMPY SISTER,[88]

It is with great pleasure I now sit down to you informing you that we are all tolerable well exclusive of bad colds, and it is my desire that these lines may find you and brother Edward and little Parthenia Brown in health as health is the greatest temporal blessing we enjoy. I received your affectionate letter dated 26th September 1811 which gave me great satisfaction. I took delight in perusing it as it was from my dear little sister who lives beyond those Mountains, Valleys, Rocks, and Rivers that separate us.

You wrote me these words, I think of you often, often indeed, and many times with tears in my eyes do I recollect the morning I parted with all and I know not that we shall ever meet again in this vale of tears, pray for me that if we never see each others faces again here-below, we may meet in heaven where parting will be no more—. Which almost if not brought tears in my eyes. I felt melted down on

[87] Peter Pelham, Jr.

[88] Sarah (Pelham) Dromgoole.

perusing your friendly letter. You thank'd me for my letter. you are very welcome my dear sister for the few indif[f]erent lines I wrote to you—

I have no doubt in my mind that you have heard of the departure of our dear Sister Elizabeth or I would have given you an account of her death in the Commencement of my letter. She went off shouting Glory Glory Glory as long as she was heard to utter a word. She gave us all the hope and belief imaginable that she was going to rest. We expect war with Britain and the Savage tribes.[89] Governor Meigs[90] is now making up an army in this state[.] the soldiers are now collecting together at Dayton and geting ready to march to Detroit at a moments warning, and we expect that there will be another Draught soon for to get more men to hold themselves in readiness in case they should be wanting....[91]

Mr. Sanford and his Lady Mr Gregg and his lady are now in the neighbourhood. they came from Chillicothe to Mr Davis's on a visit for the first since last July. they are all well and Mrs Sanford has a fine fat daughter. she calls her name Hester Ann. Mr Sanford arrived in the neighbourhood last night [a] week and has preached three times and preaches just like he used to—they expect to start home to morrow.

Miss [....] Grover has been up to see her relations[.] she was well and appear'd to [be] very hearty. Our Neighbours are generally well. Miss Polly Maxey was married last fall to Mr James Loyd[.] perhaps you have heard of it, if so you may call. Taylors news—Mr Josiah Wright is living at Mr Dromgools farm[.] him and his family are well and Mr Samuel Wright is living at Brother Jesse's place and are well except T. Coke.[92] he has the ague and fever yet, though not so severe as he had when he first came to the Country. Mr Owens is

[89] For several Methodist preachers' reactions to the approaching hostilities see Utter, *op. cit.,* p. 85.

[90] Return Jonathan Meigs (1765–1825), native of Connecticut and a Yale graduate, served in the United States Senate, 1809–10; as governor of Ohio, 1810–14; and as postmaster-general of the United States, 1814–23 (*A Biographical Congressional Directory* [1903], p. 690).

[91] In the margin at this point is written: "After concluding my letter Mama begs Brother Edward to get ready and move out with Mr. G. Wright when he comes."

[92] Thomas Coke Wright published the *Xenia* (Ohio) *Transcript* from 1829 to 1833 (*Greene County, 1803–1908,* p. 63).

living with Mr. B[ennett] Maxey and intends crossing with him this year[.] he is very poorly at present [but] the rest of the family are able to stir about. I believe they are all mighty pleas'd with the country.

We have had a great ma[n]y shocks of the Earth quake But not much damage receiv'd by them in this neighbourhood[.] about the height of them we had a little revival of religion and several got religion. among them were Mr Stone and D. Anderson Susan Price Polly Butler and Coke W[right][.] Uncle Henry Pelham mov'd home last February to keep Bachelors Hall[.] he has no companion yet to live with him and I do not expect he will get one shortly unless he will work a little more than what he has done.

I have more to communicate but cannot think of it at present[.] you must write to me shortly and inform me whether you will come out here shortly to live. do not fail writing my dear beloved Sister and the Brother E[dward] to condescend to write to me. one thing I forgot I must mention now, tell my little friend G. Coke[93] I wrote to him some time ago and cannot get a line from him and he must write to me. Give my best respects to all enquiring friends and accept the same yourself

Adieu my dear Sister

PETER A. PELHAM

[93] George Coke Dromgoole (1797–1847) was the youngest son of Edward Dromgoole, Sr. He studied law and served several years as a member of the Virginia house of representatives and senate before his election to Congress in 1835. He served three terms, covering the years 1835–37 and 1843–47 (*A Biographical Congressional Directory* [1903], p. 509).

CHAPTER VII

The Journal of Benjamin Lakin, 1794–1820

BENJAMIN LAKIN, one of the pioneer Methodist circuit-riders of the West, was born in Montgomery County, Maryland, August 23, 1767. At the age of nine he moved with his widowed mother and family to Redstone in southwestern Pennsylvania, where in the year 1791 his conversion is said to have occurred under the ministry of Richard Whatcoat. From Redstone the Lakins moved southward into Kentucky about 1793. There Lakin became convinced of a call to the ministry and, after the usual licensure, began work under the presiding elder on the Hinkstone Circuit in Kentucky in November, 1794. He was admitted on trial to the traveling connection at the Holston Conference of 1795. At this time he commenced keeping his "Journal," which he was to continue during the remainder of his active ministry.

He labored as circuit preacher in Kentucky and Tennessee until April, 1798, when preparative to his marriage with Elizabeth Roye, which took place in that month, he took a voluntary location at conference. The exigencies of frontier circuit-riding in that day largely excluded married preachers, and the bishops looked upon them as encumbrances. But Lakin felt out of his element in the two following years spent farming, and in October, 1800, he attended the first session of the newly organized Western Conference, at Bethel Academy in Kentucky. Here he received ordination as Deacon and an appointment to Limestone Circuit, Kentucky. When the Western Conference was divided in 1812, Lakin cast his lot with its northern half, the new Ohio Conference, which extended southward into Kentucky. He continued to ride circuits in the conference until 1817, when he took a supernumerary relation. The next year he is listed in the *Minutes* as a superannuate, sustaining that relation until his death in Ohio on February 5, 1849. During the last thirty years of his life he was by no means idle but supplied pulpits locally wherever there was need.

The extracts from the "Journal" here presented cover the whole range of his ministry, beginning with his labors on the circuits of northern Kentucky in 1794. In succession are reviewed his marriage and location; resumption of ministerial work in 1800; his labors on Ohio circuits such as Deer Creek, Hockhocking, and White Oak; his journey to Upper Sandusky Indian Town in 1810; and the closing years of his ministry and final retirement, 1817–20. His "Journal" is extremely introspective: his spiritual condition is constantly probed, and conflicts and doubts reported. Tokens and frontier superstitions loom large in the work, and a few of these have been included. The unusual paucity of personal names and appointments customarily found in Methodist diaries is remedied by supplemental manuscript notebooks listing his preaching appointments for each circuit he rode, together with dates of visitation and sermon texts. Others of his papers include extensive reading extracts and sermon notes. His "Journal" and other papers are in the library of the Divinity School of the University of Chicago.

Lakin was a humble, unassuming minister. He seems never to have wished for a station higher than that of a circuit preacher; the green fields of presiding eldership and episcopacy did not appeal to his nature. But, though humility was characteristic of him, he could and did exercise strict discipline after the old-time Methodist fashion, as the "Journal" reveals. The notations of books read throughout the "Journal" reveal an interest in substantial literature, mostly religious. His education was above average for the frontier communities in which he worked, though there is no record of his having had any formal schooling.

For biographies of Lakin see his memoir in *Minutes of the Annual Conferences of the Methodist Episcopal Church,* Vol. IV: *1846–1851,* p. 385; also William B. Sprague, *Annals of the American Pulpit* (New York, 1865), VII, 267–73. James B. Finley's reminiscences of Lakin, in *Sketches of Western Methodism* (Cincinnati, 1855), pp. 178–84, add a few new incidents. For his record as a member of the Western Conference (1800–1811) see William Warren Sweet, *The Rise of Methodism in the West* (New York and Cincinnati, 1920); and for his record in the Ohio Conference (1812–26), Sweet, *Circuit-Rider Days along the Ohio* (New York and Cincinnati, 1923).

Thursd[*ay*]. *November 6, 1794.* I enterd on the traveling plan.[1] Sund. 9. met bro Gibson[2] at bro. Wilmuth[s], we traveled togather till Frid. 21. we had some comfortable times togather and parted in love. I travel'd through the cold and snow to bro. Methenier[s].

[1] Lakin began his work as a licentiate under the direction of Francis Poythress, presiding elder of the Kentucky District. It was not until the Holston Conference of 1795 that he was officially admitted on trial to the traveling connection.

[2] Tobias Gibson (1771–1804), a native of South Carolina, had been received into the traveling ministry in 1792 and was in 1794 serving Lexington Circuit, Kentucky. From 1800 until his death he labored as a missionary at Natchez, Mississippi.

Sund. 23. took Hinks[t]on[e] Circuit[3] at bro. Colemans and preached from: These things I command you that you love one another: I trust my mesage was not in vain. In the evening preachd at a new town about 3 miles from bro Colemans, to a thoughtless peopel, but they refused to open a dore to receive the Gospel.

Tuesd 25. In the evening preachd with freedom at Hinks[t]on[e] Station. My mind is calm my heart daily rejoices in the Lord. I trust that I have an eye singel to his glory.

Sat. 29. This evening at bro. Whiteakers[4] our conversation was conserning the low situation of the Church. my soul was troubled at the situation of Zion.[5]

Sund. 30. I awoke with a deep sence of low state of Zion[.] my soul wept over the church my soul was engaged for the Lord to revive his work. My mind was much exercised about the subject for the day, at last preachd from these awfull words. And in Hell he lifted up his eyes being in torments. First Spake of the subjects of the wrath of God. Second, what they shall loose [lose]. Third: their torment. Fourth, the way to escape, and preachd at night from, Therefore let us not sleep as do others, but let us watch and be sober.

Mond. Dec[ember] ye 1. Met bro Lurten[6] and bro Gibson. Our meeting was profitable. my soul was melted down in love.

Tuesd. 2. This morning I rose happy in the love of God. The waters being high I had to ride a long way to get to my appointment.

[3] Hinkstone Circuit lay in northern Kentucky and embraced the present counties of Montgomery, Clark, and Bourbon, with parts of Bath, Nicholas, and Harrison. See accompanying map, p. 205.

[4] Possibly John Whitaker, a local preacher of Harrison County, Kentucky, whose son Josiah (1779–1850), a native of Maryland, entered the Ohio Conference in 1818 (William E. Arnold, *A History of Methodism in Kentucky,* Vol. I: *1783–1828* [Louisville, Ky., 1935], pp. 172, 409).

[5] For a local example, membership on the Hinkstone Circuit had declined from 281 white and 4 colored, as reported in 1793, to 270 white and 5 colored in the following year (*Minutes of the Annual Conferences of the Methodist Episcopal Church,* Vol. I: *1773–1828,* pp. 52, 57). Arnold (*op. cit.,* p. 128) cites as reasons for the general decline in membership the fact that the O'Kelley schism was only then penetrating Kentucky and also the Indian troubles of 1794. The *Minutes* of 1794 and 1795 proclaim general fast-days of humiliation and prayer to heighten the spiritual tone of the church.

[6] Jacob Lurton was appointed to Cumberland Circuit, Tennessee, in 1794. In the following year he located, settling in Jefferson County, Kentucky. He died in Illinois (Arnold, *op. cit.,* I, 115, 175).

MAP III

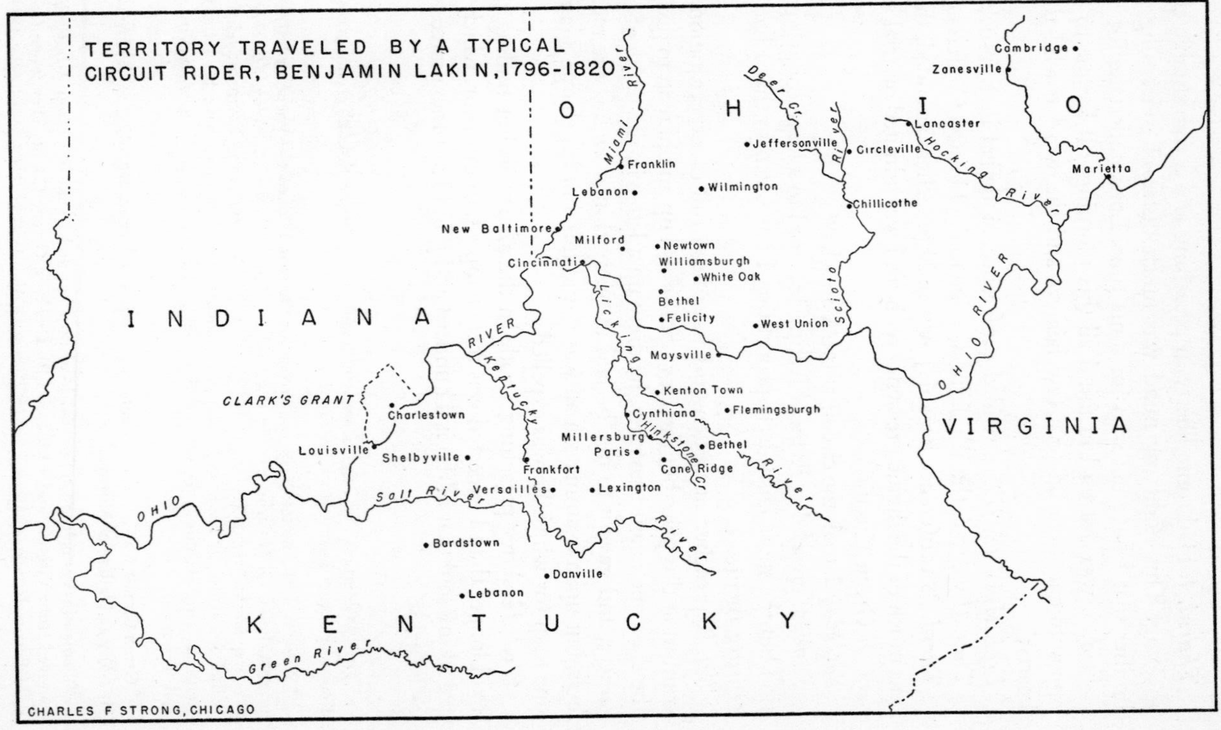

TERRITORY TRAVELED BY A TYPICAL CIRCUIT RIDER, BENJAMIN LAKIN, 1796-1820
OHIO
INDIANA
KENTUCKY
VIRGINIA
CLARK'S GRANT
Miami River
Deer Cr.
River
Hocking River
Scioto
OHIO RIVER
RIVER
Kentucky
Licking
Hinkstone Cr.
River
River
Salt River
OHIO
Green River
Cambridge
Zanesville
Lancaster
Marietta
Jeffersonville
Circleville
Franklin
Lebanon
Wilmington
Chillicothe
New Baltimore
Milford
Newtown
Williamsburgh
White Oak
Cincinnati
Bethel
Felicity
West Union
Maysville
Kenton Town
Flemingsburgh
Charlestown
Cynthiana
Millersburg
Bethel
Paris
Cane Ridge
Louisville
Shelbyville
Frankfort
Versailles
Lexington
Bardstown
Danville
Lebanon
CHARLES F STRONG, CHICAGO

Thursd. 4. Had some liberty in preaching and a comfortable class meeting. This night my mind was much distressd concerning my brother that I have not seen for some time. Lord undertake for me.

Frid. 5. was distressd in mind all this morning, till I came to my appointment, preachd to a few hearers and the word reachd their hearts;

Frid. April 17, 1795 attended conference, at Bethel in Kentuckey.

Tues. 21 we took the Wilderness[7] to go to the Holston Conference.[8]

Tuesd. 28 conference began[.] About 20 preachers attended, there was much of the divine preasence with us. I was admited on trial and sent to Green Circuit.[9]

Sat. May 2. took the circuit at bro Vanpelts[10]

Sund. 3. preachd at Evines Meeting H[ouse] to a large congr[eg]ation but the most Disorderly peopel that I have seen so that I had to reprove them.

Sat. 9. preached at Collenses. I have been full of expe[c]tation of comfort at this place but the Devil hath raisd up an old man to divide the class one against another, he drew up a letter in the name of the society, and gave it to me, he laid in many things against the members, but upon examination all was found fals, but his charge against one man for which he was expelled.

Wed. 13. After preaching I rode in the afternoon but finding the road longer than I expected was sorly tempted, to murmur, which so paind my soul that alltho it Thunderd and raind I at times scarce felt or heard it.

[7] The "Wilderness" was the famous trace laid out by Boone through Tennessee and Kentucky some twenty years previously.

[8] William Burke writes: "The conference for the year 1795 met at Ebenezer Earnest's neighborhood, on Nolachucky, the last week in April" (James B. Finley, *Sketches of Western Methodism* [Cincinnati, 1855], p. 45). The conference Lakin attended at Bethel Academy, in Jessamine County, Kentucky, would seem to have been for the Kentucky circuits; this latter was for those in the Holston region of western Virginia and Tennessee.

[9] Green Circuit was in eastern Tennessee. Lakin's colleague, according to the *Minutes* (I, 62),was Nathaniel Munsy.

[10] Benjamin Vanpelt, an influential local preacher and friend of Bishop Asbury, had removed from Virginia and settled on Lick Creek, in Greene County, Tennessee (John B. McFerrin, *History of Methodism in Tennessee,* Vol. I: *1783–1804* [Nashville, 1888], p. 290).

Mond. 18. In reading the life of Mr Wesley my soul was drawn out to seek more of the same spirit, of that man of God.

June. 5. preachd from Acts 3. v[e]rce 19. the Lord was preasent one man was made to cry out in such a manner that it astonished me.

From Thursd. 18 to sund. 21. was with bro. Kobler[11] and found it to be a precious and a profitable time. I saw my weakness in such a manner that it was with fear and trimbling that I afterward preachd.

Wed. 24. Rode through the rain to my appointment and gave an exortation. In the evening my soul was drawn out in prayer and praise.

Sat. 27. This morning my soul was deeply sencible of my dependance on the Lord, and longs to know and do his will.

Sund. 28. My mind is in deep exercise. I feare I spoke some ungarded word and I know what it is. My temtation is great. I find it hard strugling with nature.

Tuesd. July 7. My soul was cast down by reason of disputes ariseing in one of the classes.

Wed. 8. My soul was in great heaviness. This night distress was on my mind.

Thursd. 9. Found it good to give myself to reading and studying the Scriptures.

Satd. 11. This night my soul was paind on account of the Church of God.

Sund. 12. This morning spent about five hours in reading and prayer.[12] my soul was humbled before the Lord.

Wed. 15. I have been in heaviness for some days. I know not of any sin that I have commited.

Thursd. 16. As I rode examining myself. I find the heaviness of my soul is brought on for the want of watchfullness and prayer. I have fears of sore judgments on the nation, and pe[r]secution on the Church.

Sat. 18. My soul was cast down but at the sight of bro Whiteaker my heart rejoiced, and found a spirit of prais to God.

[11] John Kobler (1768–1843), a native of Virginia, was a pioneer preacher of the West. He had been admitted on trial to the traveling connection in 1789 and was in 1795 presiding elder of the Holston District, which included Lakin's circuit.

[12] The *Discipline* of 1784 advised the preachers: "From six in the morning till twelve (allowing an hour for breakfast) to read in order with much prayer first the Christian Library and other pious books."

Wed. 22. This morning was so temted that I [was] forced to leve the House, and cry to the Lord for deliverance. I rode to my appointment in deep exercise, and found liberty in preaching and meeting the class. In the evening found myself humbled before the Lord.

Thursd. 23. This day receivd an account of a wicked man that intended to send his Daughter that was about 8 or 9 years old to the Danceing School. But the Lord prevented his design by takeing the child to himself. The child often calld on them to pray for her, telling them they ware [were] old enough, to know how to pray, she was too young, and made her Mothe[r] read to her and her F[a]ther set by her and when he wanted to go away she would not suffer him, and told him he did not love to hear it but she loved it. This was the substance of her talk till her Spirit returnd to the hands of God that gave it.

Frid. 24. Preachd at Mr Williams and was sorely temted all the time of preaching and on my way to bro Vanpelts vissited a sick woman, prayd with them and spoke separtely to every one preasent. In the evening at the hour of retirement, I began to consider it is now near Four years since I began to seek the salvation of my soul.[13] I am ashamed to see the small progress I have made in religion. had I been as faithfull as I aut [ought], how much Holier might I have Been.

Sat. 25. Reading the preface to Whitbeys Comment, on the New Testament, was much affected at his quotations from the History of Josephes, to see the Lord hath given the Jews a downfall that the Gentiles might come in. My soul lays humbled in the dust at the thoughts of it, and find a willing ness to lay at the feet of the Jews if it would but profit them.

Sund. 26. Was much engaged for a deeper work of grace. I wept and prayed to the Lord to clense my heart from all sin. In the evening, the enemy began to exercise my mind about the beginning of God. I soon saw his device, and fled to the Lord by prayer, and he deliverd me. I am often temted but find no other refuge but the Lord Jesus.

Mond. 27. A poor profane sinner that was swareing I reproved, and told him he must give an account for these things before the

[13] Lakin was converted and joined the Methodist Episcopal church in 1791, supposedly under Richard Whatcoat (William B. Sprague, *Annals of the American Pulpit* [New York, 1865], VII, 268).

Lord. He in a blasphemous manner swore that if he had whiskey he could stand well enough before God. My soul trembled at such horrid wickedness.

Thursd. 30. Rode about 20 miles at times sorely temted to impatience. when I came to my appointment there was too [two] Baptist preachers present. I felt a man fearing spirit, and was temted to change my subject, I cried to the Lord and he gave me strength to stand in his name, I had liberty in preaching and one of them gave an exortation.

Sund. August 2. My mind is much shut up and [I] find a backwardness to reading and the other duties of religion.

Mond. and Tuesd. 3 and 4. was days of heavy trials, the last it seemd to be giveing the word away and to have no part myself. While I held a saviour forth to others my own heart was hard and unmoved. At night I examined myself and I fear I preach myself too much.

Sat. and Sund. 8 and 9 Quarter meeting was at Hufakers[.] I found my spirit to revive, and to drink in the word.

Mond. 10. I never knew till now what Christian fellowship could do. In the morning when parting with bro. Hufakers family, my heart felt united to them in love; In the evening, came to bro. Riggins where the friend[s] came to see us. I felt the bonds of love uniteing my heart to the Lords peopel. I was unable to converse much with them by reason of sorrow of heart to think of seeing them no more in time, may the Lord bring us to meet in heaven where parting is no more.

Wed. 12. Rose early this morning, filld with the spirit of prayer. Oh, how deare did Jesus appeare to me, it was delightful to p[o]ur out my soul to God in prayer.

Sund. 16. A number of our Local brethren met at 8. oclock to speak of the goodness of God and a precious time we had.[14] While our brethren was telling the goodness of God to their souls, I had some liberty in preaching. In the evening was much temted to think something of what I had don[e].

Wed. 19. Awoke early with my soul much engaged and humbled in prayer.

[14] A "lovefeast" featuring Christian testimony was the usual service opening Sunday of the early quarterly meeting, before morning preaching.

Thursd. 20. Left bro. Vanpelts to go to New River Circuit,[15] at night in crossing N[oli] Chuckey River (it being dark) I mis[s]ed the ford and fell too low and got on a fish dam, over which my horse had like to fell. I kept round the dam for fear of geting in deep water, when I got to the Bank of the River, it was so steep and high that I could not get up, I tied my Horse, and walked along the bank till I found a place to get out: then brought my Horse and went out, the bresh was so thick I could scarce get through[.] my mind was kept in peace, and felt thankfull to God. This night was much distressd in my Sleep.

Tuesd. 25. My Horse being sick, my mind was variously exercised, and was sorely temted to distrust the providence of God, but oh! the anguish of my soul, for some time I found myself to be miserable; I began to consider what God had don[e] for me, my soul was melted down in tears, and felt resined to the will of God. I preachd today at one of bro Koblers appointments and was much ashamed of my preaching. The Devil temts me various ways, sometimes, to pride, sometimes to shame and sometimes to feare!

Wed. 26. This morning pasd sweatly away, in reading, prayer, and meditation.

Mond. 31. On Satd night I was sorely distressd both Sleeping and wakeing. to Day it seems as if all the powers of darkness was upon me. At Night preachd from Hebrews 10. ve. 36. and found some deliverance.

Wed. September 2. Was in much distress and sorely temted all the morning, I preached and bro Bird[16] met the class, in the time of class meeting, I was pouring out my soul to God, for deliverance, and to make me a blessing to the peopel and then a blessing to me, the Lord met me in Mercy and set my soul at liberty; In the evening my soul was fil[l]ed with the love of God. I found that peace that is past understanding.

Frid. 11. I have not attended as close to the duties of religion as I should have don[e], it hath brought dullness on my soul, today I was

[15] New River Circuit lay west of New River, embracing parts of Virginia and Tennessee (McFerrin, *op. cit.,* I, 420).

[16] Richard Bird, a North Carolinian, was in 1795 serving New River Circuit. He had been admitted on trial in 1792 but located in 1797.

sorely temted in prayer; I looked to the Lord, and he deliverd me. I found some engagement in reading the life of Mr. Derenty.

Sund. 20. I rose early, and addressed myself to the throne of grace, and in reading the Saints [Rest] the power of the Lord was on me in such a manner as I neve[r] knew, Heaven was opend in my soul. Everything appeared to look of a heavenly nature. I seem'd emty of all things and fill'd with God. It was a sweet time to me at the Lord's table, oh! how precious was the blood of Xt [Christ] to my fainting soul.

Sat. 26. Meditateing on the Blessings that others had been to the sons of men, it was deeply impresd on my mind let no man take thy crown. I found a willingness, to be anything, or go anywhere, that Gods name may be Glorified, and souls saved;

Mond. 28. I have been some time with Brother Bird, and today we parted. I find it hard to have much conversation, even with the servants of God, and to keep that spiritual frame of mind I want. I have often felt cond[e]m[ne]d for too much conversation.[17]

Thursd. Oct. 1. My mind is much conf[u]sed, and under sore temptation to disbelieve the Doctrine of Christian perfection.

Mond. 12. After some slowness of mind, this Day intend to form myself in more evenness of Duty as to Prayer and Self-examination. At 12 oclock and at Night to exammin myself, and to Pray.

Sat. 17. Find myself condem'd for too much conversation, and am made to blush before the Lord, for my slowness to believe.

Sat. 24. Was a day of distress to my soul. My ideas was so dark that I could scerce preach.

Mond. 26. In crossing a large Mountain, my soul was much resigned to the will of God. When I came to the top of the Mountain. I cal[le]d on the Lord to direct my way and make it prosperious. I found some faith that the Lord would own my labors.

Wed. 18. Was engaged with the Lord, and had some liberty in preaching. In the evening visited a family out of which a young man died sudenly the Night before. Pray'd with, and spoke to those present to prepare to meet God. Today preachd his funeral to a large number of peopel. It is an awfull thing to see Dearth [death] enter

[17] Rule 2 for the conduct of preachers, as given in the *Discipline* of 1784, read: "Be serious. Let your motto be, *Holiness to the Lord*. Avoid all lightness, jesting, and foolish talking."

into families, whose hope is all in this world. The cries of this family (that was in this awfull state) was pierceing to all that had any feeling for the Distresses of their fellow creatures.

Mond. November. 2. Some Distress of mind lay on me. About noon I retired for prayer. My soul was melted down before the Lord, my life appeard to be unprofitable, and was made to wonder the Lord sufferd me to remain in the land of the liveing.

Tuesd. 12. This evening in prayer, and reading the life of Colonial Gardener, I was much affected at his charity to the Poor. Afterward I was meditating on the love of God to mankind. I began to examin if theire was anything in me to move the love of God toward me, I found nothing but sin and misery by nature. My soul was [so] overpower'd with the love of God, that my bodyly strenth failed.

Sat. 14. This evening my soul was fill'd with love while I had some conversation with a Black man about the dealings of God with his soul. He spake so feelingly and powerfull of the work of Grace on his soul that it much affected me.

Thursd. 19. Arose early and addressed myself to the throne of Grace. And then to serching the Scriptures and was much humbled before the Lord.

Mond. 23. Preachd twice and find myself weak in body but resignd to the will of God—I feel by the grace of God determind to preach more pointed than I ever have don[e].

Wed. December 2. I have been two or three days possesd with a backwardness to dut[y].

Thursd. 3. Rose before 5 oclock and addressd myself to the throne of grace. Then to reading the Acts of the Apostels, their manner of church government, and to compare our order with it, and believe it agrees with the government of the Apostels. I see a great beauty in being governd and subject to Superiors.[18] This evening was much tempted to wandering thoughts, borth [both] in private and family prayer.

Sund. 13. The past weak was porely in body, it often chill'd my Spirits. Oh! what an unfit time is a sick bed to make our peace with God.

Mond. 14. The last evening after P[rayer], laid down to rest, it was

[18] How different this from the attitude taken by James O'Kelley and his Republican Methodists!

as tho their [there] was voices sounding in my ears. I believd them to be from the enemy. Today after preaching twice. At night had some conversation with a Woman that a few days ago was allmost in dispare, appears to be happy in the Lord. This night I dreampt that myself and two of my brothers was removeing from on[e] place to another. And passing through an House A woman unknown to me arose from her bed and took me by the hand and shewd me a littel child, and said will you pass by without ever preaching to my child. Lord what is it.

Tuesd. 15. Crossed the Mountain and met bro. Kobler and Cole.[19] Wher bro. Kobler preachd after preaching, a man that had started to go home, turnd back and askd if I would not preach unto them. (Afterward I preached twice at that place but wheather it profited the peopel or not will be made known in the last day).

Thursd. 17. I have been much afflicted some days with a cold, today endevourd to Preach but with much difficulty—

Sund. 20. Was a day of deep exercise of soul. Today bid farewell to a hardend peopel and left them.

Tuesd. 22. Rose early and after addressing myself to the throne of Grace, and reading the Word of God; I spent some time in examming my past life, and viewing the goodness of God toward me.

Wed. 23. Preachd on Sinking Creek. And in the evening had a view of the wonderfull works of God, in creation, I had the opportunity of viewing of a cave. It went about 200 yards underground. Overhead it is one solid rock out of which there is a continual droping of water that turns to stone again.

Thursd. 24. It is a matter of contemplation to see the lofty mountains. In traveling a narrow path without geting any directions of my way, I felt a complaining Spirit, I cried to the Lord and he delivered me. In the evening at the hour of retirement, I felt some hardness of heart at first, but found some deliverance and got a Spirit of Contemplation.

Mond. 28. Preachd to a few hearers. I feel awfull apprehensions of some Judgment falling on this peopel.

Sund. January 3. 1796. Awoke early with a deep sence of my [need] of a Saviour, resolvd to spend the Day to the glory of God. Preachd

[19] Possibly Le Roy Cole (1749–1830), a native of Virginia, who had been admitted on trial to the traveling connection in 1777 but located in 1798.

with some freedom from, Whereas I was blind now I see. At night in my Sleep I had a deep sence of the corruptions of Nature that yet remain in me.

Frid. 8. Preachd in a cold and open meeting house; and then rode about 10 miles through the cold.

Sund. 10. The snow was falling very fast while I rode to bro. Addeers. I missd my road and went 3 or 4 miles out of my way. I preachd to a few persons with freedom.

Mond. 11. Last night it raind and frose to a Sleet. Today I rode an unbroken way[.] the ice cut my horses legs till the blood came.

Tuesd. 12. The ice was much harder than the Day before I started to me [my] appointment. I went about one mile and was stopt by the Ice. I had to walk before my Horse to brake [break] the way. I turned back and got to Mr Pages.

Wed. 13. With some difficulty got to brother McDonnals.

Thursd. 14. My Soul seems humbled before the Lord. I want to be lost in God. Jesus appears precious to me. I want the whole mind that was in Christ.

Sund. 17. By reason of Rain and hig[h] waters I had no meeting but read and wrote.

Mond. 18. High waters keeps me from traveling to Day. The reading [of] nelsons Journal was made a Blessing to my soul, it opend to my view the state of the peopel on Newriver; I cald on the Lord with sorrow, and opend my Bible on these words, It is of the Lords mercy that we are not consumed, because his compations fail not.

Sund. 24. I find it necesary to be very strict on the Sabath; the last was spent with less engagements than common. And the last weak was a time of trial and sore distress.

Sund. 31. Preachd in a cold house filld with smoke, so that [neither] myself nor [my] hearers had any comfort.

Mond. Feb. 1. The Epistel to Philipians came in the course of my reading to Day. I was much drawn out to consider the carractor of a Gospel Minister. oh, that God may enable me to answer the carractor.

Wed. 3. Preachd to a few hearers and felt life and Power in my own soul, glory to God[.] he is mercyfull to my unrighteousness and comforts me more than I deserve.

Thursd. 4. Was much exercised about Marrying, an object persented herself before my mind, many delights appeard in that state of life; But I believe I can serve God and be more useful in my present state.

Frid. 5. Last night was sorely tempted and in heaviness in the Morning. But found comfort, and had liberty in preaching.

Sat. 6. Been sometime sorely harresed by the devil. Oh! Lord undertake for me and deliver me from the roaring Lion.

Sund. 7. In reading Bunyans sermon on, So run that you may obtain, I was brought to examin myself, and see I come short of what I aut [ought] to be. I had liberty in preaching and comfort in visiting a sick woman.

Wed. 10. Was a day of fasting and prayer, to humble myself before the Lord. Today I read Four Sermons of Mr Yorick. They neither contain Repentance nor faith. The name of Xt was mentioned twice in the four sermons that contains about 108 pages.

Sat. and Sund. 13 and 14. At Quarter meeting, at the Lords table was troubled with hardness of heart for some time, and then found relief.

Thurs. 18. Was with bro. Bird and had liberty in preaching, and a refreshing time at the Sacrament.

Frid. March 11. Been some time under various exercise of mind. Last night was much distressd. Altho I had a long way to ride and a large Mountain to walk over; I took no refreshment; But made it a day of fasting and prayer to the Lord to direct me in the way he would have me to go. In the evening weak and w[e]ary in body, I retired to pour out my complaints to the Lord. I began to read my Bible but my exercise was so great I could not. Unable to contain myself I fell on the ground but could only vent myself in sighs and groans. The Lord answerd for himself, the eye of faith was opend [and] I saw the Lord Jesus Sweating blood and agoniseing for me. He was then set before my eyes on the cross Groaning and dieing then risen and in heaven pleading for me. My Soul was humbled and filld with love. I cried to the Lord to nail my affection to the cross. I seemd willing to suffer anything for the Lord. These Scriptures was powerfully applied to me, When I sent you without purs[e] or scrip lacked ye anything. My Soul cried nothing Lord. Then this: Lo I am with you to the end of the world.

Tuesd. 15. Had an instance of the providence of God over me.

Rideing over the Iron Mountain, a piece of bresh that lay in the road hung to my Horses legs, and struck him in the flank and set him to jumping. Borth [both] my sturrip-leathers broke, and then he threw me over his head. The first place that took the ground was the back of my head and then fell on my back. As I fell I held my Horse by the bridle [so] that I was in danger of his jumping on me. I rose and found myself safe from being much hurt. I rode to my appoint[ment] and had liberty in preaching.

Wed. 23. Rode an uneasy Horse about 30 miles and found myself resignd to the will of God, and my soul comforted.

Frid. April 1. I feel very awfull at the continual allarms of Dearth, to Day a man had his head broke to pieces by the fall of a tree, in about 7 months I've heard of 10 or 12 Sudden Deaths. Shurely the Lord is pouring out his fury on Newriver.

Sat. and Sun. 2 and 3. Quarter meeting at Honakers Meeting house. I bid fare well to the peopel of New rive[r] from Mat. 21:43. In the evening as I was going to bro Ingrams, in the road several men had been fighting withe their loaded whips. One of them was bleeding very much and looked awfull. Shurely this is a wicked peopel.

Mond. 11. This evening as I was about worship, a phlem [gathered] in my breast [so] that I was unable to speak.

Sat. 16. Convicted for too much conversation in the weak [week] that is past. This morning felt humbled before the Lord.

Sund. 17. This day dedicated to the Lord. In lovefeast my soul was humbled before the Lord.

Wed. 20. Conference began on Watages at bro. Danworths and ended on Frid. 22. I was appointed to Danville Ct Kentucky[20] where we arived Safe on Sat. 30. [May, 1796, to March, 1798, here omitted.]

. . . .

March Wed. 21 [1798].[21] Was humbled before God as I intended to alter my state of life, a subject which has some time laid with weight on my mind, and now the providence of God has opend the way

[20] Danville Circuit was an extensive charge in central Kentucky, including Boyle, Pulaski, Mercer, Garrard, Madison, Estill, and Lincoln counties. See map, p. 205.

[21] Lakin was at this time serving Limestone Circuit, which lay north of the Licking River in Kentucky and included the preaching appointments in the area between the Licking and the Ohio rivers. See accompanying map.

and has directed me to a person with whom I Believe I can live comfortably. I was much drawn out in prayer for God to bless us in our intended union and have Faith that God will grant my requests—

Mond. 26. My exercise is various and sollem[.] I long to know and do the will of God. I now feel something of a calm serenity of mind and engagement of soul. Lord keep me humble before the[e]——.

Wed. 28. Feel an akeing void the world can never fill. I cant enjoye any comfort except I feel my soul alive to God.

March Sat. 31 and Sund April 1. At Quarter meeting. My exercise was very great and my mind sorely distressed, But felt peace with God. it is a mercy of God that I am not cast of[f] forever. After traveling as an Itenerant preacher for Three Yeares and Five Months, I now gave up my place to the Conference.[22] Oh that God may keep me from sin and bless the Itenerant plan forever. Amen.

Thursd. 5. Yesterday and today feel the Lord is present with me and my soul is humble before him——

Sunday 8. Feel sorrow and shame before God for my many failings. When I view what a lump of sin and deformity I am by nature, I stand and wonder can it be possible that ever such a creature can be made an hiere (heir) of Glory and a companion for angels and Saints above—Lord Jesus I will rely on thy merits alone for Salvation.

Thursd. 12. April. Was this day maried to Betsey Roye, and had the testimony from above that it was acceptable in the sight of my heavenly Father—and God made it a day of consolation to my soul. [April, 1798, to February, 1799, omitted.]

. . . .

Sunday. February 10. 1799. This night at a prayer meeting, while the wicked made their sport of the things of God, my soul was brought into the true simplicity of the gosple. This night I dreamed that I was returning home from meeting (with some others that I would have taken with me but I was not prepared to receive them)[.] We came to a large House where I was to stay all night, Not far from which was a certain place that was haunted with evil Spirits, and neare the place was some evil beings that continually kept takeing something from those that passed that way[.] I had with me a small

[22] The *Minutes* of 1798 include Lakin's name in the list of those "who are under a location through weakness of body or family concerns." He continued to supply locally wherever needed, however.

water pail that in one moment was taken from me—I was amased, sore distressed, and trembled with feare The night was now on and I was now alone. I heard the noise of many wagons runing and they went by the House of widow Newland, she was much terifyed with feare and her husband (that was in a world of Spirits) would not suffer her to speak. When it was day I was informed the noise that I had heard ware [were] evil Spirits that were come being invited by some persons they brought many more along with them, and ware [were] prepareing a place for the destruction of the children of men. Whether I was alone or with some other person I know not. But I undertook to counter work them. I had to cross a small hollow and was very fearefull that in crossing a bridge made over it, I should be taken in the snare, I was soon informed the place they had prepared was a large frame hung up large enough to contain great numbers, at once and with it swing them of[f] and dash them to pieces. I saw they would dash to pieces thousands in a moment—I went on and came to a riseing ground where some were spliting pieces of timber to effect the purpose of preventing the desires of the evil Spirits. After a few minutes consideration I saw that would not effect the purpose[.] I passed on and began to pray. I went in a circle and held my left hand out toward the place where the evil Spirits were. I spoke as I could extend my voice untill I came to the place where they were to put their dreadfull plan into execution (after I engaged in this work my troubles and feare were all gon). The evil Spirits were all still by this time[.] my voice failed and my strength was gone. H.... N.... was now with me. I turned my right hand where my left was before and went on. we heard the voice of some singing that were on our side[.] my companion bid them be silent. We soon heard other singing, that came from the evil Spirits. I told my companion my voice failed and he must go to prayer, which he refused to do telling me I must myself. I saw him no more. The Lord appeared to me in human shape. I began to pray again, an evil spirit appeared in the shape of a red Bird, and calling to his companions, but none appeared. I reached out my right hand toward them and cried, Lord Jesus look there, in a moment the evil Spirit took his flight toward the place where they intended to destroy mankind[.] they all were vanqu[i]shed. So I awoke and it was a dream.

About the begining of May 1799 as I was one day laboring, a small bird came and sat on a saplin where I was. its attention appeared to be toward me. I stood up to see what it would do. A thought struck my mind that if the Bird should light on my head I should see trouble. as soon as the thought came into my mind, the Bird flew down by my head and sat by my feet, it flew back again to a limb (and tho other Birds of the same kind came on the Saplin it paid no attention to them). It then flew and sat on my head, then returned to the limb, which it did three or four times and the last time it gave a scratch and flew of[f] and I saw it no more. My feelings ware [were] awfull and my thoughts ware [were] various[.] I knew not what to think of it.

As I was now located I continued to labour and preach as often as my circumstances would admit. In the latter end of this year I had some serious thoughts about traveling again, we came once to a conclusion to travel. But after various thoughts and painfull exercise I gave over[.] my mind was now fully setteld. I gave out the thought of ever traveling. Accordingly moved some distance and setteled in another place where I expected to continue[.] we began the world poor[.] we laboured hard[.] the Lord blessed our labour and a prospect began to open to us of makeing something in the world. (But how soon can God bring all our schemes to naught.) After the General Conference in the year 1800, there was no preacher for Limestone Circuit, Brother Burk[23] after returning from conference, (and haveing the charge of the district at that time) wrote to me informing me of the state of the circuit and desired me to prepare to take it at Quarter-meeting which was to be held in July. the exercise of my mind was various on the occasion sometimes thinking it to be my duty to go and at other[s] thinking it not to be my duty. in this situation I continued until Quarter-meeting, and then concluded that I could not go; the circuit was without a preacher, it now came a question before the Quarter-meeting how it was to be supplied, differen[t] plans were preposed, at last Brother Lawson[24] preposed to supply the circuit untill Conference (which was to be the first of October)[.] the offer was ac-

[23] William Burke (1770–1855), a native of Virginia, was the first secretary of the Western Conference and one of the ablest of the early circuit-riders of Kentucky. In 1800 he was appointed to Hinkstone and Lexington circuits (See Burke's "Autobiography," in Finley, *op. cit.*, pp. 22–92).

[24] Jeremiah Lawson was received on trial in 1796 and located in 1799, settling in Limestone Circuit. He was readmitted to the connection at the Western Conference of 1800.

cepted and he took it. after I returned home my feelings ware [were] awfull. I fell into the debth of distress. it continually pursued me that another had taken my Crown. my life now almost became a burthen to me. my peace was gone, and scerse ever returnd except when I was preaching after which my anguish of mind returned. I was still requested by the preachers to take the circuit at Conference, as Kentuckey was like to be scerse of preachers, and maried preachers must travel or the work suffer. I began to think my situation would admit of it if any would, as we had no children. But in general I could not Beare the thought of traveling, my wife also made some objections to it. I laid the matter before the Lord by prayer and fasting. And took this for my direction, that if some difficulties were removed that appeared in the way and my wife gave her consent that it was the will of God that I should travel. My wife soon began to be much exercised about my traveling and soon not only gave her consent but also advised me to go. I still felt a reluctance to going, and my distresses ware [were] such before I gave up to travel that I was for some time in continual fear of being murdered[.] my pain was great and all wordly comfort was entirely gone. At last being fully convinced it was the will of God I gave up to travel, accordingly I attended conference at Bethel on the first of October. 1800. and took an appointment in Limestone circuit[.] after I received my appointment my mind was variously exercised. sometimes I allmost wished I had not took the appointment. I had some temporal concerns to attend to before I could take the circuit [so] that it was the first of November before I started, it was painfull to leve an effectionate wife and go out into the world and travel up and down. after I took the circuit my mind was more composed and I had the testimony that I was in the place where God had placed me. When I took the Circuit the prospect was most gloomy—but few attended preaching and those in general appear to care less about their souls, yet an impression was on my mind that God would revive his work among the people. The first Quarter I saw no fruits of my labour. But at Quarter-meeting the Lord began to work amongst the people[.] some ware [were] convicted and some converted, and from that time the work in some places began to revive. As the Circuit had been for a considerable time without Discipline being kept up I had many difficulties to encounter[.] I found in some places societies divided into parties and torn with contention[.] in endevouring to execute discipline I met with opposition and in some cases Borth [both] parties were offended with me. But I endevourd to do according to the best of my Judgment. I Believe some of the people in one place endevoured to set the President Elder[25] against me, which they accomplished, For on March 5, 1801 I received a few lines from him in which I was charged with being a mischiefmakeing person. the unjustness of the charge and contemtable manner in which it came to me, exercised my mind very much. I concluded as I did not make as great a shew in the world as some other[s], I was entirely held in contemt (and I think yet I had some reason for my conclusion) and I supposed some wished me at home again. I thought as I was appointed by conference to the circuit I could not with a cleare concience quit my appointment before the yeare was expired, But came to the conclusion after my appointment was out to desist from traveling. But when I came to inform my wife of my intentions she opposed me in my plan, and insisted that I was not traveling for the President Elder But for God and if God had called me to the work I aut [ought] not to quit it. Her reasons had weight and God made her an able counciler to me, her reasons brought me to this conclusion that if the Elder gave me any Satisfaction, and God blessed my labours it would be my duty to continue in the work. I accordingly wrote to him on the subject, and in a short time received an answer that gave me satisfaction. The work began to revive in a most glorious manner, it exceeded anything I had ever seen[.] Souls were converted to God in almost every part of the Circuit, [so] that in about Six Months, I ad[d]ed more than one Hundred to the church[26]—It bore me up under all my difficulties to see sinners comeing home to God[.] tho the Lord revived his work in a glorious manner, yet by reason of the opposition I met with in my first start in the circuit, I was not able to bring the circuit into order while I staid in it, and when I left it[,] it wanted a man of more wisdom and courage than I ever had[27]—I continued in Limestone

[25] The presiding elder of the Kentucky District at the time was William McKendree, later bishop.

[26] During the year the membership on the circuit rose from 417–20, as reported in the *Minutes* of 1801, to 523–18 in 1802 (*Minutes,* I, 97, 103). Note that this was during the most prosperous phase of the Great Revival in Kentucky.

[27] Henry Smith, a veteran preacher, and Lewis Hunt, were appointed in October, 1801.

Circuit untill the first of October 1801, and on the Third of the Month I entered on Lexington[28] and Hinkston Circuits.....

1802, January, Frid. 1. I am now one year older than I was this time last year, and that much nearer to eternity, oh; my soul art thou better prepared to meet God and be happy in him. [As] I look back [I see] the Lord hath delivered me out of many troubles, and hath hitherto provided for me in soul and body[.] in the last year I have seen something of the goodness of God in the convertion of many Souls, Yet I have been an unprofitable Servant, Lord pardon me—I look forward, and feel like endevouring to spend this year more to the glory of God than the last, and feel a hope of seeing more of the goodness and mighty works of God amongst the children of men.....

Mond. [*January*] *25* [*1802*]. Yesterday preached with some degree of energy of Spirit at Frankfor[t] on Hebrews 4:2, and in my diffinition of the gospel, I made it to include all the mind and will of God, revealed to mankind, that is nescessarry to Salvation. Today I received a few lines from the Govenor,[29] in which he informed me, that if he under[s]tood me, my deffinition confounded law and gospel, which is contrary to the whole tenor of Scripture.—I returnd in answer that I excluded both the Adamic and the ceremonial law, But included all the revealed will of God that is nescessary to the Salvation of fallen man in which I apprehend the law of liberty which we are under to Christ is included—

[28] Lexington Circuit lay south of Limestone Circuit and included all of the Kentucky appointments between the Licking and the Kentucky rivers, in the counties of Fayette, Jessamine, Woodford, Franklin, Scott, and Harrison. To the east and north lay Lakin's first circuit, Hinkstone (see map on p. 205). Lakin's manuscript list of preaching-places for the year 1801–2 included the following: "Simon Cochrans, Snegidors, Howards, Caneridge, Darnals, Wilsons, Lexington, Priers, Words, Bethel, Trimbles, Woodford, Isaac Ruddles, Frankford, Ratliff[s], Cornelious Ruddles, Redmans, Simpsons, Griffeth[s], Beries, Tuckers, Cannons, Colemans, Hendershots, Porters, Grimes, Indian Creek, Earlywines, Flat Run M[eeting] H[ouse], Nuns, Wilmots, Jacobys, Martins, Owens, Dunaways, Red River, Wilsons, Grassy Lick, Hopkins, Cl[a]rks, [and] Pointers"—forty-one in all.

[29] The governor of Kentucky at this time was James Garrard (1749–1822), a former Baptist clergyman. He was elected to the governorship in 1796 and served until 1804. Previously, as a member of the Virginia legislature, he had been influential in securing the passage of Jefferson's bill to establish religious liberty in the commonwealth (J. H. Spencer, *A History of Kentucky Baptists* [Cincinnati, 1885], I, 133). For his record as a member of the Elkhorn Baptist Association, Kentucky, see William Warren Sweet, *Religion on the American Frontier, 1783–1830,* Vol. I: *The Baptists* (New York, 1931), pp. 417 ff.

Sat. 30. This morning I awoke and began to examine myself and find I am in a dull insencible situation. I began to consider the cause and find I have given way to Philosophy, and begin to seek therein what alone is to be found in Christ. It was impressed on my mind to keep this day as a day of fasting to humble myself before God[.] I was sorely tempted to omit it, but by the grace of God I was enabled to comply. . . . .

Sun. Mar. 14 [*1802*]. . . . . Sometime since I received the following (remarkable) account, from Mr David Purvine. A young woman in the neighbourhood of Caneridge,[30] one day in family worship fell under the power of God at the same time her speech was taken from her. She could sit up but was intirely inclined to lay. in this situation she continued for nine days without takeing any refreshment, except some water that she took a few times[.] once by persuasion she took some Solid refreshment into her mouth, and her jaws immediately clinched on it [so] that she could not ate [eat] it, and they had by force to wrench her mouth open and take it out again[.] on the ninth day several religious friends (of the Prisbeterian order) met with her for prayer, after they had continued for some time in prayer, they mostly inclined to depart but Mr Purvine insisted on their again joining in preyer, which they did and in a few minutes after prayer was over her speech was restored and she arose with her usual strength, and her body in no ways emaciated, But in full flesh and vigour. Shurely it is the Lords doings and it is marvalous in our eyes.

Sat., 20. Rode through rain to Limestone Quarter-Meeting[31] and sat in an open Meeting-house in my wet clothes. I took cold and at night was very unwell, But my soul was happy—It was a time of the sweetest communion with God I have had for some time—My soul was humble next morning.—

Monday 22. We had a watchnight[.] the Lord was with us of a truth. My wife was so overpower'd she sunk in praises to God. as we returnd to Father Hintons that night she sunk again under the power

[30] At Cane Ridge, in Bourbon County, Kentucky, was the Presbyterian church of which Barton W. Stone was pastor. Under his preaching there had broken out in the summer of the previous year one of the most celebrated phases of the Great Revival in the West. Lakin's informant was doubtless David Purviance, an associate of Stone in the Springfield Presbytery.

[31] It was customary for the preachers on adjoining circuits to attend these quarterly gatherings.

of God and asked me if I did not see the light that surrounded us. I asked what light[.] she said a most butifull light that circeld all round us. and we ware [were] in it. Oh God may we ever walk in the light of the Lord—The next day in parting with our friends (to return to my circuit) at prayer the Lord gave us tender hearts and we parted in his name[.] Lord keep us all. . . . .

Sund. [*May*] *16* [*1802*]. Attended a prispeterian sacrament at Caneridge. I had some satisfaction in seeing a party spirit fall and union amongst Christians take place; But think there is some inconsistancies in their preaching. [May, 1802, to December, 1802, omitted.]

. . . .

Wed. 15 [*December*] [*1802*].[32] As I rode to my appointment it was often impressed on my mind what if you have to preach a funeral today. when I came to Brother Halls his Mother was dead and I was requested to preach on the occasion, which I did in much bodily weakness being obliged often to stop—Who can account for those impressions, may it not be by the ministry of angels.—

Sat. 25. Our Quarter-meeting for Salt River Circuit began we seteled our temporal buisness, and on Sund. 26. in the morning for the first time administered the Lords Supper. The Lord was with us both in Sacrament and preaching—In the evening found myself in a disagreeable situation. A daughter of Bro. Springers this evening went of[f] to be maried against her Fathers consent and without his knowledge. Her Father was in much trouble, and one of her brothers went in persuit of them in a great rage, we were fearefull of the consequences of his finding them—After some conversation and serious reflection on the subject I called the family togather for prayer, in time of prayer I had faith that there would be no mischief done, and things would turn out better than we expected. Some time in the night the young man returned, but could not find them, he seemed to be better reconciled than when he went after them—On Monday morning he seemed quite calm, and went to the young mans Brother's and saw them married. When her Father heard it, he seemed resolved to keep them at a distance. I retired to private prayer to ask council of

[32] In October, 1802, at the Western Conference held at Bethel Chapel, Cumberland, Lakin had been appointed with Ralph Lotspeich to the Salt River and Shelby Circuit in the Kentucky District (see map on p. 205). It was at this conference also that Lakin was ordained elder; note the reference to communion, below, December 26.

God, afterward I used my influence with the old man, and prevailed with him to send them word to come home, which they did the next day, and I left them in a fair way of piece [peace]—

1803—January, Sat. and Sun. 1 and 2. We held our Quarter-meeting for Shelby Circuit. We licensed some young preachers. On Sund. morning our situation reminded me of the time our Lord instituted the holy Sacrament, in a Borrowed upper chamber such [as] was ours and Jesus was with us. Afterward I preached from Micah 4.13. I spoke full[y] on the necessity of ministers exerting all their powers and devoteing as much of their time to the work of the ministry as their circumstances would admit. I intended it to stir up some young men to take a larger field in the ministry—

Wed. 5. Rode through heavy rain to Bro Culls and had some liberty in preaching—I had been here once before and while I was preaching from Luke 3.9. and enforceing the latter part of the text, it shall be hewn down and cast into the fire, a young man walked out of the house and began to crack nuts by the house side. I cried out it may be God['s] will soon [to] hew down that young man that is cracking nuts and cast him into the fire—I now received an account that God hath called him to give an account of his conduct—In this place there were five or six men that were bitter persecuters of religion, lately one of them runing of[f] his Horse broke his leg and had it cut off, one is dead, and another is at the point of death, Shurely these are the Judgments of God. . . .

Sat. and Sund. [April] 9 and 10 [1803]. Preached in the Ilenois [Illinois] grant[33] with some liberty, on Sund. morning. I felt God to be with me here in this wilderness, we had near 30 communicants and a melting time. This place has for some time lain on my mind. I had thoughts of takeing it into the circuit. (Which we have since done, there is a prospect of good being done. Some have been converted and others are under good impressions)—

Mond. 11. My mind is calm and in the morning had access to the throne of grace.

[33] The Illinois or Clarke Grant lay in what is now Clarke County, Indiana, bordering the Ohio River. Lakin and Lotspeich were the first traveling preachers to visit the grant. Included for several years in Salt River and Shelby Circuit, it was in 1807 incorporated in the first entire circuit in Indiana, Silver Creek (F. C. Holliday, *Indiana Methodism* [Cincinnati, 1873], pp. 8 and 37).

Frid. Yesterday met Bro. Lotspiech,[34] the account he gives me distresses my mind, (the circuit is full of trouble). Today am exercised in prayer to know how to act, I feel let others do as they will, I will try to be the Lord's.

Mond. 18. Had liberty in preaching, and the Lord was with us in class[.] one woman got so happy that she hung upon her husband in raptures of Joy. then she ran through the house. But the house could not hold her [and] she rushed out at the dore to invite others to come to Jesus. All the time her countenance Bore the most sollemn appearance. Others some were shouting and some in tears, God was with us of a truth [April, 1803, to October, 1803, omitted.]

. . . .

October, Sat. 1 [*1803*]. Our Conference began at Colemans.[35] I was exercised for some time with various temptations but still I was calm, that in some degree I could say I set calm on tumult whole. Our Conference ended on Thursday, 6, our buisness we went through in calmness, and piece [peace] reigned amongst us. We sent two preachers to Notchieze [Natchez][36] and one to Ilenoise,[37] my appointment was to Danvil Circuit.[38] We went from conference to visit our earthly relation[s.] I found among them Joy and sorrow, I am more than ever sensible that all earthly things are emty and vain.....

Sat. & Sund. [*December*] *17. 18* [*1803*]. Was Quarter-meeting. it

[34] Ralph Lotspeich, Lakin's colleague, was of German descent and a native of Virginia. He was admitted on trial in 1802 and faithfully served the Western and Ohio conferences until his death in 1813. For memoir, see *Minutes,* I, 238.

[35] At Mount Gerizim, Harrison County, Kentucky.

[36] Moses Floyd and Hezekiah Harriman; also A. Amos and Tobias Gibson, who as supernumerary residents of Mississippi Territory, were assigned to aid them (William Warren Sweet, *The Rise of Methodism in the West* [New York and Cincinnati, 1920], p. 90).

[37] Benjamin Young.

[38] Lakin had served Danville Circuit previously in 1796. His appointments for 1803–4 included: "Greens Chappel, Grassey Lick, Muddycreek M[eeting] H[ouse], Williamses, Concord M[eeting] house, Coleing ground, Irvines, Cochrans, Proctors Chappel, A Hunts, Ridwells, Big Spring, Gilberts, Andersons, R[e]ynolds, Highland, Evinses, Conaways, Jefferises, Smiths, Egertons, Spurgins, Shawney run M[eeting] H[ouse], Stampers, Winchester, Hicks's, Martins, Day's, Owens, Lawless's, Dunaways, John McMurry's, Wilsons, Landers's, Ray's, Websters, St Clere, Riggs, Thompson's, Joshua Owens, Jacobies, Howards, David Speers's, Philips, Bosley's M[eeting] H[ouse], Pott's, Johnson's, [and] Daniel Roystons."

appeared expedient for me to leve Danvil and go to Hinkston Circuit, as the preacher that was appointed to that Circuit had neglected to attend his appointment.[39] On Sunday morning we had a precious time at the Sacrament and a sollemn time in public.

Mond. 19. We left brother Thompsons and rode about 30 miles intending to reach Hinkston C[ircui]t the next day but was prevented by a storm of snow, we rode that day about 15 miles.

Wed. 21. We left Brother Irwins intending to cross Kentuckey-River. above the mouth of the Red-River (haveing bad directions) we fell into the Mountains, when night came on us we were in the hills, and had no more than a deer path to travel. we got out of the path in going up the hill, night was now on us and we were in the hills without any road or knowing which way to go. I felt sometimes a complaining spirit But my wife was all courage, she observed the Lord would not let [us] lay in the woods all night. I felt thankfull that God had given her support at this time. The first house we came to we were denyed lodging, the next intimated we had better go further[.] the third house the man would not come to the dore to give us any directions. about 3 hours in the night we came to a friends house where we were kindly entertained.

Thursd. 22. Met Bro. Blackman,[40] and the next day makeing our arangements we parted. I preached at Bro. Rays,[41] and was humble before God.

Sund. 25. Being Christmas day preach'd before day in the morning, I felt my heart tender, but was shut up in preaching. At 12. Ocloc I spoke plain, but was not in the Spirit of preaching.

Wed. 28. Preachd with some satisfaction to a simple people at the coleing ground, (near Burbin Furnace) In this Circuit I see the force of the observation, Get your name up. Brother J[ohn] A. G[renade]'s[42] name is up, though he has never been round the c[ircui]t,

[39] John A. Grenade, of whom later.

[40] Learner Blackman (1781–1815), a native of New Jersey, was in 1803 appointed to Lexington Circuit, Kentucky.

[41] One John Ray (1768–1837), a native of Virginia, had been admitted on trial to the traveling connection in 1791 but located 1801, settling in Montgomery County, Kentucky, within the bounds of Hinkstone Circuit (Arnold, *op. cit.,* I, 97–101).

[42] John Adam Grenade, an eccentric frontier preacher, was a native of North Carolina. He had been admitted on trial to the Western Conference in 1801 but located in 1804. His death occurred in 1807 (see Finley, *op. cit.,* pp. 288–96; and McFerrin, *op. cit.,* I, 382–418, for extracts from his journal).

and not one in Twenty hath ever heard him preach; Yet perhaps it will be one years work to get him a preachd out of the people.

1804. January, Sund. 8. For some time have been gloomy in Spirit, today was sensibly pained, yet my heart was tender, my exercise[s] are various and great, Lord direct me by thy providence. I had some liberty in preaching, and spoke plain.

Thurs. 12. A gloom of mind hath continued upon me; my exercises are great, but my hope is in God, and now feel more calm in spirit and find access to God; may I spend this day, and every day to his glory. When I was preaching, (to my own view) I was shut up; and sometimes thought the people would be offended at my awkward maner of preaching. after meeting a man came to me and asked me if I did not intend to preach on the same subject round the c[ircui]t, observing he had never heard a greater discourse. Our ideas concerning the discourse differed widely.

Frid. 13. This morning in reading Genesus 22 from 15 to the 19 verse was much struck with the promis of God, to Abraham for his obedience, and is not God the same God.

Sund. 15. Last evening and this Morning was with a man of a talkative turn and much given to disputation (in my view) but his ideas of things are confused, and his arguments weak. I had today liberty in preaching and ended the day in peace.

Frid. 27. For some time I have been much dejected in Spirit. Yesterday my spirit was pained, but felt a spirit of prayer, today had some liberty in preaching and had access to the throne of Grace.

Sund. 29. Found God to be present with me. I had liberty in preaching, and appeared by the countenance of the people, who with eyes Bathed raised their hands and voices to God in prayer and praise. After meeting a drunken man came along the road, and fell from his horse and lay untill two Negros went to his assistance. I had serious thoughts on the occasion. He came to our class meeting in the evening and at first was a little troublesome[.] I felt calm and my soul unmoved. Glory to God for his goodness.

Mond. 30. In seeing the people rejoiceing, this thought was impressed on my mind, that there is an impropriety in wishing always to be in such extacies, as it would prevent man from answering the end of his creation in many things. But in heaven they will be proper and perpetual.

February, Sat. 4. This morning I was disagreeably situated; the woman where I stayed had been displeased the evening before, and she still shewed something of the old bone; and the children was so noisey that I could neither read nor meditate; I felt the effects of it in preaching. I find when I am deprived of the oppertunity of reading and meditateing that in preaching my ideas are dark. So sure the means must be used to obtain the end.

Wed. 8. Some expressions in a letter I yesterday received from W. McK[endree][43] gives me some reason to think the time is comeing for me to retire to a more private life. My mind is variously exercised; but upon a close examination of myself my concience is clere, and my soul staid on God. I have changed my mind and intend going to Lexington C[ircui]t Quarter-meeting.

Sund. 12. As I returned from meeting, I spoke some words that gave me pain. In the evening my mind was burthened. But at prayer with a few friends, felt piece [peace] and comfort.

Sund. 19. Haveing taken cold it hath seteld in my Jaws [so] that for some days I have not been able to chew anything hard. preaching put my head and face to pain. But found liberty in my soul. I have been sceriously thinking on death; it seems a solemn thing to be seperated from the body and to appear before God—Lord prepare me for that hour.

Sunday. 25 [26?] Last night I had a sore conflict in my mind, this morning after conversing with Bro. McK[endree] my mind was unburdend. I had a comfortable time at Sacrament, and liberty in preaching. At night the Lord was with us, some were crying for mercy, some praising God for Justifying, and some for sanctifying grace. My soul was happy in God.

Wed. 29. I had some liberty in preaching on the subject of prayer. And hope to see good times.

March. Thursd. 1. Rode through the snow and preached a short sermon. Then rode about five miles, to Baptise some children and preached by candle light.

Sund. 4. Preached in an open house[.] the cold was very severe, by standing in the arc[h] of the door, I took cold that seteld in my back [so] that for some days it was a pain for me to go about.

Tuesd. 6. Spoke plain from Deuteronomy 26, 17. 18. and enforced

[43] McKendree was in 1803–4 Lakin's presiding elder over the Kentucky District.

the necessity of keeping God's commandments; to a mixed people, some Methodist, some prisbyterian, and some Baptist. Independant of persons it is my duty to preach the whole Gospel. [March, 1804, to August, 1808, omitted.]

. . . .

The year 1808 I was stationed on Deare Creek Circuit;[44] Though there was a good work on the circuit I think it one of the most gloomy years that I have ever known since I have been in the work of the Ministry. I now look at the state I was then in and think I had near fallen into the state of the Laodiceans, neither cold nor hot, and in proportion as I lost spirituallity of soul I lost the gift of preaching. And the cause of my falling into this state I think was 1. I began to think two highly of my gifts and power. 2. I was not as faithfull in the use of the meanes of grace for though I was constant in the use of them I rather used them as a form than in Spirit—so that I consider that I then stood in a dangerous situation. But God hath been mercifull unto me in shewing me my Danger—The year clos[e]d with signal displays of the power of God at our Camp-meetings, many were convicted and many converted at them.

About the 20 of August [1808] I left the circuit in order to attend Bishop Asbury to the Conference, which we held on the first of October in the state of Tennesee. My wife traveld in Company with us about 3 weaks, untill we came to Bro. Thomases on Hardens Creek in Kentucky. her strength would not admit of her going any further [so] that she taried in them parts untill my return from Conference.[45] When we came to the place where we were to hold our Conference, we had to encamp in the woods through the whole con-

[44] Lakin had been appointed with John Crane to Deer Creek Circuit, Ohio, at the Western Conference held at Chillicothe, Ohio, in September, 1807 (Sweet, *The Rise of Methodism in the West,* p. 137). During this conference year he attended the General Conference at Baltimore. Lakin's appointments on the Deer Creek Circuit in 1807–8, as listed in a manuscript notebook kept by him at the time, included: "Pickaway, Chilicothe, Thos. Bowdels, Ste[phe]n Timmons, Jos. Gardiners, Hotsonpilers, Jos. Petties, Jno Rushes, Thos Chinoweth[s], Lewis Fosters, Peter Paugh[s], Jno Blairs, Dennis Lanes, George Alkires, Hayses, White Brown[s], Strouders, Wm Woods, Ensleys, Nat[hanie]l Bunnels, Saml Davis[es], Jos. Waughs, Benjn. Goldsbury[s], Jno Jefferson[s], Porters, Jonathan Minshalls, Watsons, Isaac Pavey[s], [and] Noteman's."

[45] Bishop Asbury writes of the trip: "Our fare has been rough, but sister Lakin, and the preachers who accompanied us, bore the fatigues of the ride very well" (*Journal of Rev. Francis Asbury* [New York and Cincinnati, n.d.], III, 250). "On Monday (Sep-

ference.[46] In the course of the conference I made one statement to the conference of which I was in doubts of the propriety of makeing it in the manner in which I did which (though it was in no way calculated to any injury to any person or to make any alteration in things) after conference for some weaks gave me sore distress of soul, and brought me to examine my state of soul more closely than I had don[e] for some time. Now it was I saw clearely that state that I had been in the year past, and was astonished to discover the pride of heart I yet possess. It brought me low before God. I saw clearely if I ever was saved it must be by the mercies of God through the merrits of Christ. I was appointed to the Hockhocken Circuit[47] with John Johnston[48]—It was in November before I got into my circuit. I left my wife at Bro. Jesse Spurgins[49] and went on the appointments till Quarter-meeting which was held at Strouds Chappel. Though I did not feel that spirituality of Soul that I wished for; yet I felt some degree of confidence that God would do something great for me in the course of the year and that I should see good times in the circuit. I was in particular drawn out in prayer that God would restore my wife to bodily helth; it seemed to me a very small matter for that God that heals the sickness of the soul to heal the body also.

After Quarter-meeting we made choice of a house that was offered us by Jeremiah Stround (a man that has no religion) to live in. Accordingly the weak [week] of the Q[uarterly] M[eeting] I spent in

---

tember 19) I parted from sister Lakin, wife of Benjamen; so far from being a troublesome companion, she was very useful to me as a nurse and servant for Christ's sake" (*ibid.*, pp. 250–51).

[46] The Western Conference of 1808 convened at Liberty Hill, Tennessee, on October 1. Asbury writes: "Our conference was a camp-meeting, where the preachers ate and slept in tents" (*ibid.*, p. 251).

[47] The Hockhocking Circuit was in southern Ohio, in the valley of the Hocking River (see map, p. 205). Lakin's manuscript list of appointments served on the circuit in 1808–9 includes the following: "Salem M[eeting] H[ouse], Morrises, D. Coles, Strouds Chap[el], Yankee Town, Spurgins, Climers, Stephensons, Williams, Leonards, Seles, Frankling, Whites, Esq Hookers, Mickies or Betties, Culbersons, Jefferson, Emmitts, Bethel M[eeting] H[ouse], Rawlses, Rideinghours, Robucks, Monnetts, Lanchester, George Bohman[s], Brinks, J. Jones[es], Graves S[chool] House, [and] John Fords."

[48] Johnson was admitted on trial to the Western Conference this year.

[49] Spurgeon was in 1811 admitted on trial to the Western Conference.

moving my goods and fixing my wife. I could but remark some things in our comeing to this place that looked like the providence of God had pointed it out to us: 1. When we started from Kentucky to come to the circuit we had pleasant weather until I came with my wife to J. Spurgins. And the next [day] it began to rain and continued stormy till Q[uarterly] M[eeting]. (2) When I went to move our goods I had pleasent weather from the day I started till I came with them to the place and then the same night it began to rain and came a flood of waters. (3) Though in the time I was gone, by extraordinary exertions I was in a great perspiration, and in that situation had to ride the Scioto River three times the water comeing near my knees, and afterward had to ride about one mile with my wet clothes on, Yet I took no hurt thereby—And though I expected the consequence to be scerious yet the Lord preserved me unhurt—Oh! that I may render him the prais due to his name.—

After haveing made some arangements in our temporal affairs on Monday December the 5 I left home to enter fully on the work of the circuit. . . . .

Wed. [*May*] *24* [*1809*]. Yesterday left home under some scerious apprehensions that my wife is shortly to be taken from me. I was much oppressed in mind. Last night I dreamed that I was in a house, and there came a Whip-poor-Will, and fluttered along before the door, it then came into the house, selected me out from all that were in the [house] hovered round me and sat upon my head. I was much distressed in my Sleep takeing it to be a token of my wife's death—Today though I was much disordered in body I rode about 16 miles, and endeavoured to preach (though my Spirit was bowed down by the infirmity of the body) and Joined 4 in Society—

Sund. 28. Just after I came to Nevels (Pickaway Plains) there came on one of the most tremendious haricanes of wind &c that I ever knew; it took down fences, unroofed some houses, and tore the timber up by the roots &c—[so] That the roads in many places are so covered with timber that it is difficult traveling—This storm as we understand hath extended for hundreds of miles in every direction—many Beasts have been killed in it but we have heard of no men, women, or children being hurt. what a mercy of God that many lives were not lost.—

June. Sat 10. Being the day that a free intercours is again to take place between the United States of America and the British dominions[50] I preached from Psalm 116 and 12–13. And endeavoured to enforce the necessity of improveing our religious, and civil liberty to the Glory of God—I had some scerious thought when took into view the Joy that appeared among the people when the Presidents proclamation was issued declareing this day to be the day of free intercourse and how ready the people are to take the Benefits of it. But upon the other hand though there is a proclamation from the God of heaven that there is free intercouse to his throne, yet how few are willing to take the benifit of it.

Thursd. 15. Rode about 20 mile[s] to the Welsh setelment. The roads were very deep and Bad as they run principaly through Beach flats and Swamps, and the season has been rainy. I preach[ed] with plainness to a small congregation, And intend takeing them into the Circuit, Though we have about 20 miles to come to it and about the same distance to the next appointment from it and about one half the way nothing but a small trace through the woods—the setelement takes its name from the seteller[s] coming principally from Wales.

Sund. 18. Yesterday and today had preaching and Sacrament in Franklington, we had a good time and one or two converted.

Frid. 23. Am resolved to read and study divine subject[s] more than I have done. In readeing a commentary on the charactor of David I had a deep impression that God was about to take my wife from me to prevent me from placeing my affections so much on her as to draw my heart from God. The impression was almost more than I could bear[.] my strength [so] failed me that I could scerce sit in my chier [chair] I was abashed, confused, and confounded before God. I cried unto the Lord, and though it touched me in the tenderest point, resigned my all into his hands—Saying oh! Lord if it is thy will to take her hence grant me the priveledge of being present—From whatever source my fears for her life may proceed they haunt me from day to day—Lord stand by me in all that may lay before me.....

Sept. 1 [1809]. in crossing the Scioto, My Horse plunged into deep water. he swam round and came out the same side I went in at; and in geting out up a steep Bank lost my [saddle] baggs and was sometime before I could get them again. Just as I got my baggs and started

[50] On this date the restrictive provisions of the Embargo and Nonintercourse Acts of 1807, against trade with Great Britain, were relaxed.

the Ague took me[.] I rode about three Miles [with] my wet clothes on, shake [shaking], and pukeing till I puked blood. On the next morning I attended the meeting and preached. About 11 o'cl. Bishop McKendree[51] arrived at the Meeting, my weak state and the unexpected arival of an old friend was almost more than I could support under. We spent the evening togather in private and had the oppertunity of converseing on several things relative to the church.

Sund. 3. I was not able to attend the meet but had to be in bed in a camp with the Ague and fever.

On Mond. 4. After administering the Sacrament set out for home in company with J. Spurgin and N. Bright. we lodged at Bro. Monnetts.

Tuesd. 5. Set out early and was soon taken with the Ague. I had a painfull days ride for after the fever came on I could seldem ride more than two or three miles without sleeping by the road side. Bro. Spurgin continued with me till arived at home in the afternoon where I met Bishop Asbury. Though I had the Ague every other day, at Mr Asburys request on Frid. 8. we set out with him to conference.[52] we were not able to keep up with him constantly as sometimes I was not able to travel.—

On Thursd. 21. Mr Asbury gave me a sweat with a solution [of] tarter in wine, which broke the Ague and freed me from it. But on Thursd. 28. In rideing through an excessive hot sun it brought on a fever again whch continued every other day the greater part of conference.

On Mond. Oct. 9. Conference ended. The administration of the Sacrament was put off till after conference rose. But in consequence of some things I was in hast[e] to leve Cincinati I did not stay to the Sacrament which has given me such pain since that I should so lightly esteem the ordinance of the Lord. My appointment was to Hockhocken Circuit[53] again, as I had suffered much there the year before

[51] McKendree had been elected bishop at the General Conference of 1808, which Lakin attended.

[52] The Western Conference of 1809 was held at Cincinnati, Ohio.

[53] Besides the appointments served in 1808–9, Lakin during this conference year added the following to the circuit: "Coloniel Dernes, W. Hedges, H. Musselmans, Dunckans Plain, Morris Moors, Cents, Delaware, Simmons, [and] Mattoon[s]." John Manley was assigned to the circuit as junior preacher.

I had much rather had some other appointment. We went on from conference and visited mine, and my wifes friends and came to the circuit at the Pikeway Plains on Sund. 29. After makeing some temporal arangements, a room being offered us in Lanchester we accepted of it and moved there on Tuesda. November 7. and on Thursd. 9. set out on my appointments[.] on the 18. and 19. Was Q. Meeting[.] I felt a extraordinary weight on me but was much blessed at the Sacrament. I have come to the Circuit with much dejection of Spirit. I have been looking back on my afflictions and the cause of them. And I find them to be in mercy to bring me to a sence of my state. It seems as if God intended to shew me my formality that I had in some degree fallen into, and to discover what pride I was in danger of falling into—I have for some time been praying to God to humble me in his sight. This he is doing. But every blessing I hear [here] receive gives me pain. I go oppressed and burdened every day—I am thankfull to God—I feel often as if some weighty thing lay just before me, and every temporal comfort was Just about to depart from me. I try to repose my soul on God and find in him comfort. I look back and find I have not been as faithful as I should have been. I am resolved to talk less, read and pray, and take up my cross more than I have ever don[e]. I pray God to keep me little and make me unknown in the world. Sometimes my conflicts are such that it seems to strain every nerve. Surely I wrastle not only against flesh and blood but against principalities and powers yea against wicked Spirits in high places. Yet I pray God to try me to the utmost and let me know what I am.

I many times feel so ignorant that I ought not to preach yet I think God hath called me to the work and I must go on—In my reflections heaven appears delightful, hell appears Dreadfull, Gods law thunders, But Mercy pleads and the blood of Jesus turns its thunders by—

This day December 6. While I wright [write] I feel I love God, and am resolved to spend and be spent for him, And am confident that all my tryals shall be for my good and his Glory so be it.

Frid. December 8. For several days past have been rideing through rain; and Sleeping in damp beds, which hath in some degree injured my helth. Last night though I was shut up in a dirty cabbin; I had a dry bed, [so] that I slept comfortable. Today rode through rain Snow and ice, and had to swim my horse across the Scioto River. I spoke plain things to a confused Society from Gallations 6.3–5. Afterward spent about one hour with the class in hearing their complaints, and found it necessary to appoint a committee and set a time for examining into the charactor of two Exhorters, and other members.

I made this a day of solemn fasting, and took no refreshment until candle light. I felt a degree of serenity of mind, and trust that God will heare me through all my difficulties that are before me.

Sund. 10. In the morning was much affected in reading the 45. Chap[ter] of Jeremiah. And felt a confidence in God that notwithstanding all my difficulties if I am faithfull my life shall be given me for a prey[?]. I endeavoured in speaking to come home to the conscience and believe the word was not in vain—Sister Grub gave me the following relation. A man and his wife set out for religion last summer[.] They had been [so] very wicked and covetous that they would not suffer any person to have a peach out of their orchard[.] after they engaged in religion they became very free and in the season haveing plenty of peaches they [were] willing their neighbours should share with the[m] [the] woman observing that though they had plenty now, yet God was able to prevent their haveing any another year and her neighbours should shear [share] with her—Since her conversion she had several times sent flouer to some poor women; but one day geting a bag of flour she would keep that and would give none of it away to the poor women who perhaps never thanked her for it. She went and Baked herself some cakes and set down to eat, she got distressed and could eat [no] more untill she first sent some of her flour to a poor woman and then she sat down and eat hartily—Here is religion teaching the[m] to be liberal, for they had not been taught by preaching as they had not heard a sermon perhaps for five years.

December 1809—Thursday 14. Rode about 17 miles to my appointment, the snow fell moderately the most of the way, and blew in my face. There were but few attended preaching But when I attempted to preach to them such a Stupor of Spirit and drowsyness came on me that I do not remember ever to have experienced the like. I could (either in prayer or preaching) scercely keep from falling asleep. And several times I so lost my subject that I expect I sometimes spoke nonsense. The drowsiness continued one [on] me untill evening when it was succeeded by a chill and some degree of feever. Surely the corruptible body presses down the Spirit, and we need support from heaven for both. At night in reading [the] Lamentation[s] of Jeremiah I had a distant view of the distress of the Prophet for the state of the Jewis[h] Church; but could not feel for the present state of the Church as I wish to do.

Sund. 17. This morning was humble before God, for past failures, and in takeing view of the Church, and Ministry, it looks as if we were sinking into refined Epicurianism—while we eat and drink, and the more part of us seem to live more by sense than faith. I feel bound by the grace of God to bring myself under stricter mortification than I have ever don[e]. . . . .

Frid. [*April*] *13* [*1810*]. Was a day of deep exercise of mind, my wife and some of my friends seems to express a wish for me to locate and engage in teaching a school. But I do not see my way cleare, it gave me sensable pain to think that her wishes seemed to clash with [what] I felt to be duty (I am sensible there are but few in her feble situation but what would wish it) I made it a day of humiliation and prayer to God for direction in this case, I was led to pray fervently to God that if I was about to take any step in this or any other case as would be contrary to his will, rather than [that] I should sin agains[t] him to take me out of the world, I recollect what I suffered when I was formaly [formerly] located. I tremble at the idea of locateing unless I am fully convinced it is the will of [God]. I fear at present in that state I should be unhappy.

Sund. 15. Was so unwell that I could scerce keep up. But in preaching found strength of body and had some degree of liberty to speak. In the afternoon, my mind was much exercised about a subject to speak on at night, it seemed as if there was no text in the Bible that I could preach from. I had fixed upon a subject to speak from, but when I came to preach changed my subject and spoke plain from John 3.18–21.

Wed. 18. Yesterday was very unwell, today took Phisic and was weak, but at night was able to attend prayer meeting with a few friends. From my own feble situation and the situation of some others, I viewed it as one of the greatest priveledges on this side eternity, that after the pains, labours, and buisy scenes of the day, that we had the oppertunity of laying them in some degree aside, and uniteing togather to worship God. My mind drove on to the time when after death (if we are faithfull to God) we shall leve all the bustle of this word and rest with God. My soul was happy.....

Mond. [*April*] *30* [*1810*]. Have been for several days preaching twice a day, am much fatiegued in body—Today received the following account. In the neighbourhood of Thomas Morris, in Franklin County, Ohio, on the 23 day of February, a young man died. the Joiner that made the coffin was working at it late in the night, he had got it put togather (and made with duftails) between he supposes 10 or 11 Ocloc, that [when] all the cocks crew [and] the coffin droped to pieces. he was much allarmed at the circumstance. But recollecting he had heard old workmen say, that if a coffin fell apart after it was put together it was a token that there would be another made soon in the Same Shop—Accordingly on March 26, he was called on to make a second coffin, which after he had got it put together also the Joints fell apart. On April 19, He was called on to make a third coffin, which after he had made it and screwed on the lid, the screws all Broke as two or three of them did after the corp[se] was in the Coffin. Whether these are tokens of something that is [to] come to pass or no, they [are] certainly worthy of observeing to see what may follow. As the workman is Deistically inclined he cannot be thought supersticiously to favour things of this nature; and yet .... his takeing [it] as a token of what should happen is a concession that God can reveal things to men. After preaching, I aranged some matters in the class, and gave them my thoughts on the growing evil of drunkeness, and the one cause of it is the practice of haveing Spiritous liquors at house raisings &c.....

Tuesd. [*May*] *8* [*1810*]. Was in an humble frame of mind as I rode to my appointment I was considering whether it would be proper for me to make choice of a station in life for myself. I dare not chuse, I am not my own, But belong to God, the Church, and My Country and where they call I must go.....

Frid. [*June*] *29* [*1810*]. At Bro. Climers had some liberty in preaching from Luke 7.11–16. Just as I was going to meet the class I was prevented by one of Bro Charles Climers children being brought in that had fallen from the upper floor and had been taken up as dead. There were none of the family at home (they being at meeting) but the Children, they took up the child and shook it and hollowed over it but it still lay as dead. One of the children a boy (perhaps) about 10 or 12 years old made one of the other children take the Child out of the door and hold it up and he took a gun and shot over it which brought it too immediately. Perhaps the report of the gun like an electric shock gave motion to the heart and set the blood in circula-[t]ion—But how strange that a child of that age; even had he have heard of such a thing before should have had the presence of mind to have used the meanes, But how much more so haveing never heard of the like—May it not be the inspiration of the all Mighty, to turn the attention of men to the subject for wise ends, even the rescueing of others from death.—Or perhaps the fall might cause such a tention [tension] of the nerves as to unfit them for their proper functions, and of course the cessation of all motion, with the loss of Breath. but at the same time this tention being overcome by the shock given by the report of the gun might cause the nerves to vibrate, being an undulation suited to give them a proper tone and of course restored life again.

July. Frid. 6. Had an oppertunity of enquireing into the circumstances of the Indian that was killed by order of their Council on Satureday, June. 16. He received the scentance of death with calmness; tho he declared himself to be innocent of the crime he was charged with (which according to the best information I could get was Witchcraft). As there were several white people present they offered to ransom him, and offered two good horses one of them [a] stud and perhaps worth 200 or 300 Dollars but all in vain[;] he must die. He was taken in the morning and executed in the afternoon. The Indian fell on his knees and prayed, he then went to the River and washed himself and put on clean clothes, he then painted himself[,] ate a hearty meal and smoked his pipe, he then prayed again, then walked to his grave, and looked into it[,] clasped his hands togather raised his eyes to heaven and the tears ran down his cheeks, he told the people that he should go above and said when they met him their [there] they would know that he died innocent. he kneeled down and prayed again, and the old Chief that came to kill him prayed also, he then sat down put his hands over his face and received the fatal Blow with the Tomahawk. he was a long time dieing[.] the other Indians said he was a bad man long time dieing, good men die soon. In reflecting on the circumstance of the old Indians being condemned unheard, and receiveing the scentance and execution in the same day,

I felt thankfull to God for liveing under a well regulated Government where men are not to be condemned unheard, and not to be executed without time to repent.....

August 31, 1810. Our Yearly Camp meeting began: At which through Brother Jesse Spurgin, I received from Bishop McKendree a special request, that I would visit some Black people that live at the Upper Sandusky (Indian) Town.[54] After consulting Brother Sale[55] on the subject, I concluded to go: though I was convinced that it would be at the risk of my helth, if not of my life. Our Camp-meeting ended on Monday, Sept, 3. we had a good time, some were convicted, and some converted. I felt an uncommon degree of effiminacy at parting with my Hockhocking friends; haveing suffered much among them for two years, I felt my soul much united to them, and being about to part with them it seemed almost like leveing a part of my self behind. And I have observed that where I have suffered most, I always find it the hardest to part with the people.

Tuesd. 4. Left my wife at Mr Nevils and set out for the Indian Town, and called on Brothers J. Lambert and Thos. Morriss who are going with me; and according to appointment met Bro. Jesse Spurgin at Franklington.

Wed. 5. We set out before Sun rise[.] Brakefasted at bro. Graces, and called on G. Surlot, who supplies us with Jerk[56] for our Journey

[54] Upper Sandusky, in the present county of Wyandot in northwestern Ohio, was located on the Sandusky River about sixty miles south of Lake Erie. Six years after Lakin's visit, regular missionary work was begun among the Wyandot Indians by a Virginia Negro named John Stewart, who himself boasted of Indian blood. James B. Finley of the Ohio Conference was appointed missionary to the Wyandots in 1821. Finley was the first historian of the mission (see his *History of the Wyandott Mission* [1840]). Finley's other works, *Autobiography, Life among the Indians,* and *Sketches of Western Methodism,* also give material illustrative of this pioneer Methodist missionary venture. See also William Warren Sweet, *Circuit-Rider Days along the Ohio* (New York and Cincinnati, 1923), chap. iv. The Indian whose execution is described above was a Wyandot chief known as Featherlips. His execution—for refusing to join the Tecumseh Confederacy—took place on the banks of the Sciota, about ten miles north of Columbus, Ohio. Here he lies buried, with his grave marked by a granite monument erected by the Wyandotte Club of Columbus.

[55] John Sale (1769–1827), a native of Virginia who had been admitted on trial to the traveling connection in 1795, was, in 1810, Lakin's superior as presiding elder of the Miami District.

[56] Jerk (Sp.: *charqui*) was dried strips of venison or beef, a staple provision of the pioneer traveler.

and in the evening came to Bro. Hopkins in the Welsh Setelment. here we met with Bro. Robert Perry, and as he has some acquaintance in the Town we get him to go with us. We concluded to tarry on thursday to rest, and make some preparations for our journey.

Frid. 7. We set out early from the Welsh Settelment, and about 10 ocloc came to the Sandusky Plains. This plain is an open Barrans consisting of some scattering trees in most parts of the plain, and groves of timber; with a thin soil generally inclineing to wet. In traveling about 27 miles through the plains we obtained water once for ourselves but none for our Horses. A little before Sun set we came to what is called Negro Town. Here some Negroes and some Indians dwell. We stoped at the Cabbin of one George Wright, a white man that has a wife half Negro and half Indian. We were kindly received upon telling our buisness. We went into the cabbin of an old Negro that was confined with the Rhumatic Pains. He can read a little and has several Books[.] among them there is a Methodist Hymn Book: he appears desireous to save his own soul. We found about 10 or 12 person[s] that could speak English; among whome are two White men and one Woman. We collected them togather with some Indians; we told them our intentions in comeing to visit them, and sang and prayed with them. Even the Indians conformed by kneeling in time of Prayer. We were kindly invited to lodge in their Cabbins, but we found it necessary to Camp out that our Horses might graze in the Plains, as we had not been able to procure grain for them. They invited us to eat with them, but [we] promised to take Brakefast with them the next morning. In camping we found some difficulty to obtain wood as it was night before we came to the place. Which was about one mile from the Town. After sometime we obtained wood and encamped, without even a tree to shelter us from the dew which was very heavy as we encamped on the bank of the Sandusky River—We found no water among the Indians to drink but the River water which was warm and disagreeable—We let our Horses feed untill about 10 ocloc, we then tighed them till morning and then let them feed again.

Sat. 8. Came early to Town, and received from Cato, a black man the following experience, viz. That he attempted to run from De-Troit about 21 years ago, and was taken by the Indians, after he had been with them about 7 years he began to think about serveing God—

One night he Dreamed that he was traveling to a certain place along a broad road, and asked some the way, they shewed him a narrow blind path filled with blue grass, it went through an open part that he could see almost three mile[s] on each hand; at the far end stood a fine green tree like a broom, and when he came to it he went up steps till he came to a door like a great sheet, he opened it, and went in where was a Town all full of light, but he could see no Sun: he saw some siting at doors reading, and some praying; he went through the Town till he came to a fine Church, he went in and a Minister was preaching, and when he was done Preaching he knelt down and preyed [prayed] a good while. And he then awoke. The next morning he felt like he loved everybody and everything, says he my heart felt cool like when I had been in water. And from that time he went on praying. He had never heard anybody pray in that place before. Surely God can work without meanes—Another that belonged to a Baptist Preacher (I think by the name of Allen) in Kentucky being treated with great severity by his Master, he resolved to leve all his friends and acquaintance[s] and at the risk of his life to run away, which he did about 20 Years ago, and was taken by the Indians near the Mouth of Scioto, His name is Thomas Peters, he gave the following experience. viz. I was hunting Rackoons about 13 years ago, and by falling of a tree and lodging against another, I went up the tree and fell and broke my leg by my knee and lay there Seven days without water, fire, or food, and only my dog for company. After Seven days I cralled into the top of a laying down tree, and I got my Gun and tomahawk and made fire and got my Rackoon and roasted and eat it, and there it was I began to feel for my poor soul. The second night after I got fire I dreamed I saw three men in white comeing to me, one stood on my right side and one on my left and the other before me, the one on my right side said unto me you cannot go yet, you have more to suffer, and then left me. I was much troubled that I was left by those shineing ones, I so wept that I awoke, and was much troubled in mind, I thought all I ever did came upon me and that was the cause of my breaking my leg. My troubles increased till the next morning. Just as the Sun Arose I heard a band of music that appeared in the East, it drew near me and went around me and returned to the East again. The next morning I heard the same music comeing from the same quarter and returned again as before. The third morning it came again, and I believed that God had sent it for my comfort. "My heart got glad and rejoiced, my troubles left my mind and I felt so glad and so light that I thought I could go home. I stearted and crawled two miles to the road, I called and one Indian heard me and came to my help. I was [gone] 19 days and all I had to ate [eat] was one Rackoon. And I still feel the same gladness on to this day when I pray."

About 11 Ocloc I preached from Luke 2.10. I found it difficult to speak in language suited to their capacity. They appeared all attention. some Indians were present, they appeared very solemn. Bro. Lambert exhorted and prayed—I intended preaching to the Indians in their Town in the afternoon, and engaged a Black man to meet us there to interpret for us. We went on before to let our Horses feed in the Prarie. Our Black man met us in the Town according to appointment, but we saw no chance of collecting any of them as it was the day they were seting out to a great Council to be held at the big-rock near Detroit. They were generally gone, their Houses were locked up, and few or none to be seen but those that were seting out. When we returned we were told the Women and Children were in the fields watching their Corn to keep the Black-Birds from distroying it. We returned to Negro Town, where Mr Right had our suppers provided a part of which was Tea, this proved very refreshing to us—We then went to an encampment to let our Horses feed as we had nothing to give them.—

Sund. 9. About 8 Ocloc we returned to the Town, and were informed that they had received news from the Lower Sundusky Town that they were under considerable allarm in consequence of the Sinneca Indians, and others, holding Councils in the night, some other parts of their conduct also show an inclination to go to war with the Winedotts, there is also some fears of the same in the Upper Sundusky Town. It is said in one of the Sinneca Councils (that was held in the night) that some of the Winedotts came into the Council House: and the Sinnecas immediately covered the wampum and closed the Council—In consequence of which the Winedotts held a Council with [the] Sinnecas; it is said that in the course of the Council that some of the Sinnecas Indians Jumped across the Council fire and said they would join the Winedotts—

Between 9 and 10 Ocloc I preached from Acts 16.30. And by the help of a black man to Intarpret I repeated to a few Indians the substance of what I had said to the others, one Indian Woman shed tears—I appointed to preach again about 12 Ocloc—In the intervel between preaching, As Madam Squaw was dressed in her finer dress; when it is a custom among them not to do any work, Mr Right provided us some refreshment of Bread and Milk; he also gave us Some Water Melons which was refreshing to me—I preached according to appointment from Rom. 14.12. After which I spoke by the same interpreter to 6 or 8 Indians, they appeared very sollemn, some of my brethern that were with me observed one young Indian man to shed tears, and sollemnity sat on the countinances of most present. Bro. Jesse Spurgin spoke and closed our meeting. At the close of our meeting the interpreter spoke 8 or 10 Minutes to the Indians and told them that we had been praying for them and their Council. They appeared to express satisfaction—Afterward the interpreter asked the Indians how they liked it, they answered they liked it well. In the course of private conversation I told them our plan of traveling and preaching the gospel, and that while we were thus traveling and preaching we are entirely dependant on the Charity of our friends for support. Their countinances expressed the surprise that some of them felt at what I told them. I endeavoured to give them all the information that I could which I thought might be of use to them—Before we came away Cato requested me to pray in his cabbin, he said it may be Jesus Christ will heare and heal me (he has the Rhumatic pains) According to his request I prayed with him in his cabbin, this our last labour among them. We then set out to an encampment about Seven miles from the Town, we thought this the more necessary as we had but one feed of corn that we had kept for our Horses on our return home, and the encampment is a good place to grass—The Winedotts that live up on the Sundusky River have discovered that the use of Whisky is an evil in consequence of which they have entirely quit the use of it and will suffer none to be brought into their Town—In one of their Councils when they were about laying aside the use of Whiskey, they were promising the Great Spirit that they would drink no more Whisky, when this was put to one of the Chiefs, he refused to make the promis observeing that he did not know whether he could keep that promis, and if he was to tell the Great Spirit that he would drink no more whisky and then was to drink it he should tell lies to the Great Spirit, and that was too scerious a thing—He said he would try not to Drink any more and has remained firm to his resolution. The Winedott nation have of late been much reduced by sickness, which they ascribe to Witchcraft, in consequence of which they have killed many of their nation. last spring they killed a woman and then burnt her—they killed another woman about three weaks ago—They suppose they have yet many witches among them. It is said that all the Six Nations suppose that there are many witches among them and within this two or three years have killed many of their people. The Indians are under cerious impressions concerning their Souls. they have a prophet that teaches them but what his principals [principles] are I could not learn.—I discovered that they are much prejudiced against the Christian name. And no wonder considering the Charractors they have been conversant with, and with them a white man and a Christian is the same. The conduct also of some Ministers that have been sent among them as Missionaries have increaced their prejudices—From what I could discover the present plan of sending missionaries among them will be of but little use to them—The only way that appears to me to profit them would be to get Preachers and lay members from different parts to visit them, to preach to them and converse with them and let them see that there is a difference between a white man and a Christian—In order to [do] this conscianciously to avoid all tradeing with them and to make provision for themselves to be independant of them: yet to be fimiliar with them and not refuse their invitation &c. The removeing of their prejudice is not to be of a day[.] there must be perseverance in the buisness to effect anything among them.

Monday 10. Last night just at dark there came on us a heavy shower of rain, at the same time our horses started, and between secureing our Horses an[d] bagage we got considerable wet, [so] that it took us a considerable time to dry our clothes and blankets. We arose this morning before day and gave our Horses a feed of corn that we had saved for them. we also let them graze for some time and set out just before Sun rise. As we had about 17 miles to ride without water we only eat each one a biscake to prevent our suffering with thirst. About 10 Ocloc we came to Little Scioto where we made a hearty meal on the last of our Bread and Jirk, and about 3 Ocloc came to the Welsh Setelmen[t]. I was much fatieuged, but felt revived on returning to my own people. [September, 1810, to October, 1811, omitted.]

. . . .

October—Tuesd. 1 [*1811*] Conference began in Cincinnati. we had between 50 and 60 members attended. The Preachers in general were under apprehensions that we should have some distressing times in conference as we had much intricate buisness [to] lay before us.[57] The impression upon the whole I believe was profitable to the members as they in general expressed themselves to enjoy more of the presence of God in Conference than they had ever done; which was perhaps in consequence of their being more than common engaged in prayer. for my own part I was more engaged in prayer and felt more of the Spirit of religion than any conference I ever attended.—

We were several days engaged in the most intricate buisness that had ever come before our conference. we had to suspend one man,[58] and another stood so charged that the Conference ordered a committee to enquire into his conduct[.] perhaps there are few cases where as much painfull and intricate buisness is gone through as much in the Christian Spirit as it was in this Conference. The election of our members to General Conference appeared to be without any of the consequences that was feared by some as there appeared a general satisfaction on the subject in conference—The Members that are Elected are the following—S. Parker—D. Young—J. Sale—James Quin—L. Blackman—F. Stires—J. Collins—B. Lakin[59]—J. Axley—W. Pattison—Isaac Quin—W. Houston—T. Stillwell—13—Though I had considerable fatiegue, yet I was supported beyond my expectation. Yet after siting in Conference I was seldom able to attend preaching—Our Conference [adjourned] in peace on Friday. 11.—My appointment is to White Oak Circuit,[60] a station with [which]

[57] See Sweet, *The Rise of Methodism in the West*, pp. 191–207, for the proceedings of this conference.

[58] James Blair.

[59] Lakin attended this first delegated General Conference, which met at New York in 1812.

[60] White Oak Circuit was formed in 1808 out of the Miami Circuit, which Lakin had served in 1805–6. It lay in southern Ohio, in the vicinity of Clermont County. According to Lakin's manuscript list, the circuit included these appointments in 1811–12: "McCormack[s], Wards, Lights, Kerns, Dales, Gilberts, Fees M[eeting] H[ouse],

I am well pleased—We Judged it would be expedient to divide the Western Conference—And the Ohio is recommended as the division line, but this I do not think will stand.[61] we appointed (in case the Conference is divided) one conference to be held in Chillicothe the First of October next, and the other at Fountainhead in Tenesee in November—but should not the Conference be divided it is to be held in Chillicothe.....

[*Tuesday, July 7, 1812.*] I have reason to fear that too many of the preachers wish for and are seeking honour. In viewing the pains that attend an high station, and how far it cuts off more close communion with the common people I concluded I would not be a Bishop or Presideing Elder on any account—One day while on my Journey haveing a little time for retirement I fell into the following train of reflection viz. According to Hebrews 11. Faith is always founded on a command or promis, or call from God. This distinguishes it from presumption, which is destitute of either call, promis or command.

I believe that God hath called me to travel and preach the Gospel. In this way I can trust God for soul and body. My belief is founded on (1) A conviction of duty. (2) on seeing some fruit of my labours (3) on the accomplishment of Gods promises to supply my wants and to make my way clere before me, and giveing me all the satisfaction in the enjoyment of the comforts of life that in their own nature can arise from them. (4) That when located though God gave me the comforts of life he took the enjoyment of them from me—I cannot see that I could now locate in faith because (1) I am sensible that I am called to travel, (2) I am not sensible that this call is reversed by a call to locate (3) If I locate without a call there I shall be out of the order of God [and] (4) In that situation cannot expect the blessing of God—

Such reflections then passed my mind and I yet view them in the same light—I have had some scerious thoughts on my feelings con-

---

Hopewell M[eeting] H[ouse], J Sargant[s], Juds, Shingles, Lemings, Ezeker Davis[es], Strait Creek M[eeting] H[ouse], Stropf[s], Slons, Davidson[s], Cloverlick M[eeting] H[ouse], Dunams Town, Collins, Hutchison[s], Frees, Mitchels, Deals, Teals, Burditt[s], [and] Starlings Fork."

[61] The divison of the Western Conference into the Ohio and Tennessee conferences was approved by the General Conference of 1812. Lakin remained in the Ohio Conference, which included the Kentucky and Salt River districts in the state of Kentucky as well as the Ohio circuits.

cerning the War. I have had fears from my feelings runing across my Judgment that I must have lost my love to God and man. But I am not sensible of it. In converseing with some of my friends I find they have the same thoughts and feelings. [July, 1812, to January, 1814, omitted.]

. . . .

1814. January 1.[62] On our way to Shannon we mett a number of people going to buy and hire Negros. Oh the curse of Negro Slavery. yet we had a tollarable congregation, And a tollarable good time the next morning at lovefeast. I had some liberty in preaching from II Peter 1.10. E. Truett[63] preached after me[.] the congregation gave great attention[.] I think there were Women stood three hours—

Sat. 9. and Sund. 10. Had meeting at Kenton Town. Being very unwell I only preached on Sunday. We had but few to commune. I spoke plain to them on the subject and think it had its influence. At night we had a good time and one or two Backsliders professed to be reclaimed[.] Through this meeting I was so oppressed in my breast that it was with pain that I sat in the congregation, [so] that I had the most part of the time to stay in another room.

Tuesday. 12. After preaching at night at Edward Pattisons, I felt sensible pain in heareing of the cruelties exercised on the poor Slaves. The Whites About Christmas and New year had been danceing, and the Negroes in immitation of them collected one night and had a dance. one woman among them got so intoxicated that she laid out and died in the woods—The rest were taken before a majestrate and received from 10 to 35 lashes for thus brake [breaking] a law they never consented to—This is Republicanism in Kentucky—If there is Justice in the univerce, does not the blood of these people cry for vengance, and will not God soon avenge their cause on their oppressors......

[*February 9, 1814.*] This morning about daylight I set out to my appointment And rode about 22 miles through deep and heavy mud and came to Bro. Fentons in time to preach. (I had a slavish ride as it rained on me neare all the way)—I had but few hearers as I had an

[62] In 1813–14 Lakin was again serving the Limestone Circuit in Kentucky.

[63] Eli Truitt was a local preacher residing within the bounds of Limestone Circuit. He had, however, been a traveling preacher from 1808 until 1811 and later was re-admitted and became a missionary to the Indians of Michigan (Arnold, *op. cit.*, I, 319).

appointment in the neighbourhood the evening before and had not attended it, [so] that the people did not expect me—The next morning Bro. Fentons Son began to make some objections to their holding prayer meetings too long &c. I observed to him that the reason he thought them too long was that he had no disposition suited to them, And appealed to his conduct the evening before in staying at a weding until about 12 Ocloc at night—that the reason he was not so soon tired of being at the weding was he had a disposition to it—And if he had the same disposition to pray he would not be so soon tired of it—he owned it was the case....

[*Tuesday, March 15, 1814.*] I have been makeing some enquirey into the cause of the gloom that is on the minds of professors and the decline of religion. Lately an old Brother observed that he had observed for some time our preaching to begin with the fall of man, the Redemption by Jesus Christ, repentance and Justification by faith, and here we stoped and for a long time he had not heard the doctrine of sanctification enforced—I immediately began to make my observation on experiences that I heare, and for a considerable time have observed them go as far as Justification and there stop and no talk of sanctification. I have further observed that professors have loss [lost] (at least too many of them) that bright evidence of their acceptance with God they once had, and rest too much on general determinations to serve God—And as I have reason to thank God that there is as little immoral conduct among us as I could expect among so large a body I concluded the following causes have produced this effect (1) The confused state of affairs and the intrest every man takes in the event of the war—(2) We have preached the gospel but have been deficient in enforcing the doctrine of sanctification, and (3) the people stoped In a Justified state without persueing holiness—Immediately set about a reform in myself and began to preach and enforce the doctrine of holiness by shewing the state I found the people to be in and the need of perfecting holiness in the fear of God. [March, 1814, to September, 1816, omitted.]

. . . .

September—Tuesd. 3. [*1816*] Our Conference commenced.[64] we went through the buisness of our Conference with much satisfaction

[64] Louisville, Kentucky, was the seat of the conference this year.

haveing no difficulties of consequence, one young man we dismissed in consequence of his haveing maried the first of his traveling,[65] (And as it seemed to be coming common for the young men to marry immediately on seting out to travel we thought it time to do something to prevent it). But afterward gave the Presideing Elder liberty to employ him.

In consequence of some remonst[r]ances of our friends on the Subject of Free-Masonry—the Conference resolved that they considered any traveling preacher Joining with and associateing with the Masons in their lodges &c as degradeing their Charractor—and adviseing our Local Preachers and members not to Join or associate with the Masonic lodges. Though my state of helth seemed almost to require to take a Supernum[er]ary Station there were so many asking Supernumer[ar]y stations I resolved to take my station as usual and was appointed with Samuel Baker[66] to Hinkston Circuit again by my own Choice the Bishop haveing requested me to chose a circuit for myself—We had some souls converted and I trust the Conference will be made a blessing to the place—Our Conference closed on Mond. 9. I never knew the preachers to take their appointments with more satisfaction.

Tues. 10. We left Louisville and rode to Shelbyvill, the ride was too hard for me. I was scerce able to keep up for a day or two—we went the next day to Brother E. Talbots where we taried till friday. We then made short rides as we were able and came home to Bro. Wm Martins on Tuesd. 17. Where we intend makeing our home another year—

Frid. 20. I took the Circuit at Bro. Grimeses. But such is my bodily infirmities I know not whether I shall be able to fill it through the year, but the event of these things I must leve to God. If he hath anything more for me to do he will give me strength and if ye say ceas[e] to work or live I am content—This is the first Circuit I ever rode about 22. years ago—Sometimes I have thought that this year may close my life and labours on this Circuit. Be it as it may I want [so] to live that I may be always ready and be found doing the will of God.

[65] Evidently David Tickner (see Sweet, *Circuit Rider Days along the Ohio,* p. 142).

[66] Samuel Baker (1793–1823), who was born in Baltimore, Maryland, began to travel in the Ohio Conference in 1816 and continued until his early death.

Oct. Mond. 7. I returned home and met Brother Baker my Collegue. he appears to be a teachable young man, I endeavoured to give him the best instructions I could and trust that God will make him usefull on the Circuit—

Sat. 19. At Phillips Meeting House after preaching—Mr Judy the man that Brother Nelson[67] wanted to be licenced to Exhort at our last Quarter-meeting, left our Church. The reason he assigned was that he could not believe in our doctrine of Baptism and Christian Perfection and as our rules did not admit him to oppose them in public or private he left us being resolved to oppose them. Had we have licenced him we should have had our trouble with him.

Tuesd. 22. I expected to have had difficulties but had none—In preaching one woman was much affected[.] she trembled before the Lord[.] may it be lasting—The next day one that had been some time in society but was not converted in class cried aloud [and] trembled from head to foot.

Thursd. 24. At Bro. Hunts some seemed to be affected, may this buding of grace end in a glorious harvest of convertions. We continued on through the year as I was not able to attend constand [constantly] I committed the buisness of the Circuit mostly to Brother Baker and only attended to the most difficult cases, and in the third Quarter for some time my place was supplied by Brother John P. Taylor[68] who we took on the Circuit at the third Quarter-meeting and thus prepared his way into the work—We closed the year in peace and trust some good was done this year.

Though my bodily infirmities we[re] considerable I attended the Conference at Zenesville which [met] September 1817, and was appointed Supernumer[ar]y with Jonathan Stamper[69] and Richard Corwine[70] though I was not able to travel much yet I felt my heart in the work and was united to the preachers. I made my residence

[67] Thomas Nelson, who during the previous year had served Hinkstone Circuit with Lakin.

[68] Taylor was admitted on trial to the Ohio Conference this year.

[69] Jonathan Stamper (1791–1864) was a native of Kentucky who had been admitted on trial to the Western Conference in 1811. He served as circuit preacher and presiding elder during his eventful career.

[70] Richard Corwine (1789–1843), a native of Kentucky, served more than a dozen circuits during his active ministry.

this year in Bourbon County that I might be convenient to Paris and spend considerable of my time there as this was one object of my appointment, I spent this year the most of the time in the neighbourhood where we lived and Paris and trust that I was of some use in borth [both] places.

In this year I began to experience the accomplishment of Gods promises, that if we "seek first the Kingdom of God and his righteousness all these things shall be ad[d]ed unto you[.]" my friends were as tender of us as if we had been their own children and liberally contributed to our support—As the year began to draw to a close and I was not able to take a station my mind was much exercised where we should fix our home but could come to no determination but expected to go to State of Ohio and settle on a small piece of land I have there but as there was no improvement on it the prospect appeared gloomy, and my friends in the Circuit would not consent to it but insisted that I should continue in the Circuit that they might help to maintain us. we had also a pressing invitation from a few friends in Versails Woodford County to come to them and they would support us, [so] that my mind was in an entire state of suspence, but still my mind seemed most drawn to the State of Ohio. I had in my mind several reasons for to go there but the greatest was some unaccountable impression that there was something for me to do in that part. But at the last Quarter meeting from the importunity of my friends I gave up to continue a little longer in Kentuck and expected to be in Hinkson Circuit. As my helth did not admit of my attending Conference which was held at Stubanville on the 7 of August 1817 [1818]. We visited our friends in Ohio. While we were there my impressions returned with weight that that was yet to be the place for me to come too [to], and more especially in prayer and when my Soul had the nearest access to God the impression was most on my mind but the way seemed shut up—The preacher in the Fleming Circuit had appointed a Camp-meeting near Flemingsburgh on their return from Conference. We attended it and had the oppertunity of seeing many of our old friends. We had a good time and some souls were converted at the meeting. After the meeting we returned home to attend a campmeeting in Hinkson Circuit which was to commence the Second Friday in September—accordingly we attended the campmeeting and the power of the Lord was present and sinners wer converted to God many of the fine dressy ones and some of [the] taul sons of Anack came down to cry for mercy, and found the Lord. Brother Becrafts daughter was among the converted and when we returned home we found her triming off her ruffels—I have never known a greater change in dress than hath taken place in this neighbourhood since the Lord began to revive his work in it—At the Campmeeting I received a pressing request from our friends in Versails through Bro. Richard Rowland and a letter from Brother Long, to come to them and they would support us, and I might preach when I was able. Brother Roland urged the necessity of my going as the Methodist[71] were few and feble and the Baptist were opposeing and triumphing over them on every hand. As Bishop George[72] was at the meeting I laid the subject before him for his council. he advised me to go if the place would suit my state of helth. accordingly I sent them word that we would come and see them and tarry awhile, accordingly we paid them a short vissit of a few days and made arangements to return as soon as we could. When we returned to brother Becrafts we found them all in distress, his daughter had got into doubts and was crying continually, and her Mother was not in a much better situation [so] that we found work enough to comfort and get them reconciled.—As brother Becraft was gone to Maryland, we felt ourselves under obligations to tarry with his familly untill his return. In [the] time we were waiting for his return we packed up our goods and moved them to Brother Nuns to store them up till we should know what we would do, for as yet we had not concluded to continue long at Versails, only to go and see how it would suit us—Upon Brother Becrafts comeing home we immediately set out to Versails, and concluded for a while to live among our Christian friends for a time, which we did the whole year without moveing our goods. When I came to this place everything with regard to religion was gloomy, the society consisted of about Fifteen members and but few of them had the knowledge of the forgiveness of their sins and scercely any even to pray in public. The Baptist [were][73] beareing down all before them, and misrepresenting the doctrines of Methodism on all oc-

[71] "Methodist," i.e., without sounding the final *s*, was the common frontier pronunciation of the plural "Methodists." Cf. also "Baptist," below.

[72] Enoch George (1767–1828).

[73] See n. 71.

casions, [so] that the people in general considered the Methodist as an ignorant people depending on their own works to save them, [so] That before there was any prospect of doing any good the wrong impressions that were on the peoples minds must first be removed. In order to do this without attemping to enter into controversy with our opponants, and considering that produceing light was the best way to expell darkness, I began with the first principals of religion to explain our doctrine in the best manner that [I was] capable of and I think in doing this I found divine assistance. And indeed I never more felt my need of the aid of the Holy Spirit than I have since I have been in this place—The preachers on the Circuit had their difficulties to encounter, and much opposition to overcome [so] that borth [both] in this Town and in the Circuit, things wore a gloomy appearance. But towards the latter end of the year our prospects became better—In June 1819 we held a camp-meeting in the neighbourhood of Versails, (before the meeting came on many bad things were said about Campmeetings by our enemies and some of our friends were somewhat opposed to them), the Lord vissited us at our meeting[.] sinners were convicted and some converted—from this time our prospects began to be better and a new society was raised about Seven miles from Town —Our Campmeeting I have reason to believe went to remove much of the prejudice from the minds of the people in Town and Country and appeared to lay a foundation for good to be done.

In the course of the year our Society in Town had some addition to it. Our members were united and loveing, though we did not appear to have much zeal among us, yet I believe the Lord was with us and gave us divine support or we must have sunk under our difficulties.

Through the whole year my mind was undetermined as to my continuing any length of time in this place. Our friends were as kind to us as if we had been their own children, Sometimes I have felt myself oppressed by their kindness. I felt thankfull to them as the instruments and God as the author of all the temporal good things I enjoy. May we be able to improve them all to the glory of God, my own and others good. All this time I felt an unaccountable reluctance to continue here, sometimes I felt willing to stay, at other times my reluctance to staying was so great that my mind would be quite dejected, and I felt as if I could not stay any length of time, and had it not been that I was convinced that for the time present I was in the order of God I must have left the place. But in this as in many other thing[s] God hath overruled my inclinations, and I trust will in all things overrule me and all I have to his glory—If God is glorified by me, and through me, the end for which I wish to live is answered completely—it is all I want—The time of Conference which was to commence on the 7 of August 1819 was appr[o]aching, my friends were anxious to know whether I would continue with them, I let them know that if the conference gave me any station that I could fill, the relation I stood in to them bound me to take it. But if they left me in the same relation that I then stood (which was Superanuated) I would continue in Versails—The time of conference was approaching and I had been makeing my arangements to attend it. but my friends insisted I was not able to go, [so] that I declind going, and attended the last Quarter-meeting in the Circuit, where I met Bishop McKendree. he expected some important buisness to come before Conference, and he thought it necessary that as many of the old preachers as could attend ought to be there, and requested me to go if possible. accordingly I concluded to go, and returned to Versails to make some preparation that [was] necessary intending to meet the Bishop at the Licking Quarter-meeting and go on with him to Cincinnati—But afterward thought I could travel easier by going by Flemingsburgh, and on Sat. July 24. We set out for Conference and the next day preached in Paris. on Monday 26 Just as we lef Paris I was taken with a Bowel complaint, and was not able to ride more than 16 miles to Brother Riggs's, where I was confined untill Wednesday, and with much fatiegue on Friday came to Father Hintons. On the next day we went to the Campmeeting (that was held in the neighbourhood), but was obliged to lie down in a tent the most part of the day; On the next day borth [both] my self and my wife were partly confined to bed by sickness, which was our situation for several days, [so] that I was unable either to attend the meeting or go on to Conference. I felt resigned to the will of God, confident that his will in all things is best.—As I was not able to attend Conference, I was disappointed in vissiting my Brother as I intended. We concluded to tarry where we were untill we heard from Conference—When I got information it was that I was continued superanuated. Our friends in Fleming were desireous for us to come and live among them. But my word was out to return to Versails accordingly as soon as we thought ourselves able to beare the fatiegue of traveling we set out on our return. But on our way we got our Dearbourn[74] turned over, and our Horse ran off with the fore wheles, and broke the axeltree, and ran about two miles before I caught him—The following him so far on foot and repareing our carriage fatiegued me much. But we made out to get with it too Millersburgh where we got our Dearbourn repared—The same night our Horse broke out and left us, and we did not get him again for some weaks [weeks]. After we got our Carriage mended, Brother Nun sent us a Horse and we [rode] to his House to see about our goods we had left there. We staid two or three days. our friends from Versails haveing sent us another Horse, Brother Nun offered his Waggon to carry our goods. we took them and without haveing the oppertunity of vissiting any more of our friends, we returned to Versails, Where our friends furnish us a House and all we want. If God will reward a cup of cold water given in the name of a discipl[e], sure he will reward this people for all they have done for his names sake—Upon our return we found our little society in a prosperous way. in our absence they had attended to class and prayer-meeting, and appeared more in the Spirit of religion than they had ever been—May God increase it.

The Baptist in this place have [been] bitterly opposed to methodism, by misrepresenting the doctrine, and by opposeing us in almost every shape, appeared resolved to keep us out of the place if possible. One of their last efforts seemed to be made shortly after our return by a pre[a]cher by the name of Bowler. he came and preac[h]ed so severely against the Armenians [Arminians], that he gave general offence to the thinking part of the people. He went so far as to say the Armenians ought to be doubled damned, (1) for believeing such doctrines as they do, and (2) for not liveing up to their beliefs. Many of the people were so offended that they left the house. From the manner in which his appointment was made I believe he was brought for the purpose of ridiculeing the Methodist. But if he was, by his manner of doing it, it has proved more injurious to the Baptist, than the Methodist. As the Armenians had been so severely condemned (and that unheard) and some of the people were enquireing what an Armenian was. I informed the people that I would preach on the sub-

[74] A four-wheeled carriage with curtained sides.

ject, and let them know the doctrines held by the Armenians which I endeavoured to do on Sunday October 3, 1819. By stateing the substance of the doctrines established by the Synod of Dort, as contained in the following Articles—

Art. 1. Of Divine Predestination—That God, by an absolute decree hath elected to salvation a very small number of men, without any regard to their faith or obedience whatsoever, and secluded from saveing grace all the rest of mankind, and appointed them by the same decree to eternal damnation without any regard to their infidelity or impenitency.

Art. 2. Of the merit and effect of Christs Death [—] That Jesus Christ hath not suffered death for any other, but for those elect only, haveing neither had any intention nor commandment of his Father to make satisfaction for the sins of the whole world.

Art. 3. Of mans will in the state of nature.[—] That by Adam's fall his posterity lost their free will, being put to an unavoidable necessity to do or not to do whatsoever they do or do not, whether it be good or evil; being thereunto predestinated by the eternal and efectual secret decree of God.

Art. 4. Of the manner of convertion [—] That God, to save his elect from the corrupt mass, doth beget faith in them by a power equal to that whereby he created the world, and raised up the dead, insomuch that such unto whom he gives that grace cannot reject it, and the rest being reprobated cannot accept of it.

Art. 5. Of the certainty of Perseverance. [—] That such as have once received that grace by faith, can never fall from it finally or totally notwithstanding the most enormous sins they can commit.

Thes propos[i]tions I stated as points that the Armenians descent from, without makeing any comments on them. I then stated the Armenian sentiments as contained in Bucks Theological Dictionary on those points as follows: The distinguishing tenets of the Arminians may be comprised in the five following articles relative to predestination, universal redemption, the corruption of man, conversion, and perseverance, viz.

I. That God, from all eternity, determined to bestow salvation on those whome he foresaw would persevere unto the end; and to inflict everlasting punishments on those who should continue in their unbelief, and resist his divine succours; so that election was conditional and reprobation in like manner, the result of foreseen infidelity and persevering wickedness.

II. That Jesus Christ, by his sufferings and death, made an attonement for the sins of mankind in general, and of every individual in particular; that, however, none but those who believe in him can be partakers of divine benefits—

III. That the true faith cannot proceed from the exercise of our natural faculties and powers, nor from the force and operation of free will; since man in consequence of his natural corruption, is incapable either of thinking or doing any good thing; and that therefore, it is necessary, in order to his conversion and salvation, that he be regenerated and renewed by the operation of the Holy Ghost, which is the gift of God through Jesus Christ.

IV. That the divine grace or energy of the Holy Ghost begins and perfects every thing that can be called good in man, and consequently, all good works are to be attributed to God alone; that, nevertheless, this grace is offered to all, and does not force men to act against their inclinations, but may be resisted and rendered ineffectual by [the] perverse will of the impenitent sinner.

V. That God give to the truly faithfull who are regenerated by his grace the means of preserveing themselves in this state. But the regenerate may lose their Justifying faith, fall from a state of grace, and die in there [their] sins.

I made no farther observation on the doctrines of Calvanism than Just to state them that it might be seen what it was we dissented from, But endeavoured to illustrate the doctrines held by the Armenians and to establish them from Scripture—Some of the Baptist came expecting that I was going into controversy with them but as I only dwelt upon our own doctrines and let theirs alone, they were disappointed, and had nothing to say. But this was not my intention: for I was convinced that it was their design to draw us into controversy, and it was my intention to avoid it not seeing that any good at presint could result from it.

Our meetings began to have more life than heretoefore, as our members began to enter deeper into the spirit of religion. We sometimes had some shouting among us which some of the people hardly knew what to think of it. But gradually became better reconciled to it.

There began to appeare now some conviction among us, but nothing very particular appeared untill our Quarter-meeting which was held 1820. January 1 and 2. The Lord made beare his arm among us. Christians rejoiced, and sinners trembled, many came trembling to be prayed for—In the course of our meeting 8 Joined society, and others were under scerious impressions and in the course of a few weaks we had an addition of about 5 more—When I first came to this place in October 1819 our society consisted of about 15 members, it is now increased to upwards of 40. Our meeting continued to be well attended and our prospect appeared promising untill some difficulties arose with one man that acted in an immoral manner that made some disturbance in the Society. But being put back on tryal and then withdrawn we were freed from him. Yet the effect in the Society did not cease. Some were attached to him and some degree of coldness prevailed among us. But those that were in his favour after some time began to discover their error. the effects began to were [wear] off. Our meetings were kept up and well attended yet our prospects were not as good as they had been before. In this state things continued untill Our Camp-meeting was held in the neighbourhood. It commenced on the 13 of July and continued Four days, and the Lord was with us, we [had] some convertions and many convictions, amone [among] them were some young men from Town, that Joined society. The work now began to revive among us again, and some began to be under conviction and soon after some of them were converted [so] that we had an addition of 9 new members. Our meetings are now lively, and there begins to appear some prospect of doing good among the Black people.

The work among us appears to be among the young men and Boys. the more aged and heads of families seem yet unconcerned about religion [so] that I sometimes fear the Lord hath said to them as he did to Ephraim they have joined themselves to Idols, let them alone. When I first came to this place, Versails, I came with some degree of reluctance, and nothing could have induced me to have come but a conviction that it was the will of God and that I shoul[d] be in the order of providence in doing it. And altho my friends have allway[s] shewn the tenderest regard for us and have richly supplied us with every thing we want for this life yet I feel out of my element and many times much dejection of Spirit especially of late, I have been much burdened in my mind. I am no ways suited to the manners of a people that wish to appeare in the stile [style] of high life, as I view it as inconsistant with [the] spirit and simplicity of the gospel. The great prevailance of Slavery in this part damps my spirits and pains me in my feelings every day. And I many times fear by being heare I may in some degree be a partaker of the evil thereof, which my soul abhors. I am sometimes tempted to think from the opression and pride that is among the people that the preaching of the gosple is allmost useless to the greater part. And was it not that we have some fruit of our labours I could not support under it. Yet I dare not leve the place, as I think I have been here in the order of providence. I cannot remove untill I am convinced it is the will of God that I should do so—I have and still continue to lay the matter befor God in prayer in humble confidence that he will direct our way in that manner that will be most for his glory and our good.

August 26, 1820—

CHAPTER VIII

The Journals of the Illinois Annual Conference 1824–31

THIS document illustrates the actual workings of an annual conference of Methodist itinerant ministers on the midwestern frontier. Since primarily it deals with its own personnel, the individual "Journals" have been edited to show the background and careers of some of the more outstanding conference members. Key terms which recur throughout subsequent years have been annotated in the "Journal" for 1824. At each session the conference took up the "disciplinary questions," such as: Who are admitted on trial? Continued on trial? Admitted into full connection? Ordained deacon? Ordained elder? Located? Expelled? Supernumerary? Superannuated? Relations with the General Conference above, and the quarterly conferences below, are seen in the appointment of delegates to the former and in the hearing of appeals from ministerial trials held by the latter. The financial accounts of the conference reveal the methods of ministerial and episcopal support. The Illinois Conference "Journals" are particularly rich in evidences of Methodist interest and participation in the benevolent, missionary, and educational movements which were infusing new vigor into American Protestantism at the time. The lists of conference appointments, as printed in the *General Minutes* and appended to the journal for each year, will show in detail the expansion of Methodism within the conference territory.

Methodism was first planted in Illinois and Indiana, the territory embraced by the Illinois Conference during the years under discussion (1824–31), by pioneer local preachers, but the actual formation of circuits was begun by regularly appointed itinerants of the Western Annual Conference as part of their vast program of evangelizing the trans-Appalachian region. As early as 1803 the Illinois Circuit was formed, and in 1806 the Whitewater Circuit, the first in Indiana, appears in the *Minutes*. In 1808 the Indiana District of the Western Conference was set up, including the circuits of Illinois, Missouri, Maramack, Cold Water, Whitewater, and

Silver Creek. When the Western Conference was disbanded in 1812, the present states of Illinois, Missouri, and part of Indiana were included in the newly formed Tennessee Conference, while several eastern Indiana circuits (in Miami District) went with the Ohio Conference. From the Tennessee Conference was formed the Missouri in 1816, embracing Missouri, Illinois, and part of Indiana. The Missouri Conference was in turn, by the General Conference of 1824, divided at the Mississippi River into the Missouri and Illinois conferences; to the latter were reunited the Indiana circuits of the Ohio Conference. It is in this year (1824) that the present document commences, and it extends through the session of 1831, the last to include the Indiana appointments, which were set up as a separate Indiana Conference by the General Conference of 1832. From the Indiana Conference have come the North Indiana Conference in 1844, and the Southeastern Indiana in 1852, and from the former the Northwestern Indiana in 1852. From the Illinois Conference after 1832 was taken the Rock River Conference in 1840, including Wisconsin and Iowa, and the Southern Illinois in 1852. Peoria (now the Illinois) Conference was in turn detached from Rock River Conference in 1856. Thus, by 1856, there were eight Methodist conferences operating in the area which during the years 1824–31 was served by one—the Illinois.

The best single volume on early Methodism in Illinois is James Leaton's *History of Methodism in Illinois, from 1793 to 1832* (Cincinnati, 1883). For northern Illinois see A. D. Field, *Memorials of Methodism in the Bounds of the Rock River Conference* (Cincinnati, 1886), and Almer M. Pennewell, *The Methodist Movement in Northern Illinois* (Sycamore, Ill., 1942). W. P. Strickland (ed.), *Autobiography of Peter Cartwright, the Backwoods Preacher* (Cincinnati, 1856), and Stephen R. Beggs, *Pages from the Early History of the West and North-West .... with Especial Reference to the History of Methodism* (Cincinnati, 1868), are indispensable accounts of Methodist work in Illinois by those who participated in it during the formative years. For Indiana, Allen Wiley's "Introduction and Progress of Methodism in Southeastern Indiana," published in the *Western Christian Advocate,* 1845–46, and reprinted in the *Indiana Magazine of History,* Volume XXIII (1927), is a valuable contemporary account. The standard history of Methodism in the entire state is F. C. Holliday's *Indiana Methodism* (Cincinnati, 1873); an excellent general treatment is Elizabeth K. Nottingham's *Methodism and the Frontier—Indiana Proving Ground* (New York, 1941). Source materials referring to Indiana and Illinois Methodism include the "Journals" of the Western

Annual Conference for the years 1800–1811, which are printed in William Warren Sweet, *The Rise of Methodism in the West* (New York, 1920); the "Journals" of the Ohio Annual Conference from 1812 to 1824 (when the circuits in eastern Indiana were joined to Illinois Conference), published in William Warren Sweet, *Circuit-Rider Days along the Ohio* (New York, 1923); and the Indiana Conference "Journals" from 1832 to 1843, in William Warren Sweet, *Circuit-Rider Days in Indiana* (Indianapolis, 1916).

I. JOURNAL FOR 1824

The first Illenois Conference (agreeable to a late division by the General Conference of last May)

And the ninth Missouri (agreeable to adjournment) met at the house of William Padfield's S[t.] Clair County, Illenois. Saturday Oct. 23d.[1]

Bishop McKendree[2] opened the conference by reading a portion of the Sacred Scriptures, singing and prayer.[3]

[1] Since the Missouri Conference at its session in 1823, when Illinois was still included within its bounds, had voted to meet at Padfield's, Looking-Glass Prairie, Illinois, the plan was carried through, and the two conferences met together. In the *General Minutes* for 1824 the appointments in Illinois and Indiana are printed under the subheading of "Illinois Conference" and general heading of "Missouri Conference" (*Minutes of the Annual Conferences of the Methodist Episcopal Church,* Vol. I: *1773–1828* [New York, 1840], pp. 453–54).

[2] William McKendree (1757–1835) has been called the "Father of Western Methodism." He was a native of King William County, Virginia, served in the Revolutionary War, was converted to Methodism in the Brunswick Revival of 1787, and joined the traveling ministry soon thereafter. After serving circuits in the East, he was in 1800 appointed presiding elder over the Kentucky District, embracing most of the Methodist appointments west of the Appalachian Mountains. When Jesse Walker, pioneer missionary of the upper Mississippi Valley, went westward in 1806 to begin his work on his new appointment of "Illinois," McKendree rode the new territory with him, hunting out settlements and forming them into a circuit. In 1808 he was elected bishop of the Methodist Episcopal church and in that capacity presided over the Illinois Conference of 1824. The standard biography is Robert Paine, *Life and Times of William M'Kendree, Bishop of the Methodist Episcopal Church* (2 vols.; Nashville, Tenn., 1874).

[3] Devotions and preaching services were all a part of the annual conference, which was for the spiritual refreshment of the ministry as well as for the outward business of the church.

The list[4] was called and the following members were present.

Jesse Walker[5]
Jesse Haile[6]
John Scripps[7]
Thomas Wright[8]
James Armstrong[9]
John Dew[10]
Dennis Willey[11]
James Bankson[12]
William W. Redman[13]
Hackaliah Vredenburgh[14]
William McReynolds[15]

[4] The conference roll.

[5] Perhaps more than to any other pioneer preacher, Illinois Methodism is indebted to Jesse Walker (1766–1835), a native of Buckingham County, Virginia, who was admitted on trial to the Western Conference in 1802 and appointed to "Illinois" in 1806 to do pioneer missionary work. He settled his family in the Turkey Hill Settlement in St. Clair County and, in 1807, held near Edwardsville the first camp meeting in the state of Illinois. In 1813 he became presiding elder of the Illinois District, then in Tennessee Conference. Later he served as "Conference Missionary," freed to do work in sparsely settled territory. In 1820 he planted Methodism in the Roman Catholic city of St. Louis and in 1830 pioneered in the village of Chicago. His valuable work as missionary to the Potawatomi and other Indian tribes in the Midwest will be noted below (William B. Sprague [ed.], *Annals of the American Pulpit,* VII, 380–87; James Leaton, *History of Methodism in Illinois, from 1793 to 1832* [Cincinnati, 1883], pp. 48–64). Cf. Almer Pennewell, "Jesse Walker, the Daniel Boone of Methodism" (MS).

[6] Jesse Haile (? –1844) was admitted on trial to the Tennessee Conference in 1812 and sent to Missouri Circuit. In 1817–18 he was on Illinois Circuit, then in the Missouri Conference, and in 1818 became presiding elder of Illinois District. A contemporary writes that "he was an abolitionist of the Garrison type, and did not hesitate to preach against slavery, publicly as well as privately," and for this reason was transferred from the Missouri to the Illinois Conference in 1829 (Leaton, *op. cit.,* pp. 138–42; cf. W. S. Woodard, *Annals of Methodism in Missouri* [Columbia, Mo., 1893], p. 13).

[7] John Scripps (1785–1865), first secretary of the Illinois Conference, was a native of London, England, who entered the Tennessee Conference in 1814. He had attended the Virginia Academy and in 1809 removed to Cape Girardeau, Missouri, where he established a tanyard. Entering the Missouri Conference in 1816, he served as its secretary for twelve years. He was a delegate to the General Conference in 1820 and 1824. Woodard (*op. cit.,* pp. 18–19) estimated Scripps in his prime as the leading preacher in the Missouri Conference.

[8] Thomas Wright (*ca.* 1784–1825), a native of South Carolina, had joined the Western Conference in 1809. He served as presiding elder in Missouri, and Woodard (*ibid.,* pp. 10–11) speaks of him as the outstanding revivalist of the early conference. He was the first Methodist preacher who began and ended his ministry in Missouri.

[9] James Armstrong (1787–1834) was born in Ireland, converted in Philadelphia, and, on moving to Indiana, was received into the Missouri Conference in 1821. In 1824 he was appointed presiding elder of Indiana District. He attended several General Conferences ("Memoir," *Minutes,* Vol. II: *1829–1839,* p. 344).

[10] John Dew (1789–1840), a native of Virginia, joined the Ohio Conference in 1812, later transferring to the Tennessee. In 1824–25 he was appointed to Illinois Cir-

A Secretary being called for to take down the proceedings of Conference John Scripps was nominated by Brother Armstrong and was elected.

After which Bishop McKendree announced to the Conference the afflicting dispensation with which Divine Providence had afflicted the Church in taking from us our highly esteemed and beloved Bretherain in Christ, William Beauchamp[16] and Samuel Glaze, which annunciation he accompanied with some deeply interesting and affecting observations on the occasion during which the Divine presence was powerfully felt by the Conference he then concluded by giving out a

---

cuit, in 1827 became superintendent of the Potawatomi Mission, and was chosen president of McKendree College in 1837 ("Memoir," *Minutes,* Vol. III: *1839–1845,* p. 149).

[11] Dennis Willey had joined the Missouri Conference in 1812 (*Minutes,* Vol. I: *1773–1828,* p. 374).

[12] James Bankson (1795–1831), born in Oglethorpe County, Georgia, joined the Missouri Conference in 1821 and was its secretary for two years (1828–29); in 1829 he transferred to the Illinois Conference ("Memoir," *Minutes,* Vol. II: *1829–1839,* p. 214).

[13] William W. Redman (1799–1849), a native of Clark County, Indiana, was converted at a Kentucky camp meeting in 1817 and joined the Missouri Conference in 1820. He was, beginning in 1833, secretary of his conference fourteen times, served as presiding elder thirteen years, and attended as delegate three General Conferences. See his biography by the Reverend Andrew Monroe, in Thomas O. Summers (ed), *Biographical Sketches of Eminent Itinerant Ministers* .... (Nashville, 1859), pp. 367–84.

[14] Hackaliah Vredenburg (1790–1869) was a native of Westchester County, New York, but moved to Indiana in 1817. He joined the Missouri Conference in 1820 and served in the Illinois and, after 1832, in the Indiana conferences. Most of his itinerant life was spent in the Wabash Valley (Leaton, *op. cit.,* pp. 173–75).

[15] William McReynolds (1798–1868), a native of Washington County, Virginia, was converted in Kentucky and joined the Tennessee Conference in 1820. He served his first year as junior preacher on the Christian Circuit under Peter Cartwright (*ibid.,* pp. 192–94).

[16] William Beauchamp (1772–1824), a native of Kent County, Delaware, was converted at the age of sixteen. He became one of the leading Methodist preachers of his generation and was called by his contemporaries the "Demosthenes of the West." Admitted to the traveling connection in 1794, he served circuits in Maryland, Pennsylvania, New York, Massachusetts, etc. He is remembered for his *Essays on the Truth of Christianity* (1811), for editing the first Methodist periodical for the West, the *Western Christian Monitor* (Chillicothe, Ohio, 1815), and for his *Letters on .... the Itinerant Ministry* (Louisville, Ky., 1849). At the General Conference of 1824 he came within three votes of being elected bishop.

suitable hymn which was sung. After which Bishops Soule[17] and Roberts[18] severally prayed.

The Conference then proceeded to business. Bishop Roberts in the Chair.

The times of meeting and adjournment of the Conference being called for, on motion of Brother Samuel H. Thompson[19] and seconded by Brother Scripps it was carried by the unanimous voice of the members that the times of meeting be nine O'Clock A.M. and two O'Clock P.M. and of adjournment at twelve O'Clock, noon and at five P.M.

Brother Samuel H. T[h]ompson and John Dew were then nominated and elected to superintend the appointments for Divine service to be performed at the Camp Ground[20] during the Conference.

[17] Joshua Soule (1781–1867) presided over the Illinois Conference four times. His career was an unusual one. Born in Bristol, Maine, he spent his youth in that state and was admitted into the traveling connection in 1799. His marked ability made him presiding elder of Maine District in 1804. It was he who originated the plans for a delegated General Conference. Made book agent in 1816, he began in 1818 the *Methodist Magazine,* which had a long existence as the *Methodist Quarterly Review* and is continued as *Religion in Life*. He was partly responsible for founding the Missionary Society of the Methodist Episcopal Church in 1819. In 1824 he was elected bishop and, with the division over the slavery issue in 1845, went with the Southern Church, serving it as senior bishop until his death (see Horace M. Du Bose, *Life of Joshua Soule* [Nashville, 1911].

[18] Robert Richford Roberts (1778–1843) presided over the Illinois Conference eight times between the years 1824 and 1835. Born in Frederick County, Maryland, he was converted to Methodism at the age of fifteen. He joined the Baltimore Conference on trial in 1802 and served several important city stations. Elected bishop in 1816, he visited the widely scattered outposts of the church from New England to the Lower Mississippi (Charles Elliott, *The Life of the Rev. Robert R. Roberts*.... [New York, 1844]).

[19] Samuel H. Thompson (1786–1842), born of Presbyterian parentage in western Pennsylvania, had a distinguished itinerant career in the states of Ohio, Indiana, Tennessee, Kentucky, Illinois, Missouri, and Arkansas, beginning with his admission to the Western Conference in 1809. In 1810 he held in Wayne County, Indiana, the first camp meeting in the state. He served as presiding elder of several important districts, as in 1815, the Illinois; and in 1832 he was agent of Lebanon Seminary (McKendree College) (Leaton, *op. cit.,* pp. 131–38).

[20] The American conferences, held from summer until late fall, usually sponsored camp meetings in connection with their annual sessions; hence the reference to the "camp ground."

The Stewards[21] of Conference were then voted for by Ballot which resulted in the election of John Scripps Jesse Haile, and W. W. Redman.

John Dew, James Armstrong and John Scripps being severally nominated were elected a committee to write the memoirs of the Dead.[22]

Brother Scripps then introduced a resolution in writing seconded by Brother Armstrong, respectfully requesting Bishop Soule to preach at the Camp Ground to morrow at eleven O'Clock A.M. a Funeral Sermon in Memory of our much revered Father in Christ William Beauchamp on the vote being put by the president the Conference unanimously rose to their feet.

Bishop Roberts then Introduced Bishop Soule to the Conference—the Conference respectfully rose.

On motion of Br[other] S. H. Thompson seconded by Brother Scripps and carried by the unanimous vote of the Conference Bishop Roberts was respectfully requested to preach a Funeral Discourse on the Death of our much esteemed Brother Samuel Glaze

Brother Scripps then reminded the Conference that by the demise of Brother Beauchamp and absence of Br. [Samuel] Bassett he was the only remaining member of the Book Committee[23] in conse-

[21] The conference stewards were the treasurers of the conference. Ministers' salaries were paid, not directly by the circuits, but through the stewards. Their function of gathering statistics about the financial side of conference business has developed into the present office of statistician. At this first conference it was their chief service to hear reports of the collections on the various circuits and divide the appropriations from the Book Concern and Chartered Fund. Gradually they came to handle also the moneys of the Conference Missionary, Sunday school, and other benevolent enterprises.

[22] The "Memoirs" or obituaries of deceased ministers were usually sent to the editor of the *General Minutes,* an annual publication which became a valuable cumulative biographical record of American Methodism. The *Minutes* of the spring conferences of 1901 were, however, the last to contain memoirs.

[23] Methodist preachers were expected to be agents of the Methodist Book Concern, promoting its sales and aiding in the collection of debts. The annual conferences in turn profited both through discounts on books and through a division of the profits. At the General Conference of 1824 a resolution was passed that the bishops "pay strict attention to the affairs of the Book Concern at every annual conference" (*Journals of the General Conference of the Methodist Episcopal Church,* Vol. I: *1796–1836* [New York, 1855], p. 288). In carrying out these responsibilities, the conference appointed a committee to care for the interests of the Concern.

quence of which the President proceeded to appointment Brs. James Armstrong & John Dew respectfully to fill the vacancies.

Samuel H. Thompson, Jesse Walker, J. Scripps. J. Cord and J. Armstrong were then appointed by the Bishop and announced as a Committee to examine the Candidates for admission into full connexion[24]—J. Scripps requested to be exonerated from the duties of the appointment being already a member of other Committees the Bishop acceded to his request & appointed Brother Jesse Haile in his place.

The President then informed the Conference that Brs. Peter Cartwright[25] and Andrew Munroe[26] Elders of the Kentucky annual Conference were by transfer[27] become members of this Conference.

[24] When a minister had satisfactorily completed two probationary years of itinerant labors after his admission on trial to the conference, he was examined as to doctrines, ability, and conduct by a conference committee and admitted into full connection with the conference.

[25] Peter Cartwright (1785–1872), the best-known Methodist circuit-rider of the West, was born in Amherst County, Virginia. Moving with his parents to Logan County, Kentucky, he was converted during the Cumberland Revival in 1801. He joined the Western Conference in 1804, was ordained deacon in 1806, elder in 1808, and as early as 1812 was presiding elder of Wabash District. He was first elected to the General Conference in 1816 and served in twelve succeeding quadrenniums. In 1823 he moved his family to Pleasant Plains, Illinois, and for the rest of his life was identified with Indiana-Illinois Methodism. He was presiding elder from 1825 to 1869, when he was made conference missionary at his own request. His record of service is difficult to equal in the entire history of Methodism. It was he largely who was responsible for the foundation of McKendree College. His *Autobiography,* a standard document on frontier Methodism, was edited by W. P. Strickland and published at Cincinnati in 1856; an edition was published in London, 1858, under the title of *The Backwoods Preacher.* His *Fifty Years a Presiding Elder,* an enlargement and continuation of the narrative, appeared in 1871. A modern popularized biography is Helen Hardie Grant's *Peter Cartwright: Pioneer* (New York: Abingdon Press, 1931).

[26] Andrew Monroe (1792–1871) served fifty-six years as an effective itinerant minister, mostly in Missouri. He was a native of Hampshire County, Virginia. Three of his brothers were Methodist preachers. In 1815, having removed to Ohio, he was admitted on trial to the Ohio Conference, later serving in the Tennessee, Kentucky, and Missouri conferences. Until his death, he attended every General Conference except one (1820). He frequently was appointed presiding elder in Missouri, was agent of St. Charles and Central colleges, and conference missionary (Woodard, *op. cit.,* pp. 44–51).

[27] A Methodist minister was under appointment by the bishop and subject to appointment by him to any form of duty within the total church structure. The machinery was therefore favorable to the movement of ministers from East to West. Unlike many

And also introduced Uriel Hawe[28] and Edwin Ray Deacons present also transfer[r]ed to this from the Kentucky Conference together with Br. Richard J. Dungan a member on trial.

The President further informs the Conference's that they were at liberty to draw for money as follows—

The Illenois Conference on the Book Consarn[29]	$150.00
on the Chartered fund[30]	80.
The Missouri Conference on the Book Concern for	$150.00
on the Chartered fund	$ 80.00

and the Conference voted to draw accordingly.

The Conference then took up the consideration of the Second Question in our form of Discipline to wit, The examination of the Characters [of those] admitted on trial[31] last year and the following were severally considered and acted on as follows—

---

other denominations in which individual ministers in the East were obliged to seek openings themselves, Methodist ministers had only to indicate their interest in the West and the bishop completed the arrangements for a transfer. Such a change did not alter one's standing in the conference.

[28] Uriel Haw (1799–1844), who had joined the Kentucky Conference in 1822, was in 1829 made presiding elder of Arkansas District, Missouri Conference, and, in 1830, presiding elder of Cape Girardeau District. He was the son of the Reverend James Haw, first Methodist preacher appointed to Kentucky ("Memoir," *Minutes,* Vol. III: *1839–1845,* p. 588).

[29] Profits from the Methodist Book Concern were available to the annual conferences for making up deficiencies in ministers' salaries.

[30] The Chartered Fund was called at its inception, in 1784, the "Preachers' Fund," to provide relief for ministers no longer able to work. It was reorganized into the Chartered Fund in 1796, the *Discipline* for that year inquiring into the provision for "distressed Traveling Preachers, for the families of Traveling Preachers, and for the Superannuated and Worn-out Preachers, and the widows and orphans of Preachers" (David Sherman, *History of the Revisions of the Discipline of the Methodist Episcopal Church* [New York, 1874], p. 248). The funds gathered were put under trustees and the interest divided equally among the conferences. The Illinois Conference drew annually from this fund during the years 1824–31 from eighty to ninety dollars.

[31] A candidate for the ministry was required to be highly recommended by his local circuit quarterly conference. The annual conference then passed on this recommendation. Frequently in the "Journal" we read that the recommendation was not accepted but that the presiding elder had the right to employ the individual for ministerial duties on the district, with the apparent expectation that the candidate would sufficiently prove his worth to be eventually admitted on trial, or would be content to serve as a local preacher.

Andrew Lapp	William Moore
Orsenath Fisher[32]	John Miller
Edward Smith	Benjamin S. Ashby
James E. Johnson	Joseph Edmundson
William Shores	Rucker Tanner

All continued on trial[33]—

The Characters of the Deacons[34] were then respectfully considered and attended to as follows—

David Chamberlain Absent laid over

Dennis Willey	John Glanville
Ebenezer T. Webster	John Blasdell
James Bankson	

Their Characters being severally examined, were approved and passed.

The time being arrived the Conference adjourned J. Haile concluding by prayer.

2 O'Clock P.M.

Conference met according to adjournment and was opened by Bishop Soule reading the Scriptures Singing & Prayer—and the list being called proceeded to business—

[32] Orceneth Fisher (1803–80), a native of Chester, Windsor County, Vermont, after an itinerancy in the Illinois Conference, visited Texas in 1839 to regain his health, and from his observations there he published an immigrants' guide, *Sketches of Texas in 1840* (Springfield, Ill., 1840). In 1841 he transferred to the Texas Conference, where he published the *Texas Christian Advocate* (1848); and in 1855 again transferred to the Pacific Conference of the Methodist Episcopal Church, South. He founded and edited the *Pacific Methodist* (1856), and in 1858 he published at San Francisco his book, *The Christian Sacraments.* He began missionary work in Oregon in 1859, where he founded Corvalis College, now a state agricultural school (Robert E. Ledbetter, Jr., "Orceneth Fisher: Pioneer Methodist Preacher of Texas and the Pacific Coast" [unpublished thesis, University of Texas, 1938]).

[33] At the next annual conference after a minister's admission on trial, if he had proved competent, he was continued on trial for an additional year.

[34] At the time of his admission into full connection, a minister was examined and if approved, elected to ordination as a deacon, with the right "to administer the ordinance of baptism, marriage, and the burial of the dead, in the absence of an elder," as the time-honored certificate of ordination reads. For the complete form see W. P. Strickland (ed.), *Autobiography of Peter Cartwright* (Cincinnati, 1860), pp. 97–98. Consecration to this office was by the laying-on of hands by bishop and elders.

Bishop Soule in the Chair—

The Secratary requested the aid of an assistant and James Bankson being nominated was elected.

The examination of Deacons was then resumed. Isaac H. Piggsott[35] and Samuel Bassett supernumerary[36] being absent were laid over.

William W. Redman	George K. Hester
Hackaliah Vredenburgh	William McReynolds

were severally examined, approved and elected.

Recommendations were then laid before the Conference by the Respective Presiding Elders of Districts for the following persons to be admitted into the travelling connexion which were acted on as follows,

George Randle	Mount Carmel Q[uarterly] Con-[ference]			Their Characters were severally examined approved and they were admitted on trial.
Samuel Lowe	Blue River	do.	do.	
Daniel Anderson	Indiana District Con.			
James Garner	do.	do.	do.	
Jacob Varner	Honey Creek Q. Conf.			
John Fish	Flat Rock Qt. Conference			
Shadrach Casteek [Casteel]	La-moine	Q.	do.	
Cassel Harrison	Sagama [Sangamon]	do.	do.	
Green Orr	Arkansas	do.	do.	
Gilbert Clarke	do.	do.	do.	

John Havens Indianop[o]lis Qt. Conf his Character was examined and rejected.—

Recommendations were then presented for the following Local Preachers to be elected to Deacons orders.[37]

[35] Isaac H. Piggott (1792–1874) had been received on trial in the Missouri Conference in 1819. After his location this year, he took up the study of law. In 1821 he established the Grafton-Alton Ferry over the Mississippi River (Leaton, *op. cit.*, pp. 188–89).

[36] Supernumeraries were preachers who, because of some temporary cause, were unable to continue their active ministry. The *Discipline* of 1792 defined such a person as "one so worn out in the itinerant service as to be rendered incapable of preaching constantly; but at the same time is willing to do any work in the ministry which the Conference may direct, and his strength, enable him to perform" (Sherman, *op. cit.*, p. 180).

[37] A local preacher who had served satisfactorily a period of four years in the ministry, if recommended by his quarterly conference, might be elected by the annual conference for ordination to deacon's orders, with the title of "local deacon."

John Bond recommended from the Indiana District Conference his Character was examined, approved and he was elected.

Reuben Clearwater. his Character was examined but rejected.

See Page 67 2nd line from the bottom of the Missouri Journals—

The Stewards of the Conference then called on the Preachers for their respective amounts received on their circuits as quarterage which being done and adjournment being called for Br. Walker concluding by prayer Conference adjourned.

MONDAY OCT[OBER] 25TH 1824

Nine O'Clock [A.M.]

Conference met according to adjournment of Saturday and was opened agreeable to rule by Bishop Roberts, by reading singing and Prayer

Bishop Soule then took the Chair and the list being called the following members were found present—

Jesse Walker	J. Armstrong	U. Hawe
Jesse Haile	J. L. Thompson	E. Ray
S. H. Thompson	J. Dew	S. Hull
Th. Wright	H. Vredenburgh	S. R. Beggs[38]
J. Scripps	D. Chamberlain	F. B. Leach
J. Patterson	D. Willey	C. Ruddle
Th. Davis	E. T. Webster	Jesse Green[39]
J. Harriss	J. Bankson	A. Munroe
J. Cord	J. Glanville	W. W. Redman
Wm. Medford	J. Blosdell	T. Randle
Th. Rice	W. McReynolds	W. H. Smith

[38] Stephen R. Beggs (1801–96), born in Rockingham County, Virginia, joined the Missouri Conference in 1822. At the present conference (1824) he was sent to Fishing River Circuit, Missouri, but the following year transferred to Illinois Conference. He aided Jesse Walker in forming the first class in Chicago in 1830, and in 1831 he was sent as missionary to Chicago. He became a member of Rock River Conference in 1843. In 1868 he published his valuable *Pages from the Early History of the West and North-West: Embracing Reminiscences and Incidents of Settlement and Growth, and Sketches of the Material and Religious Progress of the States of Ohio, Indiana, Illinois, and Missouri, with Especial Reference to the History of Methodism* (Cincinnati, 1868).

[39] Jesse Greene (1791–1847) united with the Tennessee Conference in 1817 and transferred to the Missouri in 1823. He was a presiding elder in the latter until 1845,

The journals being read were corrected and passed[.] Bishop McKendree then feelingly addressed the Conference on the subject of Missions,[40] Sunday Schools[41] and work of God in General, tending to excite Missionary ardour and awaken the energies of the ministry—Under his address a sense of the Divine Presence was deeply experienced, at the conclusion of which the Conference proceeded to business—

The Characters of the Candidates for admission into full connexion being taken up.

Br. Samuel Hull's name was called but on motion of Brother Thompson his case was laid over to future consideration—

Stephen R. Beggs Frederick B. Leach Cornelius Ruddell Thomas Randle Wm. H. Smith	were severally examined, approved, admitted into full connexion and elected to ordination
William Ryon	on his name being called it was found that he had not gone on his circuit last year and that he had made no communications to Conference Br. S. H. Thompson moved and was seconded by Br. Scripps that Br. Ryon be discontinued—The motion prevailed—
David Chamberlain	His Character the consideration of which was laid over on Saturday being taken up was examined and passed.

---

when he entered the M.E. Church, South. He was remembered as a staunch defender of Methodism against Calvinism and Campbellism (see *Life, Three Sermons, and Some of the Miscellaneous Writings of Rev. Jesse Greene* [Lexington, Mo., 1852], edited by his widow, Mary Greene).

40 The Missouri Conference held at St. Louis in October, 1823, had appointed "Jesse Walker, missionary to the Missouri Conference, whose attention is particularly directed to the Indians within the bounds of said Conference" (*Minutes,* Vol. I: *1773–1828,* p. 426).

41 The General Conference of 1824 had resolved that "it shall be the duty of each travelling preacher in our connexion to encourage the establishment and progress of Sunday schools" and urged the publication of a catechism and assorted Sunday-school books (*Journals of the General Conference of the Methodist Episcopal Church,* Vol. I: *1796–1836,* p. 295).

Br. Bassett Superan[n]uated,[42] also laid over. A communication from him to the Conference was read Dated Feleciana State of Louisiana requesting a change in his relation to that of a Supernumer[ar]y. His character was examined & approved and his request was granted. And he was elected to Elders orders.[43]

The examination of the Characters of Elders was then attended to and

Jesse Walker
J. Haile
S. H. Thompson
J. Scripps
} were severally examined and passed.

The time being come Conference adjourned. Br. Wright concluded by prayer.

2 O'Clock P.M.

Conference met agreeable to adjournment, opened according to rule by Br. Haile in the duties of Holy devotion and the list being called attended to business.

Bishop Roberts in the Chair.

The consideration of Elders Characters was then resumed.

Th. Wright
J. Patterson
J. Harriss
Th. Davis
} were examined and approved

J. Cord was examined, approved and obtained a supernumerary relation.

Wm. Stephenson examined and approved

David Sharp examined approved and transferred to the Pittsburgh Conference

[42] Superannuated preachers are those who are permanently disabled because of age, sickness, or other causes, but who retain their relationship with the annual conference.

[43] The term "elder" designates one who exercises full powers as a minister in the Methodist church. After serving as a deacon for two years, the conference member was elected to the office of elder, "as a proper person to administer the sacraments and ordinances, and to feed the flock of Christ, so long as his spirit and practice are such as become the Gospel of Christ." For complete text of certificate of ordination to the eldership see Strickland (ed.), *op. cit.*, p. 112.

Jesse Green examined and approved
William Beauchamp Deceased.
William Cravens examined approved and Superanuated.
William Medford examined, approved and located.[44]

Thomas Rice
James Armstrong
James L. Thompson } examined and appeared.

Calvin Ruter[45] examined, approved & superanuated.
Samuel Hamilton examined, approved & transfered to the Ohio Conference.
Robert Delap examined, approved and his supernumer[ar]y relation continued.
John Dew examined and approved
Samuel Glaze Deceased.

Richard Hargrave[46] a preacher who rode the last year in the Indiana District under the Presiding Elder and William Medford and J. Armstrong informed the Conference that his Presiding Elder had obtained a recommendation for him to travel but owing to the death of Br. Beauchamp the recommendation did not come to conference. Br. Medford & Br. Armstrong pledged themselves to produce it at the next Illenois annual Conference if he should be admitted. He was admitted.

[44] In locating, a minister no longer willing or able to travel leaves the itinerant ministry and gives up his conference membership but is free to labor as a local preacher.

[45] Calvin W. Ruter (1794–1859), born at Bradford, Orange County, Vermont, was admitted on trial to the Ohio Conference in 1817, serving later in the Missouri and Illinois conferences. For many years he was conference secretary. He was one of the founders of Indiana Asbury, now DePauw University, and was for some time register of the United States Land Office at Indianapolis ("Memoir," *Minutes,* Vol. VII: *1858–59,* p. 274).

[46] Richard Hargrave (1803–79), a native of Caswell County, North Carolina, was in youth a member of the (O'Kelley) Christian church in Indiana but was licensed to preach in the Methodist church in 1823. He belonged successively to the Illinois, Indiana, North Indiana, and Northwest Indiana conferences, served seventeen years in the presiding eldership, and was a member of the General Conferences of 1848 and 1860 (see *Sacred Poems of Rev. Richard Hargrave, D.D., with a Biography of Himself. . . .* [Cincinnati, 1890], edited by his son, William P. Hargrave of the Northwest Indiana Conference).

Samuel Hull. His case being taken up. Charges of an immoral nature on the testimony of Elisabeth Wallace amounting to an attempt on her chastity and for which he now stands suspended were laid before the Conference—The circumstances of the case being duly considered together with the character of the Woman and the manner of her acting on the occasion the Conference were fully convinced of his innocence, and on motion of Br. Munroe seconded by Br. Glanville, the sentence of the committee who had suspended him was reversed His character was examined, approved and he was admitted into full connexion and elected to Deacons orders.

The conference adjourned Br. Patterson concluded by prayer.

TUESDAY OCT[OBER] 26TH 1824

Nine O'Clock A.M.

The conference met agreeable to adjournment, and was opened according to rule by Br. Munroe's Reading the Scripture, singing & prayer And the list being called the journals were read and corrected.

Bishop Soule in the Chair

On attending to business the character of George Horne a Deacon, transferred to this from the Tennessee Conference, at its last sitting—passed examination, was approved and he was located.

Isaac N. Piggott His character having been laid over yesterday was taken up examined and passed.

It was then announced from the Chair that if there were any who wished a change in their relation to the Conference it was time to make it known On which Brother Scripps arose, and requested a location, which was not granted. On his retiring Br. S. H. Thompson moved seconded by Br. Armstrong, that a superannuated relation be given him. The motion prevailed.

Brother Willey also requesting a location it was not granted. Brother Armstrong moved and it was seconded by Br. Scripps that a Supernumerary relation be given him it was granted.

A recommendation for Bennett Hancock a Local Preacher for

election to the office of a Deacon was then laid before the conference but on mature consideration was rejected.

Bishop Roberts in the Chair.

Br. Scripps then introduced a resolution seconded by Br. Armstrong respectfully requesting Bishop Soule to oblige the Conference with a copy of the Sermon he preached last Sabbath on the demise of Brother Beauchamp. The resolution was carried the Conference unanimously rising to their feet.

Jesse Walker the Missionary of the Missouri Conference then made his Report relative to his mission among the Indians[47] which being read on motion of Brother Munroe [was] accepted.

Brother Dew then offered a resolution seconded by Br. Bankson that the Illenois & Missouri Conferences now sitting in conjunction resolve it expedient to continue the mission under the patronage of the Illenois Conference The resolution was carried.

Bishop McKendree then addressed the Conference on the subject of the Motion relative to the manner of conducting missions among the Indians.

Bishop Roberts then informed the Conference that agreeable to a late regulation of the General Conference, a committee was required in each Annual Conference to unite with the Episcopacy in estimating the probable expence sustaining them[48] And a motion prevailed for such a Committee on motion of Br. Scripps Seconded by Br. Dew it was Carried to consist of Five Br. Scripps then moved that [the committee] be elected by ballott which also prevailing the Conference proceeded to the Ballotting and J. Scripps, J. Haile. S. H. Thompson, J. Dew and J. Armstrong were elected.

On motion of Br. J. Scripps the Delegates to General Conference[49] were called upon to render in the respective amounts of their expenses to and from Baltimore, together with the several amounts they had received to defray that expence as also all that held money in their

[47] The development of the Potawatomi Indian Mission, under Jesse Walker, Peter Cartwright, and others, will be annotated in future "Journals."

[48] The *Discipline* of 1800 divided the support of the episcopacy among the annual conferences; in 1824, however, the bishops were directed to draw funds from the Book Concern (Sherman, *op. cit.,* p. 251).

[49] The delegates from the Missouri Conference to the General Conference of 1824 were William Beauchamp, David Sharp, Samuel H. Thompson, John Scripps, and Jesse Walker (*Journals of the General Conference,* I, 242).

hands collected for that purpose that a settlement might be made in accordance with the resolutions made by the Committee to devise ways and means for defraying the expences of the Delegates last year and passed by the act of the Conference.

After which the Secretary read before the Conference a printed Circular from the Book Agents on the subject of promoting the interest of the concern when it was moved seconded and carried that the Conference adjourn till to morrow morning [at] Nine O'clock Br. Thompson concluded by prayer.

WEDNESDAY OCT[OBER] 27TH, [1824]

9 O'Clock A.M.

Conference met according to adjournment and was opened by Bishop McKendree performing Divine Worship.

Bishop Roberts in the Chair.

The list being called and the Journal read and corrected the Conference proceeded to business.

Bishop Roberts informed the Conference that as he could obtain no documents relative to Brother Glaze's life or death he was obliged to decline preaching his Funeral.

It was then moved by Br. Scripps and was Seconded by Br. Armstrong that the surplus of the money appropriated for the expenses of the delegates to General Conference be put into the hands of the Conference Stewards and to be appropriated by them in liquidating the deficiencies of the Preachers.

On motion of Br. Scripps seconded by Br. Armstrong amended and carried J. Scripps, J. Armstrong and J. Dew were appointed a committee to meet and determine what surplus of money was left by Br. Beauchamp of the money in his hands appropriated to defray his expence as a delegate and that they apply such surplus [to defraying: *omit*] as far as it will go to defraying the expences of his sickness & Funeral—the motion prevailed.

The number of members in the several Circuits were then given in by the respective Preachers.[50]

[50] The numbers in society reported for the previous conference year (1823–24) embracing the territory which this year was set off as the Illinois Conference were: Indiana District, 5,990 white and 17 colored members; Illinois District, 3,155 white and 57 colored members; total, 9,145 white and 74 colored (*Minutes,* Vol. I: *1773–1828,* p. 453).

Br. Piggott then appearing in the Conference and requesting a Location it was granted.

The Conference then proceeded to vote by ballott for the seat of the next Missouri Conference and Beulah Meeting House—St. Louis and Cedar Creek Camp Ground being in nomination were ballotted for carried for Beulah meeting house[51]—the Conference then adjourned. Br. Scripps concluded by Prayer.

Two O'Clock A.M.

Conference met according to adjournment was opened by Br. Armstrong reading the Scripture Singing & Prayer. Bishop Roberts took the Chair.

And the place where the next Illenois being called for five places were had in Nominations to wit

Walnut Grove	Illenois
Bloomington	Indiana
Charelstown	do
Madison	do
Forks of White River	do

On ballotting the vote prevailed for Charlestown

Br. Scripps then presented a recommendation for the readmission of Br. Alexander McAlister[52] into connexion he was readmitted.

In consequence of a motion made to reconsider the vote taken on the Location of Br. Wm. Medford Br. Medford withdrew his location.

The President then announced the time of the next Conferences to wit

Missouri	Conference	Aug. 4th.
Illenois	do	Aug. 25

[51] Balah Meetinghouse was in the New Tennessee Settlement on Saline Creek, St. Francois County, Missouri (Woodard, *op. cit.*, p. ix).

[52] Alexander McAlister (? –1834), a native of Kentucky, had joined the Missouri Conference in 1816 and served as presiding elder of Cape Girardeau, Missouri, and St. Louis districts from 1828 to 1831. After his final location he was John Scripps's partner in business in Rushville, Illinois.

Br. Scripps moved for adjournment till tomorrow [at] 9 O'Clock A.M. the motion was lost.

It was then moved by Armstrong seconded by Bro. Rice that Conference adjourn till Six O'Clock this evening—the motion was lost and on another motion of Bro. Scripps Conference adjourned till Six O'Clock A.M. to morrow

Br. McAlister concluded by prayer.

TUESDAY OCT[OBER] 28TH, [1824]

6 O'Clock A.M.

Conference met aggreable to adjournment was opened by Bishop Roberts with Singing & Prayer.

Bishop Roberts in the Chair.

The list being called & the Journals read & corrected Br. Wright introduced a motion seconded by Br. Walker that Br. John C. Harbicon,[53] late a Deacon in the traveling connexion but expelled should be restored to his official standing which motion was lost; it was then moved by Br. Dew that the Presiding Elder be instructed to demand his parchment[54] which motion prevailed. When motion was made by Br. Hail that the case of Br. McCallister should be reconsidered and lost.

The report of the Steward of Conference was presented and read Brother Armstrong then moved that the same be received which motion was prevailed.

Resolved on motion by Br. Dew that every Brother who should fail to render his account on the second day after the commencement of Conference should not be [a] partaker of the dividend

The Committee appointed to write the memoir[s] of the deceased then informed the Conference that not being able to obtain sufficient documents relative to Br. Beauchamp's life at present they wished time to obtain them & therefore requested permission to deferr the reporting on that as also on his finances till they could have an oppertunity of meeting at his house at Mt. Carmel for the purpose & from

[53] John C. Harbison, a lawyer, was the first secretary of the Missouri Conference, 1816; he was expelled from the conference in 1820.

[54] In this case, certificate of ordination as deacon.

there to forward them for publication. a motion being made to that effect & seconded was carried.

And there being no more business[55] before Conference adjournment was called for which prevailed & Conference adjourned to meet at Charleston [Indiana] on the 25th Aug. 1825.

J. SCRIPPS *Sec.* R. R. ROBERTS

[55] It is unusual that the conference secretary neglects to mention reading the appointments of the preachers for the following year. This was the most important act of the conference and was done on the last day by the presiding bishop. The appointments for the conference year 1824–25 are found in *Minutes,* Vol. I: *1773–1828*, pp. 453–54. Note that in this and the following "Journals" the Editor has written the word "District" in full; with this exception the appointments are as printed.

MADISON DISTRICT. John Strange, P. Elder.
Madison circuit, Allen Wiley, Aaron Wood.
Lawrenceburg, James Jones, Thomas S. Hitt, sup.
Whitewater, Peter Stephens, Nehemiah B. Griffeth.
Connersville, James Havens.
Rushville, Thomas Rice.
Indianapolis, John Miller.
Flat Rock, Thomas Hewson, James Garner.
Eel River, John Fish.

INDIANA DISTRICT. James Armstrong, P. Elder.
Charleston, James L. Thompson, Jacob Varner.
Corydon, George K. Hester, Dennis Willey, sup.
Salem, Samuel Low, Richard Hargrave.
Paoli, Edward Smith.
Boonsville, Orsenath Fisher.
Patoka, William H. Smith, Geo. Randle.
Vincennes, Edwin Ray.
Honey Creek, Samuel Hull.
Bloomington, Daniel Anderson, John Cord, sup.
Vermillion, Hackaliah Vredenburg, Robert Delap, sup.

ILLINOIS DISTRICT. Samuel H. Thompson, P. Elder.
Mount Carmel, Thomas Davis, Samuel Bassett, sup.
Wabash, Cornelius Ruddle.
Cash River, Josiah Patterson.
Mount Vernon, William Moore.
Kaskaskia, Thomas Randle.
Illinois, John Dew, James E. Johnson.
Mississippi, William Medford.
Sangamon, Peter Cartwright.
Shoal Creek, Ebenezer T. Webster.

Jesse Walker, missionary to the settlements between the Illinois and the Mississippi rivers, and to the Indians in the vicinity of Fort Clark.

William M'Reynolds is transferred to the Kentucky Conference.

II. JOURNAL FOR 1825

Charleston, Ind. August 25, 8 o'clock, Ante Meridian—

Conference met according to appointment—B[isho]p McKendree, Bp. Roberts, and the following members were present, To wit—

John Strange[1]	William Cravens	Dennis Willey
Allen Wyley[2]	Calvin Ruter	Edwin Ray
James Armstrong	Aaron Wood[3]	Sam'l Hull
James L. Thompson	Tho. S. Hitt	John Cord
Samuel H. Thompson	Nehemiah B. Griffith	H. Vredenburgh
Peter Cartwright	Geo. K. Hester	Robert Delap
Jesse Walker		

Bishop McKendree opened the Conference by reading, singing, & prayer, after which Bp. Roberts took the chair & proceeded to business. On motion, Martin Ruter[4] was chosen Secretary protempore.

[1] John Strange (1789–1832), a native of Virginia, moved to Ohio in boyhood and commenced his itinerant career in the Western Conference in 1810. He spent his ministerial life in Ohio and Indiana and was presiding elder of Charlestown and Indianapolis districts. An inadequate sketch of his life is included in James B. Finley's *Sketches of Western Methodism* (Cincinnati, 1855), pp. 399–405. For additional anecdotes and characteristic statements by this pioneer circuit-rider see J. C. Smith, *Reminiscences of Early Methodism in Indiana* (Indianapolis, 1879), chaps. ii–iv, pp. 23–51.

[2] Allen Wiley (1789–1848), a native of Frederick County, Virginia, "perhaps more than any other one man, molded the character of Indiana Methodism," writes F. C. Holliday (*Indiana Methodism* [Cincinnati, 1873], p. 274). Joining the traveling ministry in 1817, he spent eleven years as an itinerant on large circuits, traveled for fourteen years between the Ohio River and Lake Michigan as presiding elder, and served for five years in large stations. From 1832 to 1844 he was a delegate to each General Conference. He was a well-educated man and a founder and trustee of Indiana Asbury University; he was also a trustee of the state university at Bloomington and was once offered a professorship of Greek and Latin there. His "A Friend to Ministers" was published in the *Western Christian Advocate* in 1834–35. In 1845–46 he published in the same journal his "Introduction and Progress of Methodism in Southeastern Indiana," which has been reprinted in Vol. XXIII of the *Indiana Magazine of History* (1927) (William B. Sprague [ed.], *Annals of the American Pulpit,* VII, 569–74).

[3] Aaron Wood, D.D. (1802–87), was a native of Pendleton County, Virginia. From 1822 he traveled in the ministry of the Ohio, Illinois, Indiana, and Northwest Indiana conferences, spending thirteen years on districts and thirteen in agencies for Indiana Asbury University, the American Bible Society, and the Preachers' Aid Society, and was a member of five General Conferences. Two of his sons labored as missionaries in South America (William P. Hargrave [ed.], *Sacred Poems of Rev. Richard, D.D., with a Biography of Himself* .... [Cincinnati, 1890], pp. 253–58).

[4] Martin Ruter, D.D. (1785–1838), was a native of Charleton, Worcester County, Massachusetts. Licensed to preach in 1800, he was admitted on trial to the New York

Voted that the Conference shall open at 8 in the mornings & rise at eleven o'clock—also, that it shall open at two, and rise at 5 o'clock in the evening.

James Armstrong & James L. Thompson were appointed to superintend the appointments or preaching during the session. Conference proceeded to elect by ballot three stewards to manage their temporal concerns—whereupon John Strange, Peter Cartwright, & Calvin Ruter were elected—John Strange having declined serving as one of the Stewards on account of ill health, Edwin Ray was chosen in his stead. Martin Ruter, Peter Cartwright, & James Armstrong, were appointed a committee to examine the candidates for admission into the Connexion. The Conference proceeded to consider the second question in the Minutes, namely, Who remain on trial? John Fish, having travelled a part of his first year, and then left his circuit, was discontinued. James Garnor, Samuel Low, Richard Hargrave, Daniel Anderson, [and] George Randall, were continued. Jacob Varner was discontinued. Proceeded to examine the characters of the Deacons. Aaron Wood, Nehemiah B. Griffith, William H. Smith, & Edwin Rays, were passed. Samuel Hull located. Ebenezer T. Webster's case was laid over. Dennis Willey was elected to Elders orders, and having sustained a supernumerary relation during the last year on account of ill health, and considering himself still unable to do effective service, he proposed receiving a location, and it was granted him. Richard Hargrave's recommendation, which was promised at the last Conference, by Brother Armstrong & Brother Medford, was produced, and was satisfactory.

And then the Conference adjourned.—

Conference in 1801, serving circuits in Lower Canada and New England. In 1809 he became presiding elder of New Hampshire District, New England Conference, and in 1818 was made head of the New Market Wesleyan Academy. The General Conference of 1820 elected him book agent for Cincinnati, and he was re-elected in 1824. In 1828 he was appointed president of Augusta College, Augusta, Kentucky, and in 1833 became president of Allegheny College. In addition to his outstanding contributions to the educational movement in the Methodist Episcopal Church in the first half of the nineteenth century, he is remembered for having been in 1837–38 superintendent of the Methodist Mission in Texas. See the biography, "Martin Ruter," by his daughter, Mrs. S. R. Campbell, in Thomas O. Summers (ed.), *Biographical Sketches of Eminent Itinerant Ministers . . . .* (Nashville, 1859), pp. 321–66.

2 o'clock, Post Meridian.

Bp. Roberts opened the Conference and took the chair. The case of Ebenezer T. Webster was considered. Some objections were made on account of his having become a Free Mason.[5] On the question being put, shall he be elected to Elder's orders, it was decided in the Negative. Edward Smith, Thomas Hewson, Orsenath Fisher, & John Miller, having been examined by the Committee appointed for the purpose, were questioned and admonished by Bp. McKendree according to the Discipline, as preparatory to admission into the Connexion. After the examination, the Conference proceeded to the consideration of their case, and admitted them into the Connexion, and elected them to Deacon's orders. William Moore, being absent, but well recommended, was continued on trial. James E. Johnson's case was taken up, and after some deliberation concerning his peculiarities, he was according to his own request discontinued. The Stewards spent some time in attending to the pecuniary concerns of the Conference. Voted to draw on the Book Concern for one hundred and fifty dollars, also, to draw on the Chartered Fund for eighty. The Conference proceeded to the choice of a Secretary, and Calvin Ruter was elected—after which they adjourned.

FRIDAY [AUGUST 26, 1825]

8 o'clock [A.M.]

Conference was opened, Bp. Roberts in the chair. Conference proceeded to the examination of the characters of the Elders. John Strange, Allen Wiley, passed—the case of James Jones was taken up, and he being absent, his case was by the request of his Presiding [Elder] laid over. The case of Thomas S. Hitt was taken up, and after examination was passed and on motion it was voted that he con-

[5] At this time, during the anti-Masonic crusade in American politics, Masonry was looked on with disfavor by some individual conferences, but the church as a whole refused to condemn it (*Journal of the General Conference of the Methodist Episcopal Church,* Vol. I: *1796–1836,* p. 344). Four years later the Illinois Conference held its session in the Masonic Hall at Madison, Indiana (see "Journal, 1828"). Cf. William Warren Sweet, *Circuit-Rider Days along the Ohio* (New York, 1923), pp. 48–50, and "Resolution Condemning Masons," passed by the Ohio Conference (*ibid.,* pp. 158–59).

tinue in a supernumerary relation another year. Peter Stevens received a location. James Havens, Tho. Rice, James Armstrong, James L. Thompson, were examined & passed, and then the Conference adjourned.—

2 o'clock P.M.

Conference met, Bp. Roberts in the chair. Proceeded in examination of the characters of the Elders. Geo. K. Hester passed & received a location. John Cord, approved, and on motion was changed in his relation from being supernumerary to that of being effective. Hacaliah Vredenburg passed. Robert Delap passed and his relation was changed from supernumerary [to] that of being effective. Samuel H. Thompson & Thomas Davis, examined approved & passed. Josiah Patterson, examined and it was, on motion, voted that he sustain a supernumerary relation. John Dew, William Medford, Peter Cartwright, and Jesse Walker, passed. Wm. Cravens passed & his relation as superannuated preacher, was continued. Calvin Ruters, examined, passed, and it was on motion voted that he continue in his superannuated relation. John W. McReynolds, recommended by the Q[uarterly] M[eeting] Conference of Vermillion circuit for readmission into the travelling Connexion, was readmitted. Joseph Tarkinton,[6] recommended from Bloomville [Boonville] circuit, for admission on trial, was admitted. Eli P. Farmer,[7] recommended from Bloomington circuit for admission on trial, was admitted and then the Conference adjourned.

[6] Joseph Tarkington (1800–1891) was born at Nashville, Davidson County, Tennessee, and converted in Indiana in 1820. He filled leading stations, was presiding elder for eight years, and was agent of Indiana Asbury University. He was the grandfather of Booth Tarkington, American novelist. His *Autobiography,* with Introduction by T. A. Goodwin, D.D. (Cincinnati, 1899), is an interesting contemporary document on Indiana Methodism.

[7] Eli P. Farmer (1794–1881) was born in Virginia. He served in the War of 1812 and became a member of the Illinois legislature. His minstry was unusual in that he never asked for a contribution for himself, preferring to remain self-supporting by farming. Like Cartwright and other frontier preachers, "it was not infrequently the case that he would leave the pulpit to administer personal chastisement to the rowdies who attempted to disturb the peace of his meetings" (James Leaton, *History of Methodism in Illinois, from 1793 to 1832* [Cincinnati, 1883], pp. 250–52).

SATURDAY AUGUST 27, [1825]

8 o'clock Ante Meridian.

Conference met.—Bishop Roberts in the chair. Joseph Foulks[8] was recommended for readmission into the Travelling Connexion, and after due inquiry into his case he was readmitted. It was moved that this Conference in future require a recommendation in favour of every Local Preacher who applies for readmission into the Travelling Connexion, to be obtained from the Quarterly Conference of which he is a member—which motion prevailed.

The case of Philip Cole, who was recommended from Kaskaskia for admission on trial, was considered, & he was admitted. Joseph Barnes, recommended for admission on trial from Illinois Circuit was rejected. James Hadley, recommended from Illenois circuit, was admitted on trial. William See,[9] recommended from Mississippi circuit, was admitted on trial, Asa D. West, recommended from Cash River circuit, was also admitted on trial. William Shanks was readmitted into the Travelling Connexion. The Memorial of Andrew Beaman, an expelled Local Preacher, who had been expelled in 1823, was laid before the Conference, and after some discussion, was laid over until the Afternoon—and then the Conference adjourned.

2 o'clock P.M.

Conference met.—Bp. Roberts in the chair. The Conference proceeded to consider the memorial of Andrew Beaman—a question arising whether the Conference could legally take up the case and act upon it, it was submitted to the chair, and decided in the negative. The time having arrived for adjournment, it was voted that the Conference shall sit for half an hour longer. Joseph Arnold, a local preacher in Deacons orders was recommended for ordination to the

[8] Joseph Foulks (1786–1863), a native of Monmouth County, New Jersey, was admitted on trial to the Western Conference in 1811 but soon located. He later moved from Kentucky to Illinois (1820) as a local preacher. During this conference year he killed, in self-defense, a half-breed Indian displeased by one of his sermons but was upheld in his action by the conference (*ibid.*, pp. 240–42).

[9] William See traveled only two years, on Peoria Circuit, and was discontinued in 1827 at his own request. He was government blacksmith for the Indians, and while living in Chicago was in 1830 appointed by Stephen Beggs, the circuit-preacher, as first class-leader (*ibid.*, p. 243).

office of an Elder, and was elected. Isham West a Local Deacon was recommended for Elder's orders, and he was accordingly elected. John Havens, a Local preacher, was recommended for Deacons' orders, and the question being taken, Shall he be elected, it was decided in the negative. James Noland,[10] a Local Deacon, was recommended for Elders Orders, and it was voted that he be accordingly elected. The Conference then adjourned.

MONDAY, AUGUST 29, [1825]

8 o'clock Ante Meridian.

Conference met. Bp. Roberts in the chair. The Book Agent from Cincinnati,[11] addressed the Conference on the subject of circulating books. Bp. McKendree addressed the Conference on the subject of his health, manner of travelling, support, &c. It was moved & seconded, that the case of John Havens be reconsidered, and on taking the question it was decided in the affirmative; and after some explanation, he was elected to Deacon's orders. Jesse Walker, Conference Missionary among the Indians, submitted a Report respecting his Labours, which Report was accepted.[12] It was moved & seconded, that

[10] James Noland (*ca.* 1790– ?), a native of North Carolina, came with his parents to Monroe County, Illinois, in 1793. He is believed to have founded, in 1816–17, the first Sunday school in the state, at Columbia, Monroe County. He traveled one year (1814) in the itinerancy on Illinois Circuit (*ibid.*, p. 105).

[11] Martin Ruter.

[12] Jesse Walker addressed a letter to the Missionary Society of the M.E. Church dated October 25, 1825, sketching the beginnings of the Potawatomi (or Salem) Mission: "In the spring of 1824 I opened a communication with the Potawatome Indians, and found that they were willing to receive a mission among them; but my call to the general conference prevented me from holding a satisfactory council with them that year. Being reappointed the next autumn by bishop Roberts, superintendent of the Illinois conference, I opened a school at fort Clark, on Illinois river, which continued through the winter, and in which I had six Indian children, whose progress was extremely flattering for so short a period. In the spring of 1825, together with five white families, I proceeded to the mouth of Fox river,—shortly after which I had a most satisfactory council with five chiefs of said tribe. We immediately built cabins for the accommodation of the families. I then opened a school, into which I received fourteen Indian children; but finding that the station was not located on Indian land, I proceeded up Fox river about thirteen miles farther, selected a situation, and am now pre-

the case of Jacob Varner be reconsidered—after considerable discussion the question was taken, shall his case be reconsidered, [and] it was decided in the negative. The time having arrived for adjournment it was moved & seconded, that the Conference extend its session one hour, which motion prevailed. The Conference proceeded to fix on the place of its next session; and on counting the ballots, it was found that Bloomington had a majority of votes and was declared to be the place for the next sitting of this Conference—the Conference then adjourned.

2 o'clock, P.M.

Conference met, Bp. Roberts in the chair. The Stewards of the Conference reported, and their Report was accepted. The time of the next sitting of this Conference was appointed to be the 28th day of September, 1826. George K. Hester requested, & obtained readmission into the Travelling Connexion. Case of Cornelius Ruddle was considered, and he was, at his own request, located. The case of Ebenezer T. Webster was on motion of Samuel H. Thompson, reconsidered, and he was elected to Elders orders. Articles of agreement to be entered into between Jesse Walker & the Chiefs of the Potawatamy Indian nation, were read, & approved by the Conference. Voted that Jesse Walker be cloathed with proper authority, and furnished, with suitable instructions, as missionary among the Indians. James Jaggers, a Local Preacher, recommended for Deacon's orders, was on motion elected. Bennet Hancock, a Local Preacher, recommended for Deacon's orders was elected to that office. The case of Wm. Sterret, who was recommended for the office of a Local Deacon, was duly elected. Joseph Basey and Wm See, were severally recommended for Deacon's orders, and they were accordingly elected to that office. The Stewards having made a distribution of the dividend money to the claimants, a committee of three was appointed to appropriate a small

paring to remove to it, which I shall accomplish as soon as possible. . . . . The Indians have manifested great anxiety to have their children instructed in the arts of civilized life. I have received in support of the mission to the amount of about five hundred dollars in property, obtained by voluntary subscription, and the committee have voted, in addition, one thousand dollars, payable in quarterly instalments,—the first of which I received in cash, and have drafts on the treasurer of the Missionary Society for the remainder" (*Methodist Magazine,* IX [1826], 112–13).

balance that had been reserved to those whom they might conceave the most needy, and report their doings to the Conference—whereupon, John Strange, Samuel H. Thompson, an[d] James Armstrong, were appointed said committee. Wm. Shanks, Samuel H. Thompson, Allen Wiley, J. L. Thompson, & Edwin Ray, were nominated and elected as a committee to meet the Superintendents, and agree on the amount of money necessary, for the support of the Illinois Conference Mission among the Potawatamy Indians. And then the Conference adjourned.—

TUESDAY, AUGUST 30 [1825]

8 o'clock Antemeridian—

Conference met—Bishop Roberts in the chair. The Committee appointed on yesterday, to make a distribution of money that had been reserved, amounting to forty-four dollars, made their report, which report was accepted. Resolved on motion, that each preacher belonging to this Conference, shall in future, bring a certificate from the recording Steward of the circuit or station where he has laboured, stating how much he has received, as quarterage, how much as travelling expences, and how much for table expences.—Voted unanimously that the thanks of this Conference be presented to the citizens of Charleston for the kind reception given them & their friends during their stay in the place. Voted that James L. Thompson be a committee to convey to the people this expression of the Conference. The Conference then adjourned to give the members time to form a Conference Missionary Society,[13] and to resume their sitting so soon as the business of the Society shall be accomplished. Monday Morning 11 o'clock Conference resumed its sitting—Bp. Roberts in the Chair

[13] The Missionary Society of the M.E. Church had been organized in 1819 by Nathan Bangs and Joshua Soule. The *Discipline* of 1828 "recommended that within the bounds of each Annual Conference there be established a Conference Missionary Society, auxiliary to the Missionary Society of the Methodist Episcopal Church, with branches, under such regulations as the Conferences respectively shall prescribe. Each Conference Missionary Society shall annually transmit to the Corresponding Secretary of the Parent Society a copy of its annual report, embracing the operations of its branches, and shall also notify the treasurer of the amount collected in aid of the missionary cause, which amount shall be subject to the order of the Parent Society" (David Sherman, *History of the Revisions of the Discipline of the Methodist Episcopal Church* [New York, 1874], p. 215).

—the appointments[14] were read, and then the Conference adjourned, to meet at Bloomington, [Indiana,]. Sept. 28, 1826.

CALVIN RUTER, *Secy.* R. R. ROBERTS

[14] Appointments (*Minutes,* Vol. I: *1773–1828,* pp. 482–83):

MADISON DISTRICT. John Strange, P. Elder
Madison station, Samuel Basset.
Madison circuit, George K. Hester.
Lawrenceburg, James L. Thompson.
White Water, James Havens.
Connersville, Nehemiah B. Griffith.
Rushville, Stephen R. Beggs.
Flat Rock, James Jones, Thomas S. Hitt, sup.
Indianapolis, Thomas Hewson.

CHARLESTOWN DISTRICT. James Armstrong, P. Elder.
Charlestown circuit, Allen Wiley, George Randel.
Corydon, Samuel Low, George Locke.
Paoli, John Miller.
Bloomfield, Eli P. Farmer.
Eel River, Daniel Anderson.
Crawfordsville, Hackaliah Vredenburgh.
Bloomington, Edwin Ray.
Salem station, William Shanks.
Salem circuit, John Cord.

WABASH DISTRICT. Charles Holliday, P. Elder.
Vermilion, James Hadley.
Honey Creek, Richard Hargrave.
Vincennes, Aaron Wood.
Patoka, James Garner, Joseph Tarkington.
Boonville, William H. Smith.
Carmi, Robert Delap.
Wabash, Thomas Davis.
Mount Carmel, John W. M'Reynolds.

ILLINOIS DISTRICT. Samuel H. Thompson, P. Elder.
Illinois circuit, Ebenezer T. Webster.
Kaskaskia, William Moore.
Cash River, Philip Cole, Asa D. West.
Mount Vernon, Orseneth Fisher.
Shoal Creek, Joseph Foulks.
Sangamon, Peter Cartwright, (who is also superintendent of the Potawattomy mission,) William Chambers.
Peora, William See.
Mississippi, William Medford.
Brownsville, Josiah Patterson, sup.

Jesse Walker, missionary to the Potawattomy Indians.
John Dew and Thomas Randle, transferred to the Missouri Conference.
Thomas Rice, transferred to the Holston Conference.
Edward Smith, transferred to the Baltimore Conference.

III. JOURNAL FOR 1826

Journal of the Illinois Conference for 1826, Bloomington, Indiana, Sept*r*. 28th, 9 O'Clock A.M. Bishop Roberts & Bishop Soule, and the following members were present, to wit

John Strange	William Shanks	Nehemiah B. Griffith
James Armstrong	George Locke[2]	Stephen R. Beggs
Charles Holliday[1]	Calvin Ruter	Thomas Hewson
Peter Cartwright	Edwin Ray	

Bishop Soule opened Conference by reading, singing & prayer after which he took the Chair, & the Conference proceeded to business.

On motion Calvin Ruter was chosen Secretary, & Charles Holliday assistant Secretary.

Voted that Conference shall open at 8 O'Clock A.M. and adjourn One O'Clock P.M.

James Armstrong, Thomas Hewson, & Edwin Ray were elected as a Committee to superintend the appointments for preaching during the sitting of this Conference.

Charles Holliday, Peter Cartwright & William Shanks were elected Stewards of this Conference.

Charles Holliday, John Strange, and Peter Cartwright were nominated and elected a Committee to draught Rules for the Government of the Conference, & report as soon as convenient.

C. Holliday, W. Shanks, C. W. Ruter, P. Cartwright & J. Armstrong, were appointed a Committee to examine the Candidates for admission into full connection

[1] Charles Holliday (1771–1850), born in Baltimore, Maryland, of Presbyterian parentage, was educated for the Presbyterian ministry but became a Methodist after his marriage. Licensed to preach in 1797, he joined the Western Conference in 1809 and was soon presiding elder of Salt River District, Ohio Conference (1813), later serving in the Tennessee, Kentucky, and Illinois conferences. By the General Conference of 1828 he was elected agent of the Western Book Concern, to succeed Martin Ruter, and was re-elected in 1832 ("Memoir," *Minutes of the Annual Conferences of the Methodist Episcopal Church,* Vol. IV: *1846–1851,* pp. 528–29).

[2] George Locke (1797–1834), born in Mason County, Kentucky, of Episcopalian parentage and a descendant of the Reverend Richard Locke, an S.P.G. missionary in colonial Pennsylvania, was converted to Methodism, and joined the Tennessee Conference in 1818. He served that and the Kentucky Conference until 1825, when, because of his antislavery views, he transferred to the Illinois Conference with William Chambers, his brother-in-law, and Charles Holliday. In 1828 he was made presiding elder of Wabash District ("Memoir," *Minutes,* Vol. II: *1829–1839,* p. 344).

Conference then proceeded to take up the second question in the Minutes, to wit: Who remain on trial? And the Characters of Joseph Tarkington, Wm. See, Eli P. Farmer, & James Hadley were severally examined & continued on trial.

The Conference then proceeded to take up the 4th Question on the minutes, to wit: the examination of the Characters of the Deacons, & the Character of John Miller & John W. McReynolds were examined & approved: The Character of Thomas Hewson was examined, approved and at his own request [he was] located.

The Conference then proceeded to examine the Characters of the Candidates for Elders Orders, and Aaron Wood, Wm. H. Smith, Stephen R. Beggs, Nehemiah B. Griffith & Edwin Ray, were approved, and elected to the office of Elder.

The Character of the Elders was then taken up & John Strange, James L. Thompson, James Havens were ex[amine]d & approved: Geo. K. Hester, Samuel Bassett, & James Jones, were ex-d approved, & by request located.

The Character of Thomas H. Hitt [was] examined, approved & he is superannuated; The characters of James Armstrong, Allen Wiley, George Locke Wm Shanks, Charles Holliday, Robert Delap, [and] Thomas Davis, were examined & approved. John Cord was examined, approved & superannuated. Samuel H. Thompson was examined, approved & obtained a supernumerary relation. Conference then adjourned.

FRIDAY, SEPT[EMBER] 28TH 1826

8 O'Clock A.M.

Bishop Roberts in the Chair.

The Conference proceeded with the examination of those on trial: The case of Philip Cole was taken up, his Character approved and at his own request [he was] discontinued. The Character of Asa D. West was ex-d app[rove]d & he continued on trial. The Case of Orsenath Fisher was taken up his Character approved & he obtained a Superannuated relation. The Conference then proceeded with the examination of the Character of Elders:

The case of E. T. Webster was called & at the request of his presiding Elder was laid over—The Case of Joseph Foulks was then taken up, his Character examined & fully approved—The Case of

Peter Cartwright was then taken up his Character examined & approved—The Character of Wm. Medford was ex-d & app-d The Character of Josiah Patterson was ex-d, app-d and he continued in a supernumerary relation—the Character of Jesse Walker was exam-d, and app-d—The Character of Wm. Cravens was ex-d, app-d & he continued in a Superannuated Relation—The Character of Calvin W. Ruter [was] ex-d, app-d, & he continued in a superannuated Relation—The Character of Wm. Chambers was ex-d, app-d & at his request located. The Conference proceeded to take up the 4th question in the Minutes, to wit: Who are admitted into full Connection? James Garner, Samuel Lowe, R. Hargrave, Wm. More, Geo. Randall & Daniel Anderson, having been previously examined by the Committee appointed for that purpose, were questioned, & admonished by Bishop Soule according to the Discipline, as prepa[ra]tory to admission into the travelling Connexion—After the examination, the Conference proceeded to the Consideration of their Case, admitted them into full Connexion & elected them to Deacons orders, with the exception of Daniel Anderson, who was also admitted into full connexion, but he had been previously ordained while a local preacher. The Stewards spent some time in attending to the pecuniary Concerns of the Conference & then adjourned

SATURDAY (SEPT[EMBER] 30TH 1826)

8 O'Clock A.M.

Conference met according to adjournment—The Conference was open'd by reading a portion of the Sacred Scriptures, singing & prayer; After which the Conference proceeded to business, Bishop Soule in the Chair.

The Stewards spent sometime in attending to the pecuniary concerns of the Conference & the Conference voted to draw on the Charter fund for ninety dollars & on the Book Concern for one hundred fifty dollars

It was mov'd & seconded that the Conference reconsider the Character of Peter Cartwright: carried. His Case was then taken up, and some complaints were made thro a Member of this Conference by John Shrader a local preacher relative to the proceedings of Brother Cartwright, when acting as president of the board of trustees of the

Hopkinsville M[eeting] House in Kentucky: and after some discussion Bro Cartwright was exonerated from any Censure in this Case and his Character approved: It was then voted, that an order which was given by Bro. Cartwright as President af[ore]s[ai]d to Bro. Schrader on Bro. John Dew be returned to Brother Schrader—The Conference proceeded to take up the first question on the minutes, to wit: Who are admitted on trial? And Abner H. Chever, Daniel Newton, & Henry Buell, recommended by the Qr.M Conference of Flat Rock Circuit, Robt Burns, Local Deacon recommended by the Q. M. Conf. of White Water C[ircui]t were admitted: James Scott was re-admitted—John Hogan recommended by the Q. M. Conf-e of Baltimore City Station was admitted. Wm. Evans recommended by the Q. M. Conf-e of Salem Ct. & Thomas Files recommended by the Q. M. Conf. of Wabash Ct. were admitted. James Jaggers recommended by the Q. M. Conf-d of Carme Ct. & John Fox[3] recommended by the Q. M. Conference of M[ount] Carmel Ct. were not admitted; but the Presiding Elder is permitted to empl[o]y them if their labours are necessary. Martin Hale recommended by the Q. M. Conference of Vincennes Circuit was not admitted.

The Conference then took up the Case of Local Preachers recommended for Deacons Orders & Samuel Bellamy, Levi Poston, Samuel Morrison, Gamaliel Taylor, Thomas Lowry, Thomas C. Collins, Reuben Clearwater, & Humphrey Finch were elected. Alex[ande]r Rowan was not elected:—The Conference then proceeded to consider the Case of Local Deacons recommended to Elders Orders & Rob't Burns was elected—The Conference then resum'd the Consideration of the first Question on the minutes, & John T. Johnson Smith L. Robinson, Steth M. Otwell[4] & Isaac House were admitted. Samuel Bogart was not admitted. Conference then adjourned until Monday Morning 8 O'Clock.

[3] John Fox (1774–1846) was born in New Jersey. Joining the Philadelphia Conference in 1809, he located in 1820 and moved to Illinois, settling near Palestine ("Memoir," *Minutes,* Vol. IV: *1846–1851,* pp. 80–81).

[4] Stith Mead Otwell (1805–43), named for Stith Mead (1767–1835), a Virginia itinerant, was born in Jackson County, Georgia, but moved to Illinois in 1811. He served the Illinois Conference as head of the Macoupin Mission, as agent of McKendree College in 1836, and as treasurer of the Conference Missionary Society ("Memoir," *Minutes,* Vol. III: *1839–1845,* p. 456).

MONDAY OCTOBER 2ND 1826

8 o'Clock. A.M.

Conference met, pursuant to adjournement, and was open'd by reading a portion of the sacred Scriptures, singing & prayer. Bishop Roberts in the Chair, Conference proceeded to business. On Motion the Presiding Elder was permitted to employ Samuel Bogart should his labours be thought necessary. The Conf. proceeded to the consideration of the situation of the Potawatamie Mission & J. Strange, Wm. Shanks, C. W. Ruter & Allen Wiley, & J. Armstrong were nominated & selected a committee to meet the president of the Conference to determine on the amount which may be necessary for the support of s[ai]d Mission as the Discipline directs: The Conference voted that the money collected on yesterday, amounting to $42.75 be placed in the hands of the Stewards to be appropriated as other monies belonging to the Conference. Hackaliah Vredenburg, thru his Representative requested & obtained a location. William Allison was recommended for readmission, & on the vote being taken he was not readmitted Sam'l Lyon, local preacher was recommended to the Office of Deacon & was elected. The Conference proceeded to fix the place of its next meeting at Mt. Carmel [Illinois] on the 20th of Septr 1827.

Resolved that this Conference concur with the Mississippi Annual Conference in recommending to General Conference at its next session to alter the ratio of Representation in our form of Discipline Chap. 1st Section 3rd Question 2nd Answer 5 and figure 2 by striking out 5 & inserting 7: & striking out 7 and inserting 21, so as that the sd article may read as follows "They shall not allow of more than one Representative for every seven Members of the Annual Confe[rence] nor allow of a less number than one for every twenty one:—The Concurrence of the Confe was expressed in a rising vote in which none voted in the negative.[5]

On motion resolved that this Conference patronise the Christian

[5] Not until 1836 did the General Conference resolve that "the ratio of delegation for the next General Conference be fixed at one delegate for twenty-one members of each annual conference" (*Journal of the General Conference of the Methodist Episcopal Church,* Vol. I: *1796–1836,* p. 496).

Advocate[6] published by the Agents of the Meth. Book Concern at New York—Resolved that a Committee of two be appointed to address a letter to the Rev. John T. Hamilton[7] a member of the Committee of Correspondence of the General Assembly of the Presbyterian Church in answer to a communication which this Confe rec-d from him & on motion S. H. Thompson & John Strange were elected for that purpose.

On motion voted that the Conference reconsider the vote relative to the money collected on yesterday and on motion voted that s-d money be placed in the hands of the four presiding Elders to be appropriated to the most needy—The Stewards made their report which was accepted.

Conference then adjourned.

TUESDAY OCT[OBER] 2ND 1826

8 O'Clock (A.M.)

Conference met & was open-d by reading Singing & prayer—Conference proceeded to business Bishop Soule in the Chair.

The Stewards spent a few minutes in closing their business and on motion, voted, that a small balance remaining in the hands of the Stewards, amounting to $14,37½ be given to the preacher who may be appointed to Atlas Circuit. At the request of S. H. Thompson, he was dismissed from the Committee appointed to address a letter to the Rev. J. T. Hamilton & C. W. Ruter was nominated & elected in his place.

On motion resolved that this Conf-e continue the Potowatomie Mission,[8] & that every preacher of this Conf-e exert himself to procure

[6] The first issue of the *Christian Advocate* had appeared on September 9, 1826. It was American Methodism's first official weekly publication and was published at New York under authority of the General Conference.

[7] John T. Hamilton was at the time teaching and preaching in Indiana as a member of Salem Presbytery (Hanford A. Edson, *Contributions to the Early History of the Presbyterian Church in Indiana* .... [Cincinnati, 1898], pp. 167–68).

[8] During this year Jesse Walker reported as follows to the Missionary Society of the M.E. Church as to his labors on the Potawatomi Mission: ".... in pursuance with the instructions of Bishop Roberts, I went on as soon as possible [from conference] to the Indian country, and have made an agreement with the Patawatamies, through their chiefs, for a section of land, in conformity with the articles adopted by the Illinois Conference.... The place selected for the establishment is about 100 miles above Fort Clark, about 20 miles north of the Illinois river, and between it and Fox river. The

funds & means for the support of s-d mission & that St. Louis & Fort Clark be the places of deposit by those articles convey'd by water & Springfield, Sangama County, for those articles & monies convey'd by land. The Committee appointed to estimate the amount necessary to support s-d mission reported as follows

"We the Committee appointed by the Illinois Annual Conference to estimate the amount necessary to support the Potowatamie Mission have had the same under consideration and after mature deliberation, we are of opinion that one thousand dollars are necessary & amply sufficient for that purpose Signed by us this 3rd of Oct. 1826

JOHN STRANGE, *Ch[airman]*
JAS. ARMSTRONG
ALLEN WILEY
WM. SHANKS

CALVIN W. RUTER, *Sec-y.*

which report was concurr'd in by the Conference.

On motion the Case of C. W. Ruter was reconsidered & his Relation was changed to that of Supernumerary.

On motion resolved that this Conference patronise the Augusta College.[9]

---

soil is very good, timber plenty, and the spot well watered." He reports building a house for the missionary family, a smith's shop, a poultry house, a spring house, and a horse mill. Forty acres of land were under cultivation, seven were used as pasture, and one for garden purposes. Total expenditures on the mission were $2093.98 3/4, two-thirds of which were paid by the government, the rest by the church. A school of fifteen Indian children was in operation, with two teachers. Walker further reports: "I have talked with eight chiefs, all of whom are highly gratified with the mission, and have pledged themselves to use their influence to support it in its religious character; but cannot legislate on the subject of religion; that, they say, is a matter between the Great Spirit and the hearts of their people; but they will defend and protect the mission family, and if the Indians will give up their children to the care and tuition of the missionaries, they will be glad of it, but they cannot coerce this measure." He concludes by saying that "a door of communication to the hearts of these poor, neglected, persecuted sons of men, before we can expect among them the exercise of an evangelical faith, must be opened; we must try and bring them to habits of civilization. . . ." (*Methodist Magazine,* IX, No. 12 [December, 1826], 476–77).

[9] Augusta College, Augusta, Kentucky, was the first American Methodist college founded after the dismal failure of Cokesbury College in 1795. Its nucleus was an academy taken over in 1822 by the Ohio and Kentucky conferences, under the principalship of the Reverend John P. Finley. It was abandoned in 1844, when the church divided over the slavery issue and Transylvania College, at Lexington, Kentucky, came under the care of the Kentucky Conference.

Samuel H. Thompson was by the president appointed to obtain a Copy of the Report of the Committee of Safety, that it may be enter'd on the Journals of this Conference

The appointments[10] were read out, & Conference adjourn'd to meet again at Mount Carmel September 20th 1827

C. W. Ruter, *Secretary* R. R. Roberts
J. Soule

[10] Appointments (*Minutes,* Vol. I: *1773–1828,* p. 516):

Madison District. John Strange, P. Elder.
Madison station, Calvin W. Ruter, sup.
Madison cir., James Scott, Daniel Newton.
Lawrenceburg, James L. Thompson, Geo. Randle.
White Water, James Havens, John F. Johnson.
Connersville, Robert Burns.
Rushville, Nehemiah B. Griffith.
Flat Rock, Abner H. Chever.
Indianapolis, Edwin Ray.

Charleston District. James Armstrong, P. Elder.
Charleston, Allen Wiley, James Garner.
Corydon, George Locke, Samuel Low.
Paoli, Wm. H. Smith, Smith L. Robinson.
Eel River, Daniel Anderson, Stith M. Otwell.
Crawfordsville, Henry Buell.
Bloomington, Aaron Wood.
Salem, William Shanks, John Hogan.
Washington, William Moore.

Wabash District. Charles Holliday, P. Elder.
Vermilion, Eli P. Farmer.
Vincennes, Stephen R. Beggs.
Patoka, Asa D. West.
Boonville, Thomas Davis.
Wabash, Robert Delap.
Mount Vernon, Thomas Files.
Mount Carmel, John M'Reynolds.
Cash River, William Evans.

Illinois District. Peter Cartwright, P. Elder, and superintendent of the Potawattomy mission.
Illinois, Samuel H. Thompson, sup., John Miller.
Kaskaskia, Josiah Patterson, sup., James Hadley.
Shoal Creek, Joseph Foulks.
Sangamon, Richard Hargrave, Joseph Tarkington.
Peoria, William See.
Mississippi, Thomas Randle, Isaac House.
Atlas, William Medford.
Potawattomy mission, Jesse Walker.

IV. JOURNAL FOR 1827

Journal of the 4th Illinois Conference Mount Carmel [Illinois] September 20th 1827

Thursday morning 9 O'clock A.M.

Conference met according to appointment. Bishop Roberts being present Opened Conference by reading the Scriptures, Singing and prayer.

The list was then called, and the following being present took their seats.

John Strange	William H. Smith	Peter Cartwright
James Scott	Daniel Anderson	Samuel H. Thompson
James L. Thompson	Aron Wood	John Miller
Edwin Ray	William Shanks	Josiah Patterson
Calvin W. Rutter	William Moore	Richard Hargrave
James Armstrong	Charles Holliday	Thomas Randle
Allen Wiley	Stephen R. Beggs	Thomas S. Hitt
George Locke	Thomas Davis	Orseneth Fisher
Samuel Lowe	John W. McReynolds	John Dew

Conference then proceeded to business. Bishop Roberts in the chair.

On motion Calvin W. Rutter was elected Secretary. Voted by the Conference that the standing hours of meeting and adjournment be as follows (viz) Meet at 8 O'Clock and adjourn at eleven A.M. and meet again at 2 O'Clock & adjourn at 5 O'Clock P.M.

Charles Holliday, John W. McReynolds, and Aron Wood were appointed a Committee to appoint the preachers to preach and to superintend divine service at the Meeting House during the sitting of the Conference.

Conference then proceeded to elect by ballot three Stewards to manage their temp[o]ral concerns, whereupon Peter Cartwright, William Shanks & John Dew are elected.

The President then appointed James Armstrong, William Shanks and John Dew a committee to write the Memoirs of the dead.

The President also appointed the following persons (Viz) Samuel H. Thompson, Allen Wiley, George Locke, James Scott, and Tho-s S. Hitt a committee to examine the candidates for admission into full connexion.

The conference elected Allen Wiley George Locke & Calvin Rutter a book committee.

Conference then adjourned until 2 O'Clock P.M.

Evening Session 2 O'Clock P.M.

Conference met pursuant to adjournment. Bishop Roberts in the Chair. Conference was opened by Bro. Holliday by reading the Scriptures singing and prayer. The Journal was read and approved, and Conference then proceeded to business. The First question on the Minutes (Viz) "Who are admitted on trial?" [was read] and John Hardy recommended by the quarterly meeting conference of Rushville Ct. was admitted.

Constant B. Jones recommended by the quarterly meeting Conference of Indianopolis Ct. was admitted.

The case of John Havens and John Linville recommended by the Quarterly Meeting Conference of Connersville Circuit was taken up and neither of them were admitted: but on motion conference ordered that the Presiding Elder have leave to employ them both, if necessary.

The case of Enoch G. Wood recommended by the Quarterly Meeting Conference of Bloomington Circuit was taken up and he was admitted.

The case of Asahel Risley[1] recommended by the quarterly Meeting conference of Eel River circuit was taken up and he was admitted.

The case of Benj[amin] Stephenson recommended by the Quarterly Meeting Conference of Washington Circuit was taken up and he was admitted.

The case of John Kerns recommended by the quarterly meeting conference of Washington Circuit was then taken up, and he was admitted.

The case of William Mavity[2] recommended by the quarterly meet-

[1] Asahel L. Risley (1804–74), a native of Kentucky, transferred in 1848 to Rock River Conference and was appointed presiding elder of Chicago District. Later he retransferred to the Illinois Conference and became agent for McKendree College. At the time of his death he was a member of the Southern Illinois Conference (James Leaton, *History of Methodism in Illinois, from 1793 to 1832* [Cincinnati, 1883], pp. 288–89).

[2] William Mavity (1780–1834) was born in Franklin County, Virginia, moved to Tennessee in 1804, and until 1827 labored as a local preacher in Tennessee, Kentucky, and Indiana ("Memoir," *Minutes*, Vol. II: *1829–1839*, p. 344).

ing conference Peolia [Paoli] Circuit was taken up and he was admitted.

The case of Vance Jones recommended by the Quarterly Conference of Washington Circuit was then taken up, and he was not admitted.

The time of adjournment having arrived on motion, it was resolved that Conference continue its present session thirty minutes.

On motion, Conference Resolved, that the rule adopted by the Illinois Conference at their session of 1825 requiring of local Preachers applying for readmission into the travelling Connexion, a recommendation from the Quarterly meeting where they are members, be rescinded.

Conference then adjourned.

FRIDAY SEPTEMBER 21ST, [1827]

Eight O'clock A.M.

Conference met pursuant to adjournment Bishop Roberts in the chair. Conference was opened by Bro. Rutter, by Reading the Scriptures, singing and prayer. The list was called and the Journal read & approved, and Conference proceeded to business.

The Stewards of the Conference then called on the Preachers for the amount of quarterage received by them on their respective circuits, together with the amount collected on their circuits to meet deficiencies at Conference, which were rendered in.

The Conference proceeded with the consideration of the 1st question on the Minutes.

The case of Jacob Turman who was brought forward for readmission was then taken up and considered, and he was not readmitted.

William Echols, who was recommended by the quarterly meeting of Cash River Circuit was admitted.

Samuel C. Cooper,[3] recommended by the quarterly meeting Conference of Boonville, Ct. was admitted.

[3] Samuel C. Cooper (1799–1856), born of Methodist parentage in Baltimore, Maryland, was converted in Ohio in 1818. He served eleven years on districts, was seven years agent for Indiana Asbury University and one year for Fort Wayne Female College, and was twice a member of the General Conference. At his death he was a member of the North Indiana Conference.

James McKean, recommended by the quarterly Meeting Conference of Boonville Circuit, was admitted.

The case of William Townsend, a local Elder recommended for readmission into the travelling connexion was considered and he was not admitted.

The hour of adjournment having arrived, it was on motion resolved that the conference continue its present session thirty minutes longer.

Samuel Bogard, who was recommended by the quarterly Meeting Conference of Mississippi circuit for admission on trial, was admitted.

Isaac Scarrett,[4] Recommended for readmission into the travelling connexion from Mississippi Circuit, was readmitted.

William Chambers,[5] recommended from Sangama Circuit for readmission into the travelling connexion was readmitted.

The case of William Welch, who was recommended by the quarterly Meeting Conference of Illinois Circuit for admission on trial was taken up and he was not admitted: but on motion the Presiding Elder has leave to employ him if necessary.

Conference then adjourned.

2 O'Clock P.M.

Conference met pursuant to Adjournment. Bishop Roberts in the chair. Conference opened by reading the Scriptures, Singing and Prayer. The list was then called, and the Journal of the Morning session was read and approved, and Conference proceeded to business.

On motion it was resolved the Presiding Elder be permitted to employ Bro. William Townsend as a travelling Preacher, should he deem it expedient.

Bishop Roberts then presented a written course of reading and study[6] to be pursued by the candidates for the Ministry which was

[4] Isaac Scarritt (1775–1860), a native of Connecticut, joined the New England Conference in 1807, later locating. In 1818 he settled near Edwardsville, Illinois. The Illinois Conference appointed him in 1828 missionary to the Potawatomi Indians, and in 1830 he took charge of the Fort Clarke Mission.

[5] William Chambers (1796–1859), born in Calvert County, Maryland, of Episcopalian parentage, served in the War of 1812, joined the Kentucky Conference in 1821, and located after transferring to Illinois.

[6] The General Conference of 1816 had resolved that "it shall be the duty of the bishops, or of a committee which they may appoint at each annual conference, to point

read and on motion it was ordered that the same be spread on the journal. which was in the words following (to wit)

As it appears that the course of reading & study recommended by the Superintendents to the Missouri Annual Conference has not been entered on the Journals of the Illinois Conference: The following is now submitted as "proper course of Reading and Study for the Candidates for the ministry.["]

The Holy Ghost Saith "Study to shew thyself approved unto God, a workman that needeth not to be ashamed rightly dividing the Word of Truth—Hold fast the form of sound words which thou hast heard from me, in faith and love which is in Christ Jesus. Give attention to reading, to exhortation, to doctrine."

It is therefore recommended to Candidates for the Ministry, to study and make themselves acquainted with the following important points of doctrine: The general depravity & corruption of the Human Heart—Redemption by Christ—Repentance towards God—Justification by faith—The direct Witness of the holy Spirit—Holiness of heart & Life including Regeneration & Sanctification—The Divinity of our Lord Jesus Christ—The perseverence of those who have been Justified —Baptism—The resurrection of the Dead, & future Rewards and punishments.

It is recommended to them to Study, the nature and principles of Church Government, especially our own. The Philosophy, or Grammar of the English Language—Geography—Ancient History—Ecclesiastical History, Moral & Natural Philosophy & Logic.

To aid the Student in the acquisition of these important branches of knowledge the reading of the following Books, or as many of them as can be obtained, is recommended. The Holy Scriptures—Wesley's

---

out a course of reading and study proper to be pursued by candidates for the ministry; and the presiding elders, whenever such are presented to them, shall direct them to those studies which have been thus recommended. And before any such candidate is received into full connexion, he shall give satisfactory evidence respecting his knowledge of those particular subjects which have been recommended to his consideration" (*Journal of the General Conference of the Methodist Episcopal Church,* Vol. I: *1796–1836,* pp. 160–61). This was the beginning of formal theological education in the Methodist Episcopal church. The bishops were authorized by the General Conference of 1844 to prepare a uniform four-year course of study for candidates for deacons' and elders' orders in the traveling ministry, applicable to all conferences (*ibid., 1844,* pp. 125–26). The outline of this four-year course can be seen in the Appendix to the *Discipline* of 1848, pp. 213–16.

Notes—Benson's Coke's & Clarke's Commentaries—Wesleys Sermons —Answer to Taylor—Saints Rest—[Law's] Serious Call—Benson's Sermon's—Fletchers Checks & Appeal—Portrait of St. Paul—Watson's theological Institutes—Woods or Martindales Dictionary—The Methodist Discipline—Murrays Gramar—Morse's Geography—Rollin's Ancient History—Mosheim's Ecclesiastical history—Lock[e] on the Understanding—Paley's philosophy—Evidences—Wesley's Philosophy,—Duncan's or Watts' Logic—the Methodist Magazine.

Signed R. R. Roberts

The Committee appointed, at the last session of the Illinois Conference, to draught rules for the government of said Conference made their report, and the rules were then read, amended, and adopted, and ordered to be Journalized.

Rules and regulations for the government of the Illinois annual Conference.

1st. Each session of the conference shall be opened by reading a Portion of Scripture, singing, and Prayer

2nd. The President shall attend precisely at the hour to which the Conference shall have adjourned, and call the Conference to order, & proceed to business.

3rd. The President may decide on all questions of order; but if any member of the Confer[e]nce differ in Opinion from the President, on questions of order, he may appeal from said decision to the Conference, which appeal when seconded, shall be decided without debate.

4th. When two or more members shall rise to speak at the same time the President shall announce the speaker that is in order.

5th. The President shall have the oversight of all the Conference papers, correct the Journals, and at the commencement of each session shall cause the Journals of the preceeding session to be read.

6th. All committees shall be appointed by the President unless otherwise directed by the Conference.

7th When any matter is to be delivered by any member of conference, he shall rise and respectfully address the President.

8th. No speaker shall be allowed to speak longer than fifteen minutes at any one time, nor more than once (except to explain) on the same question till all have spoken, who may wish to speak, unless by permission.

9th No person shall pass about the room, when any member is speaking nor between the speaker and the President while any person is addressing the President.

10th Each member of conference shall be punctual in attending at the hour to which conference adjourned, and no member shall be absent during any of the sessions, unless he obtain leave of absence.

11th Every member of this Conference, in his debates shall have due regard to the feelings of his brethren, and avoid all personality

12th No member shall prefer a complaint against another member of the Conference unless he has spoken to him on the subject, first out of Conference

Sept. 21st 1827 — PETER CARTWRIGHT, CHARLES HOLLIDAY, JOHN STRANGE } *Comm[ittee]*

Brother Cartwright presented a Petition, from certain Citizens of Green County State of Illinois, to conference on the subject of a conference seminary,[7] which on motion was referred to a committee of three, with instructions to report to this conference; and John Dew Allen Wiley & John Fox were appointed that committee

The conference then took up the 2nd question in the minutes (to wit) Who remain on trial? and the Characters of Abner H. Chever Henry Buell, John Hogan, Thomas Files, Smith L Robinson, Isaac House, Daniel Newton Robt Burns, William Evans, John T. Johnson, & Stith M. Otwell were severally examined, and they were continued on trial. Whereupon Conference adjourned.

SATURDAY SEPT[EMBER] 22ND 1827

8 O'Clock A.M.

Conference met pursuant to adjournment Bishop Roberts in the Chair.

Bro Wiley opened conference by reading the scriptures Singing and prayer, after which conference proceeded to business

The Journal was read and approved.

[7] The General Conference of 1820 resolved that "it be, and is hereby recommended to all the annual conferences, to establish, as soon as practicable, literary institutions [1824: 'seminaries of learning'], under their own control, in such way and manner as they may think proper" (*Journals of the General Conference,* Vol. I: *1796–1836,* pp. 208, 295).

The committee appointed on yesterday to take into consideration the petition of certain citizens of Green County Ill. on the subject of a conference seminary made their report which was accepted & on motion it was resolved that a committee of five be appointed whose duty it shall be to obtain all the information they can, on the subject of a conference seminary during the ensuing year & report the result of their enquiries to the next conference The appointment of which committee was reserved by the president to a future period of the conference.

The conference then proceeded to take up the 3rd. question on the minutes (to wit) "Who are admitted into full connexion?" and Eli P. Farmer, Asa D. West, James Hadley, and Joseph Tarkington having been previously examined by the committee appointed for that purpose were called in, and questioned, and admonished by Bishop Roberts as the discipline directs, were admitted into full connexion and elected to deacons orders & Asa D. West received a location at his own request.

The Case of Wm. See was call-d & he not being present, at his own request thro his representations [representatives] was discontinued.

The Conference took up the 4th question on the minutes (to wit) who are the Deacons? & the characters of James Garner & Richard Hargrave were ex-d and app-d & Bro. Hargrave, at the Suggestion of his representative, rec-d a superannuated Relation.—George Randall's character was ex-d & he located.—The Character of Samuel Lowe & William Mow [Moore] were ex-d & app-d—The Character of J. W. McReynolds John Miller, & Orsenath Fisher, were ex-d app-d & they were elected to Elders Orders: Bro. Fisher continued in a superannuated Relation.

The superintendent and missionary of the Potowattomy mission at Salem on Fox River, presented their report which was read & accepted.

The time of adjournment having arrived, it was on motion resolved, that the Conference continue its present sitting 15 minutes: On motion resolved, that a Committee of 5 be appointed to take into Consideration the State of the Potowatemy Mission & the expediency of continuing said Mission, and report to the Conference: Whereupon the President appointed the following persons as that Committee (to wit) Wm. Shanks, Sam-l H. Thompson, James Armstrong, Allen Wiley & Peter Cartwright.

Whereupon Conf-e adjourn'd.

2 O'Clock P.M.

Conference met according to adjournment Bishop Roberts in the chair. Conference opened by Reading the Scriptures Singing and prayer, and then proceeded to business.

The conference then proceeded to the consideration of the case of local preachers recommended for Deacons orders: and Charles W. Morrow, Elijah McDaniel, [and] Alfred J. Cotton recommended from the Madison District and Daniel Dillings recommended from Charlestown District: John Givens from the Wabash District: and Thornton Peeples, William Meldrum and Lorenze Edwards recommended from the Illinois District were severally elected to Deacons orders.

The Conference then took up the case of Local Deacons recommended for Elders orders, and Robert Ray, recommended from Madison District; Hezekiah Holland and Ebenezer Jones recommended from Charleston [District], were severally elected to Elders orders.

The conference then proceeded to the examination of the characters of the Elders: & the characters of John Strange, & Calvin W. Ruttur were examined & approved, and said Ruter's Supernumerary relation continued. The case of James Scott was then called, and some objections being made relative to some doctrines, by him advanced it was, in motion resolved that a committee of five be appointed to wait on Bro. Scott & obtain his views on certain doctrines by him advanced & report to this Conference, whereupon the President appointed the following persons as that committee: Charles Holliday, George Lock, Peter Cartwright, James Armstrong & Samuel Low. Whereupon Conference adjourned.

MONDAY SEPT[EMBER] 24TH 1827

8 oclock A.M.

Conference met pursuant to adjournment; and was opened by reading the Scriptures, Singing and prayer. Conference then proceeded to business Bishop Roberts in the Chair.

The Committee appointed on Saturday to obtain the views of Bro. James Scott on certain doctrines by him advanced presented their report, & a motion made to accept the report, and after some discussion, the time of adjournment having arrived, it was on motion resolved that the Conference continue its present session until the case now under consideration be disposed of.

On motion resolved that the future consideraton of the report of the committee in the case of Bro. Scott be postponed until the next annual examination of Characters before the Conference and that he be admonished by the President not to disseminate his particular views on the points of doctrine referred to in the report of the committee & the Character of Bro. Scott was further examined & passed.

Whereupon Conference Adjourned.

2 OClock P.M.

Conference met pursuant to adjournment, and was opened by reading the Scriptures Singing and Prayer. Conference proceeded to business, Bishop Roberts in the Chair. The Journal of the morning session was read, and Bro. Charles Slocumb[8] was brought forward for readmission and he was readmitted.

The Conference then proceeded with the examination of the Characters of the Elders, and the Characters of James L. Thompson, James Havens, N. B. Griffith, Edwin Ray, James Armstrong, Allen Wiley, George Locke Wm. H. Smith, Dan-l Anderson, Aaron Wood, Wm. Shanks, Charles Holliday, Stephen R. Beggs, Thomas Davis, Rob-t Delap, P. Cartwrigth, [and] Samuel H. Thompson, were severally ex-d & app-d

Robert Delap Rec-d a superannuated Relation & Samuel H. Thompson continued in the supernumerary Relation

The Character of Josiah Patterson & Joseph Foulks were ex-d and app-d & Bro. Patterson continued in a supernumerary Relation & Bro. Foulks at his own request received a location.

The Character of Tho-s Randle, Wm. Medford, at his own Request (as suggested by his Representative) rec-d a location.

[8] Charles Slocumb (? –1844) had been originally received on trial in the Missouri Conference at its first session, but located in 1821. A contemporary described him as "especially strong on the baptismal controversy" (quoted in Leaton, *op. cit.*, p. 155).

The Character of Thomas S. Hitt was ex-d & app-d & at the suggestion of his Representative, his Relation was alter'd from a superannuated Relation to that of an effective man—The Conf-e then proceeded to take the numbers in the several Circuits and then on motion Conference adjourned.

TUESDAY [SEPTEMBER 25, 1827]

8 O'Clock, A.M.

Conference met pursuant to adjournment, & was open'd by Reading, Singing & Prayer; after which the Conf-e proceeded to business, Bishop Roberts in the Chair.

The Committee appointed to take into Consideration the Situation of the Potowatomy Mission,[9] presented their report which was read, & on motion accepted, & ordered to be spread on the Journals of the Conference, which Report is as follows, to wit:—

Your Committee to examine the State of the Potawatomy Mission, beg leave to make the following Report: At the Illinois Conference, held in Charlestown 1825, an allowance of one thousand Dollars was made for the support of the Mission, and put into the hands of the Missionary: From our recollection of the missionary Report to the Conference of 1826, that money was laid out for the Mission; & a debt contracted of $1208:80

Cash on hand to meet the Debt, 150:00

Which leaves the Mission in Debt 1058:80

At the Conference of 1826, an allowance was made for the support of the Mission of one thousand Dollars & put in the Hands of the Superintendants of the Mission: From the Report to this Conference, it appears that the money has been laid out for the Mission—No debts have been contracted the past year.

[9] Peter Cartwright, in a letter dated "Sangamon, Ill., September 15, 1827," states in regard to the Potawatomi (Salem) Mission: "Our school yet remains small, but the children are orderly, learn fast, and give a satisfactory attention to the worship of God. One adult native has professed a change of heart, and has been baptized . . . . Our farm is in a prosperous state . . . . We have endured great hardships this year, but the God of missions has supported us, and with the appropriations made by our bishops, we have met the current expenses of the year" (*Methodist Magazine,* XI, No. 1 [January, 1828], 37).

According to the Report to this Conference, the Mission property amounts to $ 303:25

The Crop, as valued in the Report, amounts to 502:00

The property offered in the Report, and which we advise the Conference to accept & make Missionary Property amounts to 250.00

If the Conference accepts this Property, then the Property and Crop belonging to the Mission will amount to 1055:25

But little has been effected, as yet by the Mission, when compared to the expence, labours & Sufferings of the Missionary & his Family; but when we consider what it has cost, and the probability of its being less expensive in the future, we cannot advise its discontinuance, until further trial is given it.

As it respects the debt now against the Mission, it is our opinion that a man had better be appointed, whose duty it shall be to make Collections in the Bounds of the Conference and else where to pay that debt

All of which is respectfully submitted

Wm. Shanks

in behalf of the Committee

and on motion the same persons were appointed as a committee in conjunction with the President of the conference to estimate the amount necessary to support the mission, and report to this conference.

On motion Bro. Lock was exhonorated from serving on the book committee in consequence of the afflictions of his family, and Thomas S. Hitt elected in his place.

The Stewards of Conference then presented their report, which was read, and on motion accepted On motion the case of Bro. Josiah Patterson was reconsidered and his relation changed from supernumerary, to a Superannuated relation. The conference then proceeded to fix the place of its next session & on counting the votes, the Town of Madison [Indiana] having a Majority, was fixed on as the place of the next session of this Conference, which will commence on the Ninth day of October 1828.

The Conference then proceeded to elect their delegates to the next general Conference, [and] on counting the votes, it appeared that John Strange, Peter Cartwright, James Armstrong, Charles Holliday, Samuel H. Thompson & John Dew were duly elected.

On motion resolved that the collections to be lifted from the Several circuits, Stations & Districts to defray the expenses of the delegates to the general Conference, be deposited with the several delegates in the conference, & by them carried on to General Conference. Whereupon on motion conference adjourned.

2 O'clock P.M.

Conference met pursuant to adjournment and was opened by reading the Scriptures, singing and Prayer. After which Conference proceeded to business Bishop Roberts in the chair.

On motion resolved that the person who shall be appointed to make collections for the Potowatomy Mission be styled the superintendant of said mission.

The committee appointed to write the memoirs of the dead presented their report containing the memoirs of The Rev. William Cravens and John Cord deceased which was read and after being amended was adopted.

The pres[iden]t appointed John Strange, James Armstrong, Charles Holliday, Peter Cartwright, and William Shanks, as a committee to obtain all the information they can, on the subject of the Conference seminary the ensuing year; according to a previous resolution of this Conference.

The Collections made during the past year for the Pottawatomy Mission were presented, and on motion resolved that the money and property collected be placed in the hands of the superintendant of s-d Mission.

Whereupon on motion Conference adjourned until tomorrow morning [at] 6 oclock.

WEDNESDAY [SEPTEMBER 26, 1827]

6 oclock A.M.

Conference met pursuant to adjournment & was opened by reading singing & prayer.

The conf- then proceeded to business Bp. Roberts in the chair. The book committee presented their report—

The Stewards of the conference then spent a few minutes in completing their business

On motion the following resolution was adopted.

Resolved by the Illinois Conference, that each Preacher belonging to the conference, be requested to present in writing to the next conference a succinct account of the time and place of his birth, the most important incidents of his life; when and by what means he was brought to the knowledge of Salvation, with any other important matter which may concern him, and that the same be kept on file among the papers of conference.[10]

On motion resolved that the Secretary of this conference be respectfully requested to forward a list of the appointments of the Preachers belonging to this conference to the Editors of the Christian Advocate & Journal for publication.

On motion resolved that a vote of thanks be given to the citizens of Mount Carmel for their kindness to the Members of this conference during its present session and that Bro. Charles Holliday publish the same the first opertunity in the Meeting House in this Town.

On motion resolved that a vote of thanks be given to the president, for his patience & Promptitude in discharging the arduous duties of the chair, during the present session.

On motion resolved that a vote of thanks be given to the Secretaries of this conference for the faithful discharge of the duties assigned them during the present session.

On motion the vote of William Chambers who was readmitted into the travelling connexion during the pressent session was reconsidered and his recommendation withdrawn by his representative.

The appointments[11] of the Preachers were then read & there [be-

[10] The Baltimore Conference of 1811 was one of the first to urge the collection of historical data by and about ministers and their charges. (James Edward Armstrong, *History of the Old Baltimore Conference* .... [Baltimore, 1907], pp. 163–64). The death of Bishop Asbury in 1816 and the first complete publication of his *Journal* in 1821 made the whole church conscious more than ever of its history, and it is doubtless this that inspired the action taken by the Illinois Conference this year.

[11] Appointments (*Minutes,* Vol. I: *1773–1828,* pp. 549–50):

MADISON DISTRICT. J. Strange, P. Elder.

Madison station, Edwin Ray.

Madison circuit, James Garner, Abner H. Chever.

Lawrenceburg circuit, Allen Wiley, D. Newton.

Lawrenceburg station, James L. Thompson.

ing] no other business Conference adjourned to meet again at Madison Indiana October 9th, 1828.

C. W. Ruter, *Sec-y* R. R. Roberts

V. JOURNAL FOR 1828

Journal of the 5th Illinois Annual Conference Madison [Indiana] Oct 9 1828.

Thursday morning 9 oclk A.M.

Conference met according to appointment. Bishop Roberts being present opened the Conference by reading the Scriptures, singing and

---

Whitewater, Thomas S. Hitt, James Scott.
Wayne, S. R. Beggs, William Evans.
Connersville, Robert Burns.
Rushville, James Havens.
Columbus, Constant B. Jones.
Indianapolis, Nehemiah B. Griffith.
Vernon, Henry Buell.

Charlestown District. James Armstrong, P. Elder.
Charlestown circuit, G. Locke, C. W. Ruter, sup., Enoch G. Wood.
Corydon, John W. M'Reynolds, S. Low, sup.
Paoli, William Moore, James M'Kean.
Eel River, William H. Smith, Benjamin Stephenson.
Crawfordsville, Eli P. Farmer.
Bloomington, Daniel Anderson, S. M. Otwell.
Salem, William Shanks, John Hardy.
Washington, Thomas Davis.

Wabash District. C. Holliday, P. Elder.
Vermilion, John Fox.
Vincennes, J. Miller, Asahel Risley.
Patoki, Charles Slocumb.
Boonville, William Mavity.
Wabash, James Hadley.
Mount Vernon, Thomas Files.
Mount Carmel, Aaron Wood.
Cash River, Samuel C. Cooper.

Illinois District. P. Cartwright, P. Elder.
Illinois, S. H. Thompson, J. Hogan.
Kaskaskia, William Echols.
Shoal Creek, T. Randle, J. Kerns.
Sangamon, Joseph Tarkington, Isaac S. House.
Peoria, Smith L. Robinson.
Apple Creek, Isaac Scarritt, John T. Johnson.
Atlas, Samuel Bogart.
Potawattomy mission at Salem, John Dew, superintendent and Conference collector for the mission; Jesse Walker, missionary.

prayer. The list was called and the following members being present took their seats, viz.

John Strange	Calvin W. Ruter	John Fox
James Garner.	John W. McReynolds	Aaron Wood.
Allen Wiley	Samuel Low	Samuel H. Thompson
James L. Thompson	William Moore	Joseph Tarkington
James Scott	William H. Smith	Isaac Scarritt
Thomas S. Hitt	Elie P. Farmer	John Dew
Steven R. Beggs	William Shank	Richard Hargrave
Nehemiah B. Griffeth	Thomas Davis	
James Armstrong	George Locke	

Conference then proceeded to business Bishop Roberts in the chair. On Motion C. W. Ruter was elected secretary. Voted by the Conference that the standing hours of meeting and adjournment be as follows: viz, Meet at half past eight A.M. and adjourn at 12 Meet at 2 P.M. and adjourn at half past 4 P.M. On motion the Rules adopted for the government of this conference at its last session were read and adopted as the Rules for the present session.

On motion the conference proceeded to elect by ballot three stewards of conference. On counting the votes, it appeared that A. Wiley, John Dew and Wm. Shanks were elected.—On motion J. Strange, J. Armstrong, and C. W. Ruter were appointed a committee to superintend the appointments for preaching during the session. It was moved to reconsider the motion fixing the hour of adjournment of the morning session, [but] in putting the question it was decided in the negative. The President appointed Samuel H. Thompson, John Strange, Allen Wiley, Wm. Shanks, James Armstrong, John Dew, and James Scott, a committee to examine the graduates for admission into full connexion. The Conference then proceeded to the examination of the characters of those who have been one year on trial. The characters of Constant B. Jones, Enoch G. Wood, Asahel Risley, Benjamin Stevenson, Samuel Bogart, Wm. Mavity, James McCain, Samuel C. Cooper, and John Kerns were severally examined and continued on trial. John Hardy [was] discontinued and William Echols discontinued at his o[w]n request.

Conference proceeded to the examination of the characters of deacons and the characters of Joseph Tarkington Elie P. Farmer, and

James Hadly were approved and passed. James Garner, Samuel Low, Richard Hargrave and Wm. Moore [were] approved and elected to Elders orders; and brothers E. P. Farmer, S. Low, R. Hargrave superanuated. Whereupon Conference adjourned.

2 oclock P.M.

Conference met pursuant to adjournment and was opened according to Rule. The list was called and the journals of the morning session were read and approved.

Conference then proceeded to business, Bishop Roberts in the chair. The conference then resumed the examination of characters of Deacons. and the character of Isaac Scarrett was examined approved and he elected to Elders orders. The Conference then proceeded to the examination of the characters of Elders, and the characters of John Strange Edwin Ray, Allen Wiley, James L. Thompson, Thomas S. Hitt, were severally examined, approved and passed. The case of Bro. James Scott, was taken up and the report of the committee in his case, at the last session of this conference was called up, and after some discussion the report of the s-d committee was on motion indefinitely pos[t]poned. The character of James Scott was examined approved and passed. The characters of Stephen R. Beggs, James Havens, N. B. Griffeth, James Armstrong, John W. McReynolds, Wm. H. Smith, Daniel Anderson, Wm. Shanks, Thos Davis, George Locke John Fox, and C. W. Ruter were severally examined approved and passed and a motion being made to change the relation of Bro. Ruter after some discussion, the further consideration of the motion was laid over. Whereupon conference adjourned.

FRIDAY [OCTOBER 10, 1828]

Half past 8 oclock.

Conference met pursuant of adjournment and was opened according to Rule The Conference proceeded to business Bishop Roberts in the Chair. The list was called and the journals read and approved. The Conference stewards spent some time in attending to the pecuniary concerns of the conference. A communication was read from the Book Agents in New York. The Conference voted to draw on the Book Concern for $150. and on the Chartered fund for $90. The candidates for admission into full connexion having been previously examined by the committee appointed for the purpose, were questioned and admonished by Bishop Roberts according to Discipline as preparatory to admission into the connexion after examination the conference proceeded to the consideration of their characters. Abner H. Cheeven [Chever] not being present but well recommended was on motion continued on trial. The characters of John Hogan, Thomas Files, Smith S. Robinson & Isaac House were examined, approved, and admitted into full connexion & elected to Deacons orders, and Bro. House received a superanuated relation. On motion resolved that when conference adjourns it adjourns until half past 8 oclk tomorrow morning, where upon Conference adjourned.

SATURDAY [OCTOBER 11, 1828]

Half past 8 Oclk.

Conference met pursuant to adjournment and opened according to Rule. Conference proceeded to business Bishop Roberts in the chair. A communication was read from A society denominated "The Female Domestic Missionary Society of Madison" accompanied with a donation amounting to $6.46¼. On motion resolved that a vote of thanks be given to the Female Domestic Missionary society of Madison, for their laudable zeal in support of the Gospel, and that the amount by them donated be placed in the hands of a committee of 4 to be appropriated to the most needy and the president appointed John Strange, James Armstrong, George Lock & Samuel H. Thompson as that committee. On motion resolved that the secretary be directed to furnish The Female Domestic Missionary society of Madison with a copy of the foregoing resolution. The Conference resumed the consideration of the characters of the candidates for admission into full connexion. The characters of Robert Burns, Wm Evans,— Stith M. Otwell, [and] John T. Johnson were severally examined approved and they admitted into full connexion and all Elected to Deacons orders except Bro. Burns who had been previously ordained while a local preacher. The character [of] Daniel Newton was examined approved, and at his own request communicated to the Conference by his colleague, he was Discontinued. The conference proceeded to the examination of the characters of local preachers recommended to Deacons orders, and Samuel Barrett, James Linaville, Phillip Conner, Isaac N Ellsbury, Recommended from Madison District, George Swartz, Henry Summers, Benjamin Davis, Jacob

Swartz, recommended from Charlestown District. Braston Parish, Richard Wheeler, John Dollihan, Robert Parrett, recommended from Wabash District, were severally elected. Little Page Procter, also [was] recommended from Wabash District but [not] elected. Whereupon on motion conference adjourned.

2 oclk P.M.

Conference met pursuant to adjournment and was opened according to Rule. On motion the calling of the list was dispensed with. The journals were read and approved. Conference then proceeded to business. Bishop Roberts in the chair. The conference resumed the consideration of the Local Preachers recommended for Deacons orders and David B. Carter[1] & Wm. Mills recommended from Illinois District were elected, Levin Green[2] not elected. The conference proceeded to the consideration of the case of Local Deacons recommended for Elders orders, and Thomas Silvey recommended from Madison District, John Mercer, recommended from Charlestown Distict, George A. Colbert[3] and Zadock Casey[4] recommended from the Wabash District, Anthony W. Casax and John Burns, recommended from the Illinois District were severally elected to Elders orders. The Conference resumed the case of candidates for admission into full connexion. Henry Buell having been previously examined by the committee for that purpose was questioned and admonished according to Discipline by Bishop Roberts and after examination of his character he was admitted into full connexion and elected to Deacons orders. The conference resumed the examination of the

[1] David B. Carter (1793–1840), a native of Tennessee, moved in 1827 to Sangamon County, Illinois. In 1832 he was on the Fort Edward Mission ("Memoir," *Minutes,* Vol. III: *1839–1845,* p. 240).

[2] Leven Green had served as a supply on the Maramec [Merrimac] Circuit, Missouri, in 1811. "Whilst on this circuit he married the belle of the settlement, which so enraged her numerous suitors, amongst whom was his colleague, that they did not rest until Green was expelled from the Church" (James Leaton, *History of Methodism in Illinois, from 1793 to 1832* [Cincinnati, 1883], p. 232).

[3] George A. Colbert had served in the Western and Tennessee conferences, 1810–14.

[4] Zadok Casey (1798–1862), a native of Georgia, was a local preacher for forty years. He was largely self-taught, having received only three months of formal schooling and learned to write as an adult. Despite these handicaps, he served in 1828 (and later) in the Illinois legislature, in 1830 was elected lieutenant-governor of Illinois, and beginning in 1832 served ten years in Congress. He was also a member of the Illinois constitutional convention of 1848 (*The Biographical Encyclopaedia of Illinois of the Nineteenth Century* [Philadelphia, 1875], pp. 439–40).

characters of the Elders, and the characters of John Miller Charles Slocumb, Aaron Wood, Peter Cartwright, Orsenath Fisher Samuel H. Thompson, Thomas Randle, Josiah Patterson, and Robert Delap were severally examined and passed. Bro. Thompsons relation was changed from supernumer[ar]y to affective [effective]. Josiah Patterson Orsenath Fisher and R. Delap continued in a superanuated relation, and Thomas Randle & Charles Slocumb located at their own request. Bro. Dews case was called, and on motion laid over until he shall bring in his missionary report Where upon conference adjourned.

MONDAY [OCTOBER 13, 1828]

Half past 8 oclk A.M.

Conference met pursuant to adjournment and was opened according to Rule. On motion the calling of the list was dispensed with. The Journals were read and approved. The conference proceeded to business Bishop Roberts in the chair. The conference then proceeded the consideration of the first question on the minutes (viz) who are admitted on trial? Answer John VanCleave[5] Asa Beck recommended from the Madison District Cornelius Reiddley [Ruddle] William L Deneen, Asa Phelps,[6] recommended from the Charleston District, were admitted. James Parcels, William Clarke, & Stephen Grimes also recommended from the Charlestown District—were not admitted, but on motion the P[residing] Elder has liberty to emply them if he deems it expedient with the exception of Bro. Grimes. Charles Bonner recommended from Wabash District was admitted and Asa D. West recommended for readmission, was readmitted. John French, George Tease, Miles Huffacre, Hardin A. Tarkington, John H. Benson recommended from Illinois District [were] admitted. Phillip Moore and David B. Carter not admitted, but the

[5] John Van Cleve, D.D. (1804–75), born in Shrewsbury, New Jersey, settled successively in New York (1808) and Ohio (1815), where he was converted in 1822. He was chosen presiding elder of Mount Vernon District in the Illinois Conference in 1835 and subsequently served Mount Carmel, Lebanon, and Alton districts. Four times he was a delegate to the General Conference, and he died in New York while attending a meeting of the General Missionary Committee.

[6] Asahel E. Phelps (? –1853) is remembered as a champion of Methodism against Unitarianism, Universalism, Deism, Immersionism, Mormonism, etc. In 1837 he served Peoria Mission and in 1838 became presiding elder of Mount Vernon District, later serving Peoria, Washington, and Rock Island districts in Illinois and Rock River conferences. He was also agent for the Rock River Seminary.

Presiding Elder has liberty to employ them if necessary. The time of adjournment having arrived, on motion resolved that conference continue its present session until half-past twelve. William Chambers [was] readmitted, William Medford not readmitted. David Breouet [Bruner] recommended from Charlestown District for admission on trial was admitted. Whereupon Conference adjourned.

2 oclk P.M.

Conference met pursuant to adjournment and was opened according to Rule. The journals were read and approved. Conference proceeded to business Bishop Roberts in the chair. Bro. Strange notified the conference that Thomas Biggs a Local preacher who had been expelled by the Quarterly Meeting conference of White Water Circuit, had appealed to this Conference whereupon on motion resolved that the conference keep closed doors. Conference then proceeded to the appeal of Thomas Biggs and after some examination of the papers it was on motion resolved that this case be remanded back to the Circuit from whence it came, and that the preacher who may be appointed to that circuit the ensuing year take the papers now before the conference relative to this case, and proceed as soon as convenient to a full investigation and fair trial of the charges against said Thomas Biggs. The superintendant of the Pottawatomy Mission at Salem then presented his report which was read. The time of adjournment having on motion resolved that the conference continue its session an hour. On motion the report of the superintendent of the Salem Mission was accepted. On motion resolved that a committee of five be appointed to take into consideration the verbal communication from the superintendant of Salem Mission together with the expediency of continuing said Mission whereupon the President appointed John Strange, James Armstrong, Allen Wiley, Isaac Scarrits and William Shanks, that committee. Whereupon conference adjourned.

TUESDAY [OCTOBER 14, 1828]

Half past 8 oclk. A.M.

Conference met pursuant to adjournment and was opened according to Rule. The list was called and the journals read [and] approved. Conference proceeded to business Bishop Roberts in the chair The book agent from Cincinati made a verbal communication relative to the books on hand in the bounds of the conference. The committee appointed to take into consideration the expediency of continuing the Pottawatomy mission at Salem presented their report which was read. and after some discussion, on motion the report was recommitted. The conference proceeded to take numbers in society.[7] The President called for the report of the committee appointed at the last annual Conference to take into consideration the subject of a conference Seminary[8] whereupon the committee asked and obtained further [time] to report and on motion resolved that the vacancy in the committee occasioned by the absence of Peter Cartwright be filled and the President appointed S. H. Thompson to fill that vacancy. On motion resolved to proceed to fix the place of holding the next session of this conference. By nomination and election and on the vote being called Edwardsville Madison County Illinois was fixed on as the place of holding the next session of this conference. Whereupon Conference adjourned.

2 oclock P.M.

Conference met pursuant to adjournment and was opened according to Rule.

The list was called and the journals read and approved. Conference then proceeded to business Bishop Roberts in the chair. The Stewards of this Conference then presented their report which was read and on motion accepted. The committee on the Pottawattomy Mission presented their report [which] was read and accepted. The conference resumed the examination of the characters of Elders, and the characters of John Dew, and Jesse Walker were examined approved and passed. Conference called up the case of Joseph Basey recommended for examination on trial into the travelling connexion. he was not admitted. On motion the relation of James Havens was changed from effective to that of supernumerary. On motion resolved that William Shanks receive no appointment for the ensuing year at his

[7] The total membership of Illinois Conference Methodism for the conference year 1827–28 was 18,724 white and 116 colored members, making an increase of 2,750 white and a decrease of 7 colored members over the previous year (*Minutes,* Vol. II: *1829–1839,* p. 9).

[8] Lebanon Seminary at Lebanon, Illinois, was the first higher school founded by the Methodists in the states of the Northwest Territory. Edward R. Ames, later bishop, was its first principal. Bishop McKendree in 1830 donated 480 acres of land to the institution, which that year was renamed McKendree College, the charter dating from 1834.

own request on motion resolved that C. W. Ruter sustain a superannuated relation to this Conference. On motion resolved that E. Ray sustain a superannuated relation [to] this conference. Where upon conference adjourned.

WEDNESDAY [OCTOBER 15, 1828]

Half past 8 oclk A.M.

Conference met pursuant to adjournment and was opened according to Rule. The list was called and the journals read and approved. The Conference then proceeded to business Bishop Roberts in the chair. On motion resolved that James Garner be left without an appointment the ensuing year at his own request. on motion resolved that the vote fixing the relation of Edwin Ray to this conf. be reconsidered and on motion Bro. E. Ray received a supernumerary relation.

It was moved & seconded that the committee appointed at the last session of the Illinois Conf to take into consideration the subject of a conference seminary be discharged from any further consideration of the subject which motion did not prevail.

It was then moved that said committee have leave of absence for one hour to make out their report which motion was lost. On motion resolved that a certain memorial with accompanying Documents now in the hands of Bro. Sam-l H. Thompson be read to this conference.

The s-d memorial and accompanying Documents concerning a seminary at Lebanon Illinois were read & on motion refer[r]ed to a committee of three who shall report as soon as convenient & the president appointed Sam-l H. Thompson John Strange & John Dew that committee.

The Stewards then spent a few moments in completing their business.

The committee appointed to take into consideration the address of the committee of Illinois Circuit on the subject of the Lebanon Seminary submitted their report which was read & on motion accepted.

On motion the Conference reconsidered the vote by which the report of the committee on the above named address was accepted.

On motion—resolved that the report of the above named committee be amended by striking out so much of said report a[s] recommends that this conf. at its present session proceed to appoint trustees to said seminary & on motion the report as amended was accepted.

On motion resolved that this conf. unite in requesting the Stockholders of the seminary at Lebanon to meet as soon as convenient & so to alter and amend their constitution as to designate the number of trustees for s-d institution and the manner of their appointment more definitely. On motion resolved that the secretary of this conference be instructed to furnish the committee of Illinois circuit with a copy of the resolutions of this conf. on the subject of the Lebanon seminary.

On motion resolved that a vote of thanks be presented to the citizens of Madison by the Rev. John Strange for their kind attention to the preachers during their present session.—On motion resolved that a vote of thanks be presented to the members of the masonic fraternity for the use of their hall as a conference room during its present session. On motion resolved that a vote of thanks be presented to the Minister & members of the Presbyterian church in this Town for the use of their Meeting House during the present session of this conf.

The time of adjournment having arrived on motion resolved that the conf. continue its present session until the appointments are read.

On motion resolved that each preacher belonging to this conf. who may have charge of a circuit or station—be and they are hereby required to use their best efforts to form missionary societies within their respective charges which societies when formed shall sustain to the Illinois Conf. Missionary society the relation of branch societies—

Resolved on motion that it be the duty of each member of this conf. having charge of a circuit or station to do what he can in the formation of sunday schools auxiliary to the sunday school union of the Methodist E. Church[9]

On motion resolved that a vote of thanks be presented to the president of this conf. for the patience & promptness with which he has

[9] The Sunday School Union of the Methodist Episcopal Church was organized in 1827 and reorganized and recognized by the General Conference of 1840. Its chief objects were "to promote the formation, and to concentrate the efforts, of sabbath schools connected with the congregations of the Methodist Episcopal church, and all others that may become auxiliary; to aid in the instruction of the rising generation, particularly in the knowledge of the Holy Scriptures, and in the service of God" (*Methodist Magazine,* X [1827], 368). One of its chief services was the publication and distribution of low-priced Sunday-school books and tracts. The Union was the basis for the Sunday-School Department in later Methodism (see Addie Grace Wardle, *History of the Sunday School Movement in the Methodist Episcopal Church* [New York: Methodist Book Concern, 1918]).

discharged the arduous duties of his office during the present ses-[s]ion of this Conf.

On motion resolved that a vote of thanks be presented to the secretary of this conference for the patience & diligence with which he has discharged the arduous duties of his office during the present session of this Conf.

Resolved on motion the secretary of this conf. be respectfully requested to forward a list of the stations of the preachers to the editors of the Christian Advocate & Journal & Zions Herald[10] for publication.

The Stations[11] of the preachers for the ensuing year were then read.

[10] In 1823 a New England Conference society began publishing *Zion's Herald,* a small weekly. It was purchased by the Book Concern in 1828 and united with the *Christian Advocate* (founded 1826) and published under the new title of *Christian Advocate and Journal and Zion's Herald* until 1833, when the New England Conference Methodists resecured the publication rights and adopted it as their official organ.

[11] Appointments (*Minutes,* Vol. II: *1829–1839,* pp. 9–10):

MADISON DISTRICT. Allen Wiley, P. Elder.
Madison station, Edwin Ray, sup.
Madison circuit, Cornelius Ruddell, Abner H. Chever.
Lawrenceburg, Nehemiah B. Griffith, Enoch G. Wood.
White Water, James L. Thompson.
Wayne, Robert Burns.
Connersville, William Evans.
Rushville, J. Havens, sup., J. Kerns.
Columbus, Asa Beck.
Indianapolis station, James Armstrong.
Fall Creek, Charles Bonner.

CHARLESTOWN DISTRICT. John Strange, P. Elder.
Charlestown circuit, J. W. M'Reynolds, James Scott.
Vernon. John T. Johnson.
Salem, John Hogan.
Bloomington, William Moore, John Vancleve.
White Lick, Joseph Tarkington.
Eel River, William H. Smith, G. Tease.
Crawfordsville, Stephen R. Beggs.
Washington, John Miller.
Corydon, Thomas Davis, S. M. Otwell.
Paoli, Daniel Anderson.

WABASH DISTRICT. Geo. Locke, P. Elder.
Vermilion, Henry Buell, A. Risley.
Carlisle, James Hadley, B. Stephenson.
Vincennes, Thomas S. Hill [Hitt].
Petersburg, David Bruner.
Boonville, Constant B. Jones.
Princeton circuit, Samuel C. Cooper.
Wabash, William Mavity.
Mt. Vernon, John Fox.

Whereupon Conference adjourned to meet at Edwardsville Madison County Illinois on the 18th day of September 1829.

C. W. Ruter *Sect.* R. R. Roberts

VI. JOURNAL FOR 1829

Journal of the 6th Illinois Annual Conference, Edwardsville, September 18th, 1829.

Friday morning 9 oclock Ante Meridian. Conference met according to appointment Bishop Soule being present opened the Conf-e by reading a portion of the sacred Scriptures Singing and prayer. The list was called and the following members being present took their seats as such (viz) Allen Wiley. Edwin Ray, Nehemiah B. Griffeth James Armstrong. John Strange. James Scott. John Hogan. Wm. Moore. Joseph Tarkington. Wm. Chambers. Stephen R. Beggs. Wm. Crane. Wm. Evans. George Locke, Thomas S. Hitt. John Fox. Aaron Wood. Thos Files. Peter Cartwright. Samuel H. Thompson. Jesse Walker. John Dew. Isaac Scarritt. C. W. Ruter. Robert Delap. Orsenath Fisher Jesse Hale. & Richard Hargrave.

Conference then proceeded to business, Bishop Soule in the chair. Calvin W. Ruter was nominated and elected secretary. Conference voted [that] the standing hours of meeting and adjournment be as follows (viz) meet at half past 8 oclk A.M. and adjourn at 1 oclk P.M. on each day. Conference then proceeded to elect their Conference stewards and on counting the votes John Dew Allen Wiley & Peter Cartwright were declared duly elected.

Conference then appointed Peter Cartwright, Wm. Chambers &

Mt. Carmel, Aaron Wood.
Cash River, T. Files, M. Huffaker.

Illinois District. Peter Cartwright, P. Elder.
Illinois circuit, William Chambers.
Kaskaskia, Smith L. Robinson, Asahel Phelps.
Shoal Creek, Samuel H. Thompson, Wm. L. Deneen.
Sangamon, J. M'Kain, J. H. Benson.
Peoria, Jesse Walker, H. Tarkington.
Apple Creek, S. Bogart, J. French.
Atlas, Asa D. West.
Galena, John Dew.
Potawattomy mission, at Salem, Isaac Scarritt.

William Shanks is without a station, at his own request.
James Garner without a station, at his own request.

Samuel H. Thompson, as a committee to appoint preachers to officiate in public and superintend the congregations during the session of Conference. On motion the rules and regulations for the government of the Illinois annual Conference adopted at their 4th session were read & adopted as the rules for the government of this session. The president appointed Samuel H. Thompson, Jas. Armstrong C. W. Ruter John Dew & T. S. Hitt as a committee to examine the candidates for admission into full connexion. It was moved that this Conference during its present session sit with open doors which motion was lost.[1] On motion resolved that in the examination of characters it shall be enquired concerning each presiding Elder, has he uniformly held lovefeasts[2] at his Quarterly Meetings, and concerning each travelling preacher, has he uniformly attended his appointments and met the classes. The Conference then took up the 2nd question on the minutes (viz) Who remain on trial? and the characters of John Vancleave, Asa Beck, Cornelius Ruddle, Wm. L. Deneen, Asahel Phelps, Charles Bonner, John E. French, George W. Taes [Tease], Miles Huffaker, Hardin A. Tarkington, John H. Benson & David Bruner, were severally examined and they continued on trial. except Cornelius Ruddle and David Bruner who were discontinued at their own request. The case of Robert H. Jordon who at the last Baltimore Conference was continued on trial, and transfer[r]ed to this conference was presented, and his standing and relation as such acknowledged by this conference. Where upon Conference adjourned.

SATURDAY [SEPTEMBER 19, 1829]

½ past 8 Oclk A.M.

Conference met pursuant to adjournmend and was opened according to rule. The list was called and the journals read and approved. Conference then proceeded to business Bp. Soule in the chair. The stewards spent some time in attending the temporal concern of the conference. Conference voted to draw on the book concern for 150$ and on the chartered fund for 90$ Conference then proceeded to examination of the characters of the Deacons of one year. The case of

[1] Conferences sat with closed doors all during the period under consideration. Laymen were admitted to conferences at a later date.

[2] Lovefeasts were a Moravian contribution to Methodism, adopted by Wesley. They consisted of all present partaking of bread and water, then sharing spiritual blessings, either Scripture passages or personal testimony, or song, with the group.

Henry Buell was called & some objections being made to his moral character he on motion received a location at his own request and the P. E. of the District instructed to withhold the cirtificate of his location until his case should be legally investigated. The characters of John Hogan, Thos Files, Smith L. Robison, Isaac S. House, Wm. Evans, Stith M. Otwell, John T. Johnson & Asa D. West were severally examined approved & passed. and I. S. House located at his own request and the character of Robert Burns as an Elder was also examined approved and passed.

The Conference proceeded to the examination of the characters of the candidates for Elders orders and the characters of Joseph Tarkington, Eli P Farmer, Jas Hadley, and Michael Taylor were severally examined approved and they elected to Elders orders except E. P. Farmer. On motion Bro. Farmers relation was changed from a superannuated to that of a supernumerary.

The Conference then proceeded to the examination of the characters of the Elders and the characters of Allen Wiley, Edwin Ray. N. B. Griffeth, Jas Havens, Jas Armstrong, Jas L. Thompson, John Strange, John W. McReynolds, were severally examined approved and passed, and on motion Bro. Ray received a superan[n]uated and Bro Havens continued in a supernumerary relation. The case of Bro. Jas Scott was called and a paper was presented to the conference by his P. E. containing some objections to Bro. Scott['s] administration when on Madison Circuit, and on motion resolved that the person who presented s-d paper be permitted to with draw the same, where upon Conference adjourned.

MONDAY [SEPTEMBER 21, 1829]

½ past 8 Oclock A.M.

Conference met pursuant to adjournment, and was opened according to rule; the list was called, the journals read, and approved. Conference then proceeded to business. Bp. Soule in the chair. The case of Bro. J. Scott was again called; his character examined, approved, and passed; and at his own request he received a supernumerary relation. On motion resolved that this conference elect a committee of three, to meet and confer with a committee appointed by the Missouri Conference, at its last session (and who were announced by the president to be in waiting) on the subject of a Conference Seminary, and report as soon as convenient to Conference: and John

Dew, John Strange, and Peter Cartwright were elected as that committee. On motion, the committee appointed at a previous session of this conference to take into consideration the subject of a conference Seminary & report to this conference were discharged from the performance of any further duties on that subject; they having made no report. The Conference proceeded to take up the 3rd question on the minutes. viz: Who are addmitted into full connexion? The case of Abner H. Chaever was called and he not being present, and being reported by his P. E. as in a state of affliction and altogether unable to preach, a motion was made that he be discontinued in consequence of inability to perform the duties of a preacher and after some discussion, and the question being put it was carried in the affirmative. Jas McKean, Samuel C. Cooper, Asahel L. Riley, E. G. Wood; having been previously examined by the committee appointed for that purpose, were questioned and admonished by Bp. Soule according to rule. The Conference then proceeded to the consideration of their characters, and they were severally admitted into full connexion, and elected to Deacons orders; except Bro. Mavity, who had been previously ordained while a local preacher and he having travelled two years as Deacon was elected to the office of an Elder. The case of Constant B. Jones, was then taken up: and some objections were made [to his] moral character, & his P. E. informed the Conference that he had been tried by a committee and on motion the papers in that case were read. It was then moved and seconded that Bro. Jones be drop[p]ed: and after some discussion & vote being taken, it was decided in the affirmative.

The conference then proceeded to the consideration of the case of local preachers recommended for Deacons orders, and Enoch Moore,[3] Henry Davidson, Clarke Banning, James Bristoe [and] Wm. Johnson recommended from the Illinois District were severally elected to that office. The time of adjournment having arrived it was on Motion resolved the conference continue its present session ten minutes. The conference proceeded with the consideration of the case of local

[3] Enoch Moore (1783–1848) is said to have been the first American male child born in Illinois, his birth having occurred in the blockhouse at Bellefontaine, Monroe County, February 17, 1783. He was a government surveyor, a member of the first Illinois constitutional convention, and an Illinois legislator and probate judge. In 1806 he had been converted to Methodism by Jesse Walker and became a local preacher (James Leaton, *History of Methodism in Illinois, from 1793 to 1832* [Cincinnati, 1883], pp. 64–65).

Preachers recommended for Deacons orders & the case of Charles R. Matheny[4] was brought forward and after some discussion was, on motion laid over. The case of Thomas Depoysture recommended from Wabash District was presented, he was not elected.

Whereupon Conference then adjourned.

TUESDAY [SEPTEMBER 22, 1829]

½ past 8 O. clock A.M.

Conference met pursuant to adjournment & was opened to rule; the list was called and the Journals read and approved. Conference then proceeded to business, Bp. Soule in the chair. Bro. Cartwright, asked & obtained leave to withdraw the recommendation of Charles R. Matheny which on yesterday was presented to this Conference.

On motion the conference, reconsidered the vote taken on yesterday in the case of Thos Depeysture, and after some discussion he was elected to Deacons Orders.

Conference proceeded with the consideration of the case of local preachers recommended for Deacon's orders & Joseph Curtis & Thos. Cottingham recommended from Wabash District were elected.

Charles Robinson, John Aarington, [and] Francis Brown[?], recommended from Illinois District were elected, Levin Green also recommended, was not elected. Joseph Wheeler recommended from Wabash District was not elected. John Bymes & Joseph Springer, recommended from the Wabash District were elected. Benjamin Blackstone Jacob Lopp, Ebenezer Patrick and Reuben Claypool, recommended from the Charlestown District were elected. Solomon Hurbaugh and John Hughes were not elected. John[a]than Shaw, and James McLane recommended from the Madison District were elected. John C. Archer recommended from the Wabash District was not elected. The joint Committee of Missouri and Illinois conferences,

[4] Charles R. Matheny (1786–1839), a native of Loudoun County, Virginia, was admitted on trial to the Western Conference in 1805 and, after serving the Illinois Circuit one year, was discontinued. He settled in St. Clair County, Illinois, and removed to Sangamon County in 1821, where he became county clerk. His house was for some time the Methodist preaching-place in Springfield (*ibid.*, pp. 45–46; cf. John Carroll Power, *History of the Early Settlers of Sangamon County, Illinois* [Springfield, Ill., 1876], pp. 479–81). See T. Walter Johnson, "Charles Reynolds Matheny: Pioneer Settler of Illinois, 1786–1839," *Journal of the Illinois State Historical Society*, XXIII, No. 4 (1940), 438–68.

appointed to confer on the subject of a conference Seminary made the following report:

Your committee having had this subject under consideration, after mature deliberation beg leave to report:

That in the opinion of the committee, the members and friends of the Methodist Episcopal Church, within the bounds of the two conferences are sufficiently numerous and wealthy, to establish a literary institution, that would do honor to any country: we have but to enlist the hearty cooperation of the members and friends of our Church herein. Your Committee doubts not for a moment the practicability of establishing a Seminary of Learning, which shall not only vie with, but excell, any now in operation, west of the Wabash River. Your Committee therefore respectfully Submits to your consideration the following preamble and Resolution. viz.

Whereas the the Missouri Annual Conference at its last Session did appoint a committee to confer with this conference on the subject of a seminary of learning, and did fully authorize said committee to agree upon a union between that conference and this, if in the opinion of this conference it be advisable, and to do all other matters and things on behalf of s-d Missouri conference in relation to a Joint Seminary of learning.

Resolved, Therefore that the Illinois conference do approve of a union, and by and with the consent of the Missouri Annual Conference, through their committee now present, do unite both conferences, for the purpose of establishing a seminary of learning under the patronage of the Methodist Episcopal Church. Which being read was adopted: And on motion the committe[e] was instructed to proceed to locate the site for said Seminary; and to do all things necessary for the accomplishment of the object contemplated in S-d Report, and report as soon as convenient to the conference.

On motion, Brothers John Dew & Peter Cartwright were discharged from any further duties as Conference Stewards, and Brothers Edwin Ray & James Armstrong were elected to fill the vacancies occasioned thereby. The President informed the Conference that he had received a communication from Mt. Carmel on the subject of the Conference seminary Site, and on Motion s-d communication was ordered to be put into the hands of the chairman of the committee on that subject.

The conference proceeded to the consideration of the case of Local Deacons, recommended for Elders Orders, and John Kirkpatrick,[5] James Stringfield, Pasham Randle[6] Wm. Hunter, Moses Osburn and Laurence Killebrew recommended from Illinois District were elected. Thomas Upjohn recommended from Madison District was elected. John W. Jones and David Gunn, recommended from Charlestown District were elected. A document was presented to the conference from Benjamin Watts, which was read and on motion the further consideration of s-d document was laid over untill tomorrow, whereupon on motion the conference adjourned—

WEDNESDAY [SEPTEMBER 23, 1829]

½ past 8 Oclk A.M.

Conference met pursuant to adjournment, and was opened according to rule. The list was called and the journals read and approved. Conference proceeded to business Bp. Soule in the chair. Conference called up the document which on yesterday was presented to this Conference from Benj-n Watt an expelled local preacher; the consideration of which was laid over until this day, and after some discussion it was on motion resolved that the s-d Benj-n Watt be allowed a new trial before the Quarterly Meeting Conference of which he was a member. Bro Dew asked & obtained leave of absence during the present day.[7] On motion the vote taken on yesterday in the case of John Archer a local preacher recommended for Deacons orders was reconsidered. On motion the document presented to this conference by Benj-n Watt was ordered to be returned to him. Conference resumed the examination of the characters of Elders and the characters of Wm. Moore, Wm. H. Smith, Stephen R. Beggs, John Miller, Thos Davis, Daniel Anderson, George Locke, Thos S. Hitt, John Fox,

[5] John Kirkpatrick (? –1845) had removed from Georgia to Illinois in 1802, settling near Edwardsville. Leaton (*op. cit.*, p. 38) believes him to have been the "first local preacher who received license in Illinois." Inheriting three slaves in 1829, he brought them to Illinois and manumitted them. After residing later in Springfield and in Adams County, Illinois, he settled near Ottumwa, Iowa, where his death occurred. Occasionally he supplied under the presiding elders.

[6] Parham Randle (*ca.* 1779– ?) had joined the Missouri Conference in 1821 but was discontinued at his own request in 1823. His father's house was the first Methodist preaching-place in Richmond, Virginia. Parham moved to Illinois in 1818–19, settling first near Edwardsville, Madison County (*ibid.*, pp. 181–82).

[7] According to the conference rules adopted at the session of 1827, "no member shall be absent during any of the sessions, unless he obtain leave of absence."

Aaron Wood Peter Cartwright, Wm Chambers Samuel H. Thompson, Jesse Walker, John Dew, Jas Garner, Wm. Shanks supernumerary, were severally examined approved and passed. Bro. Garner asked and obtained a location and Bro. Wm Shanks received a supernumerary relation. There were two documents presented to this Conference. One by Al Colbert, and one by Henry Allen and on motion ordered that they be permitted to withdraw the sd Documents. On motion resolved that when Conference adjourns it adjourns to meet at three oclk P.M. Whereupon Conference adjourned.

3 Oclk P.M.

Conference met pursuant to adjournment, and was opened according to rule. The list was called and the journals read and approved. Conference then proceeded to business Bp. Soule in the chair. Conference then resumed the examination of the characters of Elders & the Characters of C. W. Ruter, Robert Delap, Josiah Patterson, Orcenith Fisher, Samuel Lowe; Wm. Crane, Richard Hargrave were severally examined approved and passed. And Bros. C. W. Ruter & Patterson continued in a superannuated relation. Bro. Fisher received a supernumerary relation. Bro Lowe asked and received a location and Bros. R Delap & R. Hargrave returned effective. On motion resolved that a committe[e] of three be appointed to audit the accounts of Bro. Scarritt as Missionary to the Pottawatomy Indians; and report to this Conference. And the President appointed Samuel H. Thompson, J. Scott & Thos S. Hitt as that committe[e]. On motion resolved that whereas the Pottawatomy Indians have dispossed of their lands where the Mission was located, it is inexpedient longer to continue a mission among the Potawatomy Indians & the same is hereby discontinued.[8]

Resolved that in the opinion of this Conference, it is expedient to establish a Mission the ensuing year, in the Mining District of Country, on & near Fever River on the Upper Mississippi. To be called the *Galena Mission* and the same is hereby declared to be a Missionary station as aforesaid to be attached to the Illinois District. On motion resolved that in the opinion of this conference it is expedient to estab-

[8] The discontinuance of the Potawotami Mission did not mean the end of home missionary interest in the Illinois Conference. During this and the conference years immediately succeeding, missions played an increasing part in the winning of the West. The approved budgets for this expanding phase of the church's program as reported in the "Journals" were: 1829, $350; 1830, $1,125; and 1831, $1,675.

lish a mission the ensuing year on the rapides of the Illinois River commencing at Sandy Creek settlement, on the above named River and extending up the River including the Virmillion and Fox River settlements, and including all the settlements up s-d River to Chicago on the Lake Michigan and the same is hereby declared to be a Missionary station to be denominated The *Fox River Mission*. On motion resolved that in the opinion of this Conference it is expedient to establish a Mission in the country north and West of Crawfordsville circuit and North of the Vermillion Circuit on the Wabash River to be denominated the *Logan Port Mission* and the same is here by declared to be a Missionary station. The Conference elected P. Cartwright, S. H. Thompson & John Strange as a committee to meet the superintendant to estimate the amount necessary to support the several Missions the ensuing year whereupon Conference adjourned.

THURSDAY [SEPTEMBER 24, 1829]

½ past 8 Oclk A.M.

Conference met pursuant to adjournment and was opened according to rule. The list was called and the journals read and approved. Conference then proceeded to business Bp. Soule in the chair. The committee appointed to audit the accounts of Bro. Scarritt as missionary to the Potawatomy Indians presented their report which was read and adopted. On motion the vote by which the report of s-d committee was adopted was reconsidered & on motion the report was recommitted with instructions to the committee to add an item of expense for the use of sister Scarritts household furniture. The committee appointed to estimate the amount necessary for the support of the mission patronized by the Conference having had subject under consideration beg leave to report as follows viz Galena Mission one hundred Dollars. Fox River Mission two hundred Dollars, & Logansport Mission fifty Dollars all of which is respectfully submitted

signed P CARTWRIGHT JOHN STRANGE S. H. THOMPSON

I concur with the committee in the above estimates

JOSHUA SOULE

On motion P Cartwright J Dew J. Armstrong were elected as a committee to take [to take: *omit*] into consideration the claims of Bro. J. Walker to certain property at the Mission station among the P[otawatomi] Indians & report to the conference. The joint committee of the Missouri & Illinois Conference on the subject of a Conference Seminary presented their further report as follows viz

The joint committee of the Illinois and Missouri conferences, on the subject of a joint seminary beg leave to continue their report; Your committee have had under consideration the subject of locating the contemplated seminary, and have not come to any thing definite on that subject; but your committee have agreeed to report the following places as suitable sites for said locations; Lebanon, in St. Clair County, in this State, and Mount Salubria, one mile west of the city of St. Louis, in the State of Missouri.

Your Committee submit the following articles of confederation, as a compact between the two conferences, and recommend their adoption.

Articles of confederation and agreement by and between the Illinois and Missouri annual conferences of the Methodist Episcopal Church, for the purpose of establishing a joint Seminary of learning for both conferences, made and entered into at Edwardsville September twenty third 1829. by the Illinois conference on its own part & by Alexander McAllister, Andrew Monroe and Jesse Green, delegates empowered to act on the part of the Missouri Conference.

ART. 1. There shall be by the conferences aforesaid a seminary of learning located and established at Mt. Salubria in the state of Missouri under the following regulations and restrictions

ART. 2. The Illinois and Missouri Annual conferences shall have equal claims to all the rights, privileges and immunities belonging to or growing out of said Seminary of learning.

ART. 3. It shall be the duty of the said conferences respectively at each annual session to appoint a committee of ways and means to adopt such measures as to them may seem necessary to raise funds to carry into effect the designs of this confederation. And all monies or other means collected for the above purpose shall be subject to the order of the board of managers or Trustees as the case may be, who may be appointed to superintend said Institution.

ART. 4. Each conference shall annually elect seven trustees who shall constitute a board: who shall have authority to receive conveyances of all real estate and superintend Said Seminary, transact its business, make all necessary rules and regulations for their own government, and for the government of the Institution: to fill vacancies that may occur in their body during the year, appoint their own secretary and Treasurer, and do all other matters and things pertaining to the management of said institution: Provided nothing be done which shall in any wise infringe on the articles of this confederation.

Art. 5. Any of the foregoing articles of this confederation may be altered amended or rescinded upon the concurrent majority of each of these conferences agreeing thereto.

On motion the Conference proceeded to fill by ballot the blank in the first article of the confederation & on counting the vot[e]s it was found that Mt. Salubria Missouri had a majority & the blank filled accordingly. The character of J. Sciarritt was examined approved and passed. On motion resolved that when conference adjourn it adjourn to meet at 3 Oclk P.M. The Stewards of Conference presented Their report which was read and on motion adopted. Whereupon conference adjourned—

3 o clock P.M.

Conference met pursuant to adjournment. and was opened according to rule. The list was called the Journals read and approved. Conference preceeded [proceeded] to business. Bishop Soule in the chair. The conference then took up the first question on the minutes, to wit, who are admitted on trial and Richard S. Robinson recommended from Madison district, John Decker from Charlestown, Boyd Phelps from Wabash, David B. Carter from Illinois, Lorenzo D. Smith from Madison, Anthony G. Thompson from Illinois, Isaac N. Elsbury from Madison, George West from Wabash, Wilson Pitner[9] and Alfred Arrington[10] from Illinois, Sam-l Brenton from Madison, [and] James Latta from Illinois District were admitted. Thos Bennett, John

[9] Wilson Pitner (1806–80), a native of Tennessee, earned in the Illinois Conference a reputation for eccentricity such as Jacob Gruber had in the East. Cartwright writes of this "very singular and remarkable man": "notwithstanding his want of learning, and in common he was an ordinary preacher, yet at times, as we say in the backwoods, when he swung clear there were very few that could excel him in the pulpit" (W. P. Strickland [ed.], *Autobiography of Peter Cartwright* [Cincinnati, 1860], pp. 323–24). He had attended Illinois College but left after six months, feeling that "it was wicked for him to stay there in college, when souls were perishing all about him whom he might direct to Christ" (Leaton, *op. cit.*, p. 320). His ministerial life was spent within the bounds of Illinois, Missouri, and California conferences.

[10] Alfred W. Arrington (1810–67), a native of Iredell County, North Carolina, was an eloquent speaker and a polished scholar. He was expelled from the Missouri Conference in 1834, after which he practiced law, first in Arkansas, later in Texas. He was a member of the Arkansas legislature and judge of the Twelfth Judicial District of Texas, 1849–54. His *Sketches of the South and Southwest* appeared *circa* 1847. He died a Roman Catholic in Chicago (*United States Biographical Dictionary . . . . Illinois Volume* [1876], pp. 273–75).

Gillam John Proctor, Spencer W. Hunter, Wm. Meldrum, Jeremiah S. Williams, and John Rickey were not admitted. On motion the presiding Elders have leave to employ Brothers Richie, Williams Meldrum and Hunter should their Labors be necessary. Bro. George Randall from Madison District was readmitted. Whereupon Conference adjourned.

FRIDAY [SEPTEMBER 25, 1829]

Half-past 8 oclock A.M.

Conference met pursuant to adjournment and was opened according to rule, the list was called, the Journals read and approved. Conference proceeded to business Bishop Soule in the chair. The conference then proceeded to take the numbers in society within the bounds of this conference. Conference proceeded to fix the place of holding its next session and on counting the votes it was found that Vincennes, Indiana had a majority: and was declared to be the place where the next session of this conference shall meet on the 30th day of Sept. 1830.

Conference proceeded to the reconsideration of the case of John C. Archer recommended for Deacons orders and he was elected. On motion it was resolved that the Presiding Elder have liberty to employ Thos Bennett should his labors be needed. The committee appointed to take into consideration the claims of Brother Walker to certain property at the Potawatomy mission presented their report as follows. viz. Your committee beg leave to report that they are of opinion that Brother Walker is justly entitled to the mill, smith tools, waggon and remnant of hogs, if any, which he claims: and that these articles were purchased with his own funds; and for fuller information on this subject we refer this conference to the Journal of conference held at Mt. Carmel, all of which is respectfully submitted.

signed, J. DEW *Chm.*

On motion the above report was adopted.

On motion resolved that Brother Scarritt furnish a list of the property at the Potawatomy mission to the missionary who may be appointed to the Fox River mission, and that said missionary together with the Presiding Elder of the district to which s-d mission shall be attached take charge of said property and dispose of the same according to the best of their judgment for the use of the missionary society of the M.E.C. and report to the next session of this conference.

The committee appointed to audit the accounts of Brother Scarritt as missionary to the Potawatomy mission presented their report. Which was read and adopted. On motion the vote taken on the adoption of the foregoing report was reconsidered. and on motion the report was recommitted to the auditing committee. On motion Bro Samuel H. Thompson was relieved from the auditing committee and Allen Wiley elected to fill the vacancy occosioned thereby. The conference proceeded to fill the blanks in the remaining articles of confederation as contained in the report of the joint committe[e] of Missouri & Illinois Conference on the subject of a conference Seminary and proceed to adopt the several articles separately which being severally amended were adopted. On motion resolved that when Conference adjourn, it adjourn to meet at 3 ock P.M.

3 oclock P.M.

Conference met pursuant to adjournment and was opened according to rule. The list was called and the Journals read and approved. Conference proceeded to business Bishop Soule in the chair. On motion resolved that a certain Document which on yesterday was presented to this conference by Pierce Holly be returned to him. It was moved and seconded that the last report of the joint committee of the Illinois and Missouri conferences on the subject of a conference seminary containing articles of confederation be adopted and after some discussion it was decided in the negative, and said report and articles [were] not adopted. On motion the vote taken by which the first report of the s-d committee was adopted, was reconsidered, and on motion was rejected.[11]

The committee appointed to audit the accounts of Bro Scarritt as missionary of the Potawatomy mission, presented their report accompanied with the account of Bro Scarritt, as follows viz. The committee appointed to audit the accounts of Isaac Scarritt, Missionary of the Patawatomy mission, beg leave to report that they have paid all due attention to the same and beg leave to report the following as a correct statement of accounts.

[11] It will be noted that the extensive plans which had been considered so enthusiastically during much of the conference were now laid aside entirely. Peter Cartwright said at the time that he would rather send his children to a Calvinistic school than to one in a slave state! For the interesting bit of conference "politics" back of this rejection see Leaton, *op. cit.*, pp. 306–7.

Isaac Scarrit in account with the Potawatomy Mission.

Dr. to cash per drafts on the		Cr. By travelling expenses	$50.00
		By stock bought	130.00
Treasurer of Missionary		By bedding	50.00
Society	$800.00	By clothing	50.00
To cash obtained from		By farming utensils	20.00
Missionary property	46.00	By provisions	30.00
	———	By labor	100.00
	$846.00	By Groceries	54.00
Balance remaining	700.00	By salary for himself, wife	
	———	& child	216.00
	146.00		$700.00

which leaves in the hands of your committee a balance of $146.00 all of which is respectfully submitted. The report being read was on motion adopted; and the surplus money ordered to be put in the hands of the treasurer of the Illinois [Conference] missionary society. On motion unanimously resolved that a vote of thanks be given to the citizens of this town and its vicinity, for the hospitality manifested by them in the accommodation of this conference during its present session. and that Brother Cartwright be requested publicly, to announce the same [at] the first opportunity.

Resolved on motion, that each presiding elder in conjunction with the preachers on each circuit and station be requested to use thier utmost exertions to organize one or more Branch Missionary societies in each circuit and Station in this conference.

Resolved, that the secretary be requested by this conference to insert at the close of the minutes, transmitted to the publishers of the Christian Advocate and Journal and Zions Herald, for publication, an account of the good feeling that has existed among the members while in session, the profitable campmeeting held during conference, and the amount of the conference collection, together with the amount of missionary funds raised on the occasion. Whereupon the appointments[12] were read out and conference adjourned to meet at Vincennes [Indiana] on Sept. 30th 1830.

C. W. Ruter — Joshua Soule

[12] Appointments (*Minutes,* Vol. II: *1829–1839,* pp. 46–47):

Wabash District. George Locke, P. Elder.
Vermilion, James M'Kean.
Paris, Robert Delap, John Decker.

VII. JOURNAL FOR 1830

Journal of the 7th Illinois Annual Conference. Vincennes, Indiana, Thursday Morning 9 O'clock, September 30, 1830.

Conference met according to appointment:—And no Bishop being present, Rev. S. H. Thompson was unanimously called to the Chair,

---

Carlisle, Wm. H. Smith, B. Phelps.
Vincennes, Enoch G. Wood.
Petersburg, James Hadley.
Boonville, Thomas Davis.
Princetown, George West.
Wabash, John Fox, A. Arrington.
Mount Carmel, John Miller, A. F. Thompson.
Washington, Eli P. Farmer, sup.

KASKASKIA DISTRICT. Samuel H. Thompson, P. Elder.
Kaskaskia, Isaac Scarritt.
Brownsville, A. Risley, O. Fisher, sup.
Jonesborough, Samuel C. Cooper.
Golconda, Thomas Files.
Mount Vernon, John H. Benson, Miles Huffaker.
Shoal Creek, William Chambers, Wilson Pitner.
Shelbyville, Lorenzo Edwards.

SANGAMON DISTRICT. Peter Cartwright, P. Elder.
Lebanon, John Dew, Asahel Phelps.
Apple Creek, James Bankson.
Atlas, Samuel Bogart.
Spoon River, Asa D. West.
Sangamon, Smith L. Robinson, D. B. Carter.
Salt Creek, William L. Deneen.
Peoria, James Latta.
Fox River mission, Jesse Walker.
Galena mission, Benjamin C. Stephenson.

MADISON DISTRICT. Allen Wiley, P. Elder.
Madison station, James L. Thompson.
Madison circuit, M. Taylor, G. Randall.
Lawrenceburg, N. B. Griffith, R. S. Robinson.
White Water, James Havens, sup., L. D. Smith.
Wayne, Robert Burns, Wesley Wood.
Connersville, Amos Sparks.
Rushville, J. Tarkington, W. Evans.
Indianapolis, Thomas S. Hitt.
Fall Creek, Asa Beck.
Franklin, Richard Hargrave.
Vernon, John Kerns.

CHARLESTOWN DISTRICT. John Strange, P. Elder.
Salem, S. M. Otwell, J. Vancleave.
Charlestown, John W. M'Reynolds, James Scott.
Bloomington, J. Hale, J. E. French.

who open'd Conference by reading a portion of Scripture, singing & prayer: C. W. Ruter was then elected Secretary, & the Conference proceeded to elect a president protem. when, on counting the votes, it appeared that S. H. Thompson was duly elected.[1] The list was called and the following members being presented took their seats

Allen Wiley	Wm. Moore	Calvin W. Ruter
Neh. B. Griffeth	Aaron Wood	Elis P Farmer
Jas Havens	Wm Shanks	Stith M. Otwell
Jas Tarkington	Stephen R. Beggs	Thos Files
Thos S. Hitt	George Locke	Smith L Robertson
John Strange	John Fox	John Kerns
John W. McReynolds	Samuel H Thompson	Jas McKain
Jas Scott	Orsenath Fisher	Enoch G. Wood
Jesse Haile	Peter Cartwright	Samuel C. Cooper

Conference proceeded to fix the hours of meeting and adjournment, and after some debate it was determined that the conference meet at 8 Oclock A.M. and adjourn at 12. Meet at 2 P.M. adjourn at 5 P.M. Conference then proceeded to elect their stewards and on counting the votes Bro. Shanks E. Ray and Jas Scott were declared elected. The Conference appointed Geo. Locke E G. Wood and Thos S. Hitt. as a committee to appoint the preachers to officiate in public and to superintend the congregations during the sitting of the Conference.

Whitelick, Charles Bonner.
Greencastle, William Moore.
Rockville, William Mavity, H. A. Tarkington.
Crawfordsville, James Armstrong.
Columbus, Isaac N. Elsbury, J. T. Johnson.
Corydon, Aaron Wood, William Shanks, sup.
Paoli, Danial Anderson, S. Brenton.
Logan's Port mission, S. R. Beggs.

William Crane, John Hogan, Robert H. Jordon, and George W. Teas, transferred to the Missouri Conference.

[1] The General Conference of 1804 had enacted the following legislation, which provided for the election of S. H. Thompson as president of the conference when it was impossible for the bishop to attend: The annual conference may have a presiding elder as president, "but in case there are two or more presiding elders belonging to one conference the bishop or bishops may, by letter or otherwise, appoint the president; but if no appointment be made, or the presiding elder appointed do not attend, the conference shall, in either of these cases, elect the president by ballot, without debate, from among the presiding elders" (*Journals of the General Conference of the Methodist Episcopal Church,* Vol. I: *1796–1836,* p. 55).

The President appointed A. Wiley, J Scott, C. W. Ruter Jesse Haile and Aaron Wood as a committe[e] to examine the candidates for admission into full connexion. J. Dew, Peter Cartwright and E. Ray were nominated & elected as a committe[e] to write the memoir of Bro. Josiah Patterson Deceased a member of this conference. The Conference proceeded to consider the 2nd Question on the minutes viz who remain on trial and the characters of Richard S. Robinson, Lorenzo D. Smith, Wesley Wood, Amos Sparks, Isaac N Ellsbury, Samuel Brenton John Decker, Boid [Boyd] Phelps, examined and continued George West [was] discontinued at his own request. The character of Alfred W. Arrington and Anthony F Thompson were examined and they continued on trial—Wilson Pitner [was] discontinued. The case of Lorenzo Edwards was called and [at] the suggestion [of] his P. Elder was laid over. The character of David B. Carter was examined & he continued on trial. Jas Latter [Latta] [was] discontinued at his own request. Whereupon Conference adjourned.

2 Oclock P.M.

Conference met pursuant to adjournment and was opened according to Rule. The list was called and Journals read and approved. Conference proceeded to business Rev. S. H. Thompson in the chair. A communication from the Book Agents at N[ew] York directed to this Conference containing the report of s-d Agent to the N York Conference together with an exhibit of the pecuniary situation of the Methodist Book concern was read to the Conference. And on motion, resolved that the members of this conference do here by express their entire satisfaction with the report and address of their general book agents at N York and that we will do all in our power to aid them in [the] publishing and circulation [of] our very valuable Books. Conference then proceeded to the examination of the characters of the Deacons who were candidates for Elders orders and the characters of Elie P. Farmer, George Randle, Seth [Stith] M. Otwell, John T. Johnson, Thos Files, As[a] D. West, Smith L. Robison and Wm. Evans were severally examined and they elected to Elders orders except Bro. Randle who was not elected. Bro West asked and obtained a location. Conference then took up the case of the Deacons of one year and the characters of John Kerns Jas McKain, Enoch G Wood. Asahel Risley Samuel C. Cooper [were examined and approved], Samuel Bogart at his own request received a Location. The case of B. C. Stephenson was called and he not being present was laid over whereupon Conference adjourned.

FRIDAY [OCTOBER 1, 1830]

8 oclock [A.M.]

Conference met pursuant to adjournment and was opened according to rule. The list was called the journals read and approved. Conference proceeded to business. Rev. S. H. Thompson in the chair. The Conference Stewards occupied some time in attending to the pecuniary concerns of the Conference. Conference voted to draw on the book concern for Three Hundred Dollars and on the Chartered fund for Eighty Dollars. The case of Bro. B. C. Stephenson was called and [his] character examined approved and passed. Conference proceeded to take up the 3rd Question on the minutes to wit who are admitted into full connexion and Asa Beck, John Vancleave, John E. French, Hardin A. Tarkington, John H Benson, Miles Huffacre, Asahel Phelps, Wm. L. Deneen and Charles Bonner, Having been previously examined by the committee appointed for that purpose were Questioned and admonished by the President according to Discipline. The Conference then proceeded [to a] consideration of their characters and the characters of Asa Black, John Vancleave, John E French and Hardin A Tarkington were severally examined and they [were] admitted into full connexion and elected to Deacons orders. It was announced to this Conference that an Agent of the American Sunday School Union [was] in Town & wished an interview with the members of this Conference on motion resolved that he be permitted to attend and address the conference this afternoon. at 4 Oclock Whereupon Conference adjourned.

2 Oclock P.M.

Conference met pursuant to adjournment and was opened according to rule. The list was called and the journals read and approved Conference proceeded to business Rev. S. H. Thompson in the chair. On motion resolved the calling [of] the list on opening each session of Conference be dispensed with. Conference resumed the examination of the candidates for admission into full connexion and the Characters of John H Benson, Miles Huffacre, Asahel Phelps, Wm L. Deneen & Charles Bonner were severally examined and they were admitted into full connexion & elected to Deacons orders. Conference then proceeded to the consideration of the first Question on the minutes, viz who are admitted on trial & John C. Smith, Spencer W. Hunter & Ansel Beach recommended from the Madison District were admitted, Isaac Kimball recommended from Cincinnati Station, Ohio Conference, was admitted. Nathan Fairchild from Madison District was not admitted but on motion the Presiding Elder has liberty to empl[o]y him should his labours be deemed necessary. Wm Taylor recommended from the Charleston District was admitted. Hakaliah Vredenburg applied for readmission [but] was not readmitted. The Agent of the A[merican] Sunday School U[nion] attended according to a previous resolution of this conference and delivered an interesting address on the subject. Whereupon Conference adjourned.

SATURDAY [OCTOBER 2, 1830]

8 Oclock A.M.

Conference met pursuant to adjournment & was opened according to rule. The journals were read & approved. Conference proceeded to business Bro Thompson in the chair. On motion resolved that the stewards be instructed to allow Bro. Sam-l Bogart for one half year[']s labours only. The Conference resumed the consideration of those recommended for admission on trial and Wm. S. Crissey, Henry S. Talbott, John Richey, Jas Massey & Jas P Crawford recommended from the Wabash District were severally admitted. Josiah H. Hill, Philip T. Cordier & Simeon Walker[2] recommended from Kaskaskia District were severally admitted. Jacob T. Swafford [was] not admitted but on motion the Presiding Elder has leave to employ him should his labours be deemed necessary. Amos Prentice, Wm. D. R. Trotter,[3] Daniel M. Murphy and Edward R. Ames[4] recommended

[2] Simeon Walker (1802–80) was born in Jackson County, Georgia, but came with his parents to Illinois in 1809. On entering the Illinois Conference this year, he was sent to the Grand Prairie Mission. He served subsequently in the Southern Illinois Conference and in 1863 was chaplain of the Fifteenth Illinois Cavalry (James Leaton, *History of Methodism in Illinois, from 1793 to 1832* [Cincinnati, 1883], pp. 362–64).

[3] William David Rice Trotter (1807–80), a native of Kentucky, entered the United States Navy as a midshipman but resigned two years later on account of ill-health. While studying law, he was converted to Methodism at a camp meeting near Bowling Green and began preparing for the ministry. While on the Henderson River Mission in the Illinois Conference in 1833 he crossed the Mississippi to Burlington, Iowa, and

from the Sangamon District were severally admitted. Conference proceeded to the consideration of local Deacons recommended for Elders orders & Jas Conwell from the Madison District was elected. Conference then took up the case of Local preachers recommended for Deacons orders and Jas P. Crawford, Jesse Spradling, Harbert P. D. Bruler, Joseph Walker & Joseph Springer recommended from the Wabash District were severally elected. Barton Randle,[5] Robert Thomas & Levin Green recommended from Sangamon District were severally elected Whereup[on] on motion Conference adjourned.

2 Oclock P.M.

Conference met pursuant to adjournment & opened according to rule. The journals were read and approved. The conference proceeded to business Bro S. H. Thompson in the chair. On motion the relation of Bro. Elie P. Farmer was changed from Supernumerary to effective. Conference resumed the consideration of the case of Local Preachers recommended for Deacons orders & David Bruner, Jonathan Prosser, Francis Standaford, Benj-m Jones, Thos Evans Hardy Cain Jeremiah Sherwood, Solomon Cross & Vances Jones recommended from the Charleston District. [and] George M Hanson, Stephen C. Rentfro, Wm. Echols Simeon Walker, [and] Abraham T. Casey from the Kaskaskia District were severally elected. Jas E Johnson & John Dapew were not elected, some time was spent in discussing The subject of Sabbath schools Whereupon Conference adjourned.

---

preached one of the first Methodist sermons in the state. In 1834 he taught at Pleasant Plains Academy and in 1838 at the Ebenezer Manual Labor School. He served as presiding elder of several Illinois districts and founded and was the first editor of the *Central Christian Advocate* at St. Louis (*ibid.*, pp. 364–68).

[4] Edward Raymond Ames, D.D., LL.D. (1806–79), was a native of Amesville, Adams County, Ohio. He joined the Methodist church in 1827 and taught before his entrance into the conference this year. In 1840 he was elected Missionary Secretary for the West and in 1848 was offered the presidency of Indiana Asbury University, but declined. His election to the episcopacy came in 1852. He was especially active during the Reconstruction, advancing the interests of the Methodist Episcopal Church throughout the South. Cf. William Warren Sweet, *Indiana Asbury–DePauw University, 1837–1937* (New York, 1937), p. 62.

[5] Barton Randle (1796–1882), born in Scriven County, Georgia, was converted in Illinois at the age of sixteen. He served Henderson River and Galena-Dubuque missions, and Cartwright says of him: "He did great good in this new and rising country." He was one of the first Methodist itinerants to preach in what is now Iowa.

MONDAY [OCTOBER 4, 1830]

8 Oclock A.M.

Conference met pursuant to adjour[n]ment and was opened according to rule, the journals were read and approved. Conference proceeded to business Bro. Thompson in the chair. Conference proceeded to the examination of the character of the Elders & the characters of Allen Wiley Jas L Thompson, Michael Taylor, Neh B Griffeth, Jas Havens Jas Tarkington, Thos S. Hitt. Richard Hargrave, Jno Strange, John W. McReynolds, Jas Scott, Jesse Haile, Wm. Moore, Wm. Mavity, Jas Armstrong, Aaron Wood, Wm. Shank Dan-l Anderson, Stephen R. Beggs, George Locke. Robt Delap Wm. H. Smith, & Jas Hadley were severally examined & passed The relation of Bro Scott, was on motion changed from supernumerary to effective. Bros Jas Havens, Wm Shanks, & Robt Delap [were] superannuated. Bro. Dan-l Anderson through his representation [representatives] asked and obtained a location. The case of Robt Burns was called and laid over. The case of Thomas Davis was called [and] some objections being made in consequence of his not having attended the duties of a travelling preacher, during the last year, it was moved and seconded that he be deprived of his ministerial office and after some discussion the motion was withdrawn whereupon his character passed and his P. Elder asked and obtained for Bro. T. Davis a location. The hour of adjournment having arrived it was on motion resolved that conference continue its present session for one half hour. The character of John Fox, John Miller, Samuel H Thompson, Isaac Scarritt, Orsenath Fisher & Wm Chambers were severally examined and passed & Bro Fisher recieved a superan[n]uated relation and Bro. J. Scarritt and Wm Chambers—asked & received each a location. Whereup[on] Conference adjourned.

2 Oclock P.M.

Conference met pursuant to adjournment & was opened according to rule. Bro Thompson in the chair. On motion the reading of the journals [for] the present session be disposed with. A resolution was offered on the subject of sabbath schools which on motion was laid on the table Whereupon on motion conference adjourned until 8 Oclock tomorrow morning.

TUESDAY [OCTOBER 5, 1830]

8 Oclock A.M.

Conference met pursuant to adjournment and was opened according to rule, The journals were read and approved. Conference proceeded to business Br. Thompson in the chair. The committee appointed to write the memoirs of Bro Josiah Patterson (deceased) presented their report which was read and on motion accepted. On motion Bro John Fox received a supernumerary relation. On motion the vote by which Dan-l M Murphy was admitted on trial into the travelling connection was reconsidered and after some discussion and the question being put shall he be admitted into the travelling connexion on trial? it was decided in the affirmative. The case of Robt Burns was again called his character examined and passed and he received a superan[nu]ated relation. The case of Lorenzo Edwards was called [and] at his own request [he was] discontinued.

Conference resumed the examination of characters of Elders and the characters of Peter Cartwright John Dew, Jas Bankson, Jesse Walker, were examined and passed. On motion a committee of three were appointed to examine the Report and other communications from Bro. Walker & to report to this conference as soon as convenient & the President appointed J. Dew P Cartwright and George Locke as that committe. The character of E Ray was examined & passed and on motion his relation changed from superan[n]uated to that of supernumerary. The character of C. W. Ruter was examined and passed and his relation changed from superan[n]uated to effective. The stewards of Conference presented their report which was read and on motion adopted. On motion a small amount of unappropriated money was directed to be put into the hands of the P Elders to be by them appropriated to those persons whom they shall deem most needy. Bro Cartwright announced an appeal from Benj-n Watts an expelled local Elder which on motion was laid on the Table and made the order of the day for the after noon session. On motion the resolution on yesterday offered on the subject of the sabbath schools was called up and after some discussion and being amended a motion was made to indefinitely pos[t]pone the further consideration of s-d resolution but before the question was put Conference adjourned.

2 Oclock P.M.

Conference met pursuant to adjournment & was opened according rule; the journals [were] read and approved conference proceeded to business Bro Wiley in the chair. The appeal of Benj-n Watts was then taken up, the minutes of the trial had in this case in the Quarterly Meeting Conference of the Lebanon Circuit Sangamon District were read together with the charges proferred against him: and on which he was expelled from the church. Also the evidence in the case—the defendant being present was permitted to address the conference in his own defence, and having retired the conference proceeded to the consideration of his case. and a motion was made to affirm the decision of the Quarterly Meeting Conference by which the defendant was expelled. and after some discussion, the hour of adjournment having nearly arrived it was on motion resolved that conference continue its present session ½ an hour, and after some further remarks on the motion made relative to the case of Benj-n Watts the votes was taken and decided in the affirmative Whereup[on] on motion Conference adjourned.

WEDNESDAY [OCTOBER 6, 1830]

8 Oclock A. M.

Conference met pursuant to adjournment and was opened according to Rule. The journals were read & approved—Conference proceeded to business Bro Thompson in the chair. [The] Conference [committee] appointed to examine the documents sent here by Bro. J. Walker Missionary on the Fox River Mission presented their report which was read and on motion adopted. Which is as follows viz. The Conference [committee] appointed to examine the documents sent to this conference by Rev. J. Walker Missionary on the Fox River Mission beg leave to report that they have examined these documents and find that they contain a report of his Missionary labors during the past year an amount [account] of property belonging to the old Potawatomy Mission which has been sold by sd Walker together with a list of property belonging to sd Mission remaining unsold. Your committee would say that they are fully [in agreement] with the transactions of your Missionary & report as the proceeds of the sale the sum of 303$ which sum is now on hand and at the disposal of the Conference

JOHN DEW *Chair-n of Com-t.*

On motion resolved that there be a committe[e] appointed to settle the claims against the Potawatomy Mission & that the amount raised from the sale of the property of the Mission now on hand be appropriated to the payment of those claims in an equal proportion to the amount as far as the money will go. and Peter Cartwright was nominated and elected that committe[e].

On motion resolved that all the country lying between the little Wabash and the Kaskaskia Rivers lying on and near the state road leading from Maysville to Vandalia not included in any other circuit except those preaching places now included in the Mt Carmel circuit west of the little Wabash and those appointments included in Shoal Creek Circuit lying east of the Kaskaskia River shall be and is hereby made a Missionary Station to be called the *grand Prairie Mission*. On motion resolved that Fort Wayne and its vicinity be & the same is hereby constituted a s[t]ation to be denominated the *Fort Wayne Mission* and that it be attached to the Madison District. On motion resolved that all that country formerly included in the Brownsville Circuit except so much of the same as may now be included in the Mt Vernon and Jonesborough Circuits be and the same is hereby made a Missionary station to be called the *Brownsville Mission* and also that country embraced formerly in the Jonesboro Circuit now be made a Mission station to be called the *Jonesboro Mission*.

On motion resolved that in the opinion of the conference it is expedient to establish a mission the ensuing year to be denominated as the *Fort Clark Mission* embracing the District of Country lying on both sides of the Illinois River from Fort Clark up to the mount [mouth] of Fox & Vermillion Rivers & that it be attached to the Sangamon District. A motion was made to discontinue the Galena Mission which motion was lost. On motion J. Dew A Wiley G Locke, P Cartwright & J Strange were nominated and elected as a committee to meet the President and estimate the amount necessary for the sup-[port] of the several Missions under the direction of this conference. The case of Wm J Mayo a local Elder who had been expelled by the

Quarterly Meeting Conference of Paris Circuit Wabash District was brought forward by appeal—A motion was made to remand the case in consequence of informality, in the proceedings of the Quarterly Meeting Conference for a new trial which after some discussion was decided in the affirmative & the case remanded accordingly. The resolution on the subject of sabbath schools was called up, and the motion to [that it be] indefinitely pos[t]poned being discussed the motion was withdrawn and the Question being called for shall the resolution as amended be adopted it was dicided in the negative. On motion a committee of five was appointed to take into consideration the expending [expediency] or inexpediency of adopting McKendrian College of Illinois as the literary Institution of this conference The President appointed J. Strange P Cartwright G Locke J Dew & E Ray as that committe[e] who are to report as soon as possible. Whereup[on] Conference adjourned.....

2 oclock P.M.

Conference met pursuant to adjournment and was opened according to rule. The journals were read and approved. Conf proceeded to business Bro. Thompson in the chair. Conference proceeded to appoint the place of holding its next session and on counting the votes Indianapolis having a majority was announced as the place of holding our next conference which will meet October 4th 1831 The committee appointed to take into consideration the subject of a conf. seminary submitted their report which was read and on motion adopted which is as follows to wit. The com-t appointed to take into consideration the expediency or inexpediency of adopting the McKendrean college of Illinois established at Lebanon report that they have had that subject under consideration and recommend to this conf the following resolutions—

1st That this conf- accede to the proposal of the managers of the McKendrean college of Illinois in Lebanon and now agree to adopt the s-d college as a Conf- seminary.—

2nd That a committee of three be appointed by this conf. to appoint a president whose literary and religious qualifications are such as will [do] credit to the institution.

3rd That each Preacher of this conf be required to open subscriptions & solicit donations from the friends of literature within their respective charges, which monies when collected shall be paid to the person who may be loyally [legally] appointed either by this Conf or the managers, to superintend the monied concerns of said institution

J. Strange *ch-m Com.*

On motion J. Dew. Peter Cartwright & Sam-l H. Thompson were nominated and elected as a committee to appoint a president to the above named institution pursuant to the 2nd. resolution in the above report & on motion resolved that the foregoing committee in discharging the duties assigned them meet in conjunction with the managers of said institution. and on motion the s-d committee were instructed as soon as practicable to address a circular to each member of this conf giving such information as they shall deem necessary. On motion the case of George Randall was reconsidered and he was Elected to Elders orders.

On motion resolved that a committee of five be appointed to make enquiry within the limits of Indiana respecting a suitable site where[on] to Establish an institution of lear[n]ing[6] and also as to the amount of money that can be obtained in the vicinity of such site to aid in the erection of suitable Buildings & for the purpose, and report to the next session of this Conf to be held Oct. 1831 and the Pres-t appointed John Strange C. W. Ruter, James Armstrong E. Ray & A Wiley that committee.—On motion the vote by which Isaac Scarritt was located was reconsidered. The secretary asked and obtained leave to read the Journals of the present session which were accordingly read and approved whereupon on motion Conference adjourned.—

THURSDAY [OCTOBER 7, 1830]

8 Oclock A.M.

Conference met pursuant to adjournment and was opened according to rule. Conference proceeded to business Bro S. H. Thompson in the chair. On motion resolved that the Thanks of this conference be presented to the citizens of this place for their hospitality and kindness manifested in that plentiful provision they have for our accommoda-

[6] This is the earliest reference to the movement which led in 1837 to the founding of Indiana Asbury, now DePauw University, at Greencastle, Indiana. Further action was taken at the first session of the Indiana Conference (1832), when C. W. Ruter, Allen Wiley, and James Armstrong were appointed a committee "to take into consideration the propriety of building a Conference Seminary" (Sweet, *op. cit.*, chap. ii, pp. 25–41).

tion during our present session, and that a copy of this resolution be furnished the preacher of the station which shall be read to the congregations when convenient.

On motion resolved that in the opinion of this conference it is expedient to form a Mission from the mouth of Fox & Vermillion Rivers including all the settlements up the Illinois River to the Lake Michigan to be denominated the *Chicago Mission*.[7] On motion the vote by which Dan-l Anderson was reconsidered and on motion he was superan[n]uated. On motion the Fox River Mission was discontinued. The committe[e] appointed to estimate the amount necessary for the support of the several missions established by this conference presented their report which was read and on motion adopted which is as follows to wit:

Fort Wayne Mission		$150
Grand Prairie	do	100
Brownsville	do	75
Jonesboro	"	50
Galena	"	250
Fort Clarke	"	200
Chicago	"	250
Logans Pont	"	50

Signed John Dew *Ch-m*
Sam-l H. Thompson

Whereupon the appointments[8] were read out and then conference adjourned to meet at Indianapolis October 4th 1831

C. W. Ruter *sec.* Sam-l H. Thompson *Pres. Protem.*

[7] The Chicago Mission took the place of Fox River Mission, which was discontinued (see below and Leaton, *op. cit.*, p. 341).

[8] Appointments (*Minutes*, Vol. II: *1829–1839*, pp. 127–28):

Madison District. Allen Wiley, P. Elder.
Madison, Benjamin C. Stephenson.
Vevay, Joseph Tarkington, George Randle.
Lawrenceburg, John W. M'Reynolds, A. Arrington.
White Water, Michael Taylor, Isaac Kimble.
Wayne, Asa Beck, Richard S. Robinson.
Connersville, Ancil Beach, Wesley Wood.
Rushville, Amos Sparks, J. C. Smith.
Vernon, John Kerns.
Fort Wayne mission, N. B. Griffith.

[Appointments continued on facing page]

CHARLESTOWN DISTRICT. John Strange, P. Elder.
Charlestown circuit, J. L. Thompson.
Albany, Calvin W. Ruter.
Corydon, William Moore, John Decker.
Paoli, John T. Johnson, William S. Crissey.
Petersburg, James Massey.
Salem, Asahel L. Risley, H. S. Talbott.
Columbus, to be supplied.
Bloomington, Enoch G. Wood, Isaac N. Elsbury.

INDIANAPOLIS DISTRICT. James Armstrong, P. Elder.
Indianapolis, Thomas S. Hitt.
Franklin, James Scott.
Fall Creek, William Evans, C. Bonner.
White Lick, Eli P. Farmer.
Greencastle, James Hadley, J. H. Hill.
Rockville, William Mavity, Lorenzo D. Smith.
Crawfordsville, Samuel C. Cooper, Samuel Brenton.
Logansport, Harden A. Tarkington.

WABASH DISTRICT. George Locke, P. Elder.
Vermilion, James M'Kean, John E. French.
Paris, Wm. H. Smith.
Terre-Haute, Edwin Ray, sup.
Carlisle, Richard Hargrave, Daniel M. Murphy.
Vincennes, Aaron Wood.
Washington, William Taylor.
Princeton, John Richey.
Boonville, Samuel Julian.
Wabash, Thomas H. Files, Philip T. Cordier.
Mount Carmel, John Miller, John Fox, sup.

KASKASKIA DISTRICT. S. H. Thompson, P. Elder.
Kaskaskia, John Vancleave.
Brownsville mission, Anthony F. Thompson.
Jonesborough mission, Boyd Phelps.
Golconda, James P. Crawford.
M'Leansborough, Amos Prentice.
Mount Vernon, John H. Benson.
Shoal Creek, John Dew, E. R. Ames.
Shelbyville, Miles Huffaker.
Grand Prairie mission, S. Walker.

SANGAMON DISTRICT. Peter Cartwright, P. Elder.
Lebanon, Stith M. Otwell, William L. Deneen.
Apple Creek, Wm. D. R. Trotter, Wm. H. Askins.
Jacksonville, John Sinclair.
Atlas, Spencer W. Hunter.
Spoon River, James Bankson.
Tazewell, Stephen R. Beggs.
Salt Creek, Asahel E. Phelps.
Sangamon, J. Hale, D. B. Carter.
Galena mission, Smith L. Robinson.
Chicago mission, Jesse Walker.
Fort Clark mission, Isaac Scarritt.

VIII. JOURNAL FOR 1831

Journal of the 8th Illinois Annual Conference Indianapolis Ind-a October 4th 1831 Tuesday 9 oc[l]ock Ante Meridian

Conference met according to appointment Bishop Roberts and the following members were present:

Allen Wiley	James L. Thompson,	James Armstrong,
Joseph Tarkington,	Calvin W. Ruter,	James Scott,
George Randall,	William Moore	Charles Bonner,
John W. McRenolds	William Shanks,	William Mavity,
Michael S. Taylor,	John T. Johnson,	Peter Cartwright,
John Kerns	Asahel L. Risley,	John Sinclair,[1]
John Strange,	Enoch G. Wood,	Jesse Haile.

Conference was opened by reading a portion of the Sacred Scriptures Singing and prayer.

Conference then proceeded to business Bp. Roberts in the chair. C. W. Ruter was nominated and elected Secretary

Conference voted to meet at 8 oclock A.M. & adjourn at 12 meet at 2 oclock P.M. and adjourn at 5.

On motion, Brothers James Armstrong, & Thomas S. Hitt were appointed a committee, to appoint the Preachers to Preach, and Superintend the Congregations during Conference.—Conference proceeded to Elect three Stewards, & on counting the votes, it was found that Brothers Peter Cartright, Wm. Shanks, & James Scott, were Elected—Brothers John Dew, Allen Wiley, & Wm. Shanks, were nominated & Elected a Committee to write the memoirs of the Dead. On motion, resolved that funerals of Brother Edwin Ray & James

[1] John Sinclair (1793–1861) was a native of Loudoun County, Virginia, settling successively in Tennessee and Kentucky, where in 1824 he was received into the Kentucky Conference. In 1830, feeling that "the existence of slavery in the State of Kentucky was a serious thing, and dreading its consequences upon after generations" (Stephen R. Beggs, *Pages from the Early History of the West and Northwest* [Cincinnati, 1868], p. 306), he transferred to the Illinois Conference. In 1833 he was made presiding elder of Chicago District, which then "embraced all the settlements now embraced in the Rock River, Central Illinois, Upper Iowa, and Wisconsin Conferences, and some in the Illinois Conference" (James Leaton, *History of Methodism in Illinois, from 1793 to 1832* [Cincinnati, 1883], p. 359). After 1840 he was a member of the newly formed Rock River Conference and represented it at the General Conference of 1844.

Bankson Dec[eased], be Preached at some convenient time during the Session of Conference.

The President then appointed Samuel H. Thompson, Peter Cartright, James Armstrong, Calvin W. Ruter, James L Thompson, & Allen Wiley, a Committee to examine the Candidates for admission into full connexion.—

A communication & address from the Book Agents, at New York accompanied with an exhibits of the State of the Book concern was then re[a]d to the Conference—. And the Agent from Cincinnati,[2] being present addressed the Conference, and made a Statement of the Situation of the concern at Cincinnati.

On motion, resolved that a Committee of Two be appointed to attend to the business of our periodicals, and the President appointed, Brothers George Locke, & Michael S. Taylor, that Committee.

Conference then proceeded to the 2nd Question on the minutes, to Wit; Who remain on trial, & the Characters of John C. Smith, Spence[r] W. Hunter, Ancil Beach, Isaac Kimball, Wm. Taylor, Wm S. Crissy, Henry S. Talbott, John Richie, James Massey, James P. Crawford, & Josiah H Hill were severley [severally] examined, and they Continued on trial; Whereupon Conference adjourned.

2 Oclock P.M.

Conference Met pursuant to adjournment, and was opened according to rule.—Conference then proceeded to business. Bp. Roberts in the chair. Conference proceeded with the consideration of the 2nd Question on the minutes; and the characters of Philip T. Cordier, Edward R. Ames, Simeon Walker Amos Prentice, Wm. D. R. Trotter, & Daniel M. Murphy, were severley [severally] examined, & they continued on trial.

Conference then proceeded to the examination of the characters of the Deacons of one year, & the characters of Asa Beck, John Vancleave, John E. French, John H. Benson, Miles Huffacre, Asahel E Phelps, Wm. L. Deneen, Charles Bonner, Samuel Julian, & Hardin. A. Tarkington, were severally examined, and passed, & Hardin A Tarkington asked & obtained a Location.

Conference then proceeded to the examination of the characters of

[2] Charles Holliday.

Deacons who were candidates for Elders Orders, & John Kearns, James McKean, Enoch G. Wood, Asahel L. Risley, Samuel C. Cooper, & Banjamin C. Stephenson, were severally examined approved, & they elected to that office On motion, Samuel Julian was elected to the Office of an Elder.—Conference then proceeded to the examination of the Characters of Elders, The characters of Allen Wiley, Joseph Tarkington, John W. McReynols, Michael Taylor, Nemiah G. Griffith, John Strange, James L. Thompson, Calvin W. Ruter, Wm. Moore, James Armstrong, Thos S. Hitt, & James Scott were severley [severally] examined approved, and passed, and Bro James L. Thompson asked, & obtained a Location, & Bro James Scott, received a Superanuated relation. Where upon Conference Adjourned—.

WEDNESDAY [OCTOBER 5, 1836]

8 Oclock A.M.

Conference met persuant, to adjournment, & was opened according to rule.

The list [was] called, & the journals re[a]d and approved.

Conference proceeded to business Bp. Roberts in the chair.

Conference resumed the examination of the Characters of Elders & the case of James Hadley was called, and some objections being made to him in consequence of neglecting in some degree his appointments, it was on motion resolved that his character pass, but that he be admonished on that subject by the President of the Conference.

The characters of Wm. Mavity, George Locke, Wm. H. Smith, were examined approved & passed.

The name of Bro. Edwin Ray, was called & his P. E. gave us a short account of his affliction & death, stating that he died in peace & on motion Bro A[lexander]. McAllister, of the Missouri Conference was added to the Committee, which on yester[day] was appointed to write the memoirs of the dead.

The characters of Richard Hargrave, Aaron Wood, John Miller, John Fox, Samuel H. Thompson, John Dew, Peter Cartright, John Sinclair, Stephen R. Beggs, Jesse Haile, Jesse Walker, Isaac Scarriott, Eli P. Farmer, Wm Evans, John T. Johnson, Stith Meads Otwell,

Thomas Files, Smith L. Robinson, George Randall, James Havens, Robert Burns, Wm. Shanks, Daniel Anderson, Orceneth Fisher, Robert Delap, & Wm. H. Askins, were severley [severally] examined approved & passed. Aaron Wood, Isaac Scarriott, & George Randall asked & obtained a Location. and James Havens, Robt Burns, & Wm Shanks [were] made Supernumerary, and Daniel Anderson made affective; Orceneth Fisher, & Robt Delap [were] superan[n]uated, the name of Bro. James Bankson was called, & [his] P.E. & Bro A McAlister gave us an affecting account of his affliction & Death, by which he stated he died in peace at St. Louis, & on Motion Bro. McAlister was requested to bear the greatful acknowledgements of this conference, to the Brothren & friends in St. Louis, for their kindness to our lemented Bro Bankson, during his last illness.

Whereupon Conference adjourned.

2 Oclock P.M.

Conference met pursuant to adjournment & was opened according to rule. The list was called & the journals re[a]d and approved

Conference proceeded to business Bp. Roberts in the chair

The Conference took up the 1st Question on the Minutes (To wit) Who are admitted on trial. & Nathan Fairchild & George Beswick recommended from the Charlestown District were admitted & Joseph Oglesby[3] & Thomas Davis readmitted. Wm. M. Dailey James T Robe recommended from Indianapolis District were admitted Samuel Wright not admitted but on motion the Presiding Elder has liberty to employ him should he deem it expedient. Hecaliah Vereedenburg [was] readmitted. The stewards spent some time in attending to the temperal concerns of the Conference.—The time of adjournment having ar[r]ived, it was resolved on motion that the present session [continue] a half an hour. A motion was made & seconded that those

[3] Joseph Oglesby (? –1852) had been appointed to Illinois in 1804 at the Western Conference held at Mount Gerizim, Kentucky. He had joined conference in 1803 and located in 1809, after laboring in Ohio, West Virginia, Kentucky, Tennessee, and Illinois. He practiced medicine while a local preacher and became a well-known physician in Madison, Indiana (*Circuit-Rider Days in Indiana* [*Indianapolis,* 1916], p. 7). He may have been the first Methodist itinerant to preach in Missouri Territory (Leaton, *op. cit.,* pp. 41–44).

Preachers who have been employed by Presiding Elders, be considered a claiment on the Conference; which after some discussion was decided in the negative.[4] Conference then voted to draw on the charter fund $80. & on the book concern for $800., also $200. balance undrawn on the book concern last year.

Whereupon Conference adjourned.

THURSDAY [OCTOBER 6, 1831]

8 Oclock [A.M.]

Conference met pursuant to adournment & was opened according to rule

The list was called accordingly & the Journals read & approved. Conference proceeded to business Bp. Roberts in the chair.

Conference resumed the consideration of the 1st Question on the Minutes viz & Cornelius Swank recommended from Ind[i]anapolis District was admitted

Wm McHewey recommended from Wabash District was admitted Isham West not admitted Charles Slocumb was readmitted. John T. Mitchell[5] & James Walker recommended from Kaskaskea Dist were admitted Barton Randle Wm Royal and Levi Springer recommended from Sangamon District were not admitted Leven Green and James Stiker were not admitted but on motion the P. E. has leave to employ them should he deem it necessary.

A communication from Rev Samuel Sneed was read to the conference in which he requested the privilege of addressing the conference on the subject of Christian education as connected with Sunday

[4] Note that the stewards were later instructed to consider as conference claimants four men who had served as supply preachers.

[5] John Thomas Mitchell (1810–63) was born in Botetourt County, Virginia, and came with his parents to Illinois in 1817. In 1832 he was sent to Galena Mission, and in 1833 to Galena and Dubuque, under Barton Randle; he served Chicago, 1834–35. In 1840 he was made presiding elder of Chicago District in the new Rock River Conference. By the General Conference of 1844 he was elected assistant agent of the Western Book Concern and for many years served his conferences as secretary (Matthew Simpson [ed.], *Cyclopaedia of Methodism* . . . . [Philadelphia, 1898], pp. 624–25).

Schools, he being the superintending Agent of the A[merican] S[unday] S[chool] U[nion] in Ind[iana] and on motion resolved that his request be granted. And on motion resolved that the Secretary of the Conference be and he is hereby instructed to inform the Rev. Mr. Sneed that the members of this body will hear him on tomorrow at 10 Oclk A.P. in the M. E. Church in this place if it meet his views. On motion resolved that Bro. McCallaster be respectfully requested to respond to Mr Sneed if necessary & to give a general view of the claims of the Methodist S. S. Union.[6]

On motion resolved that a committee of five be appointed to examine the probable missionary ground within the bounds of this conference & report to this conference And the President appointed A Wiley J Strange G Locke J Armstrong & P Cartwright that committee.

The conference proceeded to the consideration of the third Question on the minutes and Richard S. Robinson, S. Brenton, John Decker, Boyd Phelps A. W. Arrington & I. N. Elsbury having been previously examined by the committee appointed for that purpose were called forward and examined & admonished by Bp. Roberts preparatory to their admission into full connexion after which their characters were severally examined and they were admitted into full connexion and elected to Deacons orders, except Bro Ellsbury against whom some objections being made and after some discussion and the hour of adjournment having arrived it was on motion resolved to continue the present session ten minutes Lorenzo D. Smith, Wesley Wood, Amos Sparks, Anthony F. Thompson & David B. Carter not being present but well reported of they were continued on trial. The case of Bro. Ellsbury was laid over till afternoon.

On motion resolved that when conf. adjourn it adjourn till ½ past 2 oclock. P.M. *Whereupon Conf. adjourned.*

[6] The General Conference of 1832 was to resolve that "we regard the establishment of Bible, Sunday-school and Tract Societies under our control, separate and distinct from similar associations denominated national or American, as highly expedient, necessary, and salutary, and demanding the united support and hearty cooperation of all our preachers, travelling and local, as well as all the members and friends of our Church" (*Journals of the General Conference of the Methodist Episcopal Church,* Vol. I: *1796–1836,* p. 410).

½ past 2 Oclock P. M.

Conference met pursuant to adjournment & was opened according to rule The list was called & the journals read and approved Conference proceeded to business Bp Roberts in the chair. Conference resumed the consideration the case of Bro Isaac N. Ellsbury a motion was made to continue him [on] trial and that the Preacher who shall be sent to Bloomington Circuit proceed to settle the difficulty as soon as possible and after some discussion it was decided in the affirmative & he continued on trial accordingly.

The committee appointed to examine the Missionary ground within the bounds of this Conference

Presented their report which was in part considered when the hour of adjournment having arrived the further consideration of its report was laid over until to morrow morning whereup[on] Conference Adjourned

FRIDAY [OCTOBER 7, 1831]

8 oclock A.M.

Conference met pursuant to adjournment & was opened according to rule

The list was called the Journals re[a]d and approved Conference proceeded to business Bp Roberts in the chair

Conference resumed the consideration of the report of the Committee appointed to examine the Missionary ground within the bounds of this Conference which after read was as follows

We the committee appointed to report the grounds within the limits of this Conference which should be reported as missionary ground beg leave to report as follows

That it is expedient to appoint Missionaries to the following fields of labour To wit

Logans port Ft Wayne Iroquoise South Bend Grand Praira Jonesboroagh Brownsview Macoupin Deplain Chic[a]go Ft Clark Galena Rock Iland All of which is respectfully submitted Signed in behalf of the Committee

PETER CARTWRIGHT *Ch[airman]*

Which after being considered in its various parts was adopted in full. On motion resolved that the Conference Stewards be instructed to consider Joseph Oglesby Nathan Fairchild Levin Green & Barton Randle as legal claimants on this Conference in proportion to their labors render[e]d as travelling preachers the last year On motion the vote formerly taken in case of Bro James Hadley was reconsidered on motion his character was approved and passed. Whereupon Conference adjourned.

2 Oclock P.M.

Conference met persuant to adjournment and was opened according to rule

The list was called the Journals re[a]d and approved

Conference proceeded to business Bp Roberts in the chair

A communication was re[a]d from a committee appointed by the Marrion County Temperance Society & on motion was orde[re]d to lay on the table to be called up tomorrow.

Conference then proceeded to the Election of 9 delegates to the ensuing General Conference & on counting the votes it was found that J. Strange Allen Wiley George Locke James Armstrong Samuel H. Thompson John Dew Wm Shanks Peter Cartwright [and] Calvin W. Ruter were duely elected. On motion the Conference proceeded to elect four Persons to be considered as Alternates that in [case] any of the Elected delegates should fail and not be able to attend the general Conference that they shall go in the place of those who may fail in the following order (Viz) The Bro who shall get the highest no of votes to be taken first and so on. And on counting the votes they were found as follows Thomas S. Hitt. James Scott, Joseph Oglesby, & Jesse Haile, who were declared duely Elected accor[dingly]

On motion [Motion: *omit*] resolved that each P. E. and every Preacher in charge be required to lift a collection in their respective charges and hand to some one of the delegates who are elected to the General Conference to be by them taken in to General Conference for the purpose of defraying the expenses of the delegates to the General Conference

Conference proceeded to fix the place of the next annual Conference and Jacksonville Morgan County Ill being nominated and a rising vote being called for and a large majority rising it was accordingly fixed apon as the place of the Setting of the next session of this conference. Time of adjournment having arived it was on motion resolved that the Conference continue its present session ten minutes.

[As to] The Committee which was appointed last year to liquidate and make some payments to those that had demands on the potawatomy mission. On motion Bro Peter Cartwright was reappointed as a committee to endeavor to liquidate s-d claims

On motion resolved that a committee of five be appointed to meet the Superintendent and estimate the amount necessary to support the several Missions established and the President appointed John Strange Allen Wiley George Locke J Armstrong & Peter Cartwright that Committee.

On motion resolved that a vote of thanks, by this Conf. be returned to Bro. A. McAlister of St. Louis for the course he took with the American S. S. Agent for saying what he did & for saying no more than he did. J. L. Thompson

Where upon Conference Adjourned.

SATURDAY [OCTOBER 8, 1831]

8 oclock [A.M.]

Conference met persuant to adjournment & was opened according to rule.

The list was called the Journals were re[a]d & approved

Conference proceeded to business Bp Roberts in the chair

On motion resolved that in course [case] any of the delegates fail of going to the General Conference timely notice be given to the present Secretary of this conference; whose duty it shall be to notify the alternates in the order contemplated in the resolution for their Election

The committee appointed to estimate the amount necessary to Support the Preachers that are to employ [occupy] the several Missionary fields of labour within the bounds of this conference reported as follows Viz The committee appointed to estimate the amount of money necessary to Support the men that are to occupy the Several

Missionary fields of labour beg leave to make the following report/ To wit/

Logans port	$100	Macoupin	$100
Ft. Wayne	$ 75	Deplain	$250
Irequois	$200	Chicaaigo	$200
South Bend	$ 75	Ft Clark	$100
Grand Prairie	$100	Galena	$250
Jonesborough	$100	Rock I[s]l[and]	$ 75
Brownsview	$ 50		

all of which is respec[t]fully submitted Oct the 7th 1831

PETER CARTWRIGHT *ch*

approved R R ROBERTS

which was re[a]d and on motion adopted

Rev Peter Cartwright stated to the Conference that in consequence of Bro Isaac Scarriott who was last year appointed to the Ft Clark Mission having failed in part of discharging the duties assigned him he [the] s-d Cartright with held one the drafts in favor of S-d Scarriott amounting to fifty Dollars which he presented to the Conference and on motion S-d draft was ordered to be destroyed which was done accordingly.

The Committee previously appointed by this conference on Periodicals presented their report which was re[a]d & on motion recommitted. The committee appointed to write memoirs of the dead presented the Memoirs of Bro E Ray which was read and on Motion adopted & on motion the s-d committee had further time given to write the memoirs of Bro J. Bankson & that the Committee forward on S-d Memoirs as soon as convenient. The superintendent announced the time of the setting of this conference informing that it will meet on the 25 of Sept 1832.

Conference then proceeded to the consideration of the case of Local Preachers recomended for Deacons orders & Thos T Spillman & Stephen Liddle recommended from Mad[ison] Dist[rict] was Elected. The P E. of s-d Dis[trict] presented a recommendation for Dilton Bridges but at the request of the P. E he was permitted to withdraw it

John Hughes John Cook Hull Tower [and] Nathan Fairchild from the Charlestown District were severally Elected. Wm Clark & Henry Rammill recommended from Indianapolis Dist were Elected

John Cartwright Daniel Hascoat [and] Wm Taylor recommended from Wabash District were Elected. James Walker recommended from Kask[ask]ia District were [was] elected. John Jackson recommended from the S-d Dist was not Elected—

Conference then proceeded to the consideration of the case of Local Deacons recommended for Elders orders & Gamalial Taylor recommended from M[a]d[ison] Dist [was] Elected. Israel G Lewis recommended from Ind[ianapolis] Dist was Elected. Samuel Hull recommended from Wabash Dis was Elected a recommendation for Thos C. Calling [Collins] was presented and [after] some discussion was laid over till afternoon.

On motion Wm L Deneen was appointed to receive any money which any of the Preachers may have on hand for Bro James Bankson Dec-d.

On motion resolved that when Conf. adjourn it adjourn to meet at 3 oclock P.M. Whereupon Conf adjourned—

3 oclock P.M.

Conference met persuant to adjournment, and was opened according to rule, The list was called the Journals re[a]d & approved

Conference proceeded to business Bp Roberts in the chair

Conference resumed the consideration of Thos C. Collins & after some discussion he was elected to elders orders Jeremiah Dadson recommended from Madison Dist was also elected. The conference Stewards presented their report which was re[a]d & on motion after some discussion was also adopted. The following resolution was offered to wit Resolve that in the opinion of this Conference it is inexpedient for any of our travelling Preachers to except of an Agency in the American S[unday] School Union; which resolution was on motion laid on the table untill Monday Morning

The Communication on yesterday received from a Committee appointed by the Marrion County temperance Society requesting the attendance of this Conference at a meeting of s-d Society on Monday next. and after some discussion it was on Motion resolved that the temperance Society of Marrion County have the best wishes and h[e]arty cooperation of the Members of this Conference in the advancement of the temperance cause. and regret that such is their press of business that they cannot as a conference conventeently [conveniently] attend with the Society on Monday the 10th Inst and the Sec of this Conference communicate the resolve of this Conference on the subject to the committee which addressed the conf.

On motion the vote which J L Thompson was Located was reconsidered

On Motion the Committee appointed to Liquidate the claims against the fromier [former] Potawatamy Mission was instructed to proceed in s-d settlement as he should deem most condusive to the ends of Justice.

The Delegates Elected to the General Conf. asked an expression of the mind of the conference on the Subject of the division of this conference[7] & a rising vote being [given: *omit*] called for with the exception of two votes was unanimous in favor of a Division. Bro Lorenzo D Smith having arrived, after being examined by the committee appointed for that purpose was called forward & examined and admonished by Bp Roberts preparitory to admission into full connexion after which his character was examined & he admitted into full connexion & elected to Deacons orders.

On motion the vote taken on the communication from the committee appointed by the Marrion County temperance Society was reconsidered.

And on motion resolved that Bro Hitt in form the committee that we can meet with them on Monday the 10 Inst. at the lighting of the candle & if it meet their approbation anounce the same from the Pulpit on tomorrow. Where uppon Conf Adjourned

MONDAY [OCTOBER 10, 1831]

8 oclock A.M.

Conference met persuant to adjournment and opened according to rule. The list was called the Journals re[a]d and approved. Conference proceeded to business Bp Roberts in the chair. On motion the Stewards of the Conf. were directed after taking 8.28½ cents from the Public collection lifted in Public congregation in this Town on yesterday to pay the ballance to Bro James Harvey.

[7] At the General Conference of 1832 it was decided that "Indiana Conference shall include the state of Indiana, (except so much as is included in the Illinois Conference,) Elizabethtown in the state of Ohio, and the St. Joseph's and Kalamazoo missions in Michigan Territory"; and "Illinois Conference shall include the state of Illinois, and Paris and Eugene circuits in the state of Indiana, and the Northwestern Territory" (*ibid.*, p. 389).

The resolution offered on Saturday on the subject of S. S. Agencies was called up & the following amendment was offered (To wit) to ad[d] without the consent of his P E. & the consent of the Quarterly Meeting Co[n]f. of which he is a member & after some discussion a rising vote being called for on the amendment it was decided in the negative. and after some discussion on the original Motion. and a rising vote being taken on the original resolution it was decided in the affirmative. One member only in the negative. Bp Roberts informed the conference that its Stewards of our last Conf. making the dividends appropriated a larger amount to the Super[in]tendants than they claimed of s-d Conf. which over plus he was prepared to return. And on motion resolved that the Super[in]tendants be requested to retain the s-d sum respectively. The following resolution was offered (To Wit) Resolved as a matter of expedeinent [expediency] this conference have a special agent or agents to promote the interest of the benevolent Institutions of our Church namely the Sunday School the Tracts the Missionary & Bible Societies.

And that the agent or agents receive twenty p[e]rcent on all the moneys collected by him for Sunday School purchases to defray his travelling expences and to pay his Salery provided he do not receive more than his allowance as a travelling Preacher. Resolved on Motion that we have but one such Agent

Peter Cartwright Allen Wiley

which was on motion adopted.

The following resolution was offered Viz. Resolved that every member of this Conf. in their charges respectively use [during] the ensuing year their best efforts to organize and Promote the intrests of Methodist Sunday Schools and all other benevolent institutions of our Church as far as it is Practicable

Peter Cartwright

which was re[a]d and on Motion adopted.

The following preamble & resolution was offered To wit.)

Where as the General Conf. has become so large as to be burthensome to the Brethren where it sets; to be slow in its proceedings & expensive to the Church to defray the travelling expences of the delegates And also to draw from the book money that would be otherwise employed in their respective fields of labour Resolved that this Conf. recommend to the next Gen-l Conf. an alteration of that part of our Discipline that requires one delegate from every Seven Members of

Our Annual Conf. So as to lessen the number of Delegates which was on Motion adopted

Wm. L. Denneen
S. M. Otwell

On motion Bro. P. Cartwright was appointed to receive any monies collected for the Lebanon Siminary of Illinois Conf. and that he forward the Same to the trustees of S-d Siminary.

On motion the Conf. Nominated & Elected J Strange as [Conference] Vice Pres[ident] of the M E Church Mission Society of M. E. Church. Whereupon Conf Adjourned.

2 Oclock P.M.

Conf[erence] met persuent to adjournment & was oppened according to rule Bp [Roberts] in the chair.

A communication from Henry Buell was presented to this Conf. in which he complaines of some greviences and after some discussion and the time of adjournment having arrived it was on motion resolved that the present session be continued one hour.

A motion was made that the Memorial be considered out of order which was lost.

On motion resolved that Henry Buel be tried by a committee of travelling Preachers as the discipline Direct[s] & that the P Elder who may be appointed in charge to [of] that district in the bounds of which the charges originated proceeded to try him as soon as convenient.

P. Cartwright
R Hargrave

On motion, unanimously resolved that a vote of thanks be given to the citizens of Indianapolis for their kindness & hospitality to the Members of this Conf. During its present Session. & that notice there of be announced to the congregation by the Preacher Who may be stationed here at the first convenient opportunity

C. W. Ruter
A. L. Risley

The committee on periodicals presented their report which was on motion accepted.

Resolved that this Conf approved the procedings of George Locke in the trial of Henry Bewel believing that he acted according to the instruction given him

The appointments[8] were read out, whereupon Conference adjourned to meet in Jacksonville, Morgan County, Illinois, September 25th A.D. 1832

C. W. RUTER. *Sec.* R. R. ROBERTS

[8] Appointments (*Minutes,* Vol. II: *1829–1839,* pp. 127–28):

MADISON DISTRICT. Allen Wiley, P. Elder.
Madison sta[tion], Thomas S. Hitt.
Vevay, John T. Johnson, Alfred W. Arrington.
Lawrenceburg, Joseph Oglesby, John C. Smith.
Whitewater, John W. M[c]Reynolds, Wm. M. Daily.
Wayne, Joseph Tarkington, James T. Robe.
Newcastle, Ancil Beach.
Connersville, Asa Beck.
Greensburg, Isaac Kimball, Josiah H. Hill.
Mississinaway, Robert Burns, sup.
Fort Wayne mission, Richard S. Robinson.

CHARLESTOWN DISTRICT. William Shanks, P. Elder.
Charlestown cir[cuit], William Moore, D. M. Murphy.
Lexington, John Kearns.
New-Albany sta., C. W. Ruter.
Corydon, John Miller, A. F. Thompson.
Paoli, Thomas Davis.
Salem, Michael S. Taylor, George Beswick.
Bedford, Henry S. Talbott.
Petersburg, John Decker.
Vernon, I. N. Ellsbury.

INDIANAPOLIS DISTRICT. J. Strange, P. Elder.
Indianapolis sta., Benj. C. Stephenson.
Fall Creek, Nathan Fairchild.
Rushville, Charles Bonner, Cornelius Swank.
Franklin, Eli. P. Farmer.
Bloomington sta., James L. Thompson.
Greencastle, Daniel Anderson, L. D. Smith.
White Lick, to be supplied.
Columbus, Amos Sparks.

CRAWFORDSVILLE DISTRICT. James Armstrong, P. Elder.
Crawfordsville cir., Richard Hargrave.
La Fayette, Boyd Phelps, Wesley Wood.
Pine Creek, Samuel C. Cooper.
Frankfort, Miles Huffaker.
Eugene, Asahel L. Risley.
Paris, Jesse Hale.
Rockville, Wm. H. Smith, Samuel Brinton.
Logansport miss[ion], Hakaliah Vredenburg.
South Bend miss., N. B. Griffith.
Iroquois mission, Wm. Mavity.

WABASH DISTRICT. George Locke, P. Elder.
Vincennes, E. R. Ames.
Carlisle and Terre Haute, E. G. Wood, Wm. Taylor.
Mount Carmel, James M'Kean, John Fox.
Booneville, Samuel Julian.
Wabash, Thomas Files, Jas. Massey.
Princeton, John Richie.
Washington, James Hadley.
Shawneytown, Charles Slocumb.

KASKASKIA DISTRICT. S. H. Thompson, P. Elder.
Kaskaskia cir., Wm. S. Deneen.
Brownesville miss., John E. French.
Jonesborough, James P. Crawford.
Golconda, Wm. Evans.
M'Leansborough, Wm. M'Henry.
Mount Vernon, James Walker.
Shoal Creek, John H. Benson.
Shelbyville, Barton Randle.
Grand Prairie miss., S. Walker.

SANGAMON DISTRICT. Peter Cartwright, P. Elder
Lebanon, John Dew, W. D. R. Trotter.
Apple Creek, John Vancleave, Levi Springer.
Jacksonville, Wm. Askins, J. T. Mitchell.
Atlas, Spencer W. Hunter.
Spoon River, David B. Carter.
Tazewell, Wm. S. Crissy.
Salt Creek, Amos Prentice.
Sangamon, John Sinclair, Asahel E. Phelp[s]
Maccoupen miss., Stith M. Otwell.

MISSION DISTRICT. J. Walker, superintendent.
Deplain, Jesse Walker, missionary.
Chicago, Stephen R. Beggs.
Fort Clarke, William Royal.
Galena, Smith L. Robison.
Rock Island, Philip T. Cordier.
James Havens, sup., Conference agent.

CHAPTER IX

The Journal of James Gilruth, 1834–35

JAMES GILRUTH, presiding elder of the Detroit District, Ohio Conference, from 1832 to 1836, was well equipped to be the supervisor of a group of Methodist circuits in the pioneering stage. Born of Scotch parentage on the Virginia side of the Ohio River on January 29, 1793, he removed with his family in 1797 to Scioto County, Ohio, and there in the backwoods where there were no schools, no preaching or religious meetings of any sort, he grew up. He was "ten years old before he heard a sermon or saw an ear of growing wheat." Gilruth was converted in 1818–19, which was a year of revivals in nearly all of the Ohio circuits. Apparently deciding at once to enter the ministry, he was received on trial by the Ohio Conference in August, 1819, and thus began a career if not of distinction at least of great usefulness. He remained in the active ministry in Ohio and Michigan until 1850, when he moved to Iowa, where he died on June 2, 1873, as a superannuate of the Upper Iowa Conference.

Like many of the early Methodist itinerants, James Gilruth kept a daily "Journal," of which nineteen manuscript volumes are now in the possession of a grandson, Mr. Root A. Gilruth of Chicago, Illinois. The section of the "Journal" selected for inclusion in this volume is that for the conference year 1834–35, which was Gilruth's third year as presiding elder of the Detroit District. Previous to that time he had been in the active ministry for fifteen years. Twelve of those years he was preaching on Ohio circuits, while in the year 1827–28 he was associated with James B. Finley as head of the Wyandot Mission at Upper Sandusky, Ohio. This carefully kept "Journal" furnishes us an interesting day-by-day record of a faithful circuit-rider in a pioneer setting.

The years in which Gilruth was presiding elder of the Detroit District (1832–36) coincide with the period of Michigan's most rapid growth in population. Michigan had been organized as a territory in 1805 and became a state in January, 1837. Early reports of Michigan had discouraged settlement. It was labeled "Interminable Swamp" in Jedidiah Morse's *Geography,* then widely used in the schools. It was not until Lewis Cass explored Michigan and pronounced it good, settled there himself, and became the first territorial governor that Michigan began to come into its own. In 1820 Michigan's population was 8,765; in 1830 it was 31,640. In the years 1832–34 a rush of settlers into the territory, the majority coming from New York and New England, brought the population to 87,278. This population was located in the counties in the southeastern section, the region over which Gilruth traveled in the supervision of the Methodist circuits.

Methodism had been introduced into Michigan in 1804 when Nathan Bangs came into the region from Canada. In 1809 William Case was sent to Detroit by the New York Conference. Methodist work in Michigan was suspended for three years during the War of 1812, but, beginning with 1816, Methodist preachers were sent year after year into the territory. In 1820 Michigan was included in the Ohio Conference, and in 1825 the Detroit District was created. When Gilruth was placed over the Detroit District in 1832, it included the following appointments: Detroit, Mount Clemens, Farmington, Ypsilanti, Ann Arbor, Tecumseh, Monroe, and the St. Clair, Saginaw, and Calhoun missions, with a membership of 1,671 whites and 8 Negroes. In 1835, after the detachment of the Maumee District including the circuits of Huron and Monroe, there were nine appointments and 2,114 white members, 9 Negroes, and 12 Indians. In 1836 the Ann Arbor District was formed, and the General Conference of that year created the Michigan Conference. In the early thirties an agitation was begun to establish a seminary in Michigan, and this resulted in the opening of Spring Arbor Seminary, which in 1861 became Albion College. Gilruth's "Journal" here printed records his part in securing the charter and constitution.

For Michigan Methodist history see Elijah Holmes Pilcher, *Protestantism in Michigan, Being a Special History of the Methodist Episcopal Church and Incidentally of Other Denominations; Notices of the Origin and Growth of the Principal Towns and Cities of the State; Biographical Sketches of the Many Prominent Pastors and Laymen Connected with the Birth and Growth of Protestantism in Michigan* (Detroit, 1878). A good bibliography of Michigan Methodism is contained in William R. Prescott's *The Fathers Still Speak: A History of Michigan Methodism* (Lansing, Mich., 1941). Biographical material on Gilruth can be found in Stephen N. Fellows, *History of the Upper Iowa Conference of the M.E. Church, 1856–1906* (1907), pp. 118–119; *The Old Northwest Genealogical Quarterly,* XV (1912), 104–5; and James B. Finley, *History of the Wyandott Mission, etc.* (Cincinnati, 1840), p. 366.

MAP IV

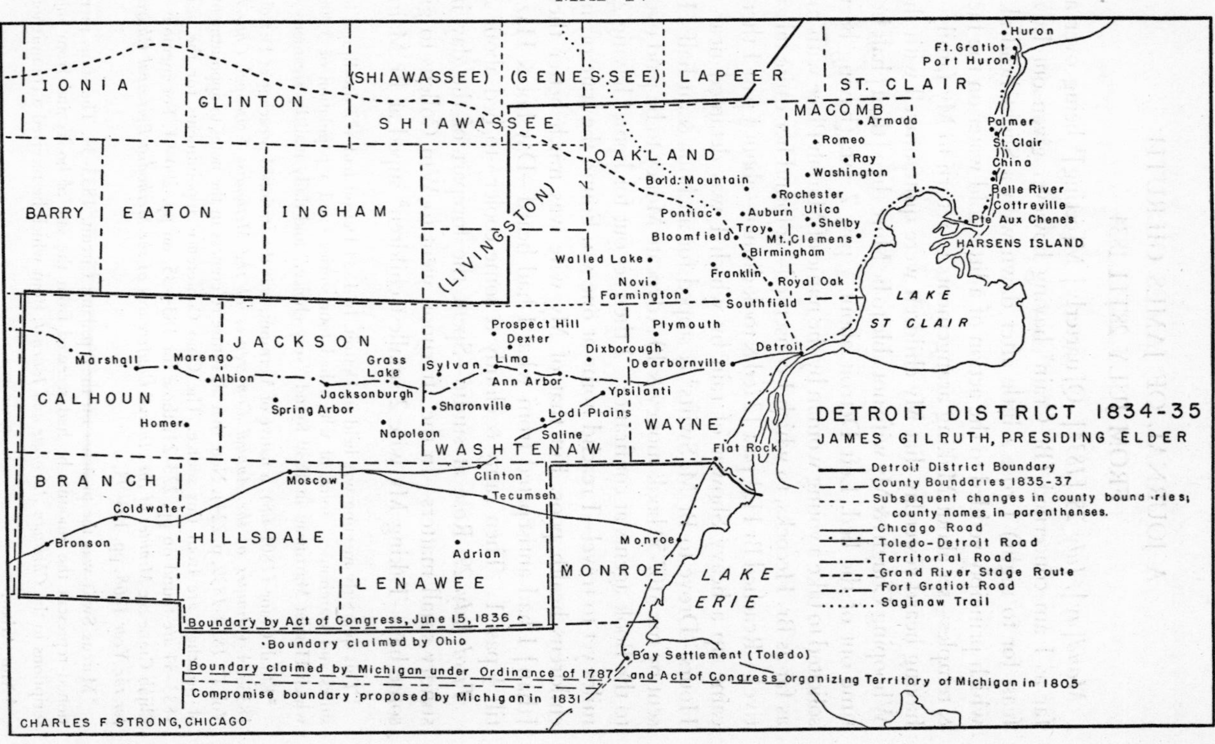

DETROIT DISTRICT 1834-35
JAMES GILRUTH, PRESIDING ELDER
Detroit District Boundary
County Boundaries 1835-37
Subsequent changes in county boundaries; county names in parentheses.
Chicago Road
Toledo-Detroit Road
Territorial Road
Grand River Stage Route
Fort Gratiot Road
Saginaw Trail
IONIA
GLINTON
(SHIAWASSEE)
(GENESSEE)
LAPEER
ST. CLAIR
SHIAWASSEE
MACOMB
OAKLAND
BARRY
EATON
INGHAM
(LIVINGSTON)
JACKSON
CALHOUN
WASHTENAW
WAYNE
BRANCH
HILLSDALE
LENAWEE
MONROE
LAKE ST CLAIR
LAKE ERIE
HARSENS ISLAND
Huron
Ft. Gratiot
Port Huron
Palmer
St. Clair
China
Belle River
Cottreville
Pte Aux Chenes
Armada
Romeo
Ray
Washington
Rochester
Utica
Shelby
Mt. Clemens
Auburn
Troy
Birmingham
Bold Mountain
Pontiac
Bloomfield
Walled Lake
Franklin
Royal Oak
Novi
Farmington
Southfield
Prospect Hill
Dexter
Plymouth
Dixborough
Dearbornville
Detroit
Lima
Sylvan
Ann Arbor
Ypsilanti
Marshall
Marengo
Albion
Grass Lake
Jacksonburgh
Spring Arbor
Sharonville
Lodi Plains
Saline
Napoleon
Homer
Flat Rock
Moscow
Clinton
Tecumseh
Coldwater
Bronson
Adrian
Monroe
Boundary by Act of Congress, June 15, 1836
Boundary claimed by Ohio
Bay Settlement (Toledo)
Boundary claimed by Michigan under Ordinance of 1787 and Act of Congress organizing Territory of Michigan in 1805
Compromise boundary proposed by Michigan in 1831
CHARLES F STRONG, CHICAGO

A JOURNAL OF JAMES GILRUTH FROM JULY 28TH 1834

Mond[*ay*], *July 28* [*1834*]. Q[uarterly] M[eeting][1] being over as far as I am concerned (Br Crain[2] having however given out Love feast for to night) I rose a little after dawn with a Slight head ake which principly yeilded to the action of a little cold water on the face & temples—set about Making arangements to return to My family—having heard yesterday that My children were quite unwell with the Whooping Cough: & My wife not able to be More then [than] half her time out of the bed. Left Detroit about ½ past 7 AM. (having been solicited to take a young woman by the name of Mariah Place with me as far as Br. Hecocks, to which I consented—& found her quite talkative)—Reached Br H. ½ past 12 fed & took dinner—about ½ past 1 there came up a heavy Shower of rain by which I was detained near 2 Hours—Drove to Br M. Swifts[3] & stoped for an hour & an half He sent by me $107-50 book money & 10 Advocate Money to be paid over to the Book agents at confirance I then set out for home[4] having 23 miles yet to travel—I reachd home at one AM. Found the state of my childrens health poor. But that of My wife was much better then [than] I had antisepated from what I had heard—Day hot & Hazy till ½ past 1 Then rainy & cloudy & some cooler—to bed about 2.

Tusd July 29. Rose at sunup—Spent the forepart of the day in sundry small matters—In the afternoon went to Wm Collens to git some hay—Taking My wife 2 smallest children[5] suped at Br Main-

[1] This quarterly meeting was held in Detroit. In 1834 Detroit had 477 dwellings, 64 stores and warehouses—some of which had four stories—and a population of 5,000, which Harriet Martineau in 1830 found "very choice," and daily mail by steamer.

[2] Elijah Crane (1801–68), a native of Vermont, was the stationed preacher at Detroit, 1833–34 (*Minutes of the Annual Conferences of the Methodist Episcopal Church*, Vol. II: *1829–1839*, p. 224). Note that all future references in the notes to appointments of preachers are from this source. The Ohio Conference appointments for the year 1833–34 are found on pp. 223–24; those for 1834–35, on pp. 290–91. For memoir of Elijah Crane see *Minutes of the Annual Conferences of the Methodist Episcopal Church for the Year 1868*, pp. 193–94.

[3] Marcus Swift was the preacher on the Ypsilanti Circuit, 1833–34. The sums mentioned represent the amounts he had received from the sale of books and from subscriptions to the *Christian Advocate and Journal*, from which he received a commission.

[4] Ann Arbor.

[5] Naomi and Matilda.

ards[6] & returned home a little before sundown Day clear & pleasant to bed about 9.

Wed July 30. Rose about sun rise—spent the morning till 10 in sundry small chores—tended the funeral of Mr Welshs infant—halled wood in the afternoon Day as yesterday—to bed about 10

Thursd July 31. Rose about 6—Spent the day in aranging my papers money etc for Conferance (Giting my horse shod and making the necessary preparations—counting tracts till ½ past 10—Day as yesterday—to bed at 11—

Frid Aug 1st. Rose at a little past 5.—Paid Mrs E. Page for the tuition of Harriet[7] for one qur. $3.—Paid Mrs Mills $10 for house rent—Baptised Mrs Prucia child—& having been closely employed till near half past one I took leave of My companion & set out for Q M at Smoth Rock intending, after having attended this to procede to Confirance by the way of Ft Finley.[8]—Drove to Ypsilanti stoped & fed at Br Norris—Saw Br John Sayre who wishes to labour on some appointment. I gave him to understand that upon the division of Ypsilanti cir[cuit] he might be employed.—Drove on to B Hitchcocks & put up, Just as the sun went down: having drove 21 miles since half past one. day clear for the most part and agreeably cool—to bed at 10 & slept soundly.

Sat Aug 2. Rose a few minuts after sun up—Read B Ps, Emorys Defense of the fathers[9] till 7.—Rode to smoth Rock & put up with Jacob Vrelandt—Preached at one P.M. from Matt XXII.39. with some liberty. after which I held Q M. conferance The business of which was conducted with sattisfaction. Br. Church Preached at ½ past 5 after which held a short prayer meeting—day clear & warm—spent the evening in conversasion till 10

Sund Aug 3d— . . . . Read "The defence of the fathers." till 9.—

[6] Deacon Maynard's was a favorite stopping place for Gilruth, about halfway between Ann Arbor and Ypsilanti (see E. H. Pilcher, *Protestantism in Michigan* [Detroit, 1878]). Gilruth usually refers to this favorite neighbor as "Old Bro. Mainard."

[7] Harriet, the oldest daughter at home.

[8] Fort Finley, now Finley, Ohio, where his daughter Helen Duduit lived.

[9] John Emory's *A Defense of "Our Fathers," and of the Original Organization of the Methodist Episcopal Church* (New York, 1828) was directed against the Methodist Protestant "Reformers." In this book Emory, who was elected a bishop in 1832, defends the three orders of the clergy—deacons, elders, and bishops. Gilruth (cf. below) reviews the book and takes issue with Emory on this point.

Attended Love feast.—after which I admenistered the ordenance of baptism to 7 adults 3 by immersion & 4 by pouring—(This was done at 2 in the river) Br. Samuel Bibbins. preached at 11 at the close of which Br Elias Patte[10] took a collection for the meeting house which amounted to upwards of 30$. (This being a new house & not yet clear of debt) After which we administered the sacrement to perhaps 40 communicants. At 5 P.M. Br. Church preached a short discourse & After he had finished I preached through an interpreter to the Indians[11]—Thus closed our Q M & Thus closes My labour on the District for this year.—. . . . .

Mond Aug 4th. . . . . Br. Bibbins being on his way to conferance for ordaination we concluded to Rig my waggon for two horses, accordingly we went to work & by 10 Made a pair of doubletrees & a tongue & neck yoke—harnised in & got under way—fed by the way, our own provender—Reached Monroe by 3 PM. fed and dined at Br Garwoods[12] & I bought some small articles for My daughtor at Ft Finley—we then set out & reached the Bay settlement[13] & put up with Br hall by dusk having made about 33 miles according to the road we traveled. . . . . Spent the evening in the familey agreably conversing on common subjects—

Tusd Aug 5 . . . . after brakefast we set out driving leasuraly—fed and dined at Br. Keelers (he was not at home being on a visit to Bufalow.) We then Drove on to Perrys burgh & put up with Mr Keys. spent the evening agreeably as circumstances would alow his wife not being at home she being gone to Portland. We bathed in the Maumee at night, & had a comfortable nights rest—Day Warm and for the most part clear yet a kind of dusky hays [haze] the affect of hot dry wether—. . . . .

Wed Aug 6. . . . After an early brakefast we set out: having relinquished the plan of going through by Ft Finley from this place; we took the road for lower sandusky—we fed at Widow Millers on Portage River, on corn furnished by Mr Keys—and then set forward

[10] Elias Pattee was a superannuated preacher, formerly the preacher at Detroit, 1823–24.

[11] The Wyandots.

[12] Joseph G. Garwood (? –1854), a prominent Methodist citizen of Monroe.

[13] Bay Settlement, now Toledo. The name "Toledo" was first used in 1833, when the two towns of Port Lawrence and Vistula united.

& a little before sundown Reached Br Emersons 3 Miles above lower Sandusky. & put up.—on our way I finished Reading B.P., Emorys "Defence of the fathers." He has done well, in risquing from sencure the characters of those whom he undertook to defend—But as far as the Doctrine of three orders of Ministers is maintained I shall choose to Judge for Myself. Nor Will I Regard any thing on this subject but the testemony of Gods word.....

Thursd Aug 7..... Read some in the Bible—After an earley brakefast we set out & by taking the direct rout in order to save distance had some Miles of Most unpleasent road. Fed, & dined with Br Andrew Love From whom I had a confirmation of the following circumstance told me some years ago by his brother Wm Love of Rushville Ohio.

"In Bloom township, Columbia Co. Pensylvania lived Martin Tweed whose familey vainly esteemed themselves of the better sort & by living above their income, in order to show as they wished, were always in cramped circumstances. Near them lived a pious old Methodist (An englishman) by the name of James Graham, a man of considerable property but who had no familey. On a certain occassion one of Tweeds daughters (Nearly a young woman) was sent to G——s to borrow some flower [flour]. When G went to give her the flower [flour] she handed him a thin gause like handkerchief to put it in. said he, My child that is not fit to carry flower [flour] in said she We have nothing better. Ah Child, said the old man, if you would lay out your money for good substantial articles they would be much more to your proffit then such things as this.—When the girl went home, she Reported the old mans Remark: which insteed of being received with the kindness that it was given, was viewed as an insult, & remembered for vengence. Some time afterward one of Ts daughters got married; on which occasion they made a considerable of a feast. Toward the close, as T. was lying on his bed, as one in a museing Mood, he sudenly rose up, saying, It is decreed that I should whip G——. And calling his son John. A lad about 14 years old, to accompany him, he set off immediately. On the way he cut 3 hickory sprouts, about the sise of a man finger—The wether being very cold; when he came to the house he was considerably chiled: G—— received him kindly, seting him a chair by the fire. He sat, & warmed himself for sometime, conversing on ordinary matters:—Rising up, said he, It is decreed that I should whip you: with that he took one of the rods & began:—& when he had worn that out, he took the second, & when that was worn out he took the 3d & wore out the top; then turned the But. G all this time neither resisting, nor complaining. But when he turned the But end of the 3 Rod. said G. in a calm and solemn manner, I charge you at the peril of your soul, not to Murder me. On which T stoped. but by this time the blood was runing off G.s heels along the floor as from a slaughtered beast. When T stoped G. went to a spring pump before the door & commenced washing himself. T remained a little time in the house to regain breath—Tucking the buts of his rods under his arm, he came out, & as he was passing by, said G. How did you git a cross the creek (fishing creek) to which T. answered roughly, I waded a cross. Said G Whatever you do, by no means attempt to wade back for you are in such a persperation, you will catch your death of cold. Go to the stable & take one of my horses & ride over. Thes words accompanied with a kind *manner* & *tone,* came like thunder on the conciance of guilty T. He stood—he Looked on his bloody victim with a deep sense of his own wikedness in abusing a man of so much goodness Overwhelemed with remorse he approached G—— saying shall I wash you? said G you may aid if you please—This done, said T shall I help you put on a clean shirt? If you see proper. This done T. Returned home sad, & comfortless; esteeming himself & familey forever disgraced by his treatment of this good man—under these feelings he determined to Move out of the countray, & accordingly removed to the Genesee countray (about 100 Miles): but a sense of guilt accompanied him; & remained in such a manner as to entirely distroy his peace. In hopes of relief he determined on returning the whole way to ask G——s pardon On his doing which G kindly told him that he had laid up nothing against him. All this only encreased his wretchedness to think that he had abused so good a man G told him to ask Gods pardon & all would be well. With this T. complied: & shortly after obtained Mercy with the evidence of his sins forgiven."

O what an instance of Christian patience & crossbearing did this pious old man exibit!! O how few of us Methodists (of Aug 7. 1834.) would do as he did! That his conduct was acceptable to God is evidenced by the result. And such an act of christian goodnes & forbearance deserves to be remembered by future generations—

We drove on for upper sandusky—on the way I read Br B My

Community[14] constitution, & the introduction. with the whole of which he seemed pleased but thought it should more distinctly recognise obediance to the M.E.C.—Would be a member if no familey embarisment prevented etc. Reached M.P. or the Mission[15] about 9 & was kindly Received by Br Thompson.[16] The Missonary.—This day 15 years ago I was admitted a probation[er] in the traveling connection a raw & inexpereanced man: But God has been good; & to him I owe all—very little to Men—.....

Frid Aug 8.....Made arangement to set out on horseback for Ft Finley—Br Bibbins hors having become lame I set off alone about 9 uncouth like enough having 3 bed quilts & 5 lb cotten to carry beside great coat etc—I fed at Mr Sergants at the Big Spring—And in the afternoon rode to Finley & found My children well My daughter had been delivered of a child on the 4th of July but by the ignorent & bruital conduct of the Midwife the child was killed I spent the evening conversing with them on these & other matters till near 10—

Sat Aug 9.....spent ½ an hour assisting Frederik[17] to catch a Raccoon that had come into his corn—And the rest of the morning in looking at his improvements & in conversation till about 8 AM. when we all set off for campmeeting 2 ½ miles distent—I preached with great liberty at 11 from John iii 5 & then called for Mourners a nomber presented themselves for the prayers of the righteous & it was said that two of them experienced peace. I preached again at 4 from Ps. cxix.1. with clearness and some power.—& again at candlelight from Matt xxii 39. with some power—In all my labour to day I was favoured with the attention of the people & the comfort of the spirit. At this I again called for Mourners some came and Prayer meeting continued for some time. Day hot with some thunder showers passing about—one of whom fill [fell] on us; accompanied by a pretty severe wind that broke down some timber very near the camp ground. To bed about 9. pretty tired.

[14] One of Gilruth's numerous plans for human betterment was the establishment of a community. The first half of the nineteenth century was the heydey in America of socialistic and religious community experiments.

[15] The Wyandot Mission at Upper Sandusky, Ohio, of which Gilruth had once been superintendent. See William Warren Sweet, *Circuit-Rider Days along the Ohio* (New York, 1923), chap. iv.

[16] Thomas Thompson, appointed to the Wyandot Mission, 1833–34.

[17] Frederick Duduit, Gilruth's son-in-law.

Sund Aug 10. .... Br Newson[18] Preached at 8. I preached at 11 from Luke xvi. 31. with some liberty lifted a publick collection riseing of 23$. Baptised 10 adults 9 by sprinkling & pouring & one by immersion —Br E Day[19] preached at 3 P.M. After which I administered the sacrement to something like 100 persons being assisted by Br. E.D.—I preached again at night with some liberty from Heb xii.14.15 The exercises were then turned to prayer & the power of God was present to heal .... to bed about 11. all in a foam of sweat & quite weried. having laboured excessively hard during the meeting.

Mond Aug 11. Rose at sunrise—Called the congregation together—Baptised a number of children—Gave an exhortation etc & dismissed the Meeting—Went home with My children—Wrote a letter to My wife intending to set out immediately for Ft. McArthur. But upon the perswasion of My Daughter altered My plan & determined to stay with them that day—Frederick & I went to work, & made a wash board, & Slab table—Went to town, & put the Letter I had writen to My wife, in the office. Read & talked till 10.....

Tus Aug 12. .... set out for Ft McArthur; but after traveling a few miles I took a wrong road which at least cost me 6 Miles additional travel in a very bad road. Fed and dined at a Br. Tanners & after resting about 3 hours I again set forward & a Most wearisome ride reached Ft McArthur about sun set having rode at least 36 Miles through some of the worst of roads.—Put up with Mr McGoldrick—spent the evening principly in talking about the countray; & the Measures that had been addopted to move the county seat. Day very hot with thunder showers passing about one of whom I bearly escaped by finding a house.....

Wed Aug 13. .... Went with Mr. McGoldrick to view My land, & see the improvements.—Had some talk of selling—would have done it if he could have made sufficient payment down—perhaps I may yet, though I do not much care at present.

I was much pleased at the fact of this man & his old father in law Mr ——s raising a very heavy hewed log house by themselves Logs 7 inches thick & some 18 browd. 34 ft long mostly green beech. The manner was this. lay 2 long smoth skeeds [skids] one end on the house

[18] Joseph Newson (1808–62), a native of Washington County, Maryland, was in 1833–34 appointed to Fort Finley Circuit, Ohio ("Memoir," *Minutes, 1862,* p. 186).

[19] Elam Day was Newson's colleague on the Fort Finley Circuit.

& the other extending out on the ground—one foot on the outside of each skeed lay a long smoth log near a foot in diameter on the ground parilell with the skeed—bring the house log on these paralill logs & a little way up the skeeds—then apply a long fork to the house log, at each end, sufficiently stiff.—with a chain hitch a span of horses to the fork 3 feet from the end so that the ground end of the fork may slide on the ground on the inside of the long paralill Logs—then start one end with the horses as far as proper then fasten the end of this fork & hitch to the other fork in like manner & start that end of the log & so alternately till the log is shoved up. The following is a rough drawing of the plan

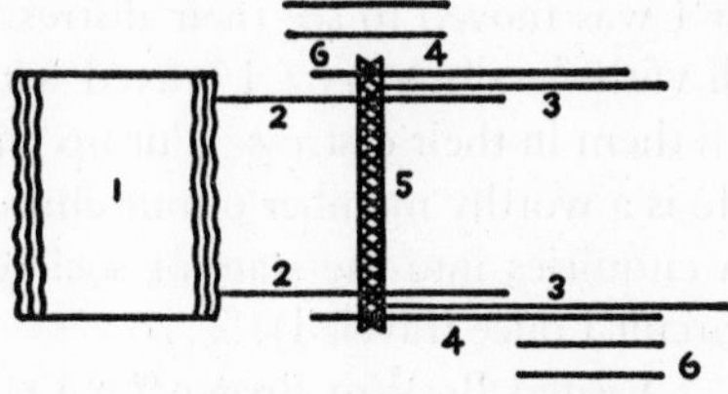

1 is the house *2* are the skeeds *3* the long forks *4* the long paralill logs on the ground to prevent the end of the forks drawing round by the pulling of the teem [team] *5* is a house log in the act of pushing up. *6* is the place for the teem to walk. The skeeds can be raised as needed at the upper end by means of a chain & handspike pry —Thus by this simple contrivence two men can Raise the heavyest log lailding at their leasure. but to do it actively there ought to be two teems [teams] (or one stout horse at each end will do) two drivers & four corner men.—set out at 9 Rode to *Kenton* the county seat 3 Miles below my land—& got a shoe put on My horse he having lost one yesterday—This is a much more pleasant situation then My land would have afforded but not more so then the exact center of the county would have afforded. I now see that when I entered my lot I did err 1st in not taking the exact center of the co. or in not laying out a town & improving it—This latter error, I owe to being engaged in the itenerent life—I never felt that I had time to leave the work of God for this business. & my error then ley in not having it done—If I had the whole to do now I could do better. but I am content yet astonished that this town was not put on the state land at the center of the county —but party intrest does everything wrong.—I intended on leaving this place to have passed down the scioto to the Urbana road & then take that to W Sandusky—but I mistook a new rode that strikes the U Road at Tyamochty—by this rout I had more mud But was much pleased to find so much good land through here. Fed at C Merimans & rested till near 6—Reached the Mission about 9 Man & horse both pretty tired.....

Thursd Aug 14..... Wrote a letter to my wife—spent the day till 12 at the Mission—being detained by thundershowers till 10—We then harnised up & set out for Bucyrus My business this rout being to preach a funeral sermon for the wife of Br James Dorland on Broken sword creek.—We stoped near an hour with an old friend Br. M. Messenger I was moved to see their distress: two children at the point of death with the disentery I prayed with them, & parted sympathising with them in their distress—Put up with Mr Bengemin Wilch. whose wife is a worthy member of our church. Spent the evening principly in enquiries into the state of society. (This being in the bounds of a circuit I once traveled).....

Frid Aug 15..... Visited Br Wm Brown[20] a Local Pr now living in this Neighborhood (formerly a school teacher at the Sandusky Mission) and spent a couple of hours quite agreeably conversing principly on the study of Medicine in which he is now engaged having furnished himself with a pretty good Medical Library—Called a moment to see My old friend Br Welch—Returned to Mr B. W.—Set out about 8 & reached Bucyrus a little before 12.—Stoped with Wm Earley And to my astonishment found that he & several others who were once pillers of Methodism in this place had joined the Protestant Reformed Methodists[21]—I had some talk with him but he still seemed of an exolent spirit yet this cannot but be a short lived state of feeling. Division is the sure parent of contention.—I went to the Land Office to enter a 40 acre lot that joins my land on the Maumee but found that an other had taken it.—While in town got my License to Solemnize Marriage recorded—Br Bibbens having found out some old acquaintances was desirous of visiting them I according left my wagon & things in his care & took horse for Br. Dorlands—Learned that since the death of his wife, he had broken up house keeping & lived

[20] Evidently William Brown was a friend of his former Indian Mission days.

[21] The Methodist Protestant church.

with his father;—whose house I reached about sundown—This was one of My preaching places when I traveled Delaware cir.....

Sat Aug 16..... Spent the day till 2 P.M. Reading Bucks Theological Dixonary[22] & in sleeping—While eating dinner My horse brok out of the stable & ran off: he had been gone but a short time before it was discouvered But before horses could be got [and] persuit be made he had goten a good way ahead (bearing south) Jas D. & I persued & about six miles off overtook him by means of a brother who saw me ride by on frid—Knowing the horse [he] stoped him & put him in the stable. We returned by Cornelius Dorlands & took supper for it was now night about 10 we returned to old Br Dorland but as there had not been the expected preparation made to seat the ground on which it was calculated to hold meeting next day James D & I wrought till midnight to effect this which we did tolerably well.....

Sund Aug 17..... spent the morning reading & taking some not[e]s on the life & death of etc Unice Dorland whose funeral I came to preach—Preached at 10 to large & attentive congragation—I immidiately set out for my other appointment at My old friends Br Isaac Monetts 12 Miles dist. Jas D accompanying me we stoped & fed & dined at br John Maxfields: and he accompanied us as far as Bucyrus passed by where Br Bibbens was waiting for me—by 6 we reached Br Monnetts I immediately commenced preaching & spoke with great liberty and power from Matt xvi.26.27. The whole congregation was much moved—Spent the evening principly conversing with Br Jas Dorland on the subject of a community—he is still disposed thereto but not sanguinly.....

Mond Aug 18..... Made preparation to set out on our journey for conferance. After brakefast we got under way but the road was rendered mudy & the way on run heavy by reason of rain last night & this morning—a little after one we reached Norton Fed & dined with Br Henry Smith.—passed through Delaware about 6 but made no halt in the village except to buy an inkstand having broken mine last Saturday. I also called at Mr *Mansers* a moment (But we went by the Sulphur Spring & drank of its waters. This place is under going great improvement & will shortly be the resort of all classes of the in-

[22] Charles Buck, *A Theological Dictionary .... Enlarged and Improved, from the Last London Edition with American Subjects Added* (Philadelphia, 1824).

habitents of this villiage.) We reached Br Travises 5 miles below with whom we put up.—felt drowsey—slight head ake, with a tendency to loosness in My bowels.....

Tusd Aug 19..... After brakefast we set out & drove to Columbus —fed & dined with a Br Kelley—rested till two set out & drove to within 6 Miles of Circleville & put up with a stranger. This is the first time that I have had to pay for Lodging since I left home & here only 37½ a piece.—.... fell in with Br E Day & all put up to gither—to bed about 10 had but a poor rest—

Wed Aug 20..... set out immediately & drove in to Circleville a little after 6—Put up with a Br More—Conferance opened at 9 A.M. Bishop Soul[23] in the chair—attended faithfully to business till 12—The P[residing] Elders were called to the B[ishop]s room at a qu past 4 when we adjourned—I had a considerable conversasion with Pr S Hamelton[24] on his state of Widowhood I felt to sympathize with him—spent the evening till 9 Making out the new circuits.....

Thurd Aug 21..... Spent the morning writing a letter to My wife—In conferance a probationer Robert Graham was expelled—In the afternoon The stewards received the amount of claims & payment & then adjourned after which the conferance Missionary Society Meet—1 spent from 7 till 9 with the P.Es & Bp Regulating the Districts.....

Frid Aug 22..... Spent the day in conferance dilegently attending to business—after the afternoon session was over I Met the PEs to arange the circuits, & districts. & from 7 till 10 laboured in the stationing business along with the P Es & Bishop..... Found my Mind some disturbed with others but more especially with Myself. To bed about ½ past 10 but did not sleep till near 12.

Sat Aug 23..... attended conferance business faithfully till 12.—We had a short session in the afternoon.—I intended going to hear preaching, but Passing the bishops boarding place & not being certain but that he had required the attendance of the P Es I called & found him busiley employed preparing the parchments for the preachers to

[23] Joshua Soule, D.D. (1781–1867), a native of Maine, was elected bishop in 1824. With the separation of 1845, he cast his lot with the Southern Methodists.

[24] Samuel Hamilton (1791–1854) was a native of West Virginia who had removed in 1806 to the Muskingum Valley of Ohio, where he joined the Ohio Conference in 1814 (James B. Finley, *Sketches of Western Methodism* [Cincinnati, 1855], pp. 445–65).

be ordained & setting beside him Br David Young.[25] he kindly asked me to be seated—I soon became engaged as his assistant at which I laboured faithfully till 11. This I esteemed a favourable oppertunity to propose some questons in rifferance to our law. I preposed the following question "supose A is notefied to trial on charges of immorality—dos not attend—is condemned.—demands an appeal on the ground of the 5th ristriction rule page 21.[26] Is objected to on the ground of a Conferance Law Page 89 part 5 What decision should a P.E. give in such a case of Law." Ans by D Young & B. P. Soul both. "The prohibition to appeal (page 89) should take precedency—it existed before the ristriction rules were in being" These are not perhaps their exact words, but they contain the Ideas I received of them. I was silent as to objection but it dose [does] appear to me they would both feel ashamed to have this idea of Methodist Law go down to posterity as their own. I forbear to comment—Returned to my lodgings—..... Musing on the various conversasions I had with the B.P. & D Young on the powers & nature of our government O how Monarkal their views!

Sund Aug 24..... immediately set out for my appointment (one I had made) 6 Miles out in the countray by the pressing invitation [of] a Br Ricard Berry a man who was in the Army in 1814 with me & who I have not seen since, till I came to this conf.—I preached with much liberty, & some power at 11 from Ps 119.1. Returned to Br Bs & took dinner—he then Rode with me to the canal aquaduct—(Went in the evening to hear Br Fielding one of the professors in Agusta Coladge)[27] But it was with difficulty I could keep from a stupid drowsiness.....

[25] David Young (1779–1858), a native of Bedford County, Virginia, was a leading member of the Ohio Conference. He was a traveling preacher from the time of his admission to the Western Conference in 1805. He was one of the trustees of Ohio University at Athens (see "Sketch of Rev. David Young," in W[illiam] P. Strickland [ed.], *Autobiography of Rev. James B. Finley; or, Pioneer Life in the West* [Cincinnati, 1855], pp. 407–18; also William B. Sprague, *Annals of the American Pulpit* [New York, 1865], VII, 427–34).

[26] The Fifth Restrictive Rule, adopted 1808, reads: "The General Conference shall not do away the privileges of our ministers or preachers, of trial by a Committee, and of an appeal" (David Sherman, *History of the Revisions of the Discipline of the Methodist Episcopal Church* [New York, 1874], p. 134).

[27] Augusta College was founded in 1822 on the Kentucky side of the Ohio River near Cincinnati, under the joint control of the Ohio and Kentucky conferences. It closed

Mond Aug 25..... Spent the day in conferance business & the evening till 10 with the Bishop & Elders in the stationing business.... to bed ½ past 10 but through anxiety on the stationing business could not sleep for some time.

Tus Aug 26..... [Similar to Monday, August 25.—EDITOR.]

Wed Aug 27..... [Also similar.—EDITOR.]

Thursd. Aug 28..... the Bishop was too unwell to perform any part of this work this evening It was finished however by the elders —good or bad as the appointments may be Thus it is.....

Frid Aug 29. Rose at 5—Met with the Bishop & P. Elders at 6 to read over the stations & see that none were left out & for the Bishops approval this done—The standing committy on Missions (of whom I am one) Met and Made our appropriations to the several Missions—Confer met as usual & after finishing its business we received our appointments about ½ past 10—I with the rest of the superintendants of the Missions Repaired to the Bishops room with the Treasurer of the Ohio conf. Miss. Society & Receid our 1st qur enstalment—After much solisitude, I came to the conclusion not to visit My mother etc this fall but return to my family at Ann Arbor, principly because the Cholera[28] Rages at this time along the towns on the Lake The Lord direct, & sustain me in my duty—About 2 We got under way (Br Bibbins & myself) & reached Columbus by dusk (25 miles) & put up with Br Robert Cloud (a son of old Robert Cloud of Ky one of the early Methodist Prs lately dead).....

Sat Aug 30..... spent the morning till 12 obtaining some anti-spasmodics for the cholera should I find occasion,—in viewing the new penitentiary—& in endeavoring to have an error (by which I paid the tax on a certain peice of land twice last year) corrected—perhaps I shall git my money again & perhaps not—having dined we left Columbus ½ past twelve & reached Delaware at dusk—Put up with My old friend Moses Bixby—tended meeting & heard E H Pilcher[29] preach.....

---

as a result of the Methodist schism in 1844. John H. Fielding, mentioned by Gilruth, was professor of mathematics there in 1834–35.

[28] There were cholera epidemics in Michigan in 1832 and 1834.

[29] Elijah Holmes Pilcher (1810–87), a native of Ohio, was in 1834–35 appointed to Farmington, Michigan. He studied law and medicine but spent his life as a circuit preacher and presiding elder in West Virginia, Ohio, and Michigan. From 1848 to

Sund Aug 31..... Spent the morning till near 11 writing letters to My mother & Motherinlaw—preached at 11 with good liberty & reproved sin with authority—heard L. D. Whitney at 2 & A Billings at candlelight after whom Curtis Godard[30] exhorted.....

Mond Sept 1..... visited the grave of our beloved Mary[31] buried here 30 of June 1828—After brakefast we set out & drove to Marion fed & dined at Br Williams—then Drove on to upper sandusky—put up at the Mission—I was so unfortunate as to lose my tarbucket[32] sumtime before I reached this place but I did not notice it till next morning—.... Bro Pilcher & Whitney staid here also—

Tus Sept 2..... discouvered I had lost My tar bucket & went back some distance for it but was unsuccessfull—of Br Thompson I bought 7 & ½ lb wool for My Daughter at Finley—after brakefast drove to Mccutchinville & left it in the care of Giorge Nessel & wrote them a letter—drove on fed & dined at A Loves near Tiffin—Reached Br. Emmersons a little before sunset—put up—Spent the evening conversing on cholera etc.....

Wed Sept 3—.... after an earley brakefast set out & Drove on to a tavern 13 Miles from Perysburgh fed:—& dined on bread & small beer—passed through Perrysbourgh about 5 (stoped & paid my land tax) Reached Br Whitneys at dark, & put up. Br Billings put here also.....

Thurd Sept 4..... drove to Br Wilkinsons for brakefast, through a slight shower of rain. Roads good—passed through Monroe a little before 12 but drove on to Swan creek (10 miles) & fed & dined It

---

1852 he was a member of the Book Committee of the Western Book Concern at Cincinnati. After a trip to the Holy Land with William X. Ninde, later bishop, in 1867, he became professor of belles-lettres and history in Albion College, Michigan. He is remembered for his *Protestantism in Michigan* (Detroit, 1878), chiefly relating to Methodism; and for his *Index* to the *Methodist Magazine* and *Methodist Quarterly Review* from 1818 to 1881. For memoir see *Fall Minutes, 1887,* p. 353; also James E. Pilcher, *Life and Labors of Elijah H. Pilcher* (1892).

[30] This is a group of preachers on their way from conference, spending Sunday at Delaware, Ohio. Luther D. Whitney was the preacher on the Mount Clemens Circuit, Curtis Goddard had taken a "location" at conference, and Alvin Billings was appointed to Elyria.

[31] Evidently a daughter of Gilruth's.

[32] "Tarbucket," a wooden bucket hung from the rear axle of the wagon, containing axle grease.

was a time of distress in Monroe between the cholera & other sickness. from swan creek we reached smoth Rock a little before sundown the place of Br Bibbins & I setting out from on the 3d of Aug. we put up with Jacob Vreeland—Here I met with Br Wm H Brockway[33] who informed me that the cholera & other sickness were raging at Ann Arbour & that himself was just raised from deaths door— . . . .

Frid Sept 5—fixed my wageon for one horse again—having brought Br E Pattes dividend of the conf funds (Marked $72.80) I put it into the hands of Br Brokway to deliver to him About 9 Brs Billings Bibbins & myself set out each on his own conveyance & after traveling 6 Miles together I parted from them forded Huron & drove to Ypsylanti —fed & dined at Br Norris (he was at Detroit) While my horse was eating I wrote to Br Crain & Frazee[34] informing C of his reappointment to Detroit & F of his transfer to Kentucky Also to Br Barris[35] Requesting him travel on Tecumseh circuit with Br. Wiley—set out for home which I reached a little before sunset & much Rejoiced once more to find all well—A nomber have died in this since I left here. Some I fear illy prepared for the change of worlds. . . . .

Sat Sept 6 . . . . halled some water etc etc—spent the day till 12 visiting & praying with the sick when I discouvered I was attacted with fever I returned home a sick man—took 20 grs of calomel which wrought well I found some relief—At night I lay with my feet to the fire & found much relief—

Sund Sept 9. . . . . felt comfortable but a slight feverish taste in my mouth a something unpleasant at the stomach perhaps for want of food having eating nothing but a small peice of tosted bread since yesterday morning—Wrote some in my journal—& coppied some of the Minnuts of Conferance which I took while at Conf. which will be found on this Journal from page 31 to 57.

[PAGES 31–57]

Minutes of the 23 Ohio Annuel Conferance held in Circleville Ohio Taken by Myself. James Gilruth.

[33] William H. Brockway (1813–1891), a native of Vermont, was in 1834–35 appointed to Ypsilanti Circuit.

[34] Bradford Frazee is described by Pilcher (*Protestantism in Michigan,* p. 283) as extremely fastidious and refined, so that he could hardly bear to eat and sleep with his parishioners.

[35] William Barrus and wife were among the first members of the Methodist society at Adrian in 1830.

Aug 20 Wed. Morning 8 O.Clock.

Conferance was opened by Bishop Soul by Reading the scriptures singing & prayer—The role was called & Joseph M Trimble[36] was appointed secretary & Wm. Herr[37] and Isaac C Hunter[38] assistent secterys Bishop Soul[39] addressed the Confirance on the following particulars—the extencive increase of Methodism,—explained the reason of Bishop Andrews Absence, vis familey affliction & that he came in his place; That the bishops were generally well—the preachers Also,—the necessity of promptness in confirance business. Hinted the necessity of small committies—the necessity of keeping the spirit of Religion, and to pray for the families etc where we board. Conferance then proceded to fix the times of Meeting: vis. . . . . On Motion . . . . appointed Conferance stewards— . . . . appointed a committy to Regulate the times of preaching & appoint the preachers to the pulpit during Conferance . . . . appointed a committy to write the memoirs of the dead . . . . appointed a book committy to settle accounts with the preachers . . . . committy . . . . to draft a request, solisitating suport for the Western Christian Advocate; to be laid before the several Western Conferances . . . . committy . . . . to take into consideration the state of our accadamies etc. . . . . committy . . . . to enquire into the state of the Meeting houses & parsonages—If built & occupied according to Our Discipline—15 . . . . committy . . . . to enquire into the expediency of establishing Theological institutions. 16. . . . . 17 . . . . committee . . . . necessitous cases. 18 . . . . committy . . . . Sabbath schools. 19 . . . . A communication from the Norwalk seminary was read praying to have E Chaplin[40] reappointed to the presidency of that institution . . . . he was

[36] Joseph M. Trimble, D.D. (1807–91), a native of Woodford County, Kentucky, and son of Governor Allen Trimble (1783–1870) of Ohio, joined the Ohio Conference in 1829 after graduating from Ohio University, and became professor of mathematics at Augusta College, Kentucky (1836–40). From 1834 until 1865 he was secretary of the Ohio Conference (Matthew Simpson [ed.] *Cyclopaedia of Methodism* [Philadelphia, 1878], pp. 870–71).

[37] William Herr was appointed at this conference to Mount Vernon Circuit, in Wooster District.

[38] Isaac C. Hunter (1798–1842), was a native of central Pennsylvania, admitted on trial to the Ohio Conference in 1819. For memoir see *Minutes,* Vol. III: *1839–1846,* p. 349.

[39] The official *Minutes* of the conference omit the digest of Bishop Soule's address.

[40] Jonathan Edwards Chaplin (1789–1846), a native of Mansfield, Connecticut, and a great-grandson of Jonathan Edwards, Sr., graduated from Yale in 1808. After prac-

committed to the committy on seminaries. 20 . . . . reconsider the vote appointing a committy . . . . on Sabbath schools . . . . resolution originating the appointment of said committee by on the table—21. An exibit of the Book Concern at N York was read (which showed on hand upwards of $141,000 worth of books) . . . . . 22. A communication from Thomas A Morris[41] concerning the reason of his not attending conferance—& in relation to his remaining in the Editorship of the Western Christian Advocate . . . . refered to the committy on the western paper etc.—23 . . . . adjourned.

Afternoon Session B Soul in the chair

1 James Quin[42] opened the conferance by Reading the scripture singing & prayer—2 . . . . Role . . . . called . . . . journals read . . . . 3 by-laws . . . . 4 . . . . 5 committy . . . . on periodicals . . . . 6 . . . . "Who remain on trial" . . . . sit with closed doors . . . . (Duncan McGrigor Droped) . . . . 7 On Motion James Quin Jacob Young,[43] William Simmons[44] were apointed a committy for some purpose I did not Recolect, so as to be able to note it.[45]—8 . . . . Adjourned.

---

ticing law in Connecticut and western New York and serving in the War of 1812, he removed in 1818 to Ohio, where he was converted to Methodism in 1830. He was principal of Norwalk Seminary, 1833–37, and joined the Ohio Conference in 1834 (see Sprague, *op. cit.*, VII, 797–802).

[41] Thomas A. Morris, D.D. (1794–1874), a native of West Virginia, was at this time editor of the *Western Christian Advocate*, with offices in Cincinnati. He was elected bishop in 1836.

[42] James Quinn (1775–1847), a native of Washington County, Pennsylvania, was converted to Methodism in 1792 and joined conference in 1799, laboring as circuit preacher and presiding elder in West Virginia and Ohio. In 1807 he became judge of the Court of Common Pleas for Fairfield County, Ohio (see John F. Wright, *Sketches of the Life and Labors of James Quinn* [Cincinnati, 1851]; cf. Sprague, *op. cit.*, VII, 314–21).

[43] Jacob Young, D.D. (1776–1859), a native of western Pennsylvania, was in 1834–35 appointed to Athens Circuit, in Zanesville District. His interesting life as a frontier circuit-rider is chronicled in his *Autobiography of a Pioneer* (Cincinnati, 1857).

[44] William Simmons (1798–*ca.* 1870), a native of Mason County, Kentucky, had been admitted on trial to the Ohio Conference in 1820. In 1834–35 he was appointed to Dayton, Ohio. Later he became president of the board of trustees of Xenia College. In his semicentennial sermon (1870) he claimed to have "traveled more than 100,000 miles, preached more than 5000 times, and seen more than 10,000 conversions and additions to the church" (Simpson, *op. cit.*, pp. 799–800).

[45] This committee included also Jacob Delay, Alfred M. Lorain, Ebenezer B. Chase, E. H. Pilcher, E. H. Field, and George W. Walker. The committee was to investigate

Aug 21 Thurd Morning. 1. Jacob Young opened conferance.... 2....3 A Motion was made to recind a certain resolution passed at a former conferance which disaproved of the Bishops transfering any person to this conferance unless they shall judge it necessary for the good of the work which after some debate was lost. A Motion was then made to amend the resolution by adding "Except he have been a member of our conferance which was carried—4....5 A Motion was then read to publish the Resolution in referance to transfering Prs to this conferance in the Christian Advocate which was lost—6 "Who remain on trial"....resumed....But Robert Graham, had been suspended on a charge of immorality[46] The facts appeared to be the huging of two different women—kissing them—afterwards denying that he huged them but owned that he laid his arm around one the history of the act was the same but a v[ar]i[a]ble differance in wording it. He was expelled—Conferance acting precipitately—7 "Who are the deacons"....James F Davison....Thomas Wiley....8 "Who are the Elders"....Bradford Frazee....Elnathan C Gavitt....elected ....Afternoon Session....1 James B Finley[47] opened Conferance ....2....The Conf stewards called for the amount of claims each preacher laid for quarterage & what each had received.[48]—....adjourned. After which conferance Resolved itself into a conferance Missionary society—Received the Annual subscription vis $1.00 per member & then elected her officiry—of which I was elected one of the Managers.

---

the state of meetinghouses and parsonages. Another committee on academies and Augusta College was appointed, and William H. Raper and James B. Finley were a committee to investigate the propriety of establishing a theological seminary.

[46] The official *Minutes* state only that Graham was expelled for immorality.

[47] James Bradley Finley (1781–1856), a native of North Carolina, was at this time an outstanding leader of American Methodism. In 1834–35 he was presiding elder of Chillicothe District, Ohio Conference. He was converted at the famous Cane Ridge Camp Meeting in 1801 and joined the Western Conference in 1810. It was he who proposed to the General Conference of 1844 the resolution requiring Bishop Andrew to desist from the exercise of his office until he had freed his slaves. Finley's labors among the Wyandots in the Sandusky Valley of Ohio are told in his *History of the Wyandott Mission at Upper Sandusky, Ohio* (1840) and his *Life among the Indians* (1857). His *Memorials of Prison Life* (1850) is drawn from his experience as chaplain to an Ohio penitentiary. Most valuable of his works are his *Autobiography* (1855)—a classic document of frontier life—and his *Sketches of Western Methodism* (1855). For a brief biographical sketch see the *Dictionary of American Biography*, VI, 389–90

[48] Gilruth's claim was $200, of which he received the full amount.

Aug 23 Friday Morning. . . . . 1 Arthur W Elliott[49] opened conferance. . . . . 2 . . . . 3 . . . . dividend assigned last conf. by the stewards to Wm. S Thornburg be forwarded to him in Mississippi conf. he being transfered there. 4. John M Daily having a counterfit $10. Note given him in his appropriation last year anounced it: & on Motion it was ordered that the stewards receive it back & make him his appropriation up in good money.—5 . . . . committy of three, were appointed to enquire into the causes of the deficiency of the fift collection (E g the collection for superanuated Prs etc. . . . . 6 . . . . committy . . . . to assertain the names of the several Post offices with each circuit etc & report to the Book agents at N York.—7. The candidates for admission into full connection were then called for & examined by the Bishop. On page [. . . .] of the Discipline . . . . (Eliakin Zimmerman was continued on trial after much debate) . . . . Wm Westlake, an elder; . . . . Luther D Whitney . . . . Arthur B Elliott . . . . elected to decons orders.—8 The Bishop announced that the conferance might draw on the chartered fund for $75 & on the Book Concern for $600, which on Motion was drawn . . . . Afternoon session. . . . . 1 Agustus Edy opened conference . . . . 2 . . . . 3 . . . . 4 The case of Benjamin Allen was taken up but for imprudent conduct in courting etc he was discontinued—4 . . . . reconsidered . . . . vote . . . . by which Robert Graham was discontinued . . . . he was discontinued— . . . .

Aug 24 Sat. Morning. . . . . 1 Levi White opened conferance . . . . 2 . . . . 3 . . . . who are elected to elders orders traveling preachers . . . . 4. Candidates for deacons orders among the Local Preachers . . . . Samuel Bibbins . . . . elected. . . . . Sat Afternoon session . . . . opened conferance. . . . . 3 candidates for elders orders among the Local Preachers. . . . . Wm Barris . . . . elected . . . . 4. Resolution . . . . requesting the Bishop to take Measures to perfect the course of study for young preachers. . . . .

Aug 26 Mond Morning. . . . . James McMahan opened conferance. . . . . the following Resolution was adopted "Resolved that it is improper for our preachers to leave the congregation till the servises are closed" (the conduct of nombers of the preachers on Sabath (last) give rise to this resolution which was intended as a Rebuke). . . . . 6 Isaac C Hunter (the only one of the committy appointed to visit

[49] Arthur W. Elliott (1784–1858) was at this time one of the "fathers" of the Ohio Conference, having joined it in 1818. He was a native of Baltimore County, Maryland ("Memoir," *Minutes, 1858*, p. 296).

Augusta College, who attended,) Made his Report: which on Motion was laid on the table. (this report showed the institution to be in debt —that a nomber of the schollars had become drunkards—that there *had* been wrangling among the professors—) 7 The Resolutions of the N York conf. Requiring Presiding Elders & Preachers to use all due means to recover all debts due the book concern, sell our books and establish sabbath school liberarys .... addopted..... examination of the characters of the Elders .... Joseph M Trimble (he being solicitated to take a professorship in the Ohio university laid the case before the conferance for advice 9 A Motion was made advising him not to accept said invitation which after a warm debate was lost by a vote of 51 to 62. 10 It was then moved "That conferance decline advising or requesting the Bishop to appoint Joseph M Trimble to the Ohio University which after some altrecation was laid on the table .... adjourned to attend to the Annual Conferance Missionary society.

Missionary Society met at 11 A.M. in the Methodist M.H. Opened by Jacob Young—Report was read—Adressed 1 by Wm H Raper,[50] 2 by Samuel A Latter,[51] Report adopted. The following Resolution was offered "That we make encreased exertions for the Missionary cause; that we tender our thanks to those who have contributed to the aid of this cause; Addressed 1 by Edmon W Sehon 2 by James B Finley who took up a collection which he commenced by proposing to be one of 10 who would give $5. It was a moving time—The whole amount of collections for Missions in the bounds of this conf this year is $2.471.78½ —4 young men volunteered for Missouri conf

---

Monday afternoon..... A Brother Clark opened conferance..... examination of character.... Leonidas L Hamline[52] .... admitted into full connection ....

[50] William H. Raper (1793–1852), a native of western Pennsylvania who had entered the Ohio Conference in 1819, was in 1834–35 appointed to the Urbana District (see Finley, *Sketches of Western Methodism* [Cincinnati, 1855], pp. 466–475; Sprague, *op. cit.*, VII, 617–21).

[51] Samuel A. Latta, M.D. (1804–52), a native of the Muskingum Valley of Ohio, had been admitted on trial to the Ohio Conference in 1829, and in 1834–35 was appointed to Lebanon, Ohio. In 1831 he had served as agent for the American Colonization Society. After 1845 he favored the Southern Church and edited the *Methodist Expositor* in Cincinnati (Simpson, *op. cit.*, pp. 526–27).

[52] Leonidas Lent Hamline, D.D. (1797–1865), was elected a bishop of the Methodist Episcopal church at the General Conference of 1844. He was a native of Connecticut

Tuesday Morning Aug 27..... David Young opened conference. .... The Bishop ordained Leonidas L Hamline a deacon .... stewards report .... 5 committy on necessitous cases .... report .... 6 A communication (what it was, I did not distinctly note) was presented, which was committed to the committee on colleges.[53] 7. The Committy .... to assertain the Nombers of post offices in each circuit asked to be dismissed, & that the Preachers on the circuits collect & report them by the end of the first qur. to the Presiding Elders: & that they forward them to the book agents at N York..... 8 Conferance then took up the motion laid on the table yesterday Refusing to request the Bishop to appoint Joseph M Trimble to the Ohio University; which motion was after some remarks withdrawn; 9 And a Motion was Made Requesting the bishop to appoint J M T to the O University: But upon the Bishops making some remarks it was also withdrawn 10 And a Motion was then offered "That this conferance approve of Joseph M Trimbles accepting an appointment in the Ohio university on his own responsibility; which was agreed to[54]— .... examination of characters of the elders..... Russel bigalow[55] (a moving letter was read from him to the conf. he was made supperanuated)..... Curtis Goddard (asked & obtained a Location) .... John P Taylor .... (& on motion ordered that he have his claimes in future) superated..... Elias Pattee superant.....

---

and of Congregational ancestry. Entering the practice of law in Ohio, he came under Methodist influence and was converted. He relinquished his law practice in 1832 to enter the Ohio Conference. In 1836 he became assistant editor of the *Western Christian Advocate*. He was the first editor of the *Ladies Repository*, established in Cincinnati in 1840, one of the earliest literary periodicals in the West (see Walter C. Palmer, *Life and Letters of Leonidas L. Hamline, D.D.* [New York, 1866]; F. G. Hibbard, *Biography of Rev. Leonidas L. Hamline* [New York, 1880]; *Dictionary of American Biography*, VIII, 198–99).

[53] This was a communication from Norwalk Seminary, a Methodist school.

[54] The question here involved was whether a member of a conference could accept a place on a state university faculty and remain on the active roll. The General Conference in 1820 adopted a rule permitting the bishops to appoint traveling preachers as officers and teachers in colleges. There was evidently still a great deal of reluctance on the part of the western conferences to permit this being done.

[55] Russell Bigelow (1793–1835), a native of Cheshire County, New Hampshire, had been admitted on trial to the Ohio Conference in 1814. In 1827 he was missionary to the Wyandots and, in 1835, chaplain to the state prison at Columbus, Ohio (Finley, *Sketches of Western Methodism*, pp. 411–27; Sprague, *op. cit.*, VII, 540–46).

Tusd Afternoon Session.....Wm H Raper opened conf..... conf reconsidered the case of Stephen A Rathbun he having been discontinued; And on motion he was continued on trial (by an overwhelming majority) The question who are admited on trial.[56].... Single or maried designated by S or M.....S Lorenzo Davis 22.....

Aug 28. Wed Morning.....committy on memoirs.....4 At this time the two young men from Pitsburg conf & the four from this who were transfered to Missouri Conf took a formal leave of our conf it was a Moving scean.....committy appointed to draft an address[57] to the Western Christian Advocate.....Read this address....approved & ordered to be published in the Western Christian Advocate..... The Committy on Theological Seminaries Read their report (decidedly in opposition to such institutions) which was addopted..... "who are admitted on trial.....

Wed Afternoon session.....Samuel Hamelton opened conf..... reception of candidates on trial.....S Lucien Berry[58] 19.....

Aug 29 Thursd Morning.....1 James Gilruth Opened Conferance. ....3 committy on colleges....report....adopted—4.....were appointed a committee to nominate a board of trustees for the Norwalk Seminary—5. On motion it was ordered that the funds subscribed of the Prs last conf to endow the McKendree professorship in the Augusta college, be deposited by the treasurer with the Book agents at Cincinnatti; that the Book Concern pay the Intrest to Augusta College—and that Arthur W Elliott....be treasurer for the ensuing year. ....6 A ressolution was offered That the preachers who were not prepared to pay their first instalment pay the intrest & keep the principle for this year, which resolution was lost—7 The committy appointed last conf consisting of the Presiding Elder of Detroit Dist

[56] The list of those admitted on trial is omitted (see *Minutes,* Vol. II: *1829–1839,* p. 288). Forty-three were admitted.

[57] The "address" was a series of resolutions, one of which was that the editor of the *Western Christian Advocate* admit temperate articles on the subject of theological seminaries (see photostat *Minutes of the Ohio Conference for 1835* in the University of Chicago Libraries).

[58] Lucian W. Berry, D.D. (1815–58), was a native of Vermont. In 1838 he entered the Indiana Conference and in 1849 was elected the second president of Indiana Asbury University, now DePauw University (see William Warren Sweet, *Indiana Asbury–DePauw University* [New York, 1937], p. 63). He was later president of Iowa Wesleyan University and of a college at Jefferson City, Missouri ("Memoir," *Minutes, 1859,* p. 126).

with the Prs in charg To exam into the practacability—& receive proposels for the location of a seminary of learning etc Reported favourably of its practicaluity & in favour of a site at Spring Arbour which was accepted & the P. Elder & preachers in charge in said Dist. were appointed a committy to nominate T[r]ustees—& assist to obtain a charter simular to those obtained for our Institutions of learning in other stat[e]s; & that they assist in raising subscriptions to endow it—8 The presiding elders were apponted a committy to nominate who should be entitled to gratuitous Instruction in the August[a] college—9 The committy .... [on a] More perfect course of Reading for the young Prs .... Report, with a course of studies .... accepted & ordered to be published in the Western Christian Advocate[59]—10 The committy apointed last conf. to corrispond with Wm Burk[60] of Cincinatti (he having made some proposals to be ristored to the M E Church from which he had been expelled, that were not distinctly understood) Read their corrispondence .... accepted .... farther consideration .... laid over .... til next conf—11 The committy .... to find the cause of the deficiency in the 5th collection & point out a cure; Read their Report with some resolutions appended The Report was adopted but the resolutions were not—Bp Soul then spoke his views freely and warmly on this subject and among other things remarked "That is as much our duty as *Methodist* preachers to take up the 5th collection as to meet a class or preach"—"I pray you in the name of God not to let the institutions of Methodism go down in your hands" (His eyes suffused with tears while making these Remarks!) 12 An appeal of a Local Preacher was Brought forward by his P.E. A Eddy, But he having failed to give notification of his intention to appeal, was bard, his appeal by the rule of Discipline on the appeal of local Preachers—.....

[59] The "Course of Study" was published in the *Western Christian Advocate*, September 5, 1834.

[60] William Burke's appeal was introduced year after year and was "laid over" regularly until late in life, when he was finally restored to conference membership. He had been the secretary of the Western Conference from 1800 until 1811. He asked for supernumerary relations in 1813 and became postmaster of Cincinnati. He continued to preach and administer the sacraments and, while in this relationship, was accused of treating an elder with contempt and was expelled in 1820, undoubtedly very unjustly (see Finley, *Sketches of Western Methodism*, pp. 22 ff.; also Sweet, *Circuit-Rider Days along the Ohio*, pp. 53–54).

Thurd Afternoon session.....1 Daniel D Davison[61] opened conf ....2....3....4 On Motion Conf ordered, to leave Lorenzo Bivens without an appointment, with a view to his being transfered to Elenoies conf—5 On Motion It was determined to appoint a agent to collect funds for the Norwalk Semenary;....Henry O Sheldon[62] was appointed....6....nombers in society.....But the Bp being unwell he called James Quin to the chair & retired during the rest of the afternoon—62,696 & the net encrease for the last year 5 451 Wt, 55 col.....7....place of next session....which on the 3d balloting was determined to be at Springfield Ohio.....

Frid. Aug 29 Jas Quin in the chair (the Bp being unwell his business was retarded so as to render him late....) 1 Edmon W Sehon opened conf.....2....3....resolution of thanks to the citizens of Circleville....4 The Bishop now assumed the chair and announced the time of Next conference to be Aug. 19th *1835*—5....Wyandot Missionary....report....6....Huron Missionary....report.... 7....Report of committy on meeting houses....(The first resolution appended....Requirs the Presiding Elder & Preacher in charge at Detroit to Use their influence to have a deed executed to the M E Church for the M. Meeting house there according to our discipline & to use their influence to have the seats made free[63] & report to this conf at its next session The 3 Resolution appended was That all preachers of this conf be instructed to line their Hymns in all our publick congregations) which report etc was adopted after an interesting Debate of some length—8....Treasurer of the Fund subscribed by the preachers to endow the McKendree professorship of Moral sciance in the augusta College Reported that he had received of the Preachers $760.75 cts!!! besides about $40 which had been Paid James

[61] Daniel D. Davison (1785–1870) had joined the Western Conference in 1811. He was in 1834–35 appointed to Sydney Circuit, in Urbana District.

[62] Henry O. Sheldon (1799–1882), a native of Hartford, Connecticut, had entered the Ohio Conference in 1825 and was this year (1834–35) appointed agent for Norwalk Seminary. In 1836 he "located" to found a Christian Community, which failed financially, and he turned to education, helping to found Baldwin Institute, Berea, Ohio. He was readmitted in the North Ohio Conference in 1851 ("Memoir," *Fall Minutes*, 1883, p. 319).

[63] The official *Minutes* make this resolution of more general character, against all pew rents. Another resolution urged that "the use of instrumental music be prudently and perseveringly dispensed with and discountenanced in all our worshipping assemblies."

B Finley last year while treasurer!!! (*sic!!!* There should have been $2500 paid at this conf.)—9 A Resolution was offered exempting the poor preachers from paying the principle [principal] for three years but that they pay the int[e]rest annually which was lost—10.... Resolved to Keep the first Friday in April as a day of Publick fasting etc & that it be published in the W. Christian Advocate—..... Bishop announced.... committy of examination of candidates at next conf—.... And.... a visiting committy to Augusta College—.... And.... a visiting committy to Norwalk seminary.... After singing & prayer the Appointments were read..... Conf adjourned

JAMES GILRUTH

Thus closed one of the longest & most labourious conferances I ever attended—I am not positive of the correctness of every part of the above Minutes as I had not the advantage of having them corrected by reading them to others

Mond Sept 8..... wrote for some time copying off My Minutes but found Myself attackted with the Ague & fever[64] so that this day I spent in bed—at night I took 30 gr[ains] of Epicecuhana which wrought pretty well except it did not effect the bile as much as I could wish I again lay with My feet to the fire, but had not a very Comfortable nights rest.....

Tus Sept 9. Rose early & commenced taking quinine, No 6 & Tinct of Cucumber (true)—Kept the house all day Again slept with my feet to the fire (considerably bilious stools).....

Wed Sept 10 Continued takeing the above tonics: had some head ake of a heavy, num, stupid character—felt better in the afternoon Wrote some at My Minutes—& spent sometime looking over My scripture collections[65] Again slept with My feet to the fire—.....

[64] Ague and fever was a common frontier complaint, especially prevalent in the autumn. Many a preacher came to conference after a month's tussle with the ague, "and some of them kept up the shake habit every other day during conference" (William Warren Sweet, *Circuit-Rider Days in Indiana* [Indianapolis, 1916], p. 75).

[65] In his "Journal" for August 10, 1831, Gilruth states: "About a year ago it came to my mind to collect the whole duty of a christian from the scriptures: which I determined to do for my own benefit..... This I have found a very profitable imployment." Later he conceived the idea of collecting the doctrines of revelation "under their respective heads" for the purpose of uniting "all true saints in faith and practice."

Thurd Sept 11..... wrote some etc etc took my wife & children & paid a visit to Br Mcdowel—employed My time in writing—Returned home in the even felt well—Halled a barrel of water etc after dark. .... smart frost to night

Frid Sept 12..... finished my Minutes & wrote some in My journal —Went to Br Mcdowels about noon & cut some oats for horse feed.....

Sat Sept 13..... attended to sundry things in the forenoon Milling etc. And in the afternoon Went to Br Barrs for hay.....

Sund Sept 14..... preached at 10 & Met class—heard Br Colclazer[66] at 2 P.M.....

Mond Sept 15..... spent the day giting some lumber & fixing a floor in My stable.....

Tusd Sept 16..... spent the day principly in fixing My stable & in whoping [hooping] a couple of water barels.....

Wed Sept 17..... Spent the day writing off My scripture collections.....

Thurd Sept 18.... (similar).

Frid Sept 19..... wrote a little—got my horse shod—Preached a funeral (at Almandingers Metting house) at 4 P.M. a Mr. Smith a lutheren Minister having first preached in dutch.[67]

Sat Sept 20..... took My wife & children & paid a visit to Col. White.....

Sund Sept 21—spent the morning Reading & writing—Preached at ½ past 10—took My familey & rode down to Mr Collens & preached at 4 staid All night with him—Read the Books of Tobit & Judeth.[68]....

Mond Sept 21 .... Returned home—halled & cut wood till 3 P.M.....

Tusd Sept 23..... spent the day till 11 A.M. Preparing to set out for Maumee with a view to geting some work done on My land there—At 11 I left home—Rode to Ypsilanti stoped with Br Norris While I wrote some letters to the preachers on the district to Meet at Ypsilanti on the 24 of Next Oct. at 1 P.M. to Make the necessary arangements to

[66] Henry Colclazer was the preacher on the Ann Arbor Circuit, 1834–35.

[67] Germans were more numerous in Washtenaw than in neighboring counties. Their first church in Michigan was two miles west of Ann Arbor, the one mentioned here (George N. Fuller, *Economic and Social Beginnings of Michigan* [Lansing, Mich., 1916], p. 241). F. Schmidt came to Ann Arbor in 1832, sent by the Mission House at Basel, Switzerland.

[68] Apocryphal books.

obtaining a charter for our contemplated seminary[69] etc Also to take measures for the promotion of sunday schools. When I had finished these I judged it too late to reach the place I had intended when I set out so I contented myself to stay at Yp. Staid over night with Br Church Wrote at My s[cripture] collections.... had some conversasion on the necessity of strict discipline in the Church.....

Wed Sept 24..... After brakefast set out reading Rollins Antinet History[70]—dined at Br. Jas Waits—Reached Monroe a little before sundown feeling tired I put up with Br. Garwood.—spent the evening in part examining the price of certain things & in part religeous conversasion.....

Thurd Sept 25..... Went to the land office to see if certain lands in Branch County M[ichigan] T[erritory] were bought yet but could obtain no information as these lands have been lately transfered to Calamazoo Land Office[71] But I discouvered an unentered qur Near My land on the Maumee which I determined to explore—Rode to Br Halls Bay settlement Dined & fed—on My way there Met Br Sprague[72] who paid me $8 of Money he had borrowed of me at conferance & promised to send me the balance by Male [mail] to Maumee—After dinner I rode to Br [H——] some Miles up & found Str H sick of a fever Ten Miles Creek—There I Met with Br Sylvester Southern who is traveling on Monroe cir—visited Br Titsworth & spent the evening till near 9 talking about the country Returned.....

Frid Sept 26..... Went back to Br Titsworth & took brakefast—After which he went with me to show me the vacant land that I mentioned as lying not far from Mine—spent the day till 2 P.M. looking at it it is perhaps worth entering situated where it is at least it would be so to me if I should settle on my land as I have contemplated—Rode down to the saw mill on Swan creek below the turnpike & got my horse fed & a cold dinner—I then rode up to Maumee in company

[69] Spring Arbor Seminary was chartered by the territorial legislature on March 23, 1835. In 1839 its name was changed to Wesleyan Seminary at Albion, and in 1861 it became Albion College (Simpson, *op. cit.*, pp. 21–23).

[70] Charles Rollins' *Ancient History* was one of the books recommended in the "Course of Study" for young preachers. It was widely used at this time and was published by at least five different publishers.

[71] The Kalamazoo Land Office was established in 1834; the Monroe Office in 1823.

[72] William Sprague was the preacher on the Monroe Circuit, which was now in the Maumee District. In 1833–34 it had been in Gilruth's Detroit District.

with Mr Hawk from near Ann Arbour & put up with Br. Jackson—Spent the evening talking on religeous subjects—Retired to bed about 10 but before I lay down I took down a book "Paul Clifferd"[73] & began looking over some of its contents—I diped into it & actualy never closed My eys till daybrake next morning—.....

Sat Sept 27. Left my bed between dawn & sunrise none the more refreshed for my last nights work.—The day became rainy & after brakefast I crost the river & put up with Aurora Spafford & spent the day writting off My scripture collections This is a Most tedious work. But I hope it will prove to be labour well spent—Felt something drousey at times—day rainy & cool—to bed about 8. It having cleared off about sundown there was a smart frost tonight

Sund Sept 28. Rose about 5. Wrote till ¾ past 10 Rode to Perrysburgh & preached with good liberty & a clear voice from Ps cxix.i. to a verry attentive congregation Went home with Mr James Keys & took dinner—Having an Appointment over at Maumee at 3 P.M. I rode over as fast as I conveniently could for fear of being late, and after all was a few minutes lacking the time but when I arived found no one at the place but two little children 4 or 5 years old I felt some shegrined but sat down & waited till ½ past 3 No one coming in but a lad & seeing nothing stiring about the street that looked like attendance I took up my saddlebags & walked out to my horse & Just as I was about to Mount[,] Mr Hunt (one of the citizens) came out observing that he had "been waiting for some time to hear the bell ring—That the people were in the habit of waiting for the ringing of the bell"—These remarks only tended to deepen the feelings of shegrin I already experianced I calmly remarked that I had waited for the people till I concluded best to wait no longer—said he "What time have you by your watch[?]" I told him. He replied "The people expect preaching & are waiting to hear the bell ring that a good many would be disappointed" etc. Said I Are you in the habit of waiting till the preacher comes & then ring for the people to come. "No" said he. said I, I am not disposed to treat people with neglect nor am I disposed to be so treated. after bid[d]ing him the time of day rode off—to Mr Key & put up. What did they mean I had left my appointment at 3? Why did none ring at 3? Why wait ½ an hour past the time &

[73] One of the novels of E. L. Bulwer, published by Harper and Brothers, in paper covers, for twenty-five cents.

then talk about ringing? If I have been wrong I can not mend it now But when I am so treated I shall be every apt to quietly go off.

As I was conversing with My wife sometime since I spoke of the advantage of having the N. Testement printed, on the one page according to the common orthography & on the other the same chapt according to Walkers pronounciation[74] She proposed as a better plan to have the dictionary aranged in words of one, two, & three sylables etc & spell the children therein untill they acquired the correct pronounciation of every word—Her remarks continued to recommend themselves to My attention ever since & while reflecting on the subject this morning The following plan of instruction suggested itself to My Mind which I should like much to know of its utility—

1 For the improvement of Education

To form a proper spelling book, Of real use to the schollar

I *Make it a Dictionary*—1 Take all the words of one sylable alphabetically aranged & set them down according to the common orthography; then how pronounced according as Walker etc. marking the part of speach to which they belong 2 Take all the words of two sylables & set them down in like manner & so all the words according to their number of sylables

II *Of the Mode of instruction*

1 (After the schollars have studied their lesson) I spell the class seeing that they pronounce correctly—having those that excel stand above them that Miss in spelling in order to excite an intrest.

II Then resolve them into a *sense class* & give out the words just as you did to be spelled; & have the schollars give the sense; & those that excel stand above as in the spelling class. III Then resolve them into a grammer class giving out the words as above & they nameing the part of speach the word belongs to. Having those that excell stand above as in the other casses.

When next exercised have them stand in the commencement just as they stood when you left off in each class when last exercised. This plan for a community school—

J. & M. Gilruth. Sept. 28. 1834.

Spent the evening reading N.P.s & in conversasion.....

[74] J. Walker, *Dictionary of the English Language,* then in common use. Noah Webster's *Dictionary* appeared in 1828.

Mond Sept 29..... After brakefast went to visite a sick man—Then to see a young man by the name of Peter Coop with a view to engage him to clear me some land but he had partially engaged to another so I failed—returned to Mr Keyes & He & I rode down to some land his uncle owns joining Mine in order to run the lines that he Might see on whose land some Ship carpenters had been trasspassing—I also showed him where I wanted some clearing done.—Returned—visited Br Jackson who is sick; & then Br Chadwick—stayed at Ks & spent the evening in writting some in my journal etc.....

Tus Sept 30..... after brakefast I set out for the neighborhood of Adrian having failed in ingaging any one to do the clearing on My land that I wanted—stoped at Br Jacksons to see them—found that my going off without preaching last sunday at Maumee[75] had greatly offended Hunt & others he had declaired that he would never hear me again, etc—Stoped a short time at a cabben on Judge Woolcuts place in which lived David Hutten & his wife etc. The woman was very communicative (he not being in) from whom I learned that they had been concerned in a little common stock society—that some of its leaders had attempted to introduce a change of wives etc & that therefore they had left it etc that they were still full of the faith of community They were Quakers—I also found that their society had been composed of discordant materials, & that corruption in principle had proved its downfall—Rode down to Delaware run & Marked out a peice of ground that I wanted cleared; But it commenced Raining so I did not finish Marking it out as I intended—It came into My Mind that perhaps Hutten would live on the place, at least for a time—I also wished to show them my plan of a common-stock with these views I returned—introduced the subject—preposed his going & building a cabben—I paying for it—& his having it free till next fall etc. We made no engagement but the matter was left free if he should see proper—Read them My preface & Constitution The woman seemed pretty well pleased; but David, I thought rather hung off from the constitution because it did not sufficiently specify liberty to preach etc. I set out & rode to Br Whitneys through a heavy rain & did not reach there till dark—got very wet—& took a severe cold—....

Wed Oct 1..... wrote a letter to Br Sprague & in it enclosed another to Mr Keys with discriptions of the land I wanted cleared & how, &

[75] Fortunately, Maumee was no longer in Gilruth's district.

what I would give, etc. Then set out for Adrian following nearly the expected rout[e] of the railroad[76]—found the countray very level—& generally, where there were openings, verry poor sandy land. There is a tract of exolent land lying a long a small lake & what is called the cottenwood swamp[77] if it could be made dry enough would Make the best of land—fed My horse near the North end of the lake—Reached Br Milton Foot (1 Mile from adrian a local Pr) about dark, with whom I put up.....

Thursed Oct 2d..... spent the day till 9 P.M. writing off my scripture collections.....

Frid Oct 3d..... spent the day as yesterday till 4 P.M. when I finished My scripture collections with the exception of transcribing them & Making some alterations in the arangements—Then rode 3 Miles to Br Nathen Cumstock (formerly a quaker) and put up with him for the night—spent the eveing principly on experimental Religion.....

Sat Oct 4..... wrote some in my journal—& read A Hist. till 12.—Diner—Rode to adrian (our q M being there) & preached with some liberty from Rev II 1.2.3.4.—after which I held q.M. conferance—which was harmonious (our q.M. was held in the presbyterian M H)

After Meeting I went with Br Bangs to a Sister Johars & took supper: her husband is a universalian & lives as might be expected: he was once a Presbyterian & then a Methodist & now a sinner—Held prayer Meeting at candle light which was a comfortable season—Returned to Br Foots & tarried for the night—.....

Sund Oct 5..... Read the scriptures till ½ past 8. Walked to Adrian (a Mile) & tended love feast, which was a pleasent season.—Preached at 11 with some liberty from John vi.44.—Administered the sacrement to an orderly well behaved people—dined with Br Phavis Sutton son in law to Br Foot.—Walked to Br Foots & tended to my horse—Read some; but was dull & drousey—Returned & preached with some liberty from 1 Cor xvi.22.—a prayer Meeting with an invitation to

[76] The Adrian and Port Lawrence (Toledo) Railroad was started in 1833 and opened in 1836, the first railroad in the West. It was a "strap" Railroad, at first operated by horsepower but in 1837 by steam (Fuller, *op. cit.*, pp. 79–82).

[77] This swamp is described by Fuller (*ibid.*, p. 253). In 1828 a pioneer started from Sandusky, Ohio, wading knee-deep through this swamp leading his horse, and reached the Carey Mission (established by Isaac McCoy, a Baptist) in Berrien County in southwestern Michigan, after two weeks, without seeing any sign of human habitation (*Michigan Historical Society Collections*, I, 123–24).

Mourners (only one came) closed the Meeting—Returned to Br Foots. .... Slept with a young man by the name of Charles Thompson who professes sanctification & is a community man in his views—

Mond Oct 6th..... Spent the morning till 8 at Br Foots. Set out for home & rode to Br Joseph Bangs & dined—on My way there, I saw some Men thrashing with a thrashing mashien. I had curiosity to see the opperation & so turned aside to take a view thereof. They were thrashing at the rate of 20 sheaves of wheat per minute & I concluded that the machien would conveneant thrash 2 doz sheaves per minute This certainly was rappid work; & it did well. It however takes say 5 horses to drive it & about 10 men to attend it. It might however be placed so as to take fewer by being sat on the brow of a bank where the straw would leave the mashien without trouble. Altho it takes so many Men to attend it, it will thrash as Much in one hour as they could thrash in a whole day by hand, & will thrash much cleaner. If the machine were placed in a suitable situation there Might be arangements to clean the grain at the same time & by the same power which would be no small gain.—— As I passed through Clinton viliage I learned the following melancholy circumstance—Two young men were out picking cranberries in a Marsh near this place last sabbath (for amusement) one by the name of bracker Barker & the other the name Henry St Johns. A man by the name of Strobeck was hunting & seeing Henry St Johns in a stooping possition took him for a bear & fired on him & killed him on the spot—This accident Might have taken place on any day: but one naturely concludes, when they hear of such tragedies on the sabbath, that attention to the laws of God & man would have prevented the evil.—fed & suped with Br. Bird at *Saline*—Reached home about 9 found all well.....

Tusd Oct 7..... spent the day at home doing small erands & reading N Ps about 10 A.M. Brs Lorenzo Davis[78] & Richard Lawrence[79] came to see me—Lawrence had been sick & wished to gain my consent to spend the winter in N.Y. This I refused 1 because I was perswaded

[78] Lorenzo Davis was the first Michigan convert to become an itinerant. He was converted in Ypsilanti, and joined conference this year (1834), being appointed to Plymouth Mission.

[79] Richard Lawrence was appointed to Calhoun Mission in 1834–35. See Gilruth's opinion of Lawrence's preaching, below, January 4, 1835.

he would be able this winter to attend to the circuit 2 because his labours were needed.—He concented to take the cir.—I preached at night with some liberty, in rather an unconnected manner, yet there appeared some feeling in the congregation. Br Colclazer was present & gave a short exhortation & held a short prayer Meeting—one (girl) came forward as a mourner but as Prayer M began to be dull Meeting was dismissed.....

Wed Oct 8..... Spent the morning in making preparations to attend q M. on Calhoon Mission. At 2 P.M. I set out with My wife & youngest child.—Drove to Br. A Bennett's & put up we were kindly received & treated by this family.....

Thursd Oct 9 Rose at 5—spent the morning Reading & conversing After brakefast we set out—fed at Mr Allens at Grass Lake—Reached Jackson burgh[80] about sundown & put up with Br Thompson—spent the evening in conversasion of the countray sickness—Read a little.— ....

Frid Oct 10..... After an earley brakefast we set out & drove to Br Facetts, fed & dined. Then set forward & reached Marshal Just as the sun was setting—Put up with Br Sidney Ketchums familey (he being absent on a journey to Boston Maessetusetts) Here I met with Br J F Davisson[81] who put up here also..... We were both afflicted with Diareaha—occassioned by eating some fresh Pork.....

Sat Oct 11..... preached at 11 with liberty from 1 John iii.25. Met the q M conferance—Ajourned it till 4 P.M. because of the small No[.] present & having the case of Br Alen Tibbits A locle Pre to try—Met at four found T guilty & took away his licence & order the P E to admonish him—preached again at night with liberty from Matt xvi.27.—Set up & read N. Ps till twelve.....

Sun Oct 12..... held love feast at 9.—Preached with liberty from Mark I.15 at 11—Administered the sacrement to a few communicants —Spent the afternoon at Br Hoberts (with my wife) Br J. F. Davisson preached at night & thus closed our q M—whoever were made sensable of their need of a saviour we know not but we had no evidence that any were converted—Day cloudy in part & smoky—.....

[80] Jacksonburgh, now Jackson. Ketchums and Hobarts, mentioned by Gilruth, figure in Pilcher's *Protestantism in Michigan.* Allen Tibbetts was licensed as a local preacher in Plymouth in 1830.

[81] James F. Davisson, appointed with Richard Lawrence to Calhoun Mission in 1834–35.

Mond Oct 13..... Attended to some stewards business with Br J F Davisson (There being no steward present) After brakefast we set out intending to go to Cold Water in the St Joseph Country but before we had got out of sight of Martial [Marshall] we concluded to give up this rout so turned & took the road for Jacksonburgh—fed, & dined in our waggon on some articals furnished by the kind providence of Str Ketchum etc. Reached Br Facets a little before sundown. They had been expecting us, & in antisipation of My coming had appointed a Temperance Meeting To whom I delivered a short address with good feeling & I trust to some good effect.....

Tusd Oct 14..... after brakefast we set out—passed Jackson about 11 fed on the road; & eat a little bread & butter etc. Put up with Br Hecocks—There being some men here looking for land The conversasion principly partook of simular subjects.....

Wed Oct 15..... Drove to Br Aruna Bennetts fed & dined—.... called a few minutes at Br John Thompsons—Reached Ann Arbour a few minutes after sundown—found all well.—suped at Br Nobles. ....

Thursd Oct 16..... spent the day fixing a chicken Ruste—Stairway in the house—going to Mill Post office etc. Tended Prayer Meeting at night.....

Frid Oct 17..... Spent the day principly searching at lawyers offices to find a college charter; from which I might obtain some data to draft a Charter for our contemplated seminary at Spring Arbour, but was by no means as successful as I could wish. I have my fears I shall have too much of this business on My hands—Read N.Ps till 11.....

Sat Oct 18..... distant thunder in the N.W. Made ready to go to q M at Dexter set out with my daughter Harriet at 9 & drove through a heavy rain—Reached Dexter at 11 & put up with Doc. C. Nichle.—preached at 1 P.M. with some life from Heb. iv.12—Held q M conferance—Br Facet preached at night—Day rainy till 12 then blustery wind turning north.....

Sund Oct 19 .... held love feast at 9 preached at 11 with good liberty from Mark I.15. Administered the sacrement—Asisted by Brs Colclazer & Facet—Baptised one child & three adults one of whom was by immersion—Preached again at night from Matt xvi.27—held a short Prayer Meeting—Day windy with particles of snow.....

Mond Oct 20..... tended preaching by Br Facet at sunrise—after brakefast set out for home (Br L Gee with me) Reach home about 11 & about 1 P.M. Went down to Br Mcdowels to git some oats in the sheef & cut them—(also got a little hay of Friend Collens) Returned by a little after dusk.....

*Tus Oct 21.....*Spent the day principly in fixing a place for our chickens & in building a stairway in our house.....

*Wed Oct 22.....*Rode out 4 M. & preached a funeral at Mathew Jennings on the death of a babe at 12 had good liberty—.....

*Thursd Oct 23.....*The day was principle [principally] spent in sundry itams (One was the Making of an ax handle) Reading etc. Attended Meeting in the evening & heard Br Crain preach.....

*Frid Oct 24.....*at 10 set out for Ypsilanti accompanied by Br Elliott[82] to attend a meeting of the Brs in charge on this Dist to take measures for obaining a charter for our contemplated seminary at Spring Arbour. Reached Yp at 12—put up with Justis Norris—Committy met about two—Br Crain Colclazer & myself were appointed to draft a pe[ti]tion & bill which having been previously prepaired we soon returned & presented them—they were amended in committy of the whole so as to seecure that two thirds of the trustees be Members of the ME. church. & then adopted—of this I have My doubts But it is the Policy of Methodist Prs to have full control or not have anything to do with any such matter[83]—Br Colclazer preached at night—....

Sat Oct 25..... determined on sending Br Richard Lawrence onto Ann Arbour circuit instead of Calhoon Miss[ion] & accordingly wrote a line to Br Facet whom I had employed to go round Ann Arbour cir to go round Calhoon Miss.—Attended Preaching at sun rise by Thos Willey[84]—Br Jas F Davison preached at 1 P.M. after which I held q M conf which was a pleasant business season—Br Elliott preached at night after which we held prayer Meeting 5 or 6 come forward to be prayed for—one found peace—day rainy & cold but the meetings were well attended—staid with Br Sayre—.....

[82] A. B. Elliott was appointed to St. Clair Circuit in 1834–35.

[83] Gilruth was unusually undenominational for his time. For example, he co-operated with the Baptists and respected the Presbyterians. He did, however, call Episcopalian services "mummery" and had nothing to do with the liberal sects of the day. In his "Journal" he wrote that a Universalist he knew was living "as might be expected."

[84] Thomas Wiley was appointed to Tecumseh Circuit in 1834–35.

Sund Oct 26.....held love feast at 9 in which we had an exolent season—preached at ½ past 10 in the Presbyterian M H. while Thos Wiley did in the S[chool] H[ouse]. I had pretty good liberty in showing the superiority of the gosple to reform sinners, from Luke xvi.31. Returned to the S.H. and administered the sacrement to about 100 communicants being assisted by the Prs Br J F D preached at 3 P.M. but I did not attend—I preached in the S H at night from Matt v.4. then held a Prayer M—some experiance religion—About 1 PM I went into the stable to feed my horse another kicked me so as to lame me a little for which reason I did not attend the afternoon meeting.....

Mond Oct 27.....went to Br Church & took brakefast etc Then set out for home On the way called at Br Mcdowel & got some articles of food—found all well at home—went to Mill—visited with Mr George Allen—

Tusd Oct 28 Spent the day principly halling wood.....

Wed Oct 29.....about 12 took my wife and an other sister to visit a Br Smith but they not being at home we went & spent the afternoon with Old Br Mainard—Returned in the evening, & Wrote the history of our familey Mariages, berths & deaths in the Large familey Bible.[85]....

Thursd Oct 30.....about 2 PM took My wife to see the Printing office in this place, This being the first time she ever saw a paper printed.[86] -tended Prayer Meeting at night which was rather dull then [than] otherwise.....

Frid Oct 31.....Spent the day in various itams preparatory to tending qM on Plymoth cir & Miss[ion]. writing letters etc etc wrote some.....

Sat Nov 1.....Rode 19 Miles & preached at 11—with good liberty—Held qM conf had two appeals both of which were laid over to the

[85] Gilruth had purchased this Bible on October 10, 1831, for $4.25.

[86] The paper printed at this office was the *Western Immigrant.* Of this paper, Harriet Martineau says in her *Society in America* (1836), I, 319: "At Ypsilanti, I picked up an Ann Arbor newspaper. It was badly printed; but its contents were pretty good; and it could happen no where out of America, that so raw a settlement as that at Ann Arbor, where there is difficulty in procuring decent accomodations, should have a newspaper." However, in 1836 there were two newspapers in the town, for the *Ann Arbor Argus* began to appear in 1835, and this may have been the paper referred to by Harriet Martineau.

next qM.—Put up with a Br Patcher (he however was not at home) was detained from Meeting till late by some business I had to settle with Br M. Swift.[87] We then went to the S H where Meeting was held. Br Dolittle had just done preaching & commenced a prayer Meeting—which continued ½ an hour longer—Returned to My lodgings several Preachers put up there also—.....

Sund Nov. 2d..... tended Love feast at 9 in the S.H. Preached in a barn not far dist. at 11 with liberty from Matt xvi.26.27. After which, I with the assistance of the other ministers administered the sacrement to about 100 people after which I baptised one by immersion (having baptised 2 just before) I felt Myself in an awkward situation just at the commencement of the Administration of the sacrement by reason of accidently touching one of the tumblers & spilling a part of the consecrated wine. But instantly reflecting that it was accidental I calmed My Mind & proceeded with the service as tho nothing had happened.—At candle light Br L Davis preached he is but a new beginer—I exhorted after him & Br Swift after me—& thus closed our qM. Many attended but none were converted of which I had any knowledge—I went home and staid with a Br Patterson (Br D. also) spent the evening till late discoursing on the scripture.....

Mond Nov 3..... After brakefast I returned to B Patchens—& from thence set out for home—stopt at Plymoth Corners & got a shoe put on my horse—Dined at Wid. Hawkins—Reached home a little before sundown.....

Tusd Nov 4..... choped wood till 12. did some little business of one kind & an other Wrote some etc day pleasent—to bed about 10.

Wed Nov 5..... imbanked around our house to keep out the cold —with a nomber of other itams   Wrote some letters—& having again commenced to transcribe My scripture collections I spent the evening at this work.

Thurd Nov 6..... Having to leave home to day to attend several q Meetings before I return the morning was spent in business of different Kinds till 12—at ½ past 1 I set out & drove to Coopers Corners & put up with Br Lyons Preached at candle light with but little liberty from 1 John III.9.

Sometime last spring I received a note from a Brother Benjemin Allen of $5.00 on Br Lyons to collect—I for got the Matter till re-

[87] Marcus Swift was now on the Plymouth Mission, with Lorenzo Davis.

minded of it in conferance I then paid the 5$ & took the note But previous to My receiving the note for collection Br Allin had writen to Br Lyons to send him the Money in a letter. By P.O. delinquencies Br Lyons did not receive this letter till near 2 Months after it was sent When he did receive it he sent the money as directed Now it appears this letter never reached Allen or he has not been honest to sell Me the note—Thus it stands a lesson of experiance to me.....

Frid Nov 7..... Read Rollen A[ncient] Hist till brakefast—drove to Esq Meads & dined—thence to Doc. Parks in bloomfield & put up with him—spent the evening writing off My scripture collections till 12.....

Sat Nov 8 Rose about ½ past 5—wrote some in My journal—Read some—& about 10 set out for Auburn, accompanied by a young woman who had been keeping school at Doc. Parks. but whose name I have not goten at preasent I talked some with her on the subject of a community toward which she manifested some inclination—put up with Br John K Smith—preached with good liberty & feeling from Heb iv.11.—held qM.c.—a Br. Earles preached at night after which we spent some time in prayer.....

Sund Nov 9..... held love feast at 9 which was a moderate season—preached with some liberty & point on Tit II.2—After which we administ[er]ed the sacrement—Br Pilcher preached at 8 PM. & Br patredge at night Br Whitney exhorted after him—Meeting somthing interesting—stayed with Esq Benj. Phelps. Br Whitney staid here also: & after we were in bed he told me that he was ingaged to be Married to a sister *Aroline Perrin* I was not prepared to hear this it being so lately since the death of sister Rebecca Brown[88] to whom it was publickly known that he was engaged—however sister Aroline May better fill the void in his heart then the widowed affections for Rebecca—did not sleep till Midnight—....

Mond Nov 10 Rose about ½ an hour before sunrise—Wrote till 10. When I attended, & managed a trial in society a Br Wm Judd was accused of Perjury he came with a Lawyer to assist him & they preposed swaring witnesses I dismised the gentleman of the bar as an

[88] Rebecca Brown was a member of the Methodist society at Ann Arbor. Pilcher states (*op. cit.,* p. 230) that "her very presence in a congregation was an inspiration to the minister." Gilruth must have felt so, too; he wept at her death, which occurred in May (see "Journal," III, 129).

unnecessary appendage to a Methodist Court—Rejected all Swearing of witnesses alledging that 1 Christ nowhere encouraged but forbid it—2 that our discipline did not recognise such a course in the trial of our members—3 That it was not Matters involving civil rights or proper[t]y but a standing in a Relgeous society—4 that Govrnment had a right to proscribe the course of proceding in civil cases—so the church had the right to proscribe her own course—I believe the trial gave general sattisfaction as to its Management & decision it lasted near all Day—Judd was acquitted.—staid at Br Torrys—sat up conversing till past 12.....

Tusd Nov 11 Rose about sunrise—saw Br Judd & advised him to desist from attempting to prosicute Br Fox at the civel law—took brakefast with Br J K Smith—had a request from some of the principle [principal] citizens of the village to write My sermon on evil speaking & they would be at the expence of publishing it—I could not consent for the want of time.—About 10 I set out to Visit Calvin Perrin on Mt Clemens cir.—dined with Br Jesse Lee stout.—Reached Br P.s about 3 P.M.—he was just fixing to go to Detroit—but the first suitable oppertunity he got he told me of Br Whitneys going to Marry his daughter—he set off about Dark—& I spent the evening till 10 writing off My scripture collectings—....

Wed Nov 12..... Spent the day & the evening till 10 Copying off My collections.....

Thursd. Nov 13..... as yesterday—preached at candlelight with liberty from Ps.cxix.1 to about 40 souls who assembled to hear me.—Then continued writing till 11.....

Frid Nov 14..... wrote till 3 P.M. then left & went to Br Jesse L Stouts & staid all night spent the evening principly in reading Rollin A. Hist. day cloudy & turned cold in the evening so that Ice was Made on the Mouth of a large Iron kettle an inch & quarter thick.....

Sat Nov 15..... scripture collections till 12. During which time, Brs. Whitney, & Brockway, came, ½ past one we set out for the place of meeting vis at Niles S.H.—at ½ past one I preached with some life & liberty from John vi.44. after which I held qM conferance—Br Pi[l]cher & I went to old Br Downers & put up—Pilchor preached at night & we concluded with a prayer Meeting—Returned to Br D—wrote till 11.....

Sund Nov 16..... held Love feast at 9—preached with some power at 11 from Eph vi.13–18 at the close of sermon I baptised one woman by sprinkling & three children.—Went with Brs Whitney & Brockway to a Br Glazers & put up—Returned to Meeting at candlelight Br Patredge preached & Brs R. Smith & J J Young exhorted & Meeting Closed—Returned to Br Gs Spent the evening till nere 12 Reading hymns & conversing with Brs W. & B. on sundry itams of criticism etc etc etc. For near a week past I have had remarkable freedom from temptation & nearly perfect victory Why this? is it a calm before a storm? O God lead me not into temptation—to bed about 12 But Slept very little— . . . .

Mond Nov 17. Rose a little after day with a slight head ake & a very bad cold—Spent the day till 11 P.M. Copying off My S. collections having a room where I could keep up a persperation I succeeded in throwing off my cold—Day turned milder toward 10 AM & rained from that on—to bed about 11 but was much haresed with filthy dreams—

Tusd Nov 18. Rose a little after day—full of filthy temptations—Resorted to watching & prayer & gained some victory—Wrote some in My journal & other Messilany Then went to copying off my script col*ns*. till 2 PM Then set out for Utica at which place I arived about sundown—put up with Br. Scott—preached at c[a]ndle light in the S H with some liberty from Rev. xxii.17.—Read Rollen An. hist. till 10— . . . .

Wed Nov. 19. . . . . Read Rollen till 9—set out toward St Clair—drove to Br E. Tuckers & put up spent the evening copying off My S.C. till 10. . . . . to bed about 10 Under some temptations of the flesh—

Thurd Nov 20. . . . . drove on to s[is]t[e]r Fairchilds but finding the road very Mudy I left my wagon (having borrowed an old saddle of Br T) I set out on horse back—Rode to pine river & put up with a bro. Henderson whom I found to be of a community spirit—set up talking & reading till past 11. . . . .

Frid Nov 21. Rose before day—head aked considerably—after brakefast set out for St clair—Reached there about 10 & Put up with Br Phillips but took my horse to Br Stewards—Wrote till 10 PM. . . . . This day I invented a Manner of using the Alphabet to write what I please without the posibility of any ones reading it without instruction & yet it is very simple.

Sat Nov 22. . . . . Walked up to the county seat through a heavy rain

& preached with good liberty & feeling, to a few attentive souls in the Court House. After which I held qM conferance—Returned to see to My horse—& then walked up again at even & preached in rather a rambling manner from Rev.xxii.17. to a few hearers—staid with Br H Jerome (who now lives in this village) Spent the evening till near 11 conversing, & reading in My bible—....

Sund Nov 23..... held Love feast at 9—preached at 11 with great plainness of speach from Eph vi.11 to 19. After which we administered the sacrement to a few souls.—staid at Br Jeromes till eveing Meeting Reading N.P.—Br Elliott preached after whom I exhorted & then opened the door of admission—three joined society.—Walked down to Br Phillips—spent the evening till 11 talking on the matters of other years.—day colder with some snow showers which continued through the night—....

Mond. Nov 24..... settled with the stewards—set out to see Br Clark Wordan—spent an hour or more very agreeably with Br ——— Bayington who has bought out Br James Ogden & is now living where he did.—rode down to Br Wordens & put up ½ past 12. & set to writting—Wrote till bed time, but to poor advantage. Day stormy with snow showers—.....

Tusd Nov 25..... Rode up to Br Boyingtons & mended my shoes—then to Br Phillips & while My horse was eating visited Br Ogdens etc—dined with Br P family & then set out on My return toward Detroit Rode to Pine river Mills & put up with a Br Pulsover This was an uncomfortable situation without light or conveniances either to read or write.....

Wed Nov 26..... rode to Wd Fairchilds where I left my wagon—dined & fed & then drove to Br Tuckers Reading on My way Rollen—find that My strength is perfect weakness—But God is My saviour.....

Thursd Nov 27..... drove to Mt Clemens—stoped & heard Elder Booth preach a thanks giving sermon—drove on to Br Porters (Reading Rollen) & put up—preached in rather a dull manner at candleligh[t] to a few hearers—from Heb. iv.11.—....

Frid Nov 28.... set out for Detroit accompanied by Mr Booth[89] a

[89] John Booth (1796–1869), a native of England, was ordained a Baptist minister in New Jersey in 1825 and came to Michigan territory in 1829 as an agent of the American Baptist Home Missionary Society. He was the first secretary of the Michigan Baptist Association, organized in 1836 (George H. Waid, *Centennial History of the Michigan Baptist Convention* [Lansing, Mich., 1936], pp. 6, 9, 35).

baptist Minister—spent the time conversing on the causes of church decensions I trust in some degree profitably—Reached Detroit about 12 I Put up with Br Jerry Dean.[90] Spent the afternoon looking at some stoves.—tended Prayer Meeting at Night.....

Sat Nov 29..... small Itams—except a short time spent at 10 attending the place of a prayer meeting at which Br. Crane, one woman & Myself Met!—I preached with some plainness but not Much feeling at 2—held qM conferance. In which I had my feelings Much hurt by some remarks in referance to quarterage & house rent. Which grew out of a quston put to me by Br. Crane With respect to My proportion of qu[a]r[terage]. with his, this led Me to explain that part of My support came from the Mission society—That I had never asked anything for My Children.[91] because I believed the part of the work where I had laboured did not justify it etc. At this Br Crane took the liberty to openly censur My course, & why, that, was seting a bad presedent—etc And Br Owen, remarked that the Ohio Conferance had imposed upon them etc. This he said in referance to what I know not—This discourse I encouraged rather than otherwise to see what it would amount to—O the Love of Money!! The love of Money!! Love feast was held at night Without any attention to see who came in—it was Wholey Managed by Br Crain dull & uninteresting. At the close of which he gave a long lecture on deviding the classes etc: & when he was done took up a collection to pay for some stove pipe. I closed by prayer—Returned to Br Deans & spent the evening till about 11 principly conversing with str. Dean upon the devision of churches. But I am inclined to think that I had as well have spared My breath for other purposes—day stormy with some rain—to bed about 11. rather dissattisfyed then [than] otherwise

Sund Nov. 30..... determined to keep this as a day of fasting & prayer as well as other religeous labour—Preached at ½ past 10 from Tit II 3d with Much plainness of speach—again at 3 from 2 Pet.III.17. On backsliding in a plain close Manner—& again at Night from Eph vi.11 to 18 in a pointed & cuting Manner. Altho I have eaten nothing to day, My strength failed not in the least I feel also that I have done My duty but I am pretty certain that there has been too Much point & plainness to set well on carnal professors—staid all night with a Br

[90] Jerry Dean started the first Methodist Sunday school in Michigan.

[91] The amounts allowed were $16 a year for children under seven and $24 for children between seven and fourteen.

Wolsey who talked like a plain Man: But who is to be depended on where popularity is concerned. Day clear & delightful—to bed about 10

Mond Dec 1 Rose about dawn of day—attended to some small Maters principly purchasing of a small stove—learned that I had been too plain to please some yesterday—I felt much like being yet more so.—On Sat someone took My pocket handkerchief—This morning a young lady (Daughter of Br R Abbot) made me a present of two better ones—about 10 I set out for home—drove to Br Hecocks & put up (about dark). Spent the evening principly in conversasion (quite agreeably).....

Tusd Dec 2d—Rose about dawn & set out amediately—took brakefast with a Br Perrin (son in law to Br. M. Swift)—spent an hour with Br Swift—drove home which I reached about dark—Found my family well—spent the evening in conversasion till 9.....

Wed dec 3d.....spent the day in small itams of business.....

Thusd Dec 4.....as yesterday....tended Prayer meeting at night which was rather dull.....

Frid Dec 5.....small Itams & procuring some hay & oats of Br Mcdowel & Collens—Spent some time conversing with Br Leonard Gurley[92] P Elder of Maumee Dist. He like most of our Prs is pretty stiff in his opinions.....

Sat Dec 6.....coppying off My s-collections. Snow fell about 3 inches deep last night but the wether remained mild.....

Sunday Dec 7.....went to hear Br Gurley preach at ½ past 10. he spoke well—I preached at ½ past 1 from Heb xii.14. But I felt to be dull & uninteresting—Br G preached again at night.—after which we held prayer meeting—

Mond Dec 8. Tusd dec 9 & *Wed dec 10* Mostly spent at home writiing etc On Wed afternoon I took My wife & went to Br Mcdowels to fill an appointment for Br R. Lawrence—Preached at Collins S H on Education from Prov II 1. to 7.—spent a little time at Collens—went to Br Mc & staid all night—Read N Ps till 10.....

Thursd Dec 11.....after brakefast we set out for home but calling to see Br Mainards we tarried till after dinner—drove home—spent the evening cutting wood—wrote till 1 P.M. [A.M.].

[92] Leonard B. Gurley (1804–80) was converted in 1824 and joined the Ohio Conference in 1828. He was a son of William Gurley (1757–1848), well-known Irish local preacher of Ohio, whose biography his son Leonard wrote and published in 1854.

Frid Dec 12..... wrote & cut wood & read N Ps till 12 P.M.—

Sat Dec 13..... spent the day in fixing sundry things & the evening in preparing some sausage Meet [meat] having bought some Porke for $3 50 cts per hundred—day cloudy & thawing but turned cold in the evening.....

Sund. dec 14..... went to hear Br John Clark[93] (Member of the N York conferance & Missionary to the Indians on the upper Lakes) he spoke well—I preached at ½ past 1 from Matt xxii.39. but with less liberty then good intention—B Clark preached a Missionary sermon in the Presbyterian M House—at night—it consisted in a collection of facts—after which we took up a publick collection for Mission purposes amounting to $16 & some cents. wrote till Midnight.....

Mond Dec 15..... heard Br Clark preach in the presbyterian M.H. at night then wrote till 12.....

Tusd Dec 16..... spent this day till 3 PM cutting wood—in the evening went to Br Bares for hay & potatoes—Returned & wrote till 1 A.M.

Wed Dec 17..... cutting wood till dark—wrote till 1 AM.....

Thurd Dec 18..... spent the day reading N P.—tended prayer meeting at night—Received two Members into society.—Wrote till 2 A.M. day clear & pleasent—some fogy in the morning.....

Frid dec 19..... prepared to set out for qM on the morrow.....

Sat Dec. 20..... Br Colclazer came about 6 to lay before me the charter we are proposing to obtain for our contemplated seminary. After brakefast I set out for Saline villiage to hold qM. on Tecumseh cir. Reached there in 2 hours preached with good feeling at 11 from 2 Pet I.5.6.7.8. after which I held qM C[onference] in a room of Mr Smiths Tavern.—Br Jas. F Davison preached at 2 after whom I exhorted with good liberty it was a time of good feeling—A Br Morea preached at night. before & after which were held prayer Ms. two professed peace—during this Meeting I did not attend but was talking with david Hutton (him that I had seen at Maumee) he gave me a general history of his life & religious tour—I also drew out of him

[93] John Clark (1797–1854), a native of Washington County, New York, had joined the New York Conference in 1820. He was the father of Methodism in Wisconsin. Assigned to the Green Bay Mission in 1832, he formed the first Methodist class in Wisconsin in July of that year (see Elizabeth Wilson, *Methodism in Eastern Wisconsin* [1938]; Sprague, *op. cit.,* VII, 626–36; also letters from John Clark in the *Western Christian Advocate,* July 11, 1834, and December 19, 1835).

some particulars of his own belief vis that the world would return to its paridisical state of purety; that the true believers would cohabit with their wives only to procure offspring, & that under an impression of duty. etc I forbare farther remarks, then [than] simply to here insert what I have often of late Said. O My Bible, Every days experiance leads me to love thee more & more!!! for by thee I am taught the right way, & preserved from every false one!!! Staid with Br Bird.....

Sund Dec 21.....held love feast at 9. which was crouded & in power—preached at 11 on future judgement from 2 cor v.10. with some liberty but with an improper pitch of voice—Br Burnet Preached at 3 P.M.—after which B Wiley baptised some children & two adults one by sprinkling & one by immersion—Br J F Davison preached at nigh[t] after which was held a prayer meeting & a nomber came forward to be prayed for: but I am not certain that any found peace.....Staid by kind invitation, with Mr Risdon a Tavern keeper in this place he is a presbyterian & treated me well. to bed near 11. Br Burnet for My Bed fellow, & with whom I had some conversasion on the subject of preaching impressions, & church government.

Mond Dec 22.....went back to Br birds....after brakefast..... I set out on my way to cold water—D Hutten walked along some miles, when he had an oppertunity of riding in a wagon as we parted I gave him some Money—probably this is the last that I shall have to do with this poor, but I think in some measure mistaken man as his mind is to go to Indiana. Rode on to Br Wheelers in company with Br J F Davison. where we put up—Read the Presidents Message—I wrote till 11 P.M.....

Tusd Dec. 23.....eat brakefast & rode on together—fed at a Mr Gambels tavern.—Rode on to Blackmers & put up—Wrote till 11.....

Wed Dec 24.....after brakefast, we set out—conversing on the subject of hell, God, heaven, etc. he maintaining that hell concists in "a conscienceness of sin, & a sense of Gods wrath" & no more: and I maintaining that there is an actual lake of fire & brimstone. 1 Because we have [no] warent from Scripture to conclude that the language discribing the place of punishment is figureative. But rather that it is historical describing things as they are. 2 That all Maters of pure revelation are to be understood (absolutely) as discribed; for we possess no means by which these things can be farther investigated then what is revealed of them: And that to give them any other meaning is to charge the revealer with falsehood. He seemed to feel the force of the argument.—fed and dined at Br R Corbus, who is sick with the dropsy.—Rode on & put up with Mr. Wm Cross. Read N.Ps till 10.....

Thurd..... set out with Br Davison to see some land lying down the cold water—There is much good heavy timbered land from Aldridgs Mill down to the Mouth of Cold water, we Returned to cold water villiage & I preached with good liberty; from Ps.cxix.1—Put up with Br. Hanchet. Spent the evening conversing on the subject of Religion till 10 or 11.—....Thus has this Christmas been spent[94]

Frid. Dec. 26..... Went to Mr Cross's & spent the day in writting—preached at night with life & some power from Matt xvi.26—Returned & staid with Mr Cross.....

Sat Dec 27..... I preached about 11 with good liberty from Heb. iv.11.—held qM conferance dined with Mr Cross in company with Brs Clark, Davison, & Gering[95]—J F D preached at 3 P.M. & Br Clark at night after which we held prayer Meeting till 10.....

Sund Dec 28—held love feast at 9. Br Clark preached at 11, after which I administered the sacrement to about 15 communicants—Br C and I took some refreshment with Br Tibbits—Br C preached again at night.....

Mond Dec 29..... lost the Morning till 12 waiting on the stewards business—I then rode to Cold Water lake accompanied by Br H. Giving to look at some land—found the land to please me well in Many respects.—Returned & preached with good liberty from Heb. xii.14. at candlelight after which Br Davison formed a society of 16 members.....

Tusd Dec 30. Rose about dawn intending to set out for Ann Arbour but some conversasion taking place concerning a place said to be an exolent Mill site Mr Cross proposing to go with me to show it to me; I concluded to imbrace the opportunity & go. so this day was spent accordingly. There is Much good land, but not Mill seat: so we re-

[94] The Methodists did not observe Christmas as a Christian festival until well along in the nineteenth century.

[95] Hiram Gearing was appointed to Ann Arbor Circuit in 1834–35 with Henry Colclazer.

turned—I got my horse shod before & put up with Br Hanchett—spent the evening till near 12 relating circumstances connected with the earley Settlement of the western parts of Virginia & Ohio. . . . .

Wed Dec 31 . . . . set out for home—Rode to Lyman Blackmers & put up—spent the evening reading Rollens Antient Hist. . . . .

Thursd Jan 1st 1835. Rose about dawn—After brakefast I set out—fed at a Mr Powers tavern—While setting in his bar room I was anoyed with the profain language of a Man who had called to git some drink—he was pretty drunk, yet I thought best to reprove him, in doing which I hapened to touch him in the proper way so I had no more trouble from him for he immediately desisted.—Reached Br. Whelers & put up—wrote till 11. While on the rode today I finished reading the 1st vol of Rollens Antient Hist This has been a day of temptations & all most no strength to resist. Yet God has kept me hitherto.

Frid Jan 2d. . . . . set out—Fed at Saline with Br Bird—Reached home about sundown—Our quarterly Meeting coming on at this place—there having been an appointment given out for me I preached in the Court house with some liberty from Hab.iii.2. Read N Ps till 11. . . . .

Sat Jan 3d. . . . . preached with some liberty at ½ past 10 from Matt v.4. & again at ½ past 2 from Matt xvi.24. after which I held qM conferance—Br Presley a local Pr preached at night after which we held prayer meeting—A number came forward as seekers & several found peace. Brs Presley & Glesen put up with us. . . . . Morning 8 deg below zero.

Sund Jan 4. . . . . held love feast at 9—preached with liberty at ½ past 10 on the evidences of the scripture from John xvii.17.—After which we administered the sacrement to about 90 persons.—Br R. Lawrence preached at Night (dear young man, I [think] he will never brake [break] himself of an "eh" at the end of his sentences) When he closed I followed with an exhortation & then called for Mourners—a No. came forward with whom we laboured a while, & then dismised for the Night—day clear & cold Morning 8 deg below zero.

Mond Jan 5. . . . . preached with some liberty from Heb x 38.—spent the day choping wood—& preached again at night from John xxi.22 but I was dull by reason of a failure of voice in consequence of cold. Br Colclazer exhorted after me & called a prayer M. Many came forward as seekers—they laboured a while & Meeting was dismissed. Thus closed this qM—

Tusd Jan. 6..... Spent the day preparing to go to Monroe & from thence to My Ypsilanti q.M. Writting letters etc etc at night heard a quaker deliver a lecture on slavery in the Court house—....

Wed Jan. 7..... set out for Monroe. Rode to a Br Thompsons fed & dined & while here sister T Made Me a present of a new pair of leggens—Rode to old B J Waits & put up—spent the evening in writting till 12.....

Thursd. Jan 8..... set out for Monroe at 6—Reached there at ¼ past 9 Stoped at Br Garwoods, & found sister G in a low state by reason of the dropsey & a hurt in her ancle which had Mortefied but was now staid—Went to the land office & entered a qr sec[tion] of land in sec 7. Township 3 of the 12 Mile square reserve at the Maumee rapids—After dinner I set out for Smouth Rock, taking the direct rout accross the country; The roads being very rough it was after dark when I reached the place—I put up with Jacob Vreland—I had been there but a few minutes when a request was sent me, requesting me to preach at a protracted Meeting held by the Presbyterians to which I acceded—preached plain & I hope usefully from Heb iv.11.—Found Elias Patee here—Spent the evening till 11. conversing with J-Vreland principly on Agraculture—etc..... This days circumstances has shown me the frailty of My Memory in a Most palpable Manner.—When I went to the land office & had applied for the lots I wanted the Registir sent me to a justice of the peace to sware that there was no preemtion right on the land The justice asked me when I saw the land I told him I did not recollect but that I thought it was sometime in Nov. or Oct. but I could not tell when unless I refered to my journal he said it was not necessary, that the law did not require the specification of a certain day. So he wrote "About the 1st of Nov. Now when I came to examin my journal, I found it was on the 26 of Sept. 1834, that I examined that land.

Frid Jan 9..... Borrowed the Apoekraphel new Testament & read therein till 7.—Set out for the arsnel[96]—Dined with a Br Sutclif—Reached the arsnel about sundown—put up with a Br Daniel a Mile West. on the Chicago road. Spent the evening till 10 readin this Apocraphal N Testement.....

[96] United States Arsenal at Dearborn(ville).

Sat Jan 10..... Brs Sayre, & Church having come we walked to Dearbornvill, (The arsnel) where I preached with some liberty from Ps.cxix.1 after which we held qM conf—Br Church was appointed to preach in the evening but being taken unwell & Br. Sayre plead off I was under the necessity of preaching on the spur of the moment—which I did from Matt xi.28 but not much to my own sattisfaction; at the close of which however we held a prayer meeting—several came to the Mourners seat & I trust some found peace with God—the meeting continued till after nine—I put up with a Br Warren in the village— ....

Sund Jan 11..... We held love feast at 9 in the school H. (where our qM is held) which proved a comfortable season—several joined society—I preached with some liberty (at 11) from Rom.I.16. but I spoiled it much by bad delivery—We then administered the Holy Sacrement to a respectable No of communicants—I returned & dined with Br Warren—Br Doolittle preached at night & Br Sayre exhorted after him after which we held a prayer M till past 9   2 or 3 came to the Mourners seat but I fear it was not with broken hearts—Our faith also being weak I judge that none found peace—We returned to Br Daniels But I being solisetated to put up with a Mr Putnam (inn keeper hard by) whose wife found peace at this qM. I consented & spent the evining till past 11 discoursing & exhorting them on the things of God.....

Mond Jan 12..... went to Br Daniels—made some entries in my Journal.—& after brakefast set out for home accompanied by Br Sayre—on our way he showed me a lot of land which he has purchased with a view to make him a farm. It is poor land—such as I should not fancy for Myself.—we dined at a Br Sheldons—I reached Ann Arbour about an hour after dark—Went to the P.Office—got some N Ps & read till 10..... some rain & fine hail fell.....

Tus Jan. 13..... Reading N.Ps—Wrote.....

Wed Jan 14..... writting, Reading N Ps & choping wood—This day we sent all three of our little Daughters[97] to school, to Miss Eliza Page It being the commencement of the qur. day rainy, & smoky, there being the appearance of a thaw—to bed about 11.

Thursd Jan 15..... Much as yesterday.....

[97] Harriett, Naomi, and Matilda. Matilda was only three and a half years old.

Frid Jan 16..... Went to Br Barrs for hay.... spent the afternoon making some arangements about the house.....

Sat Jan 17. Rose before day took a slight check of victuals & set out for qM on Plymouth cir & Mis*n*—rode about 9 Ms & brakfasted—then rode on to Coopers Corners & preached with some liberty from Heb.x.38. after which we held qM conferance tried two appeals both of which resulted in the condemnation of the appelants While this was doing Br Pilcher preached—I preached at Night from Matt viii.7. with some percision & liberty after which we hald a prayer Meeting Several came to the Mourners bench & 3 found peace—I put up with Br Lyons—also Brs Swift, Pilcher, & Davis & Holms (all prs-) Spent the evening in conversasion—

Sund Jan. 18..... held love feast at 9—preached with some liberty to a crouded congregation from 2 Cor.v.13 on future judgement—Br Pilcher preached at the same time in a S.H. hard by both houses not holding the people. at the close of preaching we administered the sacrement which proved a refreshing season—returned & dined at Br L. Br Pilcher preached at night: & I exhorted for some length after him & thus closed our qM—Taried at Br L. evening I read some & Br P sung—....

Mond Jan 19..... spent the morning till 10 writing & conversing—When Br P & I set out for Ann Arbour about 3—Tended & held class Meeting in the brick S.H.....

Tusd Jan 20..... Wrote some & choped some wood.....

Wed Jan 21..... Rode down to Collens S.H. & preached with liberty from Matt.viii.7. & then held class meeting in Br Colclazers place, he being called on to Marry a couple—put up with Mr Collens.....

Thursd Jan 22 Rose before day & rode home—.... Having a pair of boots just finished I went to the shop to git them, while waiting for them A Mr Branch of this place came in & after some time I was drawn into a conversasion with him on the subject of disinterested benevolence[98] he affirming that a man ought to feel that if his eternal damnation would save the world he should be willing to be eternally damned To which I objected 1 that such feelings were no w[h]ere commanded or recommended in scripture & that the Spirit of God

[98] Disinterested benevolence was a main emphasis in Hopkinsian theology, then in great vogue among Congregationalists.

never inspired feelings of benevolence over & above what he commanded therefore all such feelings were mear delusion 2 That it was More then [than] Christ either felt or did—That he give his life a ransom for men but not his eternal glory or salvation Therefore this doctrine would have us surpass Christ in exolency of benevolence I told him plainly that his doctrine was a tissue of Romish supperioragation[!] & a miserable peice of folley—That Man was deeply interested in every act that God required him to perform—That God annexed the promiss of reward to obediance That it is absurd to talk of duty beyond the commands & promises of God. I did not treat the matter with as much mildness as I ought—which occasioned some disagreeable reflection in my mind afterward.....

Frid Jan 23.....halled some watter etc etc & at ½ past 9 sit [set] out for my qM on Farmington cir. Rode (14 Miles in 3 hours) to Br Thayres & preached in a dull manner from 1 Pet I.15.—Rode to a S H near esq Meads & preached from cxix Ps 1st v. but I had not much liberty—staid at esq Meads—read NPs.....

Sat Jan 24.....Rode to Buck Horn corners & put up with Br David Goss in whose house qM was to be held—preached at 11 from 1 Pet. I.15 with some liberty after which I held qM conferance tried an appeal & restored the appelant—& licensed 2 local preachers—Br M Swift Preached at night: after which we held prayer meeting for some time, but there not being much power we dismissed—I staid at Br G.s..... (E Pilcher bed fellow)

Sund Jan. 25.....held love feast at 9 which was tolerable—I preached at 11 with good liberty from Matt v.4.—after which we administered the sacrement—about this time it commenced a hard rain which detained the people in the house for sometime—wrote some in my Journal—Br M Swift preached at candlelight I gave a short exhortation & dismissed the Meeting—one was reclaimed at a prayer meeting held this evening at a Br Brunsons.—spent some time in pious conversasion.....

Mond Jan 26.....Rode to Br Rufus Beach (4 M) to spend the day—wrote till night—Preached at candlelight with some liberty from Matt viii.7. in a S H not far off.....

Tusd Jan 27.....Read Physic[99] till sunrise—brakfasted with a

[99] Gilruth was much interested in remedies, as his "Journal" testifies. Later he bought and read Thomas' *Practice*.

nieghbor—returned & wrote till 12. dined—& then set out toward Pontiac, but coming on a heavy rain Mingled with snow I put up with Br Harry Bruson—.....

Wed Jan 28..... studied Medicine till 9—Rode to Pontiac to file the evidence of My ordination in the Clearks office—This Mr Comstock the cleark did without fee saying I had paid him in preaching there (at the qM.) Dined with str. Sherwood—time spent in this familey conversing on religious Matters—Rode to Bloomfield & put up with Doc Park.—Spent the afternoon Reading NPs. Preached at a S H ½ M off with good liberty from Heb vi.4.5.6.7.8 Manner I The character spoken of. II Things that lead to a falling a way. III The precise character of this falling away see Heb x.27.8.9. IV The condition of such V The course to persue, to prevent aposticy—Returned to Br Parks (walking going & coming while he rode My horse, he having severely hurt his leg by his horse falling with him some days since) The evening was spent Reading N.Ps. till 11.....

Thursd Jan 29. 1835. Rose at dawn—Wrote some business letters—at ½ past 9 set out for Br Calvin Perins (in companey with Brs Pilcher & Seburn)[100] & joined in Matrimony Rev Luther D Whitney & Aroline Perin also Hiram M Perin & Eveline Hall—Then preached on familey religion from Joshua xxiv.15—Manner I The government II The piety III The instruction IV The benefit—I then wrote a letter to the book agents at N York—Rode 7 Miles accompanied by Br Brockway & put up with Br guy Phelps—spent the evening in writting to My Mother. This day I am 42 years old—have had Many thoughts in refferance to the days of other years Thanks be to God for past & present mercies.....

Frid Jan 30..... Rode to Br Elas Scotts near Utica & put up—preached at Night with some liberty from Matt vii.7. in the Utica S H.....

Sat Jan 31..... set out at 10 accompanied by Brs Scott & Whitney for Mt Clemens—preached at 1 PM. with some liberty from Heb.iv.ii. held qM conferance which was harmonious—Br Brockway preached at night after which we held a prayer meeting for sometime—put up with Mr Allen—cleared off at night & turned cold.....

Sund Feb 1..... attended love feast—preached with some feeling

[100] Frederick A. Seaborn, appointed to Farmington Circuit with Pilcher in 1834–35 (see "Journal," June 23, 1835). He was expelled from the Michigan Conference in 1837.

at 11 from Matt xvi.24.—administered the sacrement in which we had a comfortable time Spent the afternoon at Mr A Writing—Br Whitney preached at night & I exhorted after him much to my own comfort.—prayer & dismissed qM—.....

Mond Feb 2d..... spent the day about town getting my horse shod etc—visiting—& writting—at night I attended a temperance address in which I spoke with some liberty & feeling—After I was done Judge Fletcher addressed the meeting at some length.—several joined—staid at Mr A. Br Abel Warren happened in & put up here also with whom I spent the evening till 12 in conversation on the corruptions which exist in man, & in the different forms of government.....

Tusd Feb 3d..... rode out 5 M. on the gratiot Turnpike to Wd. Fairchilds & spent the day writting—preached at night in rather a lifeless manner to a small congregation.....

Wed Feb 4..... set out for Br E Tuckers on passing through Mt Clemens I stoped—Went to see a poor sick woman who is experiencing the reward of her errors—Was married—Left her husband not esteeming him her equal—had a child by an other man 2 days ago of which I doubt of her recovery—went on to Br T.—..... Br E H Pilcher[101] having engaged to go with me to My qM on St clair Met me here according to agreement—There being an appointment for meeting he preached—& I baptised 2 children—.... day cloudy cold with light snow.....

Thursd Feb 5..... Wrote till 12—We then Rode to Salt River & put up with a Mr Little where I preached from Matt vii.7. in a plain simple way; but rather dull Br P exhorted & then I baptised 2 children.....

Frid Feb 6..... Read and wrote till 9 when we set out for Point Aux chane—as we were passing along Lake St Clair the shining of the sun on the retiring clouds to the S W presented one of the Most sublime sights that nature affords like piles on piles of snow mountains standing all the grandeur of awful silence—Reached the place of our distination at 2 P.M. & put up with Br Peter Brakeman..... tended Meeting at Pt Au chane (½ M below) Br Pilcher preached will [well] after which we prayed for some time—....

Sat Feb 7..... Went to Pt Auchane & preached with some liberty

[101] Pilcher in his *Protestantism in Michigan* records this meeting with Gilruth.

from Ps xxxiv.19 after which I held qM conferance—A Br Kerr[102] from Canada conf. preached at night after which we held Prayer Meeting—But the disagreeableness of the cold rendered it necessary to dismiss— . . . . Day—severe snow storm till 11 then cloudy & bitter cold—clear at night— . . . .

Sund Feb 8. Rose about dawn—Read some in My bible—Was taken with Br P by Br Brakeman in a sleigh to the M H Held love feast at 9—But by reason of the excessive cold few attended—Removed Meeting to Br Robinsons hard by & preached from John iii.7. with some liberty—tarried at Br Robinsons till eve[n]ing Meeting when Br P preached & Br Elliott gave a short exhortation & qM closed conversasion—

Mond Feb. 9. . . . . Br P & I set out on our return—stoped & talked & prayed with a sick woman who had been a Methodist but had moved about—backslider—& is now dying with the consumption—Reached Br E Tuckers about 3 PM a distance of upwards of 20 miles with a cold wind in our face without stoping any whare to warm. . . . .

Tus Feb 10. Rose about dawn—spent the day writing till ½ past 11 PM.—altho writing on the Judgement & final happiness of the righteous & the miseries of the wicked I find that the mear subject saves me not from strong temptation & am ready to cry out surely I am "more bruitesh then [than] any man" O what need of a present saviour have I—Thank God he is at hand—Day cloudy & cold. . . . .

Wed Feb. 11. . . . . rode to Br Porters on my way to Detroit & put up. . . . .

Thursd Feb. 12. . . . . wrote all day—preached at night from Ps. 34:19. somthing impressive but rather dull in the Manner— . . . .

Frid. Feb. 13. . . . . set out for Detroit—dined at Doc Tukesberrys—rode into the city & put up with Br Crane who received me kindly—tended a prayer meeting at night—wrote till 11—day cloudy etc.

Sat Feb 14. . . . . took my horse to burn the lampus[103] out of his mout[h]—changed my mind—took him to Br Deans stable—Preached at 3 PM. from Ps 34;19. with some liberty—held qM Conferance—spent the afternoon walking about the city etc—tended prayer meet-

[102] Peter Ker was in 1834–35 appointed to Gosfield, Essex County, Ontario.

[103] Lampas is a congestion of the mucous membrane of the hard palate in horses. The condition is physiological and requires no treatment.

ing at night—staid with Br Crane & spent the evening till 12 relating my experiance.....

Sund Feb 15..... visited Br B F Wetheral & improved the time to Move him to have the seats Made free by deed & that the deed be made according to the form of the M Discipline, for the Meeting house in this city—to all which he seemed inclined—Returned held love feast which was well attended but not very lively—preached at ½ past 10 with some liberty from Josh xxiv.15 & again at 2 PM. from 2 Tim iii.16 with much plainness but not the happiest manner. After which we administered the sacrement to a good[l]y Number of communicants. Br Crain preached at night—After whom I delivered long exhortation on the subject of Religious exercises the object of which was have the Members take hold of the work freely & pay no regard to the opinions of the work, nor of carnal professors. After which I called for seekers of salvation who were mourning over unpardoned sin—a [....] came forward & knelt down we joined in prayer for them for some time but neither of them found peace. I staid with Br [....] for the night.....

Mond Feb 16..... I set out for home taking the Chicago road I dined with Br Talbert—stoped an hour & half with Br Sayre at Ypsilanti—Reached Ann Arbour about dark. & found My familey well—.....

Tusd Feb 17 & Wed 18 Spent reading N.P. Neither of which days I retired to rest before 11—cloudy—Tusd eveing I joined in matrimony Rev Henry Colclazer & sister Aseneth True. Their Deportment on the occasion was calm & dignified—After the ceremony was over a supper in hand was served round—A certain Mrs —— Requested me to be seated by the bride To which I pled an excuse—That I wished not to conform to vain ceremonies of this world.

Thurd Feb 19..... tended Prayer meeting at night.....

Frid 20th Sat 21..... as above.... some appearance of a general thaw.....

Sund Feb 22.... preached ½ past 10 from 1 John 1.5 to the end with some liberty—& at 2 from 1 John iii.9 in a very plain & simple way—wrote till 11. day cloudy & ground very mudy—but began to freeze in the afternoon—clear at night

Mond Feb 23..... writing.... NPs.... day most delightfully clear & calm.....

Tusd Feb 24 Was waked at 4 by My wife having symtoms of approaching Labour—give her 25 drops of Laudanum—Rose at dawn—give her a gentle cathartic—Spent the day with her she having fruitless pains all day—called in Doc Brigam about Dusk.—about 9 I called in some Women—but the pain was still fruitless—then doc about 12 give her a pill opium & then all lay down—I taking My position on the floor that I might be ready on the first Movement—My wife by means of the opiate got some rest—to ward morning. Day beautiful & clear till past 12..... high wind—had much trouble by reason of our stove smoking—.....

Wed Feb 25. Rose at dawn—My wife still in labour. (Spent the time in the house)—About 12 the doc took about 3 oz of blood from her arm after which her labour became stronger—The Doc as in the morning went home—Returned at ½ past 4—and the child was born at 5 PM. Another Daughter.[104] Spent the day at home & about 12 lay down by the stove in order to keep a proper tempreture of heat in the room by regularly attending to the fire.—Day cold & blustering—

Frid Feb 27..... sundry small Itams chooping wood etc.....

Sat Feb 28 Rose a little before dawn & at day brake [break] I set out for the North branch of the razin [Raisin] to attend My qM.—Reached there ½ past ten, & put up with Conrad Row.—Preached at 11 in the S H. with some liberty & then held q conferance—A local Br Preached in the afternoon & at night—we held a prayer Meeting in which 2 found peace I however did not attend the Prayer Meeting having lost much rest retired by 9.....

Sund. March 1st..... held love feast at 9—preached at 11 with some liberty—then administered the sacrement—Preached again at Night & Br Wiley commenced another Prayer Meeting 3 or 4 found peace—Returned to Br R Br N Cumstock having also put up with me here Put a number of tracks [tracts] on slavery into my hand the reading of which waked up Many feelings on the subject.....

Mond March 2..... spent the morning till 9 in social conversasion —Rode home—(reading Birneys peice on Abolition)[105]—found

[104] The second Mary Gilruth, and his sixth daughter.

[105] James G. Birney, converted Alabama slaveholder and abolitionist who was presidential candidate on the Liberty party ticket in 1840 and 1844 (see Dwight Lowell Dumond, *Letters of James Gillespie Birney* [New York, 1938], Vol. I, Introduction). Gilruth was an ardent abolitionist.

things doing well—Read [&] choped wood etc day cold—to bed about 11.

Tusd March 3 Wed March 4 Read & wrote etc days clear

Thursd March 5 do do—Married John D Dow of Dexter to Ann Moore of this place at 6 PM—Frid.....

Sat March 7 choped wood etc—all this time the wether has been clear & mild & bed time with me 11 or 12 Rising about sunrise—

Sund March 8..... at a little past 8 set out for dexter—preached at ½ past 10 from 1 John 3:9. Met class & baptised a woman by pouring—dined with Doc Nichol whith whom I put up—Preached at 2 P.M. from Matt vii.7.—spent the afternoon conversing with Judge Dexter—tended Prayer Meeting at night—then went to see the Judge to assertain the reason of his not attending his class Meeting—conversed with him till 12 on this & a variety of different subjects—Day pleasent clear in the morning but hazzy in the afternoon—cloudy at night—

Mond March 9..... Returned to Doct Nichels wrote some in my journal—visited Mr C Kingsley, & dined there but did not see him, he being detained in the mill—Returned to Doc N & read tracts etc on slavery till 4. Rode to Br Penauyers & preached from Matt xiii.18 in a plain & pointed manner—Met class closely enquiring into the practice of each—Droped one & Received one on trial, If in this I exceeded My authority (which I do not believe I did) I felt Justefied nevertheless from the state of things—Day stormy with snow till 10 A.M.....

Tusd March 10..... Went with Br P. to prospect hill from which I had a fine view of the country—encluding 5 lakes[106] & a large portion of country W N & E.—Rode to Br Stephen Lees & preached a[t] candlelight to a considerable congregation from John xxi.22. In a close pointed Manner & then met class in a simular Manner—Rectified the class paper as I also did at Penauyers—....

Wed March 11..... Rode to Br Glesons & put up—wrote till evening—Wa[l]ked a Mile to a school house & preached with some life from Heb xii.14. then met the class in the same pointed way that I have done these days past—Returned to Br Glesons & tarried all night. Read N Ps till 11.....

[106] De Tocqueville, who visited Michigan in 1833, says of this region: "From time to time a little lake (this district is full of them) shines like a white tablecloth under the green branches" ("A Fortnight in the Wilderness," in *Michigan Historical Collections,* II, 39).

Thursd March 12 Rose about sun rise & immediately set out for home where I arived about 8 AM—spent the day chopping wood.... NPs.....

Frid March 13 rose about sun rise—halled some watter—At 9 set out—fell in with Doc packard[107] going to Spring Arbour having some lode in his waggon he was walking & his son driving. he & I walked & rode alternitly (on My horse) Br Colclazer having joined us we continued thus till we reached Mill Creek (beguiling the time on a variety of subjects) when we left him & rode on to Br Arunah Bennetts fed & dined—(Br O overtook us here) Br B set out with us we Rode to grass lake—I put up with a Mr Watkins—preached from John xxi.22.—Br B preached after me from Heb III 2. Br C exhorted etc & this continued the meeting till near midnight—Returned to Mr W.s.....

Sat March 14.....Read N Ps till 9 here I came across the Procla-m[a]tion, or rather orders of Acting Governor Mason to the Militerry commandents to resist by force the Movements of Ohio in reference to a disputed peice of ground claimed by both governments[108] —O the madness & folley of wicked men!! These movements will not settle the matter supposing the parties should shed the blood of thousands. We set out about ½ past 9 & rode to Jacksonburgh—Preached with good feeling from Ps.xxxiv.19 Then held qM confer in which Br Joseph H Smith a local Br handed in his withdrawel from the church which was not received because of his being under sensure of having envayed against our discipline—Put up with Doct Stoddard—Br Bennett preached at night & I exhorted after him & then held a short prayer Meeting.....

Sund March 15.....held love feast at 9—Preached with great plainness of speach & with some power from Josh.xxiv.15 on familey Religeon At the close Br C Baptised a Man & woman by pouring—We then administered the sacrement—I spent the afternoon partly at Doc stodards & partly at Br H Thompsons. At Doc S I was led to show my reasons for not supporting the colonization society & My views of emancipation—At Br T our conversasion run on practical religeon etc—Br Colclazer preached at night—we held a short prayer meeting attempting to git mourners to come out & unite with us in

[107] Doctor Packard was one of the prime movers in the Spring Arbor Seminary.

[108] This has reference to the so-called "Toledo War," a boundary dispute between Ohio and Michigan.

prayer but in this itam we failed—Br E Bennett & I went home with Br Duran & staid all night ¾ of a mile out of town—

Mond Mr 16. .... Spent the morning principly reading Anti s[l]avery works About 9 Br B & myself rode in to Jacksonburgh & being joined by Br Colclazer—Doc Nickols & others, we set out for Ann Arbour. Br Z & I dined at Br Hecox. Br C & Dr N at Dunhams Tavern.—The rest of our journey till we reached Br Bs I intertained the company reading Anti slavery Matter & a whig circular to the people of Michigan—before Br C & I reached Ann Arbour it became dark so that it was with difficulty we could find our way—Reached home About 9 found all well—Read N Ps till 11. ....

Tusd March 17. .... choping wood etc etc preparit[or]y to leaving home. ....

Wed Mar. 18. Rose a little after 4. to set out for Detroit to endevour to have our charter for Spring Arbour Seminary pass through the Council as we wished—But My wife being unusually unwell I delayed till sun rise & on her asuring me that she thought there was no danger in her case & that she view it as my duty to go I set out first charging her that if there were any thing serious to take place with her to immediately call on Medical aid.—Rode to Ypsilanti & Brakefasted with Br Noris—Rode to Br Torberts & dined—Here I fell in with Judge Fletcher[109]—we set out for Detroit together I found him to be well accquainted with the scriptures & on the general to have (as I judge) correct views—as we rode on Br Wm. R. Thompson overtook us—we pass on conversasion becoming general—I stoped with Br Abbot a little below the city & they went on—Spent the evening conversing on the affairs of our church & was much excited at learning that the Base viol was intorduced in to our church I determined to brake [break] up this or brake [break] down in attempting it.[110]— ....

Thurd Mr 19—Rode to town put up with Br Jerry Dean.—visited Br Crane to learn the state of seminary Bill—found that it was in the hands of the committy yet—we saw some of the Members of coun-

[109] Judge Fletcher, chief justice of the Supreme Court of Michigan, and compiler of Michigan Laws, known as *Fletcher's Code.*

[110] Gilruth was always decided in his views. The conference had taken action against the use of musical instruments in churches. Pilcher records that when, in 1837, Bishop Soule was to dedicate the new church in Ann Arbor, Gilruth refused to attend as he was told musical instruments were to be used.

cil[111] & particularly Mr Mcdonald of Detroit who was the Chairman of the Committy—who immediately reported the bill back to the house as we wished it. It was then twice Read & soon after passed through the Committy of the whole. in which I got the bill amended so that the first meeting of the trustees be a month latter.—I spent the day during the session of the council in the council room Spent the rest of the day visiting Members of our church or of the Council—staid at Br Cranes & wrote till 11.....

Frid March 20..... Spent the morning as yesterday till the meeting of the Council when I attended also—found a strong disposition to strick out the Preamble which commenced "Whereas the Ohio Annal conference etc Believing that the objection lay not to the preamble so Much as the word "Ohio" & believing that the Preamble would be of use to us I suggested to some of the Members to strike out the word Ohio & then retain the preamble This took as I expected & the whole bill then passed without any difficulty The high feeling that exists at this time against Ohio for her asserting her authority over a gore of land the right to which is in dispute betwen that state & this teritory & to hold which for the time being there are Militery preparations Making on both sides—Set out for qM at Ypsilanti Rode to Br Torberts & staid for the night—Read the vicker of Wakefield—.....

Sat March 21..... set out gave my horse a slight feed at Br Sheldons tavern & Rode on to Ypsilanti—put up my horse at Br Noris—preached at 1 PM from Eph II 8 with liberty & some power—held qM conferance—staid with Br Sayre Read NPs till dark—preached with good liberty at night in the New M H The dedcation from Matt vii. 7.—held a prayer meeting—called Morners to be prayed for 4 came & 1 found peace— .... about sundown commenced a severe snowstorm accompanied with a N wind—.....

Sund Mr 22..... held Love feast at 9. preached (in the New M H) from Joshua xxiv.15 in a pointed manner.—Administered the ordenance of baptism to a couple of Adults—& then the sacrement to a goodly number of communicants I spent the afternoon at Br Sayres reading & conversing with Str Sayres—Preached at night with some liberty from [....]. After which we held a prayer meeting some presented themselves for prayers.—staid with Br Sayre. Day cold & stormy till Noon; snow fell about 8 inches deep....

[111] The Legislative Council of Michigan Territory.

Mond Mr 23. . . . . aranged business—brakfasted at Br Mcdowls—found my family well—D-H spent the day & night at My house talking about common stock—Received a letter from Mr J Key of Perysbourgh Ohio informing me that he had engaged a man to clear me some land & that it was to be done by the 20th of this month; & requesting me to come down. This I determined to do. . . . .

Tusd Mr 24. . . . . choped wood sometime Went to find a merchant to buy a Mission draft & after triying several succeeded.—About 11 set out for Maumee—Rode to Br Thompsons fed & dined—Reached Br Taylors & put up. . . . .

Wed Mr 25. . . . . Rode to Br Christopher Gee fed & brakfasted—Rode to Br Wilkinson fed & dined—Rode on Spent some time looking at My land—clearing—& the trespasses thereon—Rode up to Maumee—ferryed over & Put up with Mr Kee. Spent the evening till 10 conversing on the state of affairs & on My business down [here] etc. . . . .

Thursd Mr 26. . . . . Left $38 & an order on Br Sprague for $7 more in Mr Keys hand to pay for My clearing—left the lot in his disposal to git a crop of oats put in—about ½ past 7 set out on My return—Just below my land, met Br Sprague coming up to see me, we rode together to 10 Mile Creek—from him I had some hints concerning the management of certain xxxxx—fed & dined at Br Wilkinsons—Reached Monroe between sundown & dark Rode up to Old Br Christopher Gees & put up. . . . . Roads amazing bad. . . . .

Frid March 27. Rose at dawn & set out (called at Br Taylors & got my legans, which I left here when going down: for the lack of which I had mud enough) Rode to Br Jas Waits & brakefasted etc. fell in with a young man by the name of Sanford here who is traveling under the elder on Munroe cir. & a Doc lately come into the country with whom I conversed some time on the means of health—We rode together some Miles—fed & dined with Br Thompson—Reached Ann Arbour a little before sundown. Read N Ps. . . . .

Sat March 28. . . . . Made ready to set out a little before 9 for qM. on Plymoth cir & Mis—Put up with Br Rufus Matthews—preached in a S H Nearby from John xiii.35. with some liberty—held qM. Tried two appeals both of whom were condemned qM held till the time of Meeting & not being through we adjourned to Br Ms house—It now near past the time of Meeting I did not think proper to attend—Spent this time in conversasion principly on church government—the proper authority of receiving Members. etc I strove to convince My hearers that the errors among Methodists were chiefly attributable to us P*rs.* I felt to sustain our discipline to the letter as long as I am a Methodist.— .... heavy snowstorm in the evening.....

Sund Mar 29th..... held love feast at 9 & preached at 11 with good liberty from Joshua xxiv.15.—Baptised one woman & two children—we then administered the sacreament (Meeting today has been in Br Matthews Barn.) the servises to day were all comfortable seasons— .... Br Bibbens preached in the afternoon & meeting was dismissed—staid with Br M.....

Mond Mar 30..... Spent the morning till 9 at Br Ms reading & attending to the stewards business—Drove home—in the evening took our hiered girl[112] home (to Br Mcdowels)..... Read NPs till 10.....

Tusd March 31..... about 12 I took My wife & child to a neighbors —they were there some 2 or 3 hours. but our babe suffered Much with the colic through the night so that I got but little rest.....

Wed Ap 1..... took my wife out again today but from the suffering of the babe we were now convinced that going out affected it— .... some thunder in the afternoon. (Ther. stood at 88 in the sun at 4 P.M.)

Thurd Ap 2..... small things preparitory to leaving.....

Frid Ap 3d..... I set out about 11 for my qM on Farmington cir—fed at R. Thayres having come this far in my waggon I left it set out on horseback—Rode to Northville & put up with a Mr Clark.....

Sat Ap 4th..... took brakefast with Br Tiler—set out about 8 Rode to Henry C S Carus the neighbourhood of qM. but went to the S H & my horse was taken to Br Samuel C Burgis I preached at 11 with good liberty from 1 Thes v.23.—Held qM conferance. dined with Br S.C.B. Br Patridge preached at 3 at the close of his sermon I baptised 2 young women—I went to put up with Mr Hungerford Spent the evening writing an index to My scripture collections till 10. In the mean time the people held a Prayer M in the S.H..... (Br Pi[l]cher staid [stayed] here also)

Sund Ap 5..... held love feast at 9—preached with life & liberty

[112] There was probably a "hiered girl" only when there was a new baby; the last baby was now a month old.

from Mark I.15—Administered the sacrement—Dined with Br H C S Carus—attended preaching at 3 heard Br G Seburn—sat down in the S H & wrote some in my journal there being a few that tarried for Prayer Meeting—then went to Old Mr H & wrote till dark attended prayer meeting (which was dull with me) Day stormy with snow & wind—. . . .

Mond Ap 6. . . . rode with Br P to Br Brunsons & spent the day writting. . . .

Tus Ap 7. . . . (similar). . . .

Wed Ap 8. . . . rode to Laben Smith[113] at Pine lake (a local Pr) & put up—Read some—but spent the evening principly in conversasion—& the night till 10 fishing with a spear (or gee [gig]) But killed only 4 small fish I did not see many & they were shy. it being Bright Moon light—to bed about 12

Thurd Ap 9. . . . Wrote as above till 10 When I took it into My head to have a sail on the lake. Obtaining a sheet I soon riged out a sail & Br Smith & I spent say 3 hours saling—Br S having set some fires by reason of the wind there was much danger of his fences being distroyed I wrought an hour to prevent this & finally we succeded in our labour. . . .

Frid Ap 10 Rose at 6—Wrote till 2 P.M. When I took it in My head to have a swim in the lake which I did but it was too cold for pleasure—(Br F Seburn came here about 11 AM) Br L Smith set out about 3 PM for my Lapier q M at paint creek—Rode to Donation Chapel[114] & put up with Br Turner (on the way I beguiled the time reading Rollens Antient History) I preached at Night from Isa XI.31. with some plainness but not much power—day clear (some smoky by reason of fires). . . .

Sat Ap 11. . . . Rode to Mr Josiah Deweys & put up (qM being here) I preached with good liberty from Ps.cxix.1. in the barn floor—held q M conf in a S H hard by—Br Laben Smith Preached at 4 P.M. after which we held a short Prayer Meeting in Old Mr Apolos Deweys (father & son ar[e] congrégationalists). . . . on our rout to meet-

[113] Laban Smith had been a local preacher since 1830. At the next conference he was placed on a circuit.

[114] Donation Chapel was a log building near Pontiac built in 1829 by "Brothers Hathaway and Turner" and given to the Methodist Episcopal church, hence the name "Donation Chapel."

ing to day we went up to the top of what is called Bald Mountain[115] from the top of which I had the grandest view that I have had in Michigan. I supose this mound is 200 ft high

Sund Ap 12.....read some in the Apoc. held Love feast at 9. Preached with clearness from Josh.xxiv.15 administered the sacrement to a goodly number of serious persons—spent the afternoon till 4. reading as above—A Br Earl preached at 4 after whom I exhorted—& then we dismised—Rode home with Br Barns a Local Pr.....day pleasent & mild mostly clear.....

Mond Ap 13.....writing off my scripture collections. day some snow showers & cold hard frost at night.....

Tusd Ap 14.....as above.....Rode to Br Abel Warrens (qM) & put up—....

Wed Ap 15.....Rode 3 M & preached a funeral from Job xiv.1.2.3. with good liberty on the death of Joseph More who was drowned yesterday—he having been for sometime deranged—left his house & in attempting to cross the clinton river came to his end. he was a religious man—A Methodist. & once an exhorter—....

Thurd Ap 16.....wrote....till 11 at night. read some—day stormy.....

Frid Ap 17.....visited Br Arby Smith—& another familey—..... for the past week I have lived very abstemiously I think it profitable to My soul at least. Rode to Lazarus Greens & put up he received & treated me kindly I spent the eve[n]ing principly Conversing with him on his shaker principles[116]—I had lent him their testemony of Christs second appearing the absurdities of which I had hoped would have opened his eyes: but it only confirmed him the more*—....

Sat Ap 18.....Rode to Br Hollands the place where we were to

*This is a work of 64 pages writen by a Wm Miller & is an attempt to prove that the 1st resurection & the milenium will take place about 1843. When the wicked will be distroyed & the righteous raign with christ on the earth 1000 years What is it that folly will not attempt?

[115] Bald Mountain (see Fuller, *op. cit.,* p. 198), a hill rising some hundreds of feet above the surrounding country. The beauty of the view from its summit is mentioned by numerous pioneers.

[116] Gilruth seems to have confused the Shakers and the Millerites. Both believed in Christ's Second Coming, but the Shakers held that Christ had already appeared in the person of Ann Lee. The Millerite movement was in full swing at this time.

hold our qM—preached at 1 P.M. from Ps xxxiv 19. with good feeling & perfect liberty to a respectable congregation (in the S.H.) after which I held qr conferance—Went to Br. Duncan Mcgrigors[117] & put up—Returned to the S H at 4 to attend the Prayer Meeting—I opened it, & then left it to be carried on by themselves & returned to D McGregors & spent the time....Reading Rollins A History.....

*Sund Ap 19.....*Read in the Bible & Apoc till ½ past 8 (It having been designed to have our Meetings in Br McGrigors barn to day preparations were accordingly made for it but in consequence of a heavy snowstorm & the place being a little to one side—etc. it was concluded to hold them in the S.H.)—held Love feast at 9 which was considered a good one (4 joined society)—I preached with liberty & some power from Mark I.15 At the close of the discourse there was a general Move in the congrigation & some praised the Lord with a loud voice—I administered the sacrement (assisted by the ministers present) to a considerable number of communicants to whom it proved a blessing—went to Br Hollands & dined—Br Wm. H Brockway preached at ½ past 3 & Br Abel Warren exhorted after him—& this closed our qM.....

*Mond Ap 20.....*scripture collections—day stormy snow showers & rain.....

*Tusd Ap 21.....*Day simaler.....

*Wed Ap 22.....*as yesterday till noon—When I set out for Br Ruben R Smiths intending to pass to St Clair by the way of the Hoxy trail—Br Duncan Mcgrigor & some others of the brethren having taken it in their heads to Make me a present of a coat patren, he met me at Romeo, & performed their intention by so doing—Rode to Br R R Smiths & put up—snow & rain in the morning.....

*Thursd Ap 23.....*Read Rollin till 8—Wrote till 5 P.M. Spent the evining till 11 conversing etc with Br Smith & Br Brockway.....

*Frid Ap 24.....*at 8 I set out for st clair accompanied by Br Brockway—we had a disagreeable road till we reached the turnpike which we struck 2 Miles south of Bell river—Fed at Bell river—Reached st clair at ½ past 5.....put up with Br Phillips.....

*Sat Ap 25.....*Wa[l]ked to town, & preached with good feeling &

[117] Duncan McGregor was dropped at the previous conference. He was the first Michigan convert to become a local preacher (1832). In 1833–34 he was on the Tecumseh Circuit. Gilruth characterizes him as a "poor hypoconderic creature" ("Journal," III, 78).

liberty from John xxi.22 at 1 P.M.—held q-conferance—then walked down to Br Phillips—to attend to my horse—Returned, & heard Br Brockway preach at ½ past 4.—(Prayer Meeting was appointed at night—) Returned to Br Ps & staid for the Night . . . . (Br Brockway with me)

Sund Ap 26. . . . . . rode to town in Br Ps Waggon & held love feast at 9. A Br Evens (of Canada Conf) preached at 11. After whom I exhorted—took up the publick collection—Administered the sacrement (assisted by the Ministers present) Dined at Br Horace Jerom's—Preached at 4 with some liberty from Josh xxiv.15—Wa[l]ked down to Br Ps took supper—Walked back to town & heard Br Evens preach & thus closed our qM. . . . . day I forgot what it was.[118] . . . . to bed about 10 pretty well fatigued

Mond Ap 27. Rose about sun rise & after brakefast set out in company with Br B for Mt Clemens—stoped a couple of hours at the county seat to see a steem mill start on a new plan vis the steem introduced into the senter of an axeltree & pass out arm & let off on the reaction plan—having been in the Mill on satterday & examined the work & the principle I had told the man who was the principle [principal] in having this Mill built on this plan that I would hold the axeltree with one hand so as to prevent its starting—I now proved it before his eyes—it is all a farse it is of no account for heavy work.—Left the county seat at 10 Rode to Pine river Mills & dined at Br Jas Ogdens—fed at bell River—Reached Widow Haskins & put up at night, 2 Miles from Mt Clemens—day some cloudy. . . . .

Tusd Ap 28. . . . . . Rode down to Br Edward Tuckers, where I devoted the day till 9 at night to writting off my collections. . . . .

Wed Ap 29. . . . . . spent the day till dark writing as above & having finished what paper I had with me I was oblidged to stop writing for the present.—Went fishing with Br Ts boys There was 10 small fish caught— . . . .

Thurd Ap 30 Spent the Morning till 10 in forming characters for writing what I may not wish others to know of this I have been thinking for some days past.—Set out on my rout toward Detroit—spent an hour looking at a vessel on the stocks at Mt Clemens[119] (to be lanched this week) Got the hind shoes on my horse reset—dined at Mr Allens.

[118] I.e., the weather.

[119] Detroit, Monroe, and Mount Clemens were early shipbuilding centers.

—Rode to Br Porters & put up—This evening I finished Reading Rollins Ancient History Having read 544 Octavo pages therein, & written & prepared for the press 53 pages (on fools cap paper) of my scripture collections since I left home—besides some other reading & writing—Read in the Presbyterian confession of faith[120] till 9. day showery—to bed ½ past 9.

On my way here today I discouvered after I passed south of the Clinton river that some of the sugar trees were in blossom These are the first that I have seen this spring—

Frid May 1..... Read some in the Life [of] Andrew Jackson President of the U.S.—about 12 set out for Detroit—stoped an hour & half with Doc Tooksberry in the run of conversasion I introduced some of the leading principles of common stock. He imbraced them appearently with all his heart. I did not discouver to him that I intertained any thoughts of attempting such a subject. But his remarks greatly strengthened my mind to proceed when circumstances answer—Reached Detroit about 4 put up with Br Crain; but my horse was sent to Br Burlingames stable—Spent the afternoon in seeking for articles for a communion service for our church at Ann Arbour.[121] but failed to find any—Read Wesleys Journal till 11.....

Sat May 2d..... Spent the day till 3 PM in Reading—looking farther for the articles wanted for the communion service—but found them [not] Accidentally Met with Br L Church of Ypsilanti (on his way to N.Y. for goods) to him I have the money & directions to get them—had a pleasent interview with a Br Richardson from england a local Br looking [for] a place to live where he may do the most good—I preached with good feeling from John xxi.22—held qM Conferance had one appeal which was laid over to the next q M.—Spent the evening till 7—mostly looking for Br Church to git him to preach found him at the M H but he refused to preach so I preached from Luke xviii.1–8. with good feeling—[to] an attentive people—Staid with a Br. Kittredge.....

Sund May 3d..... Read the book of Hosea—opened love feast at 9

[120] He was evidently meeting some opposition from Congregationalists and Presbyterians.

[121] There was probably no church building at Ann Arbor at this time, as the first church was dedicated in 1837.

had power in prayer—meeting good—A Br Deen[122] of Canada conf preached ½ past 10. after whom I exhorted with some liberty. I dined with Br Burlingame with whom & said Deen I talked on the will—the affect of the body on the mind—obedience to the letter of the scripture etc till meeting time—Br Richardson preached at 2 P.M. after which Br C & I administered the sacrement—suppd with Br Woolsey— . . . . heard Br Richardson again in the evening—staid all night with Br Woolsey. . . . .

Mond May 4 . . . . set out about ½ past 8. Rode to Br J Hecox[123] Dined etc stoped a short time with Br Swift—having an appointment at Br R Thayers I reached there at dark thinking that my hour but it had been given out at 5 so the people had met & gone before I got there. . . . .

Tusd May 5. . . . . Found my horse to be quite unwell—bled him & waited till past 8 then set out & drove slowly Reached Ann Arbour about 3 P.M. found my familey well— . . . . .

Wed May 6 Thursd May 7. Frid May 8 Sat May 9 Spent reading N.P. etc with a little gardening—My horse still unwell—Generally rose about ½ past 5 & to bed at 10 . . . . got some hay at Br Bars—Read till 3 A.M.

Sund May 10. . . . . finished reading the account of "The Nun"[124] at which I read last night till 3 in the morning—Preached at 11 from Joshua xxiv.15. with some liberty but too tart—I think family religion cannot be generaley recommended—I preached again in the afternoon on 2 cor.vi.2. with good liberty & some power— . . . .

Mond May 11 I had calculated to attend the meeting of the trustees of Spring Arbour sem[inary] tomorrow at that place—but as my horse still continued unwell I had to give this up so I spent the day writting off my scripture collections & gitting some Tameract bark for my horse etc. . . . .

Tusd May 12. . . . . set out to make my wife a pair of shoes at wich with some other itams I spent this day—day hazzy—rained some. . . . .

Wed May 13 choped some wood etc Read & wrote some—

Thursd May 14 choped some wood etc

[122] Horace Dean was appointed to Gosfield, Ontario, in 1834–35.

[123] Joseph Hickox was one of the earliest Methodist preachers in Michigan. He came in 1816 and had evidently "located."

[124] *The Nun,* by C. Spindler, a novel published by Dewitt & Davenport, New York.

Frid May 15 Was on the point of setting out for Maumee but after having saddled My horse I gave it up & set to writting etc

Sat May 16 Spent the day writing & reading

Sund May 17 Preached at 10 from 1 kings xviii.21. with good liberty & at 2 from Ps xxxiv.17.—tended Pr. Meeting at 7.

Mond May 18..... Rode down to see a peice of ground designed for a camp ground—helped to clear it off etc.

Tusd May 19 Spent the day shoe mending reading writing etc

Wed [*May 20*] Wrote—heavy thunder showers in the evening.

Thurs May 21.—Wrote—heavy rain.....

Frid May 22..... set out for qM at Tecumseh. fed at a tavern ½ Mile W of Saline—Put up with Br Edward Lookwood a local Pr at Clinton. On the way read in hinds Fariary[125]—day warm & mostly clear

Sat May 23..... Rode to Tecumseh & Preached with liberty from Ps. xxxiv.19.—held qM conferance—heard A Br Young at ½ past 3—talked some time with David Huttens on common stock & the opinions of others thereat—put up with Br Burt. spent the evening till 11 writing licences for the Prs & exorters—While a Prayer Meeting etc was carried on at the S H in Brownsville the place where our qM is held—....

Sund May 24..... held love feast at 9—preached at 11. on Josh xxiv.15. with good liberty—Administered the sacrement first baptising 3 Adolts & 2 children by sprinkling—Preached again at 6 from 1 Kings xviii.21. After which Meeting closed.....

Mond May 25..... brakefasted with Br Adams—spent an hour looking at a precision water wheel in a saw mill owned by Br Burt. which to my astonishment actually more then doubled the speed of the water.—set out for home dined at Mr Lowerys on the Lodi plains —reached home about 5.....

Tusd May 26..... spent the morning in some gardening employments—set out at ½ past 10 with my wife etc to go to Dexter—but on my way learning that the business I was going on could not be attended to we returned about dusk. etc.....

Wed May 27 Rose at 5—Made ready & set out for Spring Arbour to attend the meeting of the trustees of our seminary dined at Br A Brevetts—put up with a Br Page.....

[125] J. Hinds's *Farriary*, a veterinary manual, published by G. Lippincott & Company, Philadelphia. Gilruth prescribed for his horse as well as for his family.

Thursd May 28.—Rose at 5—& immediately set out—brakefasted at Br Durans ½ M W of Jacksonbourgh—reached Spring arbour about noon—spent the ballance of the day among the trustees there was not a quorum present so they set out for an absent Member—staid with Br Packard formerly of Ann Arbour—....

Frid May 29. Rose at 5.—Spent the day till 4 P.M. attending on the trustees but nothing could be done for want of a quorum (we appointed to meet again on the 23d of June) In the evening I set out for Br Benedicts accompanied by Br B & a Br Stodard an old traveling Pr of N.Y.C. (having after a long & unyealding Solisitation from the Packard familey agreed to tarry the next week till Thursday to marry their Daughter Caroline[126] & Br E Pilcher agreed & written to my wife to this effect.) At Br Bs I found a confirmed Calvin Baptist with whom I conversed on calvinist principles till Past 2 AM. without succeeding in the least to change his notions—....

Sat May 30.....Set out for q M 2½ M dist accompanied by Br Stodard—preached with some liberty from John xiii.34.35.—Wrote some licences etc etc. Br S preached in the afternoon, after which I held q.M.C.—staid with Br Nowls & held a prayer M. an other P.M. was held near, at a Mr Murrys—....

Sund June 1.....Wrote till ½ past 8 in the barn where our M was held—when love feast commenced. This was a verry lively Meeting—Br S preached at 11. After which I assisted by others administered the sacrement: but before we got through there came on a heavy thunder shower—This ditained the people so long as to render it improper to attempt an afternoon Meeting as had been contemplated—We however had meeting at candle light, when Br Barris preached us an exulent discourse—thus closed this qM. none converted that I knew of.

Monday June 2d.....Went a Mile & half to the Calamazoo preached at a Br Beachs & then walked ½ a Mile to a suitable place & baptised a man & a woman by immersion—Returned to Br Noals & from thence went in company with Brs Davison & Gerring & staid all night with a Mr —— whose wife I baptised....

[126] The *Ladies' Repository* for January, 1841, contains a most idealized obituary of Caroline Mathilda Packard, who died at the age of twenty-two. Thus she was seventeen at the time of her marriage, which is noticed in the *Western Christian Advocate,* July 31, 1835.

Tusd June 3d.....went a mile & half & preached a funeral for a small child—in the evening came to Br M Benedicts & put up—.....

Wed June 3d.....rode to Spring Arbour & preached at 5 to a few hearers—put up with Br Wm Smith (A member of the Christian Church).....

Thurd June 4th.....at 11 I joined in matrimony Rev Elijah H Pilcher & Caroline Matilda Packard.—Drove to Grase Lake & put up with Br Page.....

Frid June 5.....set out for Ann Arbour fed & dined at Br Cadwells—Reached home about 3 P.M. as the afternoon was showery I concluded to remain at home & not attend our Camp Meeting till next day—

Sat June 6 Rose a little after day—as soon as convenient I set out with my familey for camp meeting—reached there about 9—during Morning sermon—our q M conferance was held at 1 P.M. in which Joseph Smith A local Pr was expelled for sowing & maintaining unitarianism & enveighing against disciplines—while q conferance (for Ann Arbour cir) was in session Br Sayre preached & conducted a Prayer M. in wich 7 or 8 experienced peace. from this time the work began to advance—Day cloudy & some rain—to bed about 12

Sund June 7. Rose about 5—preached at 8 from luke xiv.16–24. there was much people on the ground to day—the good work was powerfull at night—day cloudy—to bed say 2 A.M.

Mond June 8 Rose about 5 took a vote of the people concerning continuing meeting till Tusd which was carried—a good work to day & to night—some rain in the morning—day cloudy—to bed about 2 A.M.

Tusd June 9. Rose about ½ past 5—About 10 our camp meeting closed. a fairwell sermon & the receiption of Members. This camp M was held at Mallards creek Washtenaw Co. & was the joint labour of Ann Arbour, Tecumseh, & Ypsilanti circuits—there were it was supposed between 40 & 50 converted[127]—some also professed sanctification—We had some disagreeable wether in the fore part of the Meeting: but we had verry little disturbance from the Ungodly—This Meeting will tell in eternity—Returned home with my family—spent the day Repairing our garden fence—Reading etc

[127] Among the converts was probably Wellington Collins, later presiding elder of the Detroit District, who, Pilcher says, "embraced religion at a camp meeting in Washtenaw county, 1835."

Wed June 10. Rose about 5—spent the day . . . . principly in cleaning out our garden—then visited till Night—day hot 100 deg in the sun. . . . .

Thurd June 11. . . . . Went to Mill—halled wash watter etc—visited in the afternoon—spent a few minutes in the court it being in session— . . . .

Frid June 12. . . . . spent the Morning Making arangements to attend qM on Ypsilanti cir—but did not set off till after 10.—Rode to Br Sheldons 8 M E of Ypsilanti & put up. . . . .

Sat June 13. . . . . Rode to Br James danels left my horse & rode to the arsnal & preached from Jer viii.22. held qM conferance—spent the afternoon reading Weems life of Franklin[128]—preached again at candle light from 1 kings xviii.21. Called for mourners 2 came prayer —& dismissed—heavy rain in the morning day hot & cloudy (put up with a br. Jarid Sexton Br Sayre with me). . . . .

Sund June 14. . . . . held love feast.—preached at 11 from Matt xi. 28.29.30. with good liberty—Administered the sacrement—6 joined society at love feast.—Br Doolittle preached at 3.—& I at candle light from Heb.xii.14—after meeting I rode home with a Mr. Putnum (inn keeper) & tarried for the night.— . . . .

Mond June 15. . . . . spent the morning till near 8 A.M. at Br J Daniels attending to the stewards business etc—Set out for home—fed & dined at Br Sheldons—Went to see J C Smith (5 M W of Ypsilanti) on business of the Wyandot Mission but not finding him at home left in writting what I wanted)—Reached home about sundown— . . . . tended what was given out for a love feast e.g. an experimental Meeting: a number joined society— . . . .

Tusd June 16. . . . . reading N Ps. . . . .

Wed June 17. . . . . Mowed my clover lot & halled some summer firewood—

Thurd June 18 Rose ½ past 3 was busey all day shoemaking & in some other small itams— . . . .

Frid June 19. Rose at 4—spent the day shoemaking till 1 P.M.— fixed up my wagon—& wrote a letter to the trustees of the Spring Arbour seminary— . . . . to bed about 11.

Sat June 20. Rose a little past 4.—at 7 set out for My q M on Ply-

[128] Mason L. Weems, *Life of Doctor Benjamin Franklin,* first published in 1815. Weems was the author of the famous life of Washington.

mouth Miss*n* & cir but before leaving the town I visited Mr Welsh a man who I had several times visited some time ago—found him near his end with the consumption attempted to talk with him on the subject of religion, & his being prepared to meet his end: but had no liberty nor did he seem to take any interest therein—prayed—& left with a conviction that I should likely never see him more.—drove on till within 2 Mile of the Meeting, when attempting to cross a small creek, now much swolen by the late rain, & the bridge aflote & broken up My waggon came uncoupled in the streem among the bridge logs The prospect now looked rather frightful but as My horse however unpleasently situated acted gentle & was bidable—so I succeeded in giting my things out of the waggon before they got much wet & piled them on peaces of the bridge: I then striped of my cloaths & after near half an hours close application succeeded in gitting fixed & out of this place—felt grateful—Just as I got under way there came on a smart hail shower nearly couvering the ground—Reached My Appointment near an hour after the time—Br S. Bibbens had just read out his hymn to commence Meeting—I preached with good liberty & feeling from P.s. Lxxxiv.11. held q conferance—spent the afternoon till 5 writing licences—Br L Davis preached at 5—A Br Holms exhorted I then introduced a prayer meeting which was very lively & edefying—there was Pr Meeting appointed at dark but I did not attend— ....

Sund June 21..... held love feast at 9.—preached at 11 from Rom. I.16 with some liberty to a large assembly in R Thayres Barn—Administered the sacrement at the close of which baptised a woman & then administered the sacrement unto her—(In the interval this afternoon Br Bibbins got sevearly hurt by a fall down a seller [cellar] way I immediately bleed him, but I doubt of his gitting over the hurt soon) I preached again at 5 from Matt xvi.26.27. but not to much advantage (as far as my own feelings were concerned)—staid at Br Thayres— ....

Mond June 22..... did some necessary things to my waggon—I after dinner I set out for Camp Meeting on Farmington cir in West Bloomfield Township, Oakland Co.—Fed etc at Esq Meads—Put up with Br. D. Goss at buckhorn corners— ....

Tusd June 23..... after brakefast I set out & reached the place of the camp meeting just as the morning service was commencing. Br

Frederick Seburn was in the stand & while praying his mind became affected by some recollecting which for the time being so discomposed him that he could not well proceede so I immediately took his place & preached from Matt xi.28 etc with great plainness to about 40 souls—Meeting draged all day & but few on the ground.....

Wed June 24..... meeting draged—I preached on christian perfection from Eph IV.11 to 16. No stir—

Thurd June 25 Day more favourable some better feeling among the people & some professed to receive santification—held qM conferance—....

Frid June 26—.... at the 8 o c sermon took a vote of the congregation relative to continuing the Meeting—determined to break up—accordingly of the 11 o c sermon we adminstered the sacrement & dismissed (hurried by a thunder shower) not one converted to my knowledge—drove to Doc E Park East bloomfield & put up .... took with me from the camp ground 2 young women—

Sat June 27..... Set out for My q M on Lapear cir—7 M N W of Pontiac—Reached the place at 11 & preached to a few from Rom 1:16 with some liberty & power—held q M—Put up with Richard B Bray in whose house the Meeting was held—Spent the afternoon writing licenses etc a Br H Barns preached at 4. We then held a short prayer M which was lively—....

Sund 28 .... held love feast—A Br Eral preached at 11 & in 10 Minutes after him I preached on sanctifications from 1 Thes iv.3 with good liberty & perfect command of my voice—the people were all attention & much impressed—We then administered the sacrement to a few souls & clossed the Metting because of the unfavourableness of the wether.....

Mond June 29..... Drove to Auburn & put up with a Br Terry—wrote & Read Francis Barrien[129] till dark—preached in rather a cold but pointed manner in a law office from Ps Lxxxiv 11.— ....

Tusd June 30. Rose ½ past 4. spent the day writing & reading F.B. Preached at night with liberty from Ps.37:3. finished reading F. B.....

Wed July 15..... drove to Br Arba Smiths & put up (the place of q M) Spent the remainder of the day writting.....

Thurd July 2d..... Wrote the most of the day except say 3 hours

[129] *Francis Barrian or the Mexican Patriot,* a novel by Timothy Flint, the well-known frontier Presbyterian missionary.

spent fixing My waggon cover—day mostly clear—to bed about 9—Mind calm—

Frid July 3d..... Wrote all day except a couple of hours spent in fixing my horses harness—....

Sat July 4th..... q M at this place commenced today—preached at 1 P.M. from Jer viii.22 in a plain rough manner—some wept etc.—held q conferance (but the Pr in charge Br L. D. Whitney, was detained by sickness)—I preached again at 5 with much feeling & life from Matt xi.28.29.30. Many wept—we closed with a short prayer Meeting.....

Sund July 5—rose ½ past 4. Wrote licences—& in My journal till ½ past 7.—Held lovefeast at 9—Preached from Josh.xxiv.15 on family religion in a clear & forcable manner & treat of the disciplinary rules of family government showing therein the duty of the husband—the wife—the parent—the child—& treat of the devotional rules of family religion. 1 Privet 2 publick

The happy consequence 1 on individuals 2 on the familey 3 on the publick[130]—After sermon I administered the sacrement to a goodly number of devout worshipers—having no help I felt pretty tired before the close—Br Wm H Brockway preached at 5 PM after whom I delivered a rambling but in some sort moving exhortation—& closed our q M.—visited the clas leader & spent an hour in plain conversasion about class & prayer meetings etc—Returned—ta[l]ked some plain things about love feast etc—day cloudless but a smoke like indian summer.....

Mond July 6..... drove to Utica & put up with Br Elias Scott wrote till sundown—preached in the villiage S.H. at candlelight on Universalism from Prov xiv.12 I spoke calmly but plainly for near 2 hours—the people were all attention & when the meeting broke up they went away apparently thoughtful—O God distroy this pernishious error!....

Tusd July 7..... set out for st clair dined & (fed some grass) at Wd. [....] in Mt Clemens who appears like a pious woman—read N P a couple of hours—set out & drove 5 M through a pretty heavy rain—put up with Br Stephen Fairchild—....

Wed July 8..... set out & drove on past Bell river—& fed on some grass furnished by Br F.—Reached Pine river about 2.—found the

[130] This outline of Gilruth's sermon is similar to that of a series of articles on the same subject in the *Western Christian Advocate.*

road impassable for My waggon down Pine river So I left it & being furnished with a saddle, & saddle bags, by Br J Ogden I set out on horse back through a Most difficult rode—& reached St Clair County seat (Palmer)[131] a little before sundown. My horse having torn off one of his shoes I went to a shop to git it put on. The smith proved to be a Methodist & by his kind invitation & that of his wife I put up with them—In the run of conversasion I found them both Disciples of the common stock plan—his name is John Perkins.—I learned today to my great astonishment that Old Br Charles Phillips had become intemperate. O God what is man! I knew of no man in this country, that I had more confidence in his religious worth than this man. Read some in the History of the U.S.....

Thurs July 9..... set out for Br Wordens 6 M below visiting each Methodist house on the road—arived about 1. & put up.....

Frid July 10..... engaged in writting till 6 P.M. I then rode down to see Doc Amassa Hemenger (2 M) & put up spent the eve[n]ing in conversasion on a variety of subjects—....to bed about 9—but My Mind some way became exited into an intense strain of study so that sleep departed from me for a considerable part of the night—

Sat July 11..... Read some natural history—About 8 set out for Point Auchain the place of our q.M.—put up with Br John K Smith—Meeting being set for 1 P.M. I spent my time reading the history of the U.S.—preached at 1 in a plain manner on sanctification from 1 Thes iv.3. After which I held a quarterly conferance—wrote a letter to Old Br C. Phillips in the fullness of my heart—Went over to Hersons Island in a small canoe In order to take a view of its quality found it as far as I went much poorer then I expected—Returned & wrote a little—preached at candle light on brotherly love with good liberty & feeling—a prayer meeting was held just before Preaching in which was much good feeling I however was not present at it.—....

Sund July 12..... tended love feast which was only tolerable—Preached at 11 on the general duties of the christian from 2 Pet. I.5.6. 7.8. I had some liberty in speaking but was somthing discommoded by the noise of a heavy rain during sermon—After sermon, I administered the sacrement to a Number of communicants (assisted by Br Elliott)—Meeting being appointed for 5 I concluded to leave it to Br. E. & rode up to Br C Wordens (10 M) accompanied by Br D.

[131] Palmer is the old name of St. Clair.

Steward.—Having long thought of writting off the New testament according to Walkers Pronountiation I made an experiment of a verse or two & found that it would not be so ardeous a task as I had antisipated I am of opinion that if this was introduced in to the whole english litreture it would be a real improvement by removing to [the] lumber of a long dry study to acquire the knowledge of the sounds the vowls & consenants assume before & after one another in certain positions etc.....

Mond July 13..... Rode up to Br A Phillips visiting the Methodist families on the way—fed my horse & then rode up to the county seat & stoped with Br Perkins & dined—he is at present strongly in favour of a common stock so is Br Boyanton—owning the farm formerly owned by Br Jas Ogden. I read Br P. My Constitution with which both he & his wife were pretty well pleased—Rode out to the turnpike, & staid with a Br. Henderson. Preached with some plainness from John iii.5.—day cloudy & warm—to bed about ten but did not sleep for hours after lying down.

Tusd July 14. Rose about 5—& after brakefast I set out on My way toward Detroit.—fed & dined at Br. Stephen Fairchilds. having an appointment to preach, & baptise some persons at 5 P.M. Br F went with me to the place at a Mr Duglass's on the N branch of the Clinton 4 M Distant by the road—I spoke from John iii.5. with liberty & some power to a large congregation considering the newness of the settlement. & then baptised 3 Men & 2 Women by immersion It was an impressive & solemn time—Went home with Br Calab Chapple (he & his wife riding with me) & put up—spent the evening in conversasion—Day cloudy with some showers of rain like mist.....

Wed July 15—.... after brakefast set out on my way toward Detroit. Br C went with me as far as Mt Clemens—Before his conversion this man was a noted card player he told me many of the tricks used with cards—O the wicked disceptions of Gamblers!—called a few minuts in Mt Clemens at Widow Chapples & Mr Allens—drove on to Br Porters & put up.....

Thurd July 16..... about 8 set out intending to call on Doc Tuksberry but I past his place unintentionally—Reached Detroit about ½ past 10. Put up with Br. Jerry Dean—spent the afternoon in conversasion with Brs. Sprague & Gavett[132] Traveling Prs from Monroe cir. & Huron Mis. heard Br Sprague preach at night.....

Frid July 17..... Spent the Morning conversing with Br Sprague—the day till noon looking about the city & wharves—Wrote a letter to a man concerning some conversasion I had with a universalian Pr years ago in Ohio.—tended prayer meeting at night—....

Sat 18..... Walked out about ¾ of a mile to see Br R Abbott who was confined with an abscess in his thigh—Returned & preached at 3 with good liberty from Isa.II.5—held qM conferance—& at night Pr Meeting called for Mourners one poor drunk Man came O God what is man!—staid with a Br Woolsey—....

Sund July 19..... tended love feast at 9.—Preach at ½ past 10 from Prov.xiv.12 on universalism with some liberty & power dined at J Deans—preached at 3 P.M. from John vi.44 with some liberty after which we administered the sacrement.—Prayer M was appointed for evening—But I Set out for home—drove to a Mr Thomas' & put up.....

Mond July 20..... set out & drove to Br Torberts & took brakefast—called to see Br Sayre but he was not at home—dined with Br Sheldon—stoped a while at Ypsilanti & had some conversation with a Br Oscar —— about traveling under the elder next year somewhere in *Michigan*—Reached Ann Arbour about 5 P.M. & found all my family well—....

Tusd July 21..... Spent the day in preparations to set out for Conferance: intending to take My family to see our friends.....

Wed July 22..... with much diligence got ready & set out at 9 A.M. (Having nailed up our house & left it in the care of a Mr Tylar Reasoning thus if he be a good man he will do us no harm: & if he be a bad man we cannot prevent him as we will be long absent At any rate his honour May have some influence)—I called & our landlady as I passed & paid her the House rent up till about the first of Sept—Having provided some dried meat—cheese & bread etc we dined by the road side Near a Mr Juds—By diligent driving we reached Br Jas Wait & put up having come about 23 M.....

Thurd July 23 Rose a little after dawn—took brakefast & set off about 7—drove a mile past Monroe—& fed & dined by the way side—

[132] Elnathan C. Gavit. Huron Mission was now in the Maumee District.

We concluded to stop for the night in the Bay settlement & accordingly put up with Br Hall—(This was an error for we thereby lost 2 hours of time which as it afterward turned out occasioned some heard [hard] pulling for our horse)—Having heard much of a sulpher spring in a large Marsh between this & the lake I determined on visiting I accordingly borowed a canoe & took my three oldest children & one of Br H. & set out—& after a mile & half of difficult passage by reason of grass I reached it—by passing up the spring run—It is of circular form containing about the 8th of an acre & the sides sloping to the bottom somthing like a Mill hopper but steeper—is about 30 feet deep—bottom visible when the sun & sky is in a proper state to render it so—water slightly sulpher—perhaps some other medical properties—pleasent to the tast—(Saw a great many exolent fish on my passage to & from the spring)—a slugish streem isues from this spring say 25 ft wide & 3 or 4 deep—returned before sundown—Br Sprague & wife being here (at his father in laws) & the house small—He & I concluded to sleep in My waggon but the Musquitoes were so bad, we got no rest so that I may say we had a sleepless night of it— . . .

Frid July 24. . . . . set out a ½ past 7 (Br Sprague accompanied us Near a Mile) We fed & dined at Br Whitneys—soon after we stoped here there came on a heavy Thunder shower—as soon as it was over, we set out, but it May [made] the rode [road] Mudy & slippry—as I past my place at delaware run, I found that the clearing that had been undertaken for me was not yet finished—When we came to Maumee I found the water too high by reason of the wind to ford consequently we ferried—put up with Mr Jas Key— . . . .

Say July 25. . . . . set out about ¼ past 7. found the rode [road] exeeding rough through the black swamp: & till noon, considerably Mudy etc by reason of yesterdays rain. from Portage R. on it had rained but little & the road was consequently dry & smoother—fed & dined as heretofore: vis, by the roadside. Just about sun set were sudenly overtaken with a heavy thunder shower we however reached Br Bowless & put up. Day cloudy & very warm to bed about 10

Sund July 26. . . . . Read some in christian Advocate & the W. Christian Advocate—wrote some in My Journal—& spent the balance of the day writting off my scripture collections—day rainy & warm.

Mond July 27. . . . . after an earley brakefast we set out—fed & dined by the road side—stoped with A brother Andrew Love a little above Tiffin—....

Tusd July 28—....set out—fed & dined again by the road side—Reached upper Sandusky about 5—& put up at the Mission—....

Wed July 29.....having determined on visiting My Daughter at Finley. I & my wife set out on horseback through a most difficult road—however with out meeting with any disaster except My wifes creature got into a Yellow jacket nest which occasioned some prancing—we fed & dined with a Mr Sergent near the big spring—Reached Finley a little before sundown & found My Daughter & her husband, & child well—....

Thursd July 30—Spent the day with My children—My wife had a turn of the sick head ake—Mr Duduit lamed himself last evening by a snag running into his foot so that he was confined to the house to day —spent the day principly in conversasion—Finley improving fast of late—....

Frid July 31.....set off on our return for Upper Sandusky—fed & dined again with Mr Sergent—Reached the Mission about sundown pretty well fetegued—Handed over to Br Thompson $183. that I had collected for the Mission on a note dew [due] for Mission property sold in Michigan (vis Sheep) Day hot & showery—....

Sat Aug 1.....went over the Mission farm in company with Br Thompson the Missionary—The farm is in good order as it respects fences[133] etc—We set out on our journey about 8 A.M.—Called to see our old friend at the Station—Here I found Br R Lucas[134] Gov of Ohio with whom I spent an hour in which he entered as far as time would permit into an elucidation of the nature of the dispute between Ohio & Michigan—told me confidentially, of the arangements to protect the civil authorities while holding court at Toledo if it should be found necessary—etc etc. He acted with his usual urbanity—We drove on fed & dined with an old accquaintance of little sandusky (Wilson)—we reached Marrion about 5. & drove out to Br Kinnears

[133] A letter by Thompson on the state of the mission is published in the *Western Christian Advocate,* June 13, 1834, which speaks of Squire Greyeyes and the fences.

[134] Robert Lucas (1781–1853), a native of Shepherdstown, West Virginia, was elected governor of Ohio in 1832. Lucas County, in the territory in dispute in the so-called "Toledo War" with Michigan, is named for him. He was a Methodist layman, hymnist, and poet. Later he became territorial governor of Iowa (see *DAB,* XI, 487–88).

(4 M) & put up where we were received with every demonstration of kindness.....

Sund Aug 2d..... spent the morning till 8 Reading the scripture with Clarks notes[135]—Went with Br K & most of his familey to Marrion to hear Br P Nation preach his farewell sermon But nothing would do but I must preach instead of him so I spoke with good liberty & some power from John.vi.44. Returned to Br Ks & after dinner I & my wife went to see one of her cousins who lived in this neighborhood—spent a hour & returned having been furnished with horses & a guide by Br K.—....

Mond Aug 3d..... set out—fed & dined with Br Henry Smith at Norton—stoped a few minutes at Br F Welshs in Delaware—Drove on & put up with Br Travis 5 M below....

Tusd Aug 4th.... set out—fed & dined by the rode side a Mile & half above Worthington—Reached Columbus about 4 P.M. turned aside & put up with Br Mccormic—spent a couple of hours in the city wishing to see to some business concerning the tax of some land I own in Harden county. but I had not the fortune to find the Auditor of state about his office. I spent some time noticing the price of things —Learned from Br Mccormic that the publick feeling about Columbus was pretty sanguine about the boundry queston betwen Ohio & Michigan.—day clear & hot—to bed about 10.

Wed Aug 5..... set out & fed & dined at a tavern a Mile sout[h] of the crossing of Big belly (on our own provision)—Reached Circleville sun half an [hour] high & put up with Br Delamer R Kennear a coppersmith. (Son of him, with whom we staid last sunday) There being notice of My Comming an appointment was circulated for me to preach—I spoke with liberty from Ps xxxvii.3.....

Thurd Aug 6..... we set out—fed & dined again by the road side—past Chilicothee about 3 P.M.—Put up with Br Callwell (where Br Ridenour formerly lived but both he & his wife dead since I was here before).....

Frid Aug 7..... set out fed & dined again by the road side—Reached Joseph Westlakes a little before sundown—here ends My Journey with My familey for the present—.....

Sat Aug 8—spent the forepart of the day helping W to stack wheat—& the afternoon Reading & writting.....

[135] Adam Clarke's *Commentary*, the widely used Methodist work.

Sund Aug 9.... There having been an appointment circulated for me to preach, & the people being assembled, I preach[ed] with some liberty from Ps cxix.1— ....

Mond Aug 10. Rose before day by reason of the sickness of one of our Children which was taken in the night with a hot fever—Spent the whole day attending to it—The medicine having opperated it got better in the night—day clear & hot.....

Tusd. Aug 11..... After brakefast I went to Jackson (6 M. dist.) to git some Medicine—There being several of the Ws children taken ill—dined in Jackson with a Br Larry—Returned & gave emetics to 3 of Ws children, & a dose of Calomel to My own that was unwell discouvered that it was the Measles that Ws children had—Thus after all our care, by some strange fatality we have our familey compleetly in contact with this disease It was alltogether unexpected to Ws familey it being near 6 Weeks since they had had an oppertunity of being infected. O God be gracious & suffer not thy servant to be hindered in his Ministerial duty by this providence.....

Wed Aug 12..... spent the day about the house Reading NPs etc with some attendance to the sick children—.....

Thursd Aug 13..... After brakefast W & I cleaned out their spring: & then went to cutting some oats; but before we finished It was thought necessary to go for a Doc. to one of his children: (for every child he had was now down)—he brought some Medicine, & bled the last, etc.....

Frid Aug 14..... took my wife & her mother 3 M to hear Br A Hawk preach—I exhorted a little after he was done—we staid & dined with Br Samuel Mcclures. Returned in the evening— ....

Sat Aug 15..... all the children on the mend except the one above referred to—about 9 A.M. I set out in my wagon (having borrowed a creature of W) for conferance at Springfield—There having been some rain the roads were some Mudy—drove slowly: Reached Richmond a little before sundown & Put up with Br Friend Pinny calculating to attend a camp Meeting (held in the big bottam 7 or 8 Miles below).....

Sund Aug 16..... set out for camp Meeting accompanied by Br P.—Arived there just at the close of the Morning sermon—I preached at 11 with some plainness from Heb xii.14. & after the Publick Collection was taken up—administered the sacrement to the preachers &

they to the people—about 4 P.M. Br J Delay[136] preached & I exhorted after him with some power & then called for Mourners several came to the alter & while they were yet collecting I set out for richmon (taking sister Pinny with me) where I arived about sundown but I thinking it best I went on to Br Colwells (2 M) & put up.....

Mond Aug 17..... set out Drove about 17 Miles & fed by the road side. Drove on till night & put up with a Mr George Comton an Irishman who had been settled here for 30 years This was on the waters of Deer creek—.....

Tusd Aug 18..... drove 9 M: & fed, & took brakfast with a Presbyterian Minister near Bloomingsburch by the name of Dicky whom I had seen while I lived in Marrion—Drove on, & as I was going fell in with 3 or 4 Prs & dined with them at a place called Grassy Point in the house of a widow Thomas—Thomas had been a selebrated Pr among the New Lights Possesed of some poetical powers—The Prs passed on, & I drove on to a Mr Pearce 8 Ms from Springfield & put up—staying on condition that I did with out supper—....

Wed Aug 19..... set out at dawn & Drove in to Springfield & Put up with Br Joseph Sprague having for room mates Brs Wm Sprague & E. H. Pil[cher]. Conferance Opened at 8 A.M. in the Presbyterian M.H. Bishop Andrews[137] presiding—I attended closely to business (taking Minutes of Conferance) Conf proceded harmoniously & rappidly—In the evening had an interview with H. O. Sheldon he Manifested an increasing intrest in the Community business—Walked out ½ M to see My Creature—spent the evening till 10 with the Bp & P Els in aranging the cir & districts—....

Thurd Aug 20..... Met in conferance at 8—tended to business faithfully today—Met the P Es at night to arange the districts.....

Frid Aug 21..... visited Br Brockway who was labouring under an attact of the colera Morbus—brought a docter to see him—Met with conferance at 8 & attended to business faithfully..... spent the evening in the stationing business with the Bp & Elders—....

[136] Jacob Delay (1781–1845), a native of Pennsylvania, was at this time a supernumerary, but serving on Salt Creek Circuit in Chillicothe District. For memoir see *Minutes,* Vol. IV: *1846–1851,* p. 74.

[137] Bishop James Osgood Andrew, the Methodist bishop from Georgia, whose possession of slaves by marriage was, ten years later, to become one of the immediate causes of the slavery schism in Methodism.

Sat Aug 22..... Read till 8 Mis Rieds 6 Months in a convent[138]—tended conf till 12 when it was adjourned till to meet on Monday at 8 A.M. Spent from 3 till ½ past 4 in the stationing business—heard Doc Thomson[139] preach at night—was unedefied.....

Sund Aug 23..... went to hear Bp Andrews preach & witness the ordaination of the Deacons—The Service was—1 Read 1 cor 3 chapt sang hymn commencing How beauteous etc P.397. Text 1 cor.iv.1. 2.3.—Sermon—"An evil in the corinthian church. vis an idolitry of men—devisions in favour of certain teachers, that was distructive of piety—The church is in danger of this in all ages—God alone can give success—All the differant talents are for the church—Then account of us as the Ministers of Christ—stewards of the Mysteries etc—in this light they are to be regarded—They should give evidence of thinking such—The enemies of Christianity commence their efforts against these—Remove these & the sabbath, & christianity gos—Their duty To feed the flock. To dispence the Mysteries—First, & most of all the bible contains the matter to be taught—Mans apostacy—the atonement—Justification by faith—holiness—The resurre[c]tion—Judgement etc What of the flipent preacher who attemps to feed christs flock with out the bible? he is a worthless man as a minister—study the bible,—pray—go into the pulpit thus & god will give the necessary inspiration—Former Methodist preachers were Mighty in the scripturs—other studies are only to aid this one point the publick ministry of the word.—Neglect not Pastoral visiting without this Ministers may be eloquent yet their flock grow lukewarm—True Ministers, preaches, & visits—the poor as well as the rich—deals faithfully—explains difficulties—deals kindly—applies the promises—By these you learn the whole state of your charge—gain their confidence—win their love—and render them governable—Must be kind in the administration of discipline, but firm—Never court popularity (here related the following Aanacdote "Nelson being urged to preach more refinedly did so on one occasion when he came out of the pulpit sev-

[138] Rebecca Theresa Reed's *Six Months in a Convent* (Boston, 1835) was the cause of a widespread controversy and elicited several Catholic replies (see Ray Allen Billington, *The Protestant Crusade, 1800–1860* [New York, 1938], pp. 90–92).

[139] Edward Thomson (1810–70) became the minister in Detroit in 1836. He was later editor of the *Ladies Repository,* was the first president of Ohio Wesleyan University, edited the *Christian Advocate and Journal,* and was elected a bishop in 1864 (see *DAB,* XVIII, 482–83).

eral applauded his sermon as just the thing. said he "If God will forgive me for this I never will do it again—At other times when I have come out of the pulpit I have been [besought] by the penitent asking what to do to be saved but in this I only git the praise of men") Spoke of sabbath schools & religious instruction to children—Probed the conscience of the Pr concerning how they had discharged these duties—showed the emence influence they might exert—but if neglected the influence will be evil—Avoid politics do good to all—let not the world draw you into her mudy measures—What if the world esteems you untalented? it ruins the Ministry to listen to publick opinion—it is a small thing to be Judges of mans Judgment—Addressed the people on the vanity of attending the church as a Theater & neglecting duty—go to the grave with a sinners curse on their head—to the judgement with a sinners guilt upon your heart—spoke feelingly of the aged men who stood by the ark in the wilderness—folowed it few, & far between—told an anacdote of Asbury when old & very feable on his way to gen. conf. some said what will become of our church when you die? said he "The church will do very well—it can do without me"—showing the churchs supply by a young & rising ministry—Spok of the reward—a crown of glory—*It was a most exolent discourse.* J B Finley took up a publick collection—Then the ordaination took place 37 Whites & two Wyandots Squire Graeys & Jas Harrahoot[140]—Read Beachers plee for the west[141] till 3—Went to hear Thos A Morris & witness the ordaination of the elders (21)—Read as above till dark—Went to hear Brer H Mcgowan[142]— . . . .

Mond Aug 24. . . . . Tended conferance as usuel—at ½ past 9 conferance adjourned to hold the aniversary of the Missionary society—Singing & prayer by Jas Quin The Secretary Read his annual Report—& then the treasurer Read his.—had received from the Annual conferance Missionary society $ 153. & from her auxiliaries & individu-

[140] These were Christian Wyandot leaders. Harrahoot is possibly a corruption of *Herrnhut,* an indication of Moravian influence.

[141] Lyman Beecher's *A Plea for the West* (Cincinnati, 1835) conceives more widespread education, through the founding of schools and colleges and the education in the West of teachers for the West, as the solution to the contemporary problems of the Ohio and Mississippi valleys.

[142] Burr H. McCown, professor of languages, Augusta College, 1834–35.

als $ 3551.60 also some 2 or 3 silver watches. Henry B Bascom[143] then preached from Micah iv.2. the following is an outline

I show some of the more distinguishing features of the Gospel

1 Its source is devine

2 It is a system perfect in morals—to be obeyed—not mended.

3 The gospel appeals to the heart & concience of men—

4 Its influence on the hop[e]s & practice of men—

II The extent of the provisions of the Gospel.

It provides for the distruction of sin. by the removal of Ignorance—Enmity among men—War—Tyriney & oppression—Providing for universal brotherhood—& purety—

III Its means for dessemination [of] these effe[c]ts

The pulpit—& the press—light till secterianism dies & bigotry has an end—

IV The effects of the whole

1 The incalculable increas in the church

2 Its influence on the morals of the world

3 Its influence on the world—peace—War & Tyriany extinct

4 A world redeemed from sin & ignorance etc &

on the whole a Most inimatable discourse. Publick collection was lifted by Jas B Finley, which amounted to $354.25 cts A call for volunteers for the western conferances was made. Several offered & some of them Old Men & one P.E. I told these afterward that I would Veto their going to the west, jestingly but meaning to prevent it if I could.—Spent the afternoon in conferance which was mostly employed in the trial of Francis Wilson & J P Taylor for taking up goods without a probability of paying for them etc.....

Tusd Aug 25..... Tended Conf faithfully all day..... Tended to the stationing business till 9—Read Black Hawks life[144] till 11—Br Pilcher being attacted with fever I wraped myself in my great coat slept on the floor

Wed Aug 26 Rose about sunrise—having a bad tast in my mouth.

[143] Henry B. Bascom, D.D. (1796–1850), a native of New York, was one of the most eloquent of the Methodist preachers of the time. He became chaplain of the United States Senate; president of Madison College, Uniontown, Pennsylvania; president of Transylvania University; and in 1850 was elected a bishop of the Methodist Episcopal Church, South (*DAB,* II, 30–32).

[144] The *Autobiography of Black Hawk* was published at Rock Island, Illinois, in 1833.

tended conferance—every days observation showes human frailty & perhaps in none more then in myself—spent the evening in the stationing business..... again took my rest on the floor commencing about 11—

Thursd Aug 27 Rose at daylight Read the life of Black Hawk till 8—tended to the business of the conferance all day faithfully & in the stationing business again at noon & in the appropriations to the Missions I being one of the standing committy on that subject. About sundown or a little before our appointments were read out[145]—at ½ past 7 I drew my first instalment (on the treasurer of the Mission Society) for the use of the Missions in the bounds of Detroit Dist. to which I was reappointed.—Read the life of "black hawk" till 11. This man & his people have been ill treated by the whites. I do not wonder at his fighting—day cloudy again took my rest on the floor.

Frid Aug 28. Rose at daylight prepared & set out

Minnuts of the Ohio Annual Conferance held in springfield. Aug 1835.

Wed. Aug 19. Conferance met at 8 A.M. & was opened by Bp James O Andrews by reading the scriptures & prayer.....

.....were appointed a committy to take into consideration Abolitionism, & colonization & report the same to conference..... 11. Here Bp Andrews, addressed the conferance—was pleased to extend his acquantence—Methodist Prs in the essencials, the same.—Once an Annual conferance was a season of joy; a jubellee; but now they are a toil & burden;—Asked the prayers of the Prs—spoke well on the subject of examination of character, & on the doing of business—& on individual conduct in families etc—Spoke of the present state of the health of the Bps as tolerably good—Spoke feelingly on the death of Bp McKendree[146]—..... Resolved, that one of the Bps be respectfully requested to deliver us a funeral sermon.....

("Who remain on trial") .... Lorenzo Davis..... Lucien (Berry

[145] See *Minutes,* Vol. II: *1829–1839,* pp. 356–57.

[146] Bishop McKendree died in Tennessee, March 5, 1835. His democratic habits and manner made him particularly effective on the frontier. In 1834 the Lebanon Seminary at Lebanon, Illinois, was renamed McKendree College (see Robert Paine, *Life and Times of William McKendree* [2 vols.; Nashville, Tenn., 1869]; *DAB,* XII, 85–86).

good talents.—studious—discontinued for imprudent conduct in marriage)[147].....(James Wilkinson—discontinued at his own request—is pulmonary).....

Wed afternoon session Bp Andrews in the chair—James Gilruth opened conferance by Reading singing & prayer—..... Who are admited on trial..... Wm. Nast[148].....

Thursd. Aug 20. forenoon session Bp Andrews in the chair (Bp Soul also present) James Quin opened conferance..... candidates for full connection..... Richard Lawrence..... elected to Deacons orders.....

Thursd Afternoon session..... Adam Poe[149] opened conferance by prayer..... stewards called for claims.[150].... Conferance resolved itself into a conferance Missionary society.

Frid Aug 21 Morning session—Bp Andrews in the chair Bp Soul opened Conferance by the usual servises..... "who are elected elders" .... James F Davison..... Local preachers eligible to deacons orders.....

Frid Afternoon sission—.... Isaac C Hunter opened Conferance. .... conferance drew on the Book concern for $800 And on the charte[re]d fund for $90. these being the dividends from each to each annual conf..... Conferance then resumed the election of local Prs to Deacons orders.—.... Squire Gray eyes & James Harrihoot (the last two Indians from Upper Sandusky) were elected..... local Prs to elders orders..... committy .... appointed to confer with a deputa-

[147] Lucian Berry, later to become president of Indiana Asbury University (see above, n. 58) had violated the unwritten rule in marrying while still on trial. He was but nineteen years old.

[148] William Nast was a German immigrant of education, who, after a varied experience in the United States, entered the Methodist ministry and quickly became the leader of the movement to bring Methodism to the new Germans flocking into the United States at this period (see Paul F. Douglass, *The Story of German Methodism: Biography of an Immigrant Soul* [New York: Methodist Book Concern, 1939]; cf. *DAB*, XIII, 393).

[149] Adam Poe (1804–68), a native of Columbia County, Ohio, had been admitted on trial in 1827 to the Ohio Conference. He served as circuit preacher, presiding elder, and assistant book agent of the Western Book Concern at Cincinnati. He helped to "awaken" William Nast, so that he might be called the "godfather" of German Methodism in America. He was also active in founding the Ohio Wesleyan University (Simpson, *op. cit.*, pp. 725–26).

[150] Gilruth's claim was $200 for the year, of which he had received $196.75.

tion of Augusta College.....admission of candidates in to the traveling connection.....

Sat Aug 22 forenoon sesion..... Jacob Delay opened conferance. ....Resolved to abstain from the use of tobacco in the house of God.[151] 2 Mr Anthony one of the director[s] of the Ohio penitentiary was introduced & addressed the conferance; requesting the nomination of a suitable preacher to said place.....were appointed a committy to draft a Request to the Bps to appoint the time of holding the Ohio Annual conferance as near as may be to the last of Sept or first of Oct.[152] 5 On Motion Resolved that a committee of three be appointed to take into consideration a petition of the qM Conferance of Norwalk circuit, requsting an expression of the A. Conferance on the propriety of our Prs & Members attending shows etc etc....appointed....who are admitted on trial.....The examination of the characters of Deacons of one years standing.....Luther D Whitney. ....Arthur B Elliott.....characters of the elders.....But there appearing some difficulty in the characters of John H. Fielding & Burr McGown Proffessors in Augusta College they were not passed &.... were appointed a committy to inquire into the matter & report.....

Mond Aug 24. Morning Session..... David Young opened Conferance.....committy on Memoirs Reported Memoirs on....Phillip Gatch,[153] & Russel Bigalow.....On Motion a letter from R Bigalow to this conferance last year, was put into the hands of the editor of the

[151] The official *Minutes* read: "Resolved, that in view of the inconvenience, indecencies, and insalubrity of the use of that noxious weed called tobacco, all the members of this conference do pledge themselves to abstain from the use of it in the house of God." Note that there is no obligation not to use it outside the house of God, an indication of its widespread use among the preachers. A similar resolution was passed by the Indiana Conference in 1843 (Sweet, *Circuit-Rider Days in Indiana,* pp. 319–20).

[152] August was an inconvenient time, evidently, for the holding of the conference. At this session numerous preachers had asked and received leaves of absence for the balance of the session.

[153] Philip Gatch (1751–1835), a native of Maryland, had been one of the first native American Methodist preachers. He presided at the famous Fluvanna Conference in Virginia in 1779. In 1798 he came to Ohio and settled east of Cincinnati. Here he became a county judge, though he continued to preach when occasion permitted. He was readmitted into the Ohio Conference and placed in a superannuated relation. He died at the age of eighty-five (John McLean, *Sketch of Rev. Philip Gatch* [Cincinnati, 1854]).

Western Christian Advocate to dispose of as he see fit. 4 The Annual visitors of Agusta College made a favourable report of said college showing that $1500 over what was due the institution would clear it of all debts.....5. A letter was Read from John H Fielding—requesting a transfer to Masouri conferance.....confirance adjourned to attend the Aniversary of the Confirance Mission Society (at which was collected $351.25 the largest collection ever made in this conferance)

Monday Afternoon Sission....character of elders.....On motion the case of John P Taylor, & Francis Wilson was taken up. They had been suspended on a charge of taking up goods without a probability of paying for them. or the purchase of hogs as merchants.....committy to envestigate their books.....

Tusd Aug 25 Morning Session.....Augustus Eddy opened conferance.....committy on the petition from the quarterly conferance of Norwalk circuit.....Reported that it is inexpedient in our Ministers to connive at, & wrong for our members to attend shows, Manageries, theateres etc which was adopted.....necessitous cases.....The committy appointed to examin the Book & papers of Taylor & Wilson Made their report (favourably of Wilson).....Resolved that conferance disapprove of Wilsons entering into Merchantdising and of the Manner in which he conducted it....that he be reproved by the bishop before the conferance—which was done. & he made supperanuated—....Resolved that the conferance disapprove of J P Taylors entering into Merchantdising & of the Manner he conducted it. Resolved that he be suspended for one year.....8.....examination of character....(Henry E Pilcher Isaac C Hunter objected to him the refusal to pay him a note he held on him The justice of which was disputed by Pi[l]cher....appointed a committy....)....Wm Westlake....8.....On Motion a committy of 11 or one from each District to [be] nominated by the P E were appointed to take into consideration the devision of Conferance.....Elijah Crain constituted said committy.....

Tusd Afternoon Session.....Leonard B Gurley opened conferance.....examination of character.....James Gilruth.....

Wed Aug 26. Morning session.....Arthur W Elliott opened conferance.....The committy on the case of Hunter H E Pilcher, reported amicable adjustment—4 [Lorenzo] Waugh & Jesse Prior, volunteers for Masouri Conf took their leave of conferance After which Bp Soul delivered them an impressive address after which Both Bps affectionately embraced them—& a collect[ion] of between $20 & $30 was raised in conferance for them—....8 The book committy.... report....debts due the Book concern to the amount of $42.395..... 5750 subscriber for the Western Christian Advocate.....9 The committy of the case of McGowen & Fielding Reported that Mcgowens character should pass—that a committy of 5 be appointed to investigate fully the nature of some difficulties which have existed among the faculty of Agusta College in which John H Fieldings character was implicated—....laid on the table.....characters of Bur M Mcgown & John H Fielding passed with the understanding that said Fielding be retained as a member of this conferance, & that he be notified to attend the envestigation of this matter before a committy.....12 The visiting committy to Norwalk Seminary Read their report Making a very favourable report. (Showing 108 boys & 96 girls taught last season)....ordered published in the W Christian Advocate—13 The committy appointed to take into consideration the Abolition & colonization questions Made their report (which was highly favourable to coloniztion & decidedly in opposition to Abolition as proposed by the Abolition society[154]—O God!) which was adopted almost universally. 14 The Wyandot Missionary....report.—(179 Indians in society—& well of the temporal concerns.).... 15. Jas Harrahoot (Indian) addressed the conferance (confiding wholly the indian affairs to the conferance).....

Wed. Afternoon session—.....Conferance [opened] by Zacheriah Connal[155] in the usual way..... (The Neat [net] encrease of whites

[154] The resolution expressed confidence in the policy of the Methodist Episcopal church on the issue of slavery and stated that "as friends of peaceable, gradual emancipation, we regret the proceedings of the abolitionists and anti-slavery societies, and consequent excitement in the slave states." The conference approved the Colonization Society. Gilruth was a strong abolitionist and opposed the resolution. At this time the Methodist Episcopal church was under the control of the moderates. The General Conference of 1836, which met in Cincinnati, also condemned abolitionism (see John N. Norwood, *The Schism in the Methodist Episcopal Church, 1844* [Alfred, N.Y., 1923], pp. 29 ff.).

[155] Zachariah Connell (1794–1863), a native of Connellsville, western Pennsylvania, had joined conference in 1818. For memoir see *Minutes, 1864,* p. 143.

in the church was only 260—of Negros 75—of indians 11. in the Ohio Conf.) .... report .... Norwalk Seminary setting forth its temporal prosperity..... committy .... appointed to nominate the trustees for Norwalk seminary .... which reported in a few minutes—3 of whom were traveling Prs..... Conferance then took up the case of Adam Sellers—charged with having served a brother contrary to discipline. .... he was acquitted .... certain cases of suing .... refered to the decision of the Bishops..... 9 The Bishops showed their reasons for not preaching Bp McKendrees funeral sermon—Soul[e']s ill health—Andrews press of conferance business—It was then moved that Bp Soul be requested to write said sermon for publication which was universally addopted—& then conferance expressed their intire sattisfaction of the Bps reason for not preaching Bp McKendrees funeral sermon—.....

Thurd Aug 27 *Morning session*..... Wm H Raper opened Conferance .... resolution of thanks to the people of Springfield .... & to the presbyterian Minister & church for the use of their meeting house..... 2 A ressolution recognising the committy, for estemating the amount to be allowed for Bp Souls table expence[156] to be a standing committy for four years & .... John Wright[157] was added thereto in place of Russel Bigalow deceased—3 A ressolution recommending General Conferance to release James Quin of a certain old book debt[158] was concured in— .... visiting committy to Norwalk Sem-

[156] At this time the annual conferences over which a bishop presided appointed a committee to estimate the amount the bishop needed to furnish a house, for fuel, and for table expenses. The Book Concern furnished the amount needed.

[157] John Flavel Wright, D.D. (1795–*ca.* 1880), a native of North Carolina, joined the Virginia Conference in 1815 and transferred to Ohio in 1821. He served as presiding elder and, 1832–44, as book agent. During the Civil War he was chaplain of a Kentucky regiment. His son, John Reynolds Wright, of Cincinnati, was one of the early benefactors of Ohio Wesleyan University (Simpson, *op. cit.,* p. 966).

[158] Owing to numerous causes, such as charging to the presiding elders all books sent to the preachers to be sold through their circuits, some of the prominent men became hopelessly involved in debt to the Book Concern. In 1824 James Quinn owed the Concern $400, and that year the Ohio Conference resolved that in the case of James Quinn, "considering his labors and embarrassed situation, together with his doubts about part of the charges, we have thought it proper to cancel all but the above sum, viz–$269.70" ("Ohio Conference Minutes, 1824," in Sweet, *Circuit-Rider Days along the Ohio,* p. 254).

inary & also .... to Augusta College..... 8. The committy on boundries reported "the formation of a Michigan Conferance[159] embracing Michigan & the Maumee District, the ballance to be formed into two conferences divided by the national road. Report was adopted as a matter of recommendation to general conferance .... report .... made to the last Cincinatti conf (& laid on the table) concerning what relation baptised children hold to the church & what their privileges was called up and refered to General Conferance. A ressolution .... each preacher when admitted into full connection should pay $3 to the charter fund—& that those who are in full connection pay within 3 years the same..... passed—12 On Motion resolved that our delegates be instructed to use their endeavours to obtain a repeal of the law which bars the support of the wife of those preachers who marry under four years—13 A resolution, requesting of general conferance to define what relation Probationers hold to the church .... passed.[160]

Thursd Afternoon session..... 1. The report of the court to count the ballots of the election of Delegates[161] showed 11 elected Conferance then proceeded to elect the twelvth—2 .... to fix the place of holding the next conferances vis Chillicothe Mansfield & Ann Arbor provided there be three conferances but if only two Chillicothe & Mansfield— .... committy .... appointed to visit the Wyandot Mission & examin into the practicability of stocking the farm so as to render the mission independent of the Mission society. James Gilruth Henry O Sheldon & Thomas Thompson were appointed said committy..... committy for examination of candidates for .... ful connection— .... ordered that the first Friday in April be kept as a day

[159] The General Conference of 1836 created the Michigan Conference, which was to "embrace all that part of the State of Ohio not included in the Pittsburgh, Erie, Ohio, and Indiana Conferences, and all the territory of Michigan, except so much as is included in the Laporte District, Indiana Conference" (Sherman, *op. cit.,* p. 285).

[160] None of the above recommendations was enacted by the General Conference of 1836.

[161] The delegates chosen were Thomas A. Morris, editor of the *Western Christian Advocate,* who was elected a bishop; Jacob Young, David Young, Wm. H. Raper, Leroy Swormstedt, John Ferree, James B. Finley, Wm. B. Christie, James Quinn, John W. Wright, Augustus Eddy, and John H. Power. The reserve delegates were A. W. Elliott, R. O. Spencer, and James Gilruth. It is typical of Gilruth's modesty that he does not mention his selection as a reserve delegate.

of fasting & prayer.....The Bp Addressed the conference appropriately—Appointements were read—& Conferance adjourned About sundown.

Friday Aug 28. Rose about day brake—Made preparation to return to my familey—took my leave of Joseph Spragues about 9 A.M. Drove a little past [....] & fead & dined with a Mr James Pringle a presbyterian, who received me kindly—past Bluming bourgh & put up with A Mr Gillaspie Another presbyterian these took money of me for my lodging but I believe it was because they knew me not as a preacher—....

Sat Aug 29—....set off—fed by the road side—Fed & dined with a doc Clark in Oldtown who is a Brother—Left heare about 2 P.M. & shortly after was overtaken with a severe storm of wind & rain: in so much that I felt that I was exposed to considerable danger: but finding a place of low timber I halted till it passed over—it overthrew & broke down a good deal of timber—reached chillicothe about 5—put up with a Br Orr a wholesale grocer Met with, & bought Thomas' practice[162] for $3.....

*Sund Aug 30.....*preached with some liberty from Ps.119:1..... heard Br Robert O Spencer[163] preach on the Mystery of Godliness—....Heard Levi P Miller at night.....

*Mond. Aug 31.....*set out & drove to Br Colwells—fed & got brakefast—Drove to Br Groves tavern fed & dined—Reached Joseph Westlakes about ½ past 9 P.M. found his familey Well & on the mend from the Measels—& my own gone into Chiccamogga—....

*Tusd Sept 1.....*set out for Thomas Cherringtons—on my way found a collection of people to hear preaching—being pressed by the Pr (Wm Ferson a regular Baptist) I stoped & preached with good liberty & considerable feeling—Drove to Thomas Cheringtons & put

[162] Robert Thomas' *Modern Practice of Medicine,* published by Collins & Co., New York.

[163] Robert O. Spencer (1806–58), a native of Ohio, was, in 1834–35, presiding elder of Kanawha District, and was appointed by the conference of 1835 to Chillicothe. While preaching on Athens Circuit, 1827–28, he was instrumental in initiating a revival at Ohio University, at which Edward R. Ames, later bishop, and Joseph M. Trimble, were converted. For memoir see *Minutes, 1858,* pp. 298–99.

up & spent the balance of the day (vis from 3 P.M.) conversing about our friends etc.....

Wed Sept 2d Rose at day (slight frost) & set out to see Phillip Woolfersbarger with whom I took brakefast—after which I went to see Phillip Kouns[164] with whom I dined—I then set out for Samuel & Welling Westlakes reached there a little before sundown where I found my wife & children—spent the evening at Wellings till dark—when I & My wife walked over to Samuels & tarried all night. Day clear & warm.....

Thursd Sept 3..... we took our leave of Samuels & went to Wellings where we tarried till about 3 P.M.—taking our leave we went to Jacob Bosworths (where we found Mother Westlake) with whom we spent the evening—tarried all night.....Day mostly clear to bed about 10—

Frid Sept 4th..... about 9 we set out for the French Grant—W. W. & his wife accompanying us some Miles—about one we all stoped & fed our horses by the road side, & eat a social meal under the shade of the trees—Here we parted, we going on, & they returning home—We reached Vincent McCartneys on Johns Creek a little after dark here we put up for the night (found them on the eve of Moving to Ilinoise) Spent the evening till 10 principly conversing about the new countrays—day fine—.....

Sat Sept 5..... did not get off before 9—.....fed & dined on Cannons creek, near the head—soon after past 2 houses the inhabitants of which were sick with the small pox—after a hard days drive we Reached My Mothers[165] a little after dark—& found her well but learned that My brother was sick & also some of My sisters familey—Spent the evening in conversasion on a variety of subjects.....

Sund Sept 6..... visited my brother—then my sister & then went to meeting & heard Bernard A Casset & then Elijah H Field[166] preach—An appointment being given out for an evening meeting at a Br

[164] The Kounses were Gilruth's first wife's family.

[165] His mother lived on the Ohio River across from Greenupsburgh, now Greenup, Kentucky.

[166] Cassat had at the prevous conference been appointed to Burlington Circuit, in Marietta District; Field, to Chester Circuit, Marietta District.

Emorys (2 M. above) We all attend & I preached in a plain way from Heb xii.14.— ....

Mond Sept 7 Rose about sunup—spent the day till noon writting off the Minuts of conferance—visited My brother—Then Mother & myself & wife & my Br & his wife went in My waggon to see my sister—leaving them I went & got my horse shod—about dark we returned to Mothers—day cloudy—to bed at 9—

Tusd Sept 8..... about 9 I set out with my wife to see Father Kouns & the rest of my first wifes friends living in lawrence County—Reached Br Samuel Kouns about 2 P.M. here I found Father Kouns in a very infirm state—We took him in our waggon & went up to George Kouns—found them well—spent the evening conversing till 9—

Wed Sept 9..... after brakefast went up to Andrew Kouns—here we met with Nancy Shoot & Sarah Wilson (my first wifes sisters) where we all dined together—After dinner Father Kouns, & I, & my wife set out on our return to S Kouns accompanied by George Kouns & wife & N Shoot as far as their respective places—we also called to see each of G Ks daughters, 3 in No who are settled along the road—Reached S Ks about dusk—There being an appointment given out for me here I preached to [a] house full of people from Ps 119.1. but not much to my own sattisfaction—.....

Thurs Sept 10..... spent the morning viewing a tread saw-mill—Then I took leave of Father Kouns—I think for the last time in this life—he is fast failing—about 9 set out for the Grant—stoped a couple of hours at the Hanging Rocks (with Josiah Westlake a cousin of My wifes)—This is one of the principle Iron landings on the Ohio: there being a steem forge in opperation here. beside, this is the place of storage for exportation from several furnaces—arived at Mothers about dusk. day hot & hazy—to bed about 9.

Frid Sept. 11..... took My wife to see My Old farm & spend the afternoon with str Brush who is living on it.— ....

Sat Sept 12. Rose about sunrise—Spent the forepart of the day visiting some of My old neighbours—In the afternoon we had a social Meal together at Mothers All Mothers children with a number of he[r] grand children being present—perhaps this will be the last.—Spent the evening talking with my brother till 8.....

Sund Sept. 13. Rose about sunrise—Read in the Psalms & wrote in my journal till near 9—preached at 11 at Greenupsburgh in Kentucky (court house) from Rom I.16 with good liberty—& at Oaks S H on the opposite side of the Ohio at 3 P.M. from Ps 119.1 with good liberty —staid all night with my sister—Day clear & plesent.....

Mond Sept 14.....after brakefast I & my wife paid a visit to Mr Wm Duduit (My son in laws father) & after dinner we returned to my Mothers. in the afternoon we, with My Mother & Br & his wife paid a visit to Br Emorys—My brother & I also spent some time with Mr. Nathaniel Davison—Returned after dark to Mothers.....

Tusd Sept 15.....spent the day Making preparations for our return to Michigan—staid this night with Br. Wm. day clear (mostly).....

Wed Sept 16.—Rose earley—spent the day as yesterday—was on the point of setting out at 3 P.M. but concluded to tarry with Mother till Morning This perhaps will be the last nigh[t] I shall ever spend under her roof—she is failing fast in body—but I trust ripening for a better world—day pleasant—to bed about 10—....

The names of Post Offices in Detroit Dist.[167]—In

I *Farmington Circuit*

Livonia. in Wayne Co. M[ichigan] T[erritory]

Post Office	County
Farmington Franklin Pine Lake West bloomfield Paint Creek Pontiac Auburn Bloomfield Southfield Novi? Lyma Wall Lake	Oakland Co. MT.

II *In Mt Clemens circuit*

Post Office	County
Washington Romeo Ray Armanda [Armada] Salam Mt Vernon Shelby Mt Clemens	McComb County M.T.
Troy Royal Oak Oakland Rochester	Oakland Co. MT.

[167] This list is for 1834–35, made at the request of the Ohio Conference of 1834, which had appointed a committee to "collect information relative to post offices in the bounds of the Conference and transmit the same to the Agents at N. York" (MS "Minutes of Ohio Conference for 1834," photostat). Gilruth omits VI, which was Ypsilanti Circuit.

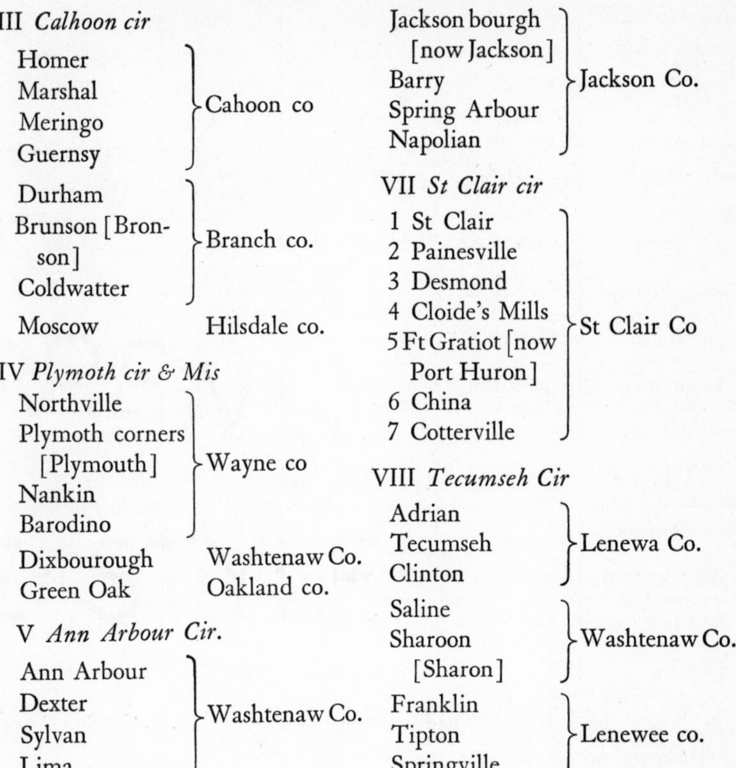

III *Calhoon cir*

Homer Marshal Meringo Guernsy	Cahoon co
Durham Brunson [Bronson] Coldwatter	Branch co.
Moscow	Hilsdale co.

IV *Plymoth cir & Mis*

Northville Plymoth corners [Plymouth] Nankin Barodino	Wayne co
Dixbourough	Washtenaw Co.
Green Oak	Oakland co.

V *Ann Arbour Cir.*

Ann Arbour Dexter Sylvan Lima	Washtenaw Co.

Jackson bourgh [now Jackson] Barry Spring Arbour Napolian	Jackson Co.

VII *St Clair cir*

1 St Clair 2 Painesville 3 Desmond 4 Cloide's Mills 5 Ft Gratiot [now Port Huron] 6 China 7 Cotterville	St Clair Co

VIII *Tecumseh Cir*

Adrian Tecumseh Clinton	Lenewa Co.
Saline Sharoon [Sharon]	Washtenaw Co.
Franklin Tipton Springville	Lenewee co.

Names of Circuits[168]	Times 1st	of 2d	qur 3d	Meetings 4th
Tecumseh	Oct 4.5	Dec.20.21	Feb.29 Mar.1	May 24.25
Calhoon Mis.	Oct 11.12	Dec.27.28	7.8.	30.31
Ann Arbour	Oct 18.19	Jan.3.4.	14.15	June 6.7
Ypsylanti	Oct 25.26	Jan 10.11	21 22	13.14
Plymoth	Nov 1.2.	17.18	28 29	20.21.
Farmington	Nov 8.9	24.25	Ap 4.5.	Camp commen Mon. June 22: 4 P.M. 27.28
Lapier			11 12	
Mt Clemens	Nov 15.16	31 J&1 Feb	18.19	July 4.5
St Clair	Nov 22.23	Feb 7.8.	25.26.	11.12
Detroit	Nov 29.30	14.15	May 2.3.	18.19

× Lapier q M Sashabaugh at Richard Brays.

[168] This was for the year 1834–35.

CHAPTER X

Letters of Orceneth Fisher, Methodist Preacher on Three Frontiers: Indiana, Texas, Oregon

THE life of Orceneth Fisher is typical of the frontier Methodist preacher in that he covered a large geographical area in his movements. For more than fifty years (1821–79) he helped to plant Methodism on three American frontiers: the Old Northwest, Texas, and the Pacific Coast. Fisher referred to himself as being "in the main a frontier man" and seems to have achieved his greatest happiness while engaged in the important task of bringing culture to the wilderness. Born of old New England stock at Chester, Windsor County, Vermont, November 5, 1803, he moved with his parents to Indiana Territory sometime before 1821. Leaving the Baptist church of his parents at the time of his conversion to Methodism, Fisher was soon called to preach and joined the Missouri Annual Conference in 1823, becoming a member of the Illinois Conference the following year. After an exploratory visit to Texas in 1839–40, he settled there in 1841 and joined the Texas Conference. Though a northerner by birth, he cast his lot with the southern church in the division of 1845 and continued to labor in Texas until 1855, when he transferred to the Pacific Conference of the Methodist Episcopal Church, South. As will be seen from the "Letters," he was instrumental in planting Southern Methodism in Oregon. His last period of active ministry (1870–79) was spent in Texas, where he died on August 28, 1880.

The letters here presented are in the possession of Fisher's descendants, Mrs. H. M. Little, Mrs. Fannie Fisher Simpson, and Thomas Asbury Fisher, of Austin, Texas; photostats are available in the library of the University of Texas. Included are two lengthy autobiographical letters, one telling of Fisher's life up to his Oregon ministry, the other of his work in Oregon. Several additional letters written during his active ministry on the Pacific Coast, although dating from the period after 1850, illustrate the continuation, on the newer American frontiers, of earlier frontier techniques of church expansion.

The most complete study of Fisher's life is the unpublished M.A. thesis by Robert E. Ledbetter, Jr., "Orceneth Fisher, Pioneer Methodist Preacher of Texas and the Pacific Coast" (University of Texas, 1938).

I

Corvallis, Oregon. Nov. 16, 1860

Rev. J. Spencer.

Dear Brother,

In brief reply to your inquiry, I state

1*st* I was born in the town of Chester, Vt. Nov. 5, 1803. My parents, Dr. David and Britania Fisher were both of the Baptist Church, rather Free Will Baptist in their belief.[1]

2*d* Of course I was not baptised in my infancy, which was a grievous stumbling block to me when I began to feel my own personal responsibility before God.

3 My early religious impressions were very early, perhaps about my seventh year. When I was about twelve years old my mother encouraged me to undertake the reading of the Bible through by course. This I did, and soon became interested in the contents; but when I came to the history of Abraham and read the terms of the covenant God made with him, and through him with all the world and sealed it with circumscision, I saw at once in the clearness of sun light, that the Gospel was the development of this great Covenant, and that Baptism now stood to men in the same relation that circumscision had formerly done, and as I was unbaptised, I was terribly afraid I was left out of the mercy of God altogether and my damnation sealed. Words cannot explain the trouble I endured on this account. I went to my mother in the anguish of my heart, but all in vain; she could give me little comfort by telling me that "Infant baptism was only a *human* invention!" etc. This very much discouraged my Bible reading; however, I still read the Bible occasionally, but tried to forget my fears and trouble as best I could. I was trained to fear God, to revere his name; to regard his Sabbath, though not so sacredly as, I think, I should have been. A little too much looseness in this department of my education, let me slide into bad company, where I was in great danger of learning bad habits. But by the mercy of God, his fear [illegible] from me. I never used His name profanely from the time

[1] In a letter to his son, Orceneth Asbury Fisher, June 6, 1868, he states further that his father was "Dr. David Fisher [Jr.]" and his mother was "Britania Chase, Daughter of Capt. Rufus Chase of Providence[,] Rhode Island. My father's father was Rev. David Fisher, of the Free Will Baptist Church."

I was old enough to know the import. I maintained a pretty fair morality; knowing however all the time that I must be born again or never inter [enter] into the Kingdom of God.

4 When between 11 and 17 years of age I was deeply convinced of my danger as a sinner in the sight of God, and especially as a *neglector* of the great Salvation. This conviction was the direct work of the Spirit of God upon my heart while at work by myself in the field. Such a flood of light all at once, (while I was musing) poured into me as fully revealed to me what I was, w[h]ither I was going, and what must be the fearful consequences if I still refused to be reconciled to God! I stood amazed, confounded, bewildered, and greatly terrified. I could not work, I could scarcely see for a time! I saw my former resolutions had been forgotten, God had been neglected, and I was taking the broad road to hell, or was at least about to do it. I tremble[d] in myself, and resolved to give myself to God at once and enter into his service. But such was my ignorance of the plan of salvation, and so unwilling was I that anyone should know that I was becoming religious, that it was several months before I felt any evidence of my acceptance with God, or any special encouragement in seeking him.

5 Having one day been discovered at secret prayer in the woods by three men who rode by me on horseback, I concluded it was useless to attempt longer to conceal my religious purposes, and began to converse on the subject with some religious friends who were Methodists. I soon found the benefit of this; they had gone that way before me and could tell much about it. Seeing the members of the church pray in their Prayer meeting, and seeing a friend of mine take up the cross and pray before he joined the church, I thought I must do so too. This was, however, a heavy cross, and the pain of it almost equal to the pain of sin. I perferred it however to the latter, and after..... [The next two pages of the manuscript are lost.]

My father of blessed memory, who had been firm in opposing me as a Methodist, up to this time, now entirely relaxed, changed his behaviour toward me, acknowledged his wrong, gave me liberty to go when and where I should think best to call sinners to repentance, and bid me God speed in the work! It came like a revelation from heaven! I took solemn leave of home to go out into the wide western world, I knew not whither, not doubting that God had a place for me some where in his vast heritage.[2]

In Smith's Settlement [Dearborn County] about seven miles from home I spent about a week. It was Christmas time [1822]. I could not pass my old friends and brethren without holding a meeting with them, and having held [one], another foll[o]wed as a matter almost of necessity, and another, and another, until the week was gone! and a glorious one it was. My own soul overflowed with the love of God incessantly day and night. Sometimes in walking out by myself my soul was so filled with the love of God that it seemed impossible to keep from shouting at the top of my voice.

The church was greatly revived during my stay here, and it was exceedingly difficult to get away from these holy and loving people. Some thought I was doing wrong to leave them. And after I had torn myself away and was gone this thing was for a short time a temptation to me, lest I disregard the voice of Providence in this matter; but having laid the whole subject before God in solemn prayer with an earnest desire to know his will and with a fixed determination by his grace to do it, the cloud soon passed away and I felt a sweet assurance within that I was in the path of duty. A few days ride brought me into the neighborhood of the camp ground where I had been in the summer before, the north end of the Charleston circuit, Mo. Conference, Jas. Armstrong preacher in charge.[3] Here I

[2] Fisher writes to his son: "I was converted to God in the town of Aurora, State of Indiana, ... joined the M.E. Church, March 1, 1821, [and] became a traveling preacher in 1822" (O. Fisher to O. A. Fisher, June 6, 1868).

One biographer says: "In February, 1821, he was converted and received into the Methodist Church by Rev. James Collard of the Ohio Conference, and shortly afterward began his ministry in the Missouri Conference when that Conference included all the territory northwest of the Ohio river" (newspaper obituary "Scrapbook" of Mrs. H. Simpson, a granddaughter). James Collard was serving the Lawrenceburg Circuit with J. P. Durbin. Aurora was one of the points on this circuit in the Miami District, Ohio Conference, in 1821 (*Minutes of the Annual Conferences of the Methodist Episcopal Church,* Vol. I: *1773–1828,* p. 367). Durbin later became one of the great leaders of Methodism. He was president of Dickinson College and was pastor of Union and Trinity churches in Philadelphia, in 1850 becoming missionary secretary. Under his leadership the great foreign missionary work was established.

[3] James Armstrong (1787–1834), a native of Ireland, had entered the ministry in 1821. Note that, at this time, Indiana and Illinois were included in the Missouri Conference, which had been erected in 1816. For memoir of Armstrong see *Minutes,* Vol. II: *1829–1839,* p. 344.

met with some acquaintances, and as I had a letter of introduction from Alexander Cummings,[4] P. E. and W. L. Draper and Wm. Lambden, preachers of the Lawrenceberg circuit,[5] to Sam'l Hamilton, P. E. of Indiana District of the Mo. Conference, I determined to wait the coming of the preachers on the circuit by whom I would find the whereabouts of the P. E.[6] In the meantime I was holding family, social, and general Prayer meetings, and God was with us in awakening and converting power. The day the preacher was to come I went to his meeting, but he was late, and the people insisted I should preach, so, tremblingly I went at it, looking every moment for the preacher, but God was with us, owned his word in power, and many hearts were deeply moved. When about two-thirds through my discourse, the preacher came and another with him. I closed rather abruptly to give place to him. He attempted to hold classmeeting, but so powerful was the work of God on the hearts of sinners and saints that some were crying aloud for mercy, and other[s] shouting for joy. Two were clearly converted.

Bro. Armstrong decided that I should remain with him until his Quarterly Meeting, (about 6 or 8 weeks) and that then he would have

[4] Alexander Cummins (1787–1823), a native of Albemarle County, Virginia, had joined the Western Conference in 1809 and was in 1822–23 presiding elder of Miami District, Ohio Conference, including eastern Indiana. For biography see *Methodist Magazine,* VII (1824), 225–227; also James B. Finley, *Sketches of Western Methodism* (Cincinnnati, 1855), pp. 372–78.

[5] Lawrenceburg Circuit, first called Enon Circuit, had been formed in 1810 out of the southern part of Whitewater Circuit. It lay in Jefferson, Dearborn, and other southeastern Indiana counties (William Warren Sweet, *Circuit-Rider Days in Indiana* [Indianapolis, 1916], p. 12). William H. Raper was assigned to the circuit in 1822–23; for biography see notes to the Gilruth "Journal" in the present volume. Lambdin (1784–1854), then a local preacher, was assigned by the presiding elder to travel with Raper. He had prevously done itinerant work in the Baltimore, Western, and Ohio conferences, and in 1825 joined the Pittsburgh Conference. At his death he was a member of the Memphis Conference of the Methodist Episcopal Church, South ("Memoir," *Minutes of the Annual Conferences of the Methodist Episcopal Church South,* Vol. I: *1845–1857,* pp. 524–25). His son, William McKendree Lambdin, became a prominent Methodist minister in Texas.

[6] For the history and personnel of the Indiana circuits in the year 1822–23 see Allen Wiley, "Methodism in Southeastern Indiana," *Indiana Magazine of History,* XXIII (1927), 266–74. These invaluable sketches, by a witness of the events, first appeared serially in the *Western Christian Advocate* from August 15, 1845, to December 11, 1846. Hamilton (1791–1854), described by Wiley as a "popular and useful" presiding elder, has been annotated in the Gilruth "Journal."

me employed with him by the Elder. We labored together a few days. At a night appointment bro. A. put me up to preach. 4 were converted. He preached the next night and 9 were converted. But soon bro. A. said I must take my own appointments, two weeks after him around the circuit. At the Quarterly Meeting, Bro. Hamilton the P. E. received me and sent me to Vincenns circuit, to supply the place of I. Ingersol, who had declined taking the work. This was another trial. About 80 had joined the church during my stay here, and I had become warmly attached to many and they as warmly attached to me. But duty had to be done and there was no time for parting. I arrived on the circuit on the 3*d* of March, 1823. It extended from Vincennes to the vicinity of Old Fort Harrision, up the Wabash river, and east into the forks of White River and up the east fork to Mt. Pleasant and above—and across the west fork near Black Creek.[7]

The circuit had been a considerable time without a preacher and was in consequence much dilapedated; I had no plan of it, and was under the necessity of hunting up the preaching places as best I could, these were sometimes far apart, and some times there were no roads, or next to none, and sometimes neither bridges nor ferries. In the spring the waters were high, and sometimes my boat was my horse, upon whom I made some serious adventures, through deep wide and rapid streams, with the water near the freezing point. One day in crossing the west fork of White river, I was in the water fording sometimes over my horse's back and sometimes swimming for about the day. But, thanks be to God, came out unharmed without the use of brandy, or any other stimulant then [than] the love of God and natural plain food.

I was on this work about seven months; filled, I believe about 26 or 28 appointments in four weeks; often preaching day and night besides holding class and Prayermeetings. Three hundred and eighteen were added to the church during that time, (a very few by letter)

[7] The area covered by the Vincennes Circuit was a considerable portion of west-central Indiana. The extent of the territory may be judged by a list of the preaching places three years later: "'In 1825, Vincennes included the following preaching places: In the county of Knox: Vincennes, Cane's, Thomas's, Snyder's, Teverbaugh's, Nicholson's, Hawkin's; in the county of Davis: Bethel Meeting-house, Stuckey's, Thomas Havill's, Widow Stone's, T. Stafford's, Ballon's; in the county of Martin: Hammond's, Clark's, Mount Pleasant, Love's, Maner's, in Green County; and back again, in Davis County, to Bratton's, Williams', Osmon's, and Florer's" (F. C. Holliday, *Indiana Methodism* [Cincinnati, 1873], p. 65).

making about 400, who had joined the church on both circuits where I had labored.

Rev. Job M. Baker,[8] and several local preachers aided me on this circuit. One of the latter, Rev. John Miller,[9] has since won a reputation as a travelling preacher. Quite a number of the converts on this circuit afterwards entered the ministry.

At the next session of the conference, which was held in St. Louis, I was received on trial and appointed to the Illinois circuit, including the towns of Bellville, Lebanon, Edwardsville, and Alton, and their vicinities, Rev. Jno. Dew, in charge, and Rev. S. H. Thompson, P. E.[10] on this circuit, we had a good work and about 150 accessions to the church. Some of these became ministers, among whom was Rev. Smith L. Robinson,[11] who served the church with great efficiency a few years, and fell at his post full of holy honors. Next year I formed the Boon[s]ville circuit, Indiana.[12] About two hundred were added to the church, among whom was Dr. A. Talbot, who became a distinguished minister. My next appointment was Mt. Vernon Circuit, Illinois.[13] Here we had a good work, but in the midst of it my health

[8] Dr. Job M. Baker (1794–1878) died in Texas after sixty years spent in the local and itinerant ministry (Homer S. Thrall, *A Brief History of Methodism in Texas* [Nashville, 1894], pp. 68–69, 186).

[9] John Miller joined the Missouri Conference in 1823, the Illinois in 1824, and the Indiana in 1832 (Holliday, *op. cit.*, pp. 264–65).

[10] This was the eighth session of the Missouri Conference and met on October 23, 1823, Bishop McKendree presiding. For biographical data on Dew and Thompson, see notes 10 and 18 to "Journal of the Illinois Conference for 1824," in the present volume.

[11] Smith L. Robinson (1806–36) was a native of Kentucky who joined the Illinois Conference in 1826 ("Memoir," *Minutes,* Vol. II: *1829–1839,* p. 572).

[12] The Conference which appointed him to the Boonsville Circuit was the joint meeting of the ninth session of the Missouri Conference and the first for the newly created Illinois Conference (see "Journal of the Illinois Conference for 1824," in the present volume).

[13] The session of the Illinois Conference at which Fisher received this appointment met at Charleston, Indiana, August 25, 1825. Fisher writes: "I was ordained Deacon by bishop McKendree in the town of Charleston Ind 1825 . . . ." (O. Fisher to O. A. Fisher, June 6, 1868). Just one month later, Fisher states that "I was married to Miss Elizabeth Watts, daughter of Rev. Benjn. Watts, (your mother) St. Clair County, Ill, Sept. 25, 1825" (*ibid.*). The ceremony was performed by Rev. Samuel H. Thompson, Fisher's presiding elder. Elizabeth Watts was born January 12, 1805, in Jackson County, Georgia. Her parents were Rev. Benjamin Watts and Elizabeth (Key) Watts, who were natives of Virginia.

(which had been failing for years under my severe labors and exposure to the severe cold of the prairies in the winter,) so far gave way that I was compelled to rest.[14] I did not again permanently resume the regular work until 1837, but as my health and strength admitted I labored far and nigh, holding camp, two-days, and other meetings, and administering baptism to hundreds (as well as the Lord's Supper) where there were no ordained ministers to do those things. In this way I often supplied the place of a presiding elder over a large extent of country. My residence was the greater part of the time in Nashville, Illinois. I believe there are few traveling preachers now who do more work than I did then, and all without fee or reward, save in a few instances, and as I had a rising family, and was myself without means it was absolutely necessary that I should labor with my own hands for my own and my family's support.[15] And as the country was new, and the climate rigorous in winter, and sickly in summer, my labors were often very heavy.[16] In 1837, I resumed the regular work and was stationed in Carlyle, the next two years on the Waterloo circuit, and in 1840 in Springfield.[17] In all these places God

[14] He was granted the superannuate relation by the Illinois Conference at Bloomington, Indiana, September 28, 1826. However, he was ordained an elder by Bishop Roberts at Mount Carmel, Illinois, September 23, 1827. His ordination parchment is in the library of the University of Texas.

[15] During his period of superannuation, five children were born to them: Mary Sophronia, in Franklin County; Electa Chase, in St. Clair County; and Orceneth Asbury, James Armstrong, and Sarah Elizabeth, in Washington County at Nashville.

[16] A biographer has this additional word to say on this period of his life: ". . . . At the close of the year [1826], his health having failed, he was granted a superannuated relation, in which he continued three years. Then, in 1829, he was sent to Brownsville Circuit as a super-numerary; but, his health being still inadequate to the work of the itinerancy, he was again placed on the superannuated list, in which he remained until 1834, when he located. He settled at Nashville, in Washington County, and engaged in the practice of medicine . . . .") James Leaton, *History of Methodism in Illinois* [Cincinnati, 1883], p. 196).

[17] An Ohio newspaper editor, after a visit to the city, described the Methodist Church as being "a modest-looking meetinghouse, which speaks more for the simple piety of the inhabitants, than the ostentatious taste of the citizens . . . ." (Paul M. Angle, *Here I Have Lived* [Springfield, 1935], p. 86). When Fisher went to Springfield, the state capitol was in process of construction, and the Senate met in his church (Randall Parrish, *Historic Illinois* [Chicago, 1905], p. 314). This is the period of the early law practice of Abraham Lincoln in the city, since he had moved there from New Salem in 1837. Fisher often related to his children that the young lawyer attended his services (John C. Simmons, *History of Southern Methodism on the Pacific Coast* [1886], p. 141).

was with us, and good was done. On Waterloo 1839 we had a glorious work, but here I fell again by sickness right in the midst of a glorious revival. In the winter of 1839–40, I visited Texas, and in 1841 received a regular transfer to that work, where I remained until the spring of 1855.[18] My last 5 appointments in Texas were on Districts in East Texas. Prior to that I had labored in the Texas Conference; three years in Houston City, where I started and edited and published the Texas Christian Advocate for the first year. During my stay of 14 years in Texas God was with us, often in great power and thousands were added to the church; about 2400 on the several districts I traveled in East Texas. I could report many instances of divine power of the most thrilling character, but it would make this article too long.[19]

In 1855 I was transferred to the Pacific Conference,[20] in which I still

[18] Upon his return from Texas and while in Springfield, Illinois, Fisher published his *Sketches of Texas in 1840*. It was an immigrant guide to the Republic, recording the observations of the author during his stay in that region. As an indication that Fisher meant to return for permanent settlement, he petitioned for and was granted a conditional certificate for 320 acres of land by the Board of Land Commissioners of San Augustine County, Texas, on December 28, 1839.

[19] During his preliminary visit to Texas, in 1839–40, Fisher served the Brazoria Circuit. In December, 1841, after removing from Illinois, he became a member of the newly formed Texas Conference and was appointed to serve Washington-on-the-Brazos. In 1844–45 he acted as senate chaplain to the Congress of the Republic of Texas. After a year of retirement he was in January, 1846, stationed in Houston by the new Western Texas Conference, returned there in 1847, and in 1848 appointed to the Houston "African Mission." In addition, he edited the *Texas Christian Advocate,* founded in 1847 by R. B. Wells, his son-in-law, at Brenham, under the title of the *Texas Christian Advocate and Brenham Advertiser;* in the following year this became the *Texas Wesleyan Banner,* organ of the Texas Conference. Becoming presiding elder of the Nacogdoches District of the East Texas Conference in 1850–51, he served successively the Palestine and San Augustine districts, until he went to California in 1855. During this first period of his Texas labors he published several tracts: the *Baptismal Catechism* (Houston, 1849); *The Christian Sacraments* (Nacogdoches, 1851); and *History of Immersion as a Religious Rite* (Rusk, 1852). His second marriage took place on May 15, 1848, to Miss Rebecca Jane Gilleland, who had come with her parents from Philadelphia to Refugio County, Texas, in 1837. Mrs. Fisher, who organized the "Daughters of the Republic of Texas" and served as its first president, has been called the "Mother of Texas," and her portrait hangs in the state capitol (see *Texas State Historical Association Quarterly,* III [1899–1900], 209–13).

[20] The Pacific Conference of the Methodist Episcopal Church, South, was organized by the General Conference of 1854 to include "all the State of California, and that part of the Territory of New Mexico west of the Rocky Mountains." From this area was taken, in 1866, the Columbia Conference, including northern California, Oregon, and Washington Territory and, in 1870, the Los Angeles Conference (P. A. Peterson,

labor. My appointments have been San Francisco, 1855, Stockton, 1856–7. San Francisco District 1858–59. Oregon District 1860–61. During my second year I edited and pu[blished the *Pacific Methodist,* which still] lives and flourishes under the editorial skill of Rev. O. P. Fitzgerald.[21] God has given me many souls in California and Oregon. And as in my former fields of labor, so here, some have already entered the ministry and are bringing other[s] to God.

Oregon is a new field of labor for Southern Methodists, where we meet with a good deal of opposition, and yet also of encouragement. We have already between 300, and 400 members, and hope for a rich harvest. It will be seen by the preceeding narative that I have been in the main a frontier man. Of course I have not enjoyed those facilities for acquiring literature that those who have remained among the Colleges and Libraries have enjoyed. Still I have made some acquaintances with the Hebrew and Greek Languages, and have written and published several works, one on Baptism and the Lord's Supper and the History of Immersion, a large octavo, which has received the approval of several of our Bishops, and several of our conferences, besides the commendation of several distinguished and learned ministers of other denominations; among whom I have the pleasure of naming W A. Scott D. D.[22] of the Presbyterian Church, San Francisco, Cal. I could say much more, but perhaps I have already drawn out these sketches too far. My purpose is still to work for God while I live. I have suffered much in the flesh with several courses of fever in Illinois which reduced me to a mere skeleton of skin and bone, with a deep consumption and yellow fever in Texas, have had my bones broken, spine erreparantly [*sic*]; have been several times reported dead, and yet

---

History of the Revisions of the Discipline of the Methodist Episcopal Church, South [Nashville, 1889], p. 225). The Methodist Episcopal church had set up in the same area an Oregon and California Mission Conference in 1848, from which its Oregon Conference was set off in 1852.

[21] Oscar Penn Fitzgerald (1829–1911), author, historian, and biographer of Southern Methodism, became a bishop of the Methodist Episcopal Church, South, in 1890.

[22] William Alexander Scott, D.D., LL.D. (1813–85), a native of Bedford County, Tennessee, had graduated from Princeton Theological Seminary in 1834 and was licensed the following year by the presbytery of Louisiana, serving from 1843 to 1854 as pastor of the First Presbyterian Church, New Orleans. In 1854 he came to California as a pioneer Presbyterian preacher (Edward A. Wicher, *The Presbyterian Church in California, 1849–1927* [New York, 1927], pp. 89–95).

thank God, I am alive and so labor more in the ministry than any man of my acquaintance, To God be all the glory Amen. I hope to preach the gospel in Mexico before I die.[23]

O. FISHER

II

SAN FRANCISCO, CALA
April 30, 1855

MY DEAR ASBURY,

I have just time before the sailing of the steamer, to say that we are here by the blessing of God, in good health and good spirits, hoping to be owned of God in His good cause in this land of gold and sin. We find some good people here, Some of our own Houston and Texas acquaintances, who seem very glad indeed to see us. This is my station for this year, But we lack a house to worship in, but hope soon to overcome this difficulty. We are pleased with the country, and think we shall be more so as we become better acquainted with it. There is nothing like winter or summer here, yet we can see snow every clear day. The production[s] of the country are enormous. We were awfully seasick but that is all over now. We got here in time to meet the conference and had a pleasant meeting with the preachers.[24]

[23] During the Civil War he had opportunity to begin mission work in Mexico, but his labors there proved unsuccessful (see Letter IX, n. 44, below).

[24] When Fisher arrived in California, the 1855 session of the Pacific Conference was meeting, during which he was invited to address the body. Bishop O. P. Fitzgerald describes the occasion in this manner: "Below medium height, plainly dressed, and with a sort of peculiar shuffling movement as he went down the aisle, he attracted no special notice except for the profoundly reverential manner that never left him anywhere. But the moment he faced his audience and spoke, it was evident to them that a man of mark stood before them. They were magnetized at once, and every eye was fixed upon the strong yet benignant face, the capacious blue eyes, the ample forehead, and massive head, bald on top, with silver locks on either side. His tones in reading the Scripture and the hymns were unspeakably solemn and musical. The blazing fervor of the prayer that followed was absolutely startling to some of the preachers, who had cooled down under the depressing atmosphere of the country. It almost seemed as if we could hear the rush of pentecostal wind and see the tongues of flame. The very house seemed to be rocking on its foundations. By the time the prayer had ended, all were in a glow, and ready for the sermon. The text I do not now recall to mind, but the impression made by the sermon remains. I had seen and heard preachers who glowed in the pulpit—this man burned. His words poured forth in a molten flood, his face shone like a furnace heated from within, his large blue eyes flashed with the lightning of impassioned sentiment, and anon swam in pathetic appeal that no heart could resist. Body, brain, and spirit, all seemed to feel the mighty afflatus. His very frame seemed to ex-

I hope to get a letter from you soon—Pray all of you for us, we shall write more after a while. I have written to the Advocate, and must refer you to that for further particulars. Love to all my dear children and all of you. Your father,

O. FISHER

III

STOCKTON, CALIFORNIA
Oct. 3, 1856.

MY DEAR ASBURY,

Yours of 9th Aug. has just come to hand. I am truly glad and thankful to God that I have at least *one* son in the work of God's holy ministry.[25] I am glad you have begun at *Houston,* it will be of great advantage to you. Fear not the face of man. Put your trust in God. Let him be your strength. And nothing can stand before you. "Have faith in God," and fear not. "The path of duty is the path of safety." Yea, and of happiness too.

May God speed you, my Son, in His glorious work, and give you *thousands* of *souls* to your ministry.

The Bishop (Kavanaugh)[26] and the preachers here are very unwilling that I should leave *now.* Several preachers are talking of

---

pand and the little man who had gone into the pulpit with shuffling step and downcast eyes was transfigured before us. When, with radiant face, upturned eyes, and upward sweep of his arm, and trumpet voice, he shouted, "Halleluiah to God!" the tide of emotion broke all barriers, the people rose to their feet, and the church reechoed with their responsive halleluiahs. The new preacher from Texas that night gave some Californians a new idea of evangelical eloquence, and took his place as a burning and shining light among the ministers of God on the Pacific Coast.

" 'He is the man we want for San Francisco!' exclaimed the impulsive B. T. Crouch, who kindled into a generous enthusiam under that marvelous discourse" (*California Sketches* [Nashville, 1897], II, 133–35). Fisher was appointed to San Francisco by Bishop Andrew, who presided over the session (*Minutes* [*South*], Vol. I: *1845–1857,* p. 572).

[25] Orceneth Asbury Fisher was licensed to preach in Houston in the summer of 1856 and was admitted on trial to the Texas Conference in December, during the session at Gonzales. He served the church for more than thirty years (Macum Phelan, *A History of Early Methodism in Texas* [Nashville, 1924], p. 379).

[26] Hubbard Hinde Kavanaugh, D.D. (1802–84), was a native of Clark County, Kentucky, who joined the Kentucky Conference in 1823. He was elected bishop of the Methodist Episcopal Church, South, in 1854 (see A. H. Redford, *Life and Times of H. H. Kavanaugh, D.D.* [Nashville, 1884]).

leaving, and if I should leave now the great work would suffer. My purpose was, that, if it were necessary for me to return on Ann, and Sterlings account I would do so as soon as possible.[27] If not, I should feel it my duty to remain here for the present.

Ministers have much more to contend against here than in Texas, enough sometimes to make the stout hearts quail; but you know it never has been your father's practice to quail, or back out in times of danger and hardship. I boast not. God has enabled me to stand at my post and do my duty. But the scale is turning here. God has recently given his servants some glorious victories. We have just closed a camp-meeting about 15 miles from this place, which held for 19 days. *Seventy-nine* were added to the church, and several more converted! Such a work has never before been known, I suppose, in California. Let God have all the glory. Next Thursday, God willing, we are to commence another, about 5 miles from this city. Expectation is up, God give us great success.

I have sent Mr. Wells a power of Attorney to attend to my land business in Texas, as I have not yet obtained titles to all my lands. And I have remitted to him $100, to help meet the expenses of Anna's schooling. My desire was, if it suited all around, that Anna should live with her sister Mary, as they say they have a good school at Gatesville and the expenses, all around, would be 50 percent less, but above all, I know Mary to be a devoted Christian, and a good governess, so that I should feel that she would be safer there than anywhere else away from me. I have a great respect for, and confidence in Mr. Miller, as a *Presbyterian,* but Presbyterian religion will not do for Methodists. God has graciously revealed to us more than He has to them, *and we must not go back*. If she still remains at Mr. Miller's, I hope you will freely correspond with her, and with Sterling also, and keep them posted on the great subject of Religion. My greatest concern for my children is that they may be *saved*. Oh how I feel for those in Houston! Do they attend the M. E. Church at all? Have they entirely forgotten their gray headed father's last admonition? Have they turned away from the Lord's house to go to Balls, and parties of pleasure, the

[27] He refers to two of his children, both still in their teens, whom he had left with relatives in Texas. The spiritual state of his children troubled him during his early sojourn on the West Coast, and we find frequent mention of them. Apparently this reason, coupled with his early failure in San Francisco, led him to think of returning to Texas.

feasts of Satan? Will they wade through the prayers and admonitions and tears of their father and mother down to hell? Oh God! have mercy upon them, and undeceive them! let them see that they have turned away from their best friends and their own mercies! Their apostacy will give them poor comfort in the day of death! I hope my son you will still pray for them; and assure them that their father ceases not to pray for them in this far off land. I have written Anna, but have as yet received no answer. Is Sterling still religious? Oh! the anxiety I feel for him and Anna! Write to me soon, and write in full. I hope you will succeed in getting into the regular work at conf. Give my love to all my old friends. Ma joins me in love to all. Pray for us,
Your father

O. Fisher

IV

San Francisco, Cal.[28]
April 19, 58

My very dear Asbury,

I have just returned from a tour of my dist[rict] and read a letter from you under date of March 11*th,* and one from Sterling, dated Feb. 27*th*. I heartily thank God for his grace to both of you. Sterling seems to be truly pious and has set in to learn[ing] in earnest. May God speed him.

I am surprised by two items in the contents of your letter, and one in his. First, you both write that you have received no letter from me for a long time! And yet I have punctually answered every letter, unless the one you wrote before your conference, and then, I knew not where to address you. I believe I have written you two or three letters to Waco.

The second item in yours is the reports that you state are afloat concerning us in California! We have not the least notion of any such thing. There is here no plan on foot or any talk of a union of the two

[28] Fisher was now presiding elder of the San Francisco District, which in the conference year 1857–58 included the following charges: San Francisco Station and Oakland, San Jose, Contra Costa, Santa Clara Circuit, Gilroy and Santa Cruz, Los Angeles, Petaluma and Bodega, Russian River, Sonoma and Napa, and Suisun (*Minutes* [*South*], Vol. I: *1845–1857*, pp. 805–6).

Methodist Churches here. If the General Conference should cast us off, which I know they will not, we should not join the North, but set up for ourselves. The reason we did not send delegates to the General Conference is that it would take two of our best men away so long as to consume the whole year, and cost a large amount of money. We could not well spare either men or money, especially the men. The North preache[r]s, many of them, are doing us all the harm they can, and if a charge of ours should be left for a short time without a pastor, they would be sure to take advantage of it if possible, and try to proselyte our members. They are often raising the cry, that we cannot succeed, or that the two churches will unite soon.—that is, that the Southern Methodists will all soon join the North Church!! and so try to make proselytes. We want a few more efficient men to occupy important places, and a little more Missionary money to enable us to send men to new teritory. Dr. T. O. Ellis[29] is doing a good work in Los Angelos, the southern part of my District, 500 miles southwest of this place. But he needs at least one man to help him. We need two men for Oregon, as we hardly know ho[w] to spare a man from the work here for that purpose. We have some young men preparing for the work, but we need *now* the *strong* men. Whenever you shall see your way clear in the order of God to come to this country I shall be glad to greet you here. Sterling informs me he is likely to get the money due me in Sabine County. This will pay his board a good while and clothe him also, about ($184) one hundred and eighty four dollars. I hope he will get a good education. I confess, I feel a degree of uneasiness about Annie. I wish she were out of Houston. I have no doubt her sister will do well by her except in religion. Harvey[30] told me the last time I saw him, that he had *"no use for the Bible."* My earnest daily prayer is that God will keep her uncorrupted. I pray she may not think of marrying a man without religion and of established character. I don't want her to think of marrying at all until she is of age, unless an extraordinary opportunity should offer, You know Sarah's misfortune by a hasty marriage. I hope and believe

[29] Dr. Thomas O. Ellis was in October, 1858, made presiding elder of the new Los Angeles District (*Minutes* [*South*], *1858,* p. 91).

[30] Harvey Allen was Electa Chase Fisher's husband. He was one of the three Allen brothers who bought the land on Buffalo Bayou, laid out and named the city of Houston.

you will use your influence to keep your sister right in all things; but when she is so far away from you and so exposed, as I fear, to bad company. Be sure my son you have a fathers prayers night and day. Ma and Becca send their love to you. Fannie says, "Tell him if he don't come down here I won't give him no banquet; and if he don't write to me I won't come to see him nomore."[31] Pray for us. Write soon, love to all. Your affectionate father

O. Fisher

I have sent to N. York for an engraved likeness of myself for my book, which will delay the publication till the last of June. The work is now going through the press here. 5000 copies, 8 vo. about 300 pages. It would be useless to send it to Nashville while Dr. Summers is in the office; he admits of no rival. I could send it to Texas.[32]

V

Santa Claree Cal. Feb. 15, 1859[33]

My dear Asbury,

Yours of 3 Jan. came to hand lately. I wrote you at Waco so late you did not get it I suppose. I should have been pleased indeed if you had transferred to this con[ference]—tho—as I told you before, I did not feel at liberty even to request it on account of Annie and Sterling. Yet if you were here you could help me much in the work. I purpose, if God will, to visit Oregon in May next, and need two or three good men to go with me. I wish Bro. Kolbe[34] would be here by that time.

[31] He refers to his wife and two daughters, Rebecca and Frances. Both of the girls were born in East Texas.

[32] This concerns another edition of his book, *The Christian Sacraments,* which was published in an enlarged edition at San Francisco in 1858. Dr. Thomas O. Summers was book editor of the Publishing House of the Methodist Episcopal Church, South, with offices at Nashville, from 1850 to 1882.

[33] At the session of the Pacific Conference in October, 1858, he had been returned to the San Francisco District, which this year was enlarged to include Oregon (*Minutes* [*South*], *1858,* p. 90).

[34] John C. Kolbe was an old Texas friend. He reached California in the spring, having been transferred from the Texas to the Pacific Conference in November, 1858 (*Minutes* [*South*], *1858,* p. 78).

I am glad to hear of the progress of Sterling. I hope he still intends to go into the ministry.

I do earnestly pray that Annie will not think of marrying a wicked man or anyone out of the Methodist Church. Is she still devoted to God? Oh! how my soul yearns over her! Now is the *slippery* time of her life. May God preserve her from all evil and especially from all evil attachments, and guide her safely to glory. Pray for her and often write her. I have not had a line from her, nor Electa, nor Sarah, for a long time! Why don't they write to their father? I have answered all their letters. I fear Sterling has not received all my letters, I have answered all his.

I pray God to be with you this year my son, and to enable you to make Satan's seat so warm with heavenly fire that he shall be compelled to give the ground. What are difficulties in the way of omnipotence? Have faith in God and go ahead.

My dear wife is just getting about again after three or four months sickness, of which I wrote you before. She gave premature birth to another son, who lived only about seven hours and then quietly passed away to a better world. She now has *three* little sons in heaven, I *four* and one daughter, beside your own dear mother. How *many* and how *strong* ties to Glory! May we all meet them there in full gospel maturity! Did you get my book? How do you like it? What would it sell there?

Write by *Overland Mail.* Three cents will pay on that route. I understand the bishop intends to come by that route.[35] If you feel like coming with him, *Come along*. Pray for us. God bless you my son,

Your father
O. Fisher

Bro Ausborn Harris at Milam Texas has one hundred and ten dollars in money for me out side of that he was to pay to Sterling. I have authorized him to pay it to you for Annie's schooling. This will

[35] Bishop George Foster Pierce (1811–84), a native of Greene County, Georgia, and son of Lovick Pierce, D.D., became president of Emory College in 1848 and bishop of the Methodist Episcopal Church, South, in 1854. For his interesting account of this visit to California see George G. Smith, *The Life and Times of George Foster Pierce, DD., LL.D.* (Sparta, Ga., 1888), chap. xiv.

authorize you to draw on him for it. It is for *rent* on my land there. It is all I can do now. I hope the Bre[n]ham property will increase in value by delay. Your father

O. Fisher

VI

Santa Claree Cal.
April 8, 1859.

Rev. O. A. Fisher

My dear Son,

Yours came duly to hand and I hasten to answer.

If you will take 4 ounces of pulverized Myrrh, one ounce of best Cayenne pepper, and one pound or 1½ lb of Sugar, mix well and melt into a candy; and take a little of this frequently, it will relieve and cure your throat. If necessary moisten it with a tincture of Lobelia. This is better than anything that I have found in the Shops. Chewing and swallowing the juice of the Prickly Ash bark frequently may answer every purpose. Be cautious how you tamper with *caustics,* or poisons of any kind.

I wish you were here. I need you in my work. One of our preachers has gone home on account of affliction.

I have just closed, or rather left a good Quarterly Meeting at Redwood City, when for the first time, in that place, we organised a society of ten. We left the meeting in progress with the young preacher. Ma's health is still not very good, Your little sisters are in fine health.

Bro Kolbe and Sister Kolbe are with us in fine health.

Tomorrow I leave for another Quarterly Meeting, and have one every week. I should feel much better Satisfied to have you here, and then your conference is full compared to this. And where should the Sons work if not with their father? If God opens your way, Come, and He will bless you. Our North Brethren in Oregon and here are almost ready to swallow the ground with rage because *we* are going to Oregon! But God will make the wrath of man to praise him. All would be very glad to see you.

All send love to you. God bless you and guide you in all things.

Pray for us, Your father

O. Fisher

VII
INTRODUCTION OF SOUTHERN METHODISM INTO OREGON[36]

Rev. J. C. Simmons,
DEAR BROTHER,

At your request I send you the following sketch of my visit to and labors in Oregon by which means it pleased God to give us a foothold in that country.

In the year 1857 while I was publishing and editing the *Pacific Methodist* in the city of Stockton, Cal., I received a few names of subscribers from Oregon which opened the way for a personal corespondence by which I became aware that there was a large population in that country who were in sympathy with our Church and would rejoice to see our ministers among them. In the meantime, our lamented brother, Rev. J[ames] C. Stewart had visited that country in the interest of the Pacific Methodist College[37] and had made acquaintance of many who were longing for the blessings of Southern Methodism. At the close of the first year of the paper I retired from its management and was put in charge of the San Francisco District, as Presiding Elder. During that year, 1858, my corespondence with Oregon friends was continued until, from all the light obtained, I became fully satisfied that it was my duty to visit Oregon in the name of the Lord. Accordingly, as I was returned to the same District for the year 1859, I requested the President of the Conference to attach Oregon to my work, and named "Independence," as a circuit in Oregon.[38] This gave me authority from the Church to visit Oregon as her legal representative and to do whatever in the premises might seem proper to be done. Some of my distinguished brethren throught it "A wild goose chase." But I did not think so, but felt, after much prayer and close self-examination, that I was called of God to that work. About the first of June, 1859 I took passage at San Francisco for Oregon on the steamer Pacific,

[36] This historical sketch, in letter form, was written *ca.* 1878.

[37] The Pacific Methodist College was at Vacaville, California. It was later moved to Santa Rosa (Matthew Simpson [ed.], *Cyclopaedia of Methodism* [Philadelphia, 1878], p. 689).

[38] The president of the Pacific Conference session at Stockton, October, 1858, was the Reverend William R. Gober, as no bishop had arrived from the East.

Capt. Patterson Master. My wife and one child, Rev. J. C. Kolbe and wife, a late transfer from Texas, Rev. J. L. Porter, and Mrs. Stanley, of Sonoma, were in the company. The weather was not rough, but as we steamed out of the Golden Gate, we found ourselves litterly on the top of a "Mountain Wave." So grand a heap of water I never saw before, nor have I since. For sometime we were steaming right along on this high mountain of water! It was inexpressably grand. Then we reached the mouth of the Columbia River, the sea was too rough to cross the bar, and the Captain steamed up Puget Sound to Esquimalt. Here we remained till the evening of the next day, which was Sunday, giving us a chance to visit Her Majesty's young city, Victoria, where I made the acquaintance of Rev. Dr. George Evans[39] of the Canadian Methodist Church, who pressed me to preach for him, and afterward took us with him to lunch. It was a pleasant occasion. God was with us and we were refreshed in spirit, and the odor of it is still sweet, now after 19 years are past. May it remain forever. The scenery along the sound and around Victoria is grand and beautiful in the extreme. Old Mt. Baker, with its mantle of snow, stands out in bold solitary grandeur, while Olympus and other peakes stand around as royal guards. The islands and the mainlands are all dressed in the richest green. Here we met two of Her Majesty's ships, who exchanged the salutes with ours, both with guns and music, which echoing from the adjoining hills over the deep waters was soul stirring. Here we saw a great many half breed Indians, with their canoes, cooking and eating their salmon. These half breeds are the produce of the "Hundson Bay Company." They took no white women with them into the Indian country, and hence this mixture. I think there are very few full bloods left. Victoria is a thriving place, pleasantly located, about five miles from the landing. Sunday evening we were called aboard and the next morning we crossed the dangerous bar at the mouth of the Columbia river and steamed up that grand Mississippi of the West. It is a grand and noble river, dividing Oregon from Washington Teritory. The scenery for some distance from the mouth up is wild, rough and forbidding. Astoria is a small old town at the south side of the entrance.

[39] *Ephraim* Evans, D.D., was the Wesleyan Methodist minister at Victoria, Vancouver Island, 1858–65 (George H. Cornish, *Cyclopaedia of Methodism in Canada* [Toronto and Halifax, 1881], p. 88).

About 100 miles from the ocean we enter the mouth of the Willamette, a noble river, rising near the south line of the State and running nearly due north about 150 miles enters the Columbia. 12 miles up this brings us to Portland, the commercial emporium of the State. Here we changed steamers, and 12 miles further up the river brings us to the falls; where we change steamers again. The river here has a fall of about 50 feet, affording an immense water power. There are three ways of getting passengers over this fall. An elevator, raised and lowered by water power. 2. A long flight of outside steps. Very poorish. 3. A walk around of about one mile on foot. I ascended the steps. A mill stands on the bluff, over hanging the river below. Above the mill we found a gallant steamer waiting for us. As we moved out into the current I could but cringe at the idea of the peril we should be in if anything should stop the working of the engine! Nothing in the world could save us from going over the falls! Tradition says, "A steamer did go over, some years ago, and plunged into the deep with all aboard, and never rose again." I felt relieved in proportion as the distance between us and the falls increased. The sceenery along the river is wild and romantic. Some of the places seemed so natural I could hardly help exclaiming, "I have been here before in my dreams!" As we ascended the river we found, "Balm of Gilliad" trees along the sandy shores like young cotton woods along the Mississippi. The sun was warm and balm with its fragrant odor filled the air.

We passed the towns of Salem (the capital of the State) and Albany, and landed at Independence, I think more than 100 miles from the mouth of the river. Here I met an old California friend, Capt. Samuel Lyon, late Master of the Lodge of Masons in Stockton, Cal. I had been his Chaplain. He was now grand lecturer of the State. He was overjoyed at meeting me. Of course, we had a hearty welcome at his house. We soon made the acquaintance of Hon. B. F. Burch, a Southern Methodist, and a Mason. Bro. and Sister Kolbe went to bro. Gabriel Hardison's, one of my correspondents, where they found a pleasant home.

The meeting of the Grand Lodge of the State, at Eugene City, was approaching, and I was pressed to meet with them. Matters were soon arranged for that purpose. We took steamers to Corvallis and there procured a conveyance to Eugene City, 30 miles. It was warm and dirty, and we merely had time to wash and eat our dinner till I was requested by the unamious vote of the Grand Lodge to take the Orator's stand, he having failed to come. God was gracious in assisting me. I showed the connection between Masonry and true Religion, both before and after Christ, and impressed upon Masons the unspeakable importance of pushing their principles to secure admittance into the celestial Lodge above, where the Universal Grand Master presides. The Address was well received and a vote of Thanks presented. The installation of the Grand Officers immediately followed, and I soon found I had as many friends in Oregon at least as there were members of the Grand Lodge, and they were not few. Indeed Oregon was already quite a Masonic state. My introduction to the Fraternity here opened the way for addresses before several subordinate lodges in other places. This also opened my way for preaching the Gospel in almost every direction. I spent a few days in Eugene City, preached several times to large congregations, and then returned to Corvallis, and to Independence. Here I left bro. Kolbe to form a circuit; went to Salem, the capital of the State, where I met with bold, and determined opposition from several ministers of the North Church, who insisted that I had no business in Oregon! That country belonged to them exclusively, and that I ought to return immediately. But I had counted the cost too well before starting to be frightened off in such a way. I knew in whom I trusted, His work I came to do, and not my own, and that work, by His grace, I was bound to do at the risk of my life. It is proper for me to remark here that a false report of me and my church had preceded me to this country. Some one had written to the Pacific Christian Advocate, published at Portland, that I was coming to Oregon as a pro-slavery propagandist, and that my object was to introduce slavery into Oregon! and warning all parties to beware of "The Old Texas Ranger!" Still the people flocked to hear me preach and listened with profound attention. Even the Rev. President of the College,[40] who had scolded me publickly for perhaps an hour before preaching, listened to me with marked attention, and remarked to others that he did not expect to hear such a sermon after such a talk!

[40] Francis S. Hoyt was president of Willamette University, the northern Methodist school at Salem, Oregon, from 1850 to 1860 (Robert M. Gatke, *Chronicles of Willamette, the Pioneer University of the West* [Portland, Ore., 1943]).

I labored everywhere to disabuse the public mind in regard to those incendiary publications, (for they were coming every week,) assuring them that I was no polition [politician], had nothing to do with the Institution of Slavery, nor had my Church; we felt it our duty to Christianize the slaves to the best of our ability, but the State alone had controll of the Institution; and as a church, we believed we had no right to meddle with State affairs; that I had come to Oregon in the name of the Lord to preach the gospel of peace and good will to man, and especially to preach to that class of people, throughout the country, who would not hear the Northern preachers. They were forced to admit that there was such a class in the country who would not hear them. Several of the popular papers joined the Christian (?) Advocate in the howl against me, but there were two others who voluntarily took up my defense. So a paper war and war of words began rather in advance of my coming, and continued to rage while I stayed in Oregon. Notwithstanding the people did and would hear, and prospect of extended usefulness brightened every day. I spent about 3 months in this prospecting work, and received quite a number into the church. Our conference was to meet in September, and it was necessary I should be there. I left bro. Kolbe in charge of the work and aimed to be in Portland in time for the next steamer for San Francisco. But on arrival at Portland, we found to our embarrassment that the steamer had sailed the day before its appointed time. This detained us at a heavy expense for 9 days. In the meantime we tried to be as useful as possible, preaching and working within the Lodges. Here we did considerable work in the department of "The Good Samaritan." We had among our subjects the Grand Master of the State, the Judge of the Court, and the Judge of the Federal Court, and others. It was a pleasant and profitable time. On the return of the steamer, I called on the clerk of the Hotel for my Bill, who informed me it was *settled!* It was only $45.00. So much for that "Ancient and Honorable Society." On the steamer as we were passing down the river, I was requested to preach on board, which I did. Again we steamed up the Sound; but [illegible] I did not get the chance to preach; did not visit Victoria. We had a calm sea on our return, and arrived in San Francisco all well and in time for the meeting of the conference. We owe many thanks to Capt. Patterson and Purser Pool, for their very kind attention to us in our voyages. The first was half-fare, the second free. Bishop G. F. Pierce, wife and daughter, had come by stage from Texas to Los Angelos, and then by Steamer. Our conference met in San Francisco. I succeeded in persuading the Bishop to take Oregon into our work and make a Missionary District.

The Rev's. Jacob Gruwell, Moses Clampit, C. H. E. Newton, Jas. Kelsey, and Robert Martin were given me as helpers.[41] Bro. Gruwell had a large family, a wife and two daughters, and we took the overland route by way of Pitt and Fall rivers. We had our tents, and prepared for emigrant traveling life. We had about 700 miles before us, over some very high mountains and through a wild, hostile Indian country. But we were on God's work and our trust was in him. Our route was from San Jose over the Contra Costa Mountain, down the Livermore Valley, across the Bay of Marines and Benicia, Suisun and Sacramento Vallies, and up the Sacramento River. At Vacaville we stopped at the "Debate Campmeeting," held by the Campbellites and Southern Methodists. Revs. W. K. Gober and Morris Evans [were] on the Methodist side, the names of the others I cannot now give with certainty. One of them got sick, before our arrival, and gave his place to another. Their side was a signal failure. To make the matter worse, they had brought two candidates for immersion with them to grace their triumph at the close of the debate. But the season was dry, and there was no hole of water near of sufficient depth for immersion. All the water for the use of the meeting was obtained by boring down to the water with an auger and inserting a pump. They, however, were not to be defeated in this matter. So they dug a vault, similar to a grave, near one of the pumps and long before day had the pump at work to fill the vault. But the ground was so dry and porous that the water ran out as fast as it was pumped in! To remedy this evil they shovelled in a quantity of the earth taken out in digging, and stirred it into a loblolly to stop the leakage! Now it was not *clean water;* and the mud would not settle worth a cent! It was indeed a *muddy* affair! But they made it do, and left. I do not think anyone was deeply impressed with either the spirituality or purity of their Gospel. They did

[41] In the new Oregon District, with Fisher as presiding elder, were the following appointments: Salem Circuit, John L. Burchard; Portland Circuit, Moses Clampet; Independence Circuit, John C. Kolbe; Corvallis Circuit, to be supplied; Eugene City Circuit, Jacob Gruelle; and Umpqua, Jacksonville, Harrisburg, Fairfield, and Yamhill Circuits, all to be supplied (*Minutes* [*South*], *1859,* p. 189).

however succeed in one thing. I think they satisfied every one present that they did not believe in experimental, or spiritual Religion. They would not pray either for the pardon of sin, or the regeneration of the Soul by the Holy Ghost. They have no conversion or regeneration but that which is comprehended in immersion alone!

The meeting over, we pursued our way, we crossed the Sacramento river some distance above the town of Red-Bluff and took the mountain road via Pitt river. The second day, late, we crossed the summit and encountered a snow storm; stopped at "Lost Camp," where we met a company of Rangers under Capt. Burns, who had the Indian Queen as a prisoner. On condition of her safety she promised to lead them to the hiding place of her people. The next day we had a heavy drive of about 40 miles over a very hostile country. We had snow on the ground for some distance. At about 15 miles we reached a Military Station where we obtained an escort to the next Station, about 16 miles. This we were told, would bring us beyond all danger from these Indians. It was no very comforting report, that two waggoners had recently been murdered not far from here. It was late at night when we reached Pitt River. We got the use of a very dirty, empty room to lodge in for the night. The next morning we crossed the river just below the mouth of Fall River, which literally, *falls* into Pitt River at this place. The fall is perhaps from 30 to 50 feet perpendicular. And just below the ferry there is a cascade; I know not how long, in which the waters rush and tumble over the rocks with great fury. After crossing the ferry we had a long steep grade to ascend. Bro. Gruwell was ahead. Our road was a dug way in the steep hill side, and below us was the wild cataracts. About 2/3 of the way up, my mules concluded to go no further in that direction and set themselves back with all their force, cramping the carriage so as to run it off the bank into the roaring river below. The parapet wall on the brinks was only a log, about a foot thick! Two strong young men of our company saw my peril and sprang behind the carriage and with all their might kept it from going over, till in the last extremity, when all hope was giving way, the mules still doing their best against us, one of the breast straps parted as if it had been cut with a knife! This alone saved us! The strength of the young men was nearly exhausted, and in perhaps another minute all would have been in the rolling flood below and dashed to pieces among the rocks! I *felt* that God saved us. If he suffered the devil to get into the mules, He also sent His angels to cut the breast straps, to defeat his purpose. How satan would have triumphed if he had tumbled my team and all I had into the river and left me with my wife and little children in this wild region in a state of utter helplessness and thus defeat my Oregon Mission! But he did not succeed. Nevertheless he came so near it that nothing but the hand of God could save us. But God did save us in a way to encourage us still to trust in him alone for help and success while in His path of duty. My soul now almost shudders when I think of the peril we were in! By the assistance of bro. Gruwell's team we got safetly up the hill, and pursued our journey with thankful hearts for our deliverance. Our route for some distance was up the valley of Fall River. It is sort of prairie valley, and at the time, pretty well settled. The principle [principal] business of the settlers seemed to be saving hay for the benefit of waggoners. This is pretty near the perpetual snow line.

Our next place of note was at the cabin of Capt. [. . . .] in command of another company of Rangers. The soldiers were in camps, but the Captain was at home and gave us the use of his house. Here we met a family from Oregon on their way south. The snow fell heavily and the lookout was anything but hopeful for travellers to the north! The Capt. told us we had better make a haste to get out of that region or we might be snowed in for the winter. The snow fall here was about 7 feet, which remains all winter and till late in the spring. . . .[42]

VIII

CORVALLIS, OREGON, March 18, 1861

MY VERY DEAR ASBURY,

Your long and anxiously looked for letter of Jan 10, came to hand to day. It was truly a welcome guest. I had had no account of the Texas Conference, tho—I had both the Rio-Grande and East Texas, and felt very anxious to hear from you. I thank God that he has graciously restored your health and that you have been able to make so good a report of God's work in your conference; it is truly wonder-

[42] John C. Simmons, to whom this letter is addressed, wrote *The History of Southern Methodism on the Pacific Coast*. His account of Fisher's activities is drawn from this manuscript. Unfortunately the rest of this manuscript sketch has been lost.

ful, but only what *should* be. O that the good work may greatly increase this year also despite all outside revolution!

. . . .

It is impossible yet to tell what position this state will take in regard to the national division: and of course what effect it will have upon our church here. So far God is blessing us; and notwithstanding the work goes on slowly, yet, so far as I know, the larger number of converts to God in the state, are under our labors. The people here seem to be waiting for things to shape their course in the older states before they make any move; and then it will depend much on the position California takes. Our latest "Poney Express" news is to Feb. 25. We are anxious to know what has been done since that. A private letter just received from Mo. by one of our preachers, announces the probability of a civil war in that state, growing out of this question. Truly these are "troublous times," but our trust is in *God alone.*

It is our purpose, if God will it to visit you either in the Fall, immediately after the next session of Conference, or early in the Spring. We cannot now promise to remain there; but the path of *duty* shall be our path, 'the Lord being our helper.'

The first session of our College has just closed.[43] Your step-mother had charge of the Female department, and acquitted herself well. The Exhibition was a fine one. Ma read her Valedictory to the parents, guardians and students. It was a good article. The audiance was very large, and the speaking of the scholars, male and female, good for any country. It is the universal saying here that nothing equal to it has ever happened here before. But Ma's health is so poor that she feels compelled to retire from the Institution. Indeed we need two good teachers; a classic man to take charge of it, and a good female teacher. Both your sisters here made speeches.

[43] While presiding elder of the Oregon District, Fisher had re-established Corvallis College, at Corvallis, Oregon. This school had been chartered by a private group in 1857–58, but financial reverses came, and Fisher bought the property at a sheriff's auction on May 16, 1860, for $4,500 (Benton County, Oregon, Deed Book E, p. 651). He made the down payment and pledged the Pacific Conference for the balance; the Oregon Methodists assumed the entire debt if five hundred dollars could be raised in California. This was ultimately accomplished, and the Methodists operated the school for a number of years. Later it became Oregon State College (see John B. Horner, "History of Oregon State College, 1865–1907," *Oregon Historical Quarterly,* XXXI [1930], 42–50).

Money is so scarce here that I have been much troubled about our college debt. Only about $2500; but that is a great deal where there is so little money. My health has been poor a part of the time this winter, but not so as to keep me altogether from my work. It is now pretty good except [for] a severe cold.

Ma and the children can hardly wait for the time to come for our Texas trip. They send much love to you and to all. Pray for us. Give my love to all the brethren in the ministry and all my friends. Write soon and full. I have had nothing from Mr. Wells since last July! What is he doing?

Your affectionate father
O. Fisher

Did I frighten you out of the notion of getting married? I hope not. Surely you can find *one* good, religious girl that will help you in God's work. But ask counsel of God; and may he direct you.

IX

Stockton District, near Linden, Cal.
June 6, 1868.[44]

My dear Asbury,

Yours of March 25, has not been answered before our annual College examination at Vacaville, which I had to attend and perform the duties of president of the Board of Trustees, preach the annual sermon, &c.[45] Since then other duties have crowded upon me in regard to family, traveling, preaching, &c. Ma and Cepahs are with me now and will perhaps make the tour of the District with me. Rebecca is now in San Francisco, and Fannie is off on a vacation visit. By the breaking of a buggy wheel in this neighborhood, I am behind the time of my Quarterly Meeting, near 30 miles distance, and scratch this note to you while breakfast is preparing. I am very glad of your letter and thank God for all his mercies to you and yours. Assure your good

[44] During the Civil War, Fisher returned to California and served again as presiding elder of the San Francisco District, 1862–64. In 1864 or 1865 he began an unsuccessful mission in Mexico (see Simmons, *op. cit.,* pp. 156–57). In 1867 he again became presiding elder of Stockton District.

[45] The Pacific Methodist College at Vacaville conferred the degree of Doctor of Divinity upon him, possibly at this session.

wife that she has a childs place in my affections and prayers. I hope her affliction is all past before now. Tell my little grandchildren I love them and have them all in my heart. My health has been a little under par of late from over work and cold. I have been called on to deliver many lectures on the Prophecies, (I have 12 in my course) which is heavy work for mind and body. I have many requests to them, which I may prepare them for, if God will. I have written about 1000 hymns which Bishop Kavanaugh says ought not to be lost.[46]

. . . .

I have several letters from Texas in regard to this country. I need several preachers on my District. Pray for us. Ma and Cephas send love to you. Cephas says he wants you to come here to live. The Lord be with you all. Write soon.

Affectionately,
O. Fisher

X

Bryan City,
Oct. 11, 1871[47]

Rev. O. A. Fisher,
My dear Son,

Yours of August last, I did not see till last Friday, Having been on the wing nearly all the time since the 15*th* of Feb. last. The time of your meetings is over and of course I cannot be at them. I leave to-morrow for Huntsville, thence to Centreville, thence to Blue Ridge, and thence to Corsicana, the N. W. Conference. Thence to Crockett, Nov. 15, and thence by home to Galveston Dec. 6. I should like to be at your Conference, but as yet I have no home for my family, and shall likely have to build. I may be compelled to suspend my district labors a little until that thing can be done. I have traveled over a large por-

[46] Photostats of these hymns, which were originally written in five pocket-size note-books bound in calfskin, are in the University of Texas Library.

[47] After representing the Pacific Conference at the southern General Conference in Memphis, May, 1870, which at his instigation created the Los Angeles Conference out of the Pacific Conference to include southern California and western Arizona, Fisher transferred to the Texas Conference and was appointed Conference Sunday School Agent. He made his home in Bryan, Texas. After this he served districts and important stations, such as First Church, Austin (1873), until his superannuation in 1879.

tion of the Chappell Hill and Austin Districts of this con. and Belton and Springfield in the North West Con. God has been gracious with us. Many hundreds have been converted and added to the church. At the joint Campmeeting of Austin City and circuit 114 converts were reported. At a Campmeeting in Burleson over 80 were reported. Immediately after my debate with Carroll at Davilla Milam Co, God gave us 27 Holy Ghost conversions. Over 200 have been added to the Marlin Circuit. At the Webberville camp (I was not there) 120. These are specimens. I have been graciously sustained in an amount of exhausting labor which is amazing when I look at it and astonishing to others. I have for a month past suffered from a very severe attack of Catarrah in my head, sore throat, &c, and yet in the severest of it I have preached as much as four hours a day and that to a vast crowd of people.

I met Mr. Wells on his way from Philadelphia. His health is greatly improved but his cancer is not quite well. His daughter Jennie Saunders was quite sick at Gatesville while I was there. I had to give her medicine, and left her convalescent. All are well here. Mr. Blandford left for Houston yesterday. I left Anna at Sterlings in Burton. I have a good supply of my Sacraments on hand, have sold many in my tours, and the demand is still good. I have made no arrangements yet for the publication of other books. Still write often. Love to all. Add a little Golden Seal to the Prickly Ash, for your eyes. Bathe your temples and the back of your head with Vitalizer.

Pray for us. The Lord be with you. Affectionately your father

O. Fisher

CHAPTER XI

Methodist Indian Missions in Kansas

THE wave of renewed missionary interest which swept over the American churches in the first quarter of the nineteenth century did not fail to arouse the missionary zeal of the Methodist Episcopal church. The *Methodist Magazine,* founded in 1818, stimulated missionary interest, and the Methodist Missionary Society, established at New York in 1819, provided for a more effective reaching of destitute areas in this and, later, in foreign countries. Methodist Indian missions began with the work of John Stewart, a freeborn Virginia mulatto, among the Wyandots in the Sandusky Valley of Ohio in 1816. Three years later the Ohio Conference adopted the mission and placed the work under the general supervision of James B. Finley, presiding elder of the Lebanon District. Later in the decade 1820–30, branch missions were planted in Michigan and Upper Canada (Ontario), though the latter came under the jurisdiction of the independent Canada Conference in 1828. In what became the Illinois Conference, a mission was established among the Potawatomis on Fox River, Illinois, in 1823; and among the Iroquois and Kickapoos in 1830. The Oneidas of New York were reached in 1829; and the Sioux, Winnebagos, and Western Chippewas in 1834. In the same year Jason and Daniel Lee founded their famous mission on the Willamette River in Oregon.

In the Old Southwest the South Carolina Conference established a mission for evangelizing the Georgia Creeks in 1822, and in the same year a mission was begun by the Tennessee Conference among the Cherokees in Alabama. The Mississippi Conference appointed missionaries to the Choctaws in 1825. The removal of these southern tribes to the new Indian lands west of the Mississippi temporarily interrupted mission work, but beginnings were made again in what is now the state of Kansas in 1830. Several important tribes then roamed the Kansas plains and river valleys—the Kansas or Kaw, Osages, Shawnees, Delawares, Ottawas (Ottois), Peorias, Kaskaskias, Weas, Piankashaws, Kickapoos, Quapaws, Cherokees, Chippewas, Iowas, Sacs, Foxes, Potawatomis, Miamis, Wyandots, Munsees, and the New York Indians. Many of these had been removed from the Old Southwest and the Old Northwest in the face of the increasing white population of those areas. The Missouri Conference became interested in mission work among these tribes as early as April, 1830, when Alexander McAlister, presiding elder of the Cape Girardeau District, wrote Jesse Greene, presiding elder of the Missouri District, calling his attention to the "Caw Indians" on the borders of the latter's district and suggesting that a school be established among them. In July, 1830, the government agent among the Shawnees, George Vashon, wrote to Greene, urging the Methodist church to establish a mission among that tribe. Greene presented Vashon's letter to the conference session at St. Louis in September, and the conference took immediate action. Thomas Johnson, a Virginian, was assigned to the Shawnee Mission, and his brother, William, was sent to the Kansas or Kaw Mission. By 1832 other missions had been begun among the Delawares, Iowas, Sacs, and Peorias, so that an Indian Mission District could be established, with Thomas Johnson as superintendent. On October 23, 1844, at Tahlequah, in the Cherokee Nation, the Indian Mission Conference was organized, including the territory westward from Missouri and Arkansas, between the Missouri River on the north and the Red River on the south and the Rocky Mountains. In the division of 1845 this important missionary conference went with the Methodist Episcopal Church, South.

The letters from William and Thomas Johnson and Jerome C. Berryman, here presented, were published originally in the *Christian Advocate* and republished in the *Kansas Historical Collections,* XVI (1923–25), 227–49. They tell the story of the establishment of Methodist mission work among the Indians of Kansas, including the founding of the Manual Labor School, the visit of Bishop Roberts in 1842, Indian customs, methods of mission work, etc. Part IV, Berryman's "A Circuit-Rider's Frontier Experiences," and the records of the Missionary Society and the report of the Mission Committee in Parts V and VI throw additional light on the Kansas work.

For the history of Methodist Indian missions see J. M. Reid, *Missions and Missionary Society of the Methodist Episcopal Church* (New York and Cincinnati, 1879), Volume I. The story of the pioneer Wyandot mission is told in William Warren Sweet, *Circuit-Rider Days along the Ohio* (New York and Cincinnati, 1923); see also James B. Finley's books on mission work, including *History of the Wyandot Mission* (Cincinnati, 1840); *Sketches of Western Methodism* (Cincinnati, 1855); *Autobiography* (Cincinnati, 1855); and *Life among the Indians* (Cincinnati, 1857). For the work of Jason Lee see H. K. Hines, *Missionary History of the Pacific Northwest* (Portland and San Francisco, 1899). Invaluable for the study of the Kansas Indian missions is the article by J. J. Lutz, "The

Methodist Missions among the Indian Tribes of Kansas," *Kansas Historical Collections,* IX (1905–6), 160–235. Of additional interest for the history of the southwestern missions is the volume by William H. Goode, who spent ten years as a member of frontier conferences, *Outposts of Zion, with Limnings of Mission Life* (Cincinnati, 1863).

I. LETTERS OF WILLIAM JOHNSON

A[1]

KANZAS INDIAN AGENCY, June 26th, 1831

To the Corresponding Secretary of the Missionary Society of the Methodist Church:

REVEREND SIR—

As I was appointed at the last session of the Missouri Conference to make an effort to introduce learning and religion among the Kanzas Indians, it becomes my duty to make some communication to you, by which all who desire information respecting this new field of labour may know what is doing here for the advancement of our Redeemer's Kingdom.

When I received this appointment, I was and had been for some time in bad health. I was able to commence the discharge of my duties on the 1st of December, 1830, and on the 19th, I opened a school in a room which the agent invited me to occupy; but for three months the weather was so extremely cold that I did but little, there being but few children in a situation to attend school. At the close of the winter we prepared a school house, which I now occupy with a small school. We have preaching every Sabbath, but there are few who understand the English language well enough to be profited by hearing. As to preaching to the Indians at large, I am not at the present prepared to do much, having no suitable interpreter; this circumstance has led me to apply all my convenient time to study of their language. I have formed a vocabulary of about 600 words, and now think 600 or 800 more will enable me to speak with some fluency.

As to my school, it is composed of about ten Indians and six or seven white children. The Indian children learn well. I have five who

[1] From *Christian Advocate and Journal and Zion's Herald* (New York), V (August 5, 1831), 198.

spell in words of two syllables, and one who reads and writes very well. There is no difficulty in teaching Indians when they are placed in a situation to learn.

As to the effect which the Gospel has had upon those who hear it, I am qualified to say that some seem profited by it, though none as yet enjoy the comfort of religion. Some seem penitent, while others are vexed, and try to oppose any who try to do better than themselves.

This is a large and needy field of labour. There are about 1,500 souls in the Kanzas tribe; and in addition to these there are large neighboring tribes which speak the same language—making in all about 7,000 who cry aloud for our assistance. I say the call is loud; for I view them on the threshold of destruction. I need not attempt to describe my feelings while viewing such scenes of human degradation and misery. Suffice it is to say, that I have ardent desire to do what I can by the help of my Master to rescue my unfortunate fellow creatures from present wretchedness and impending ruin.

Could some zealous young men in other places less needy than our western forests behold for a moment the pressing wants of these children of the forest, methinks they would leave all, gladly follow Christ and bear the tidings of Salvation to the most needy people that tread American soil. Yes, how could they refuse to give a few years to that Saviour, who has given himself for them.

Can it be possible that the Macedonian cry will never reach the ears and hearts of some, who can come with ease and labour in this interesting field?

How can a man get down on his knees and say, "Thy kingdom come" unless he act his part to hasten its establishment?

Then let those who can engage in this work and those who by giving a little out of their abundance with which the Lord has blessed them, assist in the instruction of these poor dependent children of the forest.

WILLIAM JOHNSON[2]

[2] William Johnson (1805–42) was a native of Nelson County, Virginia, converted at the age of nineteen. Moving to Missouri in 1825, he was licensed to preach in 1828 and admitted on trial to the Missouri Conference. On being ordained deacon in 1830, he was appointed to labor among the Indians on the Kansas River. After twelve years' labor as missionary, superintendent, and teacher, he died at the Indian Mission Manual Labor School, Kansas, April 8, 1842 ("Memoir," *Minutes of the Annual Conferences of the Methodist Episcopal Church,* Vol. III: *1839–1845,* pp. 349–50).

B[3]

CHAUTON, Mo., August 30th, 1831

To the Corresponding Secretary of the Missionary Society of the Methodist Church:

REVEREND BROTHER—

The year of my labor having come to an end among the Kansas Indians, I will now report to you the success we have had this year. I have little to say, but yet, what I do say proceeds out of a glad heart; for the news is joyful. I informed you in my last communication that some friends were inquiring of Him of whom Moses and the Prophets did write. I can now tell you that some have found Jesus precious to their souls, and have united themselves in society with us. Those who have turned to the Lord are of the worthy family in which I live, Colonel Boone's.[4]

We have no converts among the Indians yet; though, I have thought some were under religious impressions.

My little school continued to prosper while in operation, and I am sorry I could not keep it in operation during my absence. But this was impossible as I have had no one to aid me in teaching. I still believe, that I shall soon be able, by perseverance, to preach Jesus to this hapless people.

[3] From *Christian Advocate and Zion's Herald,* VI (October 7, 1831), 22.

[4] Daniel Morgan Boone was a son of the frontiersman, Daniel Boone. The following letter, dated Salubria, April 2, 1830, from Alexander McAlister, presiding elder of the Cape Girardeau District of the Missouri Conference, to Jesse Greene, presiding elder of the Missouri District, mentions Boone and is of importance as background material for the history of the Kansas missions. McAlister writes:

"I have just time to write a few lines by Bro. Peery, in which I wish to call your attention to the Caw [Kansas] Indians on your frontiers. Col. Daniel Boon, who is the Government's farmer among those Indians, married Mrs. McAlister's sister, which circumstance has led to a correspondence between him and myself, and the Government Agent of those Indians. Boon is among them, perhaps thirty or forty miles from Fort Osage. He promises to do all he can for the support of a school among that tribe. The agent also promises to assist, as far as he can, and informs me that the Caw Indians, according to the provisions of a treaty with the Government, have a considerable sum of money set apart to support schools among themselves, and the Agent advises us to get in there immediately and secure that fund, and improve it to their benefit. I think you might visit them, and know all about it soon, and perhaps get some pious young man to go and commence a school among them before conference" (Mary Greene, *Life, Three Sermons, and Some of the Miscellaneous Writings of Rev. Jesse Greene* [Lexington, Mo., 1852], pp. 47–48).

Our progress has been small this year; but our expenditures have been equally small. I have used very little of the money appropriated for the work.

I will close in saying, that I intend to go on in the strength of the Lord of hosts. I feel no unwillingness to spend my life in this missionary cause.

Since I left the Kanzas Mission, I have attended several camp meetings. I rejoice to see the work of the Lord prosper in almost every direction. The prospect of a great revival is brighter than I have ever seen it in Missouri. We have not only witnessed the shouts of heaven born souls at our camp meetings, but at prayer meetings.

May the Lord carry on the work over opposition, until great victory shall be achieved in these western wilds.

WILLIAM JOHNSON

C[5]

To Corresponding Secretary of the Missionary Society of the Methodist Church:

DEAR BROTHER—

According to the instructions of the superintendent of this mission, I proceed to report the state of things at this point of missionary labor. You are aware that this is a new field, selected at our last annual conference, as one of importance. We could not make any beginning to improve until March. Since then we have been trying to hasten our business as fast as possible. We have now twenty acres of good soil, fenced and planted; two cabins built, and a garden nearly finished. We removed into our cabins about two weeks since.

The Indians have cleaned their little fields, and gone out to hunt for buffalo, expecting to return in five or six weeks. There are only seven or eight families left, and they are mostly old, lame and sick. Several of the sick have camped by us, for the purpose of taking medicine, and such help as we can give.

We are preparing to instruct these people as fast as we can, but shall not be able to do much before winter, as we have our dwelling house to build—also to depend upon our new farm for provision, as we are one hundred miles from the nearest white settlement. These Indians

[5] From *Christian Advocate and Journal,* X (July 15, 1836), 186.

have some corn, and but little of anything else, either food or clothing. They are emphatically poor and exceedingly ignorant.

The Kanzas Indians have no cattle or hogs, and few horses compared to the number of persons; there being about seventeen hundred of them. The efforts of the benevolent agent will doubtless prove beneficial to them. He is at this time having about three hundred acres of land fenced and planted for them.

I wish it were my privilege to say that some religious impressions were made upon the minds of these children of nature. We have no one to interpret anything on the subject of religion, and my own knowledge of their language is yet insufficient for these things; though I am learning every day, and hope ere long to be able to preach to them a crucified Jesus.

In the midst of all we see to discourage us, among a people far sunk in superstition and darkness, we have some things to encourage us to persevere. They seem willing to learn. They are fond of talking, and do not try to conceal their views on any subject. They are more serious and devoted than many other tribes, and better informed. They fast and pray and attend to many ceremonies, in a solemn manner; yet in all their worship there is no confession of sin or knowledge of a Saviour. If they only knew Jesus, in the regeneration of their souls, and would worship in His name with the same promptness that they attend to their own ceremonies, they would doubtless be a happy people.

I will [not] close this report without begging an interest in the prayers of Christians in behalf of this poor tribe of human beings. Yours in love,

W. Johnson

June 7, 1836

D[6]

To Corresponding Secretary, Missionary Society of the Methodist Episcopal Church:

Rev. and dear Sir—

This mission has been two years in operation, though on a very small scale, in no way adequate to the wants of the people for whom it was established.

[6] From *Christian Advocate and Journal,* XIII (February 12, 1839), 136.

The Kanzas Indians are located on the Kanzas River, about eighty miles above its junction with the Missouri. They number two thousand souls, and have ever maintained the greatest friendship with the American people.

They were once a large and more wealthy people; but from sickness and the destruction of the wild game, they have been reduced in number, and sank into the most degrading poverty imaginable. While in poverty and wretchedness, they carry on a perpetual war with the Pawnees, their next neighbors west; and hence dexterity in war is the only certain road to honor, according to their teachings of the wise men of the nation, whether jugglers, dreamers or warriors. This being the state of things and there being no interpreter in the nation, very little has been done in the way of preaching. But we are not left without encouragement. In all the instruction we can give, understandingly, we are prepared to say, "our labor is not in vain in the Lord."

A great change has taken place in the minds and actions of most of the nation in reference to labor. The men begin to work with the women. They are building houses out in the woods, and are preparing fences, raising stock and preparing to live like the white men—as they call it. We do not say so much about the amount of labor, as the great change in sentiment, although quite a number have proven by experience that they profit most by civilized habits. And now we find more trying to build than we can find time to teach.

We have promised ourselves, that this winter and spring would be a favorable time for imparting religious instruction; but every day seems to bring its trials. During the fall hunt, the first chief of the nation and four braves died. Though some of these died of fever, and others of whiskey, yet such is their savage sentiments, that they must shed blood or commit depredations upon some other tribe, as a satisfaction for the loss which the Great Spirit has caused them to sustain. To gratify this savage spirit nearly all the males in the nation, who can bear arms, will march in a few days against the Pawnees. We are able to prevent a few only, and a few others are unable to walk.

Four separate parties will go out, each seeking satisfaction for the respective friend or relative. In this state of darkness and wretchedness we are thankful for a few who will profit by instruction. While we have some disposed to hear us try to tell of the true God, and of a merciful saviour, we have six living in our family, whom we wish to educate. They promise well, as far as we can form an opinion.

In conclusion, I want to state a simple fact, and then leave the condition of this people with the church and with God. This people must be rescued from their wretchedness or sunk forever, and no church has undertaken for them but the Methodist Episcopal Church.

The government is doing nothing for them but furnishing a farmer and smithery. If it devolves upon us to deliver them from destruction, it is our duty to make a strong effort to break down their prejudice and superstition, which will, if unrestrained, prove their ruin. We ask an interest in the prayers of God's people of this nation. Yours in love,

WILLIAM JOHNSON

February 12th, 1839.

E[7]

To Corresponding Secretary, Missionary Society of the Methodist Episcopal Church:

DEAR BROTHER—

I am not conscious of any report of the condition of this mission having been forwarded by the superintendent,[8] and consequently conclude that he expects me to communicate to [you] such facts as might be necessary to give you a correct idea of the true state of things at this point of missionary operations. The latter part of the summer and beginning of the fall were very sickly here, both at the mission and among the Indians generally. At one time, of the two white families at this place, viz., my own and the government farmer's, numbering in all fourteen, only myself and a young lady who lives with us here were able to go about. Several cases of fever, and other diseases, continued to resist every effort we were able to make. A physician was then se[n]t for, but being about ninety miles out of the United States, it took four days and nights to obtain a physician, at which time it was too late to do anything in one of the cases, and the unfortunate sufferer, Mrs. Bensley, died the next night, leaving a husband and five little children, all sick. In the midst of this affliction

[7] From *Christian Advocate and Journal,* XV, 102.

[8] The writer's brother, Thomas Johnson (see below), was superintendent of the Indian Mission District of the Missouri Conference, 1832–41.

and sorrow one reflection consoled us; she died in peace, professing resignation to the will of God. For about three weeks after this Mrs. Johnson and our two little children lay very sick. We were uneasy for every one of them. In another room lay Mr. Greene and wife, and none to administer to them but two of us, and neither of us well, with ten sick, and two of us to do all that was done. We had no time to rest day or night. We were next called to part with our dear little daughter, Mary Frances. We had now to bear trials new to us. We know we loved our little children, but never knew how tender the ties of affection were before. But the breach was made in our little family, and we committed her to the grave, praying God to give us grace to bear it.

While we were sick at the mission, the Indians were suffering equally as much. In some families as many as five died. But few families escaped disease; and the number of deaths was great in proportion to the number sick. The awful cries of the Indians around the dead sounded in our ears nearly every day. The lack of wholesome diet and suitable medicines doubtless increased the number of deaths greatly. The Indians were gloomy, and not inclined to do anything, but prepare for their fall hunt; believing that they would be better off if scattered in the woods, where fresh meat could be obtained. In this condition they scattered, and have not yet returned, but will be at their homes in a few weeks. The last two summers have been sickly here, though we have always considered the country very healthy.

There are great barriers in the way of reforming these Indians. One is their wandering habits, and another is their propensity to war with the neighboring tribes. According to their customs, they are at home about one-third of the year, but for the last two years they have not been at home a third of the time, in consequence of fleeing from sickness twice.

When at home they are so often employed in preparing little war parties, to steal horses from the adjoining tribes, that but little can be effected among them. In this restless condition they are threatened with an entire loss of game, by being hemmed in by the tribes west of them. With hunger and poverty, and all that can render men wretched, around them, a few of them have begun to reform and seek to do better. With these we expect to labor, and try to increase the number in every way we possibly can. The task we know from experience to be arduous, but the happiness of our fellow-man induces us to engage in it, trusting in the Lord.

During the absence of the Indians we kept up regular preaching every Sabbath for those few who attend, in English. But we expect to spend the greater part of our time with the Indians when they come home, in trying to teach them religion, and to encourage them in working and preparing to live more comfortable at home.

We feel humbled in heart, and deeply sorry that we cannot report convictions and conversions among these poor people. But they are yet left in darkness and superstition, and know but little of the blessed religion of the Bible, so well calculated to elevate and save poor degraded Indians.

Yours in love,
WM. JOHNSON

December 30, 1840

F[9]

To the Corresponding Secretary of the Missionary Society of the M. E. Church:

DEAR BROTHER—

When I wrote to you last I informed you that the Kanzas Indians had not returned home from their fall hunt. As they all collected at their villages in a short time after I wrote, and brought news with them of a distressing character, I have thought proper to write to you again, and give the particulars of their late inhuman and shameful slaughter of a party of Pawnee women and children. I do not give this statement so much to attract the attention of the readers, as to give those immediately concerned in missionary operations a correct idea of the customs and wretchedness of the wild Indians, who seem intent on their own destruction; for every new occurrence confirms me in what I have long since stated to be a fact—that there is nothing necessary to complete the destruction of the Indian population than to let them alone. They need no help to hasten this melancholy event. Only let them prosecute their own savage habits, thirsting for each other's blood; and, ere we are aware of it, there will be none left to tell the melancholy tale of a once flourishing people.

It appears, from the statements of the Indians, that a party of

[9] From *Christian Advocate and Journal,* XV, 122.

Pawnee men attempted to steal horses from the Kanzas and succeeded in taking about ten horses. Two young men, failing to get horses then, continued their journey until they found another band of Kanzas, and were there overtaken, after having stolen two horses, and killed and scalped. About this time the other band of Indians (the band with which our mission is located) sent out a war party of sixty-five men to hunt for Pawnees. After traveling about ten days, they discovered a company of Pawnees on horseback, going out to kill buffalo. They immediately directed their course to a body of timber, in which the Pawnees were camped, and there found nineteen lodges, numbering, according to size of Indian families, about one hundred and fifty souls. There were but three men left, and one of them an old blind man. They fell upon these defenseless women and children, and killed and scalped about ninety-three, and took eleven prisoners, ten horses, and all the articles they could pack, out of their houses, burned the balance, and then fled. In this massacre they state that they shot some dead, and others they thrust through with the spear. Some they knocked down with a tomahawk, and others they scalped alive. The object was for all the young men to become braves by striking with the tomahawk the head of an enemy. In performing this act of bravery many infants were knocked down and scalped; and they tell one account more shameful than all the others if possible, of a woman being killed and scalped and another young man tearing an infant child out of her bowels, and then manifesting his bravery by striking it with a tomahawk. It chills my blood to write the particulars of this wretched tragedy. The whole massacre is so destitute of bravery and honor, that I would gladly have it wiped away from a tribe of people with whom I live, and for whose good I labor and toil. There are two acts of bravery connected with the transaction, but both on the part of the Pawnees. One is the case of a man, the only man on the ground (the blind man being already killed, and the other young man gone to call the men from their hunt), who took his gun, and stood up in his lodge to defend it. The order was given by the Kanzas chief not to interrupt him, lest he should shoot some of them; and no one presumed to attack this one man, though they say they believe his gun was not loaded. The other is that of a woman who stood at the mouth of her lodge, with a gun, to defend her little family. Some of the Kanzas attempted to take the gun out of her hands, and failed. They called for help, and chopped the poor woman's hands with butcher knives, until she was compelled to give up her gun. She then got a hoe, and still defended herself and family, until she was shot through her body, and fell, but soon rose up again, and was left alive with her children, in her tent. In these two instances we see Indian bravery exhibited, one resisting sixty-five armed warriors, and thereby saving their little families from being unmercifully butchered.

Since the Indians came in, the war song and scalp dance constitute their daily employment. All other matters, either of business or amusement, are laid aside. The effect of this massacre upon the tribe at large, in paralyzing all our operations, is now felt to an alarming extent. There are but few men in all the nations of the Kanzas now disposed to think of anything but a defense against the attacks of the Pawnees, now exasperated at the slaughter of their women and children.

The upper village of Kanzas have fled from their town, and expect to wander to and fro for the balance of the year. They talk of planting a little corn at their town, but even this is uncertain. The village near the mission are so elated with their past act of bravery, that they have done little else than dance since they came in. The few families who were building houses near the mission are now the subjects of laughter and sport by the new-made braves. The number who are now disposed to build houses and provide for their families is small, not more than fifteen families in all. These are poor and ignorant, and with great difficulty kept in the notion of improving, in consequence of the great dread of the Pawnees. The prospect of reforming these people is truly gloomy at present, and, without change in their habits and feelings, must continue gloomy. I have never seen the prospect for usefulness so completely hedged up with any Indians in my life as it is with these at present. It appears that much is to do, and should be done, but how to do it is more than I am able to understand. But they are in the hands of God to whom all souls belong. To him I desire to commit the whole case, trusting in his mercy and waiting for the display of his power.

Yours truly,
WM. JOHNSON

KANZAS MISSION, Jan. 30, 1841.

G. DEATH OF REV. WM. JOHNSON[10]

Dear Brother Elliott—

Since Bishop Roberts and myself left Cincinnati in February last, up to this time, we have traveled, by steamboat, on horseback, and in our carriage, nearly two thousand five hundred miles; and, as yet, the Bishop's health and strength continue unimpaired. But while his life is spared, others, much his juniors, are falling by the stroke of death.[11]

On our arrival here a few days since, we met the mournful intelligence of brother William Johnson's death. He was the superintendent of this mission district, and missionary to the Kanzas. For eleven years, last past, he labored as a missionary among the Indians—for four years amoung the Delawares and Shawnees, and seven years among the Kanzas. As a missionary, brother Johnson had few equals, and no superiors. He possessed, in an eminent degree, the prudence, patience and zeal, which a missionary among Indians has so much occasion to exercise in the prosecution of his labors.

Of all the missionaries which, from time to time for the last twenty-five years, have been employed by our Church in the Indian country, brother Johnson was the only one who ever learned an Indian language so as to be able to preach in it: He spoke the Shawnee, so as to be able to converse in it on ordinary subjects. He was probably the only white man that ever learned the Kanzas language with grammatical accuracy. This language is common, or nearly so, to several different tribes of wild Indians, numbering altogether near ten thousand souls. Sanguine hopes had been entertained that, ultimately, through brother Johnson's instrumentality, the Gospel would have found its way to many of these wandering sons of the wilderness. But, alas, death has blasted all these hopes; the work must now be de-

[10] From *Western Christian Advocate,* IX (May 13, 1842), 14.

[11] For an account of this tour by Roberts' companion, Edward R. Ames, then missionary secretary, see Charles Elliott, *The Life of the Rev. Robert R. Roberts* (New York, 1844), pp. 338 ff. Ames writes that the Indians were "delighted with the Bishop's visit. His patriarchal and venerable appearance, his kind and affectionate deportment toward them, his familiarity in visiting them, eating at their tables and lodging in their dwellings, completely won their confidence." Roberts (1778–1843) was a native of western Maryland and reared on the western Pennsylvania frontier, so that he was accustomed to frontier ways and living.

ferred for years, before another man can be qualified, equally well, for the undertaking; and it is to be feared the mission will have to be given up, though the head chief of the nation, with whom the Bishop and myself had a council today, expressed great anxiety for its continuance. But where are the funds?

I hope materials will be found among the papers of brother Johnson, from which a biography can be prepared that will do justice to his memory. His remains rest on the mission premises at this place, and Bishop Roberts will preach his funeral sermon on next Sabbath week, when it is expected that all the missionaries in this district will be present.

You will be pleased to learn, I have no doubt, that arrangements are making, which I expect to be consummated next fall, for the establishment of an Indian Manual Labor School in the southwest, on such terms as will, I trust, be highly favorable to the interests of the missionary cause in that section of the work. I found the missions among the Choctaws[12] and Cherokees[13] doing well, all things considered. Several of the missions in the district are in a flourishing condition.

I find here a noble institution which promises to be a blessing to thousands of the red men. There are now in attendance about one hundred pupils from eleven different tribes. I hear many familiar names sounding in my ears in the school-room. Here is Joshua Soule, Nathan Bangs, William Ryland, Richard Tydings, Thomas Bottomly, William Herr, William H. Raper, Samuel Gillette, &c.;[14] and to see these fine, sprightly lads, with their frank, open countenances, cheerfully employed in the school-room, the mechanic's shop, or on the farm, you would have no fears of their disgracing the names they bear. I am sure if those who have given their money to aid the cause of missions could witness the scenes that are passing here, and in other parts of the Indian country, so far from regretting their former donations, they would hereafter double both their prayers and gifts to aid this blessed work.

[12] The Choctaw Mission was then in the Arkansas Conference, which had been erected in 1836.

[13] Arkansas Conference.

[14] All of these are names of Methodist preachers, for whom the Indian boys were named.

We expect in a few days to start from here to visit the missions on the Upper Mississippi; and if no accident occurs I think I shall reach home sometime in September.

Yours truly

E. R. AMES[15]

INDIAN MANUAL LABOR SCHOOL, SHAWNEE NATION,
April 20, 1842

II. LETTERS OF REV. THOMAS JOHNSON

A[16]

To the Corresponding Secretary of the Missionary Society of the Methodist Episcopal Church:

REV. AND DEAR BROTHER—

The time has rolled round when it becomes my duty to make known to you the state and prospects of the missions on the Kanzas. If you have received the minutes of the Missouri Conference, (though I have seen no account of this,) you have learned that brother Wm. Johnson and myself were appointed to labor together among the different tribes of Indians living on and near the Kanzas river, viz., the Shawnees, Delawares, Kanzas, Peori, Piankeshaws and Weas. Our work thus laid off was called "The Missions on the Kanzas." We were instructed to occupy any part of this work that might be deemed most advisable, as it was then and is yet somewhat uncertain what can be done.

After a fatiguing journey of nearly 500 miles, we reached our field of labor on the 21st of October. We were very much discouraged; everything appeared to be in a state of confusion; the small pox was raging among different tribes, and the Indians flying in different directions; our school among the Shawnees, which had been in a flourishing condition the most of the time we were absent at conference, was suspended, with the exception of a few children that

[15] Edward R. Ames (1806–1879), a native of Adams County, Ohio, was admitted on trial in 1830 to the Illinois Conference, and became a member of the Indiana Conference in 1832. In 1840 he was elected missionary secretary, working chiefly in the West, and in 1852 was elected bishop. For his later career as one of the "war bishops" see William Warren Sweet, *The Methodist Episocpal Church and the Civil War* (Cincinnati, n.d.), pp. 150–54.

[16] From *Christian Advocate and Journal and Zion's Herald,* VI (February 10, 1832), 94.

boarded with us, and it was but seldom that we could even see an Indian to get instruction in learning the language; therefore there was no possible chance to preach to them, consequently our spirits had well sunk within us, for we felt that we had a full and heavy year's work assigned to us, and had no time to lose. But we had learned from a little experience that patience, perseverance and fortitude are essential qualifications for missionaries; we therefore determined to do the best we could.

Brother William has visited the Kanzas tribe, and stayed a short season with them. He procured an Indian to aid him in learning the language, and returned to the Shawnee mission, as the Kanzas were generally from home. He has aided some in keeping up the Shawnee school, (as our teacher has been absent nearly two months on business), and had advanced considerably in the language, and expects to be able to preach to them next summer.

We will set out for their villages next week, and will probably spend the principal part of the winter among them. They are about seventy miles from this place. We have been striving to get our houses prepared for winter, and collecting provisions for the year.

The small pox has subsided, and the Indians are now returning home. Our prospects seem to brighten a little. There are accessions to our Shawnee school almost every day, and the children learn very well. We have instructed in this school upwards of thirty Indian children, though not all at the same time. There is but little doubt but we shall have at this establishment as many as we can manage advantageously, and we hope before the year closes, to have schools in operation among the different tribes in our charge.

But the instructing of children alone does not satisfy us; this, though of great importance, is only a secondary object. Our great anxiety is to find access to those who are capable of understanding the nature and enjoying the influence of our holy religion; but here our way is hedged up yet, for want of suitable interpreters; but we are endeavoring to improve every moment we can get in learning the language ourselves. Brother William is learning the Kanzas, and I am learning the Shawnee, as with the knowledge of these two languages, we can converse and preach to six or eight different tribes of these Northwestern Indians.

We collected together a tolerably good congregation of Shawnees last Sabbath, and as it was Christmas day, we endeavored to explain to them the reason of our keeping this day in remembrance. They listened with great solemnity while we told them of Jesus Christ coming into the world to save all men, red men as well as white. They informed us afterwards that they would think about what we told them when they went home. I must conclude, for I have already lengthened out this communication beyond what I intended.

We hope that the friends of missions in general will not fail to pray that the great Head of the Church may be with us in our infant efforts to enter this vast missionary field among the numerous tribes of Northwestern Indians. I remain yours, in the bonds of a peaceful Gospel.

THOS. JOHNSON[17]

December 29, 1831.

B[18]

To the Corresponding Secretary of the Methodist Episcopal Church

REV. AND DEAR BROTHER—

Since I wrote you last I have visited the Kansas Indians. I found but few of them at home. The most of the tribe had started to hunt buffalo two days before we reached the villages. These Indians live on the Kansas river, 60 miles from its mouth, on a straight line, and have their villages on both sides of the river, but a part of the nation have removed 40 miles higher up the river, for the purpose of getting near the buffalo. I never before saw any part of the human family in so wretched a condition. They live chiefly in dirt houses. They cultivate only a small portion of ground, and this done chiefly by the women, with hoes. They do not plough. They have no fences. Their

[17] Thomas Johnson (1802–65), the elder brother of William Johnson, was a native of Virginia who joined the Missouri Conference in 1826, serving appointments in Arkansas, Missouri, and Kansas. After 1830 he served eleven years on Indian missions, mostly as superintendent. From 1847 to 1862 he was head of the Indian Manual Labor School in the Indian Mission Conference of the Methodist Episcopal Church, South. A Union man in the Civil War, he was assassinated by a band of guerrillas at his home near Westport, Missouri, in 1865. Johnson County, Kansas, is named in his honor. For biography see W. S. Woodard, *Annals of Methodism in Missouri* (Columbia, Mo., 1893), pp. 62–63; E. J. Stanley, *Life of Rev. L. B. Stateler* (Nashville, 1916), pp. 128–29; *Kansas Historical Collections,* VII, 207; IX, 161–63.

[18] From *Christian Advocate and Journal,* IX (July 31, 1835), 194.

only dependence for meat is on the chase, and the deer have entirely disappeared from their prairies. They have to go 250 miles, or farther, to find the buffalo, and then are frequently driven back by their enemies; and should they succeed in finding the buffalo, if they bring any of the meat home, it frequently has to be packed by their women, for many of them have no horses to ride; and their means of support are becoming more difficult every year, for the buffalo, like the deer, are fast retiring. Unless we can succeed in getting these people to change their habits of life, they must soon perish. We hope to be able, at the next session of our annual conference, to send missionaries among these people.

From this tribe I set out through the lonesome prairie, without any trace, for the Peori village. After a day and a half severe traveling I reached the mission at that place. That night one of the members of our society died; but she appeared to be entirely resigned to her fate, and exhorted all around never to cease in their efforts to become a Christian people. She requested them to meet at the grave, and have preaching when they buried her. This was attended to. A more solemn scene I never witnessed. The corpse was deposited in the grave, and they all seated themselves around while I explained to them the doctrine of the resurrection. They all appeared to feel thankful, while they contemplated the happiness of meeting their departed sister where death would never molest them again. When we were done talking they covered up the grave, and we returned home. This mission is doing well.

The Shawnee mission is in a prosperous condition, and is likely to accomplish much good in this nation. The school and society are both large and regular in attendance. The mechanic shop is opened at this place, and the Indians appear to be pleased with the idea of their boys becoming mechanics. A considerable number of them are engaged as regular apprentices.

The Delaware mission is still gaining ground, and the members of society appear to enjoy much of the influence of religion, though they are greatly persecuted by the pagan part of the nation.

The mission at this place (Kickapoo) has had some difficulties to encounter this year, but they are fast giving way, and I think our prospects of ultimate success are as good as they ever have been. Our school is small at this time, but there will be no difficulty in enlarging as much as we choose, when our buildings, which are now in a state of preparation, shall have been completed.

I shall not be able to visit any of the tribes west of us before conference; but I have engaged several of the officers of the dragoons, who are now on a tour to the foot of the Rocky mountains, to collect all the information in their power relative to the condition of the different tribes they may visit. I have no doubt this will be attended to promptly, for some are men of piety, who feel a deep interest in the spread of the Gospel among all people. But I have written enough for one letter and shall conclude.

I remain yours in love,

THOS. JOHNSON

June 16, 1835.

C[19]

DEAR BROTHER—

Since I last wrote you we have had several interesting meetings, and much encouragement to persevere in our labors among the poor Indians in this part of the country.[20]

. . . .

At the Kanzas mission we have not been able to do much, in consequence of the missionary having no preparations to stay with them during the winter. He visited them twice during the fall, and made all the arrangements he could for the commencement of our labors, and is now gone again, with some hands, to prepare some temporary buildings, and will move his family as soon as ready.

I think, in view of the whole matter, our prospects are encouraging through the district. It is true, we have some privations and many difficulties to encounter—and it will be unreasonable to expect to get along without them in an Indian country. But these things do not discourage us. We are determined to do the best we can, and leave the result with God.

We trust that we share in the prayers of all the friends of Missions.

T. JOHNSON

March 9, 1836.

[19] From *Christian Advocate and Journal,* X (April 22, 1836), 138.

[20] The omitted portions of this letter have to do with the work among the Shawnee, Delaware, Peoria, and Kickapoo Indians.

D[21]

To the Missouri Conference Missionary Society:

Your Board take leave to present the following exhibit of the several missions within the bounds of the Conference, as their 6th annual report.[22]

. . . .

5. *Kanzas Mission.*—But little has been done at this Mission, excepting to prepare the way for future operations; however, the prospect is by no means discouraging. One very promising young man has lately professed religion, and been baptized in the name of the Christ.

He left the nation about nine years ago, while he was a small boy, to keep from starving, for he was destitute of friends, without clothes, and no one to provide for him; he has lived among the white people until he has learned the English language, learned to work, professed religion, and is now attending school at the Shawnee Mission, and expects to go back with your missionary, to aid him in teaching his poor benighted nation.

This may be a providential arrangement for the conversion of this benighted people. May the Lord make it successful.

In view of these facts, your board would exhort you to renewed diligence and unwearied perseverance in this glorious enterprise, for we are assured that in due time we shall reap if we faint not. May the great Head of the Church crown your labors with an abundant harvest.

All of which is respectfully submitted.

J. GREENE,[23] *Pres'.*
THOS. JOHNSON, *Sec'y.*

ST. LOUIS, Sept. 19, 1836.

[21] From *Christian Advocate and Journal,* XI (December 9, 1836), 62.

[22] Accounts of the Shawnee, Delaware, Peoria, and Kickapoo missions are omitted.

[23] As presiding elder of the district in the Missouri Conference bordering on Kansas, Jesse Greene (1791–1847) was instrumental in establishing the first missions among the Indian tribes of Kansas in 1830. He was also largely responsible for organizing the missionary society of the Missouri Conference. His widow, Mary Todd Greene (1812–93), herself a former teacher at the Shawnee mission, published his *Life* at Lexington, Missouri, in 1852. The book contains some valuable letters relating to the Kansas mission work.

E[24]

February 13, 1837.

To the Corresponding Secretary, Missionary Society of M. E. Church:

DEAR BROTHER—

The Kanzas Mission comes next in order. The Kanzas Indians live on the Kanzas river, about seventy miles south-west of the Shawnee mission. They are about 1500 in number. They have a beautiful country, but it is chiefly prairie; tho there is enough of timber, if taken care of, for the nation.

These Indians are the most wretched of all human beings that I ever saw. They live in dirt houses; but seldom wear clothes, though they generally have a buffalo skin, or, sometimes a blanket, thrown over them loosely.

They frequently suffer for something to eat, for they have always been accustomed to depend upon the chase for a living. But game has become so scarce that they can no longer subsist in this way; and there is no doubt but many of them die every year for the want of something to support nature. They have to go upward of 200 miles to get the buffalo now; and this is the chief dependence for meat. When they go after the buffalo, if there are not horses enough, which is frequently the case, their women have to walk and carry their children; and as they return home, in addition to the burden of carrying their children, they have to carry the meat which has been killed. We need not think it strange that a nation is declining when they have to live in this way. These people are very ignorant, but manifest a teachable disposition.

In the fall of 1830, we made arrangements and commenced a mission among these people; but it was then thought the Kanzas were not permanently settled, and that it would not be prudent to spend money in building houses and preparing for instruction where they then lived, consequently we opened a school at the Agency, about thirty miles from the villages. Here we were able to collect together a small school; and the missionary was useful to some extent by preaching to the few whites who lived at the Agency, as well as by instructing the Indian children in the school.

[24] From *Christian Advocate and Journal,* XI, 130.

MAP V

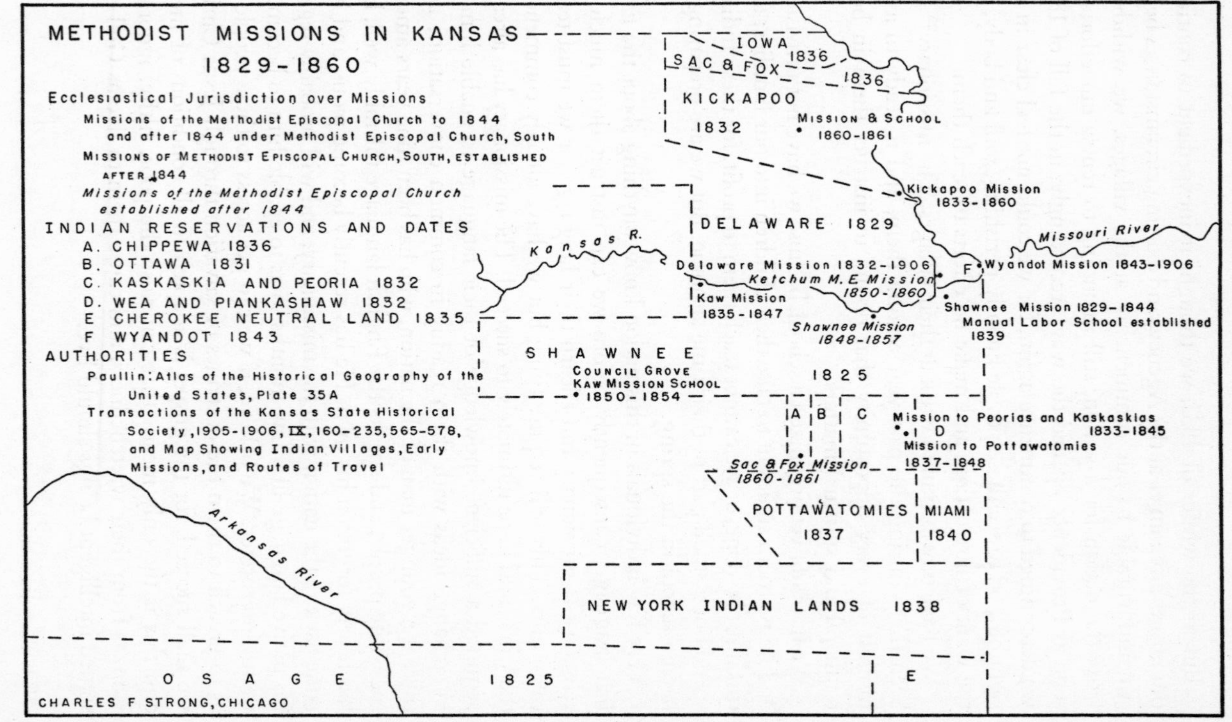
METHODIST MISSIONS IN KANSAS
1829-1860
Ecclesiastical Jurisdiction over Missions
Missions of the Methodist Episcopal Church to 1844 and after 1844 under Methodist Episcopal Church, South
Missions of Methodist Episcopal Church, South, established after 1844
Missions of the Methodist Episcopal Church established after 1844
INDIAN RESERVATIONS AND DATES
A. CHIPPEWA 1836
B. OTTAWA 1831
C. KASKASKIA AND PEORIA 1832
D. WEA AND PIANKASHAW 1832
E CHEROKEE NEUTRAL LAND 1835
F WYANDOT 1843
AUTHORITIES
Paullin: Atlas of the Historical Geography of the United States, Plate 35A
Transactions of the Kansas State Historical Society, 1905-1906, IX, 160-235, 565-578, and Map Showing Indian Villages, Early Missions, and Routes of Travel
IOWA
1836
SAC & FOX
1836
KICKAPOO
1832
Mission & School
1860-1861
Kickapoo Mission
1833-1860
DELAWARE 1829
Missouri River
Kansas R.
Delaware Mission 1832-1906
Ketchum M. E. Mission
1850-1860
F
Wyandot Mission 1843-1906
Kaw Mission
1835-1847
Shawnee Mission 1829-1844
Manual Labor School established
1839
Shawnee Mission
1848-1857
SHAWNEE
Council Grove
Kaw Mission School
1850-1854
1825
A
B
C
Mission to Peorias and Kaskaskias
1833-1845
D
Mission to Pottawatomies
1837-1848
Sac & Fox Mission
1860-1861
POTTAWATOMIES
1837
MIAMI
1840
Arkansas River
NEW YORK INDIAN LANDS 1838
OSAGE
1825
E
CHARLES F STRONG, CHICAGO

But in the winter of 1832, we thought it inexpedient to continue our efforts any longer at the Agency, and existing circumstances being still unfavorable to our commencing at the villages, we withdrew from the nation for a season, still intending to renew our efforts as soon as Providence opened the way. Accordingly, in the fall of 1835, we determined to commence again, for we could not feel clear in the sight of God to see these people literally perishing, soul and body, for the want of instruction, and make no efforts to teach them.

We have now begun to work at their villages. The missionary[25] has been there during the past year among them, and is ready to avail himself of every opportunity that occurs to instruct them in both temporal and spiritual matters.

We have not yet organized a school, because we have not provisions and house room sufficient to take their children into our families; and this must be done, or we cannot teach them to profit, for these Indians spend but a small part of their time at home. But we are preparing to open a school in the spring.

Very few individuals in this nation know anything about the English language, consequently before we can instruct them much in religion the missionary must learn their language, or we must teach them ours. This will require time; but we have already commenced the work, and hope ultimately to succeed. The missionary has already acquired a sufficient knowledge of their language to enable him to interchange ideas with them readily in common conversation; and there is a younger man of the nation, who has been nine years among the white people, and speaks the English language tolerably well, but has nearly forgotten his own. He has recently become pious, and has gone back to the nation with the missionary, and will probably regain his native language in a few months so as to enable him to become a useful interpreter. We believe, if we can get access to these people so as to preach to them the doctrines of salvation through Jesus Christ, we shall succeed, for the gospel is adapted to all conditions of men; and this is the only means that can raise the poor, filthy, ignorant Kanzas from their wretchedness, and cause them to live as God designed intelligent beings should live.

[25] William Johnson.

At this mission we have one missionary employed, and one man to cultivate the farm. The missionary is the Rev. Wm. Johnson. The members in society are three white and two Indians.

The buildings are a dwelling house, 36 feet by 18, one story and a half high, hewed logs, roof boards nailed on, not entirely finished; and also a kitchen and smoke house, each 18 feet square, under the same roof, with a ten foot passage between, roof, boards nailed on. Twenty acres of prairie, which was broken up and fenced last summer, is now ready for cultivation. No stock yet, excepting one pair of oxen.

The whole amount of property at this mission belonging to the missionary society is worth about one hundred and fifty dollars.

I remain yours, as usual,

THOS. JOHNSON

February 15, 1837.

III. LETTERS OF REV. JEROME C. BERRYMAN

A. KICKAPOO MISSION[26]

By mutual understanding among us here the reports for the missions within this district have hitherto been made to you by our superintendent, Rev. T. Johnson; but as he now requests that we all report our respective missions, I send you the following, which is under my care.

Our labors at this station have been in operation not quite one year. We opened a school on the 4th day of last March. Our general average number has been about 45. My appointment under government as teacher to this people commences with this year, the first day of which I reorganized the school in the public school house, taking in none but those who were given up to us for one year, to be taught and governed as we may think best. Under this regulation we have received upward of 50, 9 of whom, very promising boys, live with us—the rest eat dinner only. Those who now come to school are chiefly boys from ten to fifteen years of age. Some who have attended regular

[26] From *Christian Advocate and Journal,* IX (March 13, 1835), 114.

begin to read and write pretty well, and speak considerable English. We have removed to the government improvements, about a quarter of a mile from our first location. Here we intend to make all our future improvements. We are now about commencing a large and comfortable building for the use of the mission.

Our prospect of success, I have no hesitation in saying, is good. For a considerable length of time after we came here our way of access to the people in preaching to them was entirely hedged up. They, as you have heard before, have a notable religious leader of their own, who is also their chief. He is a Christian. He received his first religious impressions about twelve years ago, but by what means we have not been able precisely to ascertain. He says that he received them from God, without any human agency, which I am not disposed to doubt. Since that time he has been trying to get all his people to serve the true God, and has succeeded in getting about 400 followers. The author of a certain "annual register," published in this country, has lately said, this man "appears to have little knowledge of the doctrines of Christianity, only as his dogmas happen to agree with them."[27] But this is a great mistake, as well as others of a singular character. These people have for some years past been occasionally visited by ministers of our Church, and their leader has associated a great deal with our people previous to this mission being located among them; and by these means they have acquired considerable knowledge of the doctrines and practices of the Christian religion. But not having a missionary stationed among them until we came to them a year ago, of course their theory and practice of religion would be imperfect. Their forms of worship are both original and novel. They have in fact many religious peculiarities foreign to Christianity. Nevertheless some of them are truly pious. They are now united with us; and we frequently have very interesting meetings among them. At several of these meeting lately Ke-en-e-kuk, their leader, took the Bible in his hand, after we had preached, and told them that was God's book—that we ought to try to understand it, and that they must look to us for instruction. They seemed at first to have been afraid that we intended to introduce something new which would be injurious to

[27] Kickapoo Religious Society," in Isaac McCoy, *Annual Register of Indian Affairs* (1836), p. 31.

them; but we trust these fears are giving way to better sentiments.[28]

Besides our labors among the Indians, we preach statedly at Fort Leavenworth, at the special request of the officer in command of that post, Col. Dodge. I think the prospect for doing good here is flattering.

I am, dear brother, yours in Christ,

JEROME C. BERRYMAN[29]

January 28, 1835.

[28] John Dunbar, Presbyterian missionary, who visited the Kickapoo Mission in the summer of 1835, has left an interesting description of a worship service led by Ke-en-e-kuk on June 29, 1835:

"At 11 A.M. the hour for commencing their services, criers passed about through the village and called the people together. Their place of meeting was under some large trees in an open place in the midst of the village. First came three or four principal men, and took their places, and stood repeating prayers from their paddles till the congregation was assembled. The women and children began to assemble first. They came in following each other, and passed before these men at their prayers, shook hands with each of them, and then proceeded round to their seats, which were their blankets spread on the ground. Each individual occupies the same seat from Sabbath to Sabbath, at least this is the case with the women and children. The women were seated on the left of the speaker, the children in front, and the men on the right. After the assembly had come together, and were properly seated, the prophet came forward, took his stand, and commenced his discourse, which he continued more than an hour. He was followed by two others who spoke briefly. After prayer and singing the meeting was closed. All again passed around, shook hands, and retired to their lodges, still repeating their paddle prayers. The paddle, as it is called, is a piece of wood, wrought into a peculiar shape. In this piece of wood are cut certain hieroglyphics, which are to be learned by all the followers of the prophet, and the prayers for which they stand to be repeated at their seasons devotions. These paddles are held as peculiarly sacred to them.

"During the services at their religious meetings, several men, appointed for the purpose, went about through the assembly each with his rod in his hand, to keep order among the children and dogs, and to see that each person was in his proper place. One or more of these men attend the school and keep order among the scholars. Friday of each week is called the whipping day with them. On this day all who may have been charged with misdemeanors, during the preceding week, are tried, and if found guilty receive a flogging on the spot. Parents do not chastise their children but trust to these regulators to perform this duty for them . . . ."("Journal of John Dunbar," *Kansas Historical Collections,* XIV [1918], 586).

[29] Jerome C. Berryman (1810–1906) was a native Kentuckian who came to Missouri in 1828 and was admitted on trial to the Missouri Conference in the same year. Three other members of the "class" of 1828 became Indian missionaries also. In 1833 he was sent to the Kickapoo Mission and school, where he remained until 1847, when he became presiding elder of the Cape Girardeau District. A prominent Missouri Conference educator, he was head of Howard High School and of Arcadia High School and founder of Arcadia College. He was the last surviving member of the General Conference of 1844. Although he cast his lot with the Methodist Episcopal Church, South, he was a Union man during the Civil War (Woodard, *op. cit.,* 65–66; Stanley, *op. cit.,* pp. 129–31; "Memoir," *Minutes of the Annual Conferences of the Methodist Episcopal Church, South, 1906,* p. 46).

B. GOOD NEWS FROM THE INDIAN MANUAL LABOR SCHOOL[30]

Brother Berryman, under the date of April 4, 1842, says:

We have had a pretty good state of religion at our institution through the winter; but the native children did not seem to manifest more than an ordinary degree of feeling, until at our second quarterly meeting, held three weeks ago. At that meeting there was a general excitement which embraced every class of our congregation. Sometimes we had from thirty to forty penitents at the altar of prayer; several were converted. Several men employed as laborers at the institution have become the subjects of a work of grace, since they came among us, and have joined the church.

At our monthly concert prayer meeting for March, we proposed that all who felt like it should give one cent a week, beginning with the first of November last, up to that time, to the cause of missions. The proposition was unanimously agreed to; we received pledges for about $42, which will be paid in due time; and we intend to follow up the plan for the balance of the year.

On Monday evening, March 14th, while our quarterly meeting was still in progress, brother Wm. Osman, a young man I suppose about twenty-eight years of age, who was employed as a laboring hand on the farm, was taken sick, and continued to decline until the following Sunday afternoon, and expired about 3 o'clock. His disease was called here winter fever. He endured his affliction with patience, and died in his right mind, triumphing in the hour of death through that Savior in whom he had long trusted. He had been with us about twelve months. He came properly recommended as a member of the Methodist Episcopal Church, and continued to maintain a reputable standing among us. If I understood him correctly, he was raised near Beaver in Pennsylvania; and has some friends living in that region, though his father and mother are dead, as I learned from himself. He left some good clothing, and a small amount due him for his work; but gave no direction as to what he wished to be done with either. If any of his friends should see this, and address a letter to me at West Port, Jackson co., Mo., I will give them all the necessary information in the case.

[30] From *Western Christian Advocate,* IX (May 20, 1842), 18.

C. CLOTHING FOR MISSIONS[31]

BROTHER ELLIOTT—

I have for some time past been thinking that I ought to say something to our friends who are desirous to aid in this missionary cause, but on account of the hardness of the times are at a loss to know how to do it. And I think this is the case with many of the preachers as well as the people. I am inclined to think so more especially since our last conference in Missouri. I there heard many of them say, when called on for their missionary money, "I have none, the circuit where I traveled has from three to five hundred members; but there is literally no money in the country, and I consequently could not make missionary collections." Well, we know exactly how this matter is, and are willing to admit that these brothers would have had but little success if they *had tried* to collect missionary money on their circuits. Still there is a way for something to be done where no money can be had. Let the money come first if possible, because that is every way the most convenient for all concerned. But when the people have not got it, for the Lord's sake, let us not debar them from the privilege of giving such things as they have. I will then, with your permission, tell the readers of the *Advocate* how they can do a great deal without paying a single dollar in money. And I fancy that many who may read this, will say when they come to this part of my letter, "You are striking the right card now." Well, then, you know, Brother Elliott, that we have a large Indian School immediately on the western border of Missouri where we have for several years past averaged about one hundred scholars, or students we will call them, and we closed our last session with one hundred and twenty. In this school we are teaching the children almost every thing that they ought to learn; and thank God, with a great deal of success too. Here we have various mechanical and farming operations going on, in which the boys are employed; and spinning, weaving, knitting, and sewing, in which the girls are engaged to good effect. Our farm is large, and in harvest time, especially, we have to employ many of our adult natives to help us. And these natives can generally be paid off for this labor in clothing; this in fact is better for them than money. It takes not

[31] From *Western Christian Advocate,* X (December 1, 1843), 130. The Reverend Charles Elliott was the editor of the *Advocate* at this time.

less than fifteen hundred dollars' worth of clothing and bedding, per annum, for our school children. Besides this the teachers and mechanics about the place must have clothes from some source. All taken together, two thousand dollars' worth of dry goods would not more than supply the place one year. Now let me ask, What do our friends wear at home? Any thing of the same kind would suit us here. Could they not occasionally spare us a little? We think they could; we think they will. Establish a place of general deposit in each circuit; and one will have a pair of stockings, woolen or cotton; another a few yards of linsey or janes; another some domestic cotton; another a handkerchief or shawl; and sometimes one merchant will give you a set of knives and forks; another some spoons, another some calico or thimbles, pins and needles; and I had almost forgotten to say, some of the sisters will give a quilt or coverlet, a pair of sheets, pillow-slips, towels, table-clothes, or something of that sort. Let them all be sent to the general place of deposit; and when boxed up neatly, direct them to the Indian Manual Labor School care of Simpson & Hunter, Westport, Jackson county, Missouri. Whenever they arrive here I will vouch for the right and honest disposal of them. Or if it be preferred, let the boxes so made up be sent to any convenient place on the Ohio or Mississippi between the mouth of the Ohio and St. Louis; or to any place on the Missouri river, and let me be notified of the fact before I leave home for New York, the first of Next April; or I can be informed by letter at Pittsburgh, Cincinnati, and St. Louis, on my return about the first of June.[32]

Now, my dear brother, I do not see anything to hinder our people from doing a great deal in this way without interfering at all with the money collections. And I want you to let our people know that the bishops and others, who control these matters have brought down the appropriations until we are actually almost, yes, quite reduced to want. If our friends do not help us the "Indian Manual Labor School," the grandest enterprise ever undertaken in the Indian country, must decline, must die. Thank God, there are no symptoms of decline yet; it is vigorous and healthy: But it cannot live on empty prayers. No doubt we have enough of these; but these alone will not do. If these are all our friends will give us, we don't want them; let them appropriate these nearer home, upon their own stingy souls.

[32] Berryman was a delegate to the General Conference of 1844.

But time admonishes me to quit. I could write you a book about our school and the work generally in this mission district, but both you and your readers have so much else to do you would not be likely to read it. I will say, however, the good Lord is still with us, and Indians are being converted to God.

Your fellow-laborer in the Gospel.

J. C. Berryman

October 22, 1843.

P.S. Should any wish to write to me, let them address me at Westport, Jackson county, Missouri.

D. STATE OF THE HEATHEN[33]

Brother Berryman, in a letter to us, remarks, "Many of the heathen are dying without religion. What shall we say of them? Or what will they say of us at the bar of God, that we withheld the lamp of life from their bewildered feet? O that Christians, who are living at ease in Zion, would lay these matters to heart. O, Lord, can it be true that thousands of heathen are going to hell daily for want of the Gospel? And we, instead of sending it to them, will give our money for tea, coffee, tobacco, fine clothes, &c. May the Lord have mercy on us!"

Could we, who live in the midst of civilization be placed in the situation of brother Berryman, we should perhaps feel a little more and act somewhat differently with regard to the heathen. Millions of dollars are annually spent uselessly by professors of religion of all denominations, while unenlightened Pagans are destitute of the Gospel. God will call such professors to account at the great day of retribution. With our devoted brother we pray, "The Lord have mercy upon us."

E. ENEAS, THE CONVERTED INDIAN[34]

Dear Brother Elliott—

The death of brother Eneas, of whom I am now about to write, had nothing very peculiar connected with it, only as it is considered in connection with his life and circumstances.

I doubt not you and your associates about the Book Establishment

[33] From *Western Christian Advocate,* XI (May 10, 1844), 14.

[34] From *Western Christian Advocate,* XI (May 10, 1844), 13.

recollect brother Eneas, the Indian who accompanied me on a tour five years ago up the Ohio; and staid with you at Cincinnati while I went up to Pittsburg. I assure you he never forgot you and the numerous friends with whom he became acquainted while on that trip. Though it cannot be said that Indians are the most grateful people, it may truly be said of this man, that gratitude was one of his most prominent traits of character. As an evidence of this, I have only to produce his dying bequest. He had several hundred dollars' worth of property, which he had gathered up by economy since he became a Christian; and as he had no family dependent on him, he directed that all his little estate be divided among the missionaries, to whom he felt himself a great debtor. But as he had numerous unconverted relatives who contended for the property, it was deemed most advisable to let them have it. Indeed, we never intimated a desire to take it. Such was his ardent love for those who had shown him so much kindness, and had given him so much good counsel, when journeying with me before, that I think I should have had to use some persuasion to have reconciled him not to go with me again this spring; for he often expressed a strong desire to go, that he might be still more fully inducted into the ways of Christian life.

Eneas was of the Pottawatomie tribe by his mother, and his father was a Kickapoo. He spoke the language of both these tribes, as well as a little broken English and French. When I first became acquainted with him, ten years ago last fall, he was a devoted follower of the Kickapoo prophet, of whom and his religion I might write many things that would be interesting, especially to children, but not now. Eneas was one of this man's foremost followers, and a very important auxiliary in carrying on his scheme of proselytism. As an evidence, not only of his devotion to this prophet, but also of his sincerity, he carried many scars to his grave, which had been made by the lash on his bare back by the prophet's whippers, who were a kind of ministers or confessors, to receive confessions and administer absolution. And the penitent was taught to believe that this flagel*l*ation, voluntarily submitted to, operated in the same way that Christians believe the blood of Christ does!

These whippers, and even the prophet himself, have been known to submit to this accursed rite, with marks of the deepest penitence. But more about Eneas. It was not until Eneas had become well acquainted with me, that I seemed really to be gaining over any of his people to Christianity; and in fact not until he took the trip with me above alluded to, that he became fully decided to leave the prophet and follow Christ. Had I not relied upon a lying Frenchman to interpret for me, but taken up Eneas from the start, I believe he would much sooner have embraced Christianity; for I am confident he was a sincere inquirer after the truth all the while. But he seemed not to have been fully convinced that the prophet was himself deceived, and a deceiver of others, until the time he took the tour with me among the white people. He then had an opportunity of seeing that so many things were the contrary of what the prophet had represented, that he went home a decided Christian, and remained so, through much persecution, without wavering, till, like ripe fruit, he was gathered into the garner of God.

During the last five years of his life, Eneas was a most consistent Christian. He not only labored faithfully as an interpreter for the missionary, but, like his Master, he was ever going about doing good to his fellow-men. Having lost his wife and children by death several years ago, he had no domestic charge, and spent much of his time in my family. And often, when it was not practicable for me to accompany him, he has gone alone from house to house, and from wigwam to wigwam, teaching and preaching to the people about Jesus; but rarely without first soliciting a word of instruction from his missionary before he would start. And many whole evenings have I sat, till bedtime, with the deepest interest, and received his report of what he had said and done through the day; and I have no recollection that he ever failed to make such a report. It could hardly have been otherwise with such a man, than that he should have been constantly improving himself, while he was made a blessing to others. This was eminently the case with Eneas. God blessed him with a rapid increase in knowledge and happiness, and made him the instrument of bringing many to the knowledge of the truth as it is in Jesus.

Brother Talbott,[35] who is now the missionary at Kickapoo, testifies that our worthy brother, Eneas, was found thus faithful unto the day

[35] Nathaniel M. Talbott (1805–72), a native of Shelby County, Kentucky, spent twenty-four years in mission work and was a charter member of the Indian Mission Conference (Woodard, *op. cit.,* pp. 60–62). During the Civil War he was a chaplain in the Confederate army.

of his death, which occurred on the 29th of January 1844. His disease was something of a pleuritic character, and lasted but a few days; during which he often spoke of his state of mind and his prospects; and every word was in accordance with the undeviating Christian character he had maintained for the last five years of his life.

The wisdom of God is manifested in that providence that was preparing this man for usefulness, long before any of us knew any thing of him; and his goodness is seen in the means that were brought to bear upon him for his own conversion and salvation.

J. C. Berryman.

Indian Manual Labor School, April 1, 1844.

P.S. A number of other Christian Indians have died this winter, particularly among the Shawnees, and have given additional evidence of the truth and power of the Gospel.

IV. A CIRCUIT-RIDER'S FRONTIER EXPERIENCES

By JEROME C. BERRYMAN[36]

Arcadia, Mo., March 9, 1868

THE KICKAPOO MISSION

The [Missouri] conference sat this fall (1833) at Cane Hill camp ground in Arkansas. I attended and was appointed to establish a mission and school among the Kickapoo Indians in the neighborhood of Fort Leavenworth on the Missouri river, in what was then a part of the Indian Territory, but now the state of Kansas.....

On my return trip from the Cane Hill conference I had for traveling companions Bishop Soule, Brothers Jesse Greene, Thomas Johnson, William Johnson, Benjamin Johnson, and R. H. Jordan—seven of us in all..... Arriving at Mr. Renfro's, the name of the adventurous new settler, a little before nightfall, we found him with his family, a wife and six children, comfortably situated in a round-log or rather pole cabin which he had constructed with his own hands. The eaves of the roof just cleared our heads as we entered the door. There was no

[36] *Kansas Historical Collections,* XVI (1923–25), 177–226. Berryman began this autobiography in 1858, finishing it in December of that year. Some years later he revised and enlarged the sketches. It was from his grandson, the Hon. J. W. Berryman of Ashland, Kansas, that the Kansas Historical Society secured the manuscript for publication.

floor but about sixteen feet square of the face of mother earth. Outside of this family residence nothing was to be seen to comfort weary travelers except the luxuriant natural pasture which extended as far as we could see. The next morning, to our great discomfort, we found it extended miles beyond. Into this pasture we turned our horses, taking the precaution to bell one of them. . . . .

Bright and early in the morning we went out on the trail of our horses, and in the course of an hour we found them taking early breakfast quite a distance from the house. I mounted one of the bishop's horses, the other and my own following, and on arriving at the house the bishop met me and remarked, "You will do to go to an Indian mission. That horse was never ridden before." His horses were Canadian ponies, a beautiful match of bays.

We were soon on our way, and traveled seventeen miles before halting for breakfast at an old deserted Indian village on White river. I am here reminded that Brother A[ndrew] Monroe was one of our party, for he, I think, acted the part of cook in preparing our breakfast that morning. Probably Brother Jordan was not with us on our return trip from conference, though he journeyed with me to conference. The bishop had provided a good stock of peaches before leaving Cane Hill, but not being very well he had not eaten many of them, and as he did not wish to be encumbered with them any further he brought them out of his wagon and laid them on the ground, saying he had no further use for them. I do not remember if any but myself ate of them that morning, but my recollection is very distinct that I enjoyed them greatly while Brother Monroe was getting breakfast, for they were exceedingly delicious. It was said that I disposed of thirty-two of them, and then took my full share of the breakfast. I remember the bishop repeated his statement—"Berryman will do for an Indian missionary." I may as well remark here that all through life I have been a liberal eater, and for a number of years while we were associated in the missions it was a matter of dispute between Thomas Johnson and myself which of us, as a habit, ate the most. This abounding appetite was of no trifling advantage to me during my stay among the Indians. Often in visiting them at their wigwams and cabins it has served me a good purpose when one of a more dainty stomach would have failed to enjoy the hospitalities of his red brethren, and consequently failed to please them. I have many times sat on the ground with several of them around a large bowl or kettle of hominy, and using the same wooden spoon, passing round from hand to hand, ate as heartily of their homely fare as any one of themselves.[37]

Breakfast over at White river, we journeyed on, nothing of interest that I remember occurring for the remainder of our trip. I returned to St. Charles county, where I had left my wife, and thence to St. Louis, to purchase a few articles for an outfit for the mission, and shipping these to Fort Leavenworth by the Missouri river, I took my wife by private conveyance up to our new field of labor. We stopped for a few weeks at the Shawnee mission, the home of Brother Thomas Johnson, where we were most kindly entertained by him and his excellent wife until I could get some temporary cabins built at the settlement of the Kickapoos some thirty miles further up the Missouri river. In fact, the Kickapoos could hardly be said to have made a settlement yet in their new home, for they had just that summer been removed from Illinois to this new location. Having spent the fall in hunting, they were just returning to the vicinity of Fort Leavenworth, and our mission station served as a sort of nucleus for their subsequent settlement.

A few days after our arrival in the Indian country I went up to select a site for the Kickapoo mission, and employing some hands I soon had pretty comfortable log cabins ready for occupancy. True they were made of round logs with puncheon floors, clapboard roof and loft of the same, but they were warm, and so were our hearts. We spent two winters happily in this humble home among the savages before we got into better buildings.

The place chosen for the mission was a high bluff overlooking the Missouri river, in full view north of us, and three miles above Fort Leavenworth. This bluff, all along the river was covered by a very

[37] Peter Akers told the following story to the historian Beggs. Bishops Soule and Roberts once lost their horses in the Choctaw country of Alabama and, wandering about without provisions, came upon an old Indian squaw cooking some kind of meat. "[They] making signs of hunger, and of a wish to enjoy her hospitality, she soon placed the food before them. Bishop Roberts sat upon the ground, taking the platter in his lap, and seemed to relish his food. The other two, however, after taking a mouthful or two, seeing the filthy manner in which it was dressed and cooked, were not only compelled to refrain from eating more, but lost what they had already eaten. But the Bishop kept on eating, and laughing as heartily as he ate at the daintiness of his companions. Before they left they found that they had been served to skunk's meat" (S[tephen] R. Beggs, *Pages from the Early History of the West and North-West* [Cincinnati, 1868], pp. 274–75).

heavy growth of walnut, linn, hackberry, oak, elm, and other varieties of timber. To the south of our location was spread out an undulating prairie valley with timber-crowned hills in the distant view. Through this Eden-like valley from southwest to northeast ran a living stream of water. This pretty rivulet was named "Salt creek," I know not why. We occasionally angled successfully for fish in the shaded waters of this stream, for it was bordered by a narrow strip of wood. Never was any spot of rich earth ornamented with more beautiful carpeting of grass and flowers than this divine but still terrestial plantation. There flowers of almost countless variety began early in spring to put on their "coat of many colors," and continued to reflect the beauty of Him who made and printed the fabric until autumnal frosts drove them to winter quarters. From dawn till dark were the groves along the borders of this meadow made joyful by song birds of varied plumage. Nor had the divine Planter omitted that which gratified the appetite as well as the eye of man, for in many spots native strawberries grew and ripened to perfection. 'Tis not without grateful, though sad, recollection that memory now recalls the happy hours we used to spend, my Sarah and I, picking this juicy fruit from the vine and listening to the sweet carols which greeted us from feathered songsters chanting their evening hymns of praise to God. How could we otherwise than unite with them, as we did in heart if not in words. There also plums, grapes, crabapples, and hazelnuts grew in the "roughs," or thickets, found here and there.

Without exaggeration, such is but a meager description of the location and natural surroundings of my first mission home. And I must not forget to add that there were springs of limpid water to be found here and there, to gladden the dwellers in this miniature Paradise. But neither its new owners nor their missionary were capable of fully appreciating its near likeness to the place the poet had in his mind when he sang so sweetly in the following words:

Beautiful valley of Eden!
  Sweet is thy noontide calm;
Over the hearts of the weary
  Breathing thy waves of balm.
Beautiful valley of Eden,
  Home of the pure and blest;
How often amid the wild billows
  I dream of thy rest—sweet rest.

Let me linger here a little longer. Here all my children except one first opened their eyes to look upon surrounding scenes. Here we buried our first born, Sarah Emily, who left the earthly for the heavenly Eden at the age of three years. And twenty miles from here we buried her little brother, William Cessna, aged two years.

But enough, I must go on with the narrative. We had taken with us an excellent young woman from Missouri, Dyza Tucker, who was not merely a help for my wife but also good company for her. At the fort also, three miles below us on the river, there were several officers' families who were good neighbors for us. Indeed during our eight years' stay at this mission the loneliness of our situation was very much relieved by the society of the officers of the army and their families. I often preached to them and the soldiers at the request of the officers in command, and once, when we were about going to visit our friends in Kentucky, they presented us with a sum that more than paid the expenses of the trip.

At the mission, simultaneously with the building of our residence, I put up a schoolhouse of the same material and opened a school for Indian children very shortly after getting my family settled. I was without an assistant, and taught the school myself, my wife and Miss Tucker providing dinner for them every day. My school was quickly filled up to the number of ninety. As primitive a set of untaughts certainly as ever entered a schoolhouse. Not one of them understood a word of English, nor had then ever seen a book, unless by mere accident.

I soon discovered that to teach so large a number one by one would be an almost endless job, so taxing my inventive faculties a little, I constructed a machine by which they might at least be aided in learning the alphabet. I took four thin boards about three inches in width and six feet or less in length, and nailing them together so as to form a box I fastened it perpendicularly to the schoolroom wall. Then I took another board that would work up and down in this box and pasted the letters of the alphabet on one side of it at short intervals. I fastened a cord to the top end of this sliding board, and, passing it over a pulley above, I was enabled to take my seat at a convenient distance and by pulling the cord present each letter singly at a small opening made for this purpose in the front side of the box. I then divided my scholars into classes of convenient size, and calling these classes up one at a time caused them to form a half circle in front of my machine, and taught them the alphabet as above indicated. In two days' time I think every one knew any letter at sight. I also taught them to spell words of one syllable in the same way.

Our greatest difficulty in teaching Indian children was in getting them to understand the meaning of words after they had learned to spell them. And to overcome this difficulty we at last had to adopt the plan of taking them from their homes and into our mission families. This finally resulted in the building up of one large mission-school establishment known as the Shawnee Manual Labor School for some half-dozen neighboring tribes. This institution was located in the Shawnee nation, six miles southwest of where Kansas City now stands. It was commenced in the year 1839 under the general supervision of Brother Thomas Johnson, assisted a part of the time by Rev. Wesley Browning. Brother Johnson's health having failed, I was put in charge of this school in the fall of 1840,[38] and was succeeded at the Kickapoo mission by Rev. N. M. Talbot[t], who had previously been at the Peoria mission eight years.

KE-EN-E-KUK

Many incidents transpired during the eight years I was at the Kickapoo mission that would be interesting to relate, but I must here content myself with the recital of a few leading facts. When I went to that people I found among them a man of their own tribe by the name of Ke-en-e-kuk who exercised unlimited sway over the larger portion of the tribe, but the rest despised him. These last named, however, were opposed to any innovations upon their savage habits, and consequently opposed to missions and schools. Ke-en-e-kuk and his party were in favor of both, and gave us apparently a hearty welcome. Ke-en-e-kuk himself meant no such welcome, only as he might be able clandestinely to use us to accomplish his own ambitious ends, as we learned to our mortification after a while, but did not suspect at first. He had been preaching to his people for several years before they left Illinois to come west, and had made some of our preachers there believe he was a Christian.

[38] The list of appointments to the Indian missions of the Methodist Episcopal church for 1840 gives D. Kinnear as having charge of the Manual Labor School that year. Berryman's name first appears as head of the school in 1841.

A presiding elder there had actually given him a written license to preach. His endorsements were so satisfactory that we received him as a local preacher, and Brother Thomas Johnson, who was superintendent of our missions, employed him with a salary of two hundred dollars as a helper in our work. I had not been a great while among the Kickapoos until I baptized about four hundred of them, including Ke-en-e-kuk, the preacher, or prophet, as he was familiarly called. So far as he was concerned it was all a blind, and answered his purpose for a time. It should be stated here that this man had procured in the recent treaty his tribe had made with the government a stipulation for the building of a church house for his benefit, which stipulation was carried out by the government after our mission was established. In this house he would rarely allow us to officiate at all, pleading as an excuse that his people were yet too ignorant to be benefited by us, and promising that he would gently lead them along into our ways. He had inaugurated a peculiar mode of worship in which they were all perfectly trained, and certainly they gave strong evidence of sincerity. He had appointed men as flagellators, who carried their long, keen rods with them wherever they went. These officers whipped not only the children who violated the prophet's rules, but men and women as well. I have often seen both men and women at their public meetings for worship come forward and receive a number of lashes on their bare backs, so well laid on as to cause blood to run freely. Many of them bore visible scars on their backs, caused by former flagellations. We found out finally that this presumptuous man claimed to be the Son of God come again in the flesh, and that the Father had sent him to the red people this time as he did to the white people before! His followers were taught and they believed that this punishment which they received from the whippings was an atonement for their sins, and that the blood they shed was expiatory in its effects, hence their willing submission to the lash.

Indians generally are very much controlled by their chiefs, not so much by their hereditary or civil chiefs as by another class. These latter are aspirants, endowed by nature with somewhat more than ordinary intellect, readily perceiving and feeling their superiority. The pretensions of these savage politicians are supported in the main by appeals to the credulity of the ignorant masses. The pretenders have performed some wonderful deed, seen some dazzling vision, or received some startling revelation from the Great Spirit, all of which is received upon the bare assertion of the deceiver with a willingness proportionate to his audacity and the stupidity of his dupes. This is the way that the great leaders among savages rise to place and power. There may be now and then an honorable exception. It is the fruitful source of the miseries that have fallen upon the savage tribes of America, and would to God it were true alone of these.

Does not the heathen world groan beneath the accumulating evils which arise from ignorance, superstition and vice on the part of the many and the shrewdness, ambition, and presumptuousness of the comparatively few on the other hand? Every age has produced in every country minds of lofty aspirations, and nothing but intelligence and virtue can prevent the reckless and ruinous adventures of such minds. This class of men must be held in check by the counteracting influence of popular virtue, or they will in time barbarize the world. Our own distracted country is cursed with too many Ke-en-e-kuks today.

Among the followers of the Kickapoo prophet we found a few at length who could see that they were being deceived by an impostor. These were in every way the better class. Out of these, and a goodly number from the other portion of the nation, we had at the close of my term of service among them built up a Christian society of devoted followers of Jesus numbering about fifty. The influence of the prophet had been measurably broken, and he finally sunk away into obscurity.

Of those who separated themselves from the prophet when we discarded him, two men deserve to be remembered. These were Pes-haw-gan, a full blood Kickapoo, and Eneas, a cross of Kickapoo and Pottawatomie. Pes-haw-gun was a man endowed by nature with noble traits of mind and heart, and from the time of his conversion until his death was a shining light among his people. The same is true in the case of Eneas. But in the latter we enjoyed the additional benefit of his services as interpreter. When a young man he had had some years of association with the garrison at Bellefontaine in St. Louis county, Missouri, and by that means had gained some knowledge of English. He was an apt scholar, and by our instruction became a very reliable interpreter as well as preacher of gospel truth. His wife died several years before my removal from the Kickapoo mission. I then took him into my family, and he gave his whole time for several years to the religious instruction of his people. He visited from house to house as interpreter for me, or went alone when I could not go. He invariably asked advice from me before starting out, and when he returned he made a report of his whole day's work. The devotion and daily walk of this Christian Indian was a joy to behold and a rebuke to many who had better opportunities. Such was his love for Christ and His cause, that he left, when he died, his entire little estate to be used in the interests of the mission, and doubtless he ascended to be with the Lord.

In preaching through an interpreter much depends upon his qualifications. For instance, on one occasion I took for a text, "The Lord is my sun and shield." When my interpreter undertook to translate the passage he used the word *"no-que-thah,"* which in his native tongue meant *son,* or male child. Thus my text became "The Lord is my male child." Had I not understood enough of his language to detect the error what a sermon those Indians would have heard that morning! It is of vast importance, too, that the interpreter be in sympathy with the preacher in his mission, for if not, the very intonations of the interpreter's voice, and manner of delivery, may spoil the effect upon those who hear. We had both these disadvantages to overcome in the beginning of our labors among the Kickapoos. The only interpreter whose services we could engage for several years was a Canadian Frenchman who had intermarried with these Indians, and was no better in any respect than the worst of them. Withal he was a Roman Catholic with characteristic prejudices. This in a large measure accounted for our trouble with Ke-en-e-kuk, the prophet.

Among the Shawnees and Delawares the Johnsons readily found reliable interpreters. Lewis Rogers, a native Shawnee, had in his youth been taken to a school in Kentucky and there, besides getting some knowledge of books, had been brought under good religious influences. He at once engaged in cooperating with the missionaries. The head chief of the band to which Rogers belonged, Captain Fish by name, was also favorably disposed towards Christianity, and soon with his entire band embraced the faith. Wa-wa-la-peah, head chief of another band of that tribe, followed suit in a year or so after, and became champion in the cause of religion and education among his people. He was a man of imposing personal presence, superior intellect, and eloquent speech, mighty in exhortation and prayer, his influence was a power for good among his people. Joseph Parks and William his brother were "half-breed"; that is, their father was a white man and their mother a Shawnee woman. They both spoke English well, and had grown up to manhood under home influences as made them good men, and they with earnestness fell into ranks with Wa-wa-la-peah, and in fact took the lead in introducing the habits of Christian reform among the Shawnees. Joseph Parks was by all odds the best interpreter of a sermon or any religious discourse that was found among the tribes on and near Kansas river.

It was in the winter of 1839 that I was commissioned by the Rev. Thomas Johnson to go to Pittsburgh, Pa., to purchase materials for the Shawnee Manual Labor School. This trip to Pittsburgh was made as far as Louisville, Ky., on horseback. Taking my Kickapoo interpreter, Eneas, with me, we passed down through Missouri, Illinois, and a portion of Kentucky, giving missionary talks by the way. This put $500 or $600 in hand for the benefit of our missions. Eneas returned home from Louisville, and I made a short visit to Bishop Soule at his home in Lebanon, Ohio, before going on to Pittsburgh. The bishop's household at that time was composed of himself, Mrs. Soule, and a single daughter—as pleasant a family as it was ever my privilege to visit.

It was while on this errand I met and made the acquaintance of Rev. Wesley Browning and his excellent wife, being by them most hospitably entertained during my detention of a full month in Pittsburgh. Brother Browning was a valuable assistant to me in the purchase and shipment of what we needed, which in bulk and value amounted to a steamboat load. For the transportation of this freight I chartered a new boat just built by Captain Kizer for the Missouri river. The cargo was safely delivered by the *Shawnee,* for that was her name, at Kansas Landing, now Kansas City, and Brother Johnson was much pleased with the manner in which the trust had been discharged.

Brother Browning became so much interested in our mission work during my stay in Pittsburgh that the fall following he took a transfer, and was appointed to assist Brother Johnson in the work at Indian Manual Labor School.

EDUCATING THE SHAWNEES

In the fall of 1840 I succeeded to the superintendency of the Shawnee Manual Labor School. This institution had now got well under way by the efficient and systematic labors the preceding year of Reverends Thomas Johnson and Wesley Browning. In fact Brother Browning had been the principal of the school, while Brother Johnson had the general supervision of it, together with all our missions then connected with the Missouri conference.

The labor and care connected with this new charge were very great. With the efficient aid furnished me from time to time by my colaborers, I was enabled to give satisfaction so far as I know. In the month of June, 1844, the Indian missions within the Indian Territory were erected into a separate conference,[39] by the General Conference, and I was appointed by the bishops as general superintendent of the whole. This appointment was made in conformity with an act of the General Conference providing for such an officer in the Indian Mission Conference. I continued to fill this office until it was suspended in the fall of 1845; then I was again returned to the superintendency of the Manual Labor School. This position had been filled in the interim by Rev. E. T. Peery, a good man and true, and now gone to his rest in heaven no doubt.[40]

I have said that the management of the affairs of the Manual Labor School was hard work. I certainly found it so. With an average attendance of one hundred pupils of both sexes, all boarded, lodged, and clothed in and by the institution;[41] an extensive mechanic's de-

[39] The Indian Mission Conference.

[40] Edward T. Peery had begun his ministry in the Holston Conference but in 1832 was sent to the Shawnee Mission, Missouri Conference. He later served as a presiding elder and died near Kansas City in 1864 (Stanley, *op. cit.*, p. 128).

[41] John Dunbar, who visited the Shawnee Mission on July 5, 1835, commented on the fact that the Methodists, before the establishment of the Manual Labor School, boarded many of their students: "The Methodist Board allow their missionaries at these stations to cultivate a farm, and raise their own provisions, and to give the children, that attend their schools, their dinners, or even their entire board, as they think proper; but the Baptist Board give their mssionaries only a bare support, and instruct them to give their whole labor to communicating religious instructions, etc. cultivating no more land, than is sufficient for a garden. There is this difference in the modes of conducting the missions of their respective Boards at these stations. Which mode is, on the whole, preferable, is perhaps not easy to decide" ("Journal of John Dunbar," *Kansas Historical Collections,* XIV [1915–18], 587–88).

partment for the instruction of the boys in different branches of mechanism; a domestic department in which the girls were taught to spin, weave, sew, knit, wash, cook, etc.; a farm of some six-hundred acres in cultivation, together with grist and saw mills in operation; all to be supervised by one man; and he the general financier, bookkeeper, and official correspondent of the establishment, and having at the same time the pastoral work to do in person—all this, I repeat was work enough for one man. I did it for three and a half years consecutively, being actively employed upon an average of fourteen hours every day. I went to the place with a most vigorous and elastic constitution. It failed me to such an extent that at one time I was for months almost an invalid with lumbago, or disease of the back and hips. From this I have never fully recovered and probably never shall in this life. The duties of my office while I was general superintendent, while they required me to travel a great deal, were not a tax upon my physical energies. For although my field of operations extended from the Missouri river to Red river, running back into the interior a distance of one hunded and fifty miles from the states of Missouri and Arkansas, still the country was rather pleasant to travel over. I could make my trip rather a matter of recreation than otherwise. And I must say that with the exception of absence from my family, I enjoyed this work very much. It gave me an opportunity of exploring extensively one of the most beautiful and fertile countries on the continent. It brought me in pleasant contact with the officers of the government and the leading men of the various tribes embraced in my bounds. It also gave me much enjoyment in my association with the various missionaries and their families of our own church and others who were then engaged in the territory.

The first session of the Indian Mission conference was held in the fall of 1844 in the Cherokee nation, near Tahlequah, their seat of government, and was presided over by Bishop Thomas A. Morris. He and I boarded at the same house, indeed slept in the same bed. As the question of church division was then the absorbing topic among Methodists, of course the bishop and I talked some upon the subject. He deplored the apparent necessity for division, but acknowledged that he saw no way to avoid it. He said that from his knowledge of the whole connection, he was free to say that the purest type of Methodism existed in the Southern states. He also said that when the time for final separation should come he would be found with the Southern division, "if he could do so without unchurching himself." He further remarked, I distinctly remember, that he felt under obligations to his brethren in Ohio. At a certain time in Kentucky, he felt himself reduced to such financial straits that he was seriously meditating a location to provide for his family, when the brethren in Ohio invited him across the river and liberally provided for him. He was in fact still enjoying a home in their midst from which he could not easily separate himself. I need not say I loved Bishop Morris. Whoever knew him and did not love him? I learned to love him when I was a boy and he was "our presiding elder," and preached to us at Old Bethel church where I was raised. I must say, however, that he does furnish a very striking instance of the frequent prevalence of men's surroundings over their honest convictions. Had Bishop Morris had his home in the South he would have been a Southern bishop I think.

At this conference we elected two delegates to the Louisville convention. Rev. William H. Goode,[42] then principal of Fort Coffee Academy was one of them. He was a transfer from the Indiana conference, and had been with us a year or so. He was a fine specimen of Christian manhood. To an excellent personality he had added the graces of a good education and ministerial dignity. At the first session of Indian Mission conference we elected him to represent us at Louisville the following spring, in what is known in history as "The Louisville convention." But in due time before the assembling of that convention, he gave me official notice that he should decline to serve. Thanking us for the honor conferred by his election, he gave as his reason for accepting the honor at the time, that he had hoped to be able to use some influence in the convention to prevent the separation in the church. Now it seemed that separation was a foregone question,

[42] William H. Goode, D.D., prominent Methodist missionary and educator, had been elected principal of the New Albany Seminary, Indiana, in 1837, and in 1843 was sent among the Choctaw Indians as superintendent of the Fort Coffee Academy. In 1844 he became the first secretary of the new Indian Mission Conference. In 1854 he was made superintendent of northern Methodist missions in Kansas and Nebraska and was instrumental in organizing the Kansas and Nebraska Conference in 1855, the Nebraska Conference in 1860, and the Colorado Conference in 1864 (F. C. Holliday, *Indiana Methodism* [Cincinnati, 1873], pp. 277–81). For his own account of his missionary labors see his book, *Outposts of Zion, with Limnings of Mission Life* (Cincinnati, 1863).

and being equally certain that our conference would adhere South, he could not honorably serve us at Louisville, because he was opposed to the organization of a separate church, as was contemplated by the "plan of separation." He was at Louisville, however, when the convention met, and Bishop Morris being there also, gave him a transfer back to his former conference. Rev. Edward T. Peery, as alternate, served in Brother Goode's place. We were all sorry to lose the companionship and services of this truly good man, but he followed his honest convictions, just as the rest of us did.

The second session of the Indian Mission conference met at Shawnee Manual Labor School, Bishop Joshua Soule presiding. Here, as before stated, I was reappointed superintendent of this institution and continued to serve in this capacity until relieved in part by the appointment of Rev. William Patton, who continued in this position through the next year. In the summer of the last year of my labors at Shawnee Manual Labor School I was subjected to a trial and loss compared with which all former ones were but trifles. My wife, who had borne me six children during our stay in the Indian country, four of whom were yet living, had been in declining health more than a year. Her general health previous to this had been good, but at the birth of her last child she fell into a lingering, slow fever, from which she never fully recovered. The disease finally assumed a pulmonary character, and resulted in her death. Being left with four small children to provide for, two sons and two daughters, it became necessary in my judgment, to take them from the Indian country, which I did shortly after in the month of September, 1846. Of this I may say more further on in my narrative, but I cannot proceed in this statement of facts and incidents without stopping to pay a just tribute to her to whom I owe much more than I can express.

Sarah C. Cessna, as I have before said, was born and raised in Muhlenberg county, Kentucky. Her early training was good in all respects. She became pious in her girlhood, and I may truthfully say devoted her whole life to the service of God. She took me for her husband when we were both young, as a traveling Methodist preacher. No act of her life was unworthy of the position she occupied. In social life she was modest and retiring, respectful and dignified; she was loved by all, but most by those who were her associates. Even the poor Indians had feelings of grateful veneration for her, for they always found in her a sympathizing friend. During the thirteen years of her missionary life her services as a true helpmeet were untiring, and rendered not only without complaint, but with never ceasing cheerfulness. Her example and advice were often my chief support under discouragements, so much so that I had many times failed without them. A thousand times have I had cause to thank God for the gift of such a wife. In her personal attachment to me she was simply devoted, and one of the last things she said to me was, "Don't forget me!"

In her protracted sufferings she was at all times patient and resigned. Her religion was not passionate, but uniform, and evangelical. No clouds of doubt and fear dimmed her spiritual vision as she approached the closing scenes of life, but she met death as an expected messenger for whose coming she was fully prepared. The last Sabbath she spent on earth I remained alone with her in her room, while the rest of the household were gone to church, and so near did she seem to heaven that I almost involuntarily requested her to continue to present me to the blessed Savior in heaven until we should meet in His glorious presence. Did I do wrong? I trust not. Her pure spirit perchance has often "ministered" for me. We buried her beside her own little "Willie Cessna" in the mission burying ground, where she now lies with the Johnsons and others of precious memory. I confess that one of the strongest motives that influenced me in going so far to attend conference last fall (1867) was that it would afford me a good opportunity to visit the last resting place of the precious remains of my own Sarah.

I was accompanied from her home near Kansas City by Mrs. Peery, widow of my long tried and much loved friend, Rev. E. T. Peery, and two of her daughters. On arriving at the "mission" we met Rev. Doctor Green, of Nashville, Tenn., who was attending our conference then sitting in Kansas City, and who had taken a ride in company with other friends to see the old "Shawnee Manual Labor School." Brother Green and myself taking a little stroll together about the premises became separated after awhile, and I turned aside to seek the very room from which that sainted spirit took its flight to heaven, twenty-one years before. I soon found admission to the chamber of suffering and death, and stood or rather knelt, on the very spot where I had seen her close her eyes in her last long sleep. Oh! I cannot write on this paper what then filled my heart and made me a child again.

No, no, I can never describe the feelings inspired by my approach to the spirit-land! God heard my vows, and I believe will enable me to keep them. Oh, ye precious ones! How many of you have already gone before me. But, as another has sung:

O, what are all my sufferings here,
  If Lord thou count me meet
With that enraptured host to appear
  And worship at thy feet!
Give joy, or grief; give ease, or pain;
  Take life, or friends away;
But let me find them all again
  In that eternal day!

V. RECORDS OF THE BOARD OF MANAGERS OF THE MISSIONARY SOCIETY OF THE METHODIST EPISCOPAL CHURCH[43]

April 13, 1838: "It was mentioned that Brother [Thomas] Johnson, presiding elder and superintendent of the Shawnee Mission, with an Indian of that nation, would attend our anniversary. A committee was ordered to be appointed to take charge of the missionary lyceum; Nathan Bangs,[44] David M. Reese and George Coles constitute the committee."

May 16, 1838: "Certain documents from the Shawnee Mission having been read, they were on motion referred to a committee of five, viz.: Rev. Dr. Bangs, Rev. Dr. Luckey, Joseph Smith, Stephen Dando, and B. Disbrow."

[43] These records, copied from the originals in New York, were printed in J. J. Lutz, "The Methodist Missions among the Indian Tribes in Kansas," *Kansas Historical Collections,* IX (1905–6), 171–72.

[44] Nathan Bangs, D.D. (1778–1862), a native of Connecticut, was converted in 1800 and was in 1802 admitted into the New York Conference. He served for a time as missionary in Canada. In 1820 and 1824 he was elected book agent of the Methodist Episcopal church and subsequently edited both the *Christian Advocate* and the *Methodist Magazine.* He was one of the chief founders of the Methodist Missionary Society, and the author of its constitution. In 1836 he was appointed by the General Conference to the important post of missionary secretary. He is remembered also for his four-volume *History of the Methodist Episcopal Church* (Matthew Simpson [ed.] *Cyclopaedia of Methodism* [Philadelphia, 1878], pp. 85–86).

May 30, 1838: "Doctor Bangs, from the committee appointed at the last meeting, made the following report, which was adopted:

'The committee appointed to take into consideration certain documents presented to the board of managers respecting the necessity and expediency of establishing a large central school for the benefit of the Indian children and youth north of the Cherokee line, southwest of the Missouri river, and east of the Rocky Mountains, have had the same under consideration, and beg leave to present the following as the result of their deliberations:

'For several years past our missionaries have had schools upon a small scale among the Shawnees and other tribes of Indians in that region of country who have become in part Christianized; and though these schools have exercised a salutary influence upon those who have attended them, yet, being small, and divided among so many distant tribes, they are necessarily limited in their influence, expensive in their support, as well as difficult of management.

'It appears, moreover, that this being a part of the country ceded by the United States to the Indians for the[ir] perpetual possession, other tribes are moving into the neighborhood, to whom it is desirable to impart the benefits of religious, moral, and intellectual, as well as mechanical and agricultural instruction, that they may in due time be exalted to the benefits and immunities of a Christian and civilized community, and this is most likely to be accomplished by the employment of suitable and efficient means for the education of their children and youth.

'From the humane policy of the general government of the United States, in the efforts they made to rescue the savages of our wilderness from their state of barbarism, by means of schools, we have reason to believe, if it be determined to establish a school of a character contemplated in the documents above referred to, that pecuniary means may be obtained from the government to carry the plan into effect, and also an annuity for its support from year to year.

'Under these views and impressions, the committee submit the following resolutions for the concurrence of the board:

'*Resolved,* 1, That it be, and hereby is, recommended to the Missouri annual conference to adopt such measures as they may consider suitable for the establishment of a central manual-labor school for the special benefit of Indian children and youth, in such place and under such regulations as they may judge most fit and proper.

'*Resolved,* 2, That whenever the said conference shall so resolve, this board pledge themselves to cooperate with them in carrying the plan into effect; provided, that a sum not exceeding $10,000 shall be drawn from the treasury of the missionary society of the Methodist Episcopal Church for any one year for the support of the schools so established.

'*Resolved,* 3, That, with a view to secure the aid of the government of the United States in furnishing the pecuniary means necessary for the establishment and support of such a school as is contemplated, our corresponding secretary, or Dr. Samuel Luckey, be, and hereby is, requested to accompany our brother, the Rev. T. Johnson, to the city of Washington, and lay before the proper officer or officers having the superintendence of Indian affairs, or, if need be, submit to Congress, the plan of the contemplated school, and solicit aid in such a way and manner as may be judged most suitable for the establishment and support of said school.

All of which is respectfully submitted.

N. Bangs, *Chairman.*'

"The presiding bishop (Soule), in alluding to the call for the present meeting, gave his views fully in favor of the establishment of a central school in the Indian country. The bishop had himself been in this country, and was intimately acquainted with the tribes over whom Brother Johnson has the superintendence.

"Bishop Andrew concurred in the remarks of the presiding officer, so far as his knowledge went.

"Brother Johnson also gave his opinion as to the wants of the tribes in the southwest, their present condition and prospects.

"Letters were read from Major Cummins, the Indian agent, fully according with the representation made in the documents which have been read to this board.

"Doctor Bangs offered the following resolution, which was unanimously passed:

'*Resolved,* That our treasurer be authorized to pay to Brother Johnson the amount of his traveling expenses to and from this place, and that Brother Johnson be requested, on his return, to stop at as many of the principal places as his other engagements will allow, hold missionary meetings and take up collections for the missionary society, and account with the treasurer for the amount of said collections.' "

June 20, 1838: "Doctor Luckey stated that he had just returned from his mission to Washington city in behalf of the Southwestern Indians, and that success had attended his mission. A full report would be hereafter presented."

July 13, 1838: "Doctor Luckey presented the report of his doings at Washington, as promised at the last meeting. See documents, 'Report of Delegation on Indian Affairs,' and accompanying documents 1, 2."

VI. REPORT OF THE MISSION COMMITTEE OF THE MISSOURI CONFERENCE, 1838[45]

"WHEREAS, The board of managers of the missionary society of the Methodist Episcopal Church have recommended to the Missouri annual conference to adopt such means as they consider suitable for the establishment of a central manual-labor school for the benefit of Indian children and youth in such place and under such regulations as they may judge most fit and proper; and

"WHEREAS, The government of the United States has stipulated to aid liberally in the erection of suitable buildings for said school, and also to aid annually in its support; and

"WHEREAS, The Shawnee nation of Indians in general council assembled, and in compliance with the wishes of the government have consented to the establishment of such school on their lands near the boundary of the state of Missouri, which is deemed a most eligible situation: therefore,

"Resolved, 1, That we, fully concurring with the board of managers of the missionary society of the Methodist Episcopal church, do hereby agree to establish a manual-labor school for the benefit of Indian children and youth on the Shawnee lands near the boundary line of the state of Missouri, to be called ——.

"Resolved, 2, That a committee of three be appointed, whose duty it shall be to erect suitable buildings for the accommodation of the proposed school; second, to employ competent teachers, mechanics, a

[45] Lutz, *op. cit.,* pp. 172–73.

farmer, and such other persons as may be necessary; thirdly, to exercise a general supervision over the institution and report to this conference annually.

"*Resolved,* 3, That the above-named committee be and are hereby instructed to erect, for the accommodation of said school, two buildings, to serve as school-houses and teachers' residences, each to be 100 feet long and 30 wide and two stories high, with an ell running back, 50 feet by 20, and two stories high; thirdly, buildings for four mechanics, with shops; fourthly, such farm buildings as they may judge necesary; provided, however, that if, in the judgment of the committee, the expenses of the above-named buildings are likely to be greater than such a sum as may be estimated by the missionary committee of this conference, they may make such changes as they may think proper."[46]

[46] The location of the Shawnee Manual Labor School was on the California road in what is now Johnson County, Kansas, three miles southwest of Westport, Missouri. Johnson began work on the buildings in February, 1839. The first year he inclosed 400 acres of land, 12 of which were planted in apple trees (the first orchard set out in Kansas), and 176 acres in corn. Two large brick buildings were erected. One, 110 by 30 feet and two stories high, was used as the schoolhouse and chapel, boys' dormitory, and superintendent's home. This building was once the territorial capitol of Kansas. The second building was a large boarding-house, 100 by 30 feet, with an ell. Later blacksmith shops, wagon shops, shoemaker shops, barns, granaries, and toolhouses, a brickyard, a sawmill, and a steam flour mill were added. The school opened in October, 1839 (*ibid.,* p. 174). For the subsequent history of this important frontier institution see Martha B. Caldwell, *Annals of Shawnee Methodist Mission and Indian Manual Labor School* (Topeka, Kan., 1939).

CHAPTER XII

Quarterly Conference Records, 1808–52

I. SILVER CREEK CIRCUIT, INDIANA, 1808–11

THE Silver Creek was the first entire Methodist circuit in what is now Indiana. It was formed in 1807 with Moses Ashworth as the circuit preacher. It lay mostly in Clark's Grant, which had formerly been included in the Salt River and Shelby Circuit of the Kentucky District. Moses Ashworth closed his first year on the circuit with a camp meeting a few miles from Charlestown, which was, probably, the first camp meeting to be held in Indiana. The next year (1808) the Indiana District was formed, which included the two circuits in Indiana, the Whitewater and the Silver Creek, and four other circuits in what is now Illinois and Missouri (W. W. Sweet, *Circuit-Rider Days in Indiana* [Indianapolis, 1916], pp. 8–9).

At a Quarterly meeting Conference held at N. Robertson for Silver Creek Circuit, August 5th, 6th, 7th & 8th, 1808. Members present, Deacons, Jeremiah Stillwell, James Garner, Thomas Allen, John Evin,—Licenced preacher Jess Rowland,—Exhorters, Amos Chitwood, Nathaniel Parker,—Stewards, William Bullock and Bazil Prather, Leaders,—Dephaniah Robertson, Samuel Bullock, William Lockheart, Evin Thomas, Salathiel Newman, Edward Jacobs, Davis Floyd, George Crutchfield.

JOSIAH CRAWFORD, *Pr.*
JESSE ROWLAND, *Secy.* WILLIAM BURKE, *P.E.*

At a Quarterly meeting Conference held at Bethel meeting house Silver Creek Circuit the 8th day of April 1809:

Question, are there any appeals or complaints? *Ans.* Stephen Beman who was expelled from society for a charge laid in against him by John Lemaster for having deceived him in the sale of a mare which was not his own the case being considered by the conference and the expulsion accordingly satisfied.

JOSIAH CRAWFORD, *Pr.*
WILLIAM BULLOCK, *Sec'y pro tem.* JAMES WARD *P.E.*

At a Quarterly meeting Conference held at Salem meeting house the first day of July 1809. *Ques.* are there any appeals, complaints or applications. *Ans.* Thomas Whitson applied for other arbitration to determine the dispute between him and David Rowland which was granted by the conference.

JOSIAH CRAWFORD, *Pr.*

JESSE ROWLAND *Sec'y* JAMES WARD, *P.E.*

At a Quarterly meeting held at Robertson, Feb. 23rd, 1810. The case of George Durmint being called up, and neither him nor the conference being prepared for a hearing of the case, a motion was made by Bro. Linsey to appoint another Committee to investigate said case, which passed in the negative, the trial adjourned till the next conference.

Jacob House applied to the Conference to be received as an exhorter in this circuit, which was granted, and on motion of Bro. Linsey, whether or not J. House should be retained in full standing, passed in the affirmative.

JESSE ROWLAND, *Secy.* ISAAC LINSEY, *Pr.*

Quarterly meeting Conference 20th of Oct. 1810 Members of this conference, as follows—Barsilla Willey, E— Benjamin King D, John Eavin D, James Garner D, Thos. Allen D, Jeramiah Stilwell D, H. Noland P, Jesse Rowland P, A. Bemon P, Amos Chitwood P, William Bullock & Robt Row Etrs, William Bullock and Bazil Prather Stewards.

The Class Leaders are, Philip Monroe, William Lockheart, Samuel Bullock, John Hobson, Isaac Buskirk, Baxter Sparks, James Matheney, Elijah Hurst,—Potston, James Young, John Swartze, E. Jacobs, Rezin Picketts, Davis Floid, James Garner.

1st Question, is Bro. Beamon eligible to obtain a recommendation to the next annual conference to receive the ordination of Deacons. Voted not eligible, as the rules require as to time of probation.

2nd,—is Bro. Rowland eligible to the next annual conference for ordination to Deacon. Voted not eligible.

3rd,—is it legal that the case between Ruth Blizard and Susanna Prather in reference to a trial between them by a select meeting of a former trial be taken up in this Conference? Voted not legal.

JOHN EAVIN *Secy, Pro tem.* WILLIAM BURKE, *P.E.*

At a Quarterly meeting conference held at Salem meeting house, Silver Creek Circuit, April 21st, 1810.

Ques., Are there any appeals, complaints or applications. *Ans.,* A complaint being entered against Jeremiah Stilwell by Sally Bloom for not paying her for her work, was considered by the conference and abollished. Charge the 2nd, Bro. Stilwell you are hereby notified of the charges exhibited against you. You testified before the arbitrators at Jacobses that T. Whitson told your wife, in your hearing, that the potatoes were all ready previous to the first day of January. And before the magistrates you testified that D. Rowland told you that Whitson had told him that the potatoes were all ready previous to the first day of January. On motion made and seconded—that the vote be taken on the first charge given in the negative.

Charge 3rd By Sally Bloom as having called her a public liar and that you would prove it and said to her: if she did not acknowledge herself a liar you would send her to Jeffersonville or over the river. Also called her a mean, triffling, ill behaved girl, you also told her she had not forgotten what she had set her hand to and if she did not hush (lying) you would publish it October 24th, 1809, which charge was found true and reproved.

Sela Paine, *Pr.*

Jesse Rowland, *secy* William Burke, *P.E.*

At the Quarterly meeting conference held at Chitwood's meeting house August 4th, 1810.

Ques.—Are there any appeals, complaints or application?

Ans.—an appeal was taken from the decision of a select number of Jacobs class by Bro. Paine against Susanna Prather, who was charged of immoral language by Ruth Blizard. Bro. Paine put it to vote whether or not the conference should enter into a trial of the case or adjourn it till the next meeting in case the conference decided on entering into it now. Adjourned till Monday morning.

Jesse Rowland, *Secy.* Sela Paine, *Pr.*

At a Quarterly meeting Conference hald at Jacobs meeting house the 8th, 9th & 10th of Sept., 1809.

Members present, Deacons Jeremiah Stilwell, James Garner, John Evins,—Licenced preacher Jesse Rowland and Amos Chitwood—Exhorters Nathaniel Parker, Stewards,—William Bullock, Bazil Prather, Leaders,—Dephaniah Robertson, William Lockheart, Philip Monroe, Thomas Chapple, Edward Jacobs,— Are there any appeals, complaints or applications? *Ans.* A charge was exhibited by Jeremiah Stilwell for immoral language to Sally Bloom, also for an inconsistancy in testimony given in a suit wherein David Rowland was plaintiff and Thomas Whitson defendant.

Ordered by the conference that a Committee be appointed to examine into the same.

SAMUEL PARKER *P.E.*
JESSE ROWLAND, *Sec'y.* JOSIAH CRAWFORD, *Pr.*

At a Quarterly Conference held at Bethel Silver Creek Circuit, Jan. 5th, 1810.

The case of Jeremiah Stilwell being called up, on the introduction of J. Stillwell's letter, stating his inability to attend, whereupon J. Stillwell is postponed until the next Quarterly meeting.

On motion of Bro. Paine to reconsider the case of Stephen Beaman, in which case the opinion of the President was called for: who gave it as his opinion that S. Beaman should return to the society from which he was expelled as his remedy was there alone, which opinion was agreed to by the conference.

SELA PAINE, *Pr.*
JESSE ROWLAND, *Sec'y.* WILLIAM BURKE, *P.E.*

Quarterly meeting Conference held at Salem, May 1st, 1811.

Question, are there any complaints or appeals?

Answer, the case of George Durmint, apellant, being called up before and examined by the conference, they were of opinion Durmint was guilty and expelled him accordingly.

JESSE ROWLAND, *Secy.* WILLIAM BURKE, *P.E.*

At a Quarterly meeting held at Ebenezer meeting house, July 14th, 1811. Present William Burke, P.E. and Gabriel Woodfield, Preacher.

The case of Joseph Jones before the Conference was an appeal from the judgement of the Society at William Lockhearts where he was turned out. It is the opinion of the conference that the judgement of said Society be confirmed.

2nd,—the case of Lucy Money, and appeal from the judgement of the Society at Bethel Meeting House where she was turned out. It is the opinion of the conference that the said Society's judgement be confirmed.

3rd,—the case of Susanna Thickston, an appeal from the judgement of the Society at Ebenezars meeting house where she was turned out. It is the opinion of the conference that the judgement of the Society confirmed.

B. WHITSON *Secy pro tem.* WILLIAM BURKE

At a Quarterly meeting Conference held at Jacobs meeting house, Sept. 14th, 1811.

Are there no appeals or complaints to enter or applications to make?

Ans.,—Jacob House applied to the conference for a recommendation to the annual conference to be received as a traveling preacher. Voted in the negative.

An inquiry was made by the Elder into Robert Monroe's standing as an exhorter and certain complaints being named against him his licence was therefore taken from him.

Barzilla Willey, El, Jermiah Stilwell, James Garner, Thos. Allen, John Evins, Benjamin King, Benjamin Whitson, Deacons:—Amos Chitwood, John Nolly, William Carr, preachers.

William Bullock, Jacob House, N. Parker Exhorters.

Evin Thomas, William Lockheart, Samuel Bullock, Thos. Allen, John Hobson, Isaac Buskerk, Baxter Sparks, James Matheney, Elijah Hurst,—Patson, James Young, John Swartze, Charles Beggs, Davis Floyd Dept Robertson, Rieh Mosley, Thos. Gasaway, Leaders.

William Bullock and Bazil R. Prather Stewards.

JESSE ROWLAND, *Secy.* WILLIAM BURKE, *P.E.*

Copy of a letter to Miss Florence Robinett by I. N. Britton, relative to early Methodism in Clark County, Indiana:—

NEW WASHINGTON, INDIANA.

DEAR FRIEND:

I received your letter of recent date. Your wish to get a history of the founding of the M. E. Church in Clark County. I am indebted to your Grand Pa Andrew Mitchell for a considerable of it. He was a life long friend of mine—He was of the Colony that came from Virginia, about the beginning of this century, and settled in the neighborhood of Salem Church. He told me that he brought William Mc Kendree, the Presiding Elder of the Kentucky District across the river in a canoe, and he preached the first sermon ever preached in that place, and formed the first class ever formed in Indiana. He then took him in his canoe down opposite the "Jacobs Settlement"—went out and formed a class there—"Jacob's" is now "New Chapple" in Clark County. Thence to Louisville, Ky., and also formed a class at that point. This was in the summer of 1802.

"Old Silver Creek" was the first Circuit that was ever formed in Indiana. That was in 1807. Moses Ashworth was its first preacher. He traveled two years. In 1809 Isaac Lindsay was on it. In 1810 Sela Paine.

The first meeting house that was ever built in Indiana Territory was in 1807—The "Old Bethel Church" in what was called the "Robertson Settlement" three miles north of Charlestown, Indiana.

Your friend,
I. N. Britton

II. POMPEY CIRCUIT, NEW YORK, 1809–14[1]

The Pompey Circuit was founded in the year 1807 and was first listed in the *Minutes of the Annual Conferences of the Methodist Episcopal Church* in 1808. During 1808–9 it was situated within the bounds of the New York Conference, Cayuga District. During 1810–28 it was relocated in the Genesee Conference, first in the Cayuga District (1810–11), next in the Oneida District (1812–14), and, finally, in the Chenango District. Beginning with 1829, it was shifted to the newly formed Oneida Conference, and the name Cayuga District restored and remained as such through 1831, at which point the minutes with which we are concerned end.

The chief stations on this circuit (providing the place of quarterly conferences is a correct indication of such) are located on the accompanying map. Of the 92 recorded quarterly meetings within the circuit between the years 1807 and 1830, Pompey was host to 23, Eaton to 20, Lenox to 19, Smithfield to 9, Morrisville to 7, Sullivan to 5, Manlius to 3, and Madison to 2, while Fabius, Truxton, Nelson Flats, and Cazenovia were hosts to one each.

[1] The manuscript "Journal of Pompey Circuit, March 25, 1809, to March 12, 1814," came into the possession of the University of Chicago by purchase from a motorcycle policeman, an Irishman and a Roman Catholic, who brought it to the Editor of this volume. The pages of the minutes had been used as a scrapbook and were covered with newspaper clippings. The minutes were evidently brought to Illinois by some York stater moving west during the first half of the last century.

MAP VI

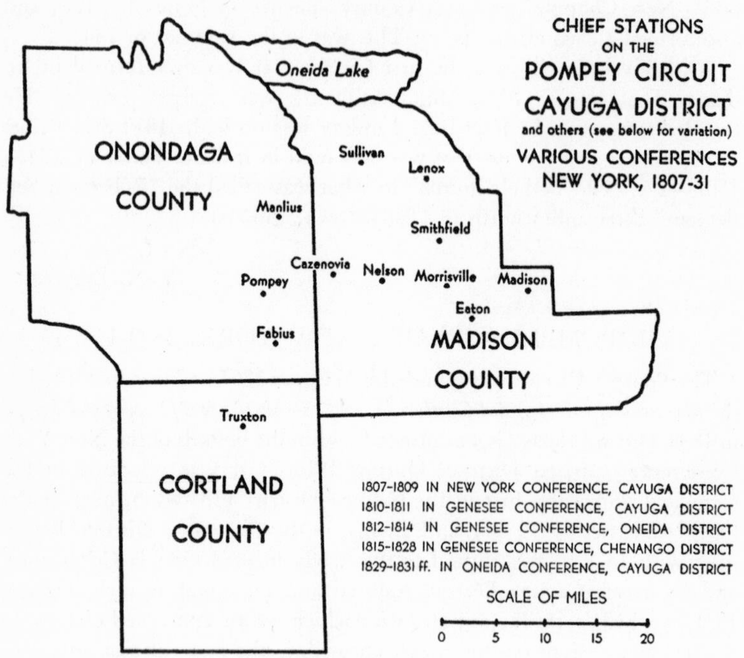
CHIEF STATIONS
ON THE
POMPEY CIRCUIT
CAYUGA DISTRICT
and others (see below for variation)
VARIOUS CONFERENCES
NEW YORK, 1807-31
Oneida Lake
ONONDAGA COUNTY
MADISON COUNTY
CORTLAND COUNTY
Sullivan
Lenox
Manlius
Smithfield
Cazenovia
Nelson
Morrisville
Madison
Pompey
Eaton
Fabius
Truxton
1807-1809 IN NEW YORK CONFERENCE, CAYUGA DISTRICT
1810-1811 IN GENESEE CONFERENCE, CAYUGA DISTRICT
1812-1814 IN GENESEE CONFERENCE, ONEIDA DISTRICT
1815-1828 IN GENESEE CONFERENCE, CHENANGO DISTRICT
1829-1831 ff. IN ONEIDA CONFERENCE, CAYUGA DISTRICT
SCALE OF MILES
0
5
10
15
20

Of the above locations, five did not appear on the circuit until 1816 or later as host to quarterly meetings, namely—Madison (1816 ff.), Morrisville (1820 ff.), Madison (1828 ff.), Nelson Flats (1829), and Cazenovia (1830). The single conferences at Fabius and Truxton were both held in 1808.

Only the legible and nonrepetitious portions of the mutilated manuscript of the minutes of this quarterly conference are here recorded—but even these brief extracts serve well in indicating the disciplinary function of the circuit conference in relation to its class members in contradistinction to the heavier matters of the Annual Conference. Also the map drawn to scale may help in giving the reader a concrete idea of the size of the early circuit (Map VII).

At Qrt. Conference Held at Smithfield March 25th 1809

Quest. 1st Who are the Members of this Conference?

Ans [List of names given.]

Qust 2d Are there any Complaints brought against any of the Members of this Conference?—

Ans Br Timothy Dewey Brought a Complaint against Br Calvin Winslow in which he charges him with falsiefying his word.—

3d Voted that there should be a Committee of five Brethren Chosen to Investigate the above Complaint (Viz) Zenas Jones, Isaac Pierson, Lemuel Stewart, Abner Camp, and Ephraham Munger.—

4th The Members of this Conference were Examined one by one.—

Qust 5th Who shall have there Licence for Preaching renewed?—

Ans James Annis, Zenas Jones, Reuben Haig, Reuben Furley, and Jabes Bigelow—

Qust 6th Who shall have there licence for Exhortation Renewed?

Ans Lemuel Stewart, Abner Camp, James Bliss, Ma[rtin] More, Timothy Prat‡—

7th Br Nathan Clark; Licence withheld—

8th Br Martin Pierson; Licence was not Renewed on account of his Being absent—

9th [Last lines unintelligible.]

At Qt Conference Held at Pompey July 22 1809

Qust 1st Who are the Members of this Conference

‡Ephraham Munger, Isaac Pierson, Benajah Williams, & Enoch Wilcox.

Ans [List of names given.]

2d The Committee that were appointed by the last Conference to Investigate the Charges Brought By Brother Timothy Dewey against Br Calvin Winslow; Report to this Conference that all the Dificulities betwixt them are happyly set[t]led

3d—Voted that Br Calvin Winslow Should have his Licence Renewed.—

4th—Br Isaac Pierson presented a Recommendation to this Conference for Licence to Preach.—

5th—Voted Br Isaac Pierson Shall have a verbil Licence to Preach until our next Qrt. Conference.—

6th—Voted that the Members of this Conference shall hereafter Duly [?] observe the Sabbath Day themselves and likewise injoin it on all they are Conversent with.—

7th—Voted that Br Martin Piersons Licence to Exhort shall be Renewed—

NEH. BATCHELLER *Secretary*

At Qrt. Conference Held at Pompey Hill October 7th 1809

Qst 1st Who are the Members of this Conference.

Ans [List of names given.]

2d Calvin Winslow Sent in a Request to withdraw from our Connection but by a Vote of the Conference it was not Granted.—

3d Voted that Calvin Winslow is Expel[l]ed from the Methodist Connection upon the following Charges 1st for Preachin Doctrins Contrary to the Methodist Discipline 2dly for throughing out hard Censures against Preachers and Members in in [*sic*] our Connection and 3dly for Drinking too fre[e]ly of Ardent Spirits—

4th Voted that Jonathan Holladay Should have verbil Licence to Exhort until our next Qrt. Conference

5th Voted that Joshua Rogers should have verbil License to Exhort until our next Qrt. Conference

6th Voted that Isaac Pierson Should have a writ[t]en Licence to Preach—

NEH. BATCHELLOR, *Secretary*

At Qrt Conference Held at Eaton Feb. 10th 1810

Qust 1st Who are the Members of this Conference?

MAP VII

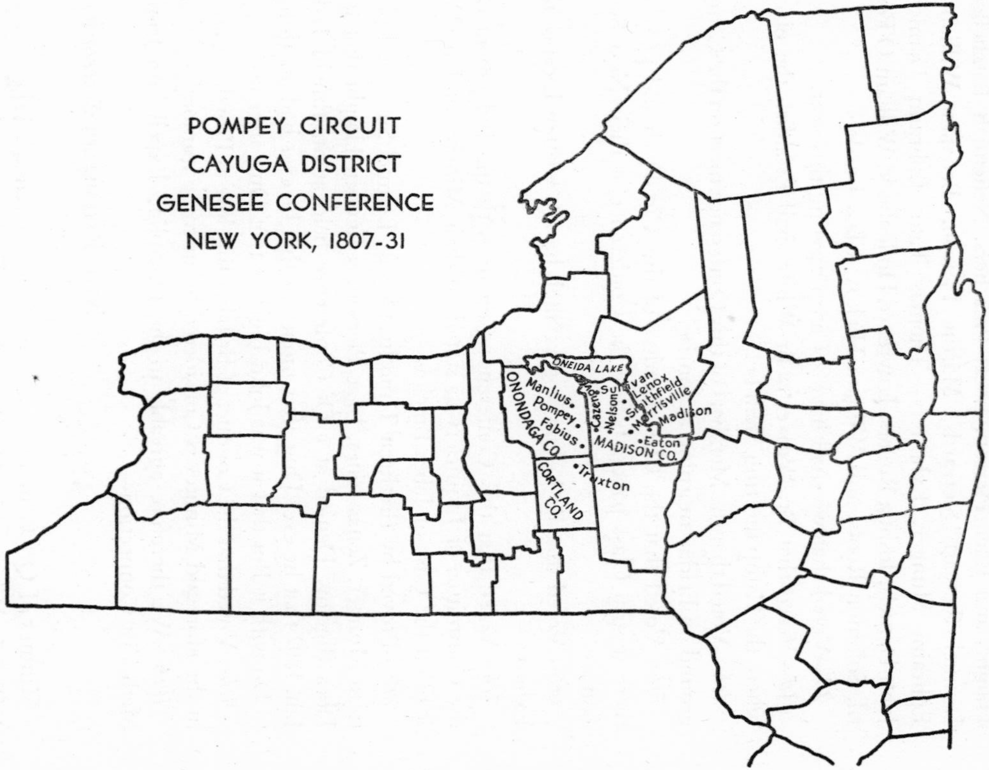
POMPEY CIRCUIT
CAYUGA DISTRICT
GENESEE CONFERENCE
NEW YORK, 1807-31
ONEIDA LAKE
Manlius
Pompey
Fabius
ONONDAGA CO.
Cazenovia
Nelson
Sullivan
Lenox
Smithfield
Morrisville
Madison
Eaton
MADISON CO.
Truxton
CORTLAND CO.

Ans. Peter Vanness Prs. Elder, John P. Weaver Preacher, Ebenezer White, James Annis, Zenas Jones, Timothy Dewey, Reuben Haight, and Isaac Pierson, Local Preachers. Nehemiah Batcheller, Lemuel Stewart Stewards, Martin Pierson, Benajah Williams, Ephraim Munger, Exhorters.—Thomas Tato, Ephraim Demich, John Daniels, Joshua Rogers, Lawrence Hollenbeck, William O'Ferril, Solomon Roots, and William Hickox, Class Leaders—

2d—Voted that we shall have a Camp meeting this year.

3d—Voted that Br. Weaver & Br White shall Establish the place where the Camp meeting Shall be.

4th—Voted that the Members of this Conference meet on the Camp ground on Friday morning at sunrise.

5th—Voted that the Class Leaders of this Circuit should present there several Class papers before the Conference at their Next Session—

6th—Voted that Br Joshua Rogers Shall have a written Licence to Exhort.—

7th—Voted that this Conference Concur with the Judgement of the Committee of Inquiriery as stated on their Minutes of Jan. 22d 1810 on the Case of Jabes Bigelow—

8th Proved by Brethren Timothy Dewey, Lemuel Stewart, Ephraim Munger, Zenas Jones, Isaac Pierson, & Reuben Haight that Br Jabes Bigelow Denied at a Qt Conference held at Smithfield 17th Jan. 1807 that he ever Dug after money or that he ever had anything to Do with it But that it was John Bigelow that Dug after it—

9th—Voted that the Conduct of Br Jabes Bigelow as Provd. & stated in the aforesaid Minutes is Considered by us to be immoral—

10th—We therefore agreable to the Discipline Expell him from Methodist Connection—

NEH. BATCHELLER *Secretary*

Minutes of Qrt Conference held at Eaton March 9th 1811

Qust 1 Who are the Members of this Conference

Ans William Case Prs. Eldr. James Kelsey Isaac Tiller Preachers. —Timothy Dewey, Zenas Jones, Isaac Pierson, Orrin Doolittle Local Preachers Ephraim Munger, Martin Pierson, James Bliss, Ebenezer Doolittle Exhorters John Daniels Ephm. Demich, Jeremiah Sailes,

Willm. Hicox, Levi Munger Thomas Fowler Class Leaders Nehemiah Batcheller, Lemuel Stewart Stewards.—

Qust 2d are there any Recommendations for a licence to exhort brought forward to this Conference

Ans None—

3d Br. James Kelsey reports to this Conference that he has [?] taken up the Charges against Br. James Annis according to his Direction at our last Conference and has Suspended him from all Publick office in this Church and Now Presents his Case to this Conference for trial—

4th James Annis calld to trial Not Present

5th Charges against Br. James Anis [*sic*] Brought forward by Mr. Daniel Woodworth—

Smithfield Dec. 21st 1810

Minutes of testimony given by Daniel Woodworth against James Annis by Request of James Kelsey 1st that he James Annis in giving Evidence between the Sd. D. W.— & S[?——] Annis Sometime in Sept. Last Said many needle[s] things with regard to the Quality of a pair of Mill Stones sold by Sd. S. Annis to the Sd. D. Woodworth which were not sound that he James Annis had got out and helped get out seven run of Mill Stones at the same quarry and that these were the best run that he ever got out that he got a Pair for Mr. Willm. Card [?] at which Mill a Man Carried a bus[h]el of Wheat and had ground which made fifty five pounds of flower and on being asked how much bran Said not more than six or Seven pounds and that these were a better pr. of Millstones than those and were the best that Could be got—

After Court and on the way home he chargd. the Sd. Daniel Woodworth with having Cheated and Defrauded his Brother and he sd. many other approbious words that he had got the millstones and now wishd. to get the Money back again and that he (J. A.) hoped the Curses of Almighty God would fall on your (D. W's.) head and bring you humble to the Dust and Bring you to Repentance and that you would take the bread out of the mouths of his Brothers wife and Children if they suffered eversomuch that on his (D. W.) reply that he would not and wished for no more than his Right he (J. A.) Said yes you would take five Hundred Dollars if you Could get it and further he hoped that almighty God would reduse [*sic*] you (D. W.) to that State of Poverty before you Die[?] that you Shall have to b[u]y your bread from Door to Door—

Daniel Woodworth

6th Br Anna's [*sic*] answer to the Charges; his plea and Justification which he made and laid before the Conference in the following Letter

REV. AND DEAR SIR

the situation of my Family is such that I cannot Safely leave them to attend Qrt. Meeting Conference if you have any Complaint Against me you must Manage them according to your own Discression the line you sent me informed me that I was suspended from all Publick office in the Church untill the next Qrt. Meeting whose Judgement I Judge to be very unjust If the question is askd. in Conference what I was suspended for you may tell them not for any Crime Commit[t]ed nor for any breach of Discipline or Gospel But for Discharging my Duty to a Devil hardened and Hell bound Man I have Considered what I said to Mr. Woodworth a long time I still feel an evidence within that I Did the man no wrong therefore I have no acknowledge[ment] to make to him nor the Conference on this Complaint therefore I submit to the Conference with this request not to Condemn me untill you Can prove that I have broken a known Gospel rule—This from your will wisher

JAMES ANNIS

NELSON March 9th 1811

7th Testimony laid before this Conference by the Committee of inquiriery who had Previous to this Conference sat upon and investigated the Case of Br. James Annis—

He (T. E.) James Annas Saith that he told Mr. Woodworth he wished if nothing else would do the Judgements of God might Come upon him and humble him so that he might know what it was to be oppressd. the reason he talk[ed] thus to Mr. Woodworth was becaus[e] he had taken such undo measures to gain his points against his Brother and he thinks he did no more than his Duty and was ready to do the same again if Mr. Woodworth wished to hear it

ZENAS JONES — *Committee*
EPHRAIM MUNGER — *of*
JEREMIAH SAILES — *Inquiery*

8th Br. James Kelsey Deposeth that Br. Annas acknowledged to him that he told Mr. Woodworth that he wishd, the Curses of God might Come upon him and Reduse him to poverty that he might know what it was to be oppressd. if nothing else would Do—

9th Voted that this Conference Consider Br. James Annas's Conversation to Mr. Daniel Woodworth to be unchristian, imprudent, and Censurable.

10th We therefore Suspend him from al[l] publick office in the Church untill our next Qrt. Conference; Nevertheless we think it Propper to appoint a Committee of four Brethren (viz) William Case, James Kelsey, Isaac Pierson and Zenas Jones to labour with him (J. Annas) who shall have Power to take off his suspention if he shall make satisfaction for his wrong and Report the same to the next Qrt Conference—

11th Voted to give Br. Ephraim Munger Licence to Preach.

12th Voted to give Br. Joshua Rogers Licence to Preach—

13th Voted to give Br. Orrin Doolittle Licence to Preach—

14th Voted that we have our next Qrt Meeting at Mr. Bliss's in Smithfield

NEH. BATCHELLER *Secretary*

Minutes of A Qrt. Conference held at Smithfield May 25th 1811

Qust 1st Who are the members of this Conference

Ans [List of names given.]

2d The Members of this Conference were particularly examined one by one in each of the following Christian ordinances and Practice—1st Baptism both Adult and the rite of Infants—2d The Lords supper—3d of Labor in their Calling—4th Experiance—5th Practise viz Family Devotion and Instruction—6 Family Habits viz Drinking spiritous liquor; Wearing of Gold and ornimintal apparal—7th Fasting—8th Support of the Gospel—9th Privileges of the Church such as Love feasts & Class meetings

3d Br. Reuben Haight and Br. Isaac Pierson have their Preaching Licence Renewed

4th Brethren Timothy Pratt, Martin Pierson, Thomas Grimes, Enoch Wilcox, & Sylvester Morris, have their Exhorting licence Renewed

5th Br Ebenezer Doolittle receivd. Licence to Preach—

6th Br. Isaac Clark Received Licence to Exhort—

7th Voted to Recommend Br Orrin Doolittle unto the Annual Conference as a Propper person to Join the Traviling Connection

8th Acording to appointment of the Qrt. Conference

We entered on our labor with Br. James Annis on Monday 11th March and Report that after requesting him (Br. Annis) to go aside with us where we first prayed to God for him and bles[s]ing on our labor we then asked Br. Annis if he did not think he had done wrong in praying the Curses of God on his Neighbor he answered that he Did not feel guilty and had no confession to make We then proved to him from our saviours words that instead of Cursing he ought to bless them that curse us to which he made no particular answer, but said he had Done the man no wrong and would make no Confession; We then informed him that he was suspended and Cited him to appear at the next conference for his trial

Wm. Case

9th This Conference Consider that the case of Br. Annis in his praying the Curses of God on his Neighbor to be very unchristian and his giving no satisfaction notwithstanding an affectionate Labor of his Brethren We therefore in the fear of God expell him from our Church

10th Voted that we have Camp Meeting at our next Qrt. at Br. O'Ferrils in Pompey—

Neh. Batcheller *Secretary*

At Qt. Conference held in Smithfield March 12th 1814

Members Present [List follows.]

2d Members examinied.—

3d An appeal presented to this Conference by Br. Benjamin Morse of Eaton.—

4# the Accusation; Falsehood.—

5# Jehial Clark deposeth that about six weeks ago he was at Br. Mors's to borrow an auger and got Br. Stewarts auger which was dull he also told Br Morse that he would bring it home at which Br. Morse told him he need not bring it home for he was a going over to his house and would git it himself

7# Br. Stewart deposeth.—that in the fore part of the winter he carried an auger to Br Morse's to be fixed and that Br Morse charg'd one Shilling for Repairing the auger in answer to which he told him he ought to have Damages inasmuch as the auger was broken he also saith that Brother Clark told him that he fill'd [*sic*] the auger and broke it. also that Brother Morse told him that he fill'd the auger himself Br. Clark saith that Br. Morse lent him the auger.

8# Br Bayley saith that he conciv'd that Br. Morse me[a]nt Br Clark should have the auger.

9# Br. Stewart saith that Br Morse told him that he had Nothing to do with the auger for Br. Clark took it without liberty.

10# Br Fowler saith that Br. Morse told him that it was his intention that Br. Clark should have the auger.

11# Resolved that this Conference Refer the Case of Br. Morse to a Committee of three to wit Brethren Timothy Dewey, John Pratt, & Isaac Pierson.—

12# From the testimony it appears to us that Br Morse is guilty of falsehood yet it may be possible that he did not design to tell a falsehood but we cannot call it any thing less than Evation—

report of the Comm.

13# Resolv'd therefore that Br Morse acknowledges to Br. Clark and the Society that he has given reason to believe that he intended falsehood and that he be Suspended three Months from the privileges of the Church and put back on triall for Six Months

14# Br Morse being cal[l]ed and the Judgement read was asked if he Conceded to it to which he replied in the Negative the Conference then Voted that three weeks be allowed him to make his Confession but if he did not in that time he should be expel[l]ed

15# Resolv'd that we advise Br Case to discharge Br Doolittle from travailing the Circuit

16# Resolv'd that we have Camp Meeting in Sept. Next—

17# Resolv'd that our next Qrt. Meeting be at the Meeting house in Lenox—

NEH. BATCHELLER *Secretary*

III. SAN AUGUSTINE CIRCUIT, TEXAS, 1837–52

Although Protestant preaching was illegal in Texas under Spanish and Mexican rule, Methodist circuit-riders from the Missouri and Mississippi conferences, beginning about 1817, occasionally preached in the Texas border settlements. In November, 1834, the Mississippi Conference, anticipating Texan independence, authorized a Texan mission in connection with its Louisiana District. Permanent circuit organization was begun in 1837, with the coming of Dr. Martin Ruter, Lyttleton Fowler, and Robert Alexander as missionaries to Texas under appointment by Bishop Elijah Hedding, who had under his charge the "foreign mission" work of the General Conference. Alexander organized the San Augustine Circuit and held its first quarterly conference on September 16, 1837. With the record of this meeting the present document begins.

The original minutes of the San Augustine Quarterly Conference are in the library of Southern Methodist University, Dallas, Texas. They give us a contemporary official record of the local organization of the first permanent Methodist circuit to be set up in Texas. The fifteen years here covered (1837–52) mark several significant milestones of Texas Methodist history: namely, the emergence of a separate Texas Conference in 1840, its division into the Eastern and Western Texas conferences in 1845, and the formation in the same year of the Methodist Episcopal Church, South. San Augustine Circuit was from 1837 to 1840 in the Mississippi Conference, from 1840 to 1845 in the Texas, and from 1845 to 1852 in the East(ern) Texas Conference. In this document the actual workings of a frontier quarterly conference are illustrated first hand: the licensing of local preachers and exhorters, the examination of character of local officials, the financial accounts including class collections and ministerial support, the camp meetings—all are mentioned on these pages. The distinctively southern touch is given by reference to "African Missions" and the licensure of colored local preachers. In short, here we have the *Methodist system locally exemplified.*

San Augustine Circuit centered in the town of San Augustine, in what is now San Augustine County, in the "Red Lands" of East Texas, with outlying appointments in Sabine, Shelby, Jasper, Nacogdoches, and other counties. As can be seen from the biographical notes concerning some of the pioneer circuit-riders and prominent laymen who are mentioned in the text, this region was settled largely from the South, the settlers representing for the most part the westward movement from the Old South through the Old Southwest, into the new slaveholding territory of Texas.

For backgrounds of Texas Methodist history the little volume by Homer S. Thrall, *A Brief History of Methodism in Texas* (Nashville, 1894), is valuable but has been largely superseded by the thorough two-volume work of Macum Phelan, *A History of Early Methodism in Texas, 1817–1866* (Nashville, 1924), and *A History of the Expansion of Methodism in Texas, 1867–1902* (Dallas, 1937). For the locale of San Augustine Circuit, George L. Crocket's *Two Centuries in East Texas: A History of San Augustine County and Surrounding Territory* (Dallas, 1932) is pertinent.

RECORDS OF THE METHODIST CHURCH, [1837]

The first quartily Conference held at Poligash Camp Ground[1] September the 16—1837 For San augustine Circuit.

Members Present

R. E. Alexander[2] Missinary......Elder
Henry Stephenson[3] ....L[ocal] Preacher
James English[4] ....L Preacher
Wm C. Crofford[5] ....Deacon
E D Johnson ....Exhorter

[1] McMahan's Campground, on Polygoch Creek, Sabine County, Texas. A permanent class was organized here in 1834 (Homer S. Thrall, *A Brief History of Methodism in Texas* [Nashville, 1894], pp. 47, 249–250).

[2] Robert Alexander, D.D. (1811–82), a native of Smith County, Tennessee, had joined the Tennessee Conference on trial in 1830, later transferring to the Mississippi Conference. In 1837 he was appointed, with Lyttleton Fowler, assistant to Dr. Martin Ruter on the Texas Mission. Alexander was the first of the group to reach Texas, crossing the Sabine on August 19, 1837. He worked in the McMahan neighborhood for a month, during which time he organized San Augustine Circuit and presided over this first quarterly conference, the earliest held in Texas. His subsequent career as minister, presiding elder, Bible agent, delegate to the Louisville Convention (1845), and president of the Texas Conference Missionary Society was so full that Thrall could write: "He has left the impress of his character upon every Methodist institution in Texas" (*ibid.*, pp. 46–47, 248–53; see also Macum Phelan, *A History of Early Methodism in 1866,* I [Nashville, 1924], 72–74).

[3] Henry Stephenson (1772–1841) was a native of Virginia, who, after moving successively to Kentucky, Missouri, Arkansas, and Louisiana, pioneered as a Methodist preacher in Texas as early as 1817. He was a member, first, of the Missouri Conference and, later, of the Mississippi Conference. Under the latter he was given charge of all the Methodist work in Texas in 1834. After his location in 1835 he settled in Jasper County, Texas (Thrall, *op. cit.,* pp. 39–41; Phelan, *op. cit.,* I, 19, 28–29, 31, 67–68).

[4] James English is said to have settled in Shelby County, Texas, in 1825 and may have planted Methodism there. He was assistant judge for the municipality of Shelby under the revolutionary government of 1836 (Phelan, *op. cit.,* I, 24–25; William C. Binkley [ed.], *Official Correspondence of the Texan Revolution, 1835–1836* [New York, 1936], II, 683).

[5] William C. Crawford was admitted on trial to the Georgia Conference in 1831, transferred in 1833 to the Alabama Conference, but located the following year and moved to Texas in 1835. He was a member of the first Methodist class in Shelby County. In 1836 he was a member of the Texas constitutional convention. His influence there is said to have kept the convention from disfranchising all preachers and from keeping them out of all public offices (Thrall, *op. cit.,* pp. 29–32; Phelan, *op. cit.,* I, 97–98).

J. P. Stevenson[6]	Deacon
S. D. Mcmahon[7]	Exhorter
George Stovoll	Exhorter
S. D. Thomas[8]	C[lass]. L[eader].
James Thompson	Exhorter

Are there any complaints or appeals[9]
Ansr. there are none
Are there any Licens to be renewed[10]

[6] James P. Stevenson (1808–85), born in Smith County, Tennessee, was a son of William Stevenson (1768–1857), the first Methodist preacher to enter Texas. James attended Augusta College, Kentucky, and was admitted into the Mississippi Conference in 1831, but located in 1835, coming to East Texas. While on the Natchitoches Circuit, Louisiana, in 1833, James P. Stevenson preached the first Methodist sermon in East Texas (Phelan, *op. cit.*, I, 26–29).

[7] Colonel Samuel D. McMahan (? –1854), a leader in the community and church, removed from Tennessee to Texas in 1831, settling about twelve miles east of San Augustine. In August, 1832, he commanded one of the battalions at Nacogdoches in the battle with Piedras. He was converted in 1832 and became the first class leader of the first Methodist class in Texas, which was organized at his home permanently in July, 1834, by Henry Stephenson, though there had been preaching there earlier. At this first quarterly conference (1837) he was licensed to exhort, and later, to preach. In 1839 the first McMahan's Chapel was erected near his home. His son, James B., was likewise a local preacher. Colonel McMahan attended as an official member almost every quarterly conference from the first one to September 12, 1850 (Thrall, *op. cit.*, p. 24; Phelan, *op. cit.*, I, 30; George L. Crocket, *Two Centuries in East Texas* [Dallas, 1932], pp. 156, 271–72).

[8] Shedrack D. Thomas, class leader and exhorter, became sheriff of San Augustine County in 1847. His father, Benjamin Thomas, had migrated from Alabama to Texas about 1821 (Crocket, *op. cit.*, pp. 83–84, 214).

[9] According to the *Discipline,* the regular business of the quarterly conference included the hearing of complaints against traveling preachers (probationers), local preachers, or members; and the reception and trial of appeals made from former judgments (David Sherman, *History of the Revisions of the Discipline of the Methodist Episcopal Church* [New York, 1874], pp. 143, 192–94).

[10] Further, the quarterly conference was [1836] "to take cognizance of all the Local Preachers in the Circuit or Station, and inquire into the gifts, labors, and usefulness of each Preacher by name; to license proper persons to preach, and *renew their license annually,* when, in the judgment of said Conference, their gifts, grace, and usefulness will warrant such renewal . . . ." (*ibid,* p. 143). Exhorters' licenses also were renewed annually.

Ansr. There are

James English Character past [passed] Licens—Renewed
S. D. Mcmahon Character past Licens—Renewed
Wm C Crofford Character past Licens—Renewed
George Stovall Character past Licens—Renewed
James P Stevenson Character past—
E. D. Johnson Character past Licens—Renewed

The following Persons were nominated and appointed Stewards (viz)

S. D. Thomas Recording Steward
S. D. Mcmahon Circuit-Steward
James English . . . . .Ditto
F McMahon . . . . .Ditto
Wm C Crofford . . . . .Ditto
James P Stevenson Circuit Steward

Approved and Signed
R. E. Alexander, *chairman*
James P. Stevenson *Se[cre]t[ar]y*

TEXIAN MISSIAN, [1838]

Quartely Meating of Nacogdoches Circuit[11] held on Mcmahons Camp Ground the 8 of Sept 1838

Persons present

Littleton Fowler[12] Preacher in charge and President
L Campbell[13] Missionary of the Conference

[11] The "Texas Mission District," under Lyttleton Fowler, presiding elder, first appears in the minutes for the Mississippi Conference of 1838, including Houston and Galveston, *Nacogdoches,* Washington, Montgomery, and Brazoria (*Minutes of the Annual Conferences of the Methodist Episcopal Church,* Vol. II: *1829–1839* [New York, 1840], p. 605). The following year San Augustine Circuit first appears by name (*ibid.,* Vol. III: *1839–1845,* p. 25).

[12] Lyttleton Fowler (1802–46) was born in Smith County, Tennessee. Converted in Kentucky in 1819, he entered the Kentucky Conference in 1826, transferring to Tennessee in 1832. In 1837 he came to Texas as an assistant to Ruter, after whose death he was appointed superintendent of the Texas Mission. He was a delegate to the General Conference of 1844 and to the Louisville Convention in 1845. For memoir see *Minutes of the Annual Conferences of the Methodist Episcopal Church, South,* Vol. I: *1845–1857,* p. 40; cf. also, William B. Sprague, *Annals of the American Pulpit* (New York, 1865), VII, 723–25.

[13] Lewell Campbell of the Kentucky Conference was appointed, at its session in 1838, missionary to Texas (*Minutes of the Annual Conferences of the Methodist Episcopal Church,* Vol. II: *1829–1839,* p. 593).

Henry Stepenson Local Preacher & Elder
Friend McMahon L Preacher
S. D. McMahon Exhortor
E. P. Chisom[14] Exhortor
James P. Irwin[15] Exhortor
George H. Stovall Exhortor
James Thompson Exhortor

Q. Are there any Complaints or appeals
Ansr. None

The conference proceeded to the examination of the Official Members

Henry Stephenson examined approved and past
James P. Stephenson examined approoved and past
E. L. Martin examined approoved and past
Wm C. Crofford examined approoved and past

Local Preachers[16]

James English examined approved and past
John R. Hubbes examined approved and past
Henderson D Palmer[17] examined approved and past and Licence Renewed
E Chisom examined approved and Licence renewed
James P Irwin examined and Licence Renewed
Elish D Johnson examined and Licence Renewed

[14] Enoch P. Chisholm was admitted on trial to the (East) Texas Conference in 1845 and located in 1857 (*ibid.*, Vol. III: *1839–1845*, p. 554; *Minutes .... South,* Vol. I: *1845–1857*, p. 797).

[15] James T. P. Irvine (? –1871), born probably in Tennessee, served in the Texas revolutionary army. He was admitted on trial to the Texas Conference in 1842 and served as presiding elder and conference secretary (Phelan, *op. cit.*, I, 378; II, 70–71).

[16] Local preachers, whose labors supplemented locally the work of the itinerant ministry, were laymen licensed to preach (*Discipline* [1816]) after an examination before the quarterly conference by the presiding elder. The time-honored form of the license reads: "——— has applied to us for liberty to preach as a Local Preacher in our Circuit, and after due inquiry concerning his gifts, grace, and usefulness, we judge he is a proper person to be licensed for this purpose, and we accordingly authorize him to preach" (Sherman, *op. cit.*, p. 181).

[17] Henderson D. Palmer (1812–69), a native of Alabama, attended LaGrange College, Alabama, and taught at Nacogdoches, Texas, before entering the ministry of the Mississippi Conference in 1839 (Phelan, *op. cit.*, I, 124, 126; II, 33).

Milton R Stringfield examined approoved and Licence Renewed
James Thompson examined not approoved and Licence not Renewed

Class Leaders[18]

Lawrence W Simpson examined and approoved
Samuel C Rose examined and approoved
William McMahon examined and approoved
S. D. Thomas examined and approoved
S. D. McMahon examined and approoved

The Conference proceded to fill the list of *Stewards*[19]

John R. Hurbert was nominated and elected
James English was nominated and elected
Harry Hamilton was nominated and elected
Milton R Stringfield was nominated and elected

Character of *Exhortors*[20]

George H Stovall character examined and approoved and Licence Renewed the next Q[uarterly] M[eeting] Conference to be at Shelbiville on the first Sunday in December

James P. Irwin (*Secretary*) Littleton Fowler *Pr*[*e*]*s*[*ident*] *Pro*[*tem*]

[18] These leaders of the local "classes" represented the lowest rank in the Methodist pastoral hierarchy, closest to the individual members. They were appointed or discharged by the circuit preacher. The *General Rules* for Methodists, prepared by the Wesleys in 1739 and inserted in the American *Discipline* of 1789, give as duties of the class leaders visitation of members, inquiring "how their souls prosper," advising, reproving, comforting, or exhorting them, and receiving collections which are deposited with the stewards (Sherman, *op. cit.*, pp. 113–14, 173; for class meetings see *ibid.*, pp. 127–29).

[19] The quarterly conference stewards were, according to the *Discipline* of 1789, to be "men of solid piety, who both know and love the Methodist Doctrine and Discipline, and of good natural and acquired abilities to transact the temporal business." The preacher in charge of the circuit nominated laymen to this office, who were then confirmed or rejected by the quarterly conference. They collected and disbursed church moneys, kept records of these receipts and expenditures, provided the elements for the Lord's Supper, and visited the needy and distressed to relieve and comfort them (*ibid.*, pp. 185–86).

[20] Exhorters were licensed by the preacher in charge. Their chief duties were holding or aiding the preachers in meetings for prayer and exhortation. As exhorters they were official members of the quarterly conference and were expected to attend (*ibid.*, pp. 179, 184–85).

We the Members of the Shelbiville Society Nacogdoches Circuit Texian Mission do hearby recommend our beloved Elisha D Johnson to the Quartily Meeting Conference as a suitable person to receive Licence to preach the Gospel in the Methodist Episcopal Church Sept 4, 1838

EDWARD L. MARTON *Sect* L CAMPBELL *P[re]s[ident] Protem*

[1838–39]

First Quartely Meeting held for San augustine Circuit in the Town of Shelbiville December 11—1838

Members Present

Littleton Fowler
Samuel A Williams[21]
John Myric

Q. Are there any complaints or appeals
Ansr. None
Quartily Meatting to nominate and elect Brother Wager Smith circuit steward
Where shall our next quartily be held
Ans. at Wm Mcmahons Feb 9th 1839

S. A. WILLIAMS (*Sect*)

LITTLETON FOWLER *Pr Protem of the Texian Mission*

Second Quartily Meeting conference held at Goodlow's Schoolhouse for Sanaugustin Circuit on the 27 Aprile 1839

Members Present

Littleton Fowler P.E.
Samuel Williams A[ppointed] P[reacher]
Goodwin Killian

[21] Samuel A. Williams (1810–66), a native of North Carolina, entered the Tennessee Conference in 1834 but became a missionary to Texas in 1838. He served as delegate to the General Conference, South, and preached actively and served as presiding elder in eastern Texas until 1863, when he was superannuated (Phelan, *op. cit.*, I, 491–93; Crocket, *op. cit.*, pp. 275–77).

George Stovall
James Irwin
John Wilson
Wager Smith
E Chisam
S. D. Thomas
Hans Hamilton

Q. Are there any complaints or appeals
A None
Q Are there any Licence to be renewed
A Br Elkins Licence renewed

Bennet Elkkins[22] appeard at Quartely Conference [and] presented his Letter of recommendation as Local Preacher

Brother Elkkins is received as a Local Preacher in the Methodist Episcopal Church Texian District

Names of the diferent societies[23]

San augustine	amt of money Re*d*	$1.50
McMahons		
Milam		
Sabbine Town		
Cartwrights School House		
Lusk		
Shelbiville		
Hammonses		
Briggses Schoolhouse		
Goodlows Schoolhouse		6.51¼
S. D. Thomas's		7.31¼
Garretts School House		5.00
Nacogdoches		3.50
Public Collection		$22.11¼

[22] Bennett Elkins (1800–1858) was a native of South Carolina. He was admitted on trial to the East Texas Conference in 1857 (Phelan, *op. cit.,* I, 418).

[23] These were the local congregations which made up San Augustine Circuit. Each "Society" included one or more "Classes." The collections listed were applied to local circuit expenses as well as to the traveling and boarding expenses of the presiding elder and circuit preachers. It is lists like this (besides, of course, detailed diaries by the circuit preachers) which inform the historian as to the actual local extent of Methodist circuits.

When and where shall our next Quarterly Meeting be held *answ* at Dugloss

LITTLETON FOWLER *P.E.*

S. D. THOMAS *Secretary & R[ecording] S[teward]*

Third quarterly Meeting for San Augustine Circuit held at Duglass August 3d 1839

Members Preasant
Littleton Fowler P.E.
S. A. Williams

Quest. i Are there any complaints or appeals
Answer None

Conference proceded to take up the case of Bro John Wilson who had been expeld in the United States and his credentials handed over to Annual conference/after deliberation and proper trial the qu[arterly] Meeting restored him and this qu conference hereby call upon the Anual conference through their proper officer for his credentials When and where shall our next qu Conference be held/at B[e]thlehem Camp ground Sept 7 & 8

Nacgdoches	$00.00
Sanaugustine	.....
Mcmahons	17.00
S Yates	.....
Dugloss	$12.50
	29.50
Milam	.....
Deduct	14 75
Sabine	.....
Ross School House	.....
Lusk	.....
Hammonds	.....
Shelbiville	.....
Briggs School House	$00.00
Goodlows	$00.00
S. D. Thomas	00.00
Garretts School House	$00.00

Minutes read and approved

S. A. WILLIAMS *Sct* LITTLETON FOWLER *P.E.*

At a *Qartely Conference* of the M E Church held at B[e]thlehem Camp Ground Sept 7 1839 and in San augustine circuit

Members present

Littleton Fowler		P.E.
S. A. Williams		A.P.
Wm C Crawford	L[ocal] D[eacon]	
Ed*d* L. Martin		
R. L. Hubert	L.P. & Stew*d*	
H. D. Parmer		
John Wilson		
James English	"	& Stew*d*
E. D. Johnson	"	
Goodwin Killian		(Ex.)
John Box		
Simon Matthews	"	
S. D. Thomas Thomas	. & Steward	
Enoc Chisholm	"	Ex)
James Irwin	"	Ex)
Samuel Box	"	Class Leader

Question 1st Any Complaints *Answ* None
" 2 Any appeals *Answ* None

Bro R. L. Hubert, having presented satisfactory credentials to the conference was duly received as a Local Preacher among us and took his Seat as a Member of this Conference.

Question 3rd Any Licence to be renewed (L.D

Ans.—Bros Wm C. Crofford & Edw. L. Martin after due examination of character were passed

Bro. S. D. Mcmahon now came in and took his Seat

Bro. Bennet Elkins L P examined and passed and license renewed
" R. L. Hubert " " "
" John Wilson " " "
" E. D. Johnson " " "
" S. D. Mcmahon " " "
" H. D. Palmer " License renewed
" renewed to Anual Conference
" James English case [w]as laid over untill the next Q*r* Conference

[Bro.] Goodwin Killian examined passed & licens renewed as Exhortor
" John Box . . . .
" Lyman Matthews " . . . .
" S. D. Thomas " " "
" Enoch Chisholme " " "
" James Irwin " " " "
" Samuel C Box " " " " as C L
" James English " English [omit] as Steward, & excused from the Steward ship & Brother Crawford Elected in his place
Bro. H. Hamilton examined & passed as Steward
" Wm S. Smith " " "
" J. T. Sanford was granted licence to Preach the gospel
" John R. Hubert was passed & renewed

Qut. 4. Where shall the next Quartely Meeting con[ference] be held

Ans at Shelbiville on the Last Saturday and Sonday in December next ensuing.

List of Appointments and classes in the Sanaugustine Circuit

Sanaugustine		
Mcmahons		
Milam		
Sabine		
Cartwrights		
Hammonds		
Sh*i*lbiville		
Briggs	in good money	1.50
Goodlows		
Thomases	in Texas money $5	
Garretts	paid Since q*r* conference	1.31¼
Nacogdoches		
Duglass	Public Collection	$20.50
Yatess		

Whereupon the Conference adjourned[*]

E. D. Johnson *Sct*

Littleton Fowler *P.E.*
S. D. Thomas (*R.S.*)

* The above quarterly conference was holden according to time and place but stands for Nacogdoches Circuit, S. D Thomas *Secr.*

This is to certify that John T. Sanford has been an acceptable Local Preacher in the Methodist E Church at Mt Pisgh Carlloton [Carrollton] ct Ala[bama] Con Novem 1st 1837

S. D. THOMAS (*R.S.*) A. P. HARRIS *P.C.*

[1840]

Fir[s]t quarterly meeting for San Augustine Circuit held in San Augustine Saturday & Sabbath March 7th 1840

Members present L. Fowler, P.E. S. A. Williams Bennett Elkins Joseph N. Kilpatrick James Ervine Enoch Chisholmn G. H. Stovall George Davis Hans Hamilton

1st Question are there any complaints or appeals *Answer* none,

We the members of the quarterly meeting of San Augustine circuit, Resolve that we will not either Drink or tolerate drinking drams unless in accordance with the Rules of our Church.[24]

Appointments

	$ cts		$ cts
San Augustine		pataroon	
paines		McMahons	3
pine Ridge Chapel			
Houson Buyo			
Sabine Town			
Lindseys			
Garretts School house			
Thomas's			
Goodloes school house		public collection	
Lows school house		on Sabbath	$16.62½
Edgar's			

[24] American Methodists had condemned the distilling of liquor in 1780 and 1783. In 1789 they adopted, as part of their *Discipline,* the Wesleyan *General Rules,* which forbade "Drunkenness, buying or selling spirituous liquors, or drinking them unless [in] cases of [extreme] necessity." The *Discipline* of 1796 ordered that "If any member of our Society retail or give spirituous liquors, and any thing disorderly be transacted under his roof on this account, the Preacher who has the oversight of the Circuit shall proceed against him as in the case of other immoralities, and the person accused shall be cleared, censured, suspended, or excluded, according to his conduct, as on other charges of immorality" (Sherman, *op. cit.,* pp. 114, 131).

W D Ratcliff nominated and elected Steward
Where shall our next quarterly meeting be held and at what time
Answer at McMahons the last Saturday & Sabbath in Aprile
Minutes Read and approved
S. A. WILLIAMS *Sectr.* LITTLETON FOWLER *P.E.*

The *Second quarterly Meeting* for San augustine Circuit was held at Col. Mcmahons' 25th Aprile 1840
*Question—1—*Are there any complaints or appeals *Answ.* None
Members Present Littleton Fowler P.E.

S. A. Williams	S D Mcmahon
J T P Irwin	George H. Stovall
E P Chishom	J. B Mcmahon

The following resolutions was brought before the Conference Amended and adopted—Resolved that We the Members of quarterly conference of San augustine Circuit will on all occasions demand the credentials or authority to preach of those strangers passing through the Republic Professing to be Methodist Preachers furthermore will not permit them to preach in our houses unl[e]ss the[y] produce certificates as is Satisfactory Amendment And all others[25]

Q When and where shall our next quarterly Meeting be held
Answ. at B[e]thlehem Camp ground on 23 & 24 August

The following Bretherin were nominated and appointed as a committee to select a suitable place for a camp ground.

G. H. Stovall Sam D Mcmahon J B. Mcmahon

The following resolutions brought forwad and adopted Resolved that the Presidig Elder be authorized to employ Brother Shook[26]

[25] In any country in process of settlement, unorganized Christian communities, eager for preaching, were sometimes imposed upon by would-be ministers, who might hold a meeting in their neighborhood, take up a collection, and move on to fleece others. In 1837 the Protestant ministry of Houston, Texas, formed a "Committee of Vigilance" to demand credentials from all unknown preachers and expose imposters (Phelan, *op. cit.*, I, 79–80).

[26] Nathan Shook was admitted on trial to the Texas Conference in 1840 but was located from the East Texas Conference in 1847 (*ibid.*, p. 150; *Minutes . . . . South,* Vol. I: *1845–1857*, p. 97).

to travel with Brother Williams the balance of the year Minutes read & approved

J T P IRVIN LITTLETON FOWLER *P.E.*

San augustine	$2.50
McMahons par $2.50 Texas $250	$2.50
Patroon	$ —
Milam	$ —
Paynes	$
Pine Wood Chappel	$ —
Killpatrick's	$ —
Sabbine Town	$ —
Lindsey's	$ —
Garrett's Schoolhouse	$ —
Thomases	$
Goodlowes Schoolhouse	$
Public Collection	$
Texas Money	
Good	$12.00
	6.50

Paid S. A. Williams par 4.12½ Texas 7-25
Paid N Shook 4-12½—7.25 Texas

The *third Qaterly Meeting Conference* For San augustine Circuit Held at B[e]thlehem Camp Ground on the 22 August 1840

Members Present

Littleton Fowler (P.E.)
Samuel A. Williams P[reacher in] C[harge] &
M Shook A.S.P.).....
John A Killian E.
H Hamilton (S)
Wm Wratliff C.L.
S. D. Thomas C.L.

Q Are there any Complaints or appeals *Answ* None
J. T. Scruggs was nominated and elected Steward

Brother Charles C. Garner's credentials presented to this Qaterly Conference and received as a Local Peacher and Lic[e]n[s]e Renewed

Local Preachers

Joseph Kilpatrick character examined and past and Licens Renewed

Samuel *B* Mcmahon's caracter Examined and past—Licens Renewed

Bennett Elkins Character examined and past....

Exhortors

J P Irwin character (E) & Past Licens Ren

E Chisom Character (E) and Past L R

George Stoval character examined his case laid over on account of some objecttions to the next Qaterly Conference

Class Leaders

John Walker Character examined and past
James Mcmahon Character examined and past
Elisha Allen Character examined and past
S. D. Thomas character examined and Past
Wm Wratliff Character examined and Past
George Davis character Examined and Past
A Lanier Character examined and Past
Samuel A. Williams P.C. character examined and past
Nathan Shook (A.P.) character examined and past.

Societies

San Augustine	$. . .
Mcmahons	$ 5.15
Milam	$
Sabbine Town	$
Howsan Bayou	$
Patroon	$
Laniers	$
Rows School House	$
S D Thomas	$
Goodlows School House	$ 1.00

Garretts School House $3.25 Texas [money] 5.00	$ 4.25
Pains School House	$
Pine Ridge Chappel	$
Lindseys	$
Public Collection at camp Bthlehem	18.97
	$29.39
	)good M[oney]
Nathan Shook Recd at Mcmahons	5 15½
at Camp Bthlehem	9 47½
	$14 63
Do do....	12½
	$14 75½
Traveling Expenses Deducted	6.00
Total Amt Recd—	8-75½
Brother Woolam Received at Camp Bethlehem	$ 9.60
Traveling Expenses	75
	$ 8-85

When and where shall our next Qaterly Conference be held
Ans. At Patroon Imbracing the 3[d] Sabbath in October next
Minutes Re[a]d and approoved
S. D. Thomas (*Sec*) & (*R.S.*) Littleton Fowler (*P.E.*

The *fourth Quarterly Meeting Conference* for San augustine circuit held at Patroon on the 17 of October 1840

Members Present

Littleton Fowler	(P E)
Samuel A Williams	(P C)
Nathan Shook	Assistant Preacher
John Wilsan	(L P)
S. D. Mcmahon	(L P)
C. C. Garner	(L P)

Exhorters

James P Irwin
E Chisom
G. H. Stovall

Class Leaders

S. D. Thomas (C L)
Jessie T Scruggs (C L)
H Hamilton (S S)

are there any complaints or appeals *Ans* None

Brother George H Stovalls case taken as layed over at Camp Bthlehem quarterly Meeting Conference was taken up character examined Licnce not renewed

Brother Nathan Shook was recommended to Qaterly Meetin Conference as a suitable parson to Preach the Gospel in the Methodist Episcopal Church and was received

Societi[e]s

San Augustine	$00.00
McMahons	00.00
Patroon	.....
Milam	.....
Sabbine Town	.....
Hauson Bayou	.....
Pine Wood Chappel	.....
Pains	.....
Linseys	.....
Garretts School House	.....
S D Thomas	.....
Goodlows School House	.....
Rows School House	.....
Cartwrights Mill	.....

When and where shall our next Quarterly conference be held *ansr.* at San augustine on the 23 and 24 of January 1841

Littleton Fowler (*PE*
S. D. Thomas (*Secret.*)

[1841]

The *first quarterly Meeting Conference* was held in the Town of San Augustine in the Masonic Casol on the 23 of Jan 1841

Members present L. Fowler P.E. F Wilson[27] P.C S.D. Thomas E Chisom J T Irwin H Griffith Secretary Elect

Brother William Craig[28] A Local preacher Presented his letter for membership and also presented charges which were made against him in Missippi by Vincent H carolson it was moved by Br F Wilson and Seconded by J. T Irwin that the charges above mentioned against Bro Craig were illegal and that this Conference would not act thereon Bro Craig was then received as a Member by Letter in his usual official Capacity it [was] Moved and Seconded that S D Thomas J T Irwin and H Griffith be a Commity to take into consideration [the] amount nessisary for the Supplying the Table Expenses of Bro F Wilson the preacher in charge and provide for the Same it was moved and Seconded and carried by unanimous Vote that the next quarterly Meeting be held in Sabine Town

L FOWLER *P.E.*

HORATIA GRIFFITH *Secty* S. D. THOMAS (*RS*)

The *Second quarterly Meeting Conference* for San Augustine circuit was held in the Town of Sabbine on the 8 May 1841 the prisideing Elder L Fowler being Sick F Wilson Presided

Members Present

F Wilson P.C.
Samuel D Mahon
Jessie F Scruggs
Jacob Crofford (E. P. Gains)
R. P. Goodhold Jessie T Scruggs was elected Sec

[27] Francis Wilson (? –1867), born in Virginia, was admitted on trial to the Virginia Conference in 1810, serving later in Kentucky and Ohio. He located from the Ohio Conference in 1839 and moved to Texas. In December, 1840, he was appointed by the newly formed Texas Conference to San Augustine Circuit. He served actively in Texas until his superannuation in 1851 and was the chief founder of Wesleyan College at San Augustine. He traveled, according to his manuscript "Memoirs," 150,000 miles, preached some 7,000 sermons, and was instrumental in converting 4,000 people, including thirty who became ministers. His death occurred in Louisiana (Crocket, *op. cit.*, pp. 277–81).

[28] William Craig (? –1865) had taken a voluntary location from the Mississippi Conference in 1839 (John G. Jones, *A Complete History of Methodism as Connected with the Mississippi Conference of the Methodist Episcopal Church, South* [Nashville, 1908], II, 426). His ministry in Texas began with his appointment to Nacogdoches Circuit in 1841; he took the superannuated relation in 1861 (*Minutes of the Annual Conferences of the Methodist Episcopal Church,* Vol. III: *1839–1845,* p. 214).

there being no complaints or appeals F Wilson give notice to the Conference that the ill health [of the Presiding Elder], and the impossibility of his being able to do the Official Buisiness of the (circuit) District at the present in all probibility for the year it being nessisary for some one to attend the quarterly Meetings Fowler had requested F Wilson to attend the quarterly Meetings in his place and to take the charge of the Same it was Mooved and Seconded by this Confr that F Wilson be Substituted by this Conferanc to take [the] District and he fill up the appointments on the Circuit by the Local Preachers when he is absent Carried unanimously there being no other buisness for the Conference tha [then] adjourned to meet on Friday the (29) 31 of July 1841. at Pine Chappel Signed and Counter Signed by

JESSIE SCRUGGS *Sec* F WILSON *A.P*

Report of Steward

McMahons Class	$3.00
Hauson Bayow	1.50
Patroon	.50
Milam & Taylors	10.30
Sabbine	7.50
Public Collection	3.81¼
	$26.61¼

8 May 1841

S D THOMAS (*R.S.*)

at the first Quartily meeting I received of Mcmahons Class

	1.81¼	
at San Augustine	12.00	Public Collection
from the 2 qu	26.81¼	
	40.62½	
Traveling Exs	6.00	
	34.62½	

F WILSON

The *third Quartily Meeting conferenc* Was held at Pine Chappel July the 31, 1841

Members present Littleton Fowler P.E. F. Wilson P.C. (William Craig, L.P.S D Mcmahon L P) [....] Mcmahon L. P. J. T. Irwin (E) E. P. Chishom (E) J. B. Mcmahon C.L. Wm D Rolliff (E) S D Thomas (E) Brother Griffith

Q Are there any complaints or appeals *A* None

J T Irwin and E P Chishom were reckommended by the Poligotch Class as purson[s] Suitable to Preach the Gospel on Motion of J. T. Irwin his examination was Laid over till the next quartily Meeting Conference On Motion of F. Wilson it was Resolved that J. T. Irwin and E P Chishom be permitted to exercise their gifts in Preachig and Exorting untill the next quartily Meeting Motion Carried

it was Motioned that a Commitee of four be appointed to layout a camp Meetin ground at the Sulfer Springs on the Attoyan Motion carried it was motioned that Wm D Ratliff Wm W. Low J Hail and [....]Griffith be appointed that Commity Motion Carried it was motiọned that Wm D Ratliff be appointed a commity of one to wait on the claimants of the Land and obtain from them a title or Relinquishment to 4 Acres of Land including the ca[m]pground Motion Carried

The *fourth quartily Meeting Conference* for San Augustine Circuit was held at Purkinses Camp Ground on the 23 Oct 1841

Members Present

Littleton Fowler	(P.*L*)	Past
F Wilson	(P.E.)	Do
William Craig	(L.E.)	Do
Samuel Mcmahon	(L.P.)	Do
Charles C. Garner	(L.P.)	Do
Bennett Elkins	(L.P.)	Do
Jacob Croffor	(L.P.)	Do
James P Irwin	Ex	Do
Enoch Chishom—	Ex	Do
Goodwin Killian	Ex	Do
Wm D Ralliff—	Ex	Do

Robert Welse—	Ex	Do
Robert Roundtree	Ex	Do
H Hamilton	S.S.	Do
Jessie T Scruggs	S.S.	Do
S D Thomas	S.S. & R Steward	
Horatio Griffiths	C.L.	Do
E P Gains—	C.L.	Do
John B Gains	C.L.	Do
Samuel Hamilton	C.L.	Do
Jacob Croffor Jun.	C.L.	Do
[....] Walker	C.L.	Do
Morgan Berry	C.L.	Do
Jonas Hale	C.L.	Do
Wm Wilson	C.L.	Do
A Nailer	C.L.	Do
H Fraser	C.L.	Do
Dr. Gudlow	C.L.	Do

[The] Character[s of all the above were] Examined [and their] Lic[e]n[se]s Renew[e]d.

Samuel *B* McMahon was reckommended to Deacons order by unanimous vote

Charles C Garner L P Character Examined and conditionally past Littleton Fowler was appointed a Commity of one to ta[l]k to Bro Garner and on condition of his promissing to do better to give him his Licnce otherwise to with hold them

Bro Jacob Crofford[29] was reckommended to this quarterly Meeting Conference as a Suitable purson to preach the Gospel in the Methodist Episcopal Church and was received and reckommended to the next anual Conference

Brothers Enoch Chishom and Irwin was reckommended to this Conference as Suitable pursons to preach the Gospel in the Methodist Episcopal Church and was received and Reckommended to the anual Conference

[29] Jacob Crawford was admitted on trial to the Texas Conference in 1841 and appointed to Penola Circuit. He located from the East Texas Conference in 1847 (*ibid.*, p. 213; *Minutes .... South*, Vol. I: *1845–1857*, p. 97).

When and Where shall our next Quartily Meeting be held *Ansr* at Mount Lebinon

S D Thomas *sec* F Wilson P.E.

Public Collection at Ayish Bayou	$13.50
Sulpher Springs	15.00
Goodlows	3.50

Paid to F. Wilson by E P Gains 25 par monney and $34 Texas

[1842]

The *first quartily Meeting* held for San Augustine Circuit at Brother Browns on the 1 January 1842

Members present

Fancis Wilson	P.E.
George West[30]	P.C.
S A Williams	S[uper]-N[umerary]
S D McMahon	L.P.
E. P. Chishome	L.P.
John Wollim	L.P.
Jess*ei* Scrugs	Stewar
John Walk*e*	Lc
A. W. Naylor	
John B Gains	C.L.
R. K. Goodlow	
N Hamilton	

Jessie T Scr[u]gs was nominated and appointed Secretary

Are there any complaints or appeals *Ansr* none The conference proceded to appoint the following persons Stewards viz James Perkins Jacob Crofford Daniel Brown Hance Hamilton removed at his own request and James Perkins appointed in his sted. When and Where Shall our next Meeting be held *Ans* San Augustine

Jessie Scrugs (*Secr*) F Wilson *P.E.*

[30] George West was admitted on trial to the Texas Conference in 1841 and superannuated in 1843, but he resumed his duties in 1845 as presiding elder of San Augustine District, East Texas Conference. He was suspended from the ministry in 1847 but again appears on the conference rolls as a superannuate in 1850 (*Minutes of the Annual Conferences of the Methodist Episcopal Church,* Vol. III: *1839–1845,* pp. 213, 426; *Minutes .... South,* Vol. I: *1845–1857,* pp. 39, 152, 297).

The *fourth Quartily Meeting Conference* for San Augustine Circuit was held at Po*r*igotch Camp ground the 24 Sept 1842

Members present

F Wilson P.E.	George West E. & P.C.		Past	
Samuel Williams	S.N.	charater E[xamined] & Past		
G Blackburn	L.P.	Ditto	Do	Do
S D Mcmahon	L.D.	Do	Do	Do
Bennet Elkins	L.P.	Do	D	Licnce Renewed
J. C. Wolom	L.P.	Do	Do	Liccce Renewed

E Chishom Exhoter character Examined and Past
Licnd to Preach ———
R Roundtree E. C[haracter] E[xamined] P[assed] Lic*nd* to Preach
Wm D Rotliff E.C.E.P. permited to preach
R. B Wells E.C.E.P. Licns Renewed
James Mcmahon E.C.E.P. Do Do
H Cohern E.C.E.P. Do—
S D Thomas E & Steward C.E.P Licens Renewed
J Crofford E & S. C.L.—C.E.P. Do Do
R. H. Goodlow E.—C.E.P. Licnsd to preach
E. P. Gains E.C.E.P. Licns renewed

Stewards

James Perkins C.L. & Steward C.E.P.
E. Gains C.E.P.
D. Brown C.E.P.
Bro Alexander C.E.P.

Class Leaders

Wm Wilson	character E.P.
Jessie Allen	Do
Bro Walker	Do
E Smith	Do
David Brown	C.E.P.
J. T. Scruggs	C.E.P.
H Fraziers	C.E.P.
John Payne	C.E.P.
J Crofford	C.E.P.

James Perkins C.E.P.
Bro Ashmore C.E.P.
Jonas Hale C.E.P.
Bro Win C.E.P.

Are there any Complaints or appeals *Ansr* There are (Moris Hill and Th*o* Jackson it is mooved and Second that Bro Jackson have an other arbitration in the above case Motion carried

Approoved

S D Thomas *Scr* F Wilson *PE*

[1843]

The *first Quarterly Meeting Conference* for San Augustine Circuit was held at Mount Lebanon on the 10th of April 1843

Present

Francis Wilson P.E.
Daniel Poe[31] C[ircuit]. P[reacher].
Samuel A. Williams A.P.
Robert K. Goodloe L.P.
James B. McMahon Ex[horter]
Francis M. Stoval Ex.
E. P. Gaines Ex.
Scott Garritt C.L.
Horatio Rowe C.L.
Leroy Miller C.L.
Daniel Brown S

[31] Daniel Poe (1809–44) was born of Presbyterian parentage in Columbiana County, Ohio, but was converted to Methodism in 1825. He attended Augusta College (Ky.) and joined the Ohio Conference in 1832. Bishop Soule appointed him missionary to the Oneida and Menominee Indians in Wisconsin in 1836. He transferred to Texas in 1842. "After his return to Texas, he endeavored to commence an institution of learning at San Augustine. The ensuing conference adopted it and gave it their patronage. Daniel was appointed to the San Augustine circuit, and commenced his labors, having some three hundred miles to travel in filling his appointments every four weeks. After the first quarter, the teacher of mathematics, in their new college, resigned, and Daniel undertook to supply his place. While filling this post, he regularly rode into the country and preached on Friday night, twice on Saturday, and twice on Sabbath, and returned so as to attend to the recitations of his classes in the college, from Monday morning to the next Friday afternoon" (James B. Finley, *Sketches of Western Methodism* [Cincinnati, 1855], pp. 495–509; see also Sprague, *op. cit.,* VII, 786–91).

Question are there any complaints or appeals—*Answer* There are none.

Brother F. M. Stovall[32] Came duly recommended as a suitable person to preach the Gospel in the M.E. Church It was moved and seconded that Brother F. M. Stovall be allowed to preach until next Quarterly Meeting Conference It was moved by D. Poe and seconded by E. P. Gaines that the Conference take into consideration the subject of education.

Resolved That this Conference cooperate with her Sister Station[33] and adjoining Circuits in erecting and establishing a literary Institution at some point hereafter to be designated

It is moved and seconded that Messrs R. E. Ratcliff and Langhom be appointed a committee for the purpose mentioned in the foregoing Resolution

On Motion W. G. Ratcliff was duly elected Steward On Motion A. W. Naylor was duly elected Steward On Motion Messrs L Fowler S. D. McMahon E. P. Gaines S. A. Williams B. Odum J. B. McMahon & James McIver be appointed Trustees to take a deed of Sister Naomi Mackey in favor of the M.E. Church to a certain tract of ground for a burying ground On Motion of the President this Conference resolved itself into a committee of the whole on finances Conference adjourned to meet at Wilsons Chapel Minutes read and approved

R. K. Goodloe *Sect.* F. Wilson *P.E.*

The *second Quarterly Meeting Conference* for San Augustine Circuit was held at Wilson's Chapel June 24th 1843 *Present*

Francis Wilson	P.E.
Daniel Poe	C.P.
Sam. A. Williams	A.P.
Bennet Elkins	L.P.
F. M. Stovall	Ex.
Thos. Sansom	C.L.

[32] Francis M. Stovall (? –1883) was admitted on trial to the Texan Conference in 1843 and appointed to Crockett Circuit, San Augustine District. At the division of the conference in 1845, he went with the Eastern Texas Conference (*Minutes of the Annual Conferences of the Methodist Episcopal Church,* Vol. III: *1839–1845,* pp. 426–27).

[33] San Augustine. The institution referred to was Wesleyan College, San Augustine.

S. D. Sansom L. E. Corne recommended from Wayne Circuit Tennessee Conference and duly declared a member of this Conference

S. D. Thomas	Ex.
W. D. Ratcliff	Ex.

Q. are there any complaints or appeals *A.* There are none

F. M. Stoval came duly recommended to this Conference as a proper person to preach the Gospel in the M.E. Church after being duly examined he was Licensed to preach as per recommendation

Resolved that the third quarterly meeting be held in conjunction with the Sanaugustine station at a campmeeting to be in September next at Perkin[s]' Camp Ground

Resolved that there shall be a camp meeting at Kendricks' Camp Ground on Ayish Bayou

Reported one Sabbath School in a flourishing condition[34]

Conference adjourned to meet again at Perkins' Camp Ground

Minutes read and approved

W. D. Ratcliff *Sec-* F. Wilson *P.E.*

The *third Quarterly Meeting* for San Augustine Circuit and Station was held at Union Camp ground September 18th 1843

Present

Francis Wilson	P.E.
S. A. Williams	A.P.
S. D. Sansam[35]	L.E.
Bennet Elkins	L.P.
S. D. Thomas	Ex.
F. M. Stovall	L.P.
B. M. Burrow	Ex.

[34] Note that this is the first reference in the document to Sabbath schools. The *Discipline* of 1840 had ordered, in answer to the question, "What shall we do for the rising generation?" that "Sunday schools be formed in all our congregations where ten children can be collected for that purpose." Each quarterly conference, as an auxiliary to the Methodist Sunday School Union, was to supervise all Sunday schools within its limits (Addie G. Wardle, *History of the Sunday School Movement in the Methodist Episcopal Church* [New York, 1918], p. 78).

[35] Samuel D. Sansom was admitted on trial to the East Texas Conference in 1851 and located in 1861 (Phelan, *op. cit.*, I, 334).

W. D. Ratliff	Ex.
Thomas L. Sansom	C.L.
A. W. Naylor	S.
Jonas Hail	C.L.
M. Wilson	C.L.

S.D. Sansom Elected Secratary

Question Are there any complaints or appeals *Answer* none

Wm. D. Ratcliff and S. D. Thomas came duly recommended as proper persons to Preach the Gospel By request of the persons recommended their business was put off untill next Quarterly Meeting Conference

Quest Where shall our next Quarterly Meeting be held

Ans at Lebanon Camp Ground on the 14th October next

Reported two Sabbath Schools containing 40 Scholars in this Circuit

Conference chose and appointed Bros. Jonas Hail S. D. Thomas J. Perkins J. C. Brooks and Theophilus Thomas Trustees for Union Camp Ground

Minutes read and approved.

S. D. Sansom *Sect.* *Signed* F. Wilson *P.E.*

The *fourth Quarterly Meeting* for San Augustine Circuit was held at Mount Lebanon Camp Ground on the 16th October 1843

Present

F. Wilson	P.E.
S. A. Williams	A.P.
B. Elkins	L.P.
S. D. McMahon	L.P.
R. Roundtree	L.P.
R. K. Goodloe	L.P.
S. D. Sansom	L.E.
F. M. Stovall	L.P.
[....] Blacburn	L.P.
W. D. Ratliff	Ex.
S. D. Thomas	Ex.
B. M. Barrow	Ex.

A. W. Naylor	Ex.
E. P. Gaines	Ex.
J. B. McMahon	Ex.
Jacob Crawford Sons	S.
Danl. Brown	S.
W Ship	S.
Jesse Scrugs—	
L. V. Sanks	
Harmon Frazer	
Scott Garrett	
Jonas Hail	
M. Watson	
M Wilson	Class Leaders
T. L. Sansom	
J. Allen	
W. Donahoe	
H. Rose	
S. Davis	

Brother Stovall was duly recommended for admission into the Texas annual Conference

Bro Ratcliff & Bro S. D. Thomas presented themselves for license to Preach in the M.E. Church as local Preachers and were licensed

Bro. Bennet Elkins character examined & license renewed

Bro. S. D. Samson Passed & license renewed

Bro. S. D. McMahon passed & license renewed

Bro. R Roundtree Character passed & license renewed

Bro. Elkins Recommended to be ordained

Bro. R. K. Goodloe's character examined and license renewed

Bro James B McMahon's character examined and after being reproved his license was renewed

Bro. E. P. Gaine's Character was examined & licens renewed

Bro. D. Brown	Character	passed
B[ro] A. W. Naylor	do	passed
Bro W Ship	—	passed
Bro J Crawford		passed
Bro Ratcliff		passed
Bro Alexander		passed

Then came the examination of *Class Leaders*

Bro Scruggs	Passed
Bro Smith	Passed
Bro Sanks	Passed
Bro. Frazer	Passed
Bro Garrett	passed
Bro Watson	passed
Bro J Hail	passed
Bro Wilson	passed
Bro Burrows	passed
Bro T. G. Sansom	passed
Bro. Allen	passed
Bro Donahoe	passed
Bro Rose	passed
Bro S Davis	passed

Bro S. A. Williams reported two Sabbath Schools of about forty members in prosperous condition

Question where shall our next Quarterly meeting be held

Answer at Col McMahons's

Minutes read & approved

HORATIO GRIFFITH *Sec* *Signed* F WILSON *P.E.*

[1844]

Minutes of the *first Quarterly conference* for the San Augustine Curcuit held at the camp ground near Col Mcmahon's on the 9th of March 1844

The following members was *Present* F Wilson P.E. D Poe C.P. C. A. Wright[36] A.P. S. D. Mcmahon L.D. F Blackburn L.E. E. P. Chisholm L.P. J V. Sanks ex D. W. Camp Ex— A W Naylor Steward John Bilbo C L James Watson C.L. Scott Garret C L

Question 1st are there any appeals *Answer* no

Question 2nd are there complaints *Answer* no

John Bilbo[37] from the Milam Society came duly recommended for

[36] Charles H. Wright was admitted on trial to the Texas Conference in 1843 and appointed to San Augustine Circuit under Daniel Poe (*Minutes of the Annual Conferences of the Methodist Episcopal Church,* Vol. III: *1839–1845,* p. 426).

[37] John Bilbo had been a traveling preacher in Alabama and Louisiana, from his admission on trial to the Mississippi Conference in 1828 to about 1834, when his name disappears from the minutes (*ibid.,* Vol. II: *1829–1839,* p. 15).

lisens to Preach And after being examined according to discipline was lisensed.

Silas W. Camp[38] from the Sabine Town Society came duly recommended for license to Preach and after being examined was licensed

Napolean W. Burks[39] from the Society at Col. Mcmahons' came duly recommended for license to preach and after being examined according to discipline was Licensed

Rev. F. Wilson Stated that the Tristees of the Wesleyan College had elected D. Poe Professor of Mathematics in said College therefore the Quarterly meeting Conference recommended D. Poe to accept the appointment

Resolutions from the Jasper Quarterly meeting Conference were presented by F Wilson recommending him to make a tour through the United States to make collections for the Wesleyan College

Resolved, That we the Members of San Augustine Quarterly Conference concur with Said resolutions Bro. Naylor offered his resignation as Steward and it was accepted the next Quarterly Meeting to be held in Judge Payn's neighborhood

D. Poe *Sec* F. Wilson *P.E.*

Third Quarterly Meeting held at Union Camp Ground Sept 7th 1844

Members present

George West	Elder
C. A. Wright	A.P.
N. W. Burks	Helper
B. Elkins	L.P.
Jonas Hail	C.L.
M. Watson	C.L.
M Wilson	C.L.
J M Odel	C.L.

[38] Silas W. Camp was admitted on trial to the (East) Texas Conference in 1845 (*ibid.,* Vol. III: *1839–1845,* p. 554).

[39] Napoleon W. Burks (1809–73), born in Green County, Kentucky, joined the (East) Texas Conference in 1845. He served as presiding elder of Clarkesville, Marshall, and Palestine districts and as president of Fowler Institute, a Methodist school at Henderson, Texas (Phelan, *op. cit.,* II, 93–94).

W. D. Ratliff nominated and elected Secratary

Question are there any Complaints or appeals *Answer* None

Resolved that it is the sense of this Conference that after examination of the character of John Bilbo L.P. that his character be not passed and his License discontinued

the next Quarterly Meeting shall be held at Mount Lebanon commencing on the last Saturday in November next

W. D. RATLIFF *Sec* CHARLES A WRIGHT
Preacher in cha[*rge*]

Minutes of the *fourth Quarterly meeting Conference* for San Augustine Circuit Texas Conference Mount Lebanon December 2nd 1844

Members Present

Members	
C. A. Wright N. B. Burks B Elkins E. P. Chisholm R Roundtree	Preachers
D. Watkins John Bilbo E. P. Gaines A. W. Naylor	Exhorters
H. Rose S. Garrett G. C. Lucas M Watson	C.L.
D. Brown G. C. Lucas E. P. Gaines	S

Question 1st are there any complaints or appeals *Ans*—none

2nd Are there any licenses to grant or renew *ans,* there are

Then came John Bilbo duly recommended and after being examined was Licensed to Preach the Gospel in the M.E. Church and recommended to the Annual Conference as a proper person to be received into the Travelling Connexion

Then came D. Watkins duly recommended for license to preach the Gospel in the M.E. Church and after being duly examined was licensed

N W Burks License renewed and recommended to the Texas Annual Conference as a proper person to be received in the Travlling Connexion

E. P. Chisholm License renewed and recommended to the Texas Annual Conference as a proper person to be received in the Travelling Connexion

B Elkins character passed and License renewed

R Roundtree character passed and License renewed
W D Ratliff character passed and license renewed
S. D. Thomas character passed and license renewed
S D McMahon character passed
R K Goodloe license not renewed
B M Burrow character not passed license no[t] renewed
Jesse Allen character passed and license renewed
L Coher character passed and license renewed
A W Naylor character passed and license renewed
E. P. Gaines character passed and license renewed

D. Brown	W. Ship	Stewards passed
L. V. Green	G. C. Lucas	
E P Gaines	C. Alexandria	
J Crawford		

Brother C Alexandria removed from the Stewardship

Bro Jesse Scruggs nomi[n]ated and elected Steward

The next Quarterly Meeting to be held at Antioch Chapel in the neighborhood of Hants

Minutes read and approved

E. P. Gaines *Sec* Charles A. Wright *P.C.*

[1845]

First Quarterly Meeting Conference for San Augustine Circuit convened at Antioch March 22nd 1845

Members Present

J. W. Fields[40]	P.C.
J. T. P. Irvine	A.P.
J. Allen	C.L.
M. Watson	C.L.

The Presiding Elder not being Present J. W. Fields took J. T. P. Irvine nominated and elected Secratary

Q. are there any complaints or appeals *A*. none

Q. Where will you hold your next Quarterly *A* at Goshen on the 14 & 15 of June next

J T P Irvine *Sec* J. W. Fields *Pres. Pro.*

The minuits of the *Second & third quarterly meetings* for 1845 has has never been plac[ed] *in the hands of the recording stewart*[41]

At a *fourth quarterly meeting* of the Methodist Episcopal Church South held at Maj[or] Augustines[42] Camp Ground on the 4th day of October 1845 was *present*

Revd F Wilson	P.E.
J. W. Fields	P.C
Jas T P. Irvin	A.P
S. D. McMahan	S.D.
B. Elkins	L.P.
George Rehm	Exhotor
N B Burks L P. & Professor in College	
John Bilbo	L P
W. D. Ratliff	L P
J Allen	Ext
[....] Smith	C L
Bro. Nailer	Extr
D. Greer	C Collector
J Haile	C L

[40] John W. Fields (1817–86) transferred from the Kentucky to the East Texas Conference in 1845 and served as presiding elder of the San Augustine District in 1847. He took the superannuated relation in 1874 (*ibid.*, I, 231; II, 272–73).

[41] Note that this was the period of transition from Methodist Episcopal Church to Methodist Episcopal Church, South.

[42] Major Henry W. Augustine was in the Battle of Nacogdoches (1832), served as delegate from San Augustine to Consultation in 1835, commanded a company in the Texan army in the Cherokee War (1838), and was a major against the Córdova rebellion in the same year (Crocket, *op. cit.*, pp. 121, 156, 172, 190).

W H Payne C L
L V Greer Stewart

The Conference then proceeded to take up the unfinished buisiness of last Conference wherupon the papers in reference to the Case of W. D. Ratliff was Coled and read before the Conference when it appeared that the Rev*d* W. D. Ratliff was charged with gross immorality —the specifications are 1st shooting and wounding Mr. Banks Burrow 2d an attempt and design to take his Burrow*s* life—On Motion the report of the Committee suspending Brother Ratliff to the quarterly Conference was sustained—Resolved that Brother Ratliff is Considered by this Conference as not guilty under all of the Circumstances of the Case as charged—Resolved that Brother Ratliff remain suspended in his ministerial capacity—

By order of Conference Brother Ratliff have the privilege at his request to withdraw from Conference and not stand as a suspended member

The case of Bro. Erasmus Elkins appealed to this Conference from the Class came up. Charged with immorality (specifications) 1st slandering Mr Jn*o* A Greer[43] 2d Lying in denying the fact when interogated. The Appellant's plea not guilty. On motion it was resolved that Bro Elkins have the privilege of withdrawing the appeal to this Conference

The Conference then entered into the examination of character
A W Nailor Ch[aracter] Approved & Licns renewed
J C Burke Ch passed not rend
[....] Coal Ch passed Lcan renewed
Revd McMahon Ch passed recomend to Conf for El?
[....] Bilbo " approved & rec to conf
Jesse Allen " " " "
George Chase " " " "
Rev B Elkins Licns renewed
Jas McMahan Licenced to Preach
O Fitzallen (Steward) Ch. appr. & passed

[43] Colonel John Alexander Greer (1802–55) was a native of East Tennessee. He settled on a farm near San Augustine, Texas, in 1837. A prominent Texas legislator, he served four terms as president of the Texas Senate. In 1845 he was appointed secretary of the Texas treasury and in 1846, 1849, andn 1851 he was elected lieutenant-governor of the state of Texas. He was a brother of Dr. Lewis V. Greer, mentioned frequently in this document (*ibid.*, pp. 239–40).

Jas Perkins [(Steward) Ch. appr. & passed]
[....] Soul " " " "
Daniel Brown " " " "
Sutton (Servint of Mr Potters) Ch. appr & L. Rend[44]
Bartlett (Svt of Garret) Ch. " " "
Edward Gaines (Steward) removed and Jno McRea fill his place.
Jacob Craford Ch. appr & passed
W Ship Ch. approve & passed
George Lucas removed & Bro F Wilson in his place
W D Ratliff removed and Maj Augustine in his place
L V Grier Ch. approved & appointed recording secty

On motion it was recommended this [that] this Circuit be divided according to discipline[45] On Motion the next quarterly meeting be at Bro McMahan for Sabin Circuit. And the first quarterly meeting for San Augustine Circuit be at Ships meeting House the Amt pd at this quarterly meeting as follows

Jonass Class	Cr By this amt		$ 2.25
Wilson Chapel	" " " "		1.00
San Augustine	" " " "		7.00
Goshan	" " " "		15.00
Public Collection			19.00
			44.25
Jas T. P. Irvin	Do To this Amt	$31.50	
J. W. Fields	Do " " "	13.00	
			$44.50

L. V. Greer[46] *Secry* F Wilson *P.E.*

[44] Provision was early made for licensing Negroes as traveling and local preachers. The *Discipline* of 1824 stipulated that "our colored Preachers and official members shall have all the privileges which are usual to others in the District and Quarterly Conferences, where the usages of the country do not forbit it" (Sherman, *op. cit.*, p. 119). This, in substance, was included in *The Doctrines and Discipline of the Methodist Episcopal Church, South* (Louisville, 1846), p. 196.

[45] In the Southern Church after 1866, division of circuits was one of the powers of the bishop rather than the presiding elder (P. A. Peterson, *History of the Revisions of the Discipline of the Methodist Episcopal Church, South* [Nashville, 1889], p. 53).

[46] Lewis V. Greer, who served as steward, recording steward, and secretary of the San Augustine Quarterly Conference, was a practicing physician and a partner in the Greer and Payne Store in San Augustine. He was a native of Tennessee (Crocket, *op. cit.*, p. 220).

[1846]

At the *first quarterly meeting Conference South* held for San Augustine Circuit at McMahans Chapel March the 7th 1846 the following *members* were *present*

Revd George West	P.E.
L. S. Marshall[47]	P.C.
J. C. Wollan[48]	A.P.
S. D. McMahan	L.D.
John Bilbo	L.P.
A Young	Extr
M Watson	Cl.
W. H. Payne	Cl.
W. B. Frazer	Cl.

L V Greer recording Stewart on Motion Brother Greer was nominated & appointed recording secatary On Motion [of] Bro Marshall Bro Core was put in nomination for St in place of Bro Shepher and Elected Bro C. Egbert to fill the place [of] Bro McRea Bro Osburn Harris to fill the place of Bro. Brown Bro Jackson to fill the place of Bro. Crawford Bro. T. P. Payne to fill the place of Bro. Garrett. Bro Saml Dorn to fill the place of Bro. F Wilson

question 1st. Are there any Complaints or appeals *Answ.* None

qs. 2d. How many members are on the circuit *A.* three hundred & forty four whites & one hundred & forty colourd[49]

qs 3d. What amount is necessary to make up the preachers allowance

A. Four hundred & forty two Dollars and seventy five cents ($442.75).

[47] Lewis S. Marshall transferred from the Kentucky to the (East) Texas Conference in 1845 and retransferred to the Arkansas Conference in 1847 (*Minutes .... South,* Vol. I: *1845–1857,* pp. 7, 98).

[48] John C. Woolam (1813–94) was admitted to the Texas Conference on trial in 1842. He was a native of Edgefield District, South Carolina, who came to Texas in 1838 and became a charter member of First Methodist Church, Houston. During the Civil War he was a chaplain in the Confederate Army. Phelan writes that "his name was known in nearly every home in East Texas. Families named their children for him, and sent for him at marriages and funerals" (*op. cit.,* II, 379–80).

[49] The colored membership of the circuits was reported to the annual conferences beginning in the year 1786 (*Minutes of the Annual Conferences of the Methodist Episcopal Church,* Vol. I: *1773–1828,* p. 26).

It is moved and seconded that Bro. S. Davis be District Stewart

qs 1 What [has] been received on the foregoing account

A $2.75) two Dollars and seventy five cents from Milom Class

qs Is there any Sunday schools on this Circuit *A* None

On Motion Resolved that the recording stewat be instructed to direct a letter to each Class setting forth the amount due from each Class

qs. When will you have your next quarterly meeting

A. At Hickory Grove on the 2d & 3d day of May next

The Conference the[n] proceded to the examination of character when the License of Jesse Payne was presented his Ch. approved & Licenc renewed

The Amount apportiond to each Class at Said Meeting as followed

McMahans Chapel	35.00
Sabine Town	$20.00
Mt Lebanon	40.00
Milam	45.00
Hickory Grove	40.00
Houson Bouyou	15.00
Deep Spring	5.00
Ships Scool House	25.00
Antyoc	20.00
New prospect	25.00
Wilson Chapel	45.00
Ironose	10.00
Goshan	35.00
Thompson	15.00
Mt Airy	10.00
Patroon	25.00
Harts	35.00

the Amt Recd from different clases at the qt meeting as folls

Milam Class		2.75
Public Collection		6.00
L S Marshall Dr To this amt	$5.87½	
J C. Wollam " " " "	2.00	
G. West	87½	
	$8.75	$8.75

At the *second Quarterly Meeting* for San Augustine Circuit held at Hickory Grove Mt. house May 2d 1846. The following *member*[s] were *present*

Revd	George West	P.E.
"	L S Marshall	P.C.
"	John C Wollam	A.P.
"	Gabriel Blackburn	L.E.
	S. D. McMahan	L.D.

Jacob Crawford Exhortor Thos Jackson (St. Michal Watson CL Charles Egbert Steward Jacob Crawford was nominated and appointed secretary

Qst 1st Are there any Complaints or appeals *A.* None

Qst 2d What was the collection for the Preachers *A.* Nothing

Q When and where shall we have the third quarterly meeting on San Augustine Circuit

A. At Mount Lebanon Camp Ground on the 29th and 30th of August Read and approved

JACOB CRAWFORD *Secy* GEORGE WEST *P.E.*

At the *third quarterly meeting Conference South* held for San Augustine Circuit August 28th 1846. At Milam the following members were present

Revd George West	P.E.
L S. Marshal	P in C
John C. Woolam	A.P.
Gabril Blackburn	L.E.
Robert Roundtree	L.P.
George Kohir	Ex
Jacob Crawford	"
Jessie Allen	"
Charles Egbert	St
Osburn Harris	St
Thomas Jackson	St
Nathaniel Hunt	C.L.
W H Payne	C L.
Jessie T. Scruggs	C.L.
Franklin Pace	C.L.

John Gilbert	C.L.
Isac Powal	—
John G. Robirts	C.L.

J. T. Scruggs was nominated & appointed Secretery
qu. 1st Are there any Complaints or Appeals *A.* none
qs 2d are there any Sabbath Schools
A There is one at Mt Lebanon preaching place. 1 Superintendent and 3 teachers and about 12 Schollars. the school is prosperous—

Col Benj Burk was nominated & appointed Steward in the place of Thomas P Payne resigned

qs 3d What has been Collected for the support of the gospel this quarter

Ans Public Collections $	$ 9.82
& quarterage	39.00

qs How has this been appropriated

Ans George West D[istric]t Travling Expenses	2.00
quarterage	3.85
L. S Marshall Traveling Expenses	13.55
quarterage	15.44
John C. Woolam Traveling Expen	6.50
" " " quarterage	7.70

qs. When and where shall the next quarterly Conference be held
Ans At Augustins Campground on the 29th day of Octbr

J. L. Scruggs George West *P.E.*

At the *fourth quarterly meeting* for the Conference for the San Augustine Circuit held at Maj Augustines Camp ground the following members were present Octb 30th 1846

Revd George West	P.E.
" L. S. Marshal	P.C.
" John C. Woolam	Ast
" Benet Elkins	L. P
" S Thomas	L. P
Bro Charles Egbert	St
Jno G. Roberts	Cl.
Wm H Payne	Cl
L V Greer	St

Wherupon L V Greer was nominated and appointed Secry

qs 1st Are there any Complaints or appeals *Ans.* None
qs 2d Are there any saboth schools on the Circuit
An none under our charge

The Conference then took up the examination of character when

Brother Blackburn ch examined & pass
Bro S D McMahan Ch examined & passed
Bro Benet Elkins examined & pased Licins renewed & recommended to Anual Conference to be ordaind Deacon also recommended to anual Conference upon trial as a traveling Preacher

Bro S Thomas ch examined & passed & Licns renewed
" George Case Exhortor examined & passed & Licnce renewed
" Jessie Allen do. Ex & passed & Licnsed renewed
" Jacob Crawford do Ex. & pasd & License renewed
" Wm Frazer Ext. Exam. & pasd & Licned renewed
" Joseph Parker Ext. Exam & passed & Licnse renewed
" L V Greer st. examined & pased
" S S Davis do. examined & pased
" C Egbert examined & pased
" C Harris examined & pasd
" T Jackson st exam & pasd
" B Burke " Exam & passd
" G Case " Examd & pasd

qs 3 What has been collected for the support of the Gospel this quarter

Ans quarterage 54.06½
Public Collection 14.75

How has this been appropriated

Ans Revd George West $ 8.44 3/4
" L Marshal 40.30
" Jn*o* C Woolam 20.06 ¼

qu When will you have your next quarterly meeting
Ans At Bro Ship on Ayish Bayou

L V Greer *Secy* George West *P.E.*

[1847]

SAN AUGUSTINE CIRCUIT ESTERN [TEXAS] CONFERENCE

At the *first quarterly meeting* for the Methodist Episcopal Church South held at McMahans Chapel on the 29th of May 1847 there were present

Revd J W Fields	P.E.
" N W Burk	P.C.
" R W Cannon	Elder
S D McMahan	L.D.
Bro A W Nailor	Ext
" George Case	Ext & St
" J Crawford	L.D.
Bro Jackson	C.L. & St
" Lucas	L.P.
" W H Payne	C.L.
" C Egbert	St & C.L.
" J T Scruggs	C.L.
" Wm B Frazer	Ext & CL
" O Harris	St
" J G Roberts	C.L. & St
" R Garrett	L S
" [....] Powell	L D
L V Greer	St

qst Brother L V Greer was appointed sec[re]tary of the Conference

qs. 1st Are there any Complaints or appeals *Ans.* None

qs 2 Is the[re] any Sabbath scools on the Circuit

Ans One at San Augustine with one superintendant, six assistants and a small library with about thirty students

qs 3 What has been done on the subject of Missions on the Circuit

Ans Nothing

qs 4 What will be done on this subject

Resolved that this Conference use all diligence in Collecting or raising as much as posible this Conference year for Missionary purposes

Resolved that Brother W H Payne be apointed Treasurer of the Centenary Missionary Society to fill the vacancy occasioned by the death of Brother James Davis

Resolved that Brother J. S. Powell be recvd into this Conference as Local Elder

Brother E Lucas was recvd from the Methodist Protestant Church as Local Decon of the Methodist Episcopal Church South

Resolved that the Letter of Brother Lucas remain in the hands of the preacher in charge

Resolved that Brother Thackers name be marked as withdrawn from Methodist Episcopal Church South

Resolved that the Licnce of Jessie Payne (a servant) be renewed

Resolved that the licence of Gideon (a servant) be renewed

Resolved that the Conference use all diligence in collecting the allowance for our Preachers this Conference year

Where will you have your next quarterly meeting

Ans At San Augustine on the 17 & 18 of July there being no futher buisiness before the Conference the minutes were then read and signed

L. V. Greer *Secy* J. W. Fields *P.E.*

Public Collection at the quartily meeting $ 12.85

N. W. Burkes Dr.	$8.50	
J. W. Fields	4.35	
	$12.85	$12.85

San Augustine July 17th 1847

The *Second quarterly meeting* for the San Augustine Circuit Estern Conference met pursuant to appointment at the Methodist Church in the town of San Augustine on the day above named Members present

J. W. Fields	P.E.
N. W. Burke	P.C.
R. W. Kennon[50]	L E

[50] Robert W. Kennon (1813–81) was the son of John W. Kennon, a Methodist circuit-rider in South Carolina and Mississippi Territory. Robert was converted in Madison County, Mississippi, in 1836 and the following year joined the Mississippi Conference, later serving in the Louisiana Conference, from which he transferred to

S. D. McMahon	L D
A. W. Nailor	Extr & Leader
George Coher	Extr & Stw
N Hunt	C.L. & St
W Frazer	Ext
M Watson	C L
J C Roberts	C L & St
W. H. Payne	C.L.
T. H. Blades	L.C.
Jesse I Allen	Ext
W. N. Harman	C.L.
Jas Odell	C.L.

On Motion R W Kennon was appointed secetary of [the Quarterly Conference].

qs 1st Are the any Complaints or appeals *A* None

qs 2. Sabath schools Reports

A Sabath schools reports was called for and a verbal one given & Received

qs 3d Do you superintend the instruction of children

A As far as I can

qs 4t Is there any special buisiness

A There is when there was read a recommendation from the society of San Augustine that W. N. Harman[51] be licensed to preach —after due examination W N Harman by motion was licnsed to preach by the Conference

5 Stewards reports was called for when Nathaniel Hunt from Antioch class reports $2.50 collected

L. V. Greer reports $10.00 from Goshan

J. C. Roberts $ 1.00 from Mt Lebonon

---

the East Texas Conference in 1847. In March, 1847, he was appointed with Foster W. Blades to Wesley College in San Augustine, but located in December. He rejoined conference in the 1850's and appears in 1852 as presiding elder of Galveston District, Texas Conference (Jones, *op. cit.*, I, 21; Phelan, *op. cit.*, II, 201; *Minutes of the Annual Conferences of the Methodist Episcopal Church*, Vol. II: *1829–1839*, p. 516; *Minutes . . . . South*, Vol. I: *1845–1857*, pp. 88, 98, 151, 424).

[51] William N. Harmon was admitted on trial to the East Texas Conference in 1848 and appointed to San Augustine Circuit. He seems to have been discontinued in 1849 (*Minutes . . . . South*, Vol. I: *1845–1857*, p. 192).

M Watson rept [$]2.00 from McMahon chapel
G Koher 1.50

there being no further buisiness before the Confn the minuts was read and signed

R W Kennon *Secy* J W Field *P.E.*

the amt of money recvd from the diferent Society at the second quarterly meeting was	$17.00
the amt collected by public collection this	9.75

It was appropriated by paying to the Preacher as below

Recd	J. W. Fields Dr.	$8.90	
	N. W. Burk	17.80	
		$26.70	$26.75

At the *third quarterly meeting* of the Eastern Texas Conference South held at Maj Augustines Camp ground the following members were present

Revd	J W Fields	P.E.
"	N W Burke	P.C.
"	F Wilson	L.P. & College Agent
"	R W Kannon	L.P.
"	W N Harman	L.P.
	Bennet Elkins	L.P.
	W H Payne	C.L.
	L V Greer	St

qs 1st Are there any Complaints or appeals *Ans.* None

qs 2 Are there any Sabbath scool reports *Ans* none

qs 3d Is there any other special buisiness *Ans* yes (yes)

Resolved that there be a meating of the missionary society at 3 ock and that the society be addresd by Brothers Fields and Wilson

qs 4 When will you have your next quarterly meeting

An At Mount Lebanon Camp ground at 8 ock on Saturday next

There being no further buisiness the minuts was then read and signed

L V Greer *Secy* J. W. Fields *P.E.*

Ship society C[...] B[...]	$ 2.50	
San Augustine	6.50	
Antioc	1.00	
Ironosi	2.50	
Public Collection	7.56	
	$20.06	
N W Burke Dr To		13.40
J W Fields		6.66¼
		$20.06¼

This meeting is by oversight in the wrong place

L V Greer *Secy*

This Circuit has paid its preachers and presiding Elder in full Decr *9th* 1847

L V Greer *Secy*

The fourth quarterly conference for the San Augustine Circuit Eastern Texas Conference of the M.E. Church South convened at Mount Lebanon Camp Ground on the 18th of Sept. 1847[52]

Members	Names
J. W. Fields	P.E.
N. W. Burks	P.C.
F. Wilson	L.E.
F. N. Blades	L E absent
R. W. Kennon	L.E.
Gabriel Blackburn	L.E. sick
Jacob Crawford	L.D.
S. D. McMann	L.D.
B. E. Lucas	L.D.
S. W. Camp	L.P.
W. N. Harman	L.P. absent
S. D. Thomas	L.P.
B. Elkins	L.P. absent
A. W. Nailor	Exhr. & leader

[52] The minutes for this meeting are taken from the fuller copy at the back of the original record book.

Acton Young	Exhr. & leader
Wm. Frazer	Exhr.
George Koher	Exhr. absent
Lewis Greer	Recg Steward absent
C. Egbert	Sted & leader
T. Jackson	Std. & leader absent
O Harris	Steward
J. C. Roberts	C.L.
Howard Garret	C.L. absent
J Scrugs	C.L. absent
F. Jace	C.L. absent
F. N. W. Forsythe	C.L. absent
J. Shipp	C.L. absent
Wm. Pearce	C.L. absent
E. Davis	C.L. absent
W. Paine	C.L. absent
J. Polk	C.L. absent

1st Q. Are there any complaints or appeals *A* none

2nd Q. Any Sabbath School Reports *A.* None

By motion the missionary society will be called this evening at 3 oclock and addressed by Rev. F. Wilson & the P. Elder.

The conference then went into the examination of character. The name of N. W. Burks was called & his character passed—F. Wilson's name was called & his character passed—F. H. Blades's name was called & his character passed—Gabriel Blackburns L E name was called, & his character passed—S. D. McMann was called, his character passed, & he Recommended to the Anual Conference for Elders Orders—B. E. Lucas was called his character passed & he Recommended to the Anual Conference for Elders Orders—Jacob Crawford was called, his character passed, & he Recommended to the Anual Conference for Elders Orders—S. W. Camp was called, his character passed, & he Recommended to the Anual Conference to Receive Deacons Orders B. Elkins was called his character passed, & his license Renewed—Wm N. Harman was called, his character passed & his license Renewed—A. W. Nailor was called, his character passed, & his license as exhorter Renewed—Wm Frazer exhorter was called, his character passed, & his license Renewed—Acton Young exhorter was called, his character passed, & his license Renewed George Koher exhorter was called, his character passed & his license Renewed—L Greer R. S. was called, & passed—O harris S. called & passed—C. Egbert S called, & passed—T. Jackson called, & passed—

The Steward's Report was then called for—from San Augustine No Report—McMann's chapel A. Young collector, $4. paid Mt. Lebanon J. G. Roberts $5. pd Milam C. Egbert col. $10.50 paid, Patroon no Report Hickory Grove No Report—Harriss O. Harris col. $8.75 Houson Bayou no Report, Deep Spring no Report—Shipps no Report—Antioch No Report Wilson's Chapel no Report Goshen No Report Ironosa no Report

The following Resolution was offered and passed—Resolved by the quarterly Conference that the preacher in charge be authorized to Renew the license of the colored preachers & exhorters in his charge at his discretion

A. W. Nailor
B. Lucas

Resolved that we the members of the quarterly conference will observe every Friday as a day of fasting or abstins & prayer, & that we Recommend the same to our brethren until the Anual Conference—

F. Wilson
C. Egbert

McMann's Chapel was selected by the conference as the place for the next quarterly meeting

The minutes were then Read & Adopted

By motion the conference then adjourned

J. W. Fields *PE*
R. W. Kennon *Sec*

20 30 Burks }
$10.10 Field } The public collection was not reported to me

L V Greer

19.50	20 30
8 75	10 10
28.25	30.40
	28 25
	2.15

Bro W. N. Harman L.P. Chr Ex. & Pasd and Licence to be renewed
Bro. S. D. Thomas L.P. Chr. Ex & Pased & Licenced to be renewed
Bro. J. T. P. Irwin Chr. Ex. & Pasd
Bro A. W. Naylor Ch Ex & Pasd & licence to be renewed
Bro. Richard Stewart Ex Char Ex & pased & licence renewed
Bro A Young Exr Char Ex & pasd License renewed
Bro. W. B. Frazer Char Ex. & pasd License renewed
Bro D M Stowall Ex char Ex & pas. & License renewed
the minuites was then read and signe[d]

CHARLES EGBERT *Scry* J. W. FIELDS *P.E.*

Stewards Report $27.25

[1848]

[No minutes recorded.]

[1849]

The proceeding of the *first quarterly meeting* for the year of Our Lord A.D. 1849 did not come into my hands

L V GREER *Recd St*

The *second quarterly Conference* for San Augustine Circuit of the Methodist Episcopal Church south held at Hickory Grove meeting house on Saturday Apr 21st 1849 there was *present*

Revd I. M. Williams[53] P.E.
" J Crawford P.C.
" J C Wollam M[issionary] to C[olored] P[eople].[54]
" W B. Frazer extr

On Motion W. B. Frazer was appointed secry
qust 1st Are there any Complaints or appeals *Ans.* None
qust 2d Are there any Sabbath school reports *Ans* none

[53] Isaac M. Williams had transferred from the Texas to the East Texas Conference in January, 1848 (*Minutes .... South*, Vol. I: *1845–1857, p.* 151). Several years later he was expelled for "immorality" (Phelan, *op. cit.*, I, 320).

[54] "Missionaries to our people of color" were provided for by appointment by the bishops (*Discipline .... South, 1846,* p. 37). Woolam was appointed to the "Red Lands Af[rican] miss[ion]" in San Augustine District in 1848 (*Minutes .... South*, Vol. I: *1845–1857*, p. 193).

qust 3d has there been anything collected this quarter for the missionary Bible and Sabbath cause *Ans* nothing

Is there any other buisiness before the quarterly Conference Bro J. C. Wollam made an encouraging report of the african mission within the bounds of this Circuit

qust What has been collected during the past quarter for the support of the ministers

Ans $4.00 from McMahans Chapel

qs how has that amt been appropriated

Ans to Bro J Crawford

qs Where shall the next quarterly meeting be held

Ans At San Augustin on the 14 & 15 of July

Attst

W. B. FRAZER *Scrt* J. M. WILLIAMS *P.E.*

At the *third quarterly meeting* of the Eastern Texas Conference South held at San Augustine July the 14th there were present

Revd.	I. M. Williams	P. Eld.
"	Jacob Crawford	P.C.
"	W. N. Harman	A.P.
"	J C Wollam	Off. Miss.
"	S Thomas	L.P.
Brother	A Young	Ex
"	D. Stovall	Ex
"	A W Nailor	Ex
"	L V Greer	St

On Motion Brot[her] L V Greer was appointed Secry, and the Conference proced to buisiness

quest 1st Are there any Complaints *Ans* none

qust 2d Are there any appeals *Ans.* none

qust 3d Have You any Sabath school reports *Ans.* None

qust 4h What has been Collected for missions the Bible Tract and sabath school cause *Ans.* Nothing

qust 5t Is there any other buisiness before the Conference

Ans there is—we want a committee appointd to receive a title to Red Land[?] church property

whereupon Brothers L V Greer Thos P. Payne N Brooks

James Hale and John W Crain was nominated and appointed a committee to receive said title—

On motion it was resolved that the licence of Jessie Crain (colourd brother) be renewed—the stewards report was then called for

qust What has been collected the past quarter for the support of the ministers

Ans

San Augustine	.50 cts
Milam	nothing
Hickory Grove	do
McMahans Chapel	do
Mt Lebanon	do
Patroon	do
Goshen	$16.00
Ironose	Nothing
Wilson Chapel	do
Deep. spring	do
Antioc	do
making in all	$ $ 16.50

qust how has it been appropriated

Ans. to the claims of Revd J Crawford

qus. where will you have your next quarterly meeting

Ans. at McMahans Chapel on the 15th & 16th of Septr next—the minuits was then read and approved

L V Greer *Secry* Isac M. Williams *P.E.*

the Public Collection was 14.85 and appropriated to I. M. Williams	2.50
J. Crawford	12.35
	$14.85

At the *fourth quarterly meeting* of the Eastern Texas Conference South held at McMahans Chapel Septr the 15th 1849 there were *present*

Revd Isaac M. Williams	P.E.
" Jacob Crawford	P.C.
" J. C. Wollam	off Miss.
S. D. McMahan	L.E.
S. D. Thomas	L.P.
A Young	Ex & C.L.

A W Nailor	[Ex & C.L.]
David Stovall	Exhortor
George Koher	"
W. B Frazer	"
Thomas P. Payne	C. Leader
Charles Egbert	C.L. & Steward

On Motion W. B. Frazer was appointed Secry and the names of the official members was called to wit J. T. Scruggs (St.) H Garrett (Steward) Thos Jackson Steward John Hunt Steward B. F. Benton St Lewis V Greer recrd Steward all absent—the Conference then proceeded to buisiness

qust 1st Are there any Complaints or appeals *Ans* None

qust 2d Are there any Sabath School reports *Ans* None

qust 3d What has been Collected for the missionary Bible and Sabath School causes the present year *Ans* Nothing

The Conference then procceed to act upon the recommendation of Broth A Young and D Stoval applicants to this Conference for licns to preach the Gospel, and after the usual Examinations Broth[ers] Young & Stoval returned after which on motion & second the Conference granted licence to Bro. Acton Young[55] to preach the Gospel of Christ—also on mottion & second the Conference Granted Licence to Bro David Stoval[56] to preach the Gospel of Christ—

The Examination of Character was taken up

Bro J. Crawford P.C. Charactr Examind & passed

S. D. McMahans L.E. " " " "

W. N. Harman L.P. " " " "

S Thomas L.P. his case was laid over in consequence [of] a personal rencounter having occured in which Br Thomas was a party and a Committe of three were appointed to wit Bro A W Naylor, Payne & S. D. McMahan to inquire into the same and report to n[e]x[t] quart meeting conference

Examination of character resumed

A W Naylor character examind & pased & Licensd renewed

George Koher Ext Examd & pasd & Licnd renewed

W B Frazer Ext C Examd & pasd & Licb renewed

[55] Acton Young (? –1873), a native of Kentucky who settled in Texas in 1841, was admitted on trial to the East Texas Conference in 1850 (Phelan, *op. cit.*, II, 93).

[56] David M. Stovall was admitted on trial to the East Texas Conference in 1851 (*Minutes .... South,* Vol. I: *1845–1857*, pp. 367, 421).

B F Benton St C. Examd & pased
J T Scruggs " " "
H Garrett " " "
Thos J Jackson " " "
John Hunt " " "
L V Greer Recd S " " "

Bro David Stoval makes application to be recommend to the Anual Conference on trial in the traveling connexion—on motion recommended

On Motion Conference adjourned untill Monday morning 7 Oclock A.M.

Monday morning Septr 17th 1849. Conference met persuant to adjourment present I M. Williams P.E. J Crawford P.C. W. N. Harman A.P. J C Wollam Off Mis S D McMahan L.E. W. B. Frazer Exhort A W Naylor T J Jackson C L & Steward C Egbert C & S.

Sutton a man of colour Exhorter character Examined and pased and Licence renewed

Gideon Greer a man of colour Exhorter Character Examend & pased & Licence renewed

Hubard a man of colour Exhorter character Examined & pased and Licenc renewed

L V Greer was nominated and appointed district Steward

Is there any other buisiness before the conference *Ans* None

What has been Collected for the support of the ministry for the present year

The Steward report

San Augustin	$50.	
Goshen	nothing	
Wilson Chapel	3.00	
McMahans	.....	
Lebanon	.....	
Patroon	.....	
Hickory Hill	.....	
Milam	5.00	
Hauson Bayou	.....	
Deep. spring	.....	
Sabine Town	Nothing	
Public Collection	$11.60	
making in all		$69-60

how has the above been appropriated
Ans

To Isac M Williams P. E.	$45.60	
" Jacob Crawford P. C.	24.00	
	$69.60	69.60

Where shall the next quarterly meeting be held
Ans at Milam Sabin County
Att W. B. Frazer
Minuits not signed by the Presiding Elder

L V Greer *Recd St*

[1850]

The *first quarterly meeting* for the San Augustine Circuit for the year A.D. 1850 was held at Milam Jany the 11th 1850. at which the following *members* were *present* (viz)

Revd S. A. Williams	P.E.
W. K. Wilson[57]	P.C.
Jacob Crawford	L.P.
Brot. Thos Burk	C.L.
" Rob Gillally	
L. V. Greer	R.S.
" C Egbert	
" J Jackson	Stds
" W. B. Frazer	Ex

On motion Bro Robt Gillally was nominated & appointed secry
qust 1 Are there any Complaints or appeals *Ans* none
qust 2d Are there any Stewards to make
Ans there is one to appoint in the place of Wm Garrett removed from the district whereup[on] Broth Ausburn Harris was elected in his place—Brother Scrugg was discontinued on account of bad health—Brother John Hunt was discontinued—Brother B F Benton is Excused and Bro John Winn Elected to fill his place—Brother A I

[57] William Kinney Wilson (1808–72), born in Georgia, was admitted on trial to the Texas Conference in 1843. He later served Woodville and San Augustine districts (Phelan, *op. cit.*, II, 79).

Mann & S. D. McMahan was elected stewards & Brother J A Winn Recording Steward

The case of Brother Thomas came up & on motion the committe appointed to enquire into the case of Bro Thomas in relation to a personal encounter in which Brother Thomas was a party was discontinued and the preacher in charge be requested to talk with Bro Thomas on the subject and report to the next quarterly Conference

qus What has been Collected during the present quarter for the support of the Ministers

Ans

1 San Augustine	00.00	
2 Goshen	$ 2.00	
3 McMahans Chapel	00	
4 Wilsons Chapel	.....	
5 Harris schoolhouse	1.00	
6 Patroon	00	
7 Hickory Hill	1.00	
8 Milam	1.50	
9 Houson Bayou	0 0 0	
10 Sabine Town	0 0 0	
11 Deep Spring	.....	
	5.50	
Public Collection	13.25	
	$18.75	
Wm K Wilson Dr. this amt expenses		$3.00
" " " quarterage		15.75
		$18.75

qs Where shall the next quarterly meeting Conference be held

Ans At Goshen on Saturday & Sunday the 9th & 10th of March

the Conference then proceeded to aportion to the diferent Society the amt due from them to the support of the preachers as follows (viz)

Goshen	$60.00
San Augustine	90.00
McMahans Chappel	40.00

Patroon		[$] 5.00
Horns schoolhouse		15.00
Milam		20.00
Hickory Grove		50.00
Houson Bayou		5.00
Deep Spring		5.00
Wilson Chapel		50.00
Claims of quarterage allowed to		
Bro W K Wilson	$216.00	
" " Table Expenses	100.00	
	$316.00	

Amt of allown Brother I A Williams	
for quarterage—	$40.00
" Table Expenses	20.00
	$60.00

Read and approved

ROBT GILLALLY *Secty* S A WILLIAM *P.E.*

March 9th 1850

The *second quarterly meeting* for San Augustine Circuit was held at Goshen The following *members present*

S A Williams P.E.	S. D. Thomas L.P.
W K Wilson P.C.	L V Greer Steward (R)
S A McMahan L.E.	Thomas Roots C.L.
Jacob Crawford Ditto	Tho. P. Payne Ditto

was elected secretary

1st question are there any Complaints or appeals *Answer* There are none

The case of Bro. S. D. Thomas was then taken up and his character examined passed and Licence renewed

The report on Sabbath Schools was then called for and there being no schools in the Circuit under our supervision there was no report

Is there any other business before the conference

The report of the stewards was then called for and the following report was made

San Augustine	nothing	amt. brot, forward	1 45
Patroon	Ditto	Goshen	10 00
Harris' S. House	Ditto	Wilsons Chapel	1 00
McMahan's Chapel	$ 1.45	Mrs. Wilson's	nothing
Milam	nothing	Irenose	Ditto
Hickory Hill	Ditto		$12 45
Sabinetown	Ditto		
Houson Bayou	Ditto		
Deep Spring	Ditto		
Carried forward	$ 1.45		

How has the above been disposed of

Answer to S. A. Williams $10.00 balance of $2.45 to W K Wilson

When shall our next quarterly meeting be held, *answer* at Hickory Hill

attested By J. Crawford S. A. Williams *P.El.*

The foregoing is a true copy left on a detached sheet of Paper by Bro. L. V. Greer for to be transcribed

Jno. A. Winn
Secty Protem

during absen of L. V. Greer

Public Collection of $9.00 appropriated to Bro. W. K. Wilson

July 10th A.D. 1850

Third quarterly meeting for San Augustine Circuit is now in session at Hickory Hill *Members present*

Bro.	S. A Williams	P.E.
"	W K Wilson	P.C.
"	Jacob Crawford	L.E.
"	C Egbert	S.
"	T. J. Jackson	S.
"	H. Harris	S.
"	B Gillally	Ex

There being no secretary present Bro. Jacob Crawford was duly elected secretary

question 1st Are there any complaints or appeals *Answer* none

No further business appearing for the consideration of the Conference

The reports of the Stewards were called for and received

San Augustine	$ 1.00	Amt brot forward	27 75
Harris	3.50	Housen Bayou	00
Patroon	-.00	Martins	00
McMahans	9.00	Deep Spring	00
Milam	14.00	Wilson's Chapel	00
Mount Airy	- 00	Red Land Church	8 50
Hickory Hill	1.25	Lovell's settlement	.00
Sabine Town	00	Public Collection	8.60
Amt. card. forwd,	$27.75		44 85

q. How was this amount appropriated

A. To Bro. W. K. Wilson

When and where shall the next quarterly meeting be held

Ans. at McMahans Chapel

McMahans Chapel
Sept. 12th A.D. 1850

The *fourth quarterly meeting Conference* for San Augustine Circuit 12th. Sept. 1850

Present S. A. Williams P. El	Jno A Winn Recd Steward
" W. K. Wilson P.C	Osburn Harris "
" S D McMahan L.E.	Chas Egbert "
" Jacob Crawford	Tho. J. Jackson "
" S. D. Thomas L.P.	Geo. Koher Exhortor
Robt. Gallally C.L.	Wm B Fraser "
Tho. Roots " "	Tho. P. Payne C.L.

Wm B Frazer was appointed Secretary

ques. 1st. Are there any complaints or appeals

Ans 1st. there are none

qus. 2. Are there any Sabbath Schools *Ans*. *2* none

qus. *3* Are there any licences to grant *Ans*. *3rd* none

The Conference then proceeded to the examination of characters of the Preachers

S. D. McMahan L.E.	Character	examined &	pased
J. Crawford L.E.	"	"	"
S D Thomas L.P.	"	"	"
Acton Young "	"	"	"
Wm. B Frazer Exhr	"	"	"
Geo. Koher "	"	"	"

The report of Stewards was next in order and being called for the following reports were submitted

San Augustine Reports	$54 20
Barbers	6 60
Patroon	0 00
Harris' Shoolhouse	4 50
McMahans Chapel	" """
Milam Reports	00 00
Hickory Grove	5 75
Sabine Town	0 00
Houson Bayou	0 00
Martins	0 00
Deep Spring	0 00
Red Land	17 00
Wilson Chapel	00 00
	$83 05

On Motion the quarterly meeting adjourned to meet on Saturday before the first Saturday in November next at the Camp ground near the city of San Augustine

ques. How was the above amount appropriated
Ans.

Bro. W K Wilson Recd.	$67 55
" I. A Williams	15 50
	$83 05

On Sabbath the Public Collection amounted to $6.95
Public col. pd. to Bro. W. K. Wilson

Wm B Frazer *Secretary* I. A. Williams *P.E.*

Camp Ground
Near San Augustine
Nov. 2nd 1850

Quarterly Meeting Conference met according to adjournment

Present S. A. Williams P.E.
" W K Wilson P.C.
" Geo Koher Exhrter
" A I Mann C L
" Tho P. Payne "
" Jno A Winn Rec Steward

J A Winn was appointed secretary whereupon the name of Wm N Harman was called and ther appearing evident dissatisfaction in his case, on motion the conference orderd that a committee be appointed to examine into the causes of complaint against said W N Harman and report theron next Monday the 4th. Qust. Bros. W K Wilson & Jno A Winn were appointed said Committee

The conference then proceeded to the examination of the character of stewards

Osborn Harris Stewd. charter exam. pass
Charls Egbert " " " "
L V Greer " " " "
J A Winn " " " "
W D McMahan " " " "

Bro. G. Jackson Exonerated from further service

Jacob Crawford elected in Bro. Jackson's place

A I Mann Exonerated by request

I P Matthews appointd in Bro Man's place

No further business appearing the Conference adjourned till Monday morning

Conference met according to adjournment

Rev. S. A. Williams P.E.

W K Wilson P.C.

A I Mann T. P. Payne and Jno A Win C L Present S D Thomas L. P. present the Committee appointed to examine the causes of complaint against Revd. W H Harman made the report hereto attached which was unanimously received and committee discharged *qs* When will you have the next qu. meeting Conference

Ans. At San Augustine commencing Saturday before 3rd Sabbath in January next

The report of Stewards being called for the following report was made

San Augustine reports	$20 00
McMahans C "	1 00
Hickory Grove	1 45
H. Bayou	2 00
Wilson's Chapel	19.50
Red Land Church	4 50
Barbar's. Patroon. Harris Cl	0 00
Milam 00—Sabin T. 00 B Creek	0 00
Deep spring	0 0
	48 45
Public Collection	40 45
	$88 90

How was this appropriated

W K Wilson Recd. 7.3	$73.40	
I. A. William	15 50	
	$88 90	$88 90

Nov. 11th/50 Bro. W K Wilson Reported $7.00 which he collected and Bro. S W Williams $2.50

Whereupon The Recording Steward examined all the reports monies received and disbursted for the year 1850

And made a perfect settlement to date with P.E. & P.C. for 1850

To W K Wilson P.C. The Rcd. Steward give a certificate for Money paid to him

For quarterage	$166 87
" Table expences	55 63
" Travelling "	3 00
Total	$225 50

To S. A. Williams

For quarterage	$33 00	33 00
" Table expencs	11 00	11 00
" Travelling "	1 00	45 00
		$270 50

JNO A WINN
Rcd. Steward

[1851]

SAN AUGUSTINE
January 24th. 1851

The *first qu. meeting* for San Augustine Circuit is now in session

Present S. A. Williams P.E.
" J. W. Shipman[58] P.C.
" T. P. Payne C.L.
" A I Mann Ditto
" L V Greer Steward
" J A Winn Rcd. Ditto and present secretary. This qt. meeting [opened] with *prayer*

qt. 1. Are there any complaints or Appeals Answ 1 none

qu. 2 Are there any Sabbath scools under our supervision *Ans. 2* none

No further business appearing the qu. conference then proceeded to assess the amount that will be due the preachers of this Circuit during this year and setting apart what each society shall pay.

[58] James W. Shipman (? –1867) joined the Arkansas Conference in 1844 and transferred to East Texas in 1850. He served as agent for the Book Depository at Galveston from 1857 to 1865 and also of the *Advocate* (*Minutes of the Annual Conferences of the Methodist Episcopal Church*, Vol. III: *1839–1845*, p. 543; Phelan, *op. cit.*, II, 9).

Claims of quarterage allowed

Bro. J. W. Shipman		$200.00		
" " " " Table Expenses			$ 80 00	
Travelling Expenses in Coming to Texas			35 00	$315.00
Amt allowed Bro. S A Williams				
Table Expenses	$35			
quarterage	35	70 00		
Total amount			385 00	

Red Land Church	pays	$45 00
San Augustine	"	90 00
McMahans	"	40 00
Patroon	"	5 00
Harris' Shool House	"	30 00
Milam	"	20 00
Hickory Grove	"	55 00
Houson Bayou	"	5 00
Deep Spring	"	5 00
Wilson's Chapel	"	60 00
Barbar's	"	10 00
Sabine Town	"	10 00
		$385 00

When will you have the next quartely meeting Conference
At Harris's Shool house Whereupon the Conference adjourned

Approved & Signed S. A. Williams *P.E.*

Public Collection on Sabbath the 25th January 1851			$16 00	$16 00
Paid S. A. Williams	$ 2.91			
" J. W. Shipman	13 09	16 00		$ 16 00

Harris' Shool House
April 5th 1851

Second qt. meeting convened at this place according to adjournment following *members present*

S. A. Williams P.E.
J. W. Shipman P.C.
J. A. Winn Stw.
L V Greer "
Chas. Egbert "
Osborn Harris "
Jacob Crawford L.E.
W B Frazer Exhot.
J A Scruggs C.L.
Robt. Galiley "

Business of qt. meeting conference asking

qt. 1st. Are there any Complaints or appeals *Ans.* none

qu. 2nd Are there any Sabbath schools Reports *Ans 2nd* none

qt. 3rd Are there any Candidates for Licenc to preach *Ans 3rd* none

On Motion of J. W. Shipman the following resolution was unanimously adopted

Resolve that the preacher in charge be and he is hereby directed to make missionary collections in every society in the bounds of this Circuit and that the qt. meeting Conference sustain him therin. No further business appearing the report of the Stewards was called for

San Augustine	$21 00	
Robinsons	00	
Barbour	00	
I Crupps	00	
Harris	00	
Milam	8 50	
Hickory Hill	5 00	
Houson Bayou	00	
Bear Creek	00	
Deep Spring	00	
McMahan's Chapel	2 20	
Red Land	00	
Wilson's Chapel	3 50	$40.20
At Q.C. Public Collection on Sabbath		10.00
		$50.20

Paid S. A. Willams	$ 9.12	
" J. W. Shipman	41.08	$50.20

When and where shall our next meeting conf be holden
Ans. at Wilson's Chapel 31st May & 1st of June next
qu. Conference then adjourned Minutes approved & signed

Attest Jno A Winn S. A Williams *P.E.*

Wilsons Chapel 31st May A.D. 1851

2nd [*3d*] *qu. Meeting* Conference met according to adjournment *Members present*

S. A. Williams P.E.
J. W. Shipman P.C.
J. P. Matthews Stewards
L V Greer
A I Mann C. L.

On motion L V Greer was appointed secty
qs. 1st Are there any complaints or appeals *Ans. 1st* none
qs. 2nd Are there any Sabbath School reports *Ans. 2* none
qs. 3rd. Are there any changes to be made in the Stewards *Ans. 3* There are

On Motion of J. P. Matthews he was discontinued as Steward and Bro. S S Davis appointed in his place

On Motion of J. W. Shipman the following the resolution was unanimously adopted

Resolved that W. D. Ratliff S. S. Davis A I Mann Wm Smith & Theo Thomas be and they are hereby appointed Trustees to receive and collect fun[d]s secure a deed to the land and erect or caused to be erected a church house for the use and benefit of the M.E. Church South in the neghbourhood of Capt. E. W. Browns and to hold said church house in trust for said church according to the Discipline thereof

The following resolutions was unanimously adopted resolved that L. V. Greer Jno A Winn Jas. Perkins Jonas Hail W D Ratliff A I Mann S. S. Davis Theo. Thomas Tho. P Payne & W E Hail be committee to take into consideration the location of a camp ground this part of the circuit and report thereon at our next qt. m Conference.

Stewards report was then called for

	San Augustine	$5.00	
	Hickory Hill	5.00	
	Red Land Chapel	10.00	
	Wilson's "	5.00	
Jun 1	Public Collection on sabbath	17.55	42.55
" "	Paid I. A. Williams	$ 8.00	
" "	" J. W. Shipman	34.55	$42.55

qt. meeting conference adjourned to meet at the camp ground near the Town of San Augustine on 27th of September next

Signed I. A WILLIAMS *P.E.*
Attest L. V. GREER *Secty*

CAMP GROUND NEAR SAN AUGUSTINE Oct. 25th A.D. 1851

Fourth Quarterly Meeting

S A Williams P. E.	J W Shipman P.C.
J. Crawford L.P.	S D Thomas L.P.
Geo. Koher ext	L V Greer steward
C Egbert Stwd.	Tho Jackson "
G. W. Sherrod ext	W B Frazer C.L.
Jas. Sharp	"

John A Winn recording steward & present secty

On motion John A Winn was elected secty are there any complaints or appeals *Ans.* [n]one—

Are there any Sabath schools under our jurisdiction *Ans.* one
How many volumes in this library *Ans.* one hundred & twenty
Superententdants one
Teachers seven
scollars Thirty
Collected ($12.00) twelve dollars which was paid for Books
The Conference then proceeded to elect Trustees for the camp-ground near San Augustine and these persons whose names appear in the deed was elected trustees

The Conference then proceeded to elect Trustees for Bluff Spring meeting house. Whereupon it was provided that Bros. J Crawford Jn.

Thomas Jackson W B Frazer A D Oliophant & J Crawford Ser [serve].

Bro. Jas. Sharp was elected steward of MaMahon Chapel society

Report of J W Shipman on the death of Revd J McMahan adopted

Bro. O. Harris at his own request was discontinued steward & Bro. W B Frazer appointed in his stead

Constitution of the Missionary society presented by J. W. Shipman read and adopted or approved

The Conference then proceeded to examine character and renewal of Licences

Bro.	J. Crawford L.E.	passed		
"	S. D. Thomas L.P.	"	Licns	R.d.
"	W B Frazer Extr	"	"	"
"	G A Sherrod "	"	"	"
"	Geo. Koher "	"	"	"

Davis steward continued
Egbert " "
Greer " "
Jackson " "
qr report of P.C.
P.C. [?] character passed

Report of Stewards

San Augustine	$45.25
Robinson's	00 00
Barbars	" 95
Scruggs	19 00
McMahans	8 95
Milam	
Bluff Spring	24 00
Sabine Town	00 00
Red Land Chapel	20 00
Wilson's Chapel	17 00

adjourned till monday morning
Conference met according to adjournment

Public Collection $40 60

paid S. A. Williams 50 cents
when and where will you have the next qt. meeting
at McMahans chapel Jany 3rd. 1852

Mony collected Red Land		$15	
" " San Augustine		10	
Wilson Chapel		6	31.00
paid S. A. Williams	$6.00		
" J. W. Shipman	25.00		
	31.00		
Paid J Shipman total		$270.11	
" S. A. Williams		57.34	

[1852]

McMahan Chapel
January 3rd 1852

Present Bro. J. T. P. Irvine P.E.
" " A Cumming[59] P.C.
" " S A Williams Ast. " (P.C.)
" " Geo Kohn Exhorter

qs. 1st Are there any Complaints or appeals *Ans* none
qs. 2 Any Sabbath School report *Ans* none
What plan shall be adopted to raise missionary money this year *Ans.* Resolved that we adopt the same resolution of our last anual Conference that each preacher in charge of circuits & stations be required to raise Missionary Collections during the month of May, the following Brethren were nominated and appointed viz.

John A Winn L. V. Greer & C. Egbert as a committee to assess the

[59] Andrew Cumming (1817–82), a native of Hawkins County, Tennessee, joined the Illinois Conference in 1843 and transferred immediately to the Arkansas Conference. He became a charter member of the new Indian Mission Conference in 1845. From the latter he transferred to the East Texas Conference in 1847 (Phelan, *op. cit.*, II, 206).

amt. of Table expenses for the Preachers viz. S. A. Williams Ast.P. the P.E. and the P. Elder to apportion on each Circuit in accordance to their ability to pay

When and where shall we have our next quarterly meetting at W D Ratcliffs time to be given hereafter

S A Williams *Secty* James T. P. Irvine *P.E.*

Public Collection	$5.65			
Paid S. A. Williams Trv. Expenses		3.65		
				5.65
" A Cumming		2.00	$5.65	5.65

W D Ratcliffs
May 27th 1852

2 qt. Meeting meet according to appointment at this place

Present J. T. P. Irvine P.E.
" A. Cumming P.C.
" S. A. Williams ast. "
" L. V. Greer Steward
" T. P. Payne C.L.
" John A Winn Rcd. Stew.

qs. 1st Are there any Complaints

Ans. 1st none

Bro. W B Frazer was discontinued by his own request as Steward

Bro. Osborn Harris elected steward

When and where will you have your next quarterly meeting Conference

At the Town of San Augustine Saturday and Sabbath June 26 & 27th

What amount is necessary to meet the claims of P. Elder P.C. and assistant for the circuit year

San Augustine	$9[?]00
Red Land Chapel	50.00
McMahans Chapel	50.00
Patroon	1[?] 00
Harriss shoolhouse	35.00

Milam	[$]35.00			
Hockory Grove - $60.00	60.00			
Houson Bayou	7.00			
Deep Spring	5.00			
Ratcliffs Chapel	50.00			
Barbars	15.00			
Sabine Town	20.00			$432.00
J.T.P. Irvine P.E. T. Expenses		$25.00		
" " " Quarterage		33.14		
			$58.14	
By Missionary Collection			7.14	51.00
A. Cumming P.C. Quarterage	$100.00			
By Missionary Col. appropriation		23.73		76.27
S. A. Williams ast T. Expenses		$140.00		
" " " Quarterage		216.00		
		356.00		
By Missionary Cr Appropriation		51.27		$304.73
				$432.00

Report of Stewards

San Augustine	$5.50	
Red Land Chapel	13.00	
McMahan's Chapel	2.00	
Patroon	0 00	
Harris' School house	3 00	
Milam	0 00	
Bluff Springs	0 00	
Houson Bayou	0 00	
Deep Spring	0 00	
amt. carried forward		$23.50
amt. brot. Forward	$23 50	
Barbars	00 00	
Sabine Town	00 00	
		$23 50

qs. How was this amt. distributed
ans. as follows

Paid J. T. P. Irvin's Travelling Expenses	$ .57	
" A Cumming " "	$ 2.00	
" S A Williams " "	2.00	
Public Collection Sabbath	$ 4.57	4 70
		$28 20
Bro. J. T. P. Irvin Dr. To T. Expt	$4.[?]	
" A. Cumming Dr. To Cash	5.00	
" S A Williams Dr. To "	14.65	
	$28.22	
	$28.22	$28 20

San Augustine
June 21st 1852

3rd qt. Meeting Conference met at this place
Present Bro. J T P Irvine P E
" " A Cumming P.C
" " S A Williams ast. "
L V Greer Steward
Jno A Winn
qs. 1st Are there any Complaints or appeals *Ans.* None
qs. 2nd What is the state and number of Sabbath Schools
Ans. no report
When and where will you have the next qt. Meeting
Ans. at Red Land Chapel November 4th A.D. 1852
Report of Stewards was then called for

San Augutine reports	$00
Red Land Chapel "	9 00
Bro. Willson's	00 -
Barbars	——
Scruggs	——
West Ferry	——

Harris's House	[$]9 50	[$]9 50
McMahans Chapel		———
Milam		7 00
Bluff Springs		0 00
H. Bayou		0 00
Bear Creek		0 00
Deep Spring		00 00
Ratliffs		1 00
		26 50
Public Collection		11 65
		$38.15

Paid A Cumming Traveling Exps	1.75	
" J T P Irvin " "	25	
" S A Williams	75	
		2 75
		$35 40

How was this amt Divided

Paid J T P Irvin	5 00	
" A Cumming	6 05	
" S. A. Williams	24 35	
	$35 40	$35 40

San Augustine
Novr. 6th 1852

The *fourth qt. Meeting* for San Augustine Circuit was held at this place

Present Bro. J T P Irvin P.E.
" " A Cumming P C
" " S A Williams ast. "

on Motion L V Greer was elected Secty

qs. Are there any Complaints or appeals *Ans.* none

Are there any Sabbath School reports

Ans. P.C. passed in a report which was recd.

When the Conference proceeded to examination of Character

Jacob Crawford L.P. passed and Licence renewed

S.D. Thomas L P Character not passed and Licence not renewed

Geo. Kohn Extr Character passed and Licence renewed

W B Frazer Character passed but Licence not renewed

Jno A Winn steward (Rcd) Character passed

C. Egbert Character passed all right.

L. V. Greer steward passed all strait

Bro. E P Gaines Elected steward in the place of Bro. Sharp Decd.

Bro. Crawford L. P. appointed Steward in place of Bro. Tho. Jackson who is no longer stwd.

Osburn Harris Char. passed

W D Ratliffs " "

Report of Stewards was then called for

San Augustine
Scruggs
Harris *O*. House
McMahans Chapel W1$ C5$ 6 00
Milam
Bluff Spring
Houson Bayou
Deep Spring
Red Land Chapel
Ratliffs
Public Collection at Camp Ground
Sulphur Springs W.490 C490 4.90 9 80

L V Greer J. T. P. Irvine *P.E.*

Where will you have next qt. meet. Conference at McMahans Chapel

CHAPTER XIII

Church Trials among the Methodists in the Early West[1]

IF YOU speak to some here about being more descent they will plead up that they are in a New Country, and have many difficulties to encounter," wrote William Colbert, one of the early Methodist preachers.[2] The rough character of a large portion of the frontier population and the rather general tendency of moral standards to break down on the frontier has long been accepted as historical fact. On the other hand, little attention has been given to those agencies of social control whch served to restrain to some degree the antisocial impulses among the people of the backwoods community. In this chapter we are concerned with the role of the church judicatory as a disciplinary agency among the people and as a purifying agency among the clergy.

The westward movement in American history began with the pushing-inland of the first settlers from the coast and came to a halt only when the plains were finally settled in the years after the Civil War. The movement reached its peak, in the decades following the War of 1812, in the "great migration" and the Jacksonian migration. "Old America seems to be breaking up and moving westward," wrote Morris Birkbeck, a European traveler, in 1817, while traveling west. "We are seldom out of sight, as we travel this grand track toward the Ohio, of family groups behind and before us."[3] In 1837 Harriet Martineau observed:

> The possession of land is the aim of all action, generally speaking, and the cure for all social evils, among men in the United States. If a man is disappointed in politics or love, he goes and buys land. If he disgraces himself, he betakes himself

[1] The originals of the documents appearing in this chapter are deposited in the Library of the Illinois Wesleyan University at Bloomington, Illinois. Mr. Paul A. Varg, a member of my seminar in the autumn of 1941, has been principally responsible for the preparation of this chapter.

[2] "A Journal of the Travels of William Colbert, Methodist Preacher, thro' Parts of Maryland, Pennsylvania, New York, Delaware, and Virginia in 1790 to 1838" (manuscript in library of Garrett Biblical Institute), I, 92.

[3] *Notes on a Journey in America* (London, 1818), p. 31.

to a lot in the west. If the demand for any article of manufacture slackens, the operatives drop into the unsettled lands. If a citizen's neighbours rise above him in the towns, he betakes himself where he can be monarch of all he surveys.[4]

Whatever the source of motivation of this migration, population figures in 1830 testify that the movement across the mountains into the Mississippi Valley had created a new section. By 1830, Ohio had a population of 937,000; Indiana, 348,000; Illinois, 157,000; Kentucky, 687,000; and Tennessee, 681,000. In the very year that Harriet Martineau was making the above observation, the sales of the General Land Office reached fifteen million acres.

The movement represented something more than a shift in population, for the frontier developed a new type of American. "In the crucible of the frontier," writes Frederick Jackson Turner, "the immigrants were Americanized, liberated, and fused into a mixed race, English in neither nationality nor characteristics."[5] Among the traits which the frontier environment tended to develop was a strong individualism. The settler, having become accustomed to complete freedom from the restraints imposed by government and the well-established customs of an old community, developed a love of freedom. Any form of restriction seemed wholly unnecessary. Old customs were strangely out of place amid the new frontier conditions. The social graces of the older community became impractical in the primitive log cabin and sod hut. Moral restraints were often left behind, too, as the frontiersman headed west, and freedom frequently ran over into license.

The backwoods environment had a way of breaking down the discipline imposed by civilization. Everett Dick, in his book *Vanguards of the Frontier,* records the following observation of a trapper: "It is easy to make a savage of a civilized man but impossible to make a civilized man of a savage in one generation."[6] This would be gross overstatement as applied to the farmers' frontier, and yet there was a tendency in that direction. The lax morals took various forms. There was excessive drinking, and this often led to rough-and-tumble fighting, when eyes were gouged out and ears torn. Barrooms prospered. Men always outnumbered the women, and this created a situation in which houses of prostitution did

[4] *Society in America* (London: Saunders & Otley, 1837), II, 31.

[5] *The Significance of the Frontier in American History: Fifth Yearbook of the National Herbart Society* (1899), p. 28.

[6] Everett N. Dick, *Vanguards of the Frontier* (New York: D. Appleton-Century Co., 1941), p. 512.

a flourishing business. While the profligate dregs of society found escape from the dull monotony of life in dram-drinking or in the company of lascivious women, the more respectable social element were guilty of lax business honor. Shady horse deals as well as loose banking practices were almost traditional.

In this western land of Sodom and Gomorrah the church had an important part to play, but it could fulfil its mission only if it accurately gauged the temper of the frontiersmen. Peter Cartwright, who so well understood the character of the westerner, wrote: "The great mass of our Western people wanted a preacher that could mount a stump, a block, or old log, or stand in the bed of a waggon, and, without note or manuscript, quote, expound, and apply the word of God to the hearts and consciences of the people."[7] The intelligentsia might be prone to term this willingness to meet the pioneer on his own level a mere pandering to primitive tastes, but the western preachers knew that their only chance of success lay in adopting unsophisticated manners and a simple emotional appeal. Thus the gospel of the Methodist circuit-riders was undiluted by any of the modern stirrings of biblical criticism or vague romanticisms about the goodness of man. Sermons were packed hard with absolutes which few questioned. There were rather well-defined moral standards, and the exhortations of the preachers were weighted with warnings against drinking, card-playing, and the need of personal salvation.

The Methodist church was decidedly moralistic in its emphasis. The *Discipline* pronounced it the duty of circuit-riders to recommend everywhere decency and cleanliness. It read: "The preachers who have the oversight of circuits are required to execute all our rules fully and strenuously against all frauds, and particularly against dishonest insolvencies, suffering none to remain in our society, on any account, who are found guilty of any fraud."[8] Special warning was given against receiving bribes from political candidates, and circuit-riders were to advise Methodists "to discountenance all treats given by candidates before or at elections." The qualification for admission to class membership was "a desire to flee from the wrath to come, and to be saved from their sins." The member would give evidence of his desire for salvation, according to the *Discipline,* in the following ways:

[7] *The Backwoods Preacher: Autobiography of Peter Cartwright* (London: Alexander Heylin, 1858), p. 208.

[8] *The Doctrines and Discipline of the Methodist Episcopal Church* (New York, 1808), p. 48.

First, By doing no harm, avoiding evil of every kind, especially that which is most generally practiced: such as

The taking of the name of God in vain:

The profaning of the day of the Lord, either by doing ordinary work therein, or by buying or selling:

Drunkenness: or drinking spirituous liquors, unless in cases of necessity:

The buying and selling of men, women and children, with an intention to enslave them:

Fighting, quarrelling, brawling, brother *going to law* with brother; returning evil for evil; or railing for railing; the *using many words* in buying or selling:

The *buying or selling goods that have not paid the duty:*

The giving or taking things on usury, i.e. unlawful interest:

Uncharitable or unprofitable conversation: particularly speaking evil of magistrates or ministers:

Doing to others as we would not they should do unto us:

Doing what we know is not for the glory of God: As

The *putting on of gold and costly apparel:*

The *taking such diversions* as cannot be used in the name of the Lord Jesus:

The *singing* those *songs,* or *reading* those *books,* which do not tend to the knowledge or love of God:

Softness, and needless self-indulgence:

Laying up treasure upon earth:

Borrowing without a probability of paying; or taking up goods without a probability of paying for them.[9]

From this code it is evident that there was to be no compromise with evil. The standards of conduct set up by the church were such as to challenge the most respectable members of the community. Lives lived in accordance with these standards were the fruit of God's grace and were not looked upon as attainable through mere human effort to live the good life. In preaching, the Methodist clergy must have done much to raise the norms of behavior.

Yet the church was not satisfied to preach against the sins common to the community. It assumed that there would be transgression by the converted and even by the clergy, for to the frontier Methodists sin was something very real. The reality of sin made it necessary to punish those who had violated the rules of the church, for only in this way could further violations be discouraged. They did not look on sin as mere mistakes of well-intentioned persons or as perverse conduct due not so much to man's depravity as to the situation in which he found himself. Sin was

[9] *Ibid.*

a fact which could not be dealt with lightly. It had to be faced realistically and just punishment meted out. The frontier Methodists did not shield either their members or their clergy. Where there were rumors abroad that some Methodist had violated a church precept, it was almost certain that the accused would come up for trial.

There was a well-established order for prosecuting offenders, although the methods of trying members and preachers differed. Elders, deacons, or preachers guilty of more serious offenses were to be summoned by the presiding elder, in the absence of the bishop, to appear before a committee of ministers. If the accused were found guilty, he was to be suspended from all official services in the church until the next annual conference, at which time his case would be taken up again. When the offense was of a less serious nature, such as cases of "improper tempers, words, or actions," the person would be reprimanded by his senior in office. In case of a second transgression "one, two, or three ministers [were] to be taken as witnesses." Another offense would result in a trial before the yearly conference, and, if the offender were found guilty, the punishment was expulsion from the church.[10]

Local preachers, local deacons, and elders were subject to a similar form of discipline. The preacher on the circuit was to summon three or more local preachers, or, in the event preachers were not available, leaders or exhorters. When such a committee adjudged the accused guilty of such a crime, or of preaching such false doctrines, as required his suspension from office, the preacher on the circuit was to suspend him from such office until the ensuing quarterly meeting. He was then tried at the quarterly meeting, and, if found guilty as charged, he could appeal to the next yearly conference.[11]

Separate provision was made for the trial of ordinary laymen. A layman was tried before the society to which he belonged, or by a few members, in the presence of a bishop, elder, deacon, or preacher. If found guilty of a transgression "sufficient to exclude a person from the kingdom of grace and glory," he was expelled. Failure to appear for trial on the part of the accused was deemed evidence of guilt. Where offences were less serious, such as imprudent conduct, private reproof was first given by a preacher or leader. A third minor offense resulted in a trial before the society or a committee. If found guilty and impenitent, he was excluded from the

[10] *Ibid.*, pp. 40 ff.

[11] *Ibid.*, p. 44.

society. A member might in all cases, except where he had absented himself from trial, appeal for a new trial before the quarterly meeting.[12]

There were a number of rules applied in all trials. Wherever possible, the accuser and the accused were to be present, and it was also required that minutes be kept. In the trials of lay members, witnesses who were not members of the church were to be admitted. In the case of preachers, it was required that testimonial should be "from the society to which he belongs, and from the stewards of the circuit, signed also by nine traveling preachers, three of whom shall be elders, three others elders or deacons; and the other three elders, deacons, or preachers."[13]

There was a set order for conducting a trial. First, there was the arraignment, which included the reading of the charges and specifications to the accused. This was followed by a reply to the charge. The accuser then called and examined his witnesses, after which these witnesses were cross-examined by the accused. The accused then submitted his evidence. Accuser and accused were permitted to present rebutting testimony. Closing arguments on both sides of the case were then heard. After the committee had reached a verdict, the presiding officer made announcement of acquittal or expulsion.[14]

An interesting question in connection with the trials is why lay members submitted to them. The church was in no position to force the accused to submit to trial, and yet there seems to have been a general willingness to so submit. Perhaps it is to be explained in part by a sense of fear of divine punishment. On the other hand, it may have been due to the desire for the approval of church and community. It seems probable that, in order to clear himself before his fellow-citizens, it was necessary for the accused to secure a verdict of not guilty from the church judiciary. Charges by the church undoubtedly became common knowledge throughout the community, and nonchurch members or those connected with other bodies were likely to hold the accused guilty until he was proved innocent. Mankind has always been interested in court trials, as is attested by the space devoted to crime and scandal by the modern newspaper. The interest in church trials was probably only less avid to the degree that the crime was less serious in the eyes of the community.

[12] *Ibid.*, p. 56.

[13] Robert Emory, *History of the Discipline of the Methodist Episcopal Church* (New York: G. Lane & P. P. Sandford, 1844), p. 169.

[14] Osmon C. Baker, *A Guide Book in the Administration of the Discipline of the Methodist Episcopal Church* (New York: Phillips & Hunt, 1881), p. 111.

Among other impressions conveyed by the documentary records of the trials is the one that they were considered extremely important by all concerned, a fact which suggests the role played by the church as a disciplinary agency. Another impression the records convey is that the early Methodist preachers were not the illiterate men they have often been pictured as being. In many cases they were excellent penmen and expressed themselves in English which would have been acceptable in the drawing rooms of the literati. Moreover, the clergy adhered strictly to formal legal procedure.

DOCUMENTS ILLUSTRATING CHURCH TRIALS AMONG THE METHODISTS ON THE FRONTIER

A. RECORD OF THE TRIAL OF THE REVEREND THOMAS W. JONES, CHARGED WITH BREACH OF MARRIAGE CONTRACT

The Reverend Thomas W. Jones was admitted on trial by the Illinois Conference of the Methodist Episcopal church in 1845. His first station was at Alton City. In February, 1850, he was tried by a committee, with the Reverend Peter Cartwright presiding, and found guilty of breach of marriage contract. He appealed his case and was tried again by the annual conference which met at Bloomington in the same year. Again he was found guilty and suspended until the next annual session of the conference.

The Jones case illustrates the check exercised by the church over clergymen who found their affections wandering. On the third day of September, 1849, he had promised to marry Miss Eliza H. Miles, a member of the Methodist church. During the fall of 1849, Jones wrote a number of letters which sounded a note of dwindling affection. By October 27, not quite two months after he had declared his intentions to Miss Miles, he testified in a letter to her that his mind was so deranged he had forgotten that he "ever made anny appointment for the consumation" although he loved her as much as he ever did. According to Jones, his uncertainty was due merely to the financial difficulty of supporting a home, and he had asked Miss Miles "to wright and let me know what you think your Father will do for you or whether you expect any assistance from him." His closing sentence implied that all might go well: "My mind is troubled in deed but the Lord is stronghold in the day of trouble I know and if he hedges up our way I hope you will be submissive." As late as December 1, Jones was still writing to Miss Miles about their engagement and testified that he looked for light from Providence. By January, 1850, Jones was married to another woman.

1. *Letter to Peter Cartwright from the preacher in charge of the Brighton Circuit and James B. Davidson, class leader of the Hopewell Society.*

BRIGHTON CIRCUIT Jany. 9 1850

Rev. P. Cartwright
DEAR BRO.

Supposing it to be our duty, painful as it is, we send you the following charge and specification against our Bro. the Rev. T. W. Jones.

Charge, Breach of Marriage Contract

Specification For on the third day of September last, in the afternoon of that day, at the residence of Mr. Jacob Miles in Upper Alton, Ills., promising to marry Miss Eliza H. Miles and since then not doing so but having married another Lady.

Miss Miles is a respectable member of our church in the Hopewell Society Simmons Neighborhood, she positively asserts to us, without any Mental reservation or hesitation that such an Engagement was made, and never afterward broken off, she has letters from Bro. Jones, close up to the time of his Marriage, after advising with several Brethren, this charge is sent, from the Excitement Created, and the Conversation about this matter, it certainly ought to be investigated it is due to the Church for if this charge is true what will be thought of us? It is due to Bro. Jones, for if these things are not so, he certainly ought not to be slandered, but sustained by his Brethren. It is certainly due to the Young Lady, a reputable Member of our church, if this charge is true, she certainly has ground of serious complaint.

We *request you* to have it tried at Hopewell, here is the scene of action, the talk, and excitement. Committing the case into your hands we are Your Bros in Christ.

HARDIN WALLACE
Pr. in Chge Brighton Ct.
JAMES B. DAVIDSON. *Class Leader at Hopewell Society in behalf of the M.E. Church*

REV P CARTWRIGHT D.D.

P.S. Please give early attention to this We send a copy to Br. Jones also at the H W same time we mail this

J. B. D.

2. *The committee of the quarterly conference meeting at Hopewell in February, 1850, submitted their conclusion in the Jones case.*

The committee after having heard the evidence, and read the foregoing letters, and duly canvassing the case, as best they could under the circumstances are of the opinion that the conduct of the Rev. T. W. Jones with Miss Eliza H. Miles has been highly censurable; but that it does not amount to a sufficient crime to exclude him from the Kingdom of grace and glory; and consequently he is not to be suspended from his ministerial function, but that the Chairman censure him severely for his conduct in this matter.

E. B. Gentry
James L. Crane

I cannot concur in the above opinion, but am of the opinion that he ought to be suspended.

William Jerome *Secretary* W. G. Moore

3. *The Jones case came up before the annual conference at Bloomington in September, 1850, and the committee reversed the decision of the committee of the quarterly conference.*

The committee to whom was referred the case of Rev. T. W. Jones, have examined the papers put into their hands and from them have come to the conclusion that the charge for "Breach of Marriage Contract" is sustained. They therefore respectfully recommend to the conference the adoption of the following resolution.

Resolved, That T. W. Jones be suspended from all his ministerial functions until the next annual session of the Conference, and that the Presiding Elder of the district where he may reside notify him to appear at the next Conference for the final adjudication of his case.

John Van Cleve
A. W. Cummings } *Committee*
C. M. Holliday

Bloomington, Sep. 24, 1850

B. RECORD OF THE TRIAL OF A. G. MEACHAM, A LAY PREACHER, CHARGED WITH IMMORAL CONDUCT

In 1836 A. G. Meacham was admitted on trial by the Illinois annual conference, and two years later he was admitted into full connection. Meacham was a doctor as well as a preacher. In May, 1839, William

Nichols brought charges against him of immoral conduct. The specification read that Meacham had made two attempts to go to bed with Malinda Nichols, daughter of the accuser. The testimony in the trial before the quarterly conference illustrates the great care with which the trials were conducted. The committee of the quarterly conference suspended Meacham. The accused then wrote to the Illinois annual conference, charging himself with immorality and high imprudence.

1. *Record of trial of A. G. Meacham before the committee of the quarterly conference at Shelbyville, Illinois, 1839.*

On the 2nd day of July A.D. 1839—

A committee consisting of Jesse Haile Wm. W. Mitchell and Barton Randle, traveling ministers, on the Lebanon District, Ill. Conference, call by Revd John Dew, P. E. met in Shelbyville, Shelby Co. Ill. to hear and consider the following charge of Immorality preferred against A. G. Meacham

Charge *Immoral* conduct

Specification—For making two attempts to go to bed to my daughter, Malinda, in my own house. Signed—William Nichols May 25th 1839

The committee met and organized by singing & prayer, and the appointment of Barton Randle to act as secretary to take the minutes of the trial.

On motion the committee adjourned to meet at 2 P.M.

At 2 o'clk P.M. the committee met pursuant to adjournment and opened with prayer—

Bro. William Hindall was added by the P. E. to the committee

Bro. Mitchell being unwell was abscent—

On motion the following was adopted as the mode of procedure in the trial

1st Each meeting of the committee shall be opened by prayer.

2nd The charge shall first be read, with the Specification, in presence of the accused to which the accused shall plead.

3rd The Testimony on part of the accusation shall be all first heard, in presence of the accused, who shall have the privilege of cross examining the witnesses, subject to the control of the President

This done

4th The Testimony on part of the defense shall be heard, subject to examination and control, as on the part of the accusation.

5th No testimony in writing, taken by one party, in the abscent of the other, shall be admitted in evidence, unless the party after due notice given, refused to attend.

6th Those witnesses, who have not been examined, shall not be present during the examination of others.

7th Each party may, if he choose, select three disinterested friends, who are members of the church; and two who are not members of the church; who may be present and witness the trial, and none others.

The committee being ready for business the parties were called in, and the charge read, to the accused, to which he pleaded Not Guilty.

The parties selected the following as witnessing friends—to wit, on part of the accusation

Amos Prentice and R. B. Ewing, members of the church.

On part of the Defence—In the church Jacob Brewer, N. R. Jones—Owen Prentice out of the church.

On part of the accusation—first witness—Malinda Nichols—said W. Meacham did come to Fathers to stay all night and went to bed and staid there about five or ten minutes, and then got up and came to my bed, and hearing Father speak to him, he returned to his bed, and at a late hour of the night he came again to my bed, and said to me that he always thought a great deal of me, and asked me if I would accept of his company—I told him no—

And again he came on another night to stay—and at a late hour of the night again came to my bed, and made an attempt to get on the bed, but said nothing—

Qs. 1—When he came to your bed the last time. Were you awake? or asleep?

Ans.—I was asleep, but awoke on his attempting to turn down the cover.

Qs.—What did you do

Ans.—I pulled the cover and tucked it under my head

Question by the *defendant*

1st About what hour did I come to your Fathers house on the first night—

Ans Dont know but it was after we had gone to bed but had not been asleep. I suppose about 8 or 9 oclock.

Qs 2nd Did I go immediately to bed on coming to your Fathers?

Ans No you sat and talked with Father a while.

Qs 3rd Were any of the Family up after my going there, and before I went to bed—

Ans If there was any person, I dont know it

Qs 4 Was it light in the house or dark

Ans I think there was not much light

Qs 5th Are you sure that no person was up before I went to bed—

Ans I think not except myself. I got up and fixed your bed, but went to bed again before you came in, to go to bed.

Qs 6 Did you go out to light a candle before you fixed the bed

Ans No the fire gave a little light through the door of the partition, by which I saw to fix the bed

Qs 7th Where does the bed stand in which I was to sleep

Ans On the right hand of the door, in going out of the large door into that in which the bed is, and close to the partition

Qs. 8 Had you been asleep when I came to your bed the 2nd time, on the first night

Ans Yes I had been asleep, but had awoke

Qs 9 Did I speak loud, when I asked you if you could accept of my company?

Ans No

Qs 10 Were you in bed alone that night?

Ans No, my youngest brother was with me

Qs 11 On the first night did I make any attempt to get to bed with you

Ans No you only asked me if I would accept of your company and on being refused went immediately away

Qs 12 Did I leave there early the next morning

Ans No you stayed until after breakfast

Qs 13th Was I in the front room in the forenoon of that day

Ans Yes you were a part of the time

Qs 14th Was there any conversation between you and I

Ans Yes

Qs 15 What was it about

Ans A young man named Carpenter Funk

Qs 16 What did I say of that young man

Ans You said he was coming out and was a cleaver young man and you wished to give me an introduction to him

Qs 17 Did I tell you that I had recommended you to him, and had promised to introduce him to you

Ans Yes I think you did

Qs 18 Did you ask me any questions about him

Ans I asked you his name and told you I did not like it and you said the person was better than the name

Qs 19 Did I tell you that I had got a letter from that young man a short time before & that he said he was coming up

Ans Yes

Qs 20 Was there any thing said at this time, between you and I about what had taken place the night before

Ans No

Qs 21st Did you feel friendly toward me at the time we had this conversation about the young man

Ans No I did not

Qs 22 What was the ground of your unfriendly feeling

Ans The manner in which you had acted the night before

Qs 23 What time in the year was it the first case of my coming to your bed occured

Ans I dont know what time it was; it was in cold weather I think before you moved down here

Qs 24 Did you come to my house while I lived at Bro. Pughs

Ans Yes I came to see your wife one day, but you were not at home, but came home, just as I sat off home, so that I did not speak to you

Qs 25 Had you been sick the week on which you say I came the second night

Ans Yes—very sick

26 Qs Did I call to see you when you were sick and by your mothers request—and did she speak to you about it before I came in

Ans She spoke to me and I told her that I cared nothing about it

Qs 27 What did I do for you

Ans You gave me a few pills, that I think done me no good

Qs 28 Did you suffer much with cold feet—Yes

Qs 29 Were you afflicted with a cold sinking state through out your cistem

Ans I dont know that I was

Qs 30 What did I do for you to relieve you of that coldness

Ans You washed my feet in something warm, pepper I think—and put some on my throat

Qs 31 Did you say to me that if you did not get better that you could not stand it long

Ans I think I may have said something like that

Qs 32 Did I ask you what your complaint was & how you were taken

Ans I think I told you something about it

Qs 33 Was it after this that you say I came to your bed the second night

Ans Yes, and I had got better and about

Qs 34 Did any other person beside yourself sleep in the room on the second night you say I came

Ans Yes—Aunt Nelly Rhodes

Qs 35 Were your bed and hers close together

Ans They were the width of the door apart one on one side and the other on the other

Qs 36 Did I tell you if you would take the medicine I had prepared for you that I would give you a Hymn book

Ans Yes—and you gave me the book at the house where you live, and I am sorry I ever took it.

2nd Witness on part of the accusation Peninah Nichols said that her Daughter never requested or agreed that W. Meacham should be sent for or called in, until she thought she was going to die, and then she agreed that he might be called in, as he was passing by—

Question by the defendent

Qs. 1 Did you ever propose to her to send for me previous to that day—

Ans Yes—a number of times, but she would not agree to it

Qs 2nd Did you ever propose to imploy any other Doctor

Ans Yes—

Qs 3th Did she agree to it

Ans No—

Qs 4th Did you send for me at any time, and by Malindas consent after I first called

Ans Yes

3d Witness William Hall Sr

Bro. Hall said that some short time after this matter was rumoured —He had a conversation with Bro. Meacham on the subject in which he neither confessed or denied the reports, and stated that for all the crimes he had committed whether many or few, he had sorely or bitterly repented and hoped he was forgiven—and when I mentioned that I had known the Young Lady from infancy and believed her to be a person of strict voracity—he said that he had nothing to say against her voracity—and that he believed her to be a decent Young Lady—

Qs 1 By the Defendant—Did you converse with Malinda on this subject

Ans Yes—in some measure—and she told me that you had gone to her bed and asked her to accept of your company—and she was so much affected that I conversed but little more with her on the subject

Qs 2 Did you ever converse with her on the subject more than the once

Ans No—

On motion the committee adjourned to meet at 8 oclk on tomorrow morning—

Wednesday morning July 3d The committee met at 8 oclock pursuant to adjournment—the meeting was opened by prayer—Bro. Mitchell continues unwell, and is abscent—The other members of the committee are present—The committee continued their investigation by calling the 4th witness on part of the accusation—Thomas Pugh

Bro. Pugh said he had a conversation with the accused on the same day that he (the accused) came in possession of the matter against him. In which conversation he said he should neither confess or deny the allegation, at that time or any other, but that there were some circumstances that might give rise to such suspicion, and that he was sorry that they had happened: but if the intention was known, that he should have no fears; he (the accused) said that he had recd. a letter from Bro. Nichols which would probably by some be thought rough but under the circumstances he did not so consider it: and that he wished the matter could be settled between them without going to the world, and wished me to use my influence to bring this about which I did but failed to accomplish it—he further said he would be willing if necessary to go on his knees to Bro. Nichols for he had nothing against him

Qs. 1 by the accuser—have you any recollection of the accused leaving your house at a late hour of the night saying that he had business with me

Ans Yes—he left my house at about 9 oclock

1st qs on part of the defence To what circumstances did you understand me to allude, in reference to the letter from Bro. Nichols—

Ans To those connected with the allegation and those with the disposition of Bro. Nichols—

Qs by the president Do you know whether the night he left your house was the night on which he should have made the first attempt of which he is accused.

Ans No I know nothing of that

Qs 2d by the defence At what season of the year should I have left your house to go as alledged above to Bro. Nichols

Ans As well as I can recollect it was before you moved here, and in the *winter*

The Evidence on part of the accusation being through

The 1st Witness on part of the defence was called Sister Ann Pugh

Qs 1st by the defendant—Do you recollect what time of the year it was that I should have left your house as alleged above to go to Bro Nichols on business

Ans I do not but my best impression is that it was sometime late in the fall or early in the winter

Qs 2nd Did you ever discover in Malinda any thing unfriendly toward me previous the commencement of the present difficulty

Ans No, not particularly so or more than to others

Qs 3d Has Malinda been frequently at my appointment for preaching at Bro Pughs & Inmans

Ans I have seen her at meeting at those places several times, but I can't say very frequently, and she remained, as I recollect, in class once, and said on being asked whether she had given up seeking religion, that she had pretty much

2nd Witness on part of defence Thos Pugh

Qs 1 Do you know whether Malindas attendance at my appointments has been about the same during the last winter up to the time of this difficulty becoming public, that it was previously

Ans I dont know that I have noticed any difference

3d Witness on part of the defence Amos Prentice

[*Qs 1*] Bro. Prentice, Was Malinda here at the Eleven oclock meeting on Sunday of the last qr. meeting when I preached

Ans I think she was; and I think she sat on the 1st or 2nd bench, on the left hand of the stand

4th Witness for the defence Betsy Nichols

Qs 1st Was Malinda with you in Love feast at this place, at the last qr. meeting

Ans Yes she was—

Qs 2nd Did Malinda go with you to my house? and did I give her a Hymn Book? and she accept of it?

Ans Yes

Qs 3d Was anything said on her receiving the H. Book

Ans No nothing

Qs 4th Did she after that tell you the reasons why I gave her the Hymn Book

Ans Yes she said you promised her the book on condition that she would take some medicine that you had prepared for her

Qs 5th Did you hear Malinda say any thing hostile about me, previous to your knowing anything of this difficulty since you came down last.

Ans Yes I have—

Qs 6 Did you last summer, when you were out her[e] before, hear her speak any thing against me

Ans Yes I heard her say she never liked you

5th Witness Sarah Inman for the defence—Not present—

6th Witness Thomas Hardy—for the defence

Qs 1st Do you recollect having seen Malinda at my appointments for preaching and class meeting

Ans I recollect to have seen her at preaching but I do not recollect to have seen her remain in class meeting

Witnesses on part of the defence: to prove that the charge has grown out of a settled enmity on part of the accuser

On motion. The committee adjourned to meet at 2 oclock this afternoon—

The committee met at 2 oclock PM pursuant to adjournment, was opened by prayer

All parties present the committee proceded with the investigation by calling 7th Witness on part of the defence—Amos Prentice

1st qs by the accused Do you recollect that Bro. Nichols wished me to bring Bro. Swaford to trial for slandering him (Nichols)

Ans I recollect that Bro. Nichols said to me, that he had requested you to bring Bro. Swaford to trial on that account

Qs 2nd Did I refuse to do it

Ans I am not positive that you refused to do it, but you did not do it; and Bro. Nichols did manifest some feeling when conversing on the subject, but I do not know that he directed this feeling toward you or toward Swaford

Qs 3d Do you remember that Maria Prentice prefered a charge against Bro. Nichols; and that I notified Nichols to trial

Ans Yes—

Qs 4th Did you not think Nichols was very angry

Ans I think his feelings were considerably rasped; but I think he might have been more angry than he was; and I think the harshest expression I heard him use, was that if you saw proper you might use your authority

qs 5th Did I argue the question with him, and was his manner somewhat abrupt,

Ans You did argue the case, and he was somewhat abrupt, and he did refuse to attend the trial

Qs 6th Did you ever hear Bro Nichols say that a house could be had for me of James Selby

Ans Yes—

Qs 7th Did Bro. Nichols ever oppose getting a house for me in town—

Ans Bro Nichols spoke against it for the reason that house-rent & fuel would come so much higher in town than in the country

Qs 8th Did you ever hear Bro. Nichols speak unfavorably of me as a man or minister

Ans Not as a man, but as a minister, I have heard him speak sometimes against both your preaching and administration

Cross examination by plaintiff

Qs 1st Did W. Meacham agree to investigate the matter of Swafords involvment

Ans Confessed by defendent

Qs 2nd Was I not active in procuring provisions for Bro. Meacham; as Steward

Ans You were—

Qs 3d Have I not manifested a willingness to make greater exertions for the support of Bro. Meacham

Ans Yes—since the last quarterly meeting

Qs 4th Did I not come to you and consult with you in reference to the course I should take in this matter, and was not the course I took the result of that consultation

Ans Yes: and I advised you to the course you took—

8th Witness on part of the defence—N. R. Jones—

Qs 1 Did I call a committee and investigate Swafords supposed involvement

Ans You did, and I sat on the committee

Question by the President Have the parties or either of them any further testimony to offer in the case—

Ans No further testimony to offer

This done—

Privilege was given the Parties to offer their Plea—Whereupon Bro. Nichols declined, submitting the case to the committee—Bro. Meacham offered his plea before the members of the committee (except Bro. Mitchell) and the witnessing friends of the parties, who chose to remain—

Bro. Meacham having concluded his plea he submitted the whole case to the committee in the name of God—

On motion the committee adjourned to meet at Bro. Prentice at early candle lighting

The committee met at Bro. Prentices at early candlelighting pursuant to adjournment—all present

The committee read over all the Testimony carfully: and came to the conclusion that the Specification under the charge was sustained by the evidence in reference to the first night

But that the Specification under the charge was not clearly sustained by the evidence in reference to the second night

The committee are unanimously of opinion therefore that the

accused should be suspended from all official services in the church, till the ensuing annual conference.

On motion the com. then adjourned Sine Die

Barton Randle *Secy* John Dew *P.E.*

Jepe Maile
Wm W Mitchell
Barton Randle
William Hindall
} *Committee*

2. *Letter of the Reverend A. G. Meacham charging himself with immorality and high imprudence.*

To the Bishop and members of the Illinois annual conference of the M.E. Church to be holden at Bloomington Sept. 11, 1839

In view of some of my past conduct, of the relation, I have, and now sustain to you and to the church, and of the best subsequent good to all concerned, I present to you against myself the following charge of immorality and high imprudence.

Specification: 1. For making two attempts with wicked intention at illicit intercourse, first with Elisabeth Sawyer of Wabash grove, and second with Malinda Williams, (now Radly) of the same place in the fall of 1838.

2nd For an act of high imprudence in going to the bedside of Malinda Nichols of Shelbyville, (or near there) for the purpose of having a word of conversation, at an improper hour at night, between 9 & 10 o'clock, when all the family were at bed.

To the above charge, in the fear of God and in view of the great day of accounts, I plead *Guilty* and, in view of justice, virtue, religion, and every equitable consideration I believe that I ought to be expelled from the M.E. Church:—and I desire that it may be done. But I ask Yours prayers that my poor soul may yet be saved for which I am intent to strive, hence forth while life shall last.

A. G. Meacham

Shelbyville 18 July 1839

C. RECORD OF THE TRIAL OF DR. SOLOMON MINEAR CHARGED WITH IMMORALITY AND IMPRUDENCE

In 1856 Dr. Solomon Minear was brought to trial. The case is of particular interest because it involved a local elder and because the accused demanded investigation of reports which were prejudicial to his character. The quarterly conference of Paris Station in the Illinois Conference appointed a committee to inquire into the reports regarding Minear and instructed the committee to prefer charges against him if they believed "said charges or any of them true and of such character as to demand investigation; . . . ." The committee, at the next quarterly conference, presented charges of immorality and imprudence against Minear. Witnesses testified that they had seen Minear in situations which were cause for suspicion. The accused was found guilty. He then appealed to the Illinois annual conference on the ground that the testimony did not sustain the specification and the specification did not sustain the charge. The annual conference reversed the decision of the Paris quarterly conference.

1. *Resolutions presented at the second quarterly conference of Paris Station in the Illinois Conference in the trial of Dr. Solomon Minear.*

Whereas for a number of years past there have been in circulation various reports prejudicial to the character of Rev.d S. Minear a Local Elder in the M.E. Church in this Sta; and whereas; said reports have and do operate to the prejudice and standing of said Minear and the best interest of the Church; and whereas, the said Minear has long since demanded an investigation of said charges or reports, therefore

Resolved, that justice to Minear and the best interest of the church, require that action on the premises be had it is

Resolved by the quart. Conference of Paris Sta. Ill. Conference that James P. Elliott, John F. Anderson, be and they are hereby appointed a committee to inquire into said reports, and what evidence can be obtained to sustain the same; and should they believe said charges or any of them true, and of such character as to demand investigation; that they prefer charges against said Minear, and prosecute the same before the Committee to be appointed to try the same, but should they after full inquiry believe the charges unfounded or not susceptable of proof that they report the same to next Quar. Conference for this station.

Resolved that in view of the feelings of members of this church and of many of the congregation who usually attend the services in this House, that the Pres. Elder and the Preacher in Charge of this Sta. be respectfully requested not to call on bro. Minear to officiate in this House until said committee report on said investigation be had.

Signed and moved by JONATHAN MAYO
Seconded by SILAS H. ELLIOTT

2. *Cross-examination of William Johnson in the trial of Dr. Solomon Minear before the quarterly conference of the Paris Station, Illinois.*

Ques. By the Prosecution. Were you acquainted with Dr. Minear and Ankey Laird and his wife and if so when did that acquaintence commence?

Ans I became acquainted with them about 15 years ago or longer, between 15 & 20 years.

Ques. Did you ever see anything that you thought imprudent conduct between Dr. Minear and Mrs. Laird and if so state what it was & when it occured?

Ans After Mr. Laird's death, and about 3 weeks before the sale I moved my family into the kitchen of the house in which Mrs. Laird lived, having brought the property of Mr Laird previous to his death. during that time Dr. Minear was frequently there both in the daytime and in the night—at late hours. The family not being sick at the time. I never saw any thing between the parties that I thought improper.

Ques What impression did the Dr visits make on your mind were they good or bad?

Ques. objected to by the defense and overruled by the chair.

Ans Well I thought there was something not right—from other circumstances.

Ques What were those circumstances?

Ans Well it was not any thing I seen within myself but from reports

Ques. What were those reports?

Here the defense objected to such testimony and were sustained by the Chair.

Ques What distance, how far is it from your residence to Dr. Minears?

Ans. About three miles.

Ques What is Dr. Minear's general character from public rumor, as to visiting houses where the females are of doubtful reputation?

Ans The rumor has been that he was guilty of visiting such places.

Ques Did such reports exist before the death of Ankey Laird?

Ans Before and since.

The above ques. and ans. objected to by the defense

Ques. By a member of Quar Conferences. What were your private feelings towards Dr Minear at the time of these reports?

Ans I had no feeling against Dr Minear only as regarded reports.

Ques. By a member of Conference. Did you ever have any personal difficulty with Dr. Minear

Ans I don't know that I have, he talked a little hard to me, but I had no difficulty with him. This took place since I saw him at Mrs Laird's house.

D. LETTER OF THE REVEREND W. B. MARK CONFESSING HIS GUILT TO THE ILLINOIS CONFERENCE

The Reverend W. B. Mark had evidently been found guilty by a quarterly meeting. Before the annual meeting of the Illinois Conference at Rushville in 1836 he wrote a letter pleading guilty to the charge of unlawful intercourse with Mrs. Eve Whitney. He had paid Mr. Whitney one thousand dollars with the understanding that it should be kept a secret. In the letter he inclosed his parchments.

1. *Letter of confession*

JULIETT July 26 1836

To the Bishop and Members of the Illinois Conference to be held at Rushville Oct. 5 1836.

REVEREND FATHERS AND BRETHREN

It is with feelings which no inocent man can conceive, no uninspired language describe, that I take up my pen to address you upon a Subject of the most painful and afflicting character—Oft have I looked forward to the Session of an Anuel conference as a kind of Jubilee—Oft have I met my ministerial brethren with reciprocal confidence and christian friendship and after spending a week or ten days in mutual converse repaired to my newly assigned field of labour, and looked forward with hope and indulged expectation that my laborers in the Lord would be attended with success. but how shall I discribe my emmotions—my *agonizing feelings* in view of the facts in my case which I know must come before you at your next session—O "that it were with me as formerly—Could my unworthy life be accepted as a Sacrifice. and blot from the memmory of Heaven and Earth my offence. How cheerfully should it be offered up—without a moment's hesitancy—What must be the feelings of those dear, those devoted men, whom I love as my own Soul, and whose confidence I have shared in an eminent degree. The Ministers of Jesus. What the feelings of my numerous friends "How will their hearts bleed..... How will infidelity triumph? O "the Church" The cause of God" My family—My Soul. Let my mournful case be a warning especially to the Young and inexperienced Herald of the cross—O "that I had strictly observed my ordination vow in reference to this Subject. Then should I have come down to the grave in peace and died without remorse—My soul hangs upon these words—

"I the chief of Sinners am
Yet Jesus died for me.

Let me ask an interest in your prayers, and as far as possible the exercise of Christian charity—With a bleeding heart, that my case may not consume time and obtrude upon the more pleasant duties of conference—though painful in the extreme I am in Justice to my own feelings compeled to prefer the following charge against myself—to which (*I trust with a broken and contrite heart*) I plead guilty

—*Charge*—

Unlawful intercourse with Mrs Eve Whitney—

At first our friendship was pure and Christian—little did I then think, it would ever degenerate to crime—but by a slow and gradual process has it thus terminated—In vain do I deprecate the fatal hour when first we yielded to temptation—

May merciful Heaven forgive, though I cannot forgive myself ———I shall make no defense—I throw myself into your hands. My name must be struck from your list. But O God forbid it should be bloted from the Lambs Book of life.

I enclose my Parchments—no longer mine—

Brothers Mitchel Sinclair and Biggs will be able to represent the District—

My feelings over come me, and I can write no more—I will only add I have done all in my power to Save the bleeding cause of Zion and make an attonement for my Sin—

I gave to Brother Whitney one thousand dollars to Settle the affair, upon the positive condition and Solemn promise that it should be kept a profound Secret. This pledge has been violated. Yet it affords me Consolation to think I gave him my earthly all. What more could I have done—but I am unworthy to intrude upon your precious time.

My Dear Brethren—Pray, pray pray for your fallen Brother

W. B. Mark

E. RECORD OF THE TRIAL OF AHMED RUCKER A LOCAL PREACHER, CHARGED WITH VIOLATING THE *DISCIPLINE*

The trial of Ahmed Rucker, a local preacher in the Sangamon Circuit, before a committee of laymen is of particular interest. In the first place, the trial occurred after the matter had been before a secular court and Rucker had been awarded one hundred dollars. Second, the records show that, when the evidence in the trial indicated a violation of the *Discipline,* the accused was duly punished though there were mitigating circumstances which would have caused less stern disciplinarians to have been satisfied to offer only a mild rebuke. Finally, the care exercised in the trial offers further evidence of the importance attached to the proper adjudication of disputes.

Rucker was charged with having violated the *Discipline* in a number of respects. Many years before, Ahmed Rucker and his wife Nelly took their infant grandson, Augustus, into their home and for twelve years they had cared for him. Their son-in-law, James Smith, father of Augustus, had gladly consented to this arrangement when the mother had died. Not until the boy reached the age of twelve did the father protest in any way. He finally decided that he wanted his son to live with him, and on a certain Sunday he and three other men removed Augustus by force from the home of his grandparents. Rucker took steps first of all to prevent the taking-away of his grandson, and later he tried to recover him both by offering prizes to certain people if they would bring the boy back and by going to court. Rucker was suspended by the committee which tried him and was later found guilty in a trial before the quarterly conference.

1. *Minutes of the charges and specifications in the trial of Ahmed Rucker in 1836.*

April 20th 1836

The charges prefered read as follows:

I Richard Smith in the fear of God and for the good of his cause, do solemnly charge Ahmed Rucker local preacher in Saugamon Circuit of the following violations of the discipline of the Methodist Church—

General Charge: Immoral Conduct

1st Specification

A profanation of the Lord's day by commencing an affray with James Smith and telling his (said Rucker) son to nock down said Smith

2nd Specification

In pursuing said Smith on the Lord's day with intention of taking from him his (said Smiths) son by violence or otherwise and offering one dollar per day to any who would accompany him in the above mentioned unchristian expedition.

3rd Specification

By offering an oath that said Smith struck his (Ruckers) son three times when the contrary is the fact and stating likewise on oath that his son was seriously injured by the assault of said Smith whereas his son was not injured at all.

4th Specification

In prosecuting said Smith at law who is a member of the Methodist episcopal church when he said Rucker and his son commenced the assault and thereby violating one of the plainest rules of our discipline

5th Specification

By offering E. Knox & P. Harrison one hundred dollars to take the said Smiths son by violence

6th Specification

In extorting from said Smith a sum of money for the support of Smiths son which is unnatural unchristian and unjust.

7th Specification

In stating to Josiah Wickersham Logan McMurray & William McMurray when requested by them to aid in building a bridge over Springcreek on said Ruckers land that the bridge would not be of much use to him, and consequently he would not aid more than 7 dol & 50 cents worth in building it and subsequently stating after the bridge was built on Bro. Wickershams land that the bridge would have been worth fifty dollars to him—

2. *Decision handed down by committee which tried Ahmed Rucker.*

The committee appointed I. M. Early C. F. Luckett & Joseph Edmundson who were appointed to investigate these the foregoing charges after hearing the testimony presented before them retired and after having deliberated upon the matter are of the opinion that in

1st Specification the accused is guilty of assisting in an affray and sabbath breaking

2nd Specification they think entirely sustained

3rd Specification in the opinion of the committee is not sustained

4th Specification is in the opinion of the committee sustained as to the prosecution

5th Specification the committee think not sustained

6th Specification the committee think is sustained

7th Specification is not sustained—

They are therefore of opinion that the said Ahmed Rucker be suspended untill the next quarterly conference.

F. TRIAL OF *YOST* V. *BURNS* INVOLVING A STOLEN PIG

In July, 1841, a trial regarding the supposed stealing of a pig took place. While the complete records of the trial are not available, a number of depositions are. The signatures of these depositions are chiefly made in the form of *X*'s.

1. *Deposition of James Martin in the* Yost *v.* Burns *trial involving the stealing of a hog.*

The question was asked Henry Yost what he was going to do with the stick which he had in his hand. And the answer was: he understood Robert Locklear said that he would muster or die. And Mr

Yost said before he would muster with a man of his color he would wear the stick out which he had in his hand. This conversation took place three years ago last April at the muster ground at John Roberts,

his
JAMES X MARTIN
mark

2. *Deposition of Cithea Locklear in the* Yost *v.* Burns *trial.*

I hereby certify that in conversation I asked Mrs Stewart if she thought the stray hog she had in possession belonged to William Burns she answered that she had no doubt of it.

her
CITHEA X LOCKLEAR
mark

G. DISCIPLINE CASES BEFORE THE QUARTERLY CONFERENCES OF THE CARROLLTON CIRCUIT

Five discipline cases are mentioned in the minutes of the quarterly conferences for the Carrollton Circuit of the Illinois annual conference from September, 1839, to May, 1850. Two members had been found guilty of indulging in sinful words and tempers and of attempting to fight. For these acts they were expelled by the committee, but the quarterly meeting reversed the decision. In another case a Miss Murphy was tried by a committee and found guilty of lying and slander. The quarterly meeting confirmed the decision of the committee. Another case involved a local preacher who had failed to comply with the order of a committee requiring him to make payment on a note. A compromise was reached between the creditor and debtor. In the fourth case the nature of the charges was not recorded, the only information given being that the quarterly conference upheld the decision of the committee which had conducted an earlier trial of the case. Finally, the preacher in charge referred the case of Keziah Meldrum, who was charged with immoral conduct, to the conference. The conference voted not to entertain the reference.

1. *Minutes of the quarterly meeting of the Carrollton Circuit for November 11, 1843, dealing with cases of discipline.*

Question 1st. Are there any complaints or appeals.

Answer Two. 1st. The case of sister ——— Murphy who was

charged of lying and slander, was found guilty, by a select committee and expelled, and who appeals to this conference, the conference after hearing the specifications, the evidence in the case and the decision of the committee read considered the same, and confirmed the decision of said committee.

2nd The case of Isaac Landis a Local preacher who was expelled for not complying with the decision of a committee, which committee required of him to execute a note in favor of G. P. Taft for a certain amount to be paid by a specified time, and he appeals to this conference, and by appointment of the chair or president of this conference. Geo. W. Allen was appointed secretary in this case, whereupon a proposition was made for the parties in this case to compromise the matter in dispute in open Conference, upon which Simon P. Taft arose and made a present of the amount claimed to the said Isaac Landiss which amount was thirty nine Dollars. Isaac Landiss then arose and proposed to give one half of said amount so claimed to the Rev. Peter Cartwright President of this conference for him to apply the same to Missionary purposes. The Conference then voted unanimously that the said Isaac Landiss be considered to sustain the same relation to the Methodist Episcopal Church and this conference that he did before the decision of the above named committee.

H. RECORD OF THE TRIAL OF THE REVEREND R. W. TRAVIS CHARGED WITH MISREPRESENTATION IN THE SALE OF LAND AND WITH REFUSAL TO COMPLY WITH THE TERMS OF A CONTRACT

There were trials involving business transactions. One of these was the Travis trial. In 1856 R. W. Travis served as presiding elder in the Griggsville District in Illinois. Two years later Rev. C. D. James charged Travis with misrepresentation in sale of land and refusal to comply with the terms of a contract. James held that Travis had charged him an excessive price for some land, but Travis introduced evidence to the contrary, and the committee decided in favor of Travis. In regard to the violation of contract, James charged that Travis had agreed to exchange with James if he wished to at a later date. This Travis admitted and gave as his reason for not complying that James refused to pay damages. The committee refused to censure Travis, holding that the contract was not unconditional. The trial is of interest in that it involved two ministers.

1. *Letter of the Reverend C. D. James listing charge against the Reverend R. W. Travis.*

GRIGGSVILLE Sept. 27th 1858

Rev. R. W. Travis
SIR

The following are the charges I prefer against you.

1st Charge Misrepresentation

Specification In selling to me in the month of May 1857 a certain tract of Land in McLean Co for fourteen hundred dollars; and afterwards claiming six hundred (600) dollars which you obtained (in a promissory note) by stating the land was worth much more than the amount for which it was sold which statement was a misrepresentation.

Withdrawn { Charge 2nd Fraud
Specification In obtaining from me a prommissory note for $600.00 by making statements to me concerning said land which statesments were not true. }

Charge 3rd Refused to comply with positive agreement.

Specification In promissing to cancel the contract concerning said Land and afterwards refusing to comply with said promise.

I am sir
Your obt servant
C. D. JAMES

2. *Decision of the committee which tried the Reverend R. W. Travis.*

After the pleadings closed, the committee decided as follows.

The specification under the first charge, not sustained by the testimony

The 1st charge not sustained—

During the consideration of the 3rd charge & specification, the following resolution was adopted (Paper B)

Resolved that while there was a verbal promise on the part of Bro Travis to Bro James touching the rescinding of their Land Contract yet it is not in evidence that it was *unconditional,* and therefore we attach no serious blame to Bro Travis because of its failure; and therefore the Specifications and 3rd Charge is not sustained in the ——— of criminality.

I. RECORD OF THE TRIAL OF THE REVEREND SAMSON SHINN, CHARGED WITH MALADMINISTRATION

Trials quite frequently dealt with charges of maladministration on the part of the clergy and with indiscretions and petty sins. Rev. Samson Shinn was brought to trial in 1852 after charges of this nature had been made by Rev. Jeremiah Ballard. Shinn had been admitted on trial by the Illinois Conference in 1843 and into full connection in 1845. He was charged with falsehood and prevarication, evil speaking, and partiality in the administration of discipline. Ballard was sharply critical of Shinn because he had not attended to certain charges Ballard had brought against a Q. B. Christie. In a letter to Ballard a Samuel Elliott quoted Shinn as saying that if Ballard would first try to settle the problem with Christie and failed, he, Shinn, would bring both up for trial. Shinn had brought Christie to the home of Ballard, and Christie confessed his error. Ballard said he would be satisfied if Christie would make a public confession before the society. Shinn was acquitted on all charges by two different committees.

1. *Rev. Mr. Ballard filed the following charges against Christie with Shinn.*

Febry 17th 1852

Brother S Shin P. C. Columbus Cirt. Ill. Confer

I hereby prefer a charge of immorality and unchristian conduct against Q. B. Christie

Specification

1st In attacking me on Sabbath, immediately after coming out of Church, in an unchristian and ungentlemanly manner.

2nd By stating that I had told Brother Thomas, that the breathren were all dissatisfied with the acknowledgement that he made and when Bro. Thomas, said he never told him so, he said I or Brother Thomas "had lyed."

3rd In charging me, as the first mover of the charges against him and charging me with interrupting the meeting here.

4th The spirit he manifested and the insulting and abusing manner in which he talked.

5th In saying that all the members were satisfied but I and Beull and our clan and that we were doing all we could to injure him.

JEREMIAH BALLARD

Witnesses
ROBERT THOMAS
JOHN A BEULL

2. *Letter of Samuel Elliott to Rev. Samson Shinn which was submitted as evidence in the trial.*

COLUMBUS Sept 9, 1852

Rev. S. Shinn
DEAR BRO.

In answer to your question "Did I show (when you were here last winter) a willing to attend to the charges which Bro. Ballard prefered against Bro Christie," You seemed disposed to think that before the matter was brought to trial Bro Ballard ought to go to Bro. Christie and see if he could not become reconciled to his Brothers, Nevertheless you did go to Bro Christies and bring him (Christie) with you to Bro Ballards at which time & place Bro Christie made such acknowledgements and confessions that Bro Ballard said if said Christie would make the same before the society of which they both were members he (Ballard) would be satisfied and perhaps added he would be satisfied with such acknowledgements & confessions if the society would be.

Yours truly
SAM'L ELLIOTT

J. RECORD OF THE TRIAL OF THE REVEREND DANIEL J. SNOW, CHARGED WITH IMMORALITY, CONTUMACY, AND UNMINISTERIAL CONDUCT

Members of the Methodist clergy were subject to careful check. At every annual conference the names of all members were read and opportunity given for any criticisms. The minutes of the annual meetings indicate that this became largely a matter of form. The censure of ministers arose with much greater frequency in another way—that of bringing charges before a committee of the quarterly or annual conference.

The trial of Rev. Daniel J. Snow offers evidence of how every act of imprudence might become the subject of an official trial. Snow, admitted to the ministry on trial in 1843, seemingly served with satisfaction until 1853, when he was brought to trial. Again in 1856 Rev. Peter Cartwright, presiding elder and famous frontier preacher, brought charges against Snow, holding that he was guilty of immorality, contumacy, and unministerial conduct. According to the specifications, he had accused Cartwright of being responsible for his being made an assistant preacher on the Sangamon Circuit. Second, Snow had said he could prove that Cartwright had called another minister "a dammed son of a Bitch." Third, he had contracted debts and had tried to avoid paying them. Another transgression consisted of having told a Mr. Roberts that the general conference had allowed him two thousand dollars when this was not true. Snow was also charged with having borrowed the records regarding an earlier trial and then refusing to return them, thereby preventing the Illinois Conference from taking action on his case. Finally, he had preached in Methodist churchs after being expelled. Snow was first found guilty before the annual conference of 1856 and again the following year. While all charges against Snow were sustained, many of the specifications were not.

1. *Charges preferred against Rev. D. J. Snow by Rev. Peter Cartwright at the Illinois Annual Conference in 1857.*

Charges preferd against Rev. D. J. Snow by P. Cartwright

1st charge Immorality

Spe. 1st Falsehood in stating in an Editorial published in a paper Edited by the said Snow "that through the influence of P. Cartwright I was removed from the charge of my work and placed as assistant preacher on Sangamon Circuit

" 2nd falsehood in saying P. Cartwright had call a certain D. D. (evidently refering to A. W. Cummings) a dammed son of a Bitch.

" 3rd falsehood in saying he could prove him (Cartwright) guilty of using the above language by Rev. A. Poe

" 4th in contracting a debt with Mrs. Forsyth of Springfield Ills. and then indeavouring to defraud her out of the amount.

" 4th Falsehood in stating to Roberts in Berlin some time in May or June of 1856 that the general conference had allowed him two thousand dollers as compensation for the time he had lost while located and expelled from the church, and that the general conference would have paid him the amount, but had not the funds on hand, but, promised him the funds as soon as they could get them.

" 6th slander Chargeing P. Cartwright with Profanity.

" 7th in violating his promise to pay money Borrowed of G. Rutledge, J. Moore, W. J. Rutledge, J. F. Jacques, Hiram Buck and others.

" 8th in contracting debts and failing to pay them.

1st a debt due Isaac ——

2nd a debt due E. M. Henkle

3rd a debt due T. Candle

Charge 2nd Contumacy

Spe 1st in withholing the documents connected with his trial of Exspulsion, therby puting it out of the Power of the dellegates of the Illinois Conference to defend the action of said conference in his Exspulsion and thus trading with contempt the authority of S*d* Conference

Spe, 2nd in Preaching in Waverly, Little York, and other Places after his Exspulsion from the church

Charge 3rd unministerial and unchristian conduct

spe 1st in wrighting insulting and abusive letters to P. Cartwright, I. C. Kimber and R. Andrews

QUINCY Oct. 21st 1856 PETER CARTWRIGHT

2. *Decision of the committee conducting the trial of Rev. D. J. Snow in 1857.*

The charges and specifications were read to the committee

1st Charge was then taken up—*Immorality*

1st Specification. *Falsehood.* In stating in an editorial published in a paper edited by the said Snow "that through the influence of P. Cartwright I was removed from the charge of my work, and placed as assistant preacher on Sangamon circuit."

The committee decided that the testimony does not sustain the Specification in the manner and form in which it is presented.

Affirmative 11 Negative 3

Specification 2nd *Falsehood* In saying that Peter Cartwright had called a certain D. D. (evidently refering to A. W. Cummings) a damned Son of a bitch.

It was sustained unanimously.

Specification 3rd Falsehood. In saying that he could prove him (Cartwright) guilty of using the above language by Rev. A. Poe.

It was sustained—unanimously—

Specification 4th. In contracting a debt with Mrs Forsythe of Springfield Ill. and then endeavoring to defraud her out of the amount.

Not sustained by 8 to 6

Specification 5th Falsehood In stating to Mr Roberts of Berlin some time in May or June of 1856 that the General Conference had allowed him two thousand Dollars as compensation for the time he had lost while located and expelled from the church, and that the General Conference would have paid him the amount, but had not the funds on hand, but promised him the funds as soon as they could get them.

Not sustained 13 to 1

Specification 6th Slander: In charging P. Cartwright with profanity.

Sustained

Specification 7th In violating his promise to pay money borrowed of George Rutledge, John Moore, Wm. J. Rutledge, J. F. Jacques, Hiram Buck and others.

Not sustained

Do the specifications that are sustained, sustain the charge of immorality?

The charge was unanimously sustained.

2nd Charge Contumacy

Specification 1st. In withholding the documents connected with his trial and expulsion, there by putting it out of the power of the delegates of the Illinois Conference to defend the action of said Conference in his expulsion and thus treating with contempt the authority of said Conference

Sustained.

Specification 2nd In preaching in Waverly, Little York and other places after his expulsion from the church.

Sustained

The specification being sustained—Do they sustain the *charge*.

The charge was unanimously sustained.

Charge 3rd Unministerial and unchristian conduct.

Specification 1st In writing insulting and unchristian letters to P. Cartwright, I. C. Kimber and R. Andrews. Unanimously sustained.

The specification being sustained does the specification sustain the charge?

Yes It was sustained.

The committee in view of all the circumstances connected with this case offer the following resolution:

That Bro D. J. Snow be and is hereby suspended from all ministerial functions in the Methodist E. Church for one year.

Adopted 10 to 3.

K. RECORD OF THE TRIAL OF THE REVEREND BENJAMIN NEWMAN, CHARGED WITH FRAUD, IMMORALITY, AND FALSEHOOD

Methodist clergymen very often were engaged in farming or business. As farmers or businessmen, they were sometimes accused of practices which were not strictly ethical. Such was the case of Benjamin Newman, who was admitted on trial by the Illinois Conference in 1843, and who first served the charge at Buckheart and in 1845 moved to Sangamon. In 1856 he was stationed at Lynnville in the Jacksonville District and the following year at Mattoon in the Paris District. In 1859 he was on trial before the Illinois Annual Conference on charges of fraud, immorality, and falsehood. Newman was accused of borrowing a revolver, of taking care of secular business on Sunday, of using profanity, of misrepresenting some horses and cows he had sold, of evading officers of the law, and of threatening to strike a man with a chair. In addition, it was specified that he made an assignment in favor of some of his creditors while not providing for others. In the trial, which lasted three days, there were more than seventy pages of testimony, while no fewer than twenty-nine witnesses appeared. After the trial several depositions were taken by the committee. While Newman was convicted on all three charges, it was held that a majority of the specifications were unsustained. Newman was suspended from all ministerial services and church privileges until the ensuing annual conference. He stated his intention to appeal. The records of a new trial are not available, but the depositions taken after he had been found guilty in 1859 are in his favor. The records of the annual conferences for 1860 reveal that Newman was stationed at Manchester, in the

Jacksonville District. Evidently the annual conference of 1860 reversed the previous verdict.

1. *Deposition of H. W. Johnson taken by the committee after the trial of the Rev. Benjamin Newman.*

The Deposition of H. W. Johnson taken at Concord August 21st 1860.

I H. W. Johnson testify and say

Q by Deft. Was not my indebtedness more than one hundred Dollars when I confessed that judgement to you.

An it was

Q by Deft. Was not that judgement made to secure my indebtedness to you and to indemnify you for other liabilities and assisting me in Redeeming my Lands that had been sold and carrying on my Buisness

Ans It was

Q By Deft. Was there any intention of Fraud manifested on my part.

Ans there was not any

Q By Deft. have you not assisted me in money and time on my Farm to a Large amount

Ans. Yes

Q By Deft. Is there any Article between you and me by Which you were to help me Settle up my buisness

Ans. Yes

Q By Deft. Was that Article to assist my Creditors or not.

Ans. It was to assist them.

Q By Deft. In what way was it to assist my Creditors

Ans. in Redeeming lands that had been sold and in Paying debts.

Q By Pros What amount of Value Received in Cash or time had Newman Received of you up to the time the Judgement was Conferred.

Ans. Two hundred and fifty three Dollars as near as I can now Recolect

Q By Pros. What is the date of that Article between you and Newman

Ans. Some time in February 1859.

Q By Pros how much money did you loan Newman and at What time.

Ans. I let Newman have forty Dollars in fifty one and fifty five Dollars in 1854.

Q By Pros What debts were you to assist Newman in Paying

Ans Such debts as were Pressing Newman Most

Q By Pros How much did Newman owe you besides that Money.

Ans One hundred and fifty Eight Dollars

Q By Deft. When was this ammt. Recovered to

Ans. the first of February 1859

Q By Deft do you conceive that any of my Creditors Could be defrauded by the Contract between you and me

Ans. I do not

Q By Deft. did I not say that my object was to Pay all my debts and to save my lands from being Sacrificed to the injury of my Creditors

Ans Yes

Q By Pros did Newman say he intended to pay all his debts

Ans. He did

Closed.

2. *The Deposition of Duttin Boyde taken by the committee after the trial of Rev. Benjamin Newman.*

The Deposition of Duttin Boyde taken at the House of D. Gigen August 23rd 1860.

Q By Deft. How long have you known me

Ans Eight years

Q By Deft. You have had considerable dealings with me in that time

Ans Yes

Q By Deft have you ever known me to avoyed paying any just debt

An No

Q By Deft What were my circumstances before the —— flood in 1858

An Well I considered it mighty good

Q By Deft What do you consider my losses by high water in 1858

An I can not say how many dollars but it would be very large

Q By Deft Did H R Gillispie opperate for me as my foreman

Ans Thats what I have heard him say

Q By Deft Do you know that he squandered a good deal of my money and property

An Yes

Q By Deft Do you know of my acting dishonorable with any body during your acquaintance with me

Ans I never did

Q By Pros What do you consider Newman worth before the high water of 1858

Ans I do not know

Q By Pros Did Gillispie tell you that he was Newmans foreman

Ans I heard him swear to it in my presence before a Justice of the Peace

Q By Deft How long have you known H R Gillispie

Ans Thirteen years

Q By Deft. What kind of a man is he considered in the naborhood

Ans he is a man that almost every body in the naborhood fears

Q By Deft Is he a law abiding man

Ans Wen it suits him wen it does not suit him he would not abide the Law

Q By Deft. Did he have a large amount of my stock pend up and would not give them up—defending them with shot guns and pistols

Ans Yes

Q By Deft. What time was this

Ans The first of March 1859

Q By Deft Would I have been safe in going about my stock and farm without arms

Ans I think not

Q By Deft Did you ever hear him threaten me in any way

Ans Yes I heard him say he would give him Hell

Q By Pros Do you know what was the cause of Gillispie making threats against Newman

Ans Because Newman wanted cattle out of the pen

Q By Pros Do you know if Newman was in debt to Gillispie

Ans I do not know that he was

Q By Pros Do you believe that Gillispie would have hurt Newman if he went where the stock was

Ans he said he would

Q By Pros had Newman and Gillispie been very friendly up to this time

Ans Yes

Q By Pros Do you know that this stock belonged to B. Newman

Ans Gillispie made oath before a Justice of the Peace that he had not to the amount of One Dollar in the stock on the farm

Q By Deft What is Gillispies character for truth in the naborhood

Ans I consider it poor

Q By Pros have you ever had any difficulty with Gillispie

Ans I never have only when he failed to fullfil his word

Q By Deft have you ever known me to misrepresent in any of my dealings

Ans I never did

DUTTIN BOYD

CHAPTER XIV

Methodist Publishing Activities and the Distribution of Literature in the West

METHODIST printing interests are nearly as old as Methodism itself, for John Wesley spent much time in preparing tracts, pamphlets, and books for publication. Beginning about 1738, he completed 371 books and pamphlets for the press before his death fifty years later. Transferred to America, Methodism found it difficult to get these books, and pirating of the texts began on the American side of the Atlantic. Robert Williams, a "plain, artless, indefatigable preacher of the gospel," reprinted several of Wesley's works after coming to Virginia in 1769. This wildcat printing was stopped by the first American Conference in 1773. By a resolution, Williams was allowed to sell the books he had on hand but enjoined to "print no more."

The centralization of printing came in 1789, when the Methodist Book Concern was organized, with John Dickins, an educated itinerant of English birth, as agent. The new agent served as pastor of St. George's Church in Philadelphia at the same time. Dickins published 114,000 books and tracts before his death in the yellow-fever epidemic of 1798. Under Ezekiel Cooper, his successor as agent, the Book Concern grew rapidly. By 1808, when Cooper retired, the business was worth $45,000, although in 1798 he had been forced to borrow $800 on his own account to continue its work. John Wilson, who had been appointed assistant to Cooper, was made agent, and Daniel Hitt, who had served for some years as Bishop Asbury's traveling companion, was made assistant. Wilson died within two years, and Hitt was named agent by the General Conference of 1812, with Thomas Ware as his assistant.

Although Methodism had been on the western scene since the 1780's, it was not until the time of Hitt and Ware that the problem arose of getting enough books distributed to the West and the money returned for their purchase. With the denomination growing from 2,800 to 175,000 members in three decades, however, a demand came from the Ohio Conference for a bookroom west of the Alleghenies. This call was not answered until 1820, when the General Conference appointed Martin Ruter, principal of the New Market Wesleyan Academy in Massachusetts, as first agent of the Western Branch, with its office in Cincinnati. Ruter sold only $4,000 worth of books the first year, but, by the time he left in 1828 to become president of Augusta College, he had done much to sow the seeds of an educated Methodist clergy and laity in the West.

Methodism's first western periodical was William Beauchamp's short-lived *Western Christian Monitor,* established at Chillicothe, Ohio, in 1816. Later the *Methodist Magazine,* established in 1818, and especially the *Christian Advocate,* a weekly religious newspaper established in 1826 for the whole denomination, both published in New York, circulated widely in the West. With the *Western Christian Advocate,* which began weekly publication at Cincinnati in 1834 under the editorship of Thomas A. Morris, a westerner, the Methodist church felt that it was possible to reach its "230,000 members and 840 traveling preachers" in the West. The hope was well founded, for the paper had 5,700 subscribers in three years, 10,000 in five, and had one of the largest periodical circulations in the country by 1840, when it boasted more than 15,000 paid subscriptions. Because of the growing power of the West, the Western Book Concern was made an independent enterprise in 1836, dependent for orders only upon the General Conference. The founding of the *Ladies Repository and Gleanings of the West* in 1840 and the schism of the church in 1844 over the slavery question marked the end of a period for the Western Book Concern. These events had demonstrated the strength of the western printing interests in Methodism and the beginning of a new period, in which its interests would become distinctly sectional in nature.

The following source materials cover the coming of the publishing interests of Methodism to the West, the general activities of the Book Concern there, and the book business as it affected particular itinerants in particular situations. For the detailed story of Methodist publishing interests in the West see the unpublished B.D. thesis of Millard G. Roberts, "The Methodist Book Concern in the West, 1800–1850" (University of Chicago, 1942).

I. THE SPREAD OF THE BOOK BUSINESS TO THE WEST

A. RULES ON PUBLISHING ADOPTED BY THE FIRST AMERICAN CONFERENCE, PHILADELPHIA, 1773[1]

None of the preachers in America [is] to reprint any of Mr. Wesley's books without his authority (when it can be gotten) and the consent of their brethren.

[1] *Minutes of the Annual Conferences of the Methodist Episcopal Church,* Vol. I: *1773–1828,* p. 5.

Robert Williams[2] [is] to sell the books he has already printed, but to print no more, unless under the above restrictions.

B. REPORT OF THE BOOK COMMITTEE TO THE GENERAL CONFERENCE OF 1792[3]

The undersigned, to whom was referred the examination of the accounts of Mr. John Dickins,[4] relative to the business of the Book Fund, respectfully report:

[2] Robert Williams had been a local preacher under Wesley in England and had come to America in October, 1769, with permission from Wesley to labor under the direction of the regular missionaries. He preached in New York and Pennsylvania and especially in Maryland and Virginia. Early Methodist literature speaks of him as the "Apostle of Methodism to Virginia." After his marriage in 1774 he ceased traveling in the ministry and died in 1775. Devereux Jarratt, with whom he worked in Virginia, spoke of him as a "plain, simple-hearted, pious man." Before 1773 he had published some of Wesley's sermons and other Methodist literature. In regard to one of these publications, Wesley wrote to Thomas Rankin on December 4, 1773; "I have written to Robert Williams and given him leave to print the *Notes* on my account; nothing on *his own.* I never knew he did till afterward" (John Telford [ed.], *The Letters of the Reverend John Wesley, A.M.* [London: 1931], VI, 57). For a biography of Williams see William B. Sprague, *Annals of the American Pulpit* (New York, 1865), VII, 11–13.

[3] This unsigned and undated paper is in the handwriting of Thomas Haskins, who, with Henry Willis, John Dickins, and the current Philadelphia preacher, made up the first Book Committee on record, appointed by the General Conference of 1792 (Lewis Curts [ed.], *The General Conferences of the Methodist Episcopal Church from 1792 to 1896* [Cincinnati and New York, 1900], p. 42).

[4] John Dickins (1746–98), a native of London, England, was well qualified to be the organizer of American Methodism's publishing interests. An exception to the generally prevailing uneducated ministry, he had a literary education which gave him a good knowledge of Latin and Greek. His name first appears in the *Minutes* as book steward in 1789, when he was pastor of St. George's in Philadelphia. It was he who published, in 1789–90, American Methodism's first periodical, the *Arminian Magazine.* The first book he issued in his capacity of book steward was Wesley's abridgment of Thomas à Kempis' *Imitation of Christ* (Philadelphia, 1789). His catalogue for 1795, a single sheet entitled "Books Published by John Dickins. . . . . For the Use of the Methodist Societies in the United States of America," included twenty-eight printed items, among which were Wesley's *Notes on the New Testament, Journals, Sermons* and other smaller treatises; the *Works of Fletcher;* the *Arminian Magazine;* the 1792 *Discipline; The Experience and Travels of Freeborn Garrettson;* devotional works by à Kempis, Doddridge, Baxter, Law, and Mrs. Rowe; the *Pocket Hymnbook; Tracts* on baptism and slavery; a children's *Catechism,* and others (Bostwick Hawley, "The Methodist Book Concern and Its Literature," *Methodist Quarterly Review,* LIV [1872], 40–54). Asbury described Dickins as "a man of great piety, [with] great skill in learning, drinks in Greek and Latin swiftly; yet prays much, and walks close with God" (*Journal of Rev. Francis Asbury, 1771–1786* [New York, 1852], I, 377).

That in their opinion (after the investigation of the accounts) the principal on which the Books were originally opened and the mode in which they have been kept by Mr. Dickins is fair and correct, that they will not only stand the test of the strictest scrutiny, but strongly mark the knowledge, industry, integrity and disinterestedness of his head and heart in the management of the whole business, and your committee is of the opinion that too much praise cannot be given Mr. Dickins when it is known under what disadvantages he has labored from the commencement of the business up to the present.

Few instances occur where an Agent or Factor has put at stake his own capital and risqued his all for the benefit of his employer and still fewer, where no compensation, or at least a very inadequate one, has been asked for the use and risque of that capital.

Yet this is a true state of facts as it respects Mr. Dickins. He began the business for the connexion on his own capital and from an accurate examination of the cash account find he has for 7½ years been in advance on an average £111..18s..0; that he has never forborne to make a charge of the whole of the legal interest justly due him, in short, our astonishment at his unexampled good conduct and management is not a little excited on the review of the whole of the business and are of opinion that the Conference will not fail to see Mr. Dickins merits all the confidence reposed in him by them and that nothing on their part will be wanting to render his situation less embarrassing, either by supplying a capital or forbearing to authorize any considerable draught from the Book Fund for 12 or 18 months to come, when in our opinion a sufficient active capital may be found for conducting the business to best advantage of the connection. We forbear to make any further remarks on the business, only that we think, in addition, to Mr. Dickins' present allowance, an additional sum of $200 might, with the greatest propriety, be added to his present allowance, with a sum to enable him to procure a room exclusively to deposit and keep the unbound impressions of the several books.... and other materials belonging to the business.[5]

[5] In 1792 Dickins' complete salary was: "1. Two hundred dollars for a dwelling-house and a book-room. 2. Eighty dollars for a boy. 3. Fifty-three and a third dollars for firewood. 4. Three-hundred-thirty-three dollars to clothe and feed family" (Curts, *op. cit.*, p. 42).

C. RESOLUTION ON THE *METHODIST MAGAZINE* GENERAL CONFERENCE OF 1796[6]

Will the Conference recommend, and engage to promote the publication of a magazine entitled *The Methodist Magazine,* which shall consist of compilations from the British magazines, and of original accounts of the experiences of pious persons, and shall be published in monthly numbers?

Ans. The Conference will recommend such a magazine, and desire that it may be printed.[7]

N.B.—The propagation of religious knowledge by the means of the press is next in importance to the preaching of the gospel. To supply the people therefore with the most pious and useful books, in order that they may fill up their leisure hours in the most profitable ways, is an object worthy the deepest attention of their pastors. On this account we are determined to move in the most cautious manner in respect to our publications. We have a great esteem for our general book-steward, and are much obliged to him for his fidelity and usefulness in his important office; but we shall in future submit our publications to the judgment of no single person.[8] The books of infidelity and profaneness with which the States at present abound demand our

[6] *Journals of the General Conference of the Methodist Episcopal Church,* Vol. I: *1796–1836* (New York, 1855), p. 17.

[7] Previously, in 1789–90, two volumes of the *Arminian Magazine: Consisting of Extracts and Original Treatises on General Redemption,* had appeared, "Printed in Philadelphia, by Prichard & Hall, in Market Street, and sold by John Dickins, in Fourth Street (East Side) near the corner of Race Street." Despite the title, it contained some surprisingly interesting American Methodist materials, such as a biography of William Adams of Virginia, Asbury's *Journal* for 1771–72, Coke's *Journal* for 1784–85, the *Address* of the Methodist bishops to President Washington in 1789 and his *Reply,* and information on the "State and Description of Cokesbury College." This magazine had failed for lack of support, and in 1797 Dickins, pursuant to the action of the General Conference of 1796 here quoted, published the first issue of the *Methodist Magazine.* It, too, failed after two volumes and was not resumed until the first volume of the new *Methodist Magazine* appeared under Soule and Mason in 1818.

[8] In 1797 a larger Book Committee was appointed, "to whom all works were to be submitted before they were published, except such as were ordered by the General Conference." The new committee included Ezekiel Cooper, who after Dickins' death in 1798 became book agent, Thomas Ware, John McClaskey, Christopher Spry, William

strongest exertions to counteract their pernicious influence; and every step shall be taken, which is consistent with our finances, to furnish our friends from time to time with the most useful treatises on every branch of religious knowledge. And the consideration, that all the profits shall be lodged in our chartered fund for the benefit of the distressed preachers, both travelling and superannuated, will, we trust, prove a considerable additional inducement to our brethren to purchase our books.[9]

D. RESOLUTIONS ON THE PRINTING AND CIRCULATION OF BOOKS, GENERAL CONFERENCE OF 1800[10]

It shall be the duty of every presiding elder, where no book-steward is appointed, to see that his district be duly supplied with books: he is to request the superintendent to send such books as are wanted, and give direction to whose care the same are to be sent; and he is to take the oversight of all the books sent to his district, and to account with the superintendent for the same: he is to have the books distributed among the several circuits in his district, in such quantities and in such a manner as he may judge proper from his own information, and keep an account with each preacher, who receives and sells the books: he is to receive the money and forward it to the superintendent. When the presiding elder is removed, he is to make a full settlement with the superintendent for all the books sold in his district, and make

---

McLenahan, Charles Cavender, Richard Swain, and Solomon Sharp. The Book Concern was then located in Philadelphia, and these men were all members of the Philadelphia Conference (*Minutes*, Vol. I: *1773–1828*, p. 77).

[9] As James Porter put it, writing on the history of the Book Concern in the *Methodist Quarterly Review* (XLIX [1867], 274), its object was *"not to make money,* but *to do good."* The Chartered Fund, to aid "distressed travelling preachers, ... the families of travelling preachers, ... superannuated and worn-out preachers, and the widows and orphans of preachers," was established by the General Conference of 1796. The profits of the Book Concern, after debts and overhead expenses were paid, were deposited in this fund (*Journals of the General Conference of the Methodist Episcopal Church*, Vol. I: *1796–1836*, pp. 20–22).

[10] *Ibid.*, pp. 45–46. These demonstrate the excellence of the Methodist type of organization for purposes of distribution and sale of literature. During the same session of the General Conference, Ezekiel Cooper (1763–1847), a native of Caroline County, Maryland, who in 1798 had succeeded Dickins as head of the book business, was officially appointed to that office. He served until 1808.

a transfer to his successor of all the books and accounts left with the preachers in the district, the amount of which shall go to his credit, and pass to the debit of his successor. Let a certificate of the amount of such transfer be sent to the superintendent.

It shall be the duty of every preacher, who has the charge of a circuit, to see that his circuit be duly supplied with books, and to take charge of all the books sent to, or that may be in his circuit, and account with the presiding elder for the same. When a preacher leaves his circuit, he must settle with the presiding elder for all the books he has disposed of, and make out an inventory of all that are remaining unsold, which must be collected at one place, the amount of which shall go to his credit and be transferred to his successor, who is to take charge of the same. In case the preacher who has the charge of a circuit be negligent in disposing of books, let the presiding elder commit the charge of the books to another.

The preachers shall be allowed for their trouble not less than fifteen, nor more than twenty-five per cent., upon the wholesale price for all the books they sell; but the per cent. shall be regulated as in the judgment of the superintendent the different impressions will afford, one-third of which the presiding elder shall have for his trouble, and the other two-thirds shall be allowed to the preachers who sell them in their different circuits.

There shall be no draft made upon the Book Concern, until the debts are discharged and a sufficient capital provided for carrying on the business, after which the profits arising from the books shall be regularly paid to the Chartered Fund, and the said profits applied, with the annual income of the funded stock, to the support of the distressed traveling preachers and their families, the widows and orphans of preachers, &c.

It shall be the duty of the preacher who travels with either of the bishops, if he be authorized by the superintendent, to act as his agent in the settlement of accounts, or in transacting any business belonging to the Concern.[11]

[11] As Asbury grew older and the work more complex, he adopted the practice of taking with him on his episcopal tours a traveling companion, usually one of the younger preachers. For instance, Jesse Lee traveled with him in 1798 and 1799. Others who served him in this capacity were Henry Boehm, Daniel Hitt, and John W. Bond. The other bishops, beginning with Whatcoat in 1800, did the same.

E. RESOLUTIONS CONCERNING BOOK BUSINESS TRANSACTIONS, OHIO ANNUAL CONFERENCE, 1829–31[12]

Minutes from September 3, 1829, Bishop Roberts presiding.

The committee appointed to settle the accounts of Presiding Elders and preachers for Books, Reported in part and on motion the report was taken up:

Jacob Young disputed a transfer purporting to have been made to him by William Swage several years since amounting to $140.55½. After hearing the explanations of Bro. J. Young and the Book Comm. it was moved, seconded and carried, that Jac. Young be and hereby is exonerated from the above transfer.

Alfred M. Loraine disputed the account against him amounting to $9.75 cts. It was moved and carried that A M Loraine be exonerated from paying the above acc't.

Minutes from September 8, 1830, Bishop Soule presiding.

Bishop Soule presented an address from the Book Agents at N.Y. and also an exhibit of the Agents to the N.Y. Ann. Conf., which was read.

It was moved and carried that G. R. Jones, J. B. Finley, I. Collins, and T. A. Morris be appointed a special comm. to examine and settle the account of D. Young with the M. Book Concern on principles of equity, and justice and report thereon.

Brother Gilruth presented a manuscript on the subject of Baptism which on the motion was referred to the Book Agent and Book Comm. in Cin[cin]n[ati] or any two of them, either to publish or return.[13]

[12] These excerpts are from the original "Journal" of the Ohio Annual Conference, Volume II (1827–40), in the library of Ohio Wesleyan University, Delaware, Ohio. Photostatic copies are available in the University of Chicago Libraries.

[13] Gilruth writes in his manuscript "Journal," May 3, 1831: "I received a letter from my old friend J. B. Finley[.] 'This day (says he) I got the committy & Book agent together on your Manuscript and all though with some alterations [we] think it would be a good work for many readers & usefull to some extent—yet it is the opinion of the committy at this time [that] the sales would not justify the Publication & that Mr Watson on that subject & other peices are sufficient for the demand of our people.' This was a Manscript on baptism which I had written for the express use of the M E Church because I knew of no work on that subject unconnected with other works in circulation, & from 11 years observation was convinced of the need of a treatice on that subject

The Comm. appointed to settle the Book Acct. of D. Young reported; and their report was approved and the Secretary directed to furnish the Agent with a copy thereof.

Following Resolution was adopted:

Resolved by the Ohio Ann. Conf. that considering the relation in which we stand to the book concern, together with the several periodicals issuing from that establishment, the aid we derive from the periodicals, an auxiliary in spreading the gospel of truth; as well as the pecuniary aid our ministry derive from the profit thereof; we view it to be our imperious duty as Methodist Ministers, and it is hereby requested of every member of this conference, to use his best endeavors:

First: to collect all the debts that are now due or may be due hereafter to the Book Concern of the M.E. Church, within his respective charge, either for books, purchased or periodicals.

Second: that every practicable exertion be used to sell the old stock of books on hand, which were issued heretofore on commission.

Third: That when any member of the Conference wishes to purchase books, either for his own use or for sale; it is improper for him to make those purchases from other establishments than our own in New York or Cincinnati: Provided the books wanted may be there obtained, and

Fourth: that we bestow a more systematic and unremmiting attention to the circulation and spread of the several periodicals issued by the Book Concern of our church in N.Y.[14]

Minutes from September 8, 1831, Bishop Hedding presiding.

A comm[unication] was rec'd from Book Agents at N.Y. enclosing a copy of the Exhibit of the state of the Concern made to the N. York Annual Conference which was read.

---

embracing the whole matter of Baptism. But these Brethren tell me of Watsons and other pieces. . . . . I suspect other reasons, then [than] its not being necessary, has governed that committee. . . . . On the whole I feel rather thankfull then [than] other wise that the work is not published—it is possible that this is for the glory of God: & this is all I mean to aim at. . . . ."

[14] At this time the Methodist Episcopal church published the following periodicals: the *Christian Advocate,* the *Youth's Instructer and Guardian,* the *Child's Magazine,* and the *Methodist Magazine and Quarterly Review.*

Bros J. B. Finley, Thomas A. Morris, and Wm. B. Christie were appointed a Book Committee.

Drafts were made on the Book Concern for $1000.

A communication from N.Y. Ann. Conf. was presented by the Presiding Bishop whereupon the following resolutions were unanimously passed:

Resolved 1st: That the members of this conference believing that the Book Concern of the M.E. Church was established primarily for the purpose of diffusing useful knowledge and scriptural holiness through the land, it is our duty to support its interests, and promote its objects by all lawful means.

Resolved 2nd: That as the profits which may arise from the sale of the Books of this establishment are directed to one of the noblest of charities, we will use our endeavors both publicly and privately, to discourage the sale of such editions of these books as are issued by those who are hostile to its interests; that we will neither purchase nor vend them ourselves, but discourage the purchasing and vending of all such books, and that we use our best exertions to promote the sale of such as are published by our Book Agents.

The following resolution was presented and on motion laid on the table.

Resolved 1st: That the Ohio Annual Conference respectfully recommends to the consideration of the next General Conference the advisability of placing the Book Agency at Cincinnati on more eligible and efficient ground.

Resolved 2nd: That this Conference recommend to the next General Conference the consideration of the propriety of establishing a Western Paper at the Book Room in Cincinnati with suitable arrangements to secure success.[15]

[15] The *Western Christian Advocate,* probably the most widely circulated periodical in the West at that time, was authorized by the General Conference of 1832. Modeled on the plan of the New York *Christian Advocate* (founded 1826), it was a weekly newspaper, with columns for "Ladies" and "Young People" as well as strictly religious intelligence. It reflected the spirit of the West in its opposition to church choirs and theological seminaries. Beginning under the editorship of Thomas A. Morris in 1834, it was served by a succession of able editors, including Charles Elliott (1836–48, 1852–56) and Matthew Simpson (1848–52). The first issue is dated May 2, 1834. For background, history, and content of this important periodical see Millard G. Roberts' unpublished thesis, "The Methodist Book Concern in the West, 1800–1850" (University of Chicago, 1942), chap. iv.

Resolved 3rd: That these resolutions be sent to the Western and Southern Conferences for their concurrence.

II. THE BOOK BUSINESS IN THE WEST

A. LETTER FROM HITT AND WARE, BOOK AGENTS IN NEW YORK CITY, TO JAMES B. FINLEY,[16] SECRETARY OF THE OHIO CONFERENCE, ASKING FOR MONEY DUE THE CONCERN

New York, October 18, 1815

Your communications of the 5th inst. were received yesterday. We readily thank you always for your hearty attention to our business, but greatly regret that you had not forwarded the money, for we are in pressing want, and made our calculations on the remitance from the Ohio Conference. And we must now suffer, unless we can borrow; which indeed is very difficult. We fear you did not receive our communication, or no doubt you would have forwarded the money immediately. This therefore, is to desire you to loose [lose] no time in procureing a draft or Treasury Notes, and forward the amount as soon as may be.

Yours in haste, but
Affection
D Hitt[17] & T. Ware[18]

[16] This and the following letters to Finley are from the "James B. Finley Letters" in the library of Ohio Wesleyan University.

[17] Daniel Hitt (? –1825), a Virginian of German extraction, had entered the itinerant ranks in 1790 and traveled in Pennsylvania, Maryland, and Virginia until his election in 1808 as assistant book agent under John Wilson, whom he succeeded in 1810. He has been described by a contemporary as a "plain and simple" preacher and "an old bachelor of the straitest sect." He seems to have secured the book agency through his close personal friendship with Asbury, whom he served as traveling companion in 1807–8. His indecision in conducting the business is seen in his failure to begin republication of the *Methodist Magazine,* a project urged by the General Conference of 1812. This he left to Joshua Soule, who succeeded him in 1816. For biographical data see the *Methodist Magazine,* IX (1826), 439–40; and Sprague, *op. cit.,* VII, 184–86.

[18] Thomas Ware (1758–1842) had been elected assistant to Hitt by the General Conference of 1812 and served until 1816.

B. LETTER FROM HITT AND WARE TO FINLEY, SHOWING THE DIFFICULTY OF COMMUNICATION AND EXCHANGE ON THE FRONTIER

Nov. 18, 1815

Our situation is more pressing at this time for money, than it has ever been before, and our not receiving the returns from your Conference laid us under the necessity to borrow, such borrowing under the necessity of returning it in twenty or thirty days, and this promise was made on the prospect of receiving from you and the Tennessee Conference. We received a communication from that conference, that the money was received and waited our order. By this mode of procedure, we are reduced to the greater straights, for we had made full calculation on receiving the money both from Ohio and Tennessee Conferences as soon as it possibly could have been conveyed, but instead of which, we are only informed that the money is subject to our order, or instruction, and in sending back these instructions and receiving an answer, there must of necessity be a lapse of several weeks or perhaps two or three months, and all this time we are pressed for the want of money. We do not make these remarks to attach any blame to you, but to evince to you the urgency of the situation and thereby justify ourselves in being this importunate. We have no calculation but that you will have to pay a premium for the accomodation, we have suggested; but a premium is no object with us, pressed as we are at this time for the want of money. Do let us hear from you. May peace and happiness attend you.

We are yours affectionately,
D. Hitt & T. Ware

C. LETTER FROM HITT AND WARE TO FINLEY, SHOWING THE FINANCIAL EXTENT OF THE BOOK BUSINESS IN THE WEST DURING 1815

January 4, 1816

Dear Brother:

Yours of the 18th ult. accompanying nine hundred fifteen dollars was duly received with its contents on the 30th of the same. Likewise, that of the 22nd ult. covering seventeen hundred and fifty dollars was duly received this day, but not in time to answer it by the return mail.

We are under obligation to you for your attention to the business and hope you will accept our sincere thanks for the same. It was wrong information you had received that Kentucky paper was at par; so far from being at par, that the brokers will not take it at less than fifteen percent discount; also promising the notes from the Western part of Pennsylvania and Ohio will be little better. Philadelphia paper is now at 5 percent below par, Baltimore, 9 percent, Washington 9, Georgetown 11. Thus the concern is obliged to sustain these great losses in circulating paper of the bank at a distance. At present we see no hope of any means to remedy these losses.

We would now just remark to you that in your former communication you stated that you had forwarded Nine Hundred and Twenty Dollars. We were very particular in counting and recounting it, and could make but Nine Hundred and Fifteen, and the parcel received to-day, you say Seventeen Hundred and forty nine; there was Seventeen Hundred and Fifty.

On the 30th ult. we received a letter from one of the preachers in Charleston, stating that Mr. Asbury was within about thirty miles of the place, and that such was his state of health, that he did not calculate on attending the Conference. From which we infer that his health becomes more and more precarious.[19]

Our prospects in this city[20] are somewhat pleasing and we hope still to see better times. May peace, happiness and success attend you. Adieu.

We are your friends,
Brethren in Christ.
HITT and WARE

D. LETTER FROM SOULE AND MASON, BOOK AGENTS IN NEW YORK, TO FINLEY, SHOWING EXTENT OF BUSINESS FOR SIX MONTHS OF 1816 IN THE WEST

October 2, 1816

DEAR BROTHER:

We have just received communications from your conference, by which we learn that there is a balance of $1777.72 cents in your hands

[19] This was only a short time before Asbury's death, which occurred on March 31, 1816.

[20] New York.

which waits our order. On the receipt of this you will please to forward the above sum by post as quick as possible, as we are in great want of it.

As it must be in bills of that county, we wish you to send no bills of banks which are not incorporated, or have not a legal charter. You will also endeavor to procure notes of the largest denomination, as it will be more convenient to us, and render the postage less expensive and dangerous. Bills on the following banks will answer our purpose best. Pittsburg, Steubenville, Marietta, Zanesville, Chillicothe, Cincinnati Exporting Company.

We are, dear brother, yours with esteem.

J. Soule[21] and T. Mason[22]

E. LETTER FROM SOULE AND MASON TO FINLEY, SHOWING THE TYPE OF LITERATURE THE BOOK CONCERN PROMOTED FOR SALE IN THE WEST

Dec. 8, 1817

Dear Brother:

Being informed by the Committee of the Ohio Conference that $173 was put in to your hands to exchange and remit to us we have waited in patient but anxious expectation of its arrival till this time and now fearing that some misfortune may have happened to it we think it proper to write.

Should you not have remitted on the reciet of this letter we entreat you to do it without delay as our demand for money is pressing in the extreme and the want of it may be attended with very unpleasant consequences both to ourselves and the Concern.

[21] Joshua Soule (1781–1687), who later was elected bishop and entered the Southern Church in the division of 1845, became book agent in 1816. By his efficient methods he rejuvenated the Book Concern and left it in good shape to Nathan Bangs, his successor, in 1820. In January, 1818, he published the first issue of the new *Methodist Magazine,* authorized by the General Conferences of 1812 and 1816. This periodical, called the *Methodist Magazine and Quarterly Review* after 1830, and the *Methodist Quarterly Review* after 1841, had a run of over a century. At his instigation, largely, the Book Committee in 1820 reported favorably on establishing a bookroom in Cincinnati for the West. For Soule's activities as book agent see Horace M. DuBose, *Life of Joshua Soule* (Nashville and Dallas, 1911), chap viii.

[22] Thomas Mason was elected Soule's assistant by the General Conference of 1816. He served as assistant again from 1832 to 1836, under Beverly Waugh, after whose election as bishop Mason succeeded as book agent (1836–44).

We have received the Letters of Dr. Coke and Mr. Fletcher from London and intend publishing as soon as the state of our funds will admit. We have on hand a fine edition of Observations by Dr. Clarke, a most valuable work in 4 volumes, and should be in the hands of every Methodist preacher.

The first number of the magazine is in the press and will be in circulation by the first of next month.

Yours in love,
SOULE and MASON

F. LETTER FROM MASON, BOOK AGENT IN NEW YORK, TO FINLEY, MISSIONARY TO THE INDIANS AT SANDUSKY, SHOWING THE USE OF THE BOOK CONCERN IN ASSISTING OTHER INTERESTS OF THE CHURCH IN THE WEST

December 22, 1823

Rev. Jas. B. Finley
DEAR BROTHER,

This day rec. a letter from Wm. Brown, cor. Secy. of the Baltimore Conference Missy. Society, saying "that a letter had been recd. from you in the City of Baltimore, in which you stated that you had recd. information from me that the Juvenile Finleyan Missy. Mite Society of Baltimore had requested that you select and take into the Missy. School another Indian Boy, to be named John Summerfield,[23] and that the Society had appropriated (or promised to give) one hundred dollars *per annum* for the maintenance and education of said Indian Boy"—If I used the term "one hundred dollars per annum" in my communication to you, it was from a misunderstanding on the subject. It is as follows—viz "The managers of the Juvenile Society have also passed a Resolution appropriating one hundred dollars ($100) for the education and maintenance of the child to be selected, and named John Summerfield,—for four years."

Mr. Brown now says "the sum appropriated is intended for the whole term of four years, being twenty-five dollars per annum, the

[23] John Summerfield (1798–1825), who had come to America from England in 1821 and joined the Troy Conference, was then at the height of his popularity as one of American Methodism's most eloquent preachers. After his death the American Tract Society published the *Memoirs of the Life and Ministry of the Rev. John Summerfield, A.M.*, by John Holland.

sum for which as the Society has been informed, a child could be supported and educated for one year."—This information I am requested to give you to prevent any mistake and embarrassment on the subject.

On the 29th Sept. we forwarded a box of clothing from the Female Missy. Society of this city, directed to you and consigned to the care of Mr. Brooks, watchmaker at Buffaloe, which I hope you have received ere this—

On the 8th Nov. we recd. a letter from John L. Meridith P.M. at Car's X Roads Coshocton County, Ohio, in which he informs us that he had been requested by a number of the members of the Methodist Church to obtain the agency of the M[ethodist] Magazine in that section of the Country, and take in Payment articles of produce for the use of the Sandusky Mission—This plan would no doubt be very accommodating to our friends who have but little money; provided you could take the articles for the use of the Mission and become accountable to the Book Concern for the amt.—We referred him to you to make the arrangement—They proposed to take the agency for every 6th copy. The Board of Managers and the Friends Mission in this City rejoice at the prosperity of your work among the Wyandote brethren, and we heartily wish you good success among others also in the name of the Lord.

Communications from you will always be acceptable to your affectionate brother

in Christ
THOMAS MASON

G. LETTER FROM MARTIN RUTER, IN CHARGE OF THE BOOKROOM IN CINCINNATI, TO FINLEY, MISSIONARY TO THE INDIANS AT SANDUSKY

CINCINNATI, February 2, 1825

DEAR BROTHER:

May grace, mercy peace and a thousand blessings be your portion. We enjoy confortable seasons here, and are moving on with a degree of prosperity. About a hundred have been added at Chillicothe, and Brother Jacob Young writes me that as many as 400 have joined in his district since Conference..... I have here a barrel of clothing for the Indian children at Sandusky, sent from a place near the Kenhawa; but I know not how to send it to you.

I received so little from the Tennessee Conf. (only the drafts, not any money), that I am not prepared to take any of the drafts that you have, and I know not that I shall be able to do it all before Conference. This is disagreeable to me, for the Agents at New York are quite disposed to find fault with their being sent there. Yet I know of no other way at present.

There is some prospect of a bank being established here, and should that be the case, I could sometimes obtain money in an emergency and later refund it. At present I cannot obtain money only when I have it of my own, and I have already, from my own funds obtained and loaned the Concern $600. But at present I have scarcely enough to support my family.

Peace and quietude I think are likely to prevail in our church. Amen. Remember me at the throne of Grace.

Yours truly in Christ,
M. RUTER[24]

H. LETTER FROM RUTER TO FINLEY, FURTHER DEMONSTRATING THE PLACE OF THE CONCERN IN THE WEST IN CHURCH ECONOMY

CINCINNATI, Jan. 19, 1826

DEAR BROTHER,

I hereby send you a draft of $50 according to your request. It is payable to your order and will require your name on the back of it.

[24] Martin Ruter (1785–1838) was principal of the New Market, New Hampshire, Wesleyan Academy when in 1820 he was elected western book agent by the General Conference and instructed to "reside in Cincinnati, and manage the Concern in the western country under the direction of the [book] editor in New-York." The Ohio Conference was authorized at the same time to appoint a committee of three, "whose duty it shall be to examine the accounts of said agents, and report to the said Conference annually" (*Journals of the General Conference of the Methodist Episcopal Church,* Vol. I: *1796–1836,* p. 225). Ruter began operations at the corner of Elm and Fifth streets, Cincinnati, "in a small office, over the door of which was placed a crude sign, 'Methodist Book Room.'" Finley tells us it was like "the log cabins of our fathers, in which kitchen, dining-room, chamber, and parlor are all in one." Here, the Book Room "comprised the depository, packing room, counting room, and Agent's office" (James B. Finley, *Sketches of Western Methodism* [Cincinnati, 1855], p. 303). Ruter, an educated New Englander, was primarily an educator, greatly concerned with raising the intellectual level of the Methodist church. As such, he proved a capable agent for the West. The "Ruter Press" at Cincinnati was named in his honor.

The balance is placed to your credit. I could not obtain a draft for you on N.Y., but this will answer about as well. I received a number of the Magazine for you, and have paid the postage and shall send it with this letter. The agents at New York ought to have directed it to Sandusky.....

I. LETTER FROM RUTER TO FINLEY OF LIKE NATURE

CINCINNATI, March 29, 1828

BROTHER FINLEY—

It may be necessary for me to say, by way of explanation that we do not sell Sunday School books to ordinary purchasers on credit, any lower than we do other books. When we sell for cash, or to Sabbath Schools by the dozen or hundred, we then sell at the prices mentioned in the Youth's Guardian—and which are mentioned also in some numbers of the Magazine. I have, therefore, charged the Sunday School books as I have the others, and when sold at the reduced prices, you must necessarily have an account kept of such sales and discounts, that it may be allowed in your credit, at settlement.

I have supplied as many books, perhaps, as may be necessary for your district until after General Conference—and you can then receive more.—

Ever yours in Christ.

M. RUTER

J. RESOLUTIONS CONCERNING THE BOOK CONCERN IN THE WEST, OHIO ANNUAL CONFERENCES, 1827–29

Conference of 1827:

The chair reported the following committee: M. Ruter, David Young, John Collins, Jacob Young, James Quinn, James B. Finley and Truman Bishop to take into consideration the propriety or impropriety of continuing a branch of the Book Concern in the Western Country.[25]

A draft was made on the Book Concern for $230.

A resolution authorizing the Book Agent in Cinn. to alter the report of the Book Comm. of the Zanesville Conf. so that instead of

[25] That there was opposition to the Western Book Concern on the part of some western preachers is seen in the fact that the Kentucky Conference in 1831 viewed "with regret and disgust the ungenerous efforts of certain individuals to undermine and ruin the Concern" (A. H. Redford, *Western Cavaliers* [Nashville, 1876], p. 69).

reading "we cancel" it shall read "we relinquish for want of sufficient grounds to establish" certain claims. Was offered, and passed.

Conference of September 18, 1828:

Draft on Book C. for $150.00.

On exhibit of the account of the members of the Ohio Conf. with the Book Concern which was filed with the papers of the Conference. It was moved and carried that the standing Book Committee of last year be continued.

Conference of September 3, 1829:

On motion John F. Wright and Thos. A. Morris were appointed a book committee. to examine the accounts of Presiding Elders and preachers and settle with them in place of the Book Agent who is absent.

Book Committee then read the account containing the balance against the preachers for books.

Draft on Book Concern for $150.

III. THE PREACHER AS BOOK AGENT IN THE WEST

A. LIST OF BOOKS SENT BY SOULE AND MASON TO FINLEY, MAY 17, 1817

RETAIL	1. 2. 3.			
1.12½	% 100	Wesley on Original Sin	92	$ 92
.50	75	Mrs. Cooper	41	30.75
.87½	50	Hervey's Medit.	73	36.50
	40	Wesley's Test.	82	32.80
.87½	500	Hymn Books	73	365.00
.12½	100	Sutcliffe's Sermons	10	10.00
1½	30	Coke's Sermons	5	1.50

B. LISTING BY FINLEY OF BOOKS FOR WHICH HE OWED THE WESTERN BOOK CONCERN AT CINCINNATI

JAMES B. FINLEY TO THE B. CONCERN——DR.

To.	12	Testaments	25	3.00
	12	do. Fullbound	31½	3.75
	36	Death of Caroline Smith	6½	2.25
	36	Sabbath occupations	3	1.08

24	Benson's Hymns	25	6
12	Sabbath School Tracts	3	.36
36	Lessons for Sab. school lerners		4.50
24	of first four numbers of The	12½	2.40
	Child's Magazine	10	
100	Father's advice to children.	6½	6.25
36	Wesley on Catechism no. 1	3	1.08
36	do. no. 2	10	3.60
36	do. no. 3	10	3.60
12	Hints for Sabbath Schools	6½	.75
152	Lessons on cards 1.50 per hundred		2.75
36	Duties of the poor	3	1.08
10	Fletcher's Address	12½	1.25
4	Cradle Hymns	12½	.50
24	Memoirs of E. Higgins	12½	3.
24	Life of 2 Ladies	12½	3.
36	Daryman's Daughter	10	3.60
36	Geo. Gilbert	3	1.08
24	Essays on Prayer	6½	1.50
100	Watts' Hymns	3	3.
36	Shepherd of Salisbury	12½	4.50
36	History of Jesus	12½	4.50
36	Token's for children	10	3.60
24	Newport's Death	6½	1.50
36	Stranger's Offering	6½	2.25
3	Nelson's Journal	43½	1.31½
6	Rules on Health	37½	1.31½
4	Bang's Letters	50	2.
6	Wesley on Original Sin	1.00	6.
6	Reformed Reformed	1.00	6.
30	Hymn Books	75	22.50
50	Sermon on Salvation	12½	6.25
36	Life of James Jones	10	3.60
			125.64½
	Discount 18		22.61½
			103.02½
36	Bundles Tracts at 50 cents		18.00
1203			$121.02½

C. TORN SHEET FROM THE BENJAMIN LAKIN CORRESPONDENCE, LISTING BOOKS SOLD, *CA.* 1812[26]

6	Appeals	70	4.20
12	Nelson's Journal	37½	4.50½
3	Directories	18 34	0.56¼
2	Truth Vindicated	31¼	0.62½
2	Lockington	37½	0.75
12	Catechisms	6¼	.75
1	Set Fletcher	500	5.00
2	Set Notes	300	6.00
2	Wesley's Jour'	100	2.00
3	S[ain]t[s'] Rest	87½	2.62½
9	Mrs Rogers	44	3.96
1	Concordance	200	2.00
18	Minuts	12¼	2.25
		Total	35.22

[back, same sheet] Showing careful check on his profits.

6	appeals	10	60
12	n. Journal	6	78
3	Directons	4	12
2	Truth vd.	5¼	10½
2	Luckington	7½	15
12	Catechisms	1¼	15
1	Set Fletcher	.75	75
2	Notes	50	100
2	W. Journal	15	30
3	St. Rest	12½	37½
9	N. Rogers	9	81
1	Concordance	25	25
18	Minuts	4	72
		comisions	5.00
		1/3 Deduct	1.96
		Remains	$3.92

[26] These accounts, and those that follow, are from manuscripts in the Benjamin Lakin Collection, Divinity School Library, University of Chicago.

D. TORN SHEET, UNDATED (PROBABLY 1816), ON WHICH LAKIN INDICATED BOOKS WHICH PEOPLE ON HIS CIRCUIT WISHED TO BUY[27]

BOOKS WANTED

John Newter	1 Appeal
N. Stevenson	W. Ser.
Samuel Reves	Benson's Yuletides
S. Tatman	1 notes
	1 pre[achers']. experience
Bray	1 Abbott's life
Bro. Bedicord	1 Baxter & Allen
Bro. Lindley	1 Hymn book
Bedicords	2 Baxter & Allen

E. PRIVATE BOOK ACCOUNTS OF LAKIN FOR THE YEARS 1813–14. MOST OF THESE ACCOUNTS WERE CROSSED OUT, INDICATING THE END OF THE TRANSACTION

BOOKS RECEIVE[D]

NOVEMBER 1, 1813

12 Hymn Books
4 Alen and Baxter
6 Disciplines
4 Nefter A Rogers
18 Catechisms
12 Hymn Books
5 Nefter A. Rogers
6 vol. Fletchers Works
3 Abbotts life
6 Christian Pattern
2 Devote Exercise
4 Nelsons Journal
3 Discipline
2 Appeals
2 Allen and Baxter
1 Preachers Experience
2 Bensons life of Fletcher
1 Wesleys Notes

NOVEMBER 29

[None]

4 Christian pattern
2 Disciplines
12 Catechisms

JANUARY 24, 1814

1 Bensons life Fletcher
1 Appeal
1 Abbott life
2 Hymn Books

FEBRUARY 21

2 Nelson Journal
2 Disiplines
1 Wesleys Notes
5 Hymn Books
2 Preachers experience
3 Abbotts life
1 Bensons life of Fletcher
1 Set Fletchers Checks
1 Allen and Baxter
5 Nester A Rogers letters
1 Rules of Composition

[27] All these are crossed out, indicating that they were ordered.

DECEMBER 2

11 Kempis
12 Nelsons Journal
6 Hymn Books
3 Allen & Baxter
5 Nester A Rogers
3 Do Letters
2 Preachers Experience
1 Wesley s Sermon

DECEMBER 27

1 Sett of Fletcher's Checks
1 Bensons life of Fletcher
1 Preachers experience
1 Abbotts life
2 Allen and Baxter
2 Hymn Books

MARCH 14

1 Preachers Experience
1 Abbotts life
2 Testaments
24 Catechisms

APRIL 18

4 Testaments
3 Disciplines
6 Important questions
2 Coats productions
1 Nester A. R. letters

MAY 16

1 Testament
1 Allen S. Baxter
3 Catechisms

F. BOOK NOTES, SHOWING THE NUMBER AND TYPE OF BOOKS RECEIVED, AND THE MEANS OF DISTRIBUTING THEM THROUGH THE ITINERANT

TAKEN OUT OF THE BOXES

9 Portraitures
1 Discipline
1 St Rest
1 Truth vindicated
2 Bound Minutes
2 Advisors
1 Set Dictionary

JUNE 19 (1814)

JULY 11

2 Setts Woods Dictionaries
2 Portraitures
2 Sts. Rest
3 Advisors

AUGUST 11

1 Set Woods Dictionary
1 Advisor

BOOKS GIVEN OUT

Susanah Shelby	1	Hymn B.
Samuel Stroud	1	Hymn B
Hugh Barns	4	Catechisms
Do-Do	1	N A Rogers
Bro. Bently	1	Discipline
Isaac Reves	1	N A Rogers
Stephen Tatman	1	Hymn Book
Nehemiah Do	1	Hymn Book
Zachariah Clinton	1	Hymn Book
Nehemiah Tatman	1	Discipline
Durken Murphy	1	Hymn Book
Michael Fenton	1	N A Rogers
Thomas Stevesson	1	Discipline
Alex. Durgan	1	Allen &
Niffen Pelham	1	Allen &
Isaac Mitchel	1	Nelson Jour. pd .25
Abraham Dugan	1	Nelson
Sally Mitchel	1	Nelson
Martha Saton	1	Nelson
Chester Pelham	2	Kempis
Abraham Dugan	1	N A Rogers
Isaac Mitchel	1	N A Rogers
George Mitchel	1	N A Rogers
	1	Benson: life of

G. RECORDS MADE IN 1814 BY LAKIN OF THE BOOKS LEFT WITH MEMBERS ON HIS CIRCUIT, WHO IN TURN SOLD THEM TO THE MEMBERS OF THE LOCAL SOCIETIES

BOOKS LEFT AT DANIEL REES DEC. 6

4 Hymn books— 3 received
3 Nelsons Journal
2 Kempes
1 Nestor A Rogers
1 Preachers Experience
1 Allen & Baxter

LEFT WITH RICH. I TILTON

12
2 Catechisms
1 Hymn Books
3 Hester A Rogers
1 Nelsons Journal
1 Discipline
1 Kempis
1 Allen and Baxter
1 Abbotts life
5 appeals
1 Catechisms

LEFT AT DAVID CLARKS

1 Nester A letters

LEFT AT ELI TRUTHS

1 Preachers Experience
1 Abbotts life
2 Allen and Baxter paid .50
4 Christian Pattern

SAMUEL REVEES	1	Bensons
MARTHA MILLIGAN	1	Nester A Rogers
BETSY BAILEY	1	Hymn Book

SENT ASBURY JONES BY BRO BANES

1 set of Fletchers checks

LEFT L. J. ARMSTRONG

1 Abbotts life

CATHERINE SAML.	1	preachers Exp.	
MOSES SUMMERS	1	Discipline	
GEORGE BENTLY	1	Testament	
DAVID D. ROSS	1	Nelsons Jour.	pd. 25
ELI TRUITT	1	Coats production	pd. 25

WITH JEREMIAH LAWSON	12	Catechisms
AT COUZENS	1	Important Question

G. MITCHELL by Spelham
1 Appeal

Left at Widow Baileys for Bro. Coulter

1 Nestor A Rogers
life and letters .75c

H. PAPER MARKED "BOOKS RETURNED," SHOWING WHAT HAPPENED TO THE UNSALABLE VOLUMES[28]

Books returned unsold

1 Sett of Fletchers checks
3 Disciplines
4 Nelsons Journal
1 Bensons life of Fletcher
1 Preachers Experience
1 Allen and Baxter
3 Abbotts life
2 Wesleys Sermon
1 Appeal
1 Allen [and Baxter]
3 Christian pattern
2 Mrs. Rogers letters
1 Coats production
1 Rule of Composition
1 Important Queftion

Into the Boxes

2 Bound Minits

I. SINGLE SHEET SHOWING THE TOTAL NUMBER AND PRICES OF BOOKS SOLD, AND THE PROFITS LAKIN MADE WHILE ON THE LIMESTONE CIRCUIT IN 1817

39	Hymn Books	$34.12½
14	Hester A Rogers life	10.50
10	Allen and Baxter	5.00
14	Disciplines	5.25
57	Catechisms	3.56½
2	Sets Fletchers Checks	10.00
7	Abbotts life	5.25
18	Kempis	5.62½

[28] These volumes were returned to the Book Concern and credited in full to the itinerant's account.

14	Nelsons Journals	5.25
2	Appeals	1.40
6	Preachers Experience	6.00
4	Bensons life of Fletcher	4.00
2	Devote Exercise	00.50
2	Sets Wesleys Notes	6.00
7	Nester A Rogers letters	1.31¼
1	Coats production	00.10½
7	Teftaments	7.00
5	Important Questions	00.31¼
11	Portraitures	11.00
3	St. Reft	3.00
1	Truth vindicated	00.31¼
6	Advisors	3.00
4	Sets Woods Dictionary	20.00
236	Total	148.58¾
	Commisions	17.83
	Neat produce	130.74¾

J. SINGLE SHEET, DATED JULY 11, 1814, GIVING A SUMMARY OF BOOK SALES BY LAKIN IN THE PRECEDING YEAR[29]

No. 2	3	6	7	8	9		
9	”	56	”	”	”	62	Dictionary
26	3	”	”	”	”	29	Bound sermons
33	2	6	”	17	”	58	Kempis
4	6	”	”	1	”	11	Roe
	—						
”	90	”	”	”	”	90	Portraiture
”	2	”	”	19	”	21	Truth vind.
”	19	”	”	”	”	19	St. Rest
”	”	”	204	209	”	413	Hymnbooks
”	15	”	”	”	61	76	Fine off Book
”	”	”	21	”	”	21	Advisers
”	”	”	”	8	497	505	Discipline
9	”	”	”	”	”	9	Coke Comm.

[29] The numbers at the top represent appointments on his circuit.

K. INVENTORY OF HOUSEHOLD EFFECTS OF LAKIN ON COMING WEST IN 1803–4[30]

Household furniture

		L	S	P
1	Set chane [China] cups	0"	10"	6
1	Table	0"	12"	0
2	bowls	0"	2"	0
2	China mugs 2/6	0"	5"	0
1	Smal pot	0"	6"	0
1	Skillett & lead	0"	7"	6
5	yds Milsin 1/6	0"	7"	6
10	yds Muslin 1/6	0"	15"	0
1	Canster 3	0"	3"	0
3¼	Muslin 2/3 yd	0"	8"	10
1	Small Trunk 18	0"	18"	0
1	Doz needles, 2 shears		1"	1
2	bowls	0"	4"	3
2	glasses		1"	6
6	plates		6"	9
1	Decanter		2"	9
Snippers			3"	0
Tea spoon set			2"	9

L. EXPENSE ACCOUNT OF LAKIN, 1807–8, SHOWING THE SMALL AMOUNT OF ACTUAL CASH HE DEALT WITH OVER A CONSIDERABLE PERIOD OF TIME

Expense Account, 1807–1808

Expence for moveing	$ 8.18
Horse shod	1.25
Shoes moved	0.25
Horse shod	0.75
Feriage	.37½
	11.37½

[30] The following documents, showing the standard of living of the itinerants in the West in the first two decades of the nineteenth century, are evidence of the substantial contribution the book profits made to their economic livelihood.

Expence	
Horse sho[d]	50
same	100
same	50
pint wine	50
Ohio and feed	1"25
feed	$18\frac{1}{2}$
pint wine	50
Cumberland	$18\frac{1}{2}$
Wine	$87\frac{1}{2}$
Ohio	50
Horse shod	1.25
	\$7"$25\frac{1}{2}$

M. EXPENSE ACCOUNTS OF LAKIN FOR HIS TRIPS TO QUARTERLY MEETINGS AND CAMP MEETINGS DURING 1809

February 25 & 26 Qu. Meet.	
Horse shod	\$ .50
Feriage	.$37\frac{1}{2}$
Feriage	.25
Qu m May 20 " 21	
2 Feriages	\$0.25
2 Feriages	25
2 Feriages	25
Horse Shod	75
2 Feriages	25
Camp Meeting Aug. 19–20	
Shoes moved	\$0.25
2 Feriages	0.25
Horse Shod	1.75
2 Feriages	25
Horses Shod	1.25

N. QUARTERAGE RECEIVED BY LAKIN IN 1812, COMPARED WITH HIS BOOK PROFITS DURING SIX MONTHS OF THE YEAR 1809

Quarteredge recived 1812

1. Quarter	$11 79
	10 25
	42½
2. Quarter	29 79
	2 50
	25
	13 32¼
3. Quarter	18 85
	1 12½
4. Quarter	27 "88¼
	4 "75
	110 94
For Horse	21 00

Book profits of Benjamin Lakin, 1809, listed by quarters

1 Quarter	$ 5 42¼	
	1 6½	
	3 50	
	0 56¼	11.15
2 Quarter	17 75	
	74	
	2 66½	
	1.05	
	1.00	
	1.60	25.60
		36.75

CHAPTER XV

Frontier Deeds, Plans of Circuits, Camp-Meeting Rules, Sermons, and Exhortations

I. FRONTIER DEEDS

THE Ebenezer Academy was the first in the long line of Methodist schools in America. The exact date of its founding is unknown, and it is possible that it dates from 1780. The building was constructed of rough stone and was two stories high with a Dutch roof and dormer windows. By 1809 it seems to have passed out of Methodist control. It will be noted that Edward Dromgoole and Peter Pelham are among the trustees. The actual establishment of the school antedated this deed by at least ten years. For a brief history of this school see H. H. Smith, "Ebenezer Academy," *Richmond Christian Advocate,* XLII, No. 24 (1934), 8. For Peter Pelham and the Pelham family see above, Part II of chapter vi.

A. THE EBENEZER SCHOOL, BRUNSWICK COUNTY, VIRGINIA, 1796[1]

This Indenture made the sixth day of August in the year of our Lord one thousand seven hundred and ninety six, between Drury Buckner Stith of Brunswick County and Fanny his wife of the one part. And Ira Ellis, Edward Dromgoole, John Paup, Aaron Brown, Henry Merritt, John Easter, Stith Parham, Peter Pelham, and Peter Robertson Trustees for Ebenezer School, for the time being, and their successors of the other part; Witneseth that the said Drury Buckner Stith for and in consideration of the sum of twenty six pounds current money of Virginia, the recipt whereof he doth hereby acknowledge, he the said Drury Buckner Stith hath granted bargained and sold aliened and confirmed and by these presents doth grant bargain and

[1] Recorded September 25, 1797, Deed Book 47, p. 165, Brunswick County Courthouse, Lawrenceville, Va.

sell alien and confirm unto the said trustees and their successors forever fifty one acres of land situate in the said County of Brunswick and Parish of Saint Andrew on both sides of Burch's Road and bounded as followeth. Beginning at a small Turkey Oak near Jack's upper spring originally called the cool spring, thence new line North seventy eight degrees, East fourteen and a half poles to a double White Oak, below Jack's lower spring, North twenty seven degrees west through cleared land 104 poles to a great White Oak on Burch's Road aforesaid, thence along the said road and crossing south thirty eight degrees west eleven poles to Joshua Lucy's corner pointers of the same, thence along his line north seventy one degrees west fifty two poles to a red oak saplin, South fifty degrees west sixty four poles to a new made corner red oak, thence along a new south sixty two and a half degrees east one hundred and twenty eight poles to a spanish oak saplin, south eighty five degrees east twenty five poles to the beginning. To have and hold the said fifty one acres of land with all and singular the appurtenances thereunto belonging unto the said trustees and their successors to the only proper use and behoof of the said trustees and their successors forever, and the said Drury Buckner Stith for him and his heirs the said parcel of fifty one acres of land and premises and every part thereof against him and his heirs and against all and every other person and persons whatsoever unto the said trustees and their successors shall and will warrant and forever defend by these presents upon trust nevertheless, and it is the true intent and meaning of the presents that the said Ira Ellis, Edward Dromgoole, John Paup, Aaron Brown, Henry Merritt, John Easter, Stith Parham, Peter Pelham and Peter Robertson trustees for Ebenezer School for the time being as aforesaid and their successors shall have and hold the said parcel of land with all the appurtenances thereunto belonging and appropriate the same to the said use and occupation of the said Ebenezer School forever. In witness whereof the said Drury Buckner Stith and Fanny his wife have hereunto set their hand and affixed their seal, the day and year above written.

Drury B. Stith (*Seal*)

B. PELHAM METHODIST CHURCH, BRUNSWICK COUNTY, VIRGINIA, 1804[2]

This Indenture made this Twenty fifth day of February one thousand eight hundred and four, Between Peter Pelham of the County of Greenville of the one part, and William Ridout, William Kennedy, Lemuel Pelham, Edmund Heath, Miles Cookrey, William Whitemore and Charles Ridout Trustees in trust for the uses and purposes hereinafter mention[ed]. All of the above parties being of the State of Virginia of the other part; Witnesseth that the said Peter Pelham for and in consideration of the love he hath to the cause of God and the Holy Religion of Jesus Christ, and also for the consideration of one dollar in hand paid, doth by these presents give, grant and confirm unto the said trustees and their successors forever, a piece or parcel of land lying and being in the County of Brunswick, bound as follows. Beginning at the forks of the old and new road leading to Brunswick Court House, thence up the old road to a new made corner, pine (above the Camp-meeting-house) thence a Northwardly course to the new road, (a new made line) thence down the new road to the beginning, being the piece or parcel of land whereon the said Camp-meeting-house stands. To have and to hold the said land with the appurtenances thereunto belonging as trustees to and for the sole use, intent and purpose as expressed in the form of an Indenture inserted in the Doctrines and Discipline of the Methodist Episcopal Church in America, as fully as if the whole intents and purposes were herein expressed, and to no other intent or purpose whatsoever. And I hereby warrant the title of the said lands to the trustees aforesaid, and to their successors as aforesaid for the purpose aforesaid, against myself, my heirs, and all persons claiming under me.

In witness whereof, I have hereunto set my hand and seal, the date first written.

Signed PETER PELHAM (*Seal*)

[2] Recorded February 27, 1804, Brunswick County Courthouse, Lawrenceville, Va. For the complete form deed to Methodist trustees see David Sherman, *History of the Revisions of the Discipline of the Methodist Episcopal Church* (New York and Cincinnati, 1874), pp. 269–71.

II. PLANS OF CIRCUITS

A. LIST OF PREACHING PLACES ON THE MIAMI CIRCUIT, OHIO, 1805–6, WITH TEXTS OF SERMONS PREACHED (BENJAMIN LAKIN, CIRCUIT PREACHER)

1805 1806		Jas. Sargants
Oct.	27	Judges. 3,20
Nov.	24	Gen. 18,23
Dec.	22	Neh. 10,38
Mar.	16	I Peter. 1,14–15
April	13	Rom. 8,29–3
May	11	Luke 13:23–24
June	8	Mat. 7:24–27
July	6	Rev. 20:12
Aug.	8	I John 3:3
Oct.	26	Amos. 3,8
Nov.	24	Prov. 27:12
Dec.	7	Ecclesiastes. 7:20
"	22	Philip. 2:3–8

1805 1806		Duncans Town Mond.
Nov.	2	Luke. 10,42
	30	James. 1,22–25
Dec.	23	Luke 17:33
Feb.	17	Job. 32:10
Mar.	17	Mark. 4:3–9
Apr.	14	II Corrin. 4,3–4
May	18	Mat. 5:20
June	15	Rom. 8:13

1805 1806		Limings. Wed.
Oct.	29	Psalm 62, 1
Nov.	27	Isaiah 53–1
Dec.	25	Psalm 2,7–8
Feb.	19	Gallatians, 6,1
Ap.	16	Rom. 5:1
May	14	Mat. 13:47–48
June	11	John 1:11–12
Oct.	27	Acts, 17:30–31
Nov.	27	Deut. 6:25

1805 1806		Crosleys. Thursd—
Oct.	30	James 1,5
Dec.	26	Mark, 4:3–9
Apr.	17	Jerem. 6:16
May.	15	Mat. 7:24–27
June	12	Psalm. 1,1–3
Nov.	25	Romans. 8:9

1805 1806		Forbus Frid.
Dec.	27	Acts 3:26
Ap.	18	II Peter 1:19
May	16	Acts, 5:31
June	13	Jonah. 1:6
Nov.	26	Luke 19:26—

1805 1806		Nelsons—Sund.
Nov.	3	Luke. 26,46–47
	11	Rev. 22,14
Dec.	1	Psalm. 37,10.11
	29	Psalm 116,12–13
Jan.	26	1 Tim. 2:8
Feb.	23	Rom. 3.20–23
Mar.	18	Mat. 6,9–13
Ap.	20	Rom. 14:10
May	18	Titus. 2:1–6
June	15	Zache. 3:9
Oct.	6	Amos, 3:8—
	31	Rom. 12:9–11
Nov.	28	Mark. 13:33
Dec.	27	2: Corrin. 6:1—

1805 1806		Williamsburgh. Mon
Nov.	4	Prov. 27,12
Dec.	2	I John. 3,3—
Jan.	27	I Peter 4:7
Feb.	24	Titus 2,11–12.
Ap	21	John, 3,36
May	19	Mark 4:3–9
June	16	I Cor. 1:21
Nov.	1	Isaiah, 55:6–7
	29	II Cor. 7:1—

1805 1806		Collins Tuesd.	
Nov.	5	Psalm. 1,1–3	
Dec.	3	Mat, 6,9–13	
—	17	Isaiah 21,11–12.	Job. 14..14.
	31	Isaiah, 1:2–3	
Januy	1	Romans. 8:29–30	
Do	29	Deut. 6:25—	
Feb.	26	Mat, 7,24–27	
Mar.	27	Psalm, 4:5.	
May	7	Exodus. 16:26–	
Aug.	2–3	Psalm 84:11—Deut. 5.29	
Oct.	23	Isaiah. 55: 10–11	
Nov.	2	Psalm 107:33–34	
	30	John, 3:18–21	
Dec.	24,, 25	Psalm. 116:12–13 &. 2,7–8	
	28	S. Songs. 2:15	

1805 1806		Dimmits—Thursd.
Nov.	6	Psalm 37,37—
Jan.	2	Mat 13:44
Do	30	Eceles— 12: 13—
Feb.	27	Micah, 2:10
Mar.	26	Mat, 7:11
Ap	24	Rev. 22:14.
May	22	Nahum. 1:7.
June	19	I Cor. 6:19–20
July.	17	Mark 4, 6–9—John. 3:3
Nov.	3	Romans 12, 9–11
Dec.	1	Genessus. 5:24—
—	29	Acts. 10:42.

1805 1806		Gatches Frid.
Nov.	7	II Pet 1,10
Dec.	6	Mat, 13,47–48.
Jan.	3	Romans. 8:13.
—	31	Nahum. 1:7–8
Feb.	20	Mat,, 7:24–27
Ap	25	Prov. 20:4
May	23	I Cor.. 16:22.
June	22	Amos 3:8
July	13	John. 20,30–31. Psalm. 37:37.
Do	20	Eph. 5:16 I Tim, 2:8
Nov.	9	Psalm. 107, 43
Jany	1	Jeremy. 28:16
—	4	Genesus. 18:23—

1805 1806		Noys. Sat—
Nov.	8	Rev. 22,14
Dec.	7	Luke. 12:32
Jan.	4	Psalm 116:7.
Feb.	1	Colloss. 3:1–4.
Mar.	11	Hebrews. 2:1—
June	21	Neh. 4:7–11.
July	19	John. 5:6.
Nov.	7	Neh. 12:1–2
Jany.	2	Luke 13:6–9—

1805 1806		Ramseys.—Sund.
Nov.	10	James 1,5.
Dec.	8	Psalm. 62:1—
Jan.	5	Acts 3:19
Feb.	2	Prov. 14:32
Mar.	2.	Isaiah. 1,2–3—
	21	Mat, 13, 3–9
May.	24:25	Rev. 12.1–2. Rom. 8:29–30
June	22	Psalm. 4:6..
July	20	John. 19:4—
Nov.	8	Revel 22:12—
Jan.	3	I Thess —5:6

1805 1806		Leonards—Mond.
Nov.	10	Psalm. 1,1–3—
Dec.	9	II Cor. 4,3–4. Mat. 7:21—
Jan.	6	Rom. 7:7 to end—Tul.
Feb.	3	II Timothy, 2:8, Mat. 5.20
Mar.	4	Psalm. 4:6
Ap	29	I Tim: 2,4–5
June	24	Mat. 5:10—
July	22	I John. 3:3— Benetts Jobe. 14:14
——		II These. 1:6–9
Nov.	11	Hebrew. 10:38
Jan.	6	Zach. 9:12

1805 1806		Davises—Tuesd.
Dec.	10	Psalm 138:6
Jan.	7	Mat, 5:8—
Feb.	5	Malachi, 3:18
March	5	John 11:26
Ap	30	Psalm 37:10–11
June	25	Ephe. 5:16
Nov.	12	Ezek. 18:32
Jan.	7	II Cor. 7,1.

1805 1806		Garrisons—Wed.
Dec.	11	Mark. 4,26–29.
Jan.	8	Gal. 6:7–8
Columbia		
Nov.	18	Acts 17:30–31.
Dec.	2	John. 3:18–21

1805 1806		Williams—Thursd
Dec.	12	Ephe. 5:16—
Jan.	9	Jeremiah. 4:14
Feb.	7	I Cor. 4:20—
Mar.	7	Job 15:20–21
May	2	2 Cor. 4:3–4.
June	27	Ecle. 8:11.
Nov.	14	I Cor. 13
Jan.	9	Psalm. 2.12

1805 1806		Sackets. Frid
Dec.	13	II John—9—
Feb.	6	Hebrew. 2:3.
Mar.	6	2 Corrin. 6:1.
		Jacob Hutchison
May	1	Eccles 12,13
June	26	2 Corrin 4:3–4.
Nov.	13	Amos. 4:12—
Jan.	8	Mat. 13, 47–48. Jas 1.22–25

1805 1806		McHerries, Sat
Dec.	14	Mark 4.3–9
Jan.	11	I Tim. 4:8
Feb.	8	Isaiah 55:10.11
May	3	John. 12,35–36—
June	28	I Chron. 4, 10
Nov.	15	I John 3:18 to the end
Jan.	10	Psalm 34:19

1805 1806	Cincinnati—Sund.
Dec. 15	Mat. 7,9–13. Genes. 18:23
Jan. 12	2 Cor. 7; 1–2. I Tim 2:8—
Feb. 9	Acts 26:23. N. Neh. 4:2.
Mar. 9	Rom. 3:20–23
May 4	I Tim. 2:4–5—II Cor. 4:3–4.
June 29	Psalm 1:1–3. Ephe. 5:16
July 26:27	Deut. 5:29—I Tim. 3:16
Oct. 19	Mark. 8:36. Acts 16: 30
Nov. 16	Neh. 10:38—Amos. 6:12
Jan. 11	Amos—3:8—Psalm 4:6

1805 1806	Whitakers—Tuesd—
Dec. 17	Mark 4,3–9.
Jan. 14	Rom. 14:12.
Feb. 11	Rom. 3.20–23
Mar. 11	1. Peter. 3:18
May 6	Luke. 21:34
July 1	II Cor. 4:3–4.
Do 29	I John. 3:3
Oct. 27	Neh. 12,1—
Nov. 20	Mat. 5:8
Dec. 18	Psalm 34:19

1805 1806	Campels. Thursd.
Feb. 13	Isaiah 55:6,7—
Mar. 12	Luke, 13:24—
Oct. 23	Ezek—12:27–28.
Nov. 21	John. 12:35–36
Dec. 19	I John. 3:2–3.

1805 1806	Wands—Mond—
Dec. 16	Psalm 2,12
Jan. 18–19	Mat. 5:16—I Pet. 1: 14,,15
Feb. 10	Luke. 6:46.
Mar. 10	Luke 13:7–9
May 5	Exodos. 16:26—
June 30	I John. 3:3—
July 28	II Thes. 2:11–12
Oct. 20	Psalm 46:10.
Nov. 17	II Corrin. 7:1—
Jan. 12	Mat. 5:16

1805 1806	Jno. Sargants. Frid
Nov. 23	Mat. 7,21
De. 20	Mark. 4:3–9
Feb. 14	II Corrin. 7:1–2
Mar. 14	Mat. 11:28
May 9	Psalm 24:3–5
June 8	I Timothy 1:15
July 6	I Peter, 4:17
Oct. 24	John 19:4—
Nov. 12	John. 3,17.
Dec. 20	John 6:27

1805 1806		Fees. Sat.
Oct.	27	James. 1–27
Nov.	22	Rev. 3,20
Dec.	21	Ezek. 18,27
Feb.	15	Rom 3:20–23
	16	2 Sam. 12:23, Jas. 1:5
Mar.	15	Psalm 97:2.
Ap.	12	Psalm 1,1–3—
May	10	II Cor. 4:3–4
June	7	Proverbs 27:12
July	5	II Kings. 4:26
Aug.	7	Psalm 89:15
Oct.	12	I Cor. 10:15–
	25	II Peter 1.10
Nov.	23	Rom. 2,4–5
Dec.	21	I Corrin. 16:22
		Woods
		Psal 90:12
		I Pet. 3:1–7
		2. Cor 13:11
		1 Tim. 3–16

1806		Clerks Mond.
Feb.	2	Psalm 116:12–13
Mar.	3	Mat, 3:10
May	26	Reve. 3:20
June	23	Psalm 138:6
July	21	Nahum, 1:7
Nov.	10	Mat. 24:44—
Jan.	5	John 3,17

[N.d.]		Sabunon. I Pet. 4:17
May	26	Rom. 3,–20–23—
June	23	Psalm 4.6
July	21	Acts. 3:19

Wells. Nahum. 1:7—

Cullumbia June 30: I Tim. 1:15

1806		Wells
June	20	Acts. 3:19—
July	18	II Cor. 4:3–4

Allisons

Nov.	3	Isaiah 55:6–7.

Fagans. Acts 17.30–37.

B. PLAN OF THE SHELBYVILLE CIRCUIT, ILLINOIS, WITH LISTS OF LOCAL PREACHERS, EXHORTERS, STEWARDS, AND CLASS LEADERS

[See insert.]

C. PLAN OF BIRMINGHAM CIRCUIT, HUNTINGDON DISTRICT, BALTIMORE CONFERENCE, 1849[3]

	Day	*Hour*	*Preaching*	*Dist from Birming.*	*No. in Society*	*Leaders*	*Stopping Places*
22	Sat	7½	Bells Forge	10	14	D. Crowl	T. Gheer, W. Chamberlain & others
23	Sun.	11	Asbury Chapel	14	38	Geo. Hartsel	Jacob Smith, D Smith, W. H. Ake "
"	"	3	Altoona	18	16	Peter Green	Andrew Green, Wm Payne
"	"	7½	Blair Furnace	15	25	Jno. Trout	J. Trout, Thos. Trout, M. Simpson
26	Wedn	7½	Ganoe's S[chool] H[ouse]	3	12	Jno. A. Stratton	James Ganoe
27	Thurs	7½	Grazier's S[chool] H[ouse]	3	9	Abr. Smith	George Guyer Sen.
28	Frid	7½	Tyrone S[chool] H[ouse]	1½	35	T.M.Calderwood	Geo. G. Given, Geo. Hatfield & others
30	Sun	11	Birmingham		31	Lew. Palmer	James Bell, Jas. Clark, Lew. Palmer
"	"	7½	Thomas Lion	6	42	C. T. Welsh	C. T. Welsh, Aaron Beyer, Abr. Beyer
			Weston's Mills	2	23	Thos. Weston	*No preaching here—only a class*
					245		

Stewards—Thos. Weston Rec.
Lewis Palmer
Aaron Beyer
C. T. Welsh
John Gheer
John Trout

Parsonage Furniture
Cooking Stove & pipe
3 Bedsteads
2 Tables—Dining
2 Setts of Chairs
Writing Table
Dotry & large iron pot

DEAR BRO. [GUYER]

The furniture you will find in Warri*e*r's Mark; the Church Register, Missionary Book, and Circuit Account Book with Bro. T.

[3] The appointments listed were in Blair and Huntingdon counties, Pennsylvania. It is of interest to note that the town of Altoona, the third appointment, had just been founded, so that Methodism was on the scene from the start. At the present time, Altoona alone has upward of twelve Methodist churches and is the head of the Altoona District of Central Pennsylvania Conference.

Weston. A suitable house has been rented for you in Birmingham. A List of Missionary & S. S. Advocate subscribers you will find in the hands of D. E. Robeson of Birmingham. Enter on your work in good heart. The Circuit has been coming up, and must prosper, if prudently managed.

Yours truly
J. S. McMurray

D. LIST OF LOCAL PREACHERS AND EXHORTERS ON THE DOVER (DELAWARE) CIRCUIT, 1793[4]

1793 Nov*r* 23

E Calob Boyer
E W*m* Thomas
L Curtis Marker
L John Farlow Dead
L Tho*s* Purnal
L Solomon Harris
I Jo*s* Farrow
John Hogens Rem[ove]d
D Majer Taylor Deacon
L Charles Connor
D Charles Cavender Travels
D Ja*s* Scotten Silanced
Ja*s* Wakman Exhorters
Jo*s* David
L Jeffery Thompson
Alixander Jackson Desists
L John Sowerd Travils

III. CAMP-MEETING RULES[5]

1 The people will be notefied of the commencement of Publick Worship from time to time by the sound of the trumpet; when all persons within the space formed by the tents, are requested to take

[4] This list, in the handwriting of Richard Whatcoat, is in the Davies Collection at Garrett Biblical Institute. "E" stands for (local) elder, "L" for local preacher (i.e., unordained), and "D" for (local) deacon.

[5] Adopted September 2, 1831, for camp-meeting in Granville Circuit, Ohio Conference ("Journal" of James Gilruth [1831–32]).

their seats in the congregation and conform to the order [of] Meeting.

2 The seats, and the grove of timber on the right hand of the stand are for the use, & retirement of the females: and the seats & grove of timber on the left hand are for the use & retirement of the men.

3 The trumpet will sound in the morning at 5 as a signal to rise & have prayer in the tents.

4 At the close of worship in the evening, the trumpet will sound as a signal of rest: when all are requested to go to their beds & be quiet; so as not to disturb others.[6] And all persons not having tents to sleep in are required to leave the encampment till morning.

5 The hours for eating will be as follows: vis, breakfast at 7, dinner at 12 and supper at 5

6 All persons commiting any act, or making any disturbence, in, or about this meting, such as are prohibited by the state laws of Ohio, will be delt with according to law.

Signed.

Benjn Pratt. Peter Thurston,
Alexander Devilbess, Samuel Carpenter,
Jacob Marten, John Jaffield,

Committy.

IV. FRONTIER SERMONS

The greatest opponents of the frontier Methodists from a theological standpoint were the Presbyterians and the Baptists. The Methodists and the Presbyterians locked horns over the doctrine of predestination and election and with the Baptists on their insistence that immersion was the only scriptural form of baptism. The three sermons here reproduced were by Benjamin Lakin, two against the doctrine of predestination and one on baptism.

[6] In connection with this rule, the following incident from the career of Jacob Gruber (1778–1850), an eccentric preacher of the Baltimore Conference, is worth repeating: "At a camp-meeting near Baltimore, after the trumpet had been blown announcing the time for closing the exercises in the praying circles, one of them, unwilling to stop, kept on singing and praying. Gruber, somewhat impatient, and evidently not pleased at their want of obedience to order, after standing near for a short time, shouted out at the top of his voice. 'That's right, brothers, blow all the fire out!'" (W[illiam] P. Strickland [ed.], *The Life of Jacob Gruber* [New York: 1860], pp. 88–89).

SERMON I [ON PREDESTINATION]

2 Pet. 1:10 "Give diligence to make your calling and election sure."

That election is a scripture doctrine no man that believes the Scripture can deny. But what this election is becomes a matter of dispute—

The calvanian opinion is that God from eternity decreed to save a part of mankind without regard to their faith or good works or anything except his own will and left the rest to perish in sins without any possibility of being saved—

The Armenian [Arminian] opinion is that God [has] chosen to eternal life all persevering believers in Jesus Christ and that he hath rejected or reprobated all impenitent unbelievers to eternal misery.

The former oppinions I cannot embrace for the following reasons

(1) because it sits the power of God in opposition to his Justice, Mercy, Goodness and truth.

(2) Because it over throws the infinite knowledge of God, and the Scripture asserts that God elects according to his foreknowledge. Romans 8:29:30 I Peter 1–2.

(3) Because it indirectly charges the sin and damnation of all the reprobates on God—

(4) Because it overthrows the day of Judgment.

I embrace the latter because it

(1) Because it harmonises the attributes of God.

(2) establishes infinite knowledge.

(3) cleares God from the sin and damnation of any.

(4) and sits the day of Judgment upon a proper principal [foundation?]

Your calling—The Calvenan idea is that the common calling that God gives, such as, the gospel, the general opperations of his spirit are ineffectual to your salvation without an irresistable call.

This opinion I cannot embrace

(1) Because the Scripture no where makes such distinction

(2) It charges God with dissimulation and makes hipocrisy a virtue,

(3) It makes God to have two wills,

(4) Because the scripture says men resist to their own distruction, and resist the Holy Ghost.

The third thing to be considered is the infalible perseverence of the

Saints, which my text makes conditional. Which the Calvanist assert to be without condition however some texts detatched from the context may seem to favour such an idea yet when taken according to the analogy of faith they do not—neither can we suppose that the Spirit of God intends to contradict such plain texts as, Ezek 18:24 and chap 33;13. But whoever fell from grace (1) Saul I Sam 10, 6 and the Spirit of the Son shall come upon thee, and he then shall prophecy with them and shall be turned into another man—verse 9 God gave him another heart. Second there is Judas according to the C.....t[?] he was chose to the ministry, and Xt [Christ] never set the example to chose Badmen etc, he was promised one of the 12 thrones, and yet lost—

But will not this make God changeable—the reverse—[The sermon is left unfinished.]

SERMON II [ON PREDESTINATION]

The scripture speak of the foreknowledge of God I Peter 1.2. Elect according to the foreknowledge of God the Father. Romans 8.29. For whome he did Forknow and that he is capable of knowing is evident, for, his understanding is infinite. Psalm 147.5. "And knoun to God are all his works from the beginning of the world." (or eternity as some render it) Acts 15:18—Hence it appears that all things are known to God before they come to pass.

But many think that this is taking these scriptures in too strong a sense to suppose them to mean that God knowes all things before they come to pass and if God does know all things Calvanism must be true. Hence some scriptures are brought to show that God does not; and some reasons that he cannot know contengient events proceeding from the will of man. These it behoves us impartially to examin. The first is in Genesis 6:6. "And it repented the Lord that he had God saw everything that he had made and behold it was very good. Genesis 1.31. And if God could have don an act that he had cause to repent off [of] he could not have given a law to his creatures relative to their conduct that would not admit of the same that was found in himself, and so all distinction between law and Gospel comes to an end.

And to take the latter clause of the text in the common sense, it would imply that God is unhappy. For grief always supposes a painful sensation, and so far as we have any painfull sensation, so far we are unhappy: Now to be pained at the heart implies the most painfull sensation that proceeds from that sense, and so God must be unhappy. This absurdity is at first view so great that we cannot for one moment admit the idea; and of course we cannot interpret the text according to the common sense of the words—The plain sense of the subject seems to be this. God haveing made man in his own image, he then saw him very good. But man by the fall lost the image of God from his soul, by transgressing his law. Then God made a covenant of grace with man, and gave him power once more to serve his God. But man abused the power God had given him, and by following his own inclination, every thought and imagination of his heart was evil continually. (and as a man convinced of the impropriety of his conduct, and grieved at heart for his disigns miscarrying, would undo the whole if in his power.) So God resolved to distroy man from the face of the earth. By an alternation of his intended goodness to them. To the execution of his righteous Judgments upon them to the extripating them from off the face of the earth. This sense is clere from this, That Noah that was perfect in his generation, and walked with God found grace in his sight. Thus the dispensation of grace to the righteous went on, and God's intention of good to him remained unalterable though the whole world was sunk in ruin. Hense it cannot stand in opposition to the infinite knowledge of God.

And in support of the limitation of the knowledge of God the following, texts are produced. Jeremiah 7,31—and 19,5 and 32,35. great stress is laid on this latter text, especially on these words, "Which I commanded them not, neither came it into my mind, that they should do this abomination. "If we attend to the term mind we shall find that though it hath different significations, yet it never hath any reference to the knowledge of future events. And when we attend to the gramatical construction of the words, we shall find their meaning to be this, it never was the intention of God that the Jews should burn their children in sacrifice to Baal, and of course that not even in his secret intentions, nor did he ever view it as a duty enjoined on them. But this does not prove that God never foresaw that this would be the case. Nor did his foreseeing of it influence it into being; any more than a man seeing the forbidden course his son is takeing will bring him to ruin has any influence on him in that course. We may observe on the texts 1 In them all there was a command given not to do. 2.

They disobeyed the command and did. 3. God clears himself of any secret intention, it never came into his heart, his mind. i.e. he had not even a secret intention that such a thing should be. But we see heare is nothing said about fore or after knowledge, these might be or not be and the text remain in its full force.

SERMON III [ON BAPTISM]

I Cor. 10, 15. I speak as to wise men: Judge what I say.

In every Controversy, an appeal is to be made to the Judgement, and not to the passions of men. This was the *Apostles* method with the Corrinthians—

There is a difference between men of knowledge, and wisdom, a man of knowledge, has a set of principals, a man of wisdom, understands the application of principals, and to those we now appeal in the Subject now before us:

THERE are two things in all controversies, which will facilitate our scerch after truth—

First that we set aside all those things wherein we are agreed, and fix our attention to that only on which a diference of oppinion may fall—And Secondly, that this difference be stated in a manner the Most plain. And to the end we may not beat the are [air] by contending about things wherein we are agreed—I shall in the FIRST place state what the subject of Controversy is. It is not whether the Baptism of believeing ADULTS, be right, for in this we agree—So that all those passages of Scripture that prove Adult Baptism to be right prove nothing but what is acknowledged on both sides. BUT whether *ye* Baptism of Infants be right, for this we affirm; and the Baptist[s] deny so we are here farely at isue—NEITHER is it whether immersion be a mode of Baptism; for in this we agree—But whether it be essential to the Baptism. THIS the Baptist[s] affirm and we deny—here again we are at isue.

THE subject being thus fairly stated it will lead us to consider FIRST, whether Infants are proper subjects of Baptism or not—and SECONDLY, Whether immersion be essential to Baptism or not.

I SHALL begin with *ye* subject of Baptism, And that we may have the clearest view of the subject under consideration I shall FIRST take into consideration the Baptist arguments against Infant Baptism—

The FIRST is—A PERSON who has a right to a positive institute, must be expressly mentioned as haveing that right: but Infants are not so mentiond, therefore they have not that right.—WHATEVER a Baptist may think of this argument, when it is tried by God's method of leading men into their duty; as it is stated in Scripture it will appeare Fals.—LET us try it (1) on Female Communion. I Cor 11, 28 Let a man &c—(2) on the Apostles command to preach the gospel to y*e* Gentiles Acts, 13, 46–47. Seeing ye Judge yourselve[s] &c—The Lord commanded—I have set y*e* a light to ye Gentiles. (3) On public worship Heb 10, 25. Not forsakeing the assembling of yourselves &C. (4) On heareing the gospel James 1, 22. Be ye doers of the word &c—Are we thus left in things of the last importance to collect our duty by inference and reject Infants because they have not more than we.

Argument 2 The scripture[s] require faith and repentance in order to Baptism; but as Infants cannot have these, they are not proper subject[s] of Baptism—They cannot repent, they cannot believe, therefore they are not to be Baptised &c. THIS is set aside by asking of whome ye Scriptures require repentance, and faith &c—what faith is necessary to Baptism Acts 19, 2–6. Every argument y*t* will prove against a known truth, or support a falshood, is a bad argument. (1) Circumcision of infants Acts 15, 24. ye must be Cir*d* and keep *ye* law Gal. 5,3. Every man—circum*d* to *do* law.—Rom. 2,25 Circumcision prof[iteth] [if thou] keep y*e* law (2) on the Baptism of Xt. (3) On the Salvation of infants Mark 16, 16 He y*t* believeth shall be saved—he that believeth not shall be damned—(4) On the temporal subsistance of infants, Isaiah 1, 19. "If ye be willing and obedient ye shall eat the good of y*e* land."

THE falacy of the argument consists in bringing more into the conclusion than was in their premices—For there should never be more in y*e* conclusion than in y*e* premises. HAVEING removed those difficulties—I proceed to give some reasons why infants should be Baptised, and in doing this I must look back to the first organiseing of y*e* Church. Gen. 12, 1–3, and Chap. 17, 7–14. This was a gospel covenant, Gal. 3, 8 And the scripture, foreseeing y*t* God would Justify y*e* heathen thrugh faith, preached before y*e* gospel unto Ab[raham], saying in thee &c. It being beyond contradiction that the Church of which infants were members, and initiated by a religious rite And that right hath never been taken from y*m* by God or men divinely inspired they must still remain in possession of y*e* same. PROCEED to shew that this right was never taken from y*m*,—But established by our lord and his Apos[tles]. Our Lord declares y*m* to be of the Kingdom of God. Mark 10, 13–15—Peter appeals to their membership Acts 2, 38–39. Then Peter said unto y*m* repent &c Household Baptism—But against this it is objected John's Baptised none but Believers, then state the difference between Johns dispensation and Xt John 3, 25 from John y*e* Baptist proceed—Not Xn Acts 19, 2–3. Then shew if the Baptist[s] have John for their foundation they come short of y*e* Xtn dispensation It is argued against infants that y*e* apostles forbid y*m* To SHEW that that [*sic*] there is no alteration in the constitution, but something aded, by observeing the Seale of the Covenant to answer the same purpose. Circumcision in stead being a sign of worldly previ*d*ledges it is "a seal of the rightiousness of faith Rom 4, 11—It lay the subject under obligation to keep the law Acts 15, 24—And Baptism lays an obligation to observe all things Xt commanded. Mat 28, 19–20. As the ordenances serve y*e* same purposes in y*e* dispensations we may conclude the[m] to have objects y*e* same THEN come to a Delima—Infants must be received &c—not without but with Baptism—Therefore &c—

SECOND on the Mode of Baptism.—Whether immersion be essential to Baptism—This y*e* Baptist[s] assert and we deny. AT this remote time all we can collect is by inference—this is cleare for y*e* Baptist[s] who are so great enemies to inference are obliged to have recorse to this on y*e* mode. THEY infer from Going into the water, and much water &c—Mat 3, 16 tho it is said Xt went up out of y*e* water it is not said how bapt[ize]d. PHILIP and y*e* Eunoch proves too much introduce Thompsons travels and so doth Rom 6, 4—Therefore we are buried &c—NOAH and his family prove nothing for immersion for every seem so is not so, THE Israelites in the Red Sea the same—IN Favour of Sprinkling the 3000 on y*e* day of penticost THE Jailor and all his—THO it is said there is no sprinkeling mentioned in Scripture, if we only attend to y*e* Scripture See Ezek 36, 25 Then will I sprinkle &c—Isaiah 52, 15 So shall he sprinkle many nations—Heb 9, 19 & 10, 2, and 11, 28—and 12, 24—pouring Isaiah 44,3 Joel 2, 28–29,

Acts 11, 17–18 Zache 12, 10. SPRINKELING OR POURING best represents the thing signified WHICH is the outpouring of the Spirit & &c

But why are children admited to Baptism and not to the Lords Supper—An*s* because Baptism is a passiv ordinance, and an infant is as capable of a passive ordinance as an Adult—and the Lords Supper is an active ordinance of which they are not as yet capable &c.

BUT what use is it to Baptise an infant the same may be said of an adult—

BUT it brings y*m* into view—and lays the Child under obligation &c &cc

V. A FRONTIER EXHORTATION

It was the custom in the new country, when two or three ministers were present, for each of them to have something to say. Usually one preached the sermon, and another followed with an exhortation, which was generally a very personal admonition to the congregation. The people thought it a waste of time to come a long distance for only a short service. Short services were later the outgrowth of thicker settlements. On this occasion a young and unknown minister had delivered the sermon, to the disappointment of the congregation, who had expected to hear James Axley. It was not uncommon for a preacher to reprove people by name in the course of his exhortation.

James Axley, a contemporary and friend of Peter Cartwright, was a renowned Methodist preacher in eastern Tennessee in the early part of the last century. Judge Hugh L. White was for many years a well-known judge in Tennessee and later served as a member of the United States Senate.

AN EXHORTATION[7]

Mr. Axley stood silently surveying the congregation, until every eye was riveted upon him. He then began:

"It may be a very painful duty, but it is a very solemn one, for a minister of the Gospel to reprove vice, misconduct, and sin, whenever and wherever he sees it. But especially is it his duty on Sunday and at church. That is a duty I am now about to attend to.

"And now," continued the reverend speaker, pointing with his

[7] This exhortation is found in William H. Milburn's *The Pioneer Preacher: or Rifle, Axe, and Saddle-Bags* (New York, 1857), pp. 72–75.

long finger in the direction indicated, "that man sitting out yonder behind the door, who got up and went out while the brother was preaching, stayed out as long as he wanted to, got his boots full of mud, came back and stamped the mud off at the door, making all the noise he could on purpose to distract the attention of the congregation, and then took his seat; that man thinks I mean him. It doesn't look as if he had been raised in the white settlements, does it, to behave that way at meeting? Now, my friend, I'd advise you to learn better manners before you come to church next time. But I don't mean him.

"And, now," again pointing at his mark, "that little girl sitting there, about half way of the house—I should judge her to be about sixteen years old—that's her with the artificial flowers on the outside of her bonnet and the inside of her bonnet; she has a breastpin on, too" (they were very severe upon all superfluities of dress); "she that was giggling and chattering all the time the brother was preaching, so that even the old sisters in the neighborhood couldn't hear what he was saying, though they tried to. She thinks I mean her. I'm sorry from the bottom of my heart for any parents that have raised a girl to her time of day and haven't taught her how to behave when she comes to church. Little girl, you have disgraced your parents as well as yourself. Behave better next time, won't you? But I don't mean her."

Directing his finger to another aim, he said, "That man sitting there, that looks as bright and 'peart' as if he never was asleep in his life and never expected to be, but who just as soon as the brother took his text, laid his head down on the seat in front of him, went sound asleep, slept the whole time, and snored; that man thinks I mean him. My friend, don't you know the church ain't the place to sleep? If you needed rest, why didn't you stay at home, take off your clothes, and go to bed? That's the place to sleep, not at church. The next time you have a chance to hear a sermon, I advise you to keep awake. But I don't mean him." Thus did he proceed, pointing out man, woman, and child who had in the slightest deviated from a befitting line of conduct; characterizing the misdemeanors, and reading sharp lessons of rebuke.

Judge White was all this time sitting at the end of the front seat, just under the speaker, enjoying the old gentleman's disquisition to the last degree; twisting his neck around to see if the congregation relished the "down comings" as much as he did; rubbing his hands, smiling, chuckling inwardly. Between his teeth and cheek was a monstrous quid of tobacco, which the better he was pleased the more he chewed; the more he chewed the more he spat, and behold, the floor bore witness to the result. At length the old gentleman, straightening himself up to his full height, continued, with great gravity:

"And now I reckon you want to know who I do mean? I mean that dirty, nasty, filthy tobacco-chewer, sitting on the end of that front seat;"—his finger meanwhile pointing true as the needle to the pole—"see what he has been about. Look at the puddles on the floor; a frog wouldn't get into them; think of the tails of the sisters' dresses being dragged through that muck." The crest-fallen judge declared that he never chewed any more tobacco in church.

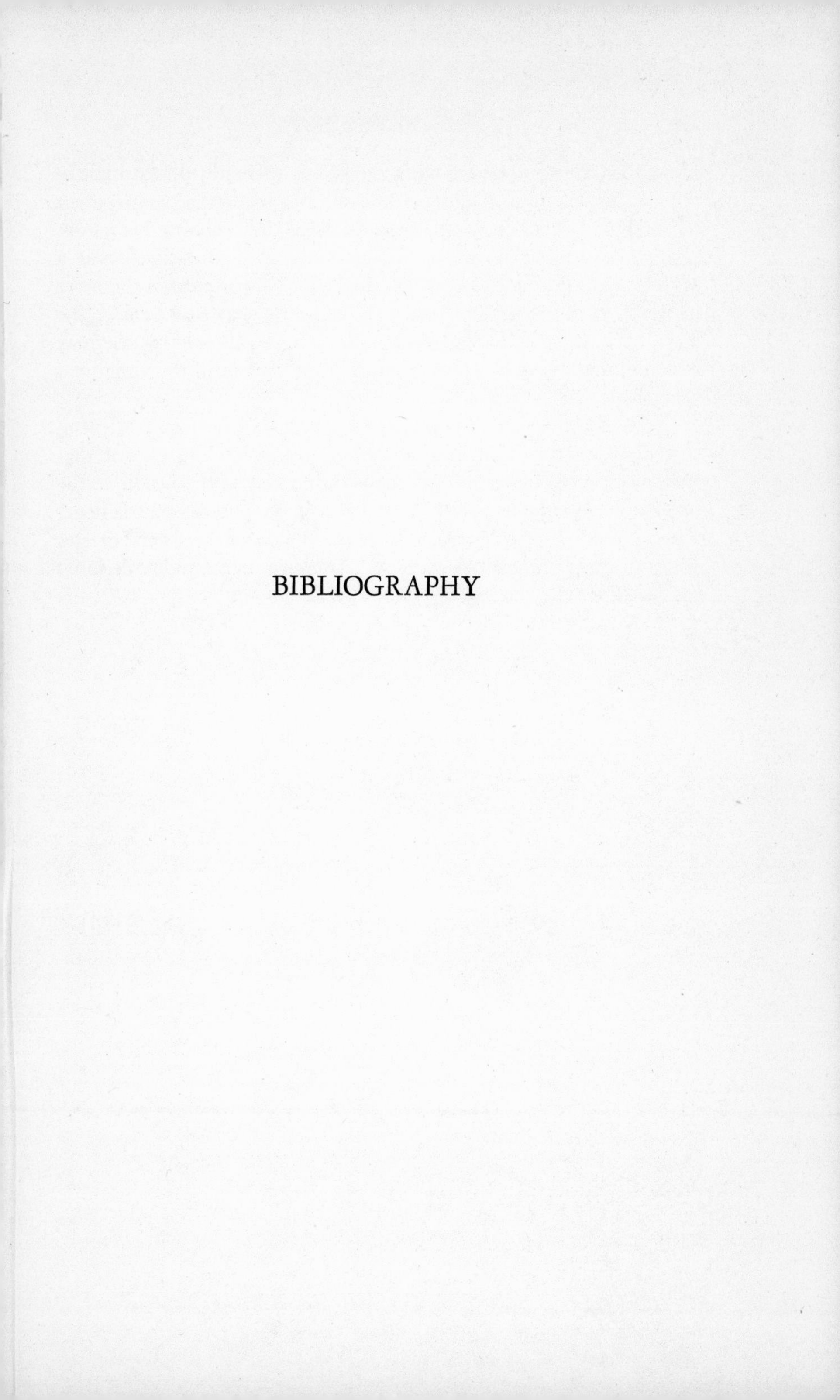

BIBLIOGRAPHY

BIBLIOGRAPHY

I. MANUSCRIPTS

I. District of Columbia

A. Library of Congress, Washington

1. "Journal of Thomas Haskins (1782–1785)." Photostat and typed copies in Divinity Library, University of Chicago.
2. "Journal of Richard Whatcoat [1792–93 and 1798–1800]." 2 manuscript booklets. Microfilm copies in Divinity Library, University of Chicago.

II. California

A. California Conference Historical Society, San Francisco

1. Diaries, biographical material, quarterly conference records, sermons of California Methodism.

B. University of Southern California, Los Angeles

1. Western Jurisdictional Conference materials.

III. Colorado

A. Iliff School of Theology, Denver

1. Western Jurisdictional Conference materials.

IV. Delaware

A. Wilmington Conference Historical Society

1. Quarterly Conference Records: "Smyrna Circuit (1800–1831)"; Milford Circuit (1804–1844)."

V. Georgia

A. Candler School of Theology, Emory University, Emory University

1. Southeastern Jurisdictional Conference materials.

VI. Illinois

A. Illinois Wesleyan, Bloomington

1. Illinois Conference Papers, including "Journal of the Illinois Conference (1824–1945)"; "Judiciary Committee Records (1838–1874)"; papers relating to the following trials of ministers: Henry Buell (1832), S. L. Robinson (1835), Elijah Knox (1836), W. B. Mack (1836), A. G. Meacham (1839), Benjamin Newman (1839), York-Parker-Green-Bond Case (1839), William Burns–Harry Yost Trial (1841), E. G. Falconer (1847), and Thomas W. Jones (1850).

2. "Central Illinois Conference Memoirs (1864–1876)."
3. Quarterly Conference Records: "Carrollton Circuit, Illinois (1839–1850)."
4. James Leaton Historical Collection, including manuscript of the supplement to his *History of Methodism in Illinois, 1793–1832;* and the unpublished draft of Vols. II and III (1833–57).

B. Divinity Library, University of Chicago, Chicago
1. "Plan of the Shelbyville Circuit, Illinois Conference (1833)." Photostat.
2. Benjamin Lakin Papers, including "Journal of Benjamin Lakin (1794–1820)," sermon and reading notes, etc.
3. Quarterly Conference Records: "Pompey Circuit, New York, 1807–1831."
4. "George Whitefield Correspondence (1739–1850)": photostats of originals in Historical Society of Wisconsin, the Library of Congress, and the Genealogical Society of Pennsylvania.
5. "Map of the Location of the First Methodist Church in Wisconsin (1835)." Photostat.
6. "James Gilruth's Journal." 19 manuscript booklets in transcript. Originals in possession of W. A. Gilruth, Chicago.

THESES

1. Edwin T. Buehrer. "The Origin and History of the Time Limit in Methodist Itinerancy" (A.M. thesis, University of Chicago, 1923).
2. ———. "Methods of Frontier Expansion in the Methodist Church in Ohio, Indiana and Illinois" (D.B. thesis, University of Chicago, 1923).
3. Elmer G. Cutshall. "The Doctrinal Training of the Traveling Ministry of the Methodist Episcopal Church of the United States" (Ph.D. thesis, University of Chicago, 1922).
4. Kenneth W. Dean. "Social and Economic Conditions in Kentucky as Reflected in the Newspapers, 1788–1804" (A.M. thesis, University of Chicago, 1925).
5. Paul H. Eller. "The Denominational Consciousness of the Albright Brethren" (A.M. thesis, University of Chicago, 1929).
6. ———. "Revivalism and the German Churches in Pennsyl-

vania, 1783–1816" (Ph.D. thesis, University of Chicago, 1933).

7. Merrill E. Gaddis. "Christian Perfectionism in America" (Ph.D. thesis, University of Chicago, 1929).
8. Dan B. Genung. "The Cultural Contributions of Methodism during the Frontier Period, 1785–1840" (D.B. thesis, University of Chicago, 1941).
9. Robert W. Goodloe. "The Office of Bishop in the Methodist Church" (Ph.D. thesis, University of Chicago, 1929).
10. W. B. Grimes. "Some Contributions of Early Methodism to American Christianity, 1729–1816" (A.M. thesis, University of Chicago, 1915).
11. W. P. Hollar. "The Early Interrelation of the Church of the United Brethren in Christ and the Methodist Episcopal Church in America" (A.M. thesis, University of Chicago, 1923).
12. Don W. Holter. "The Beginnings of Protestantism in Trans-Missouri" (Ph.D. thesis, University of Chicago, 1934).
13. Richard L. James. "Religion in Alabama, 1860–1870" (A.M. thesis, University of Chicago, 1936).
14. H. E. Jensen. "Rise of Religious Journalism" (Ph.D. thesis, University of Chicago, 1930).
15. S. F. Maine. "Early Methodism in Upper Canada" (Ph.D. thesis, University of Chicago, 1932).
16. L. E. Murphy, "Rise of the Methodist Episcopal Church in Missouri" (A.M. thesis, University of Chicago, 1921).
17. Richard Oosting. "Frontier Christianity in Michigan Territory" (A.M. thesis, University of Chicago, 1922).
18. C. J. Pardee. "Unity of American Churches from 1800 to 1840" (A.M. thesis, University of Chicago, 1929).
19. Harry E. Parker. "The Early Methodist Episcopal Church in Canada" (A.M. thesis, University of Chicago, 1928).
20. Margery Pike. "Growth of Methodism in New England, 1789–1812" (A.M. thesis, University of Chicago, 1933).
21. W. R. Rigell. "Negro Religious Leadership on the Southern Seaboard, Maryland, Virginia, North Carolina, and Georgia, 1830–1861" (A.M. thesis, University of Chicago, 1916).
22. Millard G. Roberts. "The Methodist Book Concern in the West, 1800–1850" (D.B. thesis, University of Chicago, 1942).

23. Ludd M. Spivey. "Methodist Education in America prior to 1820" (A.M. thesis, University of Chicago, 1922).
24. ———. "A Bibliography of Episcopal Methodism of America" (D.B. thesis, University of Chicago, 1922).
25. Wilbur T. Wallace. "Richard Whatcoat, Early Methodist Bishop" (A.M. thesis, University of Chicago, 1941).

C. Garrett Biblical Institute, Evanston

1. Samuel Gardiner Ayres. "Supplement to Outlines of Wesleyan Bibliography by G. Osborn, Contained in the Library of Drew Theological Seminary and the Library of Garrett Biblical Institute." N.d. Pp. 389. (Typewritten.)
2. ———. "Check List of Works by Methodist Episcopal Authors, Including Books Contained in the Library of Drew Theological Seminary and the Library of Garrett Biblical Institute." N.d. Pp. 732. (Typewritten.)
3. ———. "Check List of Works by Methodist Authors Other than M[ethodist] E[piscopal]: Also Anonymous Methodist Literature Contained in the Library of Drew Theological Seminary and the Library of Garrett Biblical Institute." 1915. Pp. 127. (Typewritten.)
4. Garrett Biblical Institute Collection: "Portraits and Autographs of Trustees and Faculty; Biographical Register (1856–1870) of Student Autobiographies."
5. Bishops' Autographs and Portraits (1789–1897): letters, etc.
6. Quarterly Conference Records: "Fall River Society (Stewards' Record) (1829–1844)"; Littleton Circuit, Illinois Conference, 1854–1872 (Field Papers)"; Newark Circuit, Rock River Conference, 1837–1849 (Field Papers)"; Sycamore Circuit, Illinois, 1837–1850"; Wheeling Circuit, Rock River Conference, 1840–1851"; Winchester Circuit, Indiana Conference, 1835—— (Field Papers)."
7. Stephen R. Beggs. "History of the Rock River Conference."
8. McKendree H. Chamberlain. "History of McKendree College, Lebanon, Illinois." 5 vols.
9. William Colbert Collection: "Journal of William Colbert (1790–1833)." 13 vols.: unfinished "Autobiography"; "Hymns"; and "Letters" from Asbury and other early preachers.
10. Ezekiel Cooper Collection: "Autobiography," "Correspondence," "Journals," "Poetry," "Notebooks," "Sermon Notes" of Cooper and others. (See *Calendar of the Ezekiel*

Cooper Collection of Early American Methodist Manuscripts [1785–1839] [Chicago: Historical Records Survey, 1941].)

11. John Davies Collection: several hundred Methodist documents, such as letters, accounts, autographs, ordination parchments.
12. Alvaro D. Field Papers: "Methodist Documents" (1 vol.); "Records of Methodist History Chiefly in Rock River Con[ference]" (1 vol.); "Correspondence on Illinois Methodist History and Biography" (2 vols.); and "Material Left out of Worthies and Workers of the Rock River Conference by A. D. Field 1896."
13. Papers of Bishop L. L. Hamline (1837–62): correspondence.
14. Papers of Bishop E. S. Janes (1831–79): correspondence, etc.
15. "Journal" of Daniel P. Kidder's early life.
16. Stephen N. Merrill Papers: "Diary" and "Autobiography."
17. Adam Miller. "A Historical Sketch of the Commencement of German Missions in the Methodist E[piscopal] Church." 1897. Pp. 100.
18. Thomas Morrell Collection: letters from Asbury and others, to Morrell.
19. "Journal" and "Autobiography" of Thomas Rankin.
20. "Autograph Album of John Scripps, Illinois Conference (1824)."
21. "Journal of John Smith, Greenbrier Circuit, Virginia (1787–1788)."
22. "Journals of Richard Whatcoat," Vol. I (1789–91); Vol. II (1794–96); and Vol. III (1797–98).

VII. Indiana

A. DePauw University, Greencastle

1. "Journals of the Indiana Conference (1832–1844)."
2. Quarterly Conference Records: "Silver Creek Circuit, Indiana, 1810——"; "Fall Creek Circuit, Indiana, 1828——"; and "Crawfordsville Station, Indiana, 1835——."

VIII. Kansas

A. Kansas Historical Society, Topeka

1. "Journals of the Kansas Annual Conference of the Methodist Episcopal Church (1856–1874)." 3 vols. Also 719 papers.
2. Quarterly Conference Records: "Wyandot Mission, Ohio and Kansas."

IX. Maryland

A. Methodist Historical Society, Baltimore

1. "Journals of the Baltimore Annual Conference (1801–1945)."
2. "Asbury Letters": 41 items.
3. "Journal of John Kobler."
4. "Journal of Nelson Reed," Vol. I (1778–79); Vol. II (1779); Vol. III (1779–81); Vol. IV (1781–82).

B. Westminister Theological Seminary, Westminster

1. Northeastern Jurisdictional Conference materials.
2. "Autobiography of William C. Lipscomb (1792)."
3. "Journal of Frederick Stier (1836–1843)."

X. Massachusetts

A. New England Methodist Historical Society, Boston

1. New England Methodist historical materials.

B. Boston University, Boston

1. Northeastern Jurisdictional Conference materials.

XI. Minnesota

A. Minnesota Historical Society, St. Paul

1. "Records of the Historical Society of the Minnesota Conference": histories and biographies.
2. "Methodist Papers from Hamline University (1823–1904)."
3. Autobiographical material, by J. Milton Akers (1836–82); Henry G. Bilbie (1859); James F. Chaffee (1857–77); J. L. Dyer (1855–60); Thomas Harwood (1857–61); Noah Lathrop (1828–66); S. J. Sterrett (1857); and W. F. Stockdill (1901).
4. "Peter Akers Papers (1776–1811)," including items of interest on Methodist missions, collected by Akers; and "Autobiography of Peter Akers to 1824" (27 pp.).
5. Alfred Brunson. "Early Methodism in St. Paul and Minnesota, 1837–1839" (9 pp.); "Minnesota Methodism in 1852" (4 pp.).
6. T. M. Fullerton. "Sketch of Chippewa Missions, 1841–1844" (20 pp.); "German and Scandinavian Methodist Episcopal Church, St. Paul, 1851–1863" (7 folders); "Indian Missions, 1840–1844" (6 pp.); "Appointments, 1841, Platteville (Minn.) Conference" (19 pp.); "Early Methodism in St. Paul and Minnesota, 1837–1853" (11 pp.); "Sketch of Scandinavian Missions (Minn.), 1851–1859" (15 pp.);

"Sketch of Methodist Missions at Stillwater (Minn.), 1853–1860" (20 pp.).

7. J. W. Hancock. "Red Wing Indian Mission, 1849–1852" (11 pp.).
8. Chauncey Hobart Historical Manuscripts.
9. C. C. Kidder. "Early History of the M. E. Church, West of Mississippi River, North of Wabashaw to Minnesota River (Minn.), 1852–1855" (19 pp.).
10. "W. P. Murray Papers (1836–1929)": concerning Methodism and Hamline University.
11. "Diaries of James Peet, Methodist Missionary at Duluth (1856–1865)." Pp. 722. (Typewritten.)
12. J. W. Powell. "A Short Sketch of Frontier Work in Southwestern Minnesota." 1900. Pp. 30.
13. Malcolm C. Shurtleff. "The Introduction of Methodism in Minnesota" (M.A. thesis, University of Minnesota, 1922). Pp. 131.

XII. Mississippi

A. Mississippi Conference Historical Society

1. "Autobiography of Learner Blackman (1800–1809)."
2. William Winans Collection, including "Journals (1812–1848)."

XIII. Missouri

A. Central Wesleyan College, Warrenton

1. "Missouri and Early Methodism, 1806–1865."

XIV. New Jersey

A. Drew Theological Seminary, Madison

1. "Journals of the General Conference of the Methodist Episcopal Church (1800–1840)."
2. "Records of the Book Committee of the Methodist Episcopal Church (1836–1868)."
3. "Archives of the Newark Annual Conference."
4. "Letters of Nathan Bangs."
5. "Journal of John Wesley Bond, Traveling Companion of Bishop Asbury."
6. "Cokesbury College Charter (1794)."
7. "Journal of George Coles, New York."
8. "Journal of George R. Crooks (1840——)."
9. John and Robert Emory Papers, including Asbury's "Letters" and unfinished "Life of Asbury."

10. Garrettson Papers: "Diary of Mrs. Catherine Garrettson (1787–1827)"; "Letters of Mrs. Catherine Garrettson" (205 items); "Biographical Sketch of Mrs. Catherine Garretson"; "Journal of Freeborn Garrettson"; "Letters of Freeborn Garrettson (1804–7)"; and "Experience of Thomas Smith (1776)."
11. "Journal of William Jessop (1788)."
12. "Journal of John B. Matthias."
13. "Journal of Thomas Morrell (1785–1792)."
14. Abel Stevens Papers: historical notes.
15. Wakeley Collection, including "Journal of J. B. Wakeley (1844–1845)" and "Biographical Sketches of Methodist Preachers," by Wakeley; examples: Francis Acuff, James Axley, William Beauchamp, John W. Bond, Thomas Branch, William Capers, John Emory, Philip Gatch, George Mair, George Pickering, George Roberts, Nicholas Snethen, John Summerfield, Peter Vannest.
16. Letters of Captain Thomas Webb.

XV. New York

A. Grosvenor Library, Buffalo
1. "Journals of the Genesee Annual Conference (1848–1897)." 3 vols.
2. "Journals of the East Genesee Annual Conference (1848–1876)." 2 vols.
3. Glezen Fillmore Collection: Genesee Conference materials, including stewards' reports, and Fillmore's "Diary" (1842–46).

B. Methodist Historical Society of the City of New York, New York
1. "Journals of the New York Annual Conference (1800–1839)." 3 vols.
2. "Records of the John Street Methodist Church, New York City (1769–1795)": marriages, births, deaths, treasurers' accounts.

C. Syracuse University, Syracuse
1. Methodist Episcopal Church Collection (1813–1900): 3,000 pieces, 70 volumes.
2. Oneida Conference Papers, including "Journals of the Oneida Conference (1829–1868)" (2 vols.); "Reports"; "Records of the Oneida Conference Missionary Society

(1846–1866)"; "Minutes of Ministerial Trials (1832–1868)" (1,500 pieces); and "Minutes of Conference Committees (1829–1870)" (1,000 pieces).

3. Quarterly Conference Records: "Scipio Circuit (1811–1826)"; "Sodus Circuit (1813–1850)"; "Western Circuit (1805, 1810–1835)."
4. Abner Chase. "Recollections of an Itinerant."

D. Troy Conference Historical Society, Troy

1. Troy Conference Papers, including "Journals of the Troy Annual Conference (1830–1929)" (10 vols.); "Minutes of Societies and Reports of Conference Committees" (39 vols.); "Ministerial Papers (1792–1945)" (2,411 pieces).
2. Quarterly Conference Records: "Vergennes Circuit (1806–1838)"; "Pittstown (1814–1829)," etc. (44 vols.).
3. "Historical Sketches of Churches in Northeastern New York, Western Massachusetts, and Vermont (1827–1903)."
4. Biographical materials, including "Biographical Data" compiled by Bostwick Hawley; "Diaries" and "Correspondence" by Matthias Swain (1790–1800); private "Record of Baptisms and Marriages" by Robert Washburn (1817–70) and John Wendell (1830–89). 81 volumes in all.

XVI. North Carolina

A. Duke University, Durham

1. "Methodist Episcopal Church, South, Papers (1759–1932)." 800 items: historical sketches, sermons, deeds, licenses, quarterly conference records, missionary society reports, etc.
2. "Allen Archer Account Books (1818–1860)." 3 vols.; Petersburg, Va.: accounts of money paid into the Methodist church at Petersburg.
3. "Fletcher Harris Archer Papers (1804–1900)." 939 items; Petersburg, Va.: including sermons of his father, Allen Leroy Archer, Methodist preacher.
4. Thomas Coke. "Sermon." Baltimore, 1785.
5. "Peter Doub Diary (1819–1834)." 1 vol.: autobiographical notes and sermon outlines of a North Carolina Methodist preacher (1796–1870).
6. "William Clark Doub Papers (1778–1899)." 314 items; Forsyth County, N.C.: family and professional correspondence of a Methodist educator (1824–1885).
7. "George Coke Dromgoole Papers (1767–1895)." 770 items;

Brunswick County, Va.: family, business, and political correspondence of Dromgoole (1797–1847), Virginia planter and member of Congress, and of his parents and children.

8. "William and Benjamin Hammett Papers (1789–1865)" 46 items; Charleston, S.C.: correspondence relating to a schism in the Methodist church, *ca.* 1791.
9. "Thomas Mann Diaries (1805–1830)." 7 vols.; Amherst County, Va.: diaries of a circuit-rider in North Carolina and Virginia.
10. "James Meacham Journals (1788–1794)." 8 vols.; Virginia and North Carolina circuits.
11. "William Ormond Journals (1791–1803)." 5 items; Tar River Circuit, N.C.
12. "Daniel Shine Papers (1793–1831)." 42 items; Louisburg, N.C.
13. "Whiteford Smith Papers (1807–1893)." 194 items; Charleston, S.C.: letters, diaries, and accounts of a South Carolina preacher and educator.
14. "John W. Young Papers (1811–1864)." 27 items; Franklin County, N.C.: correspondence of a Methodist preacher.

B. University of North Carolina, Chapel Hill

1. "Edward Dromgoole Papers."
2. "Charles Pettigrew Papers."

C. Archives of the North Carolina Historical Commission, Raleigh

1. "Richard Hugg King Papers (1767–1825)." 1 vol.: "Letters" and "Diary (1819–1823)" of a Methodist (later Presbyterian) camp-meeting preacher of North and South Carolina and Tennessee, and a manuscript "Biography" of him by Rev. Eli Caruthers (232 pp.).
2. "Robert Johnston Miller Papers (1799–1831)." 34 items: correspondence of a worker in the Methodist, Lutheran, and Episcopal churches.
3. "William Williams Stringfield Papers (1860–1914)": "Letters" and "Reminiscences" of Stringfield, son of Thomas Stringfield, Tennessee Methodist preacher.

XVII. Ohio

A. Western Reserve Historical Society, Cleveland

1. "Minutes of Cleveland District Meetings, Erie Conference (1848–1873)."

2. "Records of the Home Missionary Society of the Muskingum District (1838–1892)."
3. "Records of the Methodist Episcopal Sunday School of Ravenna, Ohio (1843–1847)."

B. Ohio Wesleyan University, Delaware

1. "Journals of the Western Annual Conference (1800–1811)."
2. "Journals of the Ohio Annual Conference": Vol. I (1812–26); Vol. II (1827–39); Vol. III (1840–67).
3. "Minutes of Preachers' Relief Society, Cincinnati Conference (1837–1849)."
4. Quarterly Conference Records: "Burlington Circuit, Ohio Conference (1820)"; "Cincinnati, Ohio Conference (1813)"; "Fairfield Circuit, Western Conference (Stewards' Record) (1805)"; "Hockhocking Circuit, Western Conference (Stewards' Record) (1804–1805)"; "Marietta Circuit, Ohio Conference (1817–1823)"; and "Paint Creek Circuit, Western Conference (1811)."
5. James B. Finley Papers (1794–1858): 1,227 letters and documents relating to Ohio Methodism and the Wyandot Mission. Indexed.
6. Benjamin St. James Fry Papers (1850–51): letters on frontier Methodism in Ohio, Indiana, and Kentucky.

XVIII. Oregon

A. Willamette University, Salem

1. "Records of Oregon Conference."
2. Miscellaneous biographical data: journals, letters, etc.

B. Oregon State Library, Salem

1. "Daybook of Henry B. Brewer, Missionary (1839–1843)." (Typewritten.)

XIX. Pennsylvania

A. Allegheny College, Meadville

1. "Journals of the Erie Annual Conference (1836–1945)."

B. Philadelphia Conference Historical Society, Philadelphia

1. "Journals of the Philadelphia Annual Conference (1800–1945)."
2. "Quarterly Conference Records and Historical Sketches of Local Churches, Philadelphia Conference."
3. "Letters of Methodist Preachers": Wesley, Clark, Asbury, Waugh, etc.
4. "Private Marriage Record of Joseph Castle (1825–1874)."

5. "Diary of John Collins (1821–1823)."
6. "Diary of David Dailey (1815–1817)."
7. "Journal of William Jessop (1790)."
8. "Journal of Joseph Pilmoor (1769–1774)." (Typewritten copy in Divinity Library, University of Chicago.)
9. "Journal of Richard Swain." (Typewritten.)

C. Historical Society of Western Pennsylvania, Pittsburgh
1. "Journals of the Pittsburgh Annual Conference (1825–1945)."
2. Daniel R. Kovar. "Social Life in Early Fayette County [Pennsylvania] as Seen Especially in Church and Court Records" (M.A. thesis, University of Pittsburgh, 1929). Pp. 128.
3. "Autobiography of John Wrenshall" (5 vols.), dealing with Pittsburgh Methodism (1796–1817).

XX. South Carolina
A. Wofford College, Spartanburg
1. Southern Methodist historical materials.

XXI. Tennessee
A. Methodist Publishing House, Nashville
1. "Journal of the General Convention (Methodist Episcopal Church, South), 1845."
2. "Journals of the General Conference of the Methodist Episcopal Church, South (1846–1870)."

XXII. Texas
A. Southern Methodist University, Dallas
1. "Quarterly Conference Records of San Augustine Circuit, Texas (1837–1857)."

B. University of Texas, Austin
1. Orceneth Fisher Papers. (Photostats.)
2. Lyttleton Fowler Papers.
3. Robert E. Ledbetter, Jr. "Orceneth Fisher, Pioneer Methodist Preacher of Texas and the Pacific Coast" (M.A. thesis, University of Texas, 1938).

XXIII. Virginia
A. Virginia Historical Society, Richmond
1. "Letterbook of Stith Mead (1793–1795)," Methodist itinerant in Virginia.

XXIV. Washington
A. College of Puget Sound, Tacoma
1. Western Jurisdictional Conference materials.

XXV. Wisconsin

A. Wisconsin Historical Society, Madison

1. "Journals and Letter Books of Alfred Brunson," Methodist circuit-rider and Indian agent.

II. OFFICIAL DOCUMENTS

Minutes of the Methodist Conferences, from the First, Held in London, by the Late Rev. John Wesley, A.M. in the Year 1744, Vol. I: *1744–1798.* London, 1812.

Minutes of the Annual Conferences of the Methodist Episcopal Church, Vol. I: *1773–1828.* New York, 1840. Vol. II: *1829–1839.* New York, 1840. Vol. III: *1839–1845.* New York, 1840–45. Vol. IV: *1846–1851.* New York, 1856.

Journals of the General Conference of the Methodist Episcopal Church, Vol. I: *1796–1836.* New York, 1855. Vol. II: *1840–1844.* New York, 1844. Vol. III: *1848.* New York, 1848. Vol. IV: *1852.* New York, 1852.

Minutes of the Annual Conferences of the Methodist Episcopal Church South, Vol. I: *1845–1857.* Richmond and Nashville, 1846–58.

Journals of the General Conference of the Methodist Episcopal Church South, Vol. I: *1846–1858.* N.p., n.d.

Minutes of the Several Conversations between the Rev. Thomas Coke, L.L.D., the Rev. Francis Asbury and Others at a Conference, Begun in Baltimore in the State of Maryland on Monday the 27th of December, in the Year 1784, Composing a Form of Discipline for the Ministers, Preachers, and Other Members of the Methodist Episcopal Church in America. Philadelphia, 1785. Subsequent editions of the Methodist *Discipline* appeared in 1786, 1787, 1788, 1789, 1790, 1791, 1792, 1797, 1798, 1800, 1801, 1804, 1805, 1808, and quadrennially thereafter.

Robert Emory. *History of the Discipline of the Methodist Episcopal Church.* New York, 1844.

David Sherman. *History of the Revisions of the Discipline of the Methodist Episcopal Church.* New York and Cincinnati, 1874.

P. A. Peterson. *History of the Revisions of the Discipline of the Methodist Episcopal Church, South.* Nashville, 1889.

William Warren Sweet (ed.). *The Rise of Methodism in the West: Being the Journal of the Western Conference (1800–1811).* New York and Cincinnati, 1920.

———. *Circuit-Rider Days along the Ohio: Being the Journals of the Ohio Conference from Its Organization in 1812 to 1826.* New York and Cincinnati, 1923.

William Warren Sweet. *Circuit-Rider Days in Indiana: The Journals of the Indiana Conference (1832–1842)*. Indianapolis, 1916.

III. METHODIST PERIODICALS

Arminian Magazine. Philadelphia, 1789–90.

Methodist Magazine. Philadelphia, 1797–98.

New England Missionary Magazine. Concord, N.H., 1815.

Western Christian Monitor. Chillicothe, Ohio, 1816.

Methodist Magazine. New York, 1818–28. Became the *Methodist Magazine and Quarterly Review,* 1830–40; the *Methodist Quarterly Review,* 1841–84; the *Methodist Review,* 1885–31; and *Religion in Life,* 1932——

Wesleyan Repository. Trenton and Philadelphia, 1821–24.

Youth's Instructer and Guardian. New York, 1823–32.

Zion's Herald. Boston, 1823——. Merged with the *Christian Advocate* (1828–33).

Mutual Rights and Methodist Protestant (now *Methodist Recorder*). Baltimore, 1824–28, 1831——.

Wesleyan Journal. Charleston, S.C., 1825–27. Merged with the *Christian Advocate.*

Christian Advocate. New York, 1826——.

Methodist Almanac. Boston, 1827.

New England Herald. N.p., 1829. Merged with the *New England Christian Herald.*

Gospel Herald. Lexington, Ky., 1829–31.

Methodist Preacher. Boston, 1830–33.

New England Christian Herald. N.p., 1831–33. Merged with *Zion's Herald.*

Christian Advocate. Nashville, 1832–1940.

Maine Wesleyan Journal. Portland, Me., 1832–41. Merged with *Zion's Herald.*

Richmond Christian Advocate. Richmond, Va., 1832–1939.

Pittsburgh Christian Advocate. Pittsburgh, 1833–1932.

Western Christian Advocate. Cincinnati, 1834–1929.

Wesleyan Christian Advocate. Atlanta, Ga., 1836——

Western Methodist. Memphis, Nashville, 1836——?.

Southern Christian Advocate. Charleston, S.C.; Columbia, S.C.; Macon, Ga., 1837——.

Methodist Recorder. Pittsburgh, 1839–1929.

Der Christliche Apologete. Cincinnati, 1839——. The *Christian Advocate* for German Methodism.

Ladies Repository. Cincinnati, 1841–76. Later the *National Repository*. Cincinnati, 1877–80.

Northern Christian Advocate. Syracuse, N.Y., 1841–1917.

American Wesleyan. Syracuse, N.Y., 1843–83?.

Wesleyan Methodist. Syracuse, N.Y., 1843——.

Texas Christian Advocate. Galveston, Dallas, 1846——. Now the *Southwestern Advocate*.

Southern Lady's Companion. Nashville, 1847–54.

Vermont Christian Messenger. Montpelier, Vt., 1847–63.

Methodist Quarterly Review. Louisville, Nashville, 1847–1930. Methodist Episcopal Church, South.

Southern Methodist Pulpit. Richmond, Va., 1848–52.

New Orleans Christian Advocate. New Orleans, 1850——

St. Louis Christian Advocate. St. Louis, 1850–1931.

Buffalo Christian Advocate. Buffalo, N.Y., 1850–1904.

Texan Wesleyan Banner. Houston, 1850–52.

California Christian Advocate. San Francisco, 1851–1932.

Northwestern Christian Advocate. Chicago, 1852–1929.

Raleigh Christian Advocate. Raleigh, N.C., 1855–1919.

Pacific Christian Advocate. Portland, Ore., 1855–1940.

Texas Methodist Historical Quarterly. 1909–11.

IV. AUTOBIOGRAPHIES

ANDREW, J[AMES] O. *Miscellanies: Comprising Letters, Essays, and Addresses, to Which Is Added a Biographical Sketch of Mrs. Ann Amelia Andrew*. Louisville, 1854.

ASBURY, FRANCIS. *Journal of Rev. Francis Asbury, Bishop of the Methodist Episcopal Church*. 3 vols. New York and Cincinnati, n.d. Vol. I: *1771–1786;* Vol. II: *1787–1800;* Vol. III: *1801–1815*.

BANGS, HEMAN. *The Autobiography and Journal of Rev. Heman Bangs*. New York, 1874.

BANGS, JOHN. *Autobiography of Rev. John Bangs, of the New York Annual Conference*. New York, 1846.

BOEHM, HENRY. *Reminiscences, Historical and Biographical, of Sixty-four Years in the Ministry*. New York, 1865.

BOYD, ROBERT. *Personal Memoirs: Together with a Discussion upon the Hardships and Sufferings of Itinerant Life*. Cincinnati, 1868.

BROOKS, JOHN. *The Life and Times of the Rev. John Brooks*. Nashville, 1848.

BROWN, GEORGE. *Recollections of Itinerant Life: Including Early Reminiscences*. Cincinnati, 1866.

Brunson, Alfred. *A Western Pioneer: or, Incidents of the Life and Times of Rev. Alfred Brunson.* 2 vols. Cincinnati, 1880.

Carroll, Andrew. *Moral and Religious Sketches and Collections, with Incidents of Ten Years' Itinerancy in the West.* Cincinnati, 1857.

Cartwright, Peter. *Autobiography of Peter Cartwright, the Backwoods Preacher,* ed. W. P. Strickland. Cincinnati, 1860.

———. *Fifty Years as a Presiding Elder.* New York, 1871.

Davis, L. D. *Life in the Laity; or, the History of a Station.* New York, 1858.

DeVinne, Daniel. *Recollections of Fifty Years in the Ministry.* New York, 1869.

Dow, Lorenzo. *The Dealings of God, Man, and Devil, as Exemplified in the Life, Experiences, and Travels of Lorenzo Dow.* Cincinnati, 1858.

———. *History of Cosmopolite; or the Writings of Rev. Lorenzo Dow.* Cincinnati, 1858.

Dunwody, James. *Reminiscences and Sermons.* Macon, Ga., 1872.

Erwin, James. *Reminiscences of Early Circuit Life.* Toledo, Ohio, 1884.

Finley, James B. *Autobiography of Rev. James B. Finley, or, Pioneer Life in the West,* ed. W. P. Strickland. Cincinnati, 1857.

———. *Life among the Indians, or, Personal Reminiscences and Historical Incidents Illustrative of Indian Life and Character,* ed D. W. Clark. Cincinnati, 1857.

Gaddis, Maxwell P. *Footprints of an Itinerant.* Cincinnati, 1874.

———. *Last Words and Old-Time Memories.* Cincinnati, 1880.

Gavitt, Elnathan Corrington. *Crumbs from My Saddle Bags: or, Reminiscences of Pioneer Life and Biographical Sketches.* Toledo, Ohio, 1884.

Giles, Charles. *Pioneer: A Narrative of the Nativity, Experience, Travels, and Ministerial Labours of Rev. Charles Giles.* New York, 1844.

Goode, William H. *Outposts of Zion, with Limnings of Mission Life.* Cincinnati, 1863.

Hobart, Chauncey. *Recollections of My Life: Fifty Years of Itineracy in the Northwest.* Red Wing, Minn., 1885.

Hudson, Thomas M. *Life and Times of Rev. Thomas M. Hudson, of the Pittsburg Annual Conference of the Methodist Episcopal Church.* Cincinnati, 1871.

Jarratt, Devereux, *The Life of Devereux Jarratt, Rector of Bath Parish, Dinwiddie County, Virginia,* . . . . ed. John Coleman. Baltimore, 1806.

Landon, S[eymour]. *Fifty Years in the Itinerant Ministry.* New York, 1868.

Lewis, David. *Recollections of a Superannuate: or, Sketches of Life, Labor, and Experience in the Methodist Itinerancy.* Cincinnati, 1857.

Lorrain, Alfred M. *The Helm, the Sword, and the Cross: A Life Narrative.* Cincinnati, 1867.

Milburn, William Henry. *The Pioneer Preacher: or, Rifle, Axe, and Saddle-Bags, and Other Lectures.* New York, 1857.

———. *Ten Years of Preacher Life: Chapter from an Autobiography.* New York, 1859.

———. *The Lance, Cross, and Canoe; the Flatboat, Rifle and Plough in the Valley of the Mississippi.* New York and St. Louis, [1892].

Miller, Adam (ed.). *Experience of German Methodist Preachers.* Cincinnati, 1859.

Miller, W. G. *Thirty Years in the Itineracy,* Milwaukee, 1875.

Moody, Granville, *Autobiography of Rev. Granville Moody,* ed. Sylvester Weeks. Cincinnati, 1890.

Morris, T. A. *Miscellany: Consisting of Essays, Biographical Sketches, and Notes of Travel.* Cincinnati, 1854.

Newell, E. F. *Life and Observations of Rev. E. F. Newell, Who Has Been More than Forty Years an Itinerant Minister in the Methodist Episcopal Church, New England Conference.* Worcester, [Mass.], 1847.

Peck, George. *The Life and Times of Rev. George Peck, D.D.* New York, 1874.

Pitezel, John H. *Lights and Shades of Missionary Life: Containing Travels, Sketches, Incidents, and Missionary Efforts, during Nine Years Spent in the Region of Lake Superior.* Cincinnati, 1857.

Smith, Henry. *Recollections and Reflections of an Old Itinerant.* New York, 1848.

Snelling, Joseph. *Life of Rev. Joseph Snelling.* Boston, 1847.

Stevens, Abel. *Sketches and Incidents; or, a Budget from the Saddle-Bags of a Superannuated Itinerant.* New York, 1855.

Stewart, John. *Highways and Hedges; or, Fifty Years of Western Methodism.* Cincinnati, 1872.

Swayze, William. *Narrative of William Swayze, Minister of the Gospel.* Cincinnati, 1839.

Tarkington, Joseph. *Autobiography of Rev. Joseph Tarkington, One of the Pioneer Methodist Preachers of Indiana.* Cincinnati, 1899.

Travis, Joseph. *Autobiography of the Rev. Joseph Travis, A.M., a Member of the Memphis Annual Conference: Embracing a Succinct History of the Methodist Episcopal Church, South; Particularly in Part of*

Western Virginia, the Carolinas, Georgia, Alabama, and Mississippi, ed. THOMAS O. SUMMERS. Nashville, 1856.

WARE, THOMAS. *Sketches of the Life and Travels of Rev. Thomas Ware.* New York, 1839.

WILEY, ALLEN. *Life and Times of the Rev. Allen Wiley,* ed. D. W. CLARK. Cincinnati, 1853.

YOUNG, JACOB. *Autobiography of a Pioneer; or, the Nativity, Experience, Travels, and Ministerial Labors of Rev. Jacob Young; with Incidents, Observations, and Reflections.* Cincinnati, 1857.

V. SECONDARY MATERIALS

BIOGRAPHIES

ALLEN, STEPHEN. *The Life of Rev. John Allen, Better Known as "Camp Meeting John."* Boston, 1888.

ANONYMOUS. *"Father Clark," or the Pioneer Preacher: Sketches and Incidents of Rev. John Clark, by an Old Pioneer.* New York, 1855.

ASBURY, HERBERT. *A Methodist Saint: The Life of Bishop Asbury.* New York, 1927.

ATKINSON, JOHN. *Memorials of Methodism in New Jersey.* Philadelphia, 1860.

BANGS, NATHAN. *The Life of the Rev. Freeborn Garrettson: Compiled from His Printed and Manuscript Journals, and Other Authentic Documents.* New York, 1832.

BROSMAN, C. J. *Jason Lee: Prophet of the New Oregon.* New York, 1932.

CANDLER, W. A. *Thomas Coke.* Nashville, 1924.

CARROLL, H. K. *Francis Asbury in the Making of American Methodism.* New York: 1923.

CARROLL, JOHN. *Case and His Cotemporaries; or, the Canadian Itinerants' Memorial: Constituting a Biographical History of Methodism in Canada, from Its Introduction into the Province, till the Death of the Rev. Wm. Case in 1855.* 5 vols. Toronto, 1867–77.

CLARK, D. W. *Life and Times of Rev. Elijah Hedding.* New York, 1855.

COOPER, EZEKIEL. *The Substance of a Funeral Discourse . . . . on the Death of Francis Asbury.* Philadelphia, 1819.

CORDERAY, EDWARD. *Father Reeves, the Model Class Leader.* Nashville, 1854.

CROOKS, GEORGE R. *Life of Bishop Matthew Simpson, of the Methodist Episcopal Church.* New York, 1890.

Dictionary of American Biography. 21 vols. New York, 1928–44.

DREW, SAMUEL. *The Life of the Rev. Thomas Coke, LLD.* London, 1817.

DUBOSE, HORACE M. *Francis Asbury: A Biographical Study.* Nashville, 1916.

———. *Life of Joshua Soule.* Nashville, 1916.

DUNHAM, ISAAC. *Memoir of Rev. Benjamin Swift, of the Reformed Methodist Connection.* Boston, 1842.

DUREN, WILLIAM LARKIN. *Francis Asbury: Founder of American Methodism and Unofficial Minister of State.* New York, 1928.

———. *The Top Sergeant of the Pioneers: The Story of a Lifelong Battle for an Ideal.* Emory University, Ga., 1930.

EDWARDS, JOHN E. *Life of Rev. John Wesley Childs.* Louisville, 1852.

ELLIOTT, CHARLES. *The Life of Bishop Robert R. Roberts.* Cincinnati, 1844.

[EMORY, ROBERT.] *The Life of Rev. John Emory, D.D., by His Eldest Son.* New York, 1841.

ETHERIDGE, J. W. *The Life of the Rev. Thomas Coke, D.C.L.* London, 1860.

FFIRTH, JOHN. *The Experience and Gospel Labours of the Rev. Benjamin Abbott, to Which Is Annexed, a Narrative of His Life and Death.* New York, 1830.

FINNEY, THOMAS M. *The Life and Labors of Enoch Mather Marvin, Late Bishop of the Methodist Episcopal Church, South.* St. Louis, 1880.

FLANIGEN, J. R. *Methodism: Old and New, with Sketches of Some of Its Early Preachers.* Philadelphia, 1880.

FLEHARTY, J. J. *Glimpses of the Life of Rev. A. E. Phelps and His Colaborers; or Twenty-five Years in the Methodist Itineracy.* Cincinnati, 1878.

FLOOD, THEODORE L., and HAMILTON, JOHN W. (eds.). *Lives of Methodist Bishops.* New York, 1882.

FRY, BENJAMIN ST. JAMES. *The Life of Rev. Richard Whatcoat.* (New York, 1852.

GADDIS, MAXWELL P. *Brief Recollections of the Late Rev. George W. Walker.* Cincinnati, 1857.

GILMORE, W. E. *Life of Edward Tiffin, First Governor of Ohio.* Chillicothe, 1897.

GORRIE, P. DOUGLASS. *The Lives of Eminent Methodist Ministers; Containing Biographical Sketches, Incidents, Anecdotes, Records of Travel, Reflections, &c, &c.* New York, 1856.

GRANT, HELEN HARDIE. *Peter Cartwright: Pioneer.* New York, 1931.

GREEN, WILLIAM M. *Life and Papers of A. L. P. Green, D.D.* Nashville, 1877.

GREENE, MARY. *Life, Three Sermons, and Some of the Miscellaneous Writings of Rev. Jesse Greene.* Lexington, Mo., 1852.

GURLEY, L[EONARD] B. *Memoir of Rev. William Gurley, Late of Milan, Ohio, a Local Minister of the Methodist Episcopal Church.* Cincinnati, 1854.

HEDGES, JOHN W. (comp.). *Crowned Victors: The Memoirs of over Four-Hundred Methodist Preachers, Including the First Two Hundred and Fifty Who Died on This Continent.* Baltimore, 1878.

HENKLE, M. M. *The Life of Henry Bidleman Bascom.* Louisville, 1854.

HIBBEN, W. W. *Rev. James Havens, One of the Heroes of Indiana Methodism.* Indianapolis, 1872.

HOLLAND, JOHN. *Memoirs of the Life and Ministry of the Rev. John Summerfield, A. M.* New York, 1830.

HOLLIDAY, F. C. *Life and Times of Rev. Allen Wiley, A.M., Containing Sketches of Early Methodist Preachers in Indiana, and Notices of the Introduction and Progress of Methodism in the State.* Cincinnati, 1853.

HOSS, E. E. *William McKendree: A Biographical Study.* Nashville, 1924.

JACKSON, THOMAS (ed.). *The Lives of Early Methodist Preachers Chiefly Written by Themselves.* 6 vols. London, 1873.

LARRABEE, WILLIAM C. *Asbury and His Co-laborers.* 2 vols. Cincinnati, 1852.

LEE, LEROY M. *The Life and Times of the Rev. Jesse Lee.* Louisville, Ky., 1848.

MCANALLY, D. R. *Life and Times of Rev. S. Patton, D.D. and Annals of the Holston Conference.* St. Louis, 1859.

MCCLINTOCK, JOHN. *Sketches of Eminent Methodist Ministers.* New York, 1854.

[MCLEAN, JOHN.] *A Sketch of the Life of Rev. John Collins, Late of the Ohio Conference.* Cincinnati, 1849.

———. *Sketch of Rev. Philip Gatch.* Cincinnati, 1854.

MAINS, GEORGE P. *Francis Asbury.* New York and Cincinnati, 1909.

MARLAY, JOHN F. *The Life of Rev. Thomas A. Morris.* Cincinnati, 1875.

MATLACK, LUCIUS C. *The Life of Rev. Orange Scott, Compiled from His Personal Narrative, Correspondence, and Other Authentic Sources of Information.* New York, 1847.

MEREDITH, WILLIAM HENRY. *Jesse Lee, a Methodist Apostle.* New York, 1909.

MITCHELL, JAMES. *Life and Times of Levi Scott.* New York, 1885.

MITCHELL, JOSEPH. *The Missionary Pioneer, or a Brief Memoir of the Life, Labors and Death of John Stewart (Man of Colour): Founder under God of the Mission among the Wyandotts at Upper Sandusky, Ohio.* New York, 1827.

MOORE, M. H. *Sketches of the Pioneers of Methodism in North Carolina and Virginia.* Nashville, 1884.

NORTHCOTT, H. C. *Biography of Rev. Benjamin Northcott, Pioneer Local Preacher of the Methodist Episcopal Church in Kentucky and for More than Sixty-three Years in the Ministry.* Cincinnati, 1875.

PADDOCK, Z[ECHARIAH]. *Memoir of Rev. Benjamin G. Paddock, with Brief Notices of Early Ministerial Associates.* New York, 1875.

PAINE, ROBERT. *Life and Times of William M'Kendree.* 2 vols. Nashville, 1874.

PALMER, WALTER C. *Life and Letters of Leonidas L. Hamline.* New York, 1866.

PHOEBUS, WILLIAM. *Memoirs of the Rev. Richard Whatcoat.* New York, 1828.

PLYLER, A. W. *The Iron Duke of the Methodist Itinerancy.* Nashville, 1925.

PRENTICE, GEORGE. *Wilbur Fisk.* Boston, 1890.

REDFORD, A. H. *Life and Times of H. H. Kavanaugh.* Nashville, 1884.

RIDGAWAY, HENRY B. *The Life of Edmund S. Janes, D.D., LL.D.* New York, 1882.

RIVERS, R. H. *The Life of Robert Paine, D.D., Bishop of the Methodist Episcopal Church, South.* Nashville, 1916.

SELLERS, CHARLES COLEMAN. *Lorenzo Dow: The Bearer of the Word.* New York, 1928.

SHERMAN, D[AVID]. *Sketches of New England Divines.* New York, 1860.

SIMS, CHARLES N. *The Life of Rev. Thomas M. Eddy, D.D.* New York and Cincinnati, 1880.

SMITH, ERNEST ASHTON. *Martin Ruter.* New York, 1915.

SMITH, GEORGE G. *The Life and Times of George Foster Pierce.* Sparta, Ga., 1888.

———. *Life and Labors of Francis Asbury, Bishop of the Methodist Episcopal Church in America.* Nashville, 1896.

SMITH, WILLIAM C. *Pillars in the Temple; or Sketches of Deceased Laymen of the Methodist Episcopal Church, Distinguished as Examples of Piety and Usefulness.* New York, 1872.

SPRAGUE, WILLIAM B. *Annals of the American Pulpit; or Commemorative Notices of Distinguished American Clergymen of Various Denominations.* Vol. VII: *Methodist.* 9 vols. New York, 1859.

STANLEY, E. J. *Life of Rev. L. B. Stateler: A Story of Life on the Old Frontier*. Nashville, 1916.

STEVENS, ABEL. *Life and Times of Nathan Bangs, D.D.* New York, 1863.

STEVENSON, EDWARD. *Biographical Sketch of the Rev. Valentine Cook, A.M.* Nashville, 1858.

STRICKLAND, W. P. *The Pioneer Bishop: or, the Life and Times of Francis Asbury*. New York, [1858].

———. *The Life of Jacob Gruber*. New York, 1860.

SUMMERS, THOMAS O. (ed.). *Biographical Sketches of Eminent Itinerant Ministers Distinguished for the Most Part, as Pioneers of Methodism within the Bounds of the Methodist Episcopal Church, South*. Nashville, 1859.

THRIFT, MINTON. *Memoir of the Rev. Jesse Lee with Extracts from His Journals*. New York, 1823.

TIPPLE, EZRA SQUIER. *Freeborn Garrettson*. New York and Cincinnati, 1910.

———. *Francis Asbury: The Prophet of the Long Road*. New York and Cincinnati, [1916].

WAKELEY, J. B. *The Heroes of Methodism, Containing Sketches of Eminent Methodist Ministers, and Characteristic Anecdotes of Their Personal History*. New York, 1856.

WATTERS, D. A. *First American Itinerant of Methodism, William Watters*. Cincinnati, 1898.

WIGHTMAN, W. M. *Life of William Capers .... Including an Autobiography*. Nashville, 1902.

WRIGHT, JOHN F. *Sketches of the Life and Labors of James Quinn*. Cincinnati, 1851.

PERIODICAL ARTICLES

A. WESTERN FRONTIER

GADDIS, MERRILL E. "Religious Ideas and Attitudes in the Early Frontier," *Church History,* II, 152–70.

GEWEHR, W. M. "Some Factors in the Expansion of Frontier Methodism, 1800–1811," *Journal of Religion,* VIII, 98–120.

JOHNSON, JESSE. "Early Theological Education West of the Alleghenies," *American Society of Church History Papers, Series II,* V, 121–30.

MILLEN, G. F. "Early Methodism and Cherokees," *Methodist Quarterly Review,* LXVI, 476–87.

MOATS, FRANCIS L. "The Rise of Methodism in the Middle West," *Mississippi Valley Historical Review,* XV, 69–88.

MODE, PETER G. "Revivalism as a Phase of Frontier Life," *Journal of Religion,* I, 337–54.

OGBURN, CAL. "The Pioneer Religious Revival," *Annals of Iowa, Series III,* XV, 483–506.

POSEY, W. B. "The Earthquake of 1811 and Its Influence on Evangelistic Methods in the Churches of the Old South," *Tennessee Historical Magazine, Series II,* I, 107–14.

RICE, J. A. "The Old-Time Circuit Rider," *Methodist Quarterly Review,* LIX, 33–47.

SHURTER, ROBERT L. "The Camp Meeting in the Early Life and Literature of the Mid-West," *Eastern Tennessee Historical Society Publications,* V, 142–49.

SWEET, WILLIAM WARREN. "The Churches as Moral Courts of the Frontier," *Church History,* II, 3–21.

———. "The First Circuit Riders in the West," *ibid.,* LXVI, 563–75.

———. "Some Salient Characteristics of Frontier Religion," *Methodist Quarterly Review,* LXXIII, 437–52.

THOMAS, J. M. "Influence of Frontier Life on American Christianity," *New Jersey Historical Society Proceedings* (N.S.), XI, 1–18.

B. ILLINOIS

BARNHARDT, J. D. "The Rise of the Methodist Episcopal Church in Illinois from the Beginning to the Year 1832," *Journal of the Illinois State Historical Society,* XII, 149–217.

BRADSHAW, ARTHUR. "The Pioneer Preacher in Illinois," *Journal of the Illinois State Historical Society,* III, 61–64.

GOODRICH, GRANT. "A Lecture Delivered in the Clark Street M. E. Church on the Rise and Progress of Methodism in Chicago," *Northwestern Christian Advocate,* Vol. I, Nos. 1–3.

HARKER, J. R. "Progress in the Illinois Conference, 1824–1924," *Journal of the Illinois State Historical Society,* XVII, 159–74.

JAMES, EDMUND J. "Reverend Colin Dew James: A Pioneer Methodist Preacher of Early Illinois," *Journal of the Illinois State Historical Society,* IX, 450–69.

NELSON, DAVID F. "The One Hundredth Anniversary of the Methodist Church of Abingdon," *Journal of the Illinois State Historical Society,* XXVI, 467–68.

SCARRITT, ISAAC. "Early Times in Chicago," *Northwestern Christian Advocate,* Vol. I, No. 26.

Scarritt, Isaac. "Early Methodism in Illinois," *ibid.*, No. 28.

Thrapp, R. F. "Early Religious Beginnings in Illinois," *Journal of the Illinois State Historical Society,* IV, 306–16.

Turnbull, E. R. "A Century of Methodism in Carlinville, Illinois," *Journal of the Illinois State Historical Society,* XXIV, 243–98.

C. INDIANA

Bridges, Albert Fletcher. "Early Methodism in Clay County," *Indiana Magazine of History,* XX, 160–73.

Iglehart, John E. "The Life and Times of John Shrader, Including the Introduction and Progress of Methodism in Southwestern Indiana," *Indiana Magazine of History,* XVII, 3–49, 117–49.

Johnson, Deidre Duff. "Moses Ashworth, Pioneer of Indiana Methodism, and His Times," *Southwestern Indiana Historical Society Proceedings, 1923,* pp. 94–118.

Leak, Roscoe R. "Salem Methodist Church (Oldest Methodist Church in Indiana)," *Indiana Magazine of History,* XXIX, 17–21.

Price, Ruth. "Indiana Methodism, 1816–1832," *Indiana Magazine of History,* XI, 231–47.

Sweet, William Warren. "Early Methodist Circuits in Indiana," *Indiana Magazine of History,* X, 359–68.

Wiley, Allen. "Methodism in Southeastern Indiana," *Indiana Magazine of History,* XXIII, 1–62, 130–216, 239–332, 393–466. Reprinted from the *Western Christian Advocate,* Vols. XII and XIII (1845–46).

Williams, J. Milton. "The Monticello Circuit of the Methodist Church, a Hundred Years of Methodist Progress," *Indiana Magazine of History,* XXXII, 38–51.

D. IOWA

Gallaher, Ruth A. "The First Church in Iowa," *Palimpsest,* VII, 1–10.

Irish, Charles W. "Some Pioneer Preachers of Iowa," *Iowa Historical Record,* X, 121–27.

Richards, W. Avery. "Early Methodism in Northwest Iowa," *Iowa Historical Record,* XI, 296–308.

E. KENTUCKY

[Hinde, Thomas S.] "Of the Rise and Progress of Methodism in the Western States by One Called Theophilus Arminius," *Gospel Herald,* Vol. II (1830).

JILLSON, WILLARD ROUSE. "Early Kentucky Church Records," *Kentucky Historical Society Register,* XXXVI, 183–85.

STAPLES, CHARLES R. "Pioneer Kentucky Preachers and Pulpits," *Filson Club Historical Quarterly,* IX, 135–57.

WELDON, J. W. "Early Methodism in Kentucky," *Kentucky Historical Society Register,* XXXII, 38–39.

F. MISSOURI

HOLTER, DON W. "The Role of the Church in Trans-Missouri," *Church History*, IV, 134–46.

MURPHY, LAWRENCE E. "Beginnings of Methodism in Missouri: 1798–1824," *Missouri Historical Review,* XXI, 370–94.

RAYMER, R. C. "The Development of Christianity in the Southwest," *Methodist Quarterly Review,* LXXVI, 69–98.

SIMMONS, LUCY. "The Rise and Growth of the Protestant Bodies in the Missouri Territory," *Missouri Historical Review,* XXII, 296–306.

G. OHIO

BRADFORD, J. E. "The Centennial Churches of the Miami Valley," *Ohio Archaeological and Historical Quarterly,* XXV, 234–58.

DAVIS, HAROLD E. "Religion in the Western Reserve, 1800–1825," *Ohio Archaeological and Historical Quarterly,* XXXVII, 475–501.

HESTER, M. M. "Methodism in the Fire Lands, from 1811 to 1881," *Fire Lands Pioneer* (N.S.), I, 71–77.

MARTZOLFF, CLEMENT L. "Early Religious Movements in the Muskingum Valley," *Ohio Archaeological and Historical Quarterly,* XXV, 183–90.

MITCHELL, MARGARET J. "Religion as a Factor in the Early Development of Ohio," *Mississippi Valley Historical Association Proceedings,* IX, 75–89.

PITEZEL, S. H. "The Early Itinerancy," *Fire Lands Pioneer* (N.S.), VI, 65–73.

SLOANE, RUSH R. "Early Methodists in Ohio," *Fire Lands Pioneer, Proceedings,* XII, 390–404.

H. PENNSYLVANIA

JOHNSON, ROY H. "Frontier Religion in Western Pennsylvania," *Western Pennsylvania Historical Magazine,* XVI, 23–27.

REYNOLDS, GRAFTON E. "The Smithfield Street Methodist Episcopal Church, Pittsburgh, Pennsylvania," *Western Pennsylvania Historical Magazine,* VI, 250–58.

SILVEUS, MARIAN. "Churches and Social Control on the Western Pennsylvania Frontier," *Western Pennsylvania Historical Magazine,* XIX, 123–34.

SLOSSER, GAIUS J. "A Chapter from the Religious History of Western Pennsylvania," *Presbyterian Church: Journal of the Department of History,* XVI, 97–125.

I. NORTH DAKOTA

WHITE, C. M. "History of Methodism in North Dakota," *North Dakota Historical Society Collections,* I, 310–18.

J. SOUTH

ALEXANDER, GROSS. "Two Chapters from the Early History of Methodism in the South," *Methodist Quarterly Review,* LXIII, 419–37.

BOYD, WILLIAM K. "Methodist Expansion in North Carolina after the Revolution," *Trinity College Historical Society Publications,* XII, 37–55.

GRISSOM, W. L. "Some First Things in North Carolina Methodism," *Trinity College Historical Society Publications,* IX, 22–32.

JOHNSON, GUION GRIFFIS. "The Camp Meeting in Ante-bellum North Carolina," *North Carolina Historical Review,* X, 15–110.

MOODY, V. ALTON. "Early Religious Efforts in the Lower Mississippi Valley," *Mississippi Valley Historical Review,* XXII, 161–76.

POSEY, WALTER B. "The Advance of Methodism into the Lower South-West," *Journal of Southern History,* II, 439–52.

PRICE, R. N. "Methodism in East Tennessee, before, during, and since the War," *Methodist Quarterly Review,* LVII, 293–303.

SMITH, L. L. "Methodism in the Albemarle Country," *Trinity College Historical Society Publications,* IX, 51–56.

WATSON, E. O. "Builders: Sketches of Methodist Preachers in South Carolina, with Historical Data," *Southern Christian Advocate* (Columbia, S.C., n.d.)

BOOKS

ALEXANDER, GROSS. *A History of the Methodist Church, South.* "American Church History Series," Vol. XI. New York, 1894.

ALLEN, STEPHEN, and PILLSBURY, W. H. *History of Methodism in Maine, 1793–1886.* Augusta, 1887.

AMES, EDWARD S. *The Psychology of Religious Experience.* Boston, 1910.

ANDERSON, JAMES A. *Centennial History of Arkansas Methodism: A His-*

tory of the Methodist Episcopal Church, South, in the State of Arkansas, 1815–1935. Benton, Ark., 1935.

[ANONYMOUS.] *Gospel News, or a Brief Account of the Revival of Religion in Kentucky and Several Other Parts of the United States.....* Baltimore, 1801.

ANTHONY, CHARLES V. *Fifty Years of Methodism: A History of the Methodist Episcopal Church within the Bounds of the California Annual Conference from 1847–1897*. San Francisco, 1901.

ARMSTRONG, JAMES EDWARD. *History of the Old Baltimore Conference from the Planting of Methodism in 1773 to the Division of the Conference in 1857*. Baltimore, 1907.

ARNOLD, W. E. *A History of Methodism in Kentucky*. 2 vols. [Louisville, Ky.], 1935–36.

ATKINSON, JOHN. *Centennial History of American Methodism, Inclusive of Its Ecclesiastical Organization in 1784 and Its Subsequent Development under the Superintendency of Francis Asbury*. New York and Cincinnati, 1884.

———. *History of the Origin of the Wesleyan Movement in America and the Establishment Therein of Methodism*. Jersey City, 1896.

ATWOOD, ANTHONY. *Causes of the Marvelous Success of Methodism in This Country within the Past Century*. Philadelphia, [1844].

BACON, L. W. *A History of American Christianity*. New York, 1897.

BAKER, GEORGE CLAUDE, JR. *An Introduction to the History of Early New England Methodism, 1789–1839*. Durham, N.C., 1941.

BANGS, NATHAN. *An Authentic History of the Missions under the Care of the Missionary Society of the Methodist Episcopal Church*, New York, 1832.

———. *A History of the Methodist Episcopal Church*. 4 vols. New York, 1838–41.

BARKER, JOHN MARSHALL. *History of Ohio Methodism*. Cincinnati, 1898.

BARNES, ANNIE M. *Scenes in Pioneer Methodism*. 2 vols. Nashville, 1892.

BASCOM, H. B. *Methodism and Slavery: Appeal of the Southern Commissioners*. Nashville, 1846.

BASHFORD, JAMES W. *The Oregon Missions*. New York, 1918.

BASSETT, ANCEL H. *A Concise History of the Methodist Protestant Church, from Its Origin*. Pittsburgh, 1877.

BEARDSLEY, FRANK GRENVILLE. *A History of American Revivals*. 2d ed. New York, 1912.

BEGGS, S. R. *Pages from the Early History of the West and North-West; Embracing Reminiscences and Incidents of Settlement and Growth, and*

Sketches of the Material and Religious Progress of the States of Ohio, Indiana, Illinois, and Missouri, with Special Reference to the History of Methodism. Cincinnati, 1868.

Bennett, P. S., and Lawson, James. *History of Methodism in Wisconsin*. Cincinnati, 1890.

Bennett, William W. *Memorials of Methodism in Virginia, from Its Introduction into the State, in the Year 1772, to the Year 1829*. Richmond, 1871.

Benson, Louis F. *The English Hymn: Its Development and Use in Worship*. London, 1915.

Boswell, John W. *A Short History of Methodism*. Nashville, 1905.

Branch, E. Douglas. *Westward: The Romance of the American Frontier*. New York, 1929.

———. *The Sentimental Years, 1830–1860*. New York, 1934.

Buckley, James M. *A History of Methodists in the United States*. "American Church History Series," Vol. V. New York, 1896.

———. *Constitutional and Parliamentary History of the Methodist Episcopal Church*. New York, 1912.

History Series," Vol. V. New York, 1896.

Burkhead, L. S. (ed.). *Centennial of Methodism in North Carolina*. Raleigh, 1876.

Burnet, J. *Notes on the Early Settlement of the Northwestern Territory*. New York, 1847.

Cannon, James. *History of Southern Methodist Missions*. Nashville, 1926.

Carroll, H. K.; Harrison, W. P.; and Bayless, J. H. (eds.). *Proceedings, Sermons, Essays and Addresses of the Centennial Methodist Conference Held in Mt. Vernon Place Methodist Episcopal Church, Baltimore, Md., December 9–17, 1884*. New York and Cincinnati, 1885.

Chaffee, A. F. *History of the Wyoming Conference of the Methodist Episcopal Church*. New York, 1904.

Chreitzberg, A. M. *Early Methodism in the Carolinas*. Nashville, 1897.

Clark, Dan Elbert. *The West in American History*. New York, 1937.

Cleveland, Catherine C. *The Great Revival in the West, 1795–1805*. Chicago, 1916.

Cole, Otis, and Baketel, Oliver S. (eds.). *History of the New Hampshire Conference of the Methodist Episcopal Church*. New York, 1929.

Conable, F. W. *History of the Genesee Annual Conference of the Methodist Episcopal Church, from Its Organization by Bishop Asbury and M'Kendree, in 1810, to the Year 1884*. New York, 1885.

Crawford, George A. (ed.). *The Centennial of New England Methodism*. Boston, 1891.

Culbreth, J. M. *Studies in Methodist History*. Nashville, 1924.

Culver, Newell. *Methodism Forty Years Ago and Now: Embracing Many Interesting Reminiscences and Incidents*. New York, 1876.

Cummings, A. W. *The Early Schools of Methodism*. New York, 1886.

Curtiss, George L. *Manual of Methodist Church History, Showing the Evolution of Methodism in the United States of America for the Use of Students and General Readers*. New York, 1893.

Curts, Lewis (ed.). *The General Conference of the Methodist Episcopal Church from 1792 to 1896*. Cincinnati and New York, 1900.

Daniels, W. H. *The Illustrated History of Methodism in Great Britain, America, and Australia, from the days of the Wesleys to the Present Time*. New York, 1884.

Davenport, Frederick M. *Primitive Traits in Religious Revivals*. New York, 1905.

Dawson, J. M. *The Spiritual Conquest of the Southwest*. Nashville, 1927.

Dimond, Sydney G. *The Psychology of the Methodist Revival: An Empirical and Descriptive Study*. London, 1926.

Dixon, James. *Methodism in America: With the Personal Narrative of the Author, during the Tour through a Part of the United States and Canada*. New York, 1849.

Dondore, Dorothy Anne. *The Prairie and the Making of Middle America: Four Centuries of Description*. Cedar Rapids, 1926.

Dorchester, Daniel. *The Why of Methodism*. New York, 1887.

———. *Christianity in the United States*. New York, 1890.

Douglass, Paul F. *The Story of German Methodism: Biography of an Immigrant Soul*. New York, 1939.

Drinkhouse, Edward J. *History of Methodist Reform Synoptical of General Methodism 1703 to 1898 with Special and Comprehensive Reference to Its Most Salient Exhibition in the History of the Methodist Protestant Church*. N.p., 1899.

DuBose, Horace M. *A History of Methodism*. Nashville, 1916.

Duncan, Watson Boone. *Studies in Methodist Literature*. Nashville, 1914.

Duren, William Larkin. *The Trail of the Circuit Rider*. New Orleans, 1936.

Duvall, Sylvanus Milne. *The Methodist Episcopal Church and Education up to 1869*. New York, 1928.

Earle, A. B. *Bringing in the Sheaves*. Boston, 1868.

Eggleston, Edward. *The Hoosier Schoolmaster*. New York, 1871.

———. *The Circuit Rider: A Tale of the Heroic Age*. New York, 1893.

ELLIOTT, CHARLES. *History of the Great Secession from the Methodist Episcopal Church in the Year 1845, Eventuating in the Organization of the New Church Entitled the Methodist Episcopal Church, South.* Cincinnati, 1855.

———. *South-Western Methodism: A History of the M. E. Church in the South-West, from 1844 to 1864.* Cincinnati, 1868.

ELSBREE, O. W. *The Rise of the Missionary Spirit in America, 1790–1815.* Williamsport, Pa., 1928.

EMORY, JOHN. *A Defense of "Our Fathers," and of the Original Organization of the Methodist Episcopal Church.* New York, 1840.

FAULKNER, JOHN ALFRED. *The Methodists.* New York, 1903.

FIELD, A. D. *Memorials of Methodism in the Bounds of the Rock River Conference.* Cincinnati, 1886.

———. *Worthies and Workers, Both Ministers and Laymen, of the Rock River Conference.* Cincinnati, 1896.

FINLEY, JAMES B. *History of the Wyandott Mission, at Upper Sandusky, Ohio, under the Direction of the Methodist Episcopal Church.* Cincinnati, 1840.

———. *Sketches of Western Methodism: Biographical, Historical, and Miscellaneous.* Cincinnati, 1854.

FISH, HENRY C. *Handbook of Revivals: For the Use of Winners of Souls.* Boston, 1874.

FITZGERALD, O. P. *The Class-Meeting.* Nashville, 1900.

FLETCHER, MIRIAM. *The Methodist: or, Incidents and Characters from Life in the Baltimore Conference.* 2 vols. New York, 1859.

FLINT, TIMOTHY. *The History and Geography of the Mississippi Valley.* 2 vols. Cincinnati, 1832.

FOOTE, J. P. *The Schools of Cincinnati and Its Vicinity.* Cincinnati, 1855.

FOREMAN, GRANT. *Pioneer Days in the Early Southwest.* Cleveland, 1926.

FOSTER, R. S. *Centenary Thoughts for the Pew and Pulpit of Methodism in 1884.* New York, 1884.

FRADENBURGH, J. N. *History of Erie Conference.* 2 vols. Oil City, Pa., 1907.

GALLAHER, J. *Western Sketch Book.* Boston, 1850.

GARBER, PAUL NEFF. *The Romance of American Methodism.* Greensboro, N.C., 1931.

GAY, THERESA. *Life and Letters of Mrs. Jason Lee, First Wife of Rev. Jason Lee of the Oregon Mission.* Portland, 1936.

GEWEHR, WESLEY M. *The Great Awakening in Virginia.* Durham, N.C., 1930.

GORRIE, P. DOUGLASS. *Episcopal Methodism, as It Was, and Is, or, An*

Account of the Origin, Progress, Doctrines, Church Polity, Usages, Institutions, and Statistics, of the Methodist Episcopal Church in the United States. Auburn [N.Y.], 1852.

———. *Black River and Northern New York Conference Memorial.* Watertown, N.Y., 1881.

Goss, C. C. *Statistical History of the First Century of American Methodism.* New York, 1866.

Gray, Marcus Lemon, *1806–1906: The Centennial Volume of Missouri Methodism, Methodist Episcopal Church, South.* Kansas City, Mo., 1907.

Gregg, Samuel. *The History of Methodism within the Bounds of the Erie Annual Conference of the Methodist Episcopal Church.* 2 vols. New York, 1873.

Grissom, W. L. *History of Methodism in North Carolina.* Nashville, 1905.

Haines, Aaron W. *The Makers of Iowa Methodism.* Cincinnati, 1900.

Hall, James. *Sketches of History, Life and Manners in the West.* 2 vols. Philadelphia, 1835.

Hall, Thomas C. *The Religious Background of American Culture.* Boston, 1930.

Hammond, Edmund Jordon. *The Methodist Episcopal Church in Georgia.* N.p., 1935.

Hart, Albert B. (ed.). *National Expansion, 1783–1845.* New York, 1901.

Henderson, Archibald. *Conquest of the Old Southwest.* New York, 1920.

Herrick, H. N., and Sweet, William Warren. *A History of the North Indiana Conference of the Methodist Episcopal Church.* Indianapolis, 1917.

Hibbard, F. G. *History of the Late East Genesee Conference of the Methodist Episcopal Church.* New York, 1887.

Hines, H. K. *Missionary History of the Pacific Northwest.* Portland, 1899.

Hobart, Chauncey. *History of Methodism in Minnesota.* Red Wing, Minn., 1887.

Holliday, F. C. *Indiana Methodism: Being an Account of the Introduction, Progress, and Present Position of Methodism in the State; and also a History of the Literary Institutions under the Care of the Church with Sketches of the Principal Methodist Educators in the State down to 1872.* Cincinnati, 1873.

Hood, Edwin Paxton. *The Great Revivals of the Eighteenth Century.* New York, 1882.

Hulbert, Archer Butler. *Frontiers, the Genius of American Nationality.* Boston, 1929.

Humphrey, E. F. *Nationalism and Religion in America.* Boston, 1924.

Humphries, A. Lewis. *The Holy Spirit in Faith and Experience.* N.p., 1911.

Hurst, John Fletcher. *The History of Methodism.* 7 vols. New York, 1902–4. (Vols. IV–VI on American Methodism.)

Hyde, A. B. *The Story of Methodism: Tracing the Rise and Progress of That Wonderful Religious Movement, Which like the Gulf Stream, Has Given Warmth to the Wide Waters and Verdure to Many Lands; and Giving an Account of Its Various Influences and Institutions of Today.* Greenfield, Mass., 1887.

Jackson, Samuel M. *A Bibliography of American Church History (1820–1893).* "American Church History Series," Vol. XII, New York, 1894.

James, William. *The Varieties of Religious Experience.* New York, 1922.

Jewell, Horace. *History of Methodism in Arkansas.* Little Rock, Ark., 1892.

Jobson, Frederick J. *America, and American Methodism.* New York, 1857.

Johnson, Herrick. *Revivals: Their Place and Their Power.* Chicago, 1882.

Jones, John G. *A Complete History of Methodism as Connected with the Mississippi Conference of the Methodist Episcopal Church, South.* 2 vols. Nashville, 1908.

Keys, Charles C. *The Class-Leader's Manual: Or, an Essay on the Duties, Difficulties, Qualifications, Motives, and Encouragements of Class Leaders.* New York, 1856.

Koch, Gustav Adolf. *Republican Religion, the American Revolution and the Cult of Reason.* New York, 1933.

Leaton, James. *History of Methodism in Illinois, from 1793 to 1832.* Cincinnati, 1883.

Lednum, John. *A History of the Rise of Methodism in America, Containing Sketches of Methodist Itinerant Preachers, from 1736 to 1785.* Philadelphia, 1859.

Lee, James W.; Luccock, Naphtali; and Dixon, James Main. *The Illustrated History of Methodism.* St. Louis, 1900.

Lee, Jesse. *A Short History of the Methodists, in the United States of America; Beginning in 1766, and Continued till 1809.* Baltimore, 1810.

Lee, Umphrey. *The Historical Backgrounds of Early Methodist Enthusiasm.* New York, 1931.

Leyburn, James G. *Frontier Folkways.* New Haven, 1935.

Lide, Anne Ayers. *Robert Alexander [1811–82] and the Early Methodist Church in Texas.* La Grange, Texas, 1935.

LINDLEY, HARLOW (ed.). *Indiana as Seen by Early Travelers: A Collection of Reprints from Books of Travel, Letters and Diaries Prior to 1830*. Indianapolis, 1916.

LUCCOCK, HALFORD E., and HUTCHINSON, PAUL. *The Story of Methodism*. New York, 1926.

MCANALLY, DAVID RICE. *History of Methodism in Missouri*. N.p., 1881.

MACDONALD, WILLIAM. *Jacksonian Democracy*. New York, 1906.

MCDONNOLD, B. W. *History of the Cumberland Presbyterian Church*. Nashville, 1899.

MCFERRIN, JOHN B. *History of Methodism in Tennessee*. 3 vols. Nashville, 1888.

MACNEMAR, RICHARD. *The Kentucky Revival: or a Short History of the Late Extraordinary Outpouring of the Spirit of God in the Western States of America*. Cincinnati, 1807.

MCTYEIRE, HOLLAND N. *A History of Methodism: Comprising a View of the Rise of This Revival of Spiritual Religion in the First Half of the Eighteenth Century, and of the Principal Agents by Whom It Was Promoted in Europe and America*. Nashville, 1898.

MAFFITT, JOHN N. *Pulpit Sketches*. Louisville, 1839.

MARTIN, ASA EARL. *The Anti-slavery Movement in Kentucky prior to 1850*. Louisville, Ky., 1918.

MATLACK, LUCIUS C. *The History of American Slavery and Methodism from 1780 to 1849, and History of the Wesleyan Connection of America*. New York, 1849.

———. *The Antislavery Struggle and Triumphs in the Methodist Episcopal Church*. New York, 1881.

MAXSON, C. H. *The Great Awakening in the Middle Colonies*. Chicago, 1920.

MEACHAM, A. G. *A Compendious History of the Rise and Progress of the Methodist Church, Both in Europe and America; Consisting Principally of Selections from Various Approved and Authentic Documents*. New York, 1835.

MECKLIN, JOHN M. *The Story of American Dissent*. New York, 1934.

MILBURN, WILLIAM H. *The Pioneers, Preachers, and People of the Mississippi Valley*. New York, 1860.

MILEY, JOHN. *Treatise on Class Meetings*. Cincinnati, 1859.

MILLER, ADAM. *Origin and Progress of the German Missions in the Methodist Episcopal Church*. Cincinnati, 1843.

MODE, PETER G. *Source Book and Bibliographical Guide for American Church History*. Menasha, Wis., 1921.

———. *The Frontier Spirit in American Christianity*. New York, 1923.

MONETTE, JOHN W. *A History of the Discovery and Settlement of the Valley of the Mississippi.* 2 vols. New York, 1846.

MUDGE, JAMES. *History of the New England Conference of the Methodist Episcopal Church, 1796–1910.* Boston, 1910.

NEELY, THOMAS B. *The Evolution of Episcopacy and Organic Methodism.* New York, 1888.

———. *History of the Origin and Development of the Governing Conference in Methodism.* New York and Cincinnati, 1892.

———. *American Methodism, Its Division and Unification.* New York, 1915.

———. *Doctrinal Standards of Methodism.* Chicago, 1918.

NIEBUHR, H. RICHARD. *The Social Sources of Denominationalism.* New York, 1929.

NORWOOD, J. N. *The Schism in the Methodist Episcopal Church, 1844: A Study of Slavery and Ecclesiastical Politics.* Alfred, N.Y., 1923.

NOTTINGHAM, ELIZABETH K. *Methodism and the Frontier: Indiana Proving Ground.* New York, 1941.

PARIS, JOHN. *History of the Methodist Protestant Church.* Baltimore, 1849.

PARKS, STEPHEN. *Troy Conference Miscellany.* Albany, N.Y., 1854.

PARRINGTON, V. L. *Main Currents in American Thought.* 3 vols. New York, 1927–30.

PAXSON, FREDERIC L. *History of the American Frontier, 1763–1893.* Boston, 1924.

PAYTON, JACOB SIMPSON. *Our Fathers Have Told Us: The Story of the Founding of Methodism in Western Pennsylvania.* Cincinnati, 1938.

PECK, GEORGE. *Early Methodism within the Bounds of the Old Genesee Conference from 1788 to 1828.* New York, 1860.

PENNEWELL, ALMER M. *The Methodist Movement in Northern Illinois.* Sycamore, Ill., 1942.

PHELAN, MACUM. *A History of Early Methodism in Texas, 1817–1866.* Nashville, 1924.

PHILLIPS, U. B. *Life and Labor in the Old South.* Boston, 1929.

PHOEBUS, GEORGE A. *Beams of Light on Early Methodism in America.* New York, 1887.

PILCHER, ELIJAH H. *Protestantism in Michigan: Being a Special History of the Methodist Episcopal Church and Incidentally of Other Denominations.* Detroit, 1878.

PLAYTER, GEORGE F. *The History of Methodism in Canada.* Toronto, 1862.

PORTER, JAMES. *A Compendium of Methodism.* Boston, 1851.

———. *A Comprehensive History of Methodism*. Cincinnati, 1876.

POSEY, WALTER BROWNLOW. *The Development of Methodism in the Old Southwest, 1783–1824*. Tuscaloosa, Ala., 1933.

PRATT, JAMES B. *The Religious Consciousness: A Psychological Study*. New York, 1920.

PRICE, R. N. *Holston Methodism*. 5 vols. Nashville, 1903–14.

RANDALL, D. B. *A Statistical History of the Maine Conference of the Methodist Episcopal Church from 1793–1893*. Portland, Me., 1893.

RAYBOLD, G. A. *Reminiscences of Methodism in West Jersey*. New York, 1849.

RED, WILLIAM STUART. *The Texas Colonists and Religion, 1821–1836: A Centennial Tribute to the Texas Patriots Who Shed Their Blood That We Might Enjoy Civil and Religious Liberty*. Austin, Tex., 1924.

REDFORD, A. H. *The History of Methodism in Kentucky*. 3 vols. Nashville, 1868–70.

———. *History of the Organization of the Methodist Episcopal Church, South*. Nashville, 1871.

———. *Western Cavaliers: Embracing the History of the Methodist Episcopal Church in Kentucky from 1832 to 1844*. Nashville, 1876.

REID, J. M. *Missions and Missionary Society of the Methodist Episcopal Church*. 3 vols. New York and Cincinnati, 1895.

RIEGEL, ROBERT E. *America Moves West*. New York, 1930.

RITSON, JOSEPH. *The Romance of Primitive Methodism*. London, 1909.

ROBERTS, GEORGE C. M. *Centenary Pictorial Album: Being Contributions of the Early History of Methodism in the State of Maryland*. Baltimore, 1866.

ROBINSON, JOHN BUNYAN. *History of Rock River Conference*. Leland, Fla., 1908.

ROOSEVELT, THEODORE. *The Winning of the West*. 6 vols. New York, 1922.

ROUSE, RUTH, and MILLER, H. CRICHTON. *Christian Experience and Psychological Processes*. N.p., 1920.

RUSK, RALPH L. *The Literature of the Middle West Frontier*. 2 vols. New York, 1925.

SANDERSON, J. E. *The First Century of Methodism in Canada*. Toronto, 1908.

SCHERMERHORN, JOHN F., and MILLS, SAMUEL J. *A Correct View of That Part of the United States, Which Lies West of the Allegheny Mountains, with Regard to Religion and Morals*. Hartford, Conn., 1814.

SCUDDER, M. L. *American Methodism*. Hartford, Conn., 1867.

SEAMAN, SAMUEL A. *Annals of New York Methodism: Being a History of the Methodist Episcopal Church in the City of New York (1766–1890)*. New York, 1892.

SELDES, GILBERT. *The Stammering Century*. New York, 1928.

SEMPLE, ELLEN C. *American History and Its Geographic Conditions*. New York, 1903.

SHIPP, ALBERT M. *The History of Methodism in South Carolina*. Nashville, 1884.

SIMPSON, MATTHEW (ed.). *Cyclopaedia of Methodism, Embracing Sketches of Its Rise, Progress, and Present Condition, with Biographical Notices and Numerous Illustrations*. Philadelphia, 1878.

SMITH, GEORGE G. *The History of Methodism in Georgia and Florida, from 1785 to 1865*. Macon, Ga., 1877.

———. *The History of Georgia Methodism from 1786 to 1866*. Atlanta, Ga., 1913.

SMITH, JOHN C. *Reminiscences of Early Methodism in Indiana Including Sketches of Various Prominent Ministers, Together with Narratives of Women Eminent for Piety Poetry and Song: Also, Descriptions of Remarkable Camp Meetings, Revivals, Incidents and Other Miscellany*. Indianapolis, 1879.

SMITH, JOHN L. *Indiana Methodism: A Series of Sketches and Incidents, Grave and Humorous concerning Preachers and People in the West*. Valparaiso, Ind., 1892.

SMITH, T[HOMAS] WATSON. *History of the Methodist Church within the Territories Embraced in the Late Conference of Eastern British America, Including Nova Scotia, New Brunswick, Prince Edward Island and Bermuda*. 2 vols. Halifax, N.S., 1877.

SMITH, WILLIAM C. *Indiana Miscellany*. Cincinnati, 1867.

SPEER, WILLIAM. *The Great Revival of 1800*. Philadelphia, 1872.

SPRAGUE, WILLIAM B. *Lectures on Revivals of Religion*. 2d ed. New York, 1833.

STEPHENSON, MRS. FREDRICK G. *One Hundred Years of Canadian Methodist Missions, 1824–1924*. Toronto, 1925.

STEVENS, ABEL. *History of the Methodist Episcopal Church in the United States of America*. 4 vols. New York, 1864–67.

———. *The Centenary of American Methodism: A Sketch of Its History, Theology, Practical System, and Success*. New York, 1866.

STREETER, BURNETT H. (ed.). *The Spirit: God and His Relations to Man*. N.p., 1919.

STRICKLAND, W. P. *The Pioneers of the West, or Life in the Woods*. New York, 1856.

SWANEY, C. B. *Episcopal Methodism and Slavery*. Boston, 1926.

SWEET, WILLIAM WARREN. *The Methodist Episcopal Church and the Civil War*. Cincinnati, 1912.

———. *The Story of Religions in America*. New York, 1930.

———. *Religion on the American Frontier*, Vol. I: *The Baptists, 1783–1830*. New York, 1931. Vol II: *The Presbyterians, 1783–1840*. New York, 1936. Vol. III: *The Congregationalists, 1783–1850*. Chicago, 1939.

———. *The Makers of Christianity, from John Cotton to Lyman Abbott*. New York, 1933.

———. *Methodism in American History*. New York, 1933.

———. *Men of Zeal: The Romance of American Methodist Beginnings*. New York, 1935.

———. *Indiana Asbury–DePauw University (1837–1937)*. New York, [1937].

———. *Revivalism in America: Its Origin, Growth and Decline*. New York, 1944.

TEES, FRANCIS H. *The Begining of Methodism in England and in America*. Nashville, 1940.

TEWKESBURY, DONALD G. *The Founding of American Colleges and Universities before the Civil War with Particular Reference to the Religious Influences Bearing upon the College Movement*. New York, 1932.

THRALL, HOMER S. *A Brief History of Methodism in Texas*. Nashville, 1894.

THRIFT, CHARLES TINSLEY, JR. *The Trail of the Florida Circuit Rider*. Lakeland, Fla., 1944.

TIGERT, JOHN J. *The Making of Methodism: Studies in the Genesis of Institutions*. Nashville, 1898.

———. *A Constitutional History of American Episcopal Methodism*. Nashville, 1916.

TOWNSEND, W. J.; WORKMAN, H. B.; and EAYRS, GEORGE. *A New History of Methodism*. 2 vols. London, 1909.

TRACY, JOSEPH. *The Great Awakening: A History of Religion in the Time of Edwards and Whitefield*. Boston, 1842.

TROLLOPE, MRS. FRANCES. *Domestic Manners of the Americans*. 2 vols. New York and London, 1832.

TURNER, FREDERICK J. *The Significance of the Frontier in American History*. Washington, 1894.

———. *The Frontier in American History*. New York, 1921.

UNDERWOOD, A. C. *Conversion, Christian and Non-Christian*. N.p., 1925.

VAN DEVENTER, CORNELIUS I. *Sketches of Methodism in Northwest Missouri*. St. Joseph, Mo., 1894.

WAKELEY, J. B. *Lost Chapters Recovered from the Early History of American Methodism*. New York, 1858.

WARDLE, ADDIE G. *History of the Sunday School Movement in the Methodist Episcopal Church*. New York, 1918.

WARING, EDMUND H. *History of the Iowa Annual Conference of the Methodist Episcopal Church*. N.p., n.d.

WEIGLE, L. A. *American Idealism*. "Pageant of America Series," Vol. X. New Haven, 1928.

WEST, ANSON. *A History of Methodism in Alabama*. Nashville, 1893.

WHITLOCK, W. F. *The Story of the Book Concerns*. Cincinnati, 1903.

WILLIAMS, SAMUEL W. *Pictures of Early Methodism in Ohio*. Cincinnati, 1909.

WILSON, ELIZABETH. *Methodism in Eastern Wisconsin (1832–1850)*. N.p., 1938.

WOODARD, W. S. *Annals of Methodism in Missouri*. Columbia, Mo., 1893.

WRIGHT, RICHARDSON. *Hawkers and Walkers in Early America*. Philadelphia, 1927.

YOUNGS, JAMES. *A History of the Most Interesting Events in the Rise and Progress of Methodism, in Europe and America*. New Haven, 1830.

INDEX

PRINTED IN U·S·A